EP Sixth Reader
Days 1-90

EP Reader Series

Volume 6

CONTENTS

ACKNOWLEDGEMENTS

Thank you to Abigail Baia for the use of her beautiful cover image.

Welcome to Easy Peasy All-in-One Homeschool's Sixth Reader Lessons 1-90

This is Easy Peasy's offline version of its assignments for the first half of Reading 6. The novels and poetry included are found in the public domain and have been gathered here along with each lesson's assignment directions. The online lessons from Easy Peasy's website have been replaced with offline lessons found in this book. Care was taken to ensure the children don't miss out on any important lessons or activities.

This book covers Lessons 1 – 90, only. The second half of the course is found in the EP Sixth Reader Lessons 91-180.

Lesson 1

1. Write the words **teeming, fathom, reverberating,** and **cumulative**. Write them on different lines so that there's room to add definitions. Pay attention to the words as you read and decide what you think they mean.
2. Read these Carl Sandburg poems. This poet was born in 1878.
3. Look at the title of the poem "Monotone." The rain is monotone and is being contrasted with a rainbow which has lots of colors. What does monotone mean? The prefix mono means one.
4. Look at the word catalpa in "Back Yard." I don't know what it is. Do you? But the poem gives us clues. It says, "grass, catalpa and oak." We know what grass is. Oak is referring to the tree, so we can assume catalpa is some sort of plant. Here's a picture of a catalpa tree.

5. Here is a picture of something like what they think a mastodon resembled. How would you imagine a mastodon moved?

6. Look the bold words up in the Answers section to find their definitions. Add the correct definition to your notebook along with the word. (Answers)

7. Choose two poems and tell or write what each poem is talking about in your own words.

Under a Telephone Pole
I am a copper wire slung in the air,
Slim against the sun I make not even a clear line of shadow.
Night and day I keep singing-humming and thrumming:
It is love and war and money; it is the fighting and the tears, the work and want,
Death and laughter of men and women passing through me, carrier of your speech,
In the rain and the wet dripping, in the dawn and the shine drying,
A copper wire.

Fog
The fog comes
on little cat feet.
It sits looking
over harbor and city
on silent haunches
and then moves on.

Flux
Sand of the sea runs red
Where the sunset reaches and quivers.
Sand of the sea runs yellow
Where the moon slants and wavers.

Monotone
The monotone of the rain is beautiful,
And the sudden rise and slow relapse
Of the long multitudinous rain.
The sun on the hills is beautiful,
Or a captured sunset sea-flung,
Bannered with fire and gold.
A face I know is beautiful-
With fire and gold of sky and sea,
And the peace of long warm rain.

Back Yard
Shine on, O moon of summer.
Shine to the leaves of grass, catalpa and oak,
All silver under your rain to-night.
An Italian boy is sending songs to you tonight from an accordion.
A Polish boy is out with his best girl;
They marry next month;
tonight they are throwing you kisses.
An old man next door is dreaming over a sheen
That sits in a cherry tree in his back yard.
The clocks say I must go-
I stay here sitting on the back porch
drinking white thoughts you rain down.
Shine on, O moon,
Shake out more and more silver changes.

Child Moon
The child's wonder
At the old moon
Comes back nightly.
She points her finger
To the far silent yellow thing
Shining through the branches
Filtering on the leaves a golden sand,
Crying with her little tongue, "See the moon!"
And in her bed fading to sleep
With babblings of the moon on her little mouth.

Docks
Strolling along
By the teeming docks,
I watch the ships put out.
Black ships that heave and lunge
And move like mastodons
Arising from lethargic sleep.
The fathomed harbor
Calls them not nor dares
Them to a strain of action,
But outward, on and outward,
Sounding low-reverberating calls,
Shaggy in the half-lit distance,

They pass the pointed headland,
View the wide, far-lifting wilderness
And leap with cumulative speed
To test the challenge of the sea.
Plunging,
Doggedly onward plunging,
Into salt and mist and foam and sun.

Lost

Desolate and lone
All night long on the lake
Where fog trails and mist creeps,
The whistle of a boat
Calls and cries unendingly,
Like some lost child
In tears and trouble
Hunting the harbor's breast
And the harbor's eyes.

Margaret

Many birds and the beating of wings
Make a flinging reckless hum
In the early morning at the rocks
Above the blue pool
Where the gray shadows swim lazy.
In your blue eyes, O reckless child,
I saw today many little wild wishes,
Eager as the great morning.

Window

Night from a railroad car window
Is a great, dark, soft thing
Broken across with slashes of light.

Lesson 2

1. Write the words **gnarled, trajectory, baritone** and **furrows** under Lesson 1's words and pay attention to them as you read. Decide what you think they mean.
2. Read the Carl Sandburg poems.
3. Look the bold words up to find their definition. Add the definitions to your notebook. (Answers)

4. Choose two poems and tell or write what each poem is talking about in your own words.

Baby Face

White moon comes in on a baby face.
The shafts across her bed are flimmering.
Out on the land White Moon shines,
Shines and glimmers against gnarled shadows,
All silver to slow twisted shadows
Falling across the long road that runs from the house.
Keep a little of your beauty
And some of your flimmering silver
For her by the window to-night
Where you come in, White Moon.

Goldwing Moth

A goldwing moth is between the scissors and the ink bottle on the desk
Last night it flew hundreds of circles around a glass bulb and a flame wire.
The wings are a soft gold; it is the gold of illuminated initials in manuscripts of the medieval monks.

Prayers of Steel

Lay me on an anvil, O God.
Beat me and hammer me into a crowbar.
Let me pry loose old walls.
Let me lift and loosen old foundations.
Lay me on an anvil, O God.
Beat me and hammer me into a steel spike.
Drive me into the girders that hold a skyscraper together.
Take red-hot rivets and fasten me into the central girders.
Let me be the great nail holding a skyscraper
through blue nights into white stars.

Improved Farmland

Tall timber stood here once, here on a corn belt farm along the Monon.
Here the roots of a half mile of trees dug their runners deep in the loam for a grip and a hold against wind storms.
Then the axmen came and the chips flew to the zing of steel and handle the lank railsplitters cut the big ones first, the beeches and the oaks, then the brush.
Dynamite, wagons and horses took the stumps--the plows sunk their teeth in--

now it is first class corn land--improved property--and the hogs grunt over the fodder crops.

It would come hard now for this half mile of improved farm land along the Monon corn belt, on a piece of Grand Prairie, to remember once it had a great singing family of trees.

Primer Lesson

Look out how you use proud words.
When you let proud words go
It is not easy to call them back.
They wear long boots, hard boots;
They walk off proud;
They can't hear you calling---
Look out how you use proud words.

Baby Toes

There is a blue star, Janet,
Fifteen years' ride from us,
If we ride a hundred miles an hour.
There is a white star, Janet,
Forty years' ride from us,
If we ride a hundred miles an hour.
Shall we ride
To the blue star
Or the white star?

Basket

Speak, sir, and be wise.
Speak choosing your words, sir,
like an old woman over a bushel of apples.

Five Cent Balloons

Pietro has twenty red and blue balloons on a string.
They flutter and dance pulling Pietro's arm.
A nickel apiece is what they sell for.
Wishing children tag Pietro's heels.
He sells out and goes the streets alone.

Good Night

Many ways to spell good night.
Fireworks at a pier on the Fourth of July

spell it with red wheels and yellow spokes.
They fizz in the air, touch the water and quit.
Rockets make a trajectory of gold-and-blue and then go out.
Railroad trains at night spell with a smokestack mushrooming a white pillar.
Steamboats turn a curve in the Mississippi crying in a baritone
that crosses lowland cottonfields to a razorback hill.
It is easy to spell good night.
Many ways to spell good night.

Harvest Sunset
Red gold of pools,
Sunset furrows six o'clock,
And the farmer done in the fields
And the cows in the barns with bulging udders.
Take the cows and the farmer,
Take the barns and bulging udders.
Leave the red gold of pools
And sunset furrows six o'clock.
The farmer's wife is singing.
The farmer's boy is whistling.
I wash my hands in red gold of pools.

Lesson 3

1. Read the Carl Sandburg poems.
2. The last poem is talking about the city of Chicago. He is saying, yes, we have problems with evil in our city, but we are still proud this is our city and we are all these great things. The first part of the second paragraph of the poem reminded me of Proverbs 7. Why? Proverbs 7:7–10 "…I noticed among the young men, a youth who had no sense. He was going down the street near her corner, walking along in the direction of her house at twilight, as the day was fading, as the dark of night set in. Then out came a woman to meet him, dressed like a prostitute and with crafty intent." (NLT)
3. **Effluvia** in the first poem means emanation or exhalation, maybe it means like the breath of the mountains. Effluvia is actually plural. Effluvium is the singular.
4. Thingamajig in "Manual System" is pronounced thing – a – ma – jig. It's just a word we use when we don't know what something is called. What do you think the thingamajig is?

Vocabulary

1. Write at least one synonym for each word. Synonyms are words that mean the same thing. If you write more than one, get a high five and/or hug. (Answers)
   - full, knobby, increasing, content, admire, cautious, understand, echoing

Languages
There are no handles upon a language
Whereby men take hold of it
And mark it with signs for its remembrance.
It is a river, this language,
Once in a thousand years
Breaking a new course
Changing its way to the ocean.
It is mountain effluvia
Moving to valleys
And from nation to nation
Crossing borders and mixing.
Languages die like rivers.
Words wrapped round your tongue today
And broken to shape of thought
Between your teeth and lips speaking
Now and today
Shall be faded hieroglyphics
Ten thousand years from now.
Sing-and singing-remember
Your song dies and changes
And is not here to-morrow
Any more than the wind
Blowing ten thousand years ago.

Manual System
Mary has a thingamajig clamped on her ears
And sits all day taking plugs out and sticking plugs in.
Flashes and flashes-voices and voices
calling for ears to pour words in
Faces at the ends of wires
asking for other faces at the ends of other wires:
All day taking plugs out and sticking plugs in,
Mary has a thingamajig clamped on her ears.

People Who Must
I painted on the roof of a skyscraper.
I painted a long while and called it a day's work.
The people on a corner swarmed
and the traffic cop's whistle never let up all afternoon.
They were the same as bugs, many bugs on their way-
Those people on the go or at a standstill;
And the traffic cop a spot of blue, a splinter of brass,
Where the black tides ran around him
And he kept the street. I painted a long while
And called it a day's work.

Potomac Town in February
The bridge says:
Come across, try me; see how good I am.
The big rock in the river says:
Look at me; learn how to stand up.
The white water says:
I go on; around, under, over, I go on.
A kneeling, scraggly pine says:
I am here yet; they nearly got me last year.
A sliver of moon slides by on a high wind calling:
I know why; I'll see you to-morrow;
I'll tell you everything to-morrow.

Sea-Wash
The sea-wash never ends.
The sea-wash repeats, repeats.
Only old songs?
Is that all the sea knows?
Only the old strong songs?
Is that all?
The sea-wash repeats, repeats.

Summer Stars
Bend low again, night of summer stars.
So near you are, sky of summer stars,
So near, a long arm man can pick off stars,
Pick off what he wants in the sky bowl,
So near you are, summer stars,

So near, strumming, strumming,
So lazy and hum-strumming.

Chicago

Hog Butcher for the World,
Tool Maker, Stacker of Wheat,
Player with Railroads and the Nation's Freight Handler;
Stormy, husky, brawling,
City of the Big Shoulders:

They tell me you are wicked and I believe them, for I have seen your painted women under the gas lamps luring the farm boys.

And they tell me you are crooked and I answer: Yes, it is true I have seen the gunman kill and go free to kill again.

And they tell me you are brutal and my reply is: On the faces of women and children I have seen the marks of wanton hunger.

And having answered so I turn once more to those who sneer at this my city, and I give them back the sneer and say to them:

Come and show me another city with lifted head singing so proud to be alive and coarse and strong and cunning.

Flinging magnetic curses amid the toil of piling job on job, here is a tall bold slugger set vivid against the little soft cities;

Fierce as a dog with tongue lapping for action, cunning as a savage pitted against the wilderness,
Bareheaded,
Shoveling,
Wrecking,
Planning,
Building, breaking, rebuilding,

Under the smoke, dust all over his mouth, laughing with white teeth,

Under the terrible burden of destiny laughing as a young man laughs,

Laughing even as an ignorant fighter laughs who has never lost a battle,

Bragging and laughing that under his wrist is the pulse, and under his ribs the heart of the people,
Laughing!

Laughing the stormy, husky, brawling laughter of Youth, half-naked, sweating, proud to be Hog Butcher, Tool Maker, Stacker of Wheat, Player with Railroads and Freight Handler to the Nation.

Lesson 4

1. Read the Robert Frost poems. Robert Frost is a very well-known poet born in 1874.
2. Find one word you don't know and write it and its definition.
3. Do you see a common thread in his poems? What is in all of his poems? (Answers)

The Pasture

I'm going out to clean the pasture spring;
I'll only stop to rake the leaves away
(And wait to watch the water clear, I may):
I sha'n't be gone long.--You come too.
I'm going out to fetch the little calf
That's standing by the mother. It's so young,
It totters when she licks it with her tongue.
I sha'n't be gone long.--You come too.

Going for Water

The well was dry beside the door,
    And so we went with pail and can
Across the fields behind the house
    To seek the brook if still it ran;
Not loth to have excuse to go,
    Because the autumn eve was fair
(Though chill), because the fields were ours,
    And by the brook our woods were there.
We ran as if to meet the moon
    That slowly dawned behind the trees,
The barren boughs without the leaves,
    Without the birds, without the breeze.
But once within the wood, we paused
    Like gnomes that hid us from the moon,
Ready to run to hiding new
    With laughter when she found us soon.
Each laid on other a staying hand
    To listen ere we dared to look,
And in the hush we joined to make
    We heard, we knew we heard the brook.
A note as from a single place,
    A slender tinkling fall that made
Now drops that floated on the pool
    Like pearls, and now a silver blade.

Fire and Ice

Some say the world will end in fire,
Some say in ice.
From what I've tasted of desire
I hold with those who favor fire.

11

But if I had to perish twice,
I think I know enough of hate
To say that for destruction ice
Is also great
And would suffice.

Good-by and Keep Cold
This saying good-by on the edge of the dark
And cold to an orchard so young in the bark
Reminds me of all that can happen to harm
An orchard away at the end of the farm
All winter, cut off by a hill from the house.
I don't want it girdled by rabbit and mouse,
I don't want it dreamily nibbled for browse
By deer, and I don't want it budded by grouse.
(If certain it wouldn't be idle to call
I'd summon grouse, rabbit, and deer to the wall
And warn them away with a stick for a gun.)
I don't want it stirred by the heat of the sun.
(We made it secure against being, I hope,
By setting it out on a northerly slope.)
No orchard's the worse for the wintriest storm;
But one thing about it, it mustn't get warm.
"How often already you've had to be told,
Keep cold, young orchard. Good-by and keep cold.
Dread fifty above more than fifty below."
I have to be gone for a season or so.
My business awhile is with different trees,
Less carefully nourished, less fruitful than these,
And such as is done to their wood with an ax
Maples and birches and tamaracks.
I wish I could promise to lie in the night
And think of an orchard's arboreal plight
When slowly (and nobody comes with a light)
Its heart sinks lower under the sod.
But something has to be left to God.

The Runaway
Once when the snow of the year was beginning to fall,
We stopped by a mountain pasture to say 'Whose colt?'
A little Morgan had one forefoot on the wall,

The other curled at his breast. He dipped his head
And snorted at us. And then he had to bolt.
We heard the miniature thunder where he fled,
And we saw him, or thought we saw him, dim and grey,
Like a shadow against the curtain of falling flakes.
'I think the little fellow's afraid of the snow.
He isn't winter-broken. It isn't play
With the little fellow at all. He's running away.
I doubt if even his mother could tell him, "Sakes,
It's only weather". He'd think she didn't know!
Where is his mother? He can't be out alone.'
And now he comes again with a clatter of stone
And mounts the wall again with whited eyes
And all his tail that isn't hair up straight.
He shudders his coat as if to throw off flies.
'Whoever it is that leaves him out so late,
When other creatures have gone to stall and bin,
Ought to be told to come and take him in.'

Lesson 5

1. The Robert Frost poem "The Road Not Taken" is his most famous.
2. What is he talking about in this poem?
3. After reading the poem, read the summary below about the poem. Do you think you were right about what you thought the poem was about? Why or why not?
    - The speaker stands in the woods, considering a fork in the road. Both ways are equally worn and equally overlaid with un-trodden leaves. The speaker chooses one, telling himself that he will take the other another day. Yet he knows it is unlikely that he will have the opportunity to do so. And he admits that someday in the future he will recreate the scene with a slight twist: He will claim that he took the less-traveled road.
    (from sparknotes.com/poetry/frost/section7.rhtml)

    The Road Not Taken
    Two roads diverged in a yellow wood,
    And sorry I could not travel both
    And be one traveler, long I stood
    And looked down one as far as I could
    To where it bent in the undergrowth;

    Then took the other, as just as fair,

And having perhaps the better claim,
Because it was grassy and wanted wear;
Though as for that the passing there
Had worn them really about the same,

And both that morning equally lay
In leaves no step had trodden black.
Oh, I kept the first for another day!
Yet knowing how way leads on to way,
I doubted if I should ever come back.

I shall be telling this with a sigh
Somewhere ages and ages hence:
Two roads diverged in a wood, and I -
I took the one less traveled by
And that has made all the difference.

Lesson 6

1. Read these Robert Frost poems.
2. Write the new vocabulary words: **foliage, flecked, knoll**.
3. Look the words up and write their definitions. (Answers)

Vocabulary

1. Read over your vocabulary words and definitions from last week. Then read quotes with these words in them.
2. "Halloo your name to the reverberate hills,
   And make the babbling gossip of the air
   Cry out 'Olivia!'" Shakespeare (He's saying to call out her name and listen to it echo.)
3. "If in this wide world, teeming with abundant supplies for human want, to thousands of wretched creatures no choice is open, save between starvation and sin, may we not justly say that there is something utterly wrong in the system that permits such things to be?" Tennessee Clafin (He's saying that it's wrong that there are those with nothing when there is so much available.)

A Patch of Old Snow
There's a patch of old snow in a corner
That I should have guessed
Was a blow-away paper the rain
Had brought to rest.

It is speckled with grime as if
Small print overspread it,
The news of a day I've forgotten
If I ever read it.

The Telephone
"When I was just as far as I could walk
From here today,
There was an hour
All still
When leaning with my head against a flower
I heard you talk.
Don't say I didn't, for I heard you say--
You spoke from that flower on the windowsill--
Do you remember what it was you said?"

"First tell me what it was you thought you heard."

"Having found the flower and driven a bee away,
I leaned my head,
And holding by the stalk,
I listened and I thought I caught the word--
What was it? Did you call me by my name?
Or did you say--
Someone said 'Come'--I heard it as I bowed."

"I may have thought as much, but not aloud."
"Well, so I came."

Hyla Brook
By June our brook's run out of song and speed.
Sought for much after that, it will be found
Either to have gone groping underground
(And taken with it all the Hyla breed
That shouted in the mist a month ago,
Like ghost of sleigh-bells in a ghost of snow)
Or flourished and come up in jewel-weed,
Weak foliage that is blown upon and bent

Even against the way its waters went.
Its bed is left a faded paper sheet
Of dead leaves stuck together by the heat
A brook to none but who remember long.
This as it will be seen is other far
Than with brooks taken otherwhere in song.
We love the things we love for what they are.

The Oven Bird

There is a singer everyone has heard,
Loud, a mid-summer and a mid-wood bird,
Who makes the solid tree trunks sound again.
He says that leaves are old and that for flowers
Mid-summer is to spring as one to ten.
He says the early petal-fall is past
When pear and cherry bloom went down in showers
On sunny days a moment overcast;
And comes that other fall we name the fall.
He says the highway dust is over all.
The bird would cease and be as other birds
But that he knows in singing not to sing.
The question that he frames in all but words
Is what to make of a diminished thing.

Birches

When I see birches bend to left and right
Across the lines of straighter darker trees,
I like to think some boy's been swinging them.
But swinging doesn't bend them down to stay.
Ice-storms do that. Often you must have seen them
Loaded with ice a sunny winter morning
After a rain. They click upon themselves
As the breeze rises, and turn many-coloured
As the stir cracks and crazes their enamel.
Soon the sun's warmth makes them shed crystal shells
Shattering and avalanching on the snow-crust--
Such heaps of broken glass to sweep away
You'd think the inner dome of heaven had fallen.
They are dragged to the withered bracken by the load,
And they seem not to break; though once they are bowed
So low for long, they never right themselves:
You may see their trunks arching in the woods
Years afterwards, trailing their leaves on the ground,

Like girls on hands and knees that throw their hair
Before them over their heads to dry in the sun.
But I was going to say when Truth broke in
With all her matter-of-fact about the ice-storm,
I should prefer to have some boy bend them
As he went out and in to fetch the cows--
Some boy too far from town to learn baseball,
Whose only play was what he found himself,
Summer or winter, and could play alone.
One by one he subdued his father's trees
By riding them down over and over again
Until he took the stiffness out of them,
And not one but hung limp, not one was left
For him to conquer. He learned all there was
To learn about not launching out too soon
And so not carrying the tree away
Clear to the ground. He always kept his poise
To the top branches, climbing carefully
With the same pains you use to fill a cup
Up to the brim, and even above the brim.
Then he flung outward, feet first, with a swish,
Kicking his way down through the air to the ground.
So was I once myself a swinger of birches.
And so I dream of going back to be.
It's when I'm weary of considerations,
And life is too much like a pathless wood
Where your face burns and tickles with the cobwebs
Broken across it, and one eye is weeping
From a twig's having lashed across it open.
I'd like to get away from earth awhile
And then come back to it and begin over.
May no fate willfully misunderstand me
And half grant what I wish and snatch me away
Not to return. Earth's the right place for love:
I don't know where it's likely to go better.
I'd like to go by climbing a birch tree
And climb black branches up a snow-white trunk
Toward heaven, till the tree could bear no more,
But dipped its top and set me down again.
That would be good both going and coming back.
One could do worse than be a swinger of birches.

The Cow in Apple Time
Something inspires the only cow of late

To make no more of a wall than an open gate,
And think no more of wall-builders than fools.
Her face is flecked with pomace and she drools
A cider syrup. Having tasted fruit,
She scorns a pasture withering to the root.
She runs from tree to tree where lie and sweeten
The windfalls spiked with stubble and worm-eaten.
She leaves them bitten when she has to fly.
She bellows on a knoll against the sky.
Her udder shrivels and the milk goes dry.

Lesson 7

1. Write **miscellany, interposed, tumultuous, keen, subdue, dilating, sanctify**. Look up the words and write their definitions. (Answers)
2. Read the Robert Frost poems.
3. In the poem "Stars," the poet mentions Minerva. She's a Roman goddess. Talking about her "marble eyes" means he's talking about a statue that's supposed to be her.
4. Pick two of the poems you read today and tell or write about what they mean.

A Girl's Garden

A neighbor of mine in the village
    Likes to tell how one spring
When she was a girl on the farm, she did
    A childlike thing.

One day she asked her father
    To give her a garden plot
To plant and tend and reap herself,
    And he said, "Why not?"

In casting about for a corner
    He thought of an idle bit
Of walled-off ground where a shop had stood,
    And he said, "Just it."

And he said, "That ought to make you
    An ideal one-girl farm,
And give you a chance to put some strength
    On your slim-jim arm."

It was not enough of a garden,
    Her father said, to plough;
So she had to work it all by hand,

But she don't mind now.

She wheeled the dung in the wheelbarrow
　　Along a stretch of road;
But she always ran away and left
　　Her not-nice load

And hid from anyone passing.
　　And then she begged the seed.
She says she thinks she planted one
　　Of all things but weed.

A hill each of potatoes,
　　Radishes, lettuce, peas,
Tomatoes, beets, beans, pumpkins, corn,
　　And even fruit trees

And yes, she has long mistrusted
　　That a cider apple tree
In bearing there to-day is hers,
　　Or at least may be.

Her crop was a miscellany
　　When all was said and done,
A little bit of everything,
　　A great deal of none.

Now when she sees in the village
　　How village things go,
Just when it seems to come in right,
　　She says, "I know!

It's as when I was a farmer--"
　　Oh, never by way of advice!
And she never sins by telling the tale
　　To the same person twice.

The Exposed Nest
You were forever finding some new play.
So when I saw you down on hands and knees
In the meadow, busy with the new-cut hay,
Trying, I thought, to set it up on end,
I went to show you how to make it stay,
If that was your idea, against the breeze,
And, if you asked me, even help pretend
To make it root again and grow afresh.
But 'twas no make-believe with you to-day,
Nor was the grass itself your real concern,

19

Though I found your hand full of wilted fern,
Steel-bright June-grass, and blackening heads of clover.
'Twas a nest full of young birds on the ground
The cutter-bar had just gone champing over
(Miraculously without tasting flesh)
And left defenseless to the heat and light.
You wanted to restore them to their right
Of something interposed between their sight
And too much world at once--could means be found.
The way the nest-full every time we stirred
Stood up to us as to a mother-bird
Whose coming home has been too long deferred,
Made me ask would the mother-bird return
And care for them in such a change of scene
And might our meddling make her more afraid.
That was a thing we could not wait to learn.
We saw the risk we took in doing good,
But dared not spare to do the best we could
Though harm should come of it; so built the screen
You had begun, and gave them back their shade.
All this to prove we cared. Why is there then
No more to tell? We turned to other things.
I haven't any memory--have you?--
Of ever coming to the place again
To see if the birds lived the first night through,
And so at last to learn to use their wings.

Stars
How countlessly they congregate
    O'er our tumultuous snow,
Which flows in shapes as tall as trees
    When wintry winds do blow!--

As if with keenness for our fate,
    Our faltering few steps on
To white rest, and a place of rest
    Invisible at dawn,--

And yet with neither love nor hate,
    Those stars like some snow-white
Minerva's snow-white marble eyes
    Without the gift of sight.

Storm Fear
When the wind works against us in the dark,
And pelts with snow
The lowest chamber window on the east,
And whispers with a sort of stifled bark,
The beast,
'Come out! Come out!'--
It costs no inward struggle not to go,
Ah, no!
I count our strength,
Two and a child,
Those of us not asleep subdued to mark
How the cold creeps as the fire dies at length,--
How drifts are piled,
Dooryard and road ungraded,
Till even the comforting barn grows far away
And my heart owns a doubt
Whether 'tis in us to arise with day
And save ourselves unaided.

A Prayer in Spring
Oh, give us pleasure in the flowers to-day;
And give us not to think so far away
As the uncertain harvest; keep us here
All simply in the springing of the year.

Oh, give us pleasure in the orchard white,
Like nothing else by day, like ghosts by night;
And make us happy in the happy bees,
The swarm dilating round the perfect trees.

And make us happy in the darting bird
That suddenly above the bees is heard,
The meteor that thrusts in with needle bill,
And off a blossom in mid air stands still.

For this is love and nothing else is love,
The which it is reserved for God above
To sanctify to what far ends He will,
But which it only needs that we fulfil.

Lesson 8

1. Write **russet, profane (profanation), peck, acquainted, luminary**.
2. Write their definitions. Look up any of these words you don't know. (Answers)
3. Read the Robert Frost poems.
4. Pick two of the poems you read today and tell or write about what they mean.

Vocabulary

1. Match the words to their definitions. Write the letters and numbers of the matches on a separate piece of paper.

1. to be full	A. reverberating
2. understand	B. miscellany
3. echoing	C. tumultuous
4. increasing	D. furrows
5. knobby	E. cumulative
6. the path of a flying object	F. gnarled
7. rut or trench	G. keen
8. marked or dotted with color	H. knoll
9. small hill	I. fathom
10. a collection of different items	J. interposed
11. interruption between two things	K. teeming
12. disorderly, loud and confused noise	L. flecked
13. eagerness, interest in	M. dilating
14. bring under control	N. trajectory
15. make or become wider, larger	O. subdue

After Apple-picking
My long two-pointed ladder's sticking through a tree
Toward heaven still,
And there's a barrel that I didn't fill
Beside it, and there may be two or three
Apples I didn't pick upon some bough.
But I am done with apple-picking now.

Essence of winter sleep is on the night,
The scent of apples: I am drowsing off.
I cannot rub the strangeness from my sight
I got from looking through a pane of glass
I skimmed this morning from the drinking trough
And held against the world of hoary grass.
It melted, and I let it fall and break.
But I was well
Upon my way to sleep before it fell,
And I could tell
What form my dreaming was about to take.
Magnified apples appear and disappear,
Stem end and blossom end,
And every fleck of russet showing clear.
My instep arch not only keeps the ache,
It keeps the pressure of a ladder-round.
I feel the ladder sway as the boughs bend.
And I keep hearing from the cellar bin
The rumbling sound
Of load on load of apples coming in.
For I have had too much
Of apple-picking: I am overtired
Of the great harvest I myself desired.
There were ten thousand thousand fruit to touch,
Cherish in hand, lift down, and not let fall.
For all
That struck the earth,
No matter if not bruised or spiked with stubble,
Went surely to the cider-apple heap
As of no worth.
One can see what will trouble
This sleep of mine, whatever sleep it is.
Were he not gone,
The woodchuck could say whether it's like his
Long sleep, as I describe its coming on,
Or just some human sleep.

Good Hours
I had for my winter evening walk--
No one at all with whom to talk,

But I had the cottages in a row
Up to their shining eyes in snow.
And I thought I had the folk within:
I had the sound of a violin;
I had a glimpse through curtain laces
Of youthful forms and youthful faces.
I had such company outward bound.
I went till there were no cottages found.
I turned and repented, but coming back
I saw no window but that was black.
Over the snow my creaking feet
Disturbed the slumbering village street
Like profanation, by your leave,
At ten o'clock of a winter eve.

Gathering Leaves
Spades take up leaves
No better than spoons,
And bags full of leaves
Are light as balloons.
I make a great noise
Of rustling all day
Like rabbit and deer
Running away.
But the mountains I raise
Elude my embrace,
Flowing over my arms
And into my face.
I may load and unload
Again and again
Till I fill the whole shed,
And what have I then?
Next to nothing for weight,
And since they grew duller
From contact with earth,
Next to nothing for color.
Next to nothing for use.
But a crop is a crop,
And who's to say where
The harvest shall stop?

For Once, Then, Something
Others taught me with having knelt at well-curbs
Always wrong to the light, so never seeing
Deeper down in the well than where the water
Gives me back in a shining surface picture
Me myself in the summer heaven godlike
Looking out of a wreath of fern and cloud puffs.
Once, when trying with chin against a well-curb,
I discerned, as I thought, beyond the picture,
Through the picture, a something white, uncertain,
Something more of the depths--and then I lost it.
Water came to rebuke the too clear water.
One drop fell from a fern, and lo, a ripple
Shook whatever it was lay there at bottom,
Blurred it, blotted it out. What was that whiteness?
Truth? A pebble of quartz? For once, then, something.

Now Close the Windows
Now close the windows and hush all the fields:
If the trees must, let them silently toss;
No bird is singing now, and if there is,
Be it my loss.
It will be long ere the marshes resume,
I will be long ere the earliest bird:
So close the windows and not hear the wind,
But see all wind-stirred.

Stopping by Woods on a Snowy Evening
Whose woods these are I think I know.
His house is in the village though;
He will not see me stopping here
To watch his woods fill up with snow.

My little horse must think it queer
To stop without a farmhouse near
Between the woods and frozen lake
The darkest evening of the year.

He gives his harness bells a shake
To ask if there is some mistake.
The only other sound's the sweep
Of easy wind and downy flake.

The woods are lovely, dark and deep,
But I have promises to keep,
And miles to go before I sleep,
And miles to go before I sleep.

Lesson 9

1. Write **rued, diffuse, agitated, fragmentary**. If you notice them while you are reading, use the context to try to figure out their meanings.
2. Read the Robert Frost poems. One word you'll come across is phoebe.
   - Here's a phoebe.

3. The poem "Mending Wall" ends with "Good fences make good neighbors." This is a common expression. What does it mean? Write your answer in a complete sentence in your notebook. To answer with a complete sentence you need to include the question. Example: The expression "good fences make good neighbors" means....
4. "To rue the day" is another common expression. What do you think it means? Remember to write your answer in a complete sentence.
5. Which poem is your favorite? Why? Tell or write your answer.

Vocabulary

1. Review your vocabulary from Lesson 8.

Dust of Snow

The way a crow
Shook down on me
The dust of snow
From a hemlock tree

Has given my heart
A change of mood
And saved some part
Of a day I had rued.

Mending Wall

Something there is that doesn't love a wall,
That sends the frozen-ground-swell under it,
And spills the upper boulders in the sun;
And makes gaps even two can pass abreast.
The work of hunters is another thing:
I have come after them and made repair
Where they have left not one stone on a stone,
But they would have the rabbit out of hiding,
To please the yelping dogs. The gaps I mean,
No one has seen them made or heard them made,
But at spring mending-time we find them there.
I let my neighbour know beyond the hill;
And on a day we meet to walk the line
And set the wall between us once again.
We keep the wall between us as we go.
To each the boulders that have fallen to each.
And some are loaves and some so nearly balls
We have to use a spell to make them balance:
"Stay where you are until our backs are turned!"
We wear our fingers rough with handling them.
Oh, just another kind of out-door game,
One on a side. It comes to little more:
There where it is we do not need the wall:
He is all pine and I am apple orchard.
My apple trees will never get across
And eat the cones under his pines, I tell him.
He only says, "Good fences make good neighbours."
Spring is the mischief in me, and I wonder
If I could put a notion in his head:

"Why do they make good neighbours? Isn't it
Where there are cows? But here there are no cows.
Before I built a wall I'd ask to know
What I was walling in or walling out,
And to whom I was like to give offence.
Something there is that doesn't love a wall,
That wants it down." I could say "Elves" to him,
But it's not elves exactly, and I'd rather
He said it for himself. I see him there
Bringing a stone grasped firmly by the top
In each hand, like an old-stone savage armed.
He moves in darkness as it seems to me,
Not of woods only and the shade of trees.
He will not go behind his father's saying,
And he likes having thought of it so well
He says again, "Good fences make good neighbours."

In Hardwood Groves

The same leaves over and over again!
They fall from giving shade above
To make one texture of faded brown
And fit the earth like a leather glove.

Before the leaves can mount again
To fill the trees with another shade,
They must go down past things coming up.
They must go down into the dark decayed.

They must be pierced by flowers and put
Beneath the feet of dancing flowers.
However it is in some other world
I know that this is way in ours.

Revelation

We make ourselves a place apart
    Behind light words that tease and flout,
But oh, the agitated heart
    Till someone find us really out.

'Tis pity if the case require
    (Or so we say) that in the end
We speak the literal to inspire

The understanding of a friend.

But so with all, from babes that play
    At hide-and-seek to God afar,
So all who hide too well away
    Must speak and tell us where they are.

Fragmentary Blue

Why make so much of fragmentary blue
In here and there a bird, or butterfly,
Or flower, or wearing-stone, or open eye,
When heaven presents in sheets the solid hue?

Since earth is earth, perhaps, not heaven (as yet)--
Though some savants make earth include the sky;
And blue so far above us comes so high,
It only gives our wish for blue a whet.

The Need of Being Versed in Country Things

The house had gone to bring again
To the midnight sky a sunset glow.
Now the chimney was all of the house that stood,
Like a pistil after the petals go

The barn opposed across the way,
That would have joined the house in flame
Had it been the will of the wind, was left
To bear forsaken the place's name.

No more it opened with all one end
For teams that came by the stony road
To drum on the floor with scurrying hoofs
And brush the mow with the summer load.

The birds that came to it through the air
At broken windows flew out and in,
Their murmur more like the sigh we sigh
From too much dwelling on what has been.

Yet for them the lilac renewed its leaf,
And the aged elm, though touched with fire;
And the dry pump flung up an awkward arm;
And the fence post carried a strand of wire.

For them there was really nothing sad.

But though they rejoiced in the nest they kept,
One had to be versed in country things
Not to believe the phoebes wept.

Lesson 10

1. Read Robert Frost's poem "Nothing Gold Can Stay."
2. What three things does he mention that were gold? (Answers)
3. What happens/ed to each of these that the gold went away? (Answers)
4. What is the mood of this poem? Happy, sad, etc. (Answers)
5. What does this poem tell you about Robert Frost as a person? (Answers)

Vocabulary

1. Match the words to their definitions. Write the letters and numbers of the matches on a separate piece of paper.

1. acquainted	A. set apart or declare holy
2. agitated	B. an amount of food, strike with a beak, light kiss
3. diffuse	C. bitterly regret
4. fragmentary	D. degrade, desecrate
5. luminary	E. spread or cause to spread over a wide area
6. peck	F. to come to know, have a fair knowledge of
7. profane	G. redish brown color, rustic
8. rued	H. artificial light, someone who inspires
9. russet	I. consisting of small parts, incomplete
10. sanctify	J. feeling troubled

Nothing Gold Can Stay
Nature's first green is gold,
Her hardest hue to hold.
Her early leaf's a flower;
But only so an hour.

Then leaf subsides to leaf.
So Eden sank to grief,
So dawn goes down to day.
Nothing gold can stay.

Lesson 11

1. Your first book this year is by a very famous author, Rudyard Kipling. He was born in 1865 in British-controlled India. He was the youngest ever recipient of the Nobel Prize in Literature and the first Englishman to be awarded the honor. He's famous for his poems, short stories and novels. He says the foundations of his literary career began in his youth when he was sent away to England to live with a family that boarded children. He was treated cruelly there. At sixteen he returned to India, and England left him, and all the memories of his early years in India flooded back to him.

2. Read these selections from a review of *The Jungle Book*. What does the review say about Kipling's view of humankind? (Answers)

3. The book is a collection of stories. Our hero is Mowgli who was raised by a pack of wolves. Can you relate these stories, especially the first described below, to his childhood?

4. "After Mowgli left his Wolf Pack, he visited a Human village and was adopted by Messua and her husband, who both believed him their own son, previously stolen by a tiger. They teach him Human customs and language and help him adjust to a new life. However, the wolf-boy Mowgli hears from Grey Brother (a wolf) that trouble is afoot against him. Mowgli does not succeed in the Human village, but makes enemies of a hunter, a priest, and others, because he denounces their unrealistic comments about the jungle and its animals. For this, he is reduced to the status of cowherd. This story suggests that perhaps the animals are more just than Humans.

    "Other favorites from this collection are 'The White Seal', the tale of a Bering Sea's seal pup that saves 1000s of his kindred from the fur trade, and 'Her Majesty's Servants', a story of the conversations heard by a man among the camp animals of the Queen's military. The entire collection observes mankind from a stance of needing improvement that is possible if they listen to animal wisdom."
    (from http://classiclit.about.com/od/junglebookkipling/fr/bl_junglebook.htm)

5. A little more background information before you begin the book: "India is an eastern country north of the Indian Ocean. At the time these stories were written, India was an English Colony. In the story, there are references to white men. At that time, virtually all the white people in India were British military men or diplomats and were viewed as people with power and greater technology. The people living in the native villages had

brown skin. India is no longer a colony, and that distinction is long outdated." (from classical-childrens-books.com/jungle-book-unit-study.html)

Lesson 12
1. Read the first part of the first chapter, "Mowgli's Brothers."
2. What is jungle law? Can you name some of its rules?
    (Questions adapted from classical-childrens-books.com/jungle-book-unit-study.html)

> Now Rann the Kite brings home the night
> That Mang the Bat sets free--
> The herds are shut in byre and hut
> For loosed till dawn are we.
> This is the hour of pride and power,
> Talon and tush and claw.
> Oh, hear the call!--Good hunting all
> That keep the Jungle Law!
> -Night-Song in the Jungle

It was seven o'clock of a very warm evening in the Seeonee hills when Father Wolf woke up from his day's rest, scratched himself, yawned, and spread out his paws one after the other to get rid of the sleepy feeling in their tips. Mother Wolf lay with her big gray nose dropped across her four tumbling, squealing cubs, and the moon shone into the mouth of the cave where they all lived. "Augrh!" said Father Wolf. "It is time to hunt again." He was going to spring down hill when a little shadow with a bushy tail crossed the threshold and whined: "Good luck go with you, O Chief of the Wolves. And good luck and strong white teeth go with noble children that they may never forget the hungry in this world."

It was the jackal--Tabaqui, the Dish-licker--and the wolves of India despise Tabaqui because he runs about making mischief, and telling tales, and eating rags and pieces of leather from the village rubbish-heaps. But they are afraid of him too, because Tabaqui, more than anyone else in the jungle, is apt to go mad, and then he forgets that he was ever afraid of anyone, and runs through the forest biting everything in his way. Even the tiger runs and hides when little Tabaqui goes mad, for madness is the most disgraceful thing that can overtake a wild creature. We call it hydrophobia, but they call it dewanee--the madness--and run.

"Enter, then, and look," said Father Wolf stiffly, "but there is no food here."

"For a wolf, no," said Tabaqui, "but for so mean a person as myself a dry bone is a good feast. Who are we, the Gidur-log [the jackal people], to pick and choose?" He scuttled to the back of the cave, where he found the bone of a buck with some meat on it, and sat cracking the end merrily.

"All thanks for this good meal," he said, licking his lips. "How beautiful are the noble children! How large are their eyes! And so young too! Indeed, indeed, I might have remembered that the children of kings are men from the beginning."

Now, Tabaqui knew as well as anyone else that there is nothing so unlucky as to compliment children to their faces. It pleased him to see Mother and Father Wolf look uncomfortable.

Tabaqui sat still, rejoicing in the mischief that he had made, and then he said spitefully:

"Shere Khan, the Big One, has shifted his hunting grounds. He will hunt among these hills for the next moon, so he has told me."

Shere Khan was the tiger who lived near the Waingunga River, twenty miles away.

"He has no right!" Father Wolf began angrily--"By the Law of the Jungle he has no right to change his quarters without due warning. He will frighten every head of game within ten miles, and I--I have to kill for two, these days."

"His mother did not call him Lungri [the Lame One] for nothing," said Mother Wolf quietly. "He has been lame in one foot from his birth. That is why he has only killed cattle. Now the villagers of the Waingunga are angry with him, and he has come here to make our villagers angry. They will scour the jungle for him when he is far away, and we and our children must run when the grass is set alight. Indeed, we are very grateful to Shere Khan!"

"Shall I tell him of your gratitude?" said Tabaqui.

"Out!" snapped Father Wolf. "Out and hunt with thy master. Thou hast done harm enough for one night."

"I go," said Tabaqui quietly. "Ye can hear Shere Khan below in the thickets. I might have saved myself the message."

Father Wolf listened, and below in the valley that ran down to a little river he heard the dry, angry, snarly, singsong whine of a tiger who has caught nothing and does not care if all the jungle knows it.

"The fool!" said Father Wolf. "To begin a night's work with that noise! Does he think that our buck are like his fat Waingunga bullocks?"

"H'sh. It is neither bullock nor buck he hunts to-night," said Mother Wolf. "It is Man."

The whine had changed to a sort of humming purr that seemed to come from every quarter of the compass. It was the noise that bewilders woodcutters and gypsies sleeping in the open, and makes them run sometimes into the very mouth of the tiger.

"Man!" said Father Wolf, showing all his white teeth. "Faugh! Are there not enough beetles and frogs in the tanks that he must eat Man, and on our ground too!"

The Law of the Jungle, which never orders anything without a reason, forbids every beast to eat Man except when he is killing to show his children how to kill, and then he must hunt outside the hunting grounds of his pack or tribe. The real reason for this is that man-killing means, sooner or later, the arrival of white men on elephants, with guns, and hundreds of brown men with gongs and rockets and torches. Then everybody in the jungle suffers. The reason the beasts give among themselves is that Man is the weakest and most defenseless of all living things, and it is unsportsmanlike to touch him. They say too--and it is true--that man-eaters become mangy, and lose their teeth.

The purr grew louder, and ended in the full-throated "Aaarh!" of the tiger's charge.

Then there was a howl--an untigerish howl--from Shere Khan. "He has missed," said Mother Wolf. "What is it?"

Father Wolf ran out a few paces and heard Shere Khan muttering and mumbling savagely as he tumbled about in the scrub.

"The fool has had no more sense than to jump at a woodcutter's campfire, and has burned his feet," said Father Wolf with a grunt. "Tabaqui is with him."

"Something is coming uphill," said Mother Wolf, twitching one ear. "Get ready."

The bushes rustled a little in the thicket, and Father Wolf dropped with his haunches under him, ready for his leap. Then, if you had been watching, you would have seen the most wonderful thing in the world--the wolf checked in mid-spring. He made his bound before he saw what it was he was jumping at, and then he tried to stop himself. The result was that he shot up straight into the air for four or five feet, landing almost where he left ground.

"Man!" he snapped. "A man's cub. Look!"

Directly in front of him, holding on by a low branch, stood a naked brown baby who could just walk--as soft and as dimpled a little atom as ever came to a wolf's cave at night. He looked up into Father Wolf's face, and laughed.

"Is that a man's cub?" said Mother Wolf. "I have never seen one. Bring it here."

A Wolf accustomed to moving his own cubs can, if necessary, mouth an egg without breaking it, and though Father Wolf's jaws closed right on the child's back not a tooth even scratched the skin as he laid it down among the cubs.

"How little! How naked, and--how bold!" said Mother Wolf softly. The baby was pushing his way between the cubs to get close to the warm hide. "Ahai! He is taking his meal with the others. And so this is a man's cub. Now, was there ever a wolf that could boast of a man's cub among her children?"

"I have heard now and again of such a thing, but never in our Pack or in my time," said Father Wolf. "He is altogether without hair, and I could kill him with a touch of my foot. But see, he looks up and is not afraid."

The moonlight was blocked out of the mouth of the cave, for Shere Khan's great square head and shoulders were thrust into the entrance. Tabaqui, behind him, was squeaking: "My lord, my lord, it went in here!"

"Shere Khan does us great honor," said Father Wolf, but his eyes were very angry. "What does Shere Khan need?"

"My quarry. A man's cub went this way," said Shere Khan. "Its parents have run off. Give it to me."

Shere Khan had jumped at a woodcutter's campfire, as Father Wolf had said, and was furious from the pain of his burned feet. But Father Wolf knew that the mouth of the cave was too narrow for a tiger to come in by. Even where he was, Shere Khan's shoulders and forepaws were cramped for want of room, as a man's would be if he tried to fight in a barrel.

"The Wolves are a free people," said Father Wolf. "They take orders from the Head of the Pack, and not from any striped cattle-killer. The man's cub is ours--to kill if we choose."

"Ye choose and ye do not choose! What talk is this of choosing? By the bull that I killed, am I to stand nosing into your dog's den for my fair dues? It is I, Shere Khan, who speak!"

The tiger's roar filled the cave with thunder. Mother Wolf shook herself clear of the cubs and sprang forward, her eyes, like two green moons in the darkness, facing the blazing eyes of Shere Khan.

"And it is I, Raksha [The Demon], who answers. The man's cub is mine, Lungri--mine to me! He shall not be killed. He shall live to run with the Pack and to hunt with the Pack; and in the end, look you, hunter of little naked cubs--frog-eater--fish-killer--he shall hunt thee! Now get hence, or by the Sambhur that I killed (I eat no starved cattle), back thou goest to thy mother, burned beast of the jungle, lamer than ever thou camest into the world! Go!"

Father Wolf looked on amazed. He had almost forgotten the days when he won Mother Wolf in fair fight from five other wolves, when she ran in the Pack and was not called The Demon for compliment's sake. Shere Khan might have faced Father Wolf, but he could not stand up against Mother Wolf, for he knew that where he was she had all the advantage of the ground, and would fight to the death. So he backed out of the cave mouth growling, and when he was clear he shouted:

"Each dog barks in his own yard! We will see what the Pack will say to this fostering of man-cubs. The cub is mine, and to my teeth he will come in the end, O bush-tailed thieves!"

Mother Wolf threw herself down panting among the cubs, and Father Wolf said to her gravely:

"Shere Khan speaks this much truth. The cub must be shown to the Pack. Wilt thou still keep him, Mother?"

"Keep him!" she gasped. "He came naked, by night, alone and very hungry; yet he was not afraid! Look, he has pushed one of my babes to one side already. And that lame butcher would have killed him and would have run off to the Waingunga while the villagers here hunted through all our lairs in revenge! Keep him? Assuredly I will keep him. Lie still, little frog. O thou Mowgli--for Mowgli the Frog I will call thee--the time will come when thou wilt hunt Shere Khan as he has hunted thee."

"But what will our Pack say?" said Father Wolf.

The Law of the Jungle lays down very clearly that any wolf may, when he marries, withdraw from the Pack he belongs to. But as soon as his cubs are old enough to stand on their feet he must bring them to the Pack Council, which is generally held once a month at full moon, in order that the other wolves may identify them. After that inspection the cubs are free to run where they please, and until they have killed their first buck no excuse is accepted if a grown wolf of the Pack kills one of them. The punishment is death where the murderer can be found; and if you think for a minute you will see that this must be so.

Father Wolf waited till his cubs could run a little, and then on the night of the Pack Meeting took them and Mowgli and Mother Wolf to the Council Rock--a hilltop covered with stones and boulders where a hundred wolves could hide. Akela, the great gray Lone Wolf, who led all the Pack by strength and cunning, lay out at full length on his rock, and below him sat forty or more wolves of every size and color, from badger-colored veterans who could handle a buck alone to young black three-year-olds who thought they could. The Lone Wolf had led them for a year now. He had fallen twice into a wolf trap in his youth, and once he had been beaten and left for dead; so he knew the manners and customs of men. There was very little talking at the Rock. The cubs tumbled over each other in the center of the circle where their mothers and fathers sat, and now and again a senior wolf would go quietly up to a cub, look at him carefully, and return to his place on noiseless feet. Sometimes a mother would push her cub far out into the moonlight to be sure that he had not been overlooked. Akela from his rock would cry: "Ye know the Law--ye know the Law. Look well, O Wolves!" And the anxious mothers would take up the call: "Look--look well, O Wolves!"

At last--and Mother Wolf's neck bristles lifted as the time came--Father Wolf pushed "Mowgli the Frog," as they called him, into the center, where he sat laughing and playing with some pebbles that glistened in the moonlight.

Akela never raised his head from his paws, but went on with the monotonous cry: "Look well!" A muffled roar came up from behind the rocks--the voice of Shere Khan crying: "The cub is mine. Give him to me. What have the Free People to do with a man's cub?" Akela never even twitched his ears. All he said was: "Look well, O Wolves! What have the Free People to do with the orders of any save the Free People? Look well!"

There was a chorus of deep growls, and a young wolf in his fourth year flung back Shere Khan's question to Akela: "What have the Free People to do with a man's cub?" Now, the Law of the Jungle lays down that if there is any dispute as to the right of a cub to be accepted by the Pack, he must be spoken for by at least two members of the Pack who are not his father and mother.

"Who speaks for this cub?" said Akela. "Among the Free People who speaks?" There was no answer and Mother Wolf got ready for what she knew would be her last fight, if things came to fighting.

Then the only other creature who is allowed at the Pack Council--Baloo, the sleepy brown bear who teaches the wolf cubs the Law of the Jungle: old Baloo, who can come and go where he pleases because he eats only nuts and roots and honey--rose upon his hind quarters and grunted.

"The man's cub--the man's cub?" he said. "I speak for the man's cub. There is no harm in a man's cub. I have no gift of words, but I speak the truth. Let him run with the Pack, and be entered with the others. I myself will teach him."

"We need yet another," said Akela. "Baloo has spoken, and he is our teacher for the young cubs. Who speaks besides Baloo?"

A black shadow dropped down into the circle. It was Bagheera the Black Panther, inky black all over, but with the panther markings showing up in certain lights like the pattern of watered silk. Everybody knew Bagheera, and nobody cared to cross his path; for he was as cunning as Tabaqui, as bold as the wild buffalo, and as reckless as the wounded elephant. But he had a voice as soft as wild honey dripping from a tree, and a skin softer than down.

"O Akela, and ye the Free People," he purred, "I have no right in your assembly, but the Law of the Jungle says that if there is a doubt which is not a killing matter in regard to a new cub, the life of that cub may be bought at a price. And the Law does not say who may or may not pay that price. Am I right?"

"Good! Good!" said the young wolves, who are always hungry. "Listen to Bagheera. The cub can be bought for a price. It is the Law."

"Knowing that I have no right to speak here, I ask your leave."

"Speak then," cried twenty voices.

"To kill a naked cub is shame. Besides, he may make better sport for you when he is grown. Baloo has spoken in his behalf. Now to Baloo's word I will add one bull, and a fat one, newly killed, not half a mile from here, if ye will accept the man's cub according to the Law. Is it difficult?"

There was a clamor of scores of voices, saying: "What matter? He will die in the winter rains. He will scorch in the sun. What harm can a naked frog do us? Let him run with the Pack. Where is the bull, Bagheera? Let him be accepted." And then came Akela's deep bay, crying: "Look well--look well, O Wolves!"

Mowgli was still deeply interested in the pebbles, and he did not notice when the wolves came and looked at him one by one. At last they all went down the hill for the dead bull, and only Akela, Bagheera, Baloo, and Mowgli's own wolves were left. Shere Khan roared still in the night, for he was very angry that Mowgli had not been handed over to him.

"Ay, roar well," said Bagheera, under his whiskers, "for the time will come when this naked thing will make thee roar to another tune, or I know nothing of man."

"It was well done," said Akela. "Men and their cubs are very wise. He may be a help in time."

"Truly, a help in time of need; for none can hope to lead the Pack forever," said Bagheera.

Akela said nothing. He was thinking of the time that comes to every leader of every pack when his strength goes from him and he gets feebler and feebler, till at last he is killed by the wolves and a new leader comes up--to be killed in his turn.

"Take him away," he said to Father Wolf, "and train him as befits one of the Free People."

And that is how Mowgli was entered into the Seeonee Wolf Pack for the price of a bull and on Baloo's good word.

Lesson 13

1. Finish reading the chapter.
2. Compare human and jungle law.

Vocabulary

1. Review your vocabulary words by going to Lesson 8.

Now you must be content to skip ten or eleven whole years, and only guess at all the wonderful life that Mowgli led among the wolves, because if it were written out it would fill ever so many books. He grew up with the cubs, though they, of course, were grown wolves almost before he was a child. And Father Wolf taught him his business, and the meaning of things in the jungle, till every rustle in the grass, every breath of the warm night air, every note of the owls above his head, every scratch of a bat's claws as it roosted for a while in a tree, and every splash of every little fish jumping in a pool meant just as much to him as the work of his office means to a business man. When he was not learning he sat out in the sun and slept, and ate and went to sleep again. When he felt dirty or hot he swam in the forest pools; and when he wanted honey (Baloo told him that honey and nuts were just as pleasant to eat as raw meat) he climbed up for it, and that Bagheera showed him how to do. Bagheera would lie out on a branch and call, "Come along, Little Brother," and at first Mowgli would cling like the sloth, but afterward he would fling himself through the branches almost as boldly as the gray ape. He took his place at the Council Rock, too, when the Pack met, and there he discovered that if he stared hard at any wolf, the wolf would be forced to drop his eyes, and so he used to stare for fun. At other times he would pick the long thorns out of the pads of his friends, for wolves suffer terribly from thorns and burs in their coats. He would go down the hillside into the cultivated lands by night, and look very curiously at the villagers in their huts, but he had a mistrust of men because Bagheera showed him a square box with a drop gate so cunningly hidden in the jungle that he nearly walked into it, and told him that it was a trap. He loved better than anything else to go with Bagheera into the dark warm heart of the forest, to sleep all through the drowsy day, and at night see how Bagheera did his killing. Bagheera killed right and left as he felt hungry, and so did Mowgli--with one exception. As soon as he was old enough to understand things, Bagheera told him that he must never touch cattle because he had been bought into the Pack at the price of a bull's life. "All the jungle is thine," said Bagheera, "and thou canst kill everything that thou art strong enough to kill; but for the sake of the bull that bought thee thou must never kill or eat any cattle young or old. That is the Law of the Jungle." Mowgli obeyed faithfully.

And he grew and grew strong as a boy must grow who does not know that he is learning any lessons, and who has nothing in the world to think of except things to eat.

Mother Wolf told him once or twice that Shere Khan was not a creature to be trusted, and that some day he must kill Shere Khan. But though a young wolf would have remembered that advice every hour, Mowgli forgot it because he was only a boy--though he would have called himself a wolf if he had been able to speak in any human tongue.

Shere Khan was always crossing his path in the jungle, for as Akela grew older and feebler the lame tiger had come to be great friends with the younger wolves of the Pack, who followed him for scraps, a thing Akela would never have allowed if he had dared to push his authority to the proper bounds. Then Shere Khan would flatter them and wonder that such fine young hunters were content to be led by a dying wolf and a man's cub. "They tell me," Shere Khan would say, "that at Council ye dare not look him between the eyes." And the young wolves would growl and bristle.

Bagheera, who had eyes and ears everywhere, knew something of this, and once or twice he told Mowgli in so many words that Shere Khan would kill him some day. Mowgli would laugh and answer: "I have the Pack and I have thee; and Baloo, though he is so lazy, might strike a blow or two for my sake. Why should I be afraid?"

It was one very warm day that a new notion came to Bagheera--born of something that he had heard. Perhaps Ikki the Porcupine had told him; but he said to Mowgli when they were deep in the jungle, as the boy lay with his head on Bagheera's beautiful black skin, "Little Brother, how often have I told thee that Shere Khan is thy enemy?"

"As many times as there are nuts on that palm," said Mowgli, who, naturally, could not count. "What of it? I am sleepy, Bagheera, and Shere Khan is all long tail and loud talk--like Mao, the Peacock."

"But this is no time for sleeping. Baloo knows it; I know it; the Pack know it; and even the foolish, foolish deer know. Tabaqui has told thee too."

"Ho! ho!" said Mowgli. "Tabaqui came to me not long ago with some rude talk that I was a naked man's cub and not fit to dig pig-nuts. But I caught Tabaqui by the tail and swung him twice against a palm-tree to teach him better manners."

"That was foolishness, for though Tabaqui is a mischief-maker, he would have told thee of something that concerned thee closely. Open those eyes, Little Brother. Shere Khan dare not kill thee in the jungle. But remember, Akela is very old, and soon the day comes when he cannot kill his buck, and then he will be leader no more. Many of the wolves that looked thee over when thou wast brought to the Council first are old too, and the young wolves believe, as Shere Khan has taught them, that a man-cub has no place with the Pack. In a little time thou wilt be a man."

"And what is a man that he should not run with his brothers?" said Mowgli. "I was born in the jungle. I have obeyed the Law of the Jungle, and there is no wolf of ours from whose paws I have not pulled a thorn. Surely they are my brothers!"

Bagheera stretched himself at full length and half shut his eyes. "Little Brother," said he, "feel under my jaw."

Mowgli put up his strong brown hand, and just under Bagheera's silky chin, where the giant rolling muscles were all hid by the glossy hair, he came upon a little bald spot.

"There is no one in the jungle that knows that I, Bagheera, carry that mark--the mark of the collar; and yet, Little Brother, I was born among men, and it was among men that my mother died--in the cages of the king's palace at Oodeypore. It was because of this that I paid the price for thee at the Council when thou wast a little naked cub. Yes, I too was born among men. I had never seen the jungle. They fed me behind bars from an iron pan till one night I felt that I was Bagheera--the Panther--and no man's plaything, and I broke the silly lock with one blow of my paw and came away. And because I had learned the ways of men, I became more terrible in the jungle than Shere Khan. Is it not so?"

"Yes," said Mowgli, "all the jungle fear Bagheera--all except Mowgli."

"Oh, thou art a man's cub," said the Black Panther very tenderly. "And even as I returned to my jungle, so thou must go back to men at last--to the men who are thy brothers--if thou art not killed in the Council."

"But why--but why should any wish to kill me?" said Mowgli.

"Look at me," said Bagheera. And Mowgli looked at him steadily between the eyes. The big panther turned his head away in half a minute.

"That is why," he said, shifting his paw on the leaves. "Not even I can look thee between the eyes, and I was born among men, and I love thee, Little Brother. The others they hate thee because their eyes cannot meet thine; because thou art wise; because thou hast pulled out thorns from their feet--because thou art a man."

"I did not know these things," said Mowgli sullenly, and he frowned under his heavy black eyebrows.

"What is the Law of the Jungle? Strike first and then give tongue. By thy very carelessness they know that thou art a man. But be wise. It is in my heart that when Akela misses his next kill--and at each hunt it costs him more to pin the buck--the Pack will turn against him and against thee. They will hold a jungle Council at the Rock, and then--and then--I have it!" said Bagheera, leaping up. "Go thou down quickly to the men's huts in the valley, and take some of the Red Flower which they grow there, so that when the time comes thou mayest have even a stronger friend than I or Baloo or those of the Pack that love thee. Get the Red Flower."

By Red Flower Bagheera meant fire, only no creature in the jungle will call fire by its proper name. Every beast lives in deadly fear of it, and invents a hundred ways of describing it.

"The Red Flower?" said Mowgli. "That grows outside their huts in the twilight. I will get some."

"There speaks the man's cub," said Bagheera proudly. "Remember that it grows in little pots. Get one swiftly, and keep it by thee for time of need."

"Good!" said Mowgli. "I go. But art thou sure, O my Bagheera"--he slipped his arm around the splendid neck and looked deep into the big eyes--"art thou sure that all this is Shere Khan's doing?"

"By the Broken Lock that freed me, I am sure, Little Brother."

"Then, by the Bull that bought me, I will pay Shere Khan full tale for this, and it may be a little over," said Mowgli, and he bounded away.

"That is a man. That is all a man," said Bagheera to himself, lying down again. "Oh, Shere Khan, never was a blacker hunting than that frog-hunt of thine ten years ago!"

Mowgli was far and far through the forest, running hard, and his heart was hot in him. He came to the cave as the evening mist rose, and drew breath, and looked down the valley. The cubs were out, but Mother Wolf, at the back of the cave, knew by his breathing that something was troubling her frog.

"What is it, Son?" she said.

"Some bat's chatter of Shere Khan," he called back. "I hunt among the plowed fields tonight," and he plunged downward through the bushes, to the stream at the bottom of the valley. There he checked, for he heard the yell of the Pack hunting, heard the bellow of a hunted Sambhur, and the snort as the buck turned at bay. Then there were wicked, bitter howls from the young wolves: "Akela! Akela! Let the Lone Wolf show his strength. Room for the leader of the Pack! Spring, Akela!"

The Lone Wolf must have sprung and missed his hold, for Mowgli heard the snap of his teeth and then a yelp as the Sambhur knocked him over with his forefoot.

He did not wait for anything more, but dashed on; and the yells grew fainter behind him as he ran into the croplands where the villagers lived.

"Bagheera spoke truth," he panted, as he nestled down in some cattle fodder by the window of a hut. "To-morrow is one day both for Akela and for me."

Then he pressed his face close to the window and watched the fire on the hearth. He saw the husbandman's wife get up and feed it in the night with black lumps. And when the morning came and the mists were all white and cold, he saw the man's child pick up a wicker pot plastered inside with earth, fill it with lumps of red-hot charcoal, put it under his blanket, and go out to tend the cows in the byre.

"Is that all?" said Mowgli. "If a cub can do it, there is nothing to fear." So he strode round the corner and met the boy, took the pot from his hand, and disappeared into the mist while the boy howled with fear.

"They are very like me," said Mowgli, blowing into the pot as he had seen the woman do. "This thing will die if I do not give it things to eat"; and he dropped twigs and dried bark on the red stuff. Halfway up the hill he met Bagheera with the morning dew shining like moonstones on his coat.

"Akela has missed," said the Panther. "They would have killed him last night, but they needed thee also. They were looking for thee on the hill."

"I was among the plowed lands. I am ready. See!" Mowgli held up the fire-pot.

"Good! Now, I have seen men thrust a dry branch into that stuff, and presently the Red Flower blossomed at the end of it. Art thou not afraid?"

"No. Why should I fear? I remember now--if it is not a dream--how, before I was a Wolf, I lay beside the Red Flower, and it was warm and pleasant."

All that day Mowgli sat in the cave tending his fire pot and dipping dry branches into it to see how they looked. He found a branch that satisfied him, and in the evening when Tabaqui came to the cave and told him rudely enough that he was wanted at the Council Rock, he laughed till Tabaqui ran away. Then Mowgli went to the Council, still laughing.

Akela the Lone Wolf lay by the side of his rock as a sign that the leadership of the Pack was open, and Shere Khan with his following of scrap-fed wolves walked to and fro openly being flattered. Bagheera lay close to Mowgli, and the fire pot was between Mowgli's knees. When they were all gathered together, Shere Khan began to speak--a thing he would never have dared to do when Akela was in his prime.

"He has no right," whispered Bagheera. "Say so. He is a dog's son. He will be frightened."

Mowgli sprang to his feet. "Free People," he cried, "does Shere Khan lead the Pack? What has a tiger to do with our leadership?"

"Seeing that the leadership is yet open, and being asked to speak--" Shere Khan began.

"By whom?" said Mowgli. "Are we all jackals, to fawn on this cattle butcher? The leadership of the Pack is with the Pack alone."

There were yells of "Silence, thou man's cub!" "Let him speak. He has kept our Law"; and at last the seniors of the Pack thundered: "Let the Dead Wolf speak." When a leader of the Pack has missed his kill, he is called the Dead Wolf as long as he lives, which is not long.

Akela raised his old head wearily:--

"Free People, and ye too, jackals of Shere Khan, for twelve seasons I have led ye to and from the kill, and in all that time not one has been trapped or maimed. Now I have missed my kill. Ye know how that plot was made. Ye know how ye brought me up to an untried buck to make my weakness known. It was cleverly done. Your right is to kill me here on the Council Rock, now. Therefore, I ask, who comes to make an end of the Lone Wolf? For it is my right, by the Law of the Jungle, that ye come one by one."

There was a long hush, for no single wolf cared to fight Akela to the death. Then Shere Khan roared: "Bah! What have we to do with this toothless fool? He is doomed to die! It is the man-cub who has lived too long. Free People, he was my meat from the first. Give him to me. I am weary of this man-wolf folly. He has troubled the jungle for ten seasons. Give me the man-cub, or I will hunt here always, and not give you one bone. He is a man, a man's child, and from the marrow of my bones I hate him!"

Then more than half the Pack yelled: "A man! A man! What has a man to do with us? Let him go to his own place."

"And turn all the people of the villages against us?" clamored Shere Khan. "No, give him to me. He is a man, and none of us can look him between the eyes."

Akela lifted his head again and said, "He has eaten our food. He has slept with us. He has driven game for us. He has broken no word of the Law of the Jungle."

"Also, I paid for him with a bull when he was accepted. The worth of a bull is little, but Bagheera's honor is something that he will perhaps fight for," said Bagheera in his gentlest voice.

"A bull paid ten years ago!" the Pack snarled. "What do we care for bones ten years old?"

"Or for a pledge?" said Bagheera, his white teeth bared under his lip. "Well are ye called the Free People!"

"No man's cub can run with the people of the jungle," howled Shere Khan. "Give him to me!"

"He is our brother in all but blood," Akela went on, "and ye would kill him here! In truth, I have lived too long. Some of ye are eaters of cattle, and of others I have heard that, under Shere Khan's teaching, ye go by dark night and snatch children from the villager's doorstep. Therefore I know ye to be cowards, and it is to cowards I speak. It is certain that I must die, and my life is of no worth, or I would offer that in the man-cub's place. But for the sake of the Honor of the Pack,--a little matter that by being without a leader ye have forgotten,--I promise that if ye let the man-cub go to his own place, I will not, when my time comes to die, bare one tooth against ye. I will die without fighting. That will at least save the Pack three lives. More I cannot do; but if ye will, I can save ye the shame that comes of killing a brother against whom there is no fault--a brother spoken for and bought into the Pack according to the Law of the Jungle."

"He is a man--a man--a man!" snarled the Pack. And most of the wolves began to gather round Shere Khan, whose tail was beginning to switch.

"Now the business is in thy hands," said Bagheera to Mowgli. "We can do no more except fight." Mowgli stood upright--the fire pot in his hands. Then he stretched out his arms, and yawned in the face of the Council; but he was furious with rage and sorrow, for, wolflike, the wolves had never told him how they hated him. "Listen you!" he cried. "There is no need for this dog's jabber. Ye have told me so often tonight that I am a man (and indeed I would have been a wolf with you to my life's end) that I feel your words are true. So I do not call ye my brothers any more, but sag [dogs], as a man should. What ye will do, and what ye will not do, is not yours to say. That matter is with me; and that we may see the matter more plainly, I, the man, have brought here a little of the Red Flower which ye, dogs, fear."

He flung the fire pot on the ground, and some of the red coals lit a tuft of dried moss that flared up, as all the Council drew back in terror before the leaping flames.

Mowgli thrust his dead branch into the fire till the twigs lit and crackled, and whirled it above his head among the cowering wolves.

"Thou art the master," said Bagheera in an undertone. "Save Akela from the death. He was ever thy friend."

Akela, the grim old wolf who had never asked for mercy in his life, gave one piteous look at Mowgli as the boy stood all naked, his long black hair tossing over his shoulders in the light of the blazing branch that made the shadows jump and quiver.

"Good!" said Mowgli, staring round slowly. "I see that ye are dogs. I go from you to my own people--if they be my own people. The jungle is shut to me, and I must forget your talk and your companionship. But I will be more merciful than ye are. Because I was all but your brother in blood, I promise that when I am a man among men I will not betray ye to men as ye have betrayed me." He kicked the fire with his foot, and the sparks flew up. "There shall be no war between any of us in the Pack. But here is a debt to pay before I go." He strode forward to where Shere Khan sat blinking stupidly at the flames, and caught him by the tuft on his chin. Bagheera followed in case of accidents. "Up, dog!" Mowgli cried. "Up, when a man speaks, or I will set that coat ablaze!"

Shere Khan's ears lay flat back on his head, and he shut his eyes, for the blazing branch was very near.

"This cattle-killer said he would kill me in the Council because he had not killed me when I was a cub. Thus and thus, then, do we beat dogs when we are men. Stir a whisker, Lungri, and I ram the Red Flower down thy gullet!" He beat Shere Khan over the head with the branch, and the tiger whimpered and whined in an agony of fear.

"Pah! Singed jungle cat--go now! But remember when next I come to the Council Rock, as a man should come, it will be with Shere Khan's hide on my head. For the rest, Akela goes free to live as he pleases. Ye will not kill him, because that is not my will. Nor do I think that ye will sit here any longer, lolling out your tongues as though ye were somebodies, instead of dogs whom I drive out--thus! Go!" The fire was burning furiously at the end of the branch, and Mowgli struck right and left round the circle, and the wolves ran howling with the sparks burning their fur. At last there were only Akela, Bagheera, and perhaps ten wolves that had taken Mowgli's part. Then something began to hurt Mowgli inside him, as he had never been hurt in his life before, and he caught his breath and sobbed, and the tears ran down his face.

"What is it? What is it?" he said. "I do not wish to leave the jungle, and I do not know what this is. Am I dying, Bagheera?"

"No, Little Brother. That is only tears such as men use," said Bagheera. "Now I know thou art a man, and a man's cub no longer. The jungle is shut indeed to thee henceforward. Let them fall, Mowgli. They are only tears." So Mowgli sat and cried as though his heart would break; and he had never cried in all his life before.

"Now," he said, "I will go to men. But first I must say farewell to my mother." And he went to the cave where she lived with Father Wolf, and he cried on her coat, while the four cubs howled miserably.

"Ye will not forget me?" said Mowgli.

"Never while we can follow a trail," said the cubs. "Come to the foot of the hill when thou art a man, and we will talk to thee; and we will come into the croplands to play with thee by night."

"Come soon!" said Father Wolf. "Oh, wise little frog, come again soon; for we be old, thy mother and I."

"Come soon," said Mother Wolf, "little naked son of mine. For, listen, child of man, I loved thee more than ever I loved my cubs."

"I will surely come," said Mowgli. "And when I come it will be to lay out Shere Khan's hide upon the Council Rock. Do not forget me! Tell them in the jungle never to forget me!"

The dawn was beginning to break when Mowgli went down the hillside alone, to meet those mysterious things that are called men.

Lesson 14
1. Read the first part of "Kaa's Hunting."
2. Describe the Bandar log. How do they act toward others?

His spots are the joy of the Leopard: his horns are the Buffalo's pride.
Be clean, for the strength of the hunter is known by the gloss of his hide.
If ye find that the Bullock can toss you, or the heavy-browed Sambhur can gore;
Ye need not stop work to inform us: we knew it ten seasons before.
Oppress not the cubs of the stranger, but hail them as Sister and Brother,
For though they are little and fubsy, it may be the Bear is their mother.
"There is none like to me!" says the Cub in the pride of his earliest kill;
But the jungle is large and the Cub he is small. Let him think and be still.

-Maxims of Baloo

All that is told here happened some time before Mowgli was turned out of the Seeonee Wolf Pack, or revenged himself on Shere Khan the tiger. It was in the days when Baloo was teaching him the Law of the Jungle. The big, serious, old brown bear was delighted to have so quick a pupil, for the young wolves will only learn as much of the Law of the Jungle as applies to their own pack and tribe, and run away as soon as they can repeat the Hunting Verse --"Feet that make no noise; eyes that can see in the dark; ears that can hear the winds in their lairs, and sharp white teeth, all these things are the marks of our brothers except Tabaqui the Jackal and the Hyaena whom we hate." But Mowgli, as a man-cub, had to learn a great deal more than this. Sometimes Bagheera the Black Panther would come lounging through the jungle to see how his pet was getting on, and would purr with his head against a tree while Mowgli recited the day's lesson to Baloo. The boy could climb almost as well as he could swim, and swim almost as well as he could run. So Baloo, the Teacher of the Law, taught him the Wood and Water Laws: how to tell a rotten branch from a sound one; how to speak politely to the wild bees when he came upon a hive of them fifty feet above ground; what to say to Mang the Bat when he disturbed him in the branches at midday; and how to warn the water-snakes in the pools before he splashed down among them. None of the Jungle People like being disturbed, and all are very ready to fly at an intruder. Then, too, Mowgli was taught the Strangers' Hunting Call, which must be repeated aloud till it is answered, whenever one of the Jungle-People hunts outside his own grounds. It means, translated, "Give me leave to hunt here because I am hungry." And the answer is, "Hunt then for food, but not for pleasure."

All this will show you how much Mowgli had to learn by heart, and he grew very tired of saying the same thing over a hundred times. But, as Baloo said to Bagheera, one day when Mowgli had been cuffed and run off in a temper, "A man's cub is a man's cub, and he must learn all the Law of the Jungle."

"But think how small he is," said the Black Panther, who would have spoiled Mowgli if he had had his own way. "How can his little head carry all thy long talk?"

"Is there anything in the jungle too little to be killed? No. That is why I teach him these things, and that is why I hit him, very softly, when he forgets."

"Softly! What dost thou know of softness, old Iron-feet?" Bagheera grunted. "His face is all bruised today by thy--softness. Ugh."

"Better he should be bruised from head to foot by me who love him than that he should come to harm through ignorance," Baloo answered very earnestly. "I am now teaching him the Master Words of the Jungle that shall protect him with the birds and the Snake People, and all that hunt on four feet, except his own pack. He can now claim protection, if he will only remember the words, from all in the jungle. Is not that worth a little beating?"

"Well, look to it then that thou dost not kill the man-cub. He is no tree trunk to sharpen thy blunt claws upon. But what are those Master Words? I am more likely to give help than to ask it"--

Bagheera stretched out one paw and admired the steel-blue, ripping-chisel talons at the end of it-- "still I should like to know."

"I will call Mowgli and he shall say them--if he will. Come, Little Brother!"

"My head is ringing like a bee tree," said a sullen little voice over their heads, and Mowgli slid down a tree trunk very angry and indignant, adding as he reached the ground: "I come for Bagheera and not for thee, fat old Baloo!"

"That is all one to me," said Baloo, though he was hurt and grieved. "Tell Bagheera, then, the Master Words of the Jungle that I have taught thee this day."

"Master Words for which people?" said Mowgli, delighted to show off. "The jungle has many tongues. I know them all."

"A little thou knowest, but not much. See, O Bagheera, they never thank their teacher. Not one small wolfling has ever come back to thank old Baloo for his teachings. Say the word for the Hunting-People, then--great scholar."

"We be of one blood, ye and I," said Mowgli, giving the words the Bear accent which all the Hunting People use.

"Good. Now for the birds."

Mowgli repeated, with the Kite's whistle at the end of the sentence.

"Now for the Snake-People," said Bagheera.

The answer was a perfectly indescribable hiss, and Mowgli kicked up his feet behind, clapped his hands together to applaud himself, and jumped on to Bagheera's back, where he sat sideways, drumming with his heels on the glossy skin and making the worst faces he could think of at Baloo.

"There--there! That was worth a little bruise," said the brown bear tenderly. "Some day thou wilt remember me." Then he turned aside to tell Bagheera how he had begged the Master Words from Hathi the Wild Elephant, who knows all about these things, and how Hathi had taken Mowgli down to a pool to get the Snake Word from a water-snake, because Baloo could not pronounce it, and how Mowgli was now reasonably safe against all accidents in the jungle, because neither snake, bird, nor beast would hurt him.

"No one then is to be feared," Baloo wound up, patting his big furry stomach with pride.

"Except his own tribe," said Bagheera, under his breath; and then aloud to Mowgli, "Have a care for my ribs, Little Brother! What is all this dancing up and down?"

Mowgli had been trying to make himself heard by pulling at Bagheera's shoulder fur and kicking hard. When the two listened to him he was shouting at the top of his voice, "And so I shall have a tribe of my own, and lead them through the branches all day long."

"What is this new folly, little dreamer of dreams?" said Bagheera.

"Yes, and throw branches and dirt at old Baloo," Mowgli went on. "They have promised me this. Ah!"

"Whoof!" Baloo's big paw scooped Mowgli off Bagheera's back, and as the boy lay between the big fore-paws he could see the Bear was angry.

"Mowgli," said Baloo, "thou hast been talking with the Bandar-log--the Monkey People."

Mowgli looked at Bagheera to see if the Panther was angry too, and Bagheera's eyes were as hard as jade stones.

"Thou hast been with the Monkey People--the gray apes--the people without a law--the eaters of everything. That is great shame."

"When Baloo hurt my head," said Mowgli (he was still on his back), "I went away, and the gray apes came down from the trees and had pity on me. No one else cared." He snuffled a little.

"The pity of the Monkey People!" Baloo snorted. "The stillness of the mountain stream! The cool of the summer sun! And then, man-cub?"

"And then, and then, they gave me nuts and pleasant things to eat, and they--they carried me in their arms up to the top of the trees and said I was their blood brother except that I had no tail, and should be their leader some day."

"They have no leader," said Bagheera. "They lie. They have always lied."

"They were very kind and bade me come again. Why have I never been taken among the Monkey People? They stand on their feet as I do. They do not hit me with their hard paws. They play all day. Let me get up! Bad Baloo, let me up! I will play with them again."

"Listen, man-cub," said the Bear, and his voice rumbled like thunder on a hot night. "I have taught thee all the Law of the Jungle for all the peoples of the jungle--except the Monkey-Folk who live in the trees. They have no law. They are outcasts. They have no speech of their own, but use the stolen words which they overhear when they listen, and peep, and wait up above in the branches. Their way is not our way. They are without leaders. They have no remembrance. They boast and chatter and pretend that they are a great people about to do great affairs in the jungle, but the falling of a nut turns their minds to laughter and all is forgotten. We of the jungle have no dealings with them. We do not drink where the monkeys drink; we do not go where the monkeys go; we do not hunt where they hunt; we do not die where they die. Hast thou ever heard me speak of the Bandar-log till today?"

"No," said Mowgli in a whisper, for the forest was very still now Baloo had finished.

"The Jungle-People put them out of their mouths and out of their minds. They are very many, evil, dirty, shameless, and they desire, if they have any fixed desire, to be noticed by the Jungle People. But we do not notice them even when they throw nuts and filth on our heads."

He had hardly spoken when a shower of nuts and twigs spattered down through the branches; and they could hear coughings and howlings and angry jumpings high up in the air among the thin branches.

"The Monkey-People are forbidden," said Baloo, "forbidden to the Jungle-People. Remember."

"Forbidden," said Bagheera, "but I still think Baloo should have warned thee against them."

"I--I? How was I to guess he would play with such dirt. The Monkey People! Faugh!"

A fresh shower came down on their heads and the two trotted away, taking Mowgli with them. What Baloo had said about the monkeys was perfectly true. They belonged to the tree-tops, and as beasts very seldom look up, there was no occasion for the monkeys and the Jungle-People to cross each other's path. But whenever they found a sick wolf, or a wounded tiger, or bear, the monkeys would torment him, and would throw sticks and nuts at any beast for fun and in the hope of being noticed. Then they would howl and shriek senseless songs, and invite the Jungle-People to climb up their trees and fight them, or would start furious battles over nothing among themselves, and leave the dead monkeys where the Jungle-People could see them. They were always just going to have a leader, and laws and customs of their own, but they never did, because their memories would not hold over from day to day, and so they compromised things by making up a saying, "What the Bandar-log think now the jungle will think later," and that comforted them a great deal. None of the beasts could reach them, but on the other hand none of the beasts would notice them, and that was why they were so pleased when Mowgli came to play with them, and they heard how angry Baloo was.

They never meant to do any more--the Bandar-log never mean anything at all; but one of them invented what seemed to him a brilliant idea, and he told all the others that Mowgli would be a useful person to keep in the tribe, because he could weave sticks together for protection from the wind; so, if they caught him, they could make him teach them. Of course Mowgli, as a woodcutter's child, inherited all sorts of instincts, and used to make little huts of fallen branches without thinking how he came to do it. The Monkey-People, watching in the trees, considered his play most wonderful. This time, they said, they were really going to have a leader and become the wisest people in the jungle--so wise that everyone else would notice and envy them. Therefore they followed Baloo and Bagheera and Mowgli through the jungle very quietly till it was time for the midday nap, and Mowgli, who was very much ashamed of himself, slept between the Panther and the Bear, resolving to have no more to do with the Monkey People.

The next thing he remembered was feeling hands on his legs and arms--hard, strong, little hands-- and then a swash of branches in his face, and then he was staring down through the swaying boughs as Baloo woke the jungle with his deep cries and Bagheera bounded up the trunk with every tooth bared. The Bandar-log howled with triumph and scuffled away to the upper branches where Bagheera dared not follow, shouting: "He has noticed us! Bagheera has noticed us. All the Jungle-People admire us for our skill and our cunning." Then they began their flight; and the flight of the Monkey-People through tree-land is one of the things nobody can describe. They have their regular roads and crossroads, up hills and down hills, all laid out from fifty to seventy or a hundred feet above ground, and by these they can travel even at night if necessary. Two of the strongest monkeys caught Mowgli under the arms and swung off with him through the treetops, twenty feet at a bound. Had they been alone they could have gone twice as fast, but the boy's weight held them back. Sick and giddy as Mowgli was he could not help enjoying the wild rush, though the glimpses of earth far down below frightened him, and the terrible check and jerk at the end of the swing over nothing but empty air brought his heart between his teeth. His escort would rush him up a tree till he felt the thinnest topmost branches crackle and bend under them, and then with a cough and a whoop would fling themselves into the air outward and downward, and bring up, hanging by their hands or their feet to the lower limbs of the next tree. Sometimes he could see for miles and miles across the still green jungle, as a man on the top of a mast can see for miles across the sea, and then the branches and leaves would lash him across the face, and he and his two guards would be almost down to earth again. So, bounding and crashing and whooping and yelling, the whole tribe of Bandar-log swept along the tree-roads with Mowgli their prisoner.

For a time he was afraid of being dropped. Then he grew angry but knew better than to struggle, and then he began to think. The first thing was to send back word to Baloo and Bagheera, for, at the pace the monkeys were going, he knew his friends would be left far behind. It was useless to look down, for he could only see the topsides of the branches, so he stared upward and saw, far away in the blue, Rann the Kite balancing and wheeling as he kept watch over the jungle waiting for things to die. Rann saw that the monkeys were carrying something, and dropped a few hundred yards to find out whether their load was good to eat. He whistled with surprise when he saw Mowgli being dragged up to a treetop and heard him give the Kite call for--"We be of one blood, thou and I." The waves of the branches closed over the boy, but Chil balanced away to the next tree in time to see the little brown face come up again. "Mark my trail!" Mowgli shouted. "Tell Baloo of the Seeonee Pack and Bagheera of the Council Rock."

"In whose name, Brother?" Rann had never seen Mowgli before, though of course he had heard of him.

"Mowgli, the Frog. Man-cub they call me! Mark my tra-il!"

The last words were shrieked as he was being swung through the air, but Rann nodded and rose up till he looked no bigger than a speck of dust, and there he hung, watching with his telescope eyes the swaying of the treetops as Mowgli's escort whirled along.

"They never go far," he said with a chuckle. "They never do what they set out to do. Always pecking at new things are the Bandar-log. This time, if I have any eye-sight, they have pecked down trouble for themselves, for Baloo is no fledgling and Bagheera can, as I know, kill more than goats."

So he rocked on his wings, his feet gathered up under him, and waited.

Meantime, Baloo and Bagheera were furious with rage and grief. Bagheera climbed as he had never climbed before, but the thin branches broke beneath his weight, and he slipped down, his claws full of bark.

"Why didst thou not warn the man-cub?" he roared to poor Baloo, who had set off at a clumsy trot in the hope of overtaking the monkeys. "What was the use of half slaying him with blows if thou didst not warn him?"

"Haste! O haste! We--we may catch them yet!" Baloo panted.

"At that speed! It would not tire a wounded cow. Teacher of the Law--cub-beater--a mile of that rolling to and fro would burst thee open. Sit still and think! Make a plan. This is no time for chasing. They may drop him if we follow too close."

"Arrula! Whoo! They may have dropped him already, being tired of carrying him. Who can trust the Bandar-log? Put dead bats on my head! Give me black bones to eat! Roll me into the hives of the wild bees that I may be stung to death, and bury me with the Hyaena, for I am most miserable of bears! Arulala! Wahooa! O Mowgli, Mowgli! Why did I not warn thee against the Monkey-Folk instead of breaking thy head? Now perhaps I may have knocked the day's lesson out of his mind, and he will be alone in the jungle without the Master Words."

Baloo clasped his paws over his ears and rolled to and fro moaning.

"At least he gave me all the Words correctly a little time ago," said Bagheera impatiently. "Baloo, thou hast neither memory nor respect. What would the jungle think if I, the Black Panther, curled myself up like Ikki the Porcupine, and howled?"

"What do I care what the jungle thinks? He may be dead by now."

"Unless and until they drop him from the branches in sport, or kill him out of idleness, I have no fear for the man-cub. He is wise and well taught, and above all he has the eyes that make the Jungle-People afraid. But (and it is a great evil) he is in the power of the Bandar-log, and they, because they live in trees, have no fear of any of our people." Bagheera licked one forepaw thoughtfully.

"Fool that I am! Oh, fat, brown, root-digging fool that I am," said Baloo, uncoiling himself with a jerk, "it is true what Hathi the Wild Elephant says: 'To each his own fear'; and they, the Bandar-log, fear Kaa the Rock Snake. He can climb as well as they can. He steals the young monkeys in the night. The whisper of his name makes their wicked tails cold. Let us go to Kaa."

"What will he do for us? He is not of our tribe, being footless--and with most evil eyes," said Bagheera.

"He is very old and very cunning. Above all, he is always hungry," said Baloo hopefully. "Promise him many goats."

"He sleeps for a full month after he has once eaten. He may be asleep now, and even were he awake what if he would rather kill his own goats?" Bagheera, who did not know much about Kaa, was naturally suspicious.

"Then in that case, thou and I together, old hunter, might make him see reason." Here Baloo rubbed his faded brown shoulder against the Panther, and they went off to look for Kaa the Rock Python.

They found him stretched out on a warm ledge in the afternoon sun, admiring his beautiful new coat, for he had been in retirement for the last ten days changing his skin, and now he was very splendid--darting his big blunt-nosed head along the ground, and twisting the thirty feet of his body into fantastic knots and curves, and licking his lips as he thought of his dinner to come.

"He has not eaten," said Baloo, with a grunt of relief, as soon as he saw the beautifully mottled brown and yellow jacket. "Be careful, Bagheera! He is always a little blind after he has changed his skin, and very quick to strike."

Kaa was not a poison snake--in fact he rather despised the poison snakes as cowards--but his strength lay in his hug, and when he had once lapped his huge coils round anybody there was no more to be said. "Good hunting!" cried Baloo, sitting up on his haunches. Like all snakes of his breed Kaa was rather deaf, and did not hear the call at first. Then he curled up ready for any accident, his head lowered.

"Good hunting for us all," he answered. "Oho, Baloo, what dost thou do here? Good hunting, Bagheera. One of us at least needs food. Is there any news of game afoot? A doe now, or even a young buck? I am as empty as a dried well."

"We are hunting," said Baloo carelessly. He knew that you must not hurry Kaa. He is too big. "Give me permission to come with you," said Kaa. "A blow more or less is nothing to thee, Bagheera or Baloo, but I--I have to wait and wait for days in a wood-path and climb half a night on the mere chance of a young ape. Psshaw! The branches are not what they were when I was young. Rotten twigs and dry boughs are they all."

"Maybe thy great weight has something to do with the matter," said Baloo.

"I am a fair length--a fair length," said Kaa with a little pride. "But for all that, it is the fault of this new-grown timber. I came very near to falling on my last hunt--very near indeed--and the noise of my slipping, for my tail was not tight wrapped around the tree, waked the Bandar-log, and they called me most evil names."

"Footless, yellow earth-worm," said Bagheera under his whiskers, as though he were trying to remember something.

"Sssss! Have they ever called me that?" said Kaa.

"Something of that kind it was that they shouted to us last moon, but we never noticed them. They will say anything--even that thou hast lost all thy teeth, and wilt not face anything bigger than a kid, because (they are indeed shameless, these Bandar-log)--because thou art afraid of the he-goat's horns," Bagheera went on sweetly.

Now a snake, especially a wary old python like Kaa, very seldom shows that he is angry, but Baloo and Bagheera could see the big swallowing muscles on either side of Kaa's throat ripple and bulge.

"The Bandar-log have shifted their grounds," he said quietly. "When I came up into the sun today I heard them whooping among the tree-tops."

"It--it is the Bandar-log that we follow now," said Baloo, but the words stuck in his throat, for that was the first time in his memory that one of the Jungle-People had owned to being interested in the doings of the monkeys.

"Beyond doubt then it is no small thing that takes two such hunters--leaders in their own jungle I am certain--on the trail of the Bandar-log," Kaa replied courteously, as he swelled with curiosity.

"Indeed," Baloo began, "I am no more than the old and sometimes very foolish Teacher of the Law to the Seeonee wolf-cubs, and Bagheera here--"

"Is Bagheera," said the Black Panther, and his jaws shut with a snap, for he did not believe in being humble. "The trouble is this, Kaa. Those nut-stealers and pickers of palm leaves have stolen away our man-cub of whom thou hast perhaps heard."

"I heard some news from Ikki (his quills make him presumptuous) of a man-thing that was entered into a wolf pack, but I did not believe. Ikki is full of stories half heard and very badly told."
"But it is true. He is such a man-cub as never was," said Baloo. "The best and wisest and boldest of man-cubs--my own pupil, who shall make the name of Baloo famous through all the jungles; and besides, I--we--love him, Kaa."

"Ts! Ts!" said Kaa, weaving his head to and fro. "I also have known what love is. There are tales I could tell that--"

"That need a clear night when we are all well fed to praise properly," said Bagheera quickly. "Our man-cub is in the hands of the Bandar-log now, and we know that of all the Jungle-People they fear Kaa alone."

"They fear me alone. They have good reason," said Kaa. "Chattering, foolish, vain--vain, foolish, and chattering, are the monkeys. But a man-thing in their hands is in no good luck. They grow tired of the nuts they pick, and throw them down. They carry a branch half a day, meaning to do great things with it, and then they snap it in two. That man-thing is not to be envied. They called me also—'yellow fish' was it not?"

"Worm--worm--earth-worm," said Bagheera, "as well as other things which I cannot now say for shame."

"We must remind them to speak well of their master. Aaa-ssp! We must help their wandering memories. Now, whither went they with the cub?"

"The jungle alone knows. Toward the sunset, I believe," said Baloo. "We had thought that thou wouldst know, Kaa."

"I? How? I take them when they come in my way, but I do not hunt the Bandar-log, or frogs--or green scum on a water-hole, for that matter."

"Up, Up! Up, Up! Hillo! Illo! Illo, look up, Baloo of the Seeonee Wolf Pack!"

Baloo looked up to see where the voice came from, and there was Rann the Kite, sweeping down with the sun shining on the upturned flanges of his wings. It was near Rann's bedtime, but he had ranged all over the jungle looking for the Bear and had missed him in the thick foliage.

"What is it?" said Baloo.

"I have seen Mowgli among the Bandar-log. He bade me tell you. I watched. The Bandar-log have taken him beyond the river to the monkey city--to the Cold Lairs. They may stay there for a night, or ten nights, or an hour. I have told the bats to watch through the dark time. That is my message. Good hunting, all you below!"

"Full gorge and a deep sleep to you, Rann," cried Bagheera. "I will remember thee in my next kill, and put aside the head for thee alone, O best of kites!"

"It is nothing. It is nothing. The boy held the Master Word. I could have done no less," and Rann circled up again to his roost.

"He has not forgotten to use his tongue," said Baloo with a chuckle of pride. "To think of one so young remembering the Master Word for the birds too while he was being pulled across trees!"

"It was most firmly driven into him," said Bagheera. "But I am proud of him, and now we must go to the Cold Lairs."

Lesson 15

1. Finish the chapter.
2. How can pride and jealousy been seen in these animals?

They all knew where that place was, but few of the Jungle People ever went there, because what they called the Cold Lairs was an old deserted city, lost and buried in the jungle, and beasts seldom use a place that men have once used. The wild boar will, but the hunting tribes do not. Besides, the monkeys lived there as much as they could be said to live anywhere, and no self-respecting animal would come within eyeshot of it except in times of drought, when the half-ruined tanks and reservoirs held a little water.

"It is half a night's journey--at full speed," said Bagheera, and Baloo looked very serious. "I will go as fast as I can," he said anxiously.

"We dare not wait for thee. Follow, Baloo. We must go on the quick-foot--Kaa and I."

"Feet or no feet, I can keep abreast of all thy four," said Kaa shortly. Baloo made one effort to hurry, but had to sit down panting, and so they left him to come on later, while Bagheera hurried forward, at the quick panther-canter. Kaa said nothing, but, strive as Bagheera might, the huge Rock-python held level with him. When they came to a hill stream, Bagheera gained, because he bounded across while Kaa swam, his head and two feet of his neck clearing the water, but on level ground Kaa made up the distance.

"By the Broken Lock that freed me," said Bagheera, when twilight had fallen, "thou art no slow goer!"

"I am hungry," said Kaa. "Besides, they called me speckled frog."

"Worm--earth-worm, and yellow to boot."

"All one. Let us go on," and Kaa seemed to pour himself along the ground, finding the shortest road with his steady eyes, and keeping to it.

In the Cold Lairs the Monkey-People were not thinking of Mowgli's friends at all. They had brought the boy to the Lost City, and were very much pleased with themselves for the time. Mowgli had never seen an Indian city before, and though this was almost a heap of ruins it seemed very wonderful and splendid. Some king had built it long ago on a little hill. You could still trace the stone causeways that led up to the ruined gates where the last splinters of wood hung to the worn, rusted hinges. Trees had grown into and out of the walls; the battlements were tumbled down and decayed, and wild creepers hung out of the windows of the towers on the walls in bushy hanging clumps.

A great roofless palace crowned the hill, and the marble of the courtyards and the fountains was split, and stained with red and green, and the very cobblestones in the courtyard where the king's elephants used to live had been thrust up and apart by grasses and young trees. From the palace you could see the rows and rows of roofless houses that made up the city looking like empty honeycombs filled with blackness; the shapeless block of stone that had been an idol in the square where four roads met; the pits and dimples at street corners where the public wells once stood, and the shattered domes of temples with wild figs sprouting on their sides. The monkeys called the place their city, and pretended to despise the Jungle-People because they lived in the forest. And yet they never knew what the buildings were made for nor how to use them. They would sit in circles on the hall of the king's council chamber, and scratch for fleas and pretend to be men; or they would run in and out of the roofless houses and collect pieces of plaster and old bricks in a corner, and forget where they had hidden them, and fight and cry in scuffling crowds, and then break off to play up and down the terraces of the king's garden, where they would shake the rose trees and the oranges in sport to see the fruit and flowers fall. They explored all the passages and dark tunnels in the palace and the hundreds of little dark rooms, but they never remembered what they had seen and what they had not; and so drifted about in ones and twos or crowds telling each other that they were doing as men did. They drank at the tanks and made the water all muddy, and then they fought over it, and then they would all rush together in mobs and shout: "There is no one in the jungle so wise and good and clever and strong and gentle as the Bandar-log." Then all would begin again till they grew tired of the city and went back to the tree-tops, hoping the Jungle-People would notice them.

Mowgli, who had been trained under the Law of the Jungle, did not like or understand this kind of life. The monkeys dragged him into the Cold Lairs late in the afternoon, and instead of going to sleep, as Mowgli would have done after a long journey, they joined hands and danced about and sang their foolish songs. One of the monkeys made a speech and told his companions that Mowgli's capture marked a new thing in the history of the Bandar-log, for Mowgli was going to show them how to weave sticks and canes together as a protection against rain and cold. Mowgli picked up some creepers and began to work them in and out, and the monkeys tried to imitate; but in a very few minutes they lost interest and began to pull their friends' tails or jump up and down on all fours, coughing.
"I wish to eat," said Mowgli. "I am a stranger in this part of the jungle. Bring me food, or give me leave to hunt here."

Twenty or thirty monkeys bounded away to bring him nuts and wild pawpaws. But they fell to fighting on the road, and it was too much trouble to go back with what was left of the fruit. Mowgli was sore and angry as well as hungry, and he roamed through the empty city giving the Strangers' Hunting Call from time to time, but no one answered him, and Mowgli felt that he had reached a very bad place indeed. "All that Baloo has said about the Bandar-log is true," he thought to himself. "They have no Law, no Hunting Call, and no leaders--nothing but foolish words and little picking thievish hands. So if I am starved or killed here, it will be all my own fault. But I must try to return to my own jungle. Baloo will surely beat me, but that is better than chasing silly rose leaves with the Bandar-log."

No sooner had he walked to the city wall than the monkeys pulled him back, telling him that he did not know how happy he was, and pinching him to make him grateful. He set his teeth and said nothing, but went with the shouting monkeys to a terrace above the red sandstone reservoirs that were half-full of rain water. There was a ruined summer-house of white marble in the center of the terrace, built for queens dead a hundred years ago. The domed roof had half fallen in and blocked up the underground passage from the palace by which the queens used to enter. But the walls were made of screens of marble tracery--beautiful milk-white fretwork, set with agates and cornelians and jasper and lapis lazuli, and as the moon came up behind the hill it shone through the open work, casting shadows on the ground like black velvet embroidery. Sore, sleepy, and hungry as he was, Mowgli could not help laughing when the Bandar-log began, twenty at a time, to tell him how great and wise and strong and gentle they were, and how foolish he was to wish to leave them. "We are great. We are free. We are wonderful. We are the most wonderful people in all the jungle! We all say so, and so it must be true," they shouted. "Now as you are a new listener and can carry our words back to the Jungle-People so that they may notice us in future, we will tell you all about our most excellent selves." Mowgli made no objection, and the monkeys gathered by hundreds and hundreds on the terrace to listen to their own speakers singing the praises of the Bandar-log, and whenever a speaker stopped for want of breath they would all shout together: "This is true; we all say so." Mowgli nodded and blinked, and said "Yes" when they asked him a question, and his head spun with the noise. "Tabaqui the Jackal must have bitten all these people," he said to himself, "and now they have madness. Certainly this is dewanee, the madness. Do they never go to sleep? Now there is a cloud coming to cover that moon. If it were only a big enough cloud I might try to run away in the darkness. But I am tired."

That same cloud was being watched by two good friends in the ruined ditch below the city wall, for Bagheera and Kaa, knowing well how dangerous the Monkey-People were in large numbers, did not wish to run any risks. The monkeys never fight unless they are a hundred to one, and few in the jungle care for those odds.

"I will go to the west wall," Kaa whispered, "and come down swiftly with the slope of the ground in my favor. They will not throw themselves upon my back in their hundreds, but--"

"I know it," said Bagheera. "Would that Baloo were here, but we must do what we can. When that cloud covers the moon I shall go to the terrace. They hold some sort of council there over the boy."

"Good hunting," said Kaa grimly, and glided away to the west wall. That happened to be the least ruined of any, and the big snake was delayed awhile before he could find a way up the stones. The cloud hid the moon, and as Mowgli wondered what would come next he heard Bagheera's light feet on the terrace. The Black Panther had raced up the slope almost without a sound and was striking--he knew better than to waste time in biting--right and left among the monkeys, who were seated round Mowgli in circles fifty and sixty deep. There was a howl of fright and rage, and then as Bagheera tripped on the rolling kicking bodies beneath him, a monkey shouted: "There is only one here! Kill him! Kill." A scuffling mass of monkeys, biting, scratching, tearing, and pulling, closed over Bagheera, while five or six laid hold of Mowgli, dragged him up the wall of the summerhouse and pushed him through the hole of the broken dome. A man-trained boy would have been badly bruised, for the fall was a good fifteen feet, but Mowgli fell as Baloo had taught him to fall, and landed on his feet.

"Stay there," shouted the monkeys, "till we have killed thy friends, and later we will play with thee--if the Poison-People leave thee alive."

"We be of one blood, ye and I," said Mowgli, quickly giving the Snake's Call. He could hear rustling and hissing in the rubbish all round him and gave the Call a second time, to make sure.

"Even ssso! Down hoods all!" said half a dozen low voices (every ruin in India becomes sooner or later a dwelling place of snakes, and the old summerhouse was alive with cobras). "Stand still, Little Brother, for thy feet may do us harm."

Mowgli stood as quietly as he could, peering through the open work and listening to the furious din of the fight round the Black Panther--the yells and chatterings and scufflings, and Bagheera's deep, hoarse cough as he backed and bucked and twisted and plunged under the heaps of his enemies. For the first time since he was born, Bagheera was fighting for his life.

"Baloo must be at hand; Bagheera would not have come alone," Mowgli thought. And then he called aloud: "To the tank, Bagheera. Roll to the water tanks. Roll and plunge! Get to the water!" Bagheera heard, and the cry that told him Mowgli was safe gave him new courage. He worked his way desperately, inch by inch, straight for the reservoirs, halting in silence. Then from the ruined wall nearest the jungle rose up the rumbling war-shout of Baloo. The old Bear had done his best, but he could not come before. "Bagheera," he shouted, "I am here. I climb! I haste! Ahuwora! The stones slip under my feet! Wait my coming, O most infamous Bandar-log!" He panted up the terrace only to disappear to the head in a wave of monkeys, but he threw himself squarely on his haunches, and, spreading out his forepaws, hugged as many as he could hold, and then began to hit with a regular bat-bat-bat, like the flipping strokes of a paddle wheel. A crash and a splash told Mowgli that Bagheera had fought his way to the tank where the monkeys could not follow. The Panther lay gasping for breath, his head just out of the water, while the monkeys stood three deep on the red steps, dancing up and down with rage, ready to spring upon him from all sides if he came out to help Baloo. It was then that Bagheera lifted up his dripping chin, and in despair gave the Snake's Call for protection--"We be of one blood, ye and I"-- for he believed that Kaa had turned tail at the last minute. Even Baloo, half smothered under the monkeys on the edge of the terrace, could not help chuckling as he heard the Black Panther asking for help.

Kaa had only just worked his way over the west wall, landing with a wrench that dislodged a coping stone into the ditch. He had no intention of losing any advantage of the ground, and coiled and uncoiled himself once or twice, to be sure that every foot of his long body was in working order. All that while the fight with Baloo went on, and the monkeys yelled in the tank round Bagheera, and Mang the Bat, flying to and fro, carried the news of the great battle over the jungle, till even Hathi the Wild Elephant trumpeted, and, far away, scattered bands of the Monkey-Folk woke and came leaping along the tree-roads to help their comrades in the Cold Lairs, and the noise of the fight roused all the day birds for miles round. Then Kaa came straight, quickly, and anxious to kill. The fighting strength of a python is in the driving blow of his head backed by all the strength and weight of his body. If you can imagine a lance, or a battering ram, or a hammer weighing nearly half a ton driven by a cool, quiet mind living in the handle of it, you can roughly imagine what Kaa was like when he fought. A python four or five feet long can knock a man down if he hits him fairly in the chest, and Kaa was thirty feet long, as you know. His first stroke was delivered into the heart of the crowd round Baloo. It was sent home with shut mouth in silence, and there was no need of a second. The monkeys scattered with cries of--"Kaa! It is Kaa! Run! Run!"

Generations of monkeys had been scared into good behavior by the stories their elders told them of Kaa, the night thief, who could slip along the branches as quietly as moss grows, and steal away the strongest monkey that ever lived; of old Kaa, who could make himself look so like a dead branch or a rotten stump that the wisest were deceived, till the branch caught them. Kaa was everything that the monkeys feared in the jungle, for none of them knew the limits of his power, none of them could look him in the face, and none had ever come alive out of his hug. And so they ran, stammering with terror, to the walls and the roofs of the houses, and Baloo drew a deep breath of relief. His fur was much thicker than Bagheera's, but he had suffered sorely in the fight. Then Kaa opened his mouth for the first time and spoke one long hissing word, and the far-away monkeys, hurrying to the defense of the Cold Lairs, stayed where they were, cowering, till the loaded branches bent and crackled under them. The monkeys on the walls and the empty houses stopped their cries, and in the stillness that fell upon the city Mowgli heard Bagheera shaking his wet sides as he came up from the tank. Then the clamor broke out again. The monkeys leaped higher up the walls. They clung around the necks of the big stone idols and shrieked as they skipped along the battlements, while Mowgli, dancing in the summerhouse, put his eye to the screenwork and hooted owl-fashion between his front teeth, to show his derision and contempt.

"Get the man-cub out of that trap; I can do no more," Bagheera gasped. "Let us take the man-cub and go. They may attack again."

"They will not move till I order them. Stay you sssso!" Kaa hissed, and the city was silent once more. "I could not come before, Brother, but I think I heard thee call"--this was to Bagheera. "I--I may have cried out in the battle," Bagheera answered. "Baloo, art thou hurt?"

"I am not sure that they did not pull me into a hundred little bearlings," said Baloo, gravely shaking one leg after the other. "Wow! I am sore. Kaa, we owe thee, I think, our lives--Bagheera and I."

"No matter. Where is the manling?"

"Here, in a trap. I cannot climb out," cried Mowgli. The curve of the broken dome was above his head.

"Take him away. He dances like Mao the Peacock. He will crush our young," said the cobras inside.

"Hah!" said Kaa with a chuckle, "he has friends everywhere, this manling. Stand back, manling. And hide you, O Poison People. I break down the wall."

Kaa looked carefully till he found a discolored crack in the marble tracery showing a weak spot, made two or three light taps with his head to get the distance, and then lifting up six feet of his body clear of the ground, sent home half a dozen full-power smashing blows, nose-first. The screen-work broke and fell away in a cloud of dust and rubbish, and Mowgli leaped through the opening and flung himself between Baloo and Bagheera--an arm around each big neck.

"Art thou hurt?" said Baloo, hugging him softly.

"I am sore, hungry, and not a little bruised. But, oh, they have handled ye grievously, my Brothers! Ye bleed."

"Others also," said Bagheera, licking his lips and looking at the monkey-dead on the terrace and round the tank.

"It is nothing, it is nothing, if thou art safe, oh, my pride of all little frogs!" whimpered Baloo.

"Of that we shall judge later," said Bagheera, in a dry voice that Mowgli did not at all like. "But here is Kaa to whom we owe the battle and thou owest thy life. Thank him according to our customs, Mowgli."

Mowgli turned and saw the great Python's head swaying a foot above his own.

"So this is the manling," said Kaa. "Very soft is his skin, and he is not unlike the Bandar-log. Have a care, manling, that I do not mistake thee for a monkey some twilight when I have newly changed my coat."

"We be one blood, thou and I," Mowgli answered. "I take my life from thee tonight. My kill shall be thy kill if ever thou art hungry, O Kaa."
"All thanks, Little Brother," said Kaa, though his eyes twinkled. "And what may so bold a hunter kill? I ask that I may follow when next he goes abroad."

"I kill nothing,--I am too little,--but I drive goats toward such as can use them. When thou art empty come to me and see if I speak the truth. I have some skill in these [he held out his hands], and if

61

ever thou art in a trap, I may pay the debt which I owe to thee, to Bagheera, and to Baloo, here. Good hunting to ye all, my masters."

"Well said," growled Baloo, for Mowgli had returned thanks very prettily. The Python dropped his head lightly for a minute on Mowgli's shoulder. "A brave heart and a courteous tongue," said he. "They shall carry thee far through the jungle, manling. But now go hence quickly with thy friends. Go and sleep, for the moon sets, and what follows it is not well that thou shouldst see."

The moon was sinking behind the hills and the lines of trembling monkeys huddled together on the walls and battlements looked like ragged shaky fringes of things. Baloo went down to the tank for a drink and Bagheera began to put his fur in order, as Kaa glided out into the center of the terrace and brought his jaws together with a ringing snap that drew all the monkeys' eyes upon him.

"The moon sets," he said. "Is there yet light enough to see?"

From the walls came a moan like the wind in the tree-tops-- "We see, O Kaa."

"Good. Begins now the dance--the Dance of the Hunger of Kaa. Sit still and watch."

He turned twice or thrice in a big circle, weaving his head from right to left. Then he began making loops and figures of eight with his body, and soft, oozy triangles that melted into squares and five-sided figures, and coiled mounds, never resting, never hurrying, and never stopping his low humming song. It grew darker and darker, till at last the dragging, shifting coils disappeared, but they could hear the rustle of the scales.

Baloo and Bagheera stood still as stone, growling in their throats, their neck hair bristling, and Mowgli watched and wondered.

"Bandar-log," said the voice of Kaa at last, "can ye stir foot or hand without my order? Speak!"

"Without thy order we cannot stir foot or hand, O Kaa!"

"Good! Come all one pace nearer to me."

The lines of the monkeys swayed forward helplessly, and Baloo and Bagheera took one stiff step forward with them.

"Nearer!" hissed Kaa, and they all moved again.

Mowgli laid his hands on Baloo and Bagheera to get them away, and the two great beasts started as though they had been waked from a dream.

"Keep thy hand on my shoulder," Bagheera whispered. "Keep it there, or I must go back--must go back to Kaa. Aah!"

"It is only old Kaa making circles on the dust," said Mowgli. "Let us go." And the three slipped off through a gap in the walls to the jungle.

"Whoof!" said Baloo, when he stood under the still trees again. "Never more will I make an ally of Kaa," and he shook himself all over.

"He knows more than we," said Bagheera, trembling. "In a little time, had I stayed, I should have walked down his throat."

"Many will walk by that road before the moon rises again," said Baloo. "He will have good hunting--after his own fashion."

"But what was the meaning of it all?" said Mowgli, who did not know anything of a python's powers of fascination. "I saw no more than a big snake making foolish circles till the dark came. And his nose was all sore. Ho! Ho!"

"Mowgli," said Bagheera angrily, "his nose was sore on thy account, as my ears and sides and paws, and Baloo's neck and shoulders are bitten on thy account. Neither Baloo nor Bagheera will be able to hunt with pleasure for many days."

"It is nothing," said Baloo; "we have the man-cub again."

"True, but he has cost us heavily in time which might have been spent in good hunting, in wounds, in hair--I am half plucked along my back--and last of all, in honor. For, remember, Mowgli, I, who am the Black Panther, was forced to call upon Kaa for protection, and Baloo and I were both made stupid as little birds by the Hunger Dance. All this, man-cub, came of thy playing with the Bandar-log."

"True, it is true," said Mowgli sorrowfully. "I am an evil man-cub, and my stomach is sad in me."

"Mf! What says the Law of the Jungle, Baloo?"

Baloo did not wish to bring Mowgli into any more trouble, but he could not tamper with the Law, so he mumbled: "Sorrow never stays punishment. But remember, Bagheera, he is very little."

"I will remember. But he has done mischief, and blows must be dealt now. Mowgli, hast thou anything to say?"
"Nothing. I did wrong. Baloo and thou are wounded. It is just."

Bagheera gave him half a dozen love-taps from a panther's point of view (they would hardly have waked one of his own cubs), but for a seven-year-old boy they amounted to as severe a beating as

63

you could wish to avoid. When it was all over Mowgli sneezed, and picked himself up without a word.

"Now," said Bagheera, "jump on my back, Little Brother, and we will go home."

One of the beauties of Jungle Law is that punishment settles all scores. There is no nagging afterward.

Mowgli laid his head down on Bagheera's back and slept so deeply that he never waked when he was put down in the home-cave.

-Road-Song of the Bandar-Log

Here we go in a flung festoon,
Half-way up to the jealous moon!
Don't you envy our pranceful bands?
Don't you wish you had extra hands?
Wouldn't you like if your tails were--so—
Curved in the shape of a Cupid's bow?
Now you're angry, but--never mind,
Brother, thy tail hangs down behind!

Here we sit in a branchy row,
Thinking of beautiful things we know;
Dreaming of deeds that we mean to do,
All complete, in a minute or two—
Something noble and wise and good,
Done by merely wishing we could.
We've forgotten, but--never mind,
Brother, thy tail hangs down behind!

All the talk we ever have heard
Uttered by bat or beast or bird—
Hide or fin or scale or feather—
Jabber it quickly and all together!
Excellent! Wonderful! Once again!
Now we are talking just like men!
Let's pretend we are ... never mind,
Brother, thy tail hangs down behind!
This is the way of the Monkey-kind.
Then join our leaping lines
that scumfish through the pines,

That rocket by where, light and high, the wild grape swings.
By the rubbish in our wake,
and the noble noise we make,
Be sure, be sure, we're going to do some splendid things!

Lesson 16

1. Read the Bible verses below. What gives someone significance in God's eyes?
   - 1 Samuel 16:7 But the Lord said to Samuel, "Do not consider his appearance or his height, for I have rejected him. The Lord does not look at the things people look at. People look at the outward appearance, but the Lord looks at the heart." (NIV)
   - Acts 13:22 After removing Saul, he made David their king. God testified concerning him: "I have found David son of Jesse, a man after my own heart; he will do everything I want him to do." (NIV)
2. Background information: "India used to have a caste system. A person was born into a particular group, and they had to stay within that group all of their lives. They could not marry anyone in a higher or lower caste. Everyone knew what everyone else's caste was, and were required to treat people differently depending on the caste. The caste determined what clothes people would wear and what jobs they would do. In this chapter Mowgli goes to live with humans. Mowgli did not understand the caste system, but everyone else did. Mowgli has grown up in the jungle. He did not try to treat people better because they were from a higher caste, or refuse to help them if they were in a lower caste." (from classical-childrens-books.com/jungle-book-unit-study.html)
3. Read the first part of "Tiger! Tiger!"
4. Who is the protagonist and who is the antagonist? (Answers)

What of the hunting, hunter bold? Brother, the watch was long and cold. What of the quarry ye went to kill? Brother, he crops in the jungle still. Where is the power that made your pride? Brother, it ebbs from my flank and side. Where is the haste that ye hurry by? Brother, I go to my lair--to die.

Now we must go back to the first tale. When Mowgli left the wolf's cave after the fight with the Pack at the Council Rock, he went down to the plowed lands where the villagers lived, but he would not stop there because it was too near to the jungle, and he knew that he had made at least one bad enemy at the Council. So he hurried on, keeping to the rough road that ran down the valley, and followed it at a steady jog-trot for nearly twenty miles, till he came to a country that he did not know. The valley opened out into a great plain dotted over with rocks and cut up by ravines. At one end stood a little village, and at the other the thick jungle came down in a sweep to the grazing-grounds, and stopped there as though it had been cut off with a hoe. All over the plain, cattle and buffaloes were grazing, and when the little boys in charge of the herds saw Mowgli they shouted and ran away, and the yellow pariah dogs that hang about every Indian village barked. Mowgli walked on, for he was feeling hungry, and when he came to the village gate he saw the big thorn-bush that was drawn up before the gate at twilight, pushed to one side.

"Umph!" he said, for he had come across more than one such barricade in his night rambles after things to eat. "So men are afraid of the People of the Jungle here also." He sat down by the gate, and when a man came out he stood up, opened his mouth, and pointed down it to show that he wanted food. The man stared, and ran back up the one street of the village shouting for the priest, who was a big, fat man dressed in white, with a red and yellow mark on his forehead. The priest came to the gate, and with him at least a hundred people, who stared and talked and shouted and pointed at Mowgli.

"They have no manners, these Men Folk," said Mowgli to himself. "Only the gray ape would behave as they do." So he threw back his long hair and frowned at the crowd.

"What is there to be afraid of?" said the priest. "Look at the marks on his arms and legs. They are the bites of wolves. He is but a wolf-child run away from the jungle."

Of course, in playing together, the cubs had often nipped Mowgli harder than they intended, and there were white scars all over his arms and legs. But he would have been the last person in the world to call these bites, for he knew what real biting meant.

"Arre! Arre!" said two or three women together. "To be bitten by wolves, poor child! He is a handsome boy. He has eyes like red fire. By my honor, Messua, he is not unlike thy boy that was taken by the tiger."

"Let me look," said a woman with heavy copper rings on her wrists and ankles, and she peered at Mowgli under the palm of her hand. "Indeed he is not. He is thinner, but he has the very look of my boy."

The priest was a clever man, and he knew that Messua was wife to the richest villager in the place. So he looked up at the sky for a minute and said solemnly: "What the jungle has taken the jungle has restored. Take the boy into thy house, my sister, and forget not to honor the priest who sees so far into the lives of men."

"By the Bull that bought me," said Mowgli to himself, "but all this talking is like another looking-over by the Pack! Well, if I am a man, a man I must become."

The crowd parted as the woman beckoned Mowgli to her hut, where there was a red lacquered bedstead, a great earthen grain chest with funny raised patterns on it, half a dozen copper cooking pots, an image of a Hindu god in a little alcove, and on the wall a real looking glass, such as they sell at the country fairs.

She gave him a long drink of milk and some bread, and then she laid her hand on his head and looked into his eyes; for she thought perhaps that he might be her real son come back from the jungle where the tiger had taken him. So she said, "Nathoo, O Nathoo!" Mowgli did not show that he knew the name. "Dost thou not remember the day when I gave thee thy new shoes?" She touched his foot, and it was almost as hard as horn. "No," she said sorrowfully, "those feet have never worn shoes, but thou art very like my Nathoo, and thou shalt be my son."

Mowgli was uneasy, because he had never been under a roof before. But as he looked at the thatch, he saw that he could tear it out any time if he wanted to get away, and that the window had no fastenings. "What is the good of a man," he said to himself at last, "if he does not understand man's talk? Now I am as silly and dumb as a man would be with us in the jungle. I must speak their talk."

It was not for fun that he had learned while he was with the wolves to imitate the challenge of bucks in the jungle and the grunt of the little wild pig. So, as soon as Messua pronounced a word Mowgli would imitate it almost perfectly, and before dark he had learned the names of many things in the hut.

There was a difficulty at bedtime, because Mowgli would not sleep under anything that looked so like a panther trap as that hut, and when they shut the door he went through the window. "Give him his will," said Messua's husband. "Remember he can never till now have slept on a bed. If he is indeed sent in the place of our son he will not run away."

So Mowgli stretched himself in some long, clean grass at the edge of the field, but before he had closed his eyes a soft gray nose poked him under the chin.

"Phew!" said Gray Brother (he was the eldest of Mother Wolf's cubs). "This is a poor reward for following thee twenty miles. Thou smellest of wood smoke and cattle--altogether like a man already. Wake, Little Brother; I bring news."

"Are all well in the jungle?" said Mowgli, hugging him.

"All except the wolves that were burned with the Red Flower. Now, listen. Shere Khan has gone away to hunt far off till his coat grows again, for he is badly singed. When he returns he swears that he will lay thy bones in the Waingunga."

"There are two words to that. I also have made a little promise. But news is always good. I am tired to-night,--very tired with new things, Gray Brother,--but bring me the news always."

"Thou wilt not forget that thou art a wolf? Men will not make thee forget?" said Gray Brother anxiously.

"Never. I will always remember that I love thee and all in our cave. But also I will always remember that I have been cast out of the Pack."
"And that thou mayest be cast out of another pack. Men are only men, Little Brother, and their talk is like the talk of frogs in a pond. When I come down here again, I will wait for thee in the bamboos at the edge of the grazing-ground."

For three months after that night Mowgli hardly ever left the village gate, he was so busy learning the ways and customs of men. First he had to wear a cloth round him, which annoyed him horribly; and then he had to learn about money, which he did not in the least understand, and about plowing, of which he did not see the use. Then the little children in the village made him very angry. Luckily, the Law of the Jungle had taught him to keep his temper, for in the jungle life and food depend on keeping your temper; but when they made fun of him because he would not play games or fly kites, or because he mispronounced some word, only the knowledge that it was unsportsmanlike to kill little naked cubs kept him from picking them up and breaking them in two.

He did not know his own strength in the least. In the jungle he knew he was weak compared with the beasts, but in the village people said that he was as strong as a bull.

And Mowgli had not the faintest idea of the difference that caste makes between man and man. When the potter's donkey slipped in the clay pit, Mowgli hauled it out by the tail, and helped to stack the pots for their journey to the market at Khanhiwara. That was very shocking, too, for the potter is a low-caste man, and his donkey is worse. When the priest scolded him, Mowgli threatened to put him on the donkey too, and the priest told Messua's husband that Mowgli had better be set to work as soon as possible; and the village head-man told Mowgli that he would have to go out with the buffaloes next day, and herd them while they grazed. No one was more pleased than Mowgli; and that night, because he had been appointed a servant of the village, as it were, he went off to a circle that met every evening on a masonry platform under a great fig-tree. It was the village club, and the head-man and the watchman and the barber, who knew all the gossip of the village, and old Buldeo, the village hunter, who had a Tower musket, met and smoked. The monkeys sat and talked in the upper branches, and there was a hole under the platform where a cobra lived, and he had his little platter of milk every night because he was sacred; and the old men sat around the tree and talked, and pulled at the big huqas (the water-pipes) till far into the night. They told wonderful tales of gods and men and ghosts; and Buldeo told even more wonderful ones of the ways of beasts in the jungle, till the eyes of the children sitting outside the circle bulged out of their heads. Most of the tales were about animals, for the jungle was always at their door. The deer and the wild pig grubbed up their crops, and now and again the tiger carried off a man at twilight, within sight of the village gates.

Mowgli, who naturally knew something about what they were talking of, had to cover his face not to show that he was laughing, while Buldeo, the Tower musket across his knees, climbed on from one wonderful story to another, and Mowgli's shoulders shook.

Buldeo was explaining how the tiger that had carried away Messua's son was a ghost-tiger, and his body was inhabited by the ghost of a wicked, old money-lender, who had died some years ago. "And I know that this is true," he said, "because Purun Dass always limped from the blow that he got in a riot when his account books were burned, and the tiger that I speak of he limps, too, for the tracks of his pads are unequal."

"True, true, that must be the truth," said the gray-beards, nodding together.

"Are all these tales such cobwebs and moon talk?" said Mowgli. "That tiger limps because he was born lame, as everyone knows. To talk of the soul of a money-lender in a beast that never had the courage of a jackal is child's talk."

Buldeo was speechless with surprise for a moment, and the head-man stared.

"Oho! It is the jungle brat, is it?" said Buldeo. "If thou art so wise, better bring his hide to Khanhiwara, for the Government has set a hundred rupees on his life. Better still, talk not when thy elders speak."

Mowgli rose to go. "All the evening I have lain here listening," he called back over his shoulder, "and, except once or twice, Buldeo has not said one word of truth concerning the jungle, which is at his very doors. How, then, shall I believe the tales of ghosts and gods and goblins which he says he has seen?"

"It is full time that boy went to herding," said the head-man, while Buldeo puffed and snorted at Mowgli's impertinence.

The custom of most Indian villages is for a few boys to take the cattle and buffaloes out to graze in the early morning, and bring them back at night. The very cattle that would trample a white man to death allow themselves to be banged and bullied and shouted at by children that hardly come up to their noses. So long as the boys keep with the herds they are safe, for not even the tiger will charge a mob of cattle. But if they straggle to pick flowers or hunt lizards, they are sometimes carried off. Mowgli went through the village street in the dawn, sitting on the back of Rama, the great herd bull. The slaty-blue buffaloes, with their long, backward-sweeping horns and savage eyes, rose out their byres, one by one, and followed him, and Mowgli made it very clear to the children with him that he was the master. He beat the buffaloes with a long, polished bamboo, and told Kamya, one of the boys, to graze the cattle by themselves, while he went on with the buffaloes, and to be very careful not to stray away from the herd.

An Indian grazing ground is all rocks and scrub and tussocks and little ravines, among which the herds scatter and disappear. The buffaloes generally keep to the pools and muddy places, where they lie wallowing or basking in the warm mud for hours. Mowgli drove them on to the edge of the plain where the Waingunga came out of the jungle; then he dropped from Rama's neck, trotted off to a bamboo clump, and found Gray Brother. "Ah," said Gray Brother, "I have waited here very many days. What is the meaning of this cattle-herding work?"

"It is an order," said Mowgli. "I am a village herd for a while. What news of Shere Khan?"
"He has come back to this country, and has waited here a long time for thee. Now he has gone off again, for the game is scarce. But he means to kill thee."

"Very good," said Mowgli. "So long as he is away do thou or one of the four brothers sit on that rock, so that I can see thee as I come out of the village. When he comes back wait for me in the ravine by the dhak tree in the center of the plain. We need not walk into Shere Khan's mouth."

Then Mowgli picked out a shady place, and lay down and slept while the buffaloes grazed round him. Herding in India is one of the laziest things in the world. The cattle move and crunch, and lie down, and move on again, and they do not even low. They only grunt, and the buffaloes very seldom say anything, but get down into the muddy pools one after another, and work their way into the mud till only their noses and staring china-blue eyes show above the surface, and then they lie like logs. The sun makes the rocks dance in the heat, and the herd children hear one kite (never any more) whistling almost out of sight overhead, and they know that if they died, or a cow died, that kite would sweep down, and the next kite miles away would see him drop and follow, and the next, and the next, and almost before they were dead there would be a score of hungry kites come out of nowhere. Then they sleep and wake and sleep again, and weave little baskets of dried grass and put grasshoppers in them; or catch two praying mantises and make them fight; or string a necklace of red and black jungle nuts; or watch a lizard basking on a rock, or a snake hunting a frog near the wallows. Then they sing long, long songs with odd native quavers at the end of them, and the day seems longer than most people's whole lives, and perhaps they make a mud castle with mud figures of men and horses and buffaloes, and put reeds into the men's hands, and pretend that they are kings and the figures are their armies, or that they are gods to be worshiped. Then evening comes and the children call, and the buffaloes lumber up out of the sticky mud with noises like gunshots going off one after the other, and they all string across the gray plain back to the twinkling village lights.

Day after day Mowgli would lead the buffaloes out to their wallows, and day after day he would see Gray Brother's back a mile and a half away across the plain (so he knew that Shere Khan had not come back), and day after day he would lie on the grass listening to the noises round him, and dreaming of old days in the jungle. If Shere Khan had made a false step with his lame paw up in the jungles by the Waingunga, Mowgli would have heard him in those long, still mornings.
At last a day came when he did not see Gray Brother at the signal place, and he laughed and headed the buffaloes for the ravine by the dhāk tree, which was all covered with golden-red flowers. There sat Gray Brother, every bristle on his back lifted.

"He has hidden for a month to throw thee off thy guard. He crossed the ranges last night with Tabaqui, hot-foot on thy trail," said the Wolf, panting.

Mowgli frowned. "I am not afraid of Shere Khan, but Tabaqui is very cunning."

"Have no fear," said Gray Brother, licking his lips a little. "I met Tabaqui in the dawn. Now he is telling all his wisdom to the kites, but he told me everything before I broke his back. Shere Khan's plan is to wait for thee at the village gate this evening--for thee and for no one else. He is lying up now, in the big dry ravine of the Waingunga."
"Has he eaten today, or does he hunt empty?" said Mowgli, for the answer meant life and death to him.

"He killed at dawn,--a pig,--and he has drunk too. Remember, Shere Khan could never fast, even for the sake of revenge."

"Oh! Fool, fool! What a cub's cub it is! Eaten and drunk too, and he thinks that I shall wait till he has slept! Now, where does he lie up? If there were but ten of us we might pull him down as he lies. These buffaloes will not charge unless they wind him, and I cannot speak their language. Can we get behind his track so that they may smell it?"

"He swam far down the Waingunga to cut that off," said Gray Brother.

"Tabaqui told him that, I know. He would never have thought of it alone." Mowgli stood with his finger in his mouth, thinking. "The big ravine of the Waingunga. That opens out on the plain not half a mile from here. I can take the herd round through the jungle to the head of the ravine and then sweep down--but he would slink out at the foot. We must block that end. Gray Brother, canst thou cut the herd in two for me?"

"Not I, perhaps--but I have brought a wise helper." Gray Brother trotted off and dropped into a hole. Then there lifted up a huge gray head that Mowgli knew well, and the hot air was filled with the most desolate cry of all the jungle--the hunting howl of a wolf at midday.

"Akela! Akela!" said Mowgli, clapping his hands. "I might have known that thou wouldst not forget me. We have a big work in hand. Cut the herd in two, Akela. Keep the cows and calves together, and the bulls and the plow buffaloes by themselves."

The two wolves ran, ladies'-chain fashion, in and out of the herd, which snorted and threw up its head, and separated into two clumps. In one, the cow-buffaloes stood with their calves in the center, and glared and pawed, ready, if a wolf would only stay still, to charge down and trample the life out of him. In the other, the bulls and the young bulls snorted and stamped, but though they looked more imposing they were much less dangerous, for they had no calves to protect. No six men could have divided the herd so neatly.

"What orders!" panted Akela. "They are trying to join again."

Mowgli slipped on to Rama's back. "Drive the bulls away to the left, Akela. Gray Brother, when we are gone, hold the cows together, and drive them into the foot of the ravine."

"How far?" said Gray Brother, panting and snapping.

"Till the sides are higher than Shere Khan can jump," shouted Mowgli. "Keep them there till we come down." The bulls swept off as Akela bayed, and Gray Brother stopped in front of the cows. They charged down on him, and he ran just before them to the foot of the ravine, as Akela drove the bulls far to the left.

"Well done! Another charge and they are fairly started. Careful, now--careful, Akela. A snap too much and the bulls will charge. Hujah! This is wilder work than driving black-buck. Didst thou think these creatures could move so swiftly?" Mowgli called.

"I have--have hunted these too in my time," gasped Akela in the dust. "Shall I turn them into the jungle?"

"Ay! Turn. Swiftly turn them! Rama is mad with rage. Oh, if I could only tell him what I need of him to-day."

Lesson 17

1. Finish the chapter.
2. Why was Mowgli rejected? (Answers)

The bulls were turned, to the right this time, and crashed into the standing thicket. The other herd children, watching with the cattle half a mile away, hurried to the village as fast as their legs could carry them, crying that the buffaloes had gone mad and run away.

But Mowgli's plan was simple enough. All he wanted to do was to make a big circle uphill and get at the head of the ravine, and then take the bulls down it and catch Shere Khan between the bulls and the cows; for he knew that after a meal and a full drink Shere Khan would not be in any condition to fight or to clamber up the sides of the ravine. He was soothing the buffaloes now by voice, and Akela had dropped far to the rear, only whimpering once or twice to hurry the rear-guard. It was a long, long circle, for they did not wish to get too near the ravine and give Shere Khan warning. At last Mowgli rounded up the bewildered herd at the head of the ravine on a grassy patch that sloped steeply down to the ravine itself. From that height you could see across the tops of the trees down to the plain below; but what Mowgli looked at was the sides of the ravine, and he saw with a great deal of satisfaction that they ran nearly straight up and down, while the vines and creepers that hung over them would give no foothold to a tiger who wanted to get out.

"Let them breathe, Akela," he said, holding up his hand. "They have not winded him yet. Let them breathe. I must tell Shere Khan who comes. We have him in the trap."

He put his hands to his mouth and shouted down the ravine--it was almost like shouting down a tunnel--and the echoes jumped from rock to rock.

After a long time there came back the drawling, sleepy snarl of a full-fed tiger just wakened. "Who calls?" said Shere Khan, and a splendid peacock fluttered up out of the ravine screeching.

"I, Mowgli. Cattle thief, it is time to come to the Council Rock! Down--hurry them down, Akela! Down, Rama, down!"

The herd paused for an instant at the edge of the slope, but Akela gave tongue in the full hunting-yell, and they pitched over one after the other, just as steamers shoot rapids, the sand and stones spurting up round them. Once started, there was no chance of stopping, and before they were fairly in the bed of the ravine Rama winded Shere Khan and bellowed.

"Ha! Ha!" said Mowgli, on his back. "Now thou knowest!" and the torrent of black horns, foaming muzzles, and staring eyes whirled down the ravine just as boulders go down in floodtime; the weaker buffaloes being shouldered out to the sides of the ravine where they tore through the creepers. They knew what the business was before them--the terrible charge of the buffalo herd against which no tiger can hope to stand. Shere Khan heard the thunder of their hoofs, picked himself up, and lumbered down the ravine, looking from side to side for some way of escape, but the walls of the ravine were straight and he had to hold on, heavy with his dinner and his drink, willing to do anything rather than fight. The herd splashed through the pool he had just left, bellowing till the narrow cut rang. Mowgli heard an answering bellow from the foot of the ravine, saw Shere Khan turn (the tiger knew if the worst came to the worst it was better to meet the bulls than the cows with their calves), and then Rama tripped, stumbled, and went on again over something soft, and, with the bulls at his heels, crashed full into the other herd, while the weaker buffaloes were lifted clean off their feet by the shock of the meeting. That charge carried both herds out into the plain, goring and stamping and snorting. Mowgli watched his time, and slipped off Rama's neck, laying about him right and left with his stick.

"Quick, Akela! Break them up. Scatter them, or they will be fighting one another. Drive them away, Akela. Hai, Rama! Hai, hai, hai! my children. Softly now, softly! It is all over."

Akela and Gray Brother ran to and fro nipping the buffaloes' legs, and though the herd wheeled once to charge up the ravine again, Mowgli managed to turn Rama, and the others followed him to the wallows.

Shere Khan needed no more trampling. He was dead, and the kites were coming for him already.

"Brothers, that was a dog's death," said Mowgli, feeling for the knife he always carried in a sheath round his neck now that he lived with men. "But he would never have shown fight. His hide will look well on the Council Rock. We must get to work swiftly."

A boy trained among men would never have dreamed of skinning a ten-foot tiger alone, but Mowgli knew better than anyone else how an animal's skin is fitted on, and how it can be taken off. But it was hard work, and Mowgli slashed and tore and grunted for an hour, while the wolves lolled out their tongues, or came forward and tugged as he ordered them. Presently a hand fell on his shoulder, and looking up he saw Buldeo with the Tower musket. The children had told the village about the buffalo stampede, and Buldeo went out angrily, only too anxious to correct Mowgli for not taking better care of the herd. The wolves dropped out of sight as soon as they saw the man coming.

"What is this folly?" said Buldeo angrily. "To think that thou canst skin a tiger! Where did the buffaloes kill him? It is the Lame Tiger too, and there is a hundred rupees on his head. Well, well, we will overlook thy letting the herd run off, and perhaps I will give thee one of the rupees of the reward when I have taken the skin to Khanhiwara." He fumbled in his waist cloth for flint and steel, and stooped down to singe Shere Khan's whiskers. Most native hunters always singe a tiger's whiskers to prevent his ghost from haunting them.

"Hum!" said Mowgli, half to himself as he ripped back the skin of a forepaw. "So thou wilt take the hide to Khanhiwara for the reward, and perhaps give me one rupee? Now it is in my mind that I need the skin for my own use. Heh! Old man, take away that fire!"

"What talk is this to the chief hunter of the village? Thy luck and the stupidity of thy buffaloes have helped thee to this kill. The tiger has just fed, or he would have gone twenty miles by this time. Thou canst not even skin him properly, little beggar brat, and forsooth I, Buldeo, must be told not to singe his whiskers. Mowgli, I will not give thee one anna of the reward, but only a very big beating. Leave the carcass!"

"By the Bull that bought me," said Mowgli, who was trying to get at the shoulder, "must I stay babbling to an old ape all noon? Here, Akela, this man plagues me."

Buldeo, who was still stooping over Shere Khan's head, found himself sprawling on the grass, with a gray wolf standing over him, while Mowgli went on skinning as though he were alone in all India.

"Ye-es," he said, between his teeth. "Thou art altogether right, Buldeo. Thou wilt never give me one anna of the reward. There is an old war between this lame tiger and myself--a very old war, and--I have won."

To do Buldeo justice, if he had been ten years younger he would have taken his chance with Akela had he met the wolf in the woods, but a wolf who obeyed the orders of this boy who had private wars with man-eating tigers was not a common animal. It was sorcery, magic of the worst kind, thought Buldeo, and he wondered whether the amulet round his neck would protect him. He lay as still as still, expecting every minute to see Mowgli turn into a tiger too.

"Maharaj! Great King," he said at last in a husky whisper.

"Yes," said Mowgli, without turning his head, chuckling a little.

"I am an old man. I did not know that thou wast anything more than a herdsboy. May I rise up and go away, or will thy servant tear me to pieces?"

"Go, and peace go with thee. Only, another time do not meddle with my game. Let him go, Akela." Buldeo hobbled away to the village as fast as he could, looking back over his shoulder in case Mowgli should change into something terrible. When he got to the village he told a tale of magic and enchantment and sorcery that made the priest look very grave.

Mowgli went on with his work, but it was nearly twilight before he and the wolves had drawn the great gay skin clear of the body.

"Now we must hide this and take the buffaloes home! Help me to herd them, Akela."

The herd rounded up in the misty twilight, and when they got near the village Mowgli saw lights, and heard the conches and bells in the temple blowing and banging. Half the village seemed to be waiting for him by the gate. "That is because I have killed Shere Khan," he said to himself. But a shower of stones whistled about his ears, and the villagers shouted: "Sorcerer! Wolf's brat! Jungle demon! Go away! Get hence quickly or the priest will turn thee into a wolf again. Shoot, Buldeo, shoot!"

The old Tower musket went off with a bang, and a young buffalo bellowed in pain.

"More sorcery!" shouted the villagers. "He can turn bullets. Buldeo, that was thy buffalo."

"Now what is this?" said Mowgli, bewildered, as the stones flew thicker.

"They are not unlike the Pack, these brothers of thine," said Akela, sitting down composedly. "It is in my head that, if bullets mean anything, they would cast thee out."

"Wolf! Wolf's cub! Go away!" shouted the priest, waving a sprig of the sacred tulsi plant.

"Again? Last time it was because I was a man. This time it is because I am a wolf. Let us go, Akela."

A woman--it was Messua--ran across to the herd, and cried: "Oh, my son, my son! They say thou art a sorcerer who can turn himself into a beast at will. I do not believe, but go away or they will kill thee. Buldeo says thou art a wizard, but I know thou hast avenged Nathoo's death."

"Come back, Messua!" shouted the crowd. "Come back, or we will stone thee."

Mowgli laughed a little short ugly laugh, for a stone had hit him in the mouth. "Run back, Messua. This is one of the foolish tales they tell under the big tree at dusk. I have at least paid for thy son's life. Farewell; and run quickly, for I shall send the herd in more swiftly than their brickbats. I am no wizard, Messua. Farewell!"

"Now, once more, Akela," he cried. "Bring the herd in."

The buffaloes were anxious enough to get to the village. They hardly needed Akela's yell, but charged through the gate like a whirlwind, scattering the crowd right and left.

"Keep count!" shouted Mowgli scornfully. "It may be that I have stolen one of them. Keep count, for I will do your herding no more. Fare you well, children of men, and thank Messua that I do not come in with my wolves and hunt you up and down your street."

He turned on his heel and walked away with the Lone Wolf, and as he looked up at the stars he felt happy. "No more sleeping in traps for me, Akela. Let us get Shere Khan's skin and go away. No, we will not hurt the village, for Messua was kind to me."

When the moon rose over the plain, making it look all milky, the horrified villagers saw Mowgli, with two wolves at his heels and a bundle on his head, trotting across at the steady wolf's trot that eats up the long miles like fire. Then they banged the temple bells and blew the conches louder than ever. And Messua cried, and Buldeo embroidered the story of his adventures in the jungle, till he ended by saying that Akela stood up on his hind legs and talked like a man.

The moon was just going down when Mowgli and the two wolves came to the hill of the Council Rock, and they stopped at Mother Wolf's cave.

"They have cast me out from the Man-Pack, Mother," shouted Mowgli, "but I come with the hide of Shere Khan to keep my word."

Mother Wolf walked stiffly from the cave with the cubs behind her, and her eyes glowed as she saw the skin.

"I told him on that day, when he crammed his head and shoulders into this cave, hunting for thy life, Little Frog--I told him that the hunter would be the hunted. It is well done."

"Little Brother, it is well done," said a deep voice in the thicket. "We were lonely in the jungle without thee, and Bagheera came running to Mowgli's bare feet. They clambered up the Council Rock together, and Mowgli spread the skin out on the flat stone where Akela used to sit, and pegged it down with four slivers of bamboo, and Akela lay down upon it, and called the old call to the Council, "Look--look well, O Wolves," exactly as he had called when Mowgli was first brought there.

Ever since Akela had been deposed, the Pack had been without a leader, hunting and fighting at their own pleasure. But they answered the call from habit; and some of them were lame from the traps they had fallen into, and some limped from shot wounds, and some were mangy from eating bad food, and many were missing. But they came to the Council Rock, all that were left of them, and saw Shere Khan's striped hide on the rock, and the huge claws dangling at the end of the empty dangling feet. It was then that Mowgli made up a song that came up into his throat all by itself, and he shouted it aloud, leaping up and down on the rattling skin, and beating time with his heels till he had no more breath left, while Gray Brother and Akela howled between the verses.
"Look well, O Wolves. Have I kept my word?" said Mowgli. And the wolves bayed "Yes," and one tattered wolf howled:

"Lead us again, O Akela. Lead us again, O Man-cub, for we be sick of this lawlessness, and we would be the Free People once more."

"Nay," purred Bagheera, "that may not be. When ye are full-fed, the madness may come upon you again. Not for nothing are ye called the Free People. Ye fought for freedom, and it is yours. Eat it, O Wolves."

"Man-Pack and Wolf-Pack have cast me out," said Mowgli. "Now I will hunt alone in the jungle."

"And we will hunt with thee," said the four cubs.

So Mowgli went away and hunted with the four cubs in the jungle from that day on. But he was not always alone, because, years afterward, he became a man and married.

But that is a story for grown-ups.

Lesson 18

1. Introduction: "Toomai is a young boy who is the fourth generation of elephant drivers in his family. The government owned elephant that he helps herd is Kala Nag, an old and loyal animal. Kala Nag and his handlers are in a camp near the jungle, helping break in the new elephants recently caught by the elephant hunters. Some men notice that Toomai has a special way with the elephants, but his father is afraid he will also become an elephant hunter that catches wild elephants in the jungle. The father feels that his status as a mahout of the plains is superior. One night, Toomai rides on Kala Nag's back as the old elephant breaks his chains and joins other elephants for a legendary dance of the elephants that no other human has witnessed."
    (from classical-childrens-books.com/jungle-book-unit-study.html)

2. Read the first part of "Toomai of the Elephants."

3. Read the poem of Kala Nag at the start of the story. What do you think domesticated animals remember about their former lives?

Vocabulary

1. Use the definitions to help you unscramble the words. Write your answers on a separate piece of paper. This continues onto the next page. (Answers)

1.	citfysan	set apart or declare holy
2.	kepc	an amount of food, strike with a beak, light kiss
3.	deru	bitterly regret
4.	naprootfina	degrade, profane or desecrate

5.	eifsfdu	spread or cause to spread over a wide area
6.	detquacina	to come to know, have a fair knowledge of
7.	suters	redish brown color, rustic
8.	maryniul	artificial light, someone who inspires
9.	marytengraf	consisting of small parts, incomplete
10.	dettaaig	feeling troubled

I will remember what I was, I am sick of rope and chain—
I will remember my old strength and all my forest affairs.
I will not sell my back to man for a bundle of sugar-cane:
I will go out to my own kind, and the wood-folk in their lairs.
I will go out until the day, until the morning break—
Out to the wind's untainted kiss, the water's clean caress;
I will forget my ankle-ring and snap my picket stake.
I will revisit my lost loves, and playmates masterless!

Kala Nag, which means Black Snake, had served the Indian Government in every way that an elephant could serve it for forty-seven years, and as he was fully twenty years old when he was caught, that makes him nearly seventy--a ripe age for an elephant. He remembered pushing, with a big leather pad on his forehead, at a gun stuck in deep mud, and that was before the Afghan War of 1842, and he had not then come to his full strength.

His mother Radha Pyari,--Radha the darling,--who had been caught in the same drive with Kala Nag, told him, before his little milk tusks had dropped out, that elephants who were afraid always got hurt. Kala Nag knew that that advice was good, for the first time that he saw a shell burst he backed, screaming, into a stand of piled rifles, and the bayonets pricked him in all his softest places. So, before he was twenty-five, he gave up being afraid, and so he was the best-loved and the best-looked-after elephant in the service of the Government of India. He had carried tents, twelve hundred pounds' weight of tents, on the march in Upper India. He had been hoisted into a ship at the end of a steam crane and taken for days across the water, and made to carry a mortar on his back in a strange and rocky country very far from India, and had seen the Emperor Theodore lying dead in Magdala, and had come back again in the steamer entitled, so the soldiers said, to the Abyssinian War medal. He had seen his fellow elephants die of cold and epilepsy and starvation and sunstroke up at a place called Ali Musjid, ten years later; and afterward he had been sent down thousands of miles south to haul and pile big balks of teak in the timberyards at Moulmein. There he had half killed an insubordinate young elephant who was shirking his fair share of work.

After that he was taken off timber-hauling, and employed, with a few score other elephants who were trained to the business, in helping to catch wild elephants among the Garo hills. Elephants are very strictly preserved by the Indian Government. There is one whole department which does nothing else but hunt them, and catch them, and break them in, and send them up and down the country as they are needed for work.

Kala Nag stood ten fair feet at the shoulders, and his tusks had been cut off short at five feet, and bound round the ends, to prevent them splitting, with bands of copper; but he could do more with those stumps than any untrained elephant could do with the real sharpened ones. When, after weeks and weeks of cautious driving of scattered elephants across the hills, the forty or fifty wild monsters were driven into the last stockade, and the big drop gate, made of tree trunks lashed together, jarred down behind them, Kala Nag, at the word of command, would go into that flaring, trumpeting pandemonium (generally at night, when the flicker of the torches made it difficult to judge distances), and, picking out the biggest and wildest tusker of the mob, would hammer him and hustle him into quiet while the men on the backs of the other elephants roped and tied the smaller ones.

There was nothing in the way of fighting that Kala Nag, the old wise Black Snake, did not know, for he had stood up more than once in his time to the charge of the wounded tiger, and, curling up his soft trunk to be out of harm's way, had knocked the springing brute sideways in mid-air with a quick sickle cut of his head, that he had invented all by himself; had knocked him over, and kneeled upon him with his huge knees till the life went out with a gasp and a howl, and there was only a fluffy striped thing on the ground for Kala Nag to pull by the tail.

"Yes," said Big Toomai, his driver, the son of Black Toomai who had taken him to Abyssinia, and grandson of Toomai of the Elephants who had seen him caught, "there is nothing that the Black Snake fears except me. He has seen three generations of us feed him and groom him, and he will live to see four."

"He is afraid of me also," said Little Toomai, standing up to his full height of four feet, with only one rag upon him. He was ten years old, the eldest son of Big Toomai, and, according to custom, he would take his father's place on Kala Nag's neck when he grew up, and would handle the heavy iron ankus, the elephant goad, that had been worn smooth by his father, and his grandfather, and his great-grandfather.

He knew what he was talking of; for he had been born under Kala Nag's shadow, had played with the end of his trunk before he could walk, had taken him down to water as soon as he could walk, and Kala Nag would no more have dreamed of disobeying his shrill little orders than he would have dreamed of killing him on that day when Big Toomai carried the little brown baby under Kala Nag's tusks, and told him to salute his master that was to be.

"Yes," said Little Toomai, "he is afraid of me," and he took long strides up to Kala Nag, called him a fat old pig, and made him lift up his feet one after the other.

"Wah!" said Little Toomai, "thou art a big elephant," and he wagged his fluffy head, quoting his father. "The Government may pay for elephants, but they belong to us mahouts. When thou art old, Kala Nag, there will come some rich rajah, and he will buy thee from the Government, on account of thy size and thy manners, and then thou wilt have nothing to do but to carry gold earrings in thy ears, and a gold howdah on thy back, and a red cloth covered with gold on thy sides, and walk at the head of the processions of the King. Then I shall sit on thy neck, O Kala Nag, with a silver ankus, and men will run before us with golden sticks, crying, 'Room for the King's elephant!' That will be good, Kala Nag, but not so good as this hunting in the jungles."

"Umph!" said Big Toomai. "Thou art a boy, and as wild as a buffalo-calf. This running up and down among the hills is not the best Government service. I am getting old, and I do not love wild elephants. Give me brick elephant lines, one stall to each elephant, and big stumps to tie them to safely, and flat, broad roads to exercise upon, instead of this come-and-go camping. Aha, the Cawnpore barracks were good. There was a bazaar close by, and only three hours' work a day."

Little Toomai remembered the Cawnpore elephant-lines and said nothing. He very much preferred the camp life, and hated those broad, flat roads, with the daily grubbing for grass in the forage reserve, and the long hours when there was nothing to do except to watch Kala Nag fidgeting in his pickets.

What Little Toomai liked was to scramble up bridle paths that only an elephant could take; the dip into the valley below; the glimpses of the wild elephants browsing miles away; the rush of the frightened pig and peacock under Kala Nag's feet; the blinding warm rains, when all the hills and valleys smoked; the beautiful misty mornings when nobody knew where they would camp that night; the steady, cautious drive of the wild elephants, and the mad rush and blaze and hullabaloo of the last night's drive, when the elephants poured into the stockade like boulders in a landslide, found that they could not get out, and flung themselves at the heavy posts only to be driven back by yells and flaring torches and volleys of blank cartridge.

Even a little boy could be of use there, and Toomai was as useful as three boys. He would get his torch and wave it, and yell with the best. But the really good time came when the driving out began, and the Keddah--that is, the stockade--looked like a picture of the end of the world, and men had to make signs to one another, because they could not hear themselves speak. Then Little Toomai would climb up to the top of one of the quivering stockade posts, his sun-bleached brown hair flying loose all over his shoulders, and he looking like a goblin in the torch-light. And as soon as there was a lull you could hear his high-pitched yells of encouragement to Kala Nag, above the trumpeting and crashing, and snapping of ropes, and groans of the tethered elephants. "Mael, mael, Kala Nag! (Go on, go on, Black Snake!) Dant do! (Give him the tusk!) Somalo! Somalo! (Careful, careful!) Maro! Mar! (Hit him, hit him!) Mind the post! Arre! Arre! Hai! Yai! Kya-a-ah!" he would shout, and the big fight between Kala Nag and the wild elephant would sway to and fro across the Keddah, and the old elephant catchers would wipe the sweat out of their eyes, and find time to nod to Little Toomai wriggling with joy on the top of the posts.

He did more than wriggle. One night he slid down from the post and slipped in between the elephants and threw up the loose end of a rope, which had dropped, to a driver who was trying to get a purchase on the leg of a kicking young calf (calves always give more trouble than full-grown animals). Kala Nag saw him, caught him in his trunk, and handed him up to Big Toomai, who slapped him then and there, and put him back on the post.

Next morning he gave him a scolding and said, "Are not good brick elephant lines and a little tent carrying enough, that thou must needs go elephant catching on thy own account, little worthless? Now those foolish hunters, whose pay is less than my pay, have spoken to Petersen Sahib of the matter." Little Toomai was frightened. He did not know much of white men, but Petersen Sahib was the greatest white man in the world to him. He was the head of all the Keddah operations--the man who caught all the elephants for the Government of India, and who knew more about the ways of elephants than any living man.

"What--what will happen?" said Little Toomai.

"Happen! The worst that can happen. Petersen Sahib is a madman. Else why should he go hunting these wild devils? He may even require thee to be an elephant catcher, to sleep anywhere in these fever-filled jungles, and at last to be trampled to death in the Keddah. It is well that this nonsense ends safely. Next week the catching is over, and we of the plains are sent back to our stations. Then we will march on smooth roads, and forget all this hunting. But, son, I am angry that thou shouldst meddle in the business that belongs to these dirty Assamese jungle folk. Kala Nag will obey none but me, so I must go with him into the Keddah, but he is only a fighting elephant, and he does not help to rope them. So I sit at my ease, as befits a mahout,--not a mere hunter,--a mahout, I say, and a man who gets a pension at the end of his service. Is the family of Toomai of the Elephants to be trodden underfoot in the dirt of a Keddah? Bad one! Wicked one! Worthless son! Go and wash Kala Nag and attend to his ears, and see that there are no thorns in his feet. Or else Petersen Sahib will surely catch thee and make thee a wild hunter--a follower of elephant's foot tracks, a jungle bear. Bah! Shame! Go!"

Little Toomai went off without saying a word, but he told Kala Nag all his grievances while he was examining his feet. "No matter," said Little Toomai, turning up the fringe of Kala Nag's huge right ear. "They have said my name to Petersen Sahib, and perhaps--and perhaps--and perhaps--who knows? Hai! That is a big thorn that I have pulled out!"

The next few days were spent in getting the elephants together, in walking the newly caught wild elephants up and down between a couple of tame ones to prevent them giving too much trouble on the downward march to the plains, and in taking stock of the blankets and ropes and things that had been worn out or lost in the forest.

Petersen Sahib came in on his clever she-elephant Pudmini; he had been paying off other camps among the hills, for the season was coming to an end, and there was a native clerk sitting at a table under a tree, to pay the drivers their wages. As each man was paid he went back to his elephant, and joined the line that stood ready to start. The catchers, and hunters, and beaters, the men of the regular Keddah, who stayed in the jungle year in and year out, sat on the backs of the elephants that belonged to Petersen Sahib's permanent force, or leaned against the trees with their guns across their arms, and made fun of the drivers who were going away, and laughed when the newly caught elephants broke the line and ran about.

Big Toomai went up to the clerk with Little Toomai behind him, and Machua Appa, the head tracker, said in an undertone to a friend of his, "There goes one piece of good elephant stuff at least. 'Tis a pity to send that young jungle-cock to molt in the plains."

Now Petersen Sahib had ears all over him, as a man must have who listens to the most silent of all living things--the wild elephant. He turned where he was lying all along on Pudmini's back and said, "What is that? I did not know of a man among the plains-drivers who had wit enough to rope even a dead elephant."

"This is not a man, but a boy. He went into the Keddah at the last drive, and threw Barmao there the rope, when we were trying to get that young calf with the blotch on his shoulder away from his mother."

Machua Appa pointed at Little Toomai, and Petersen Sahib looked, and Little Toomai bowed to the earth.

"He throw a rope? He is smaller than a picket-pin. Little one, what is thy name?" said Petersen Sahib.

Little Toomai was too frightened to speak, but Kala Nag was behind him, and Toomai made a sign with his hand, and the elephant caught him up in his trunk and held him level with Pudmini's forehead, in front of the great Petersen Sahib. Then Little Toomai covered his face with his hands, for he was only a child, and except where elephants were concerned, he was just as bashful as a child could be.

"Oho!" said Petersen Sahib, smiling underneath his mustache, "and why didst thou teach thy elephant that trick? Was it to help thee steal green corn from the roofs of the houses when the ears are put out to dry?"

"Not green corn, Protector of the Poor,--melons," said Little Toomai, and all the men sitting about broke into a roar of laughter. Most of them had taught their elephants that trick when they were boys. Little Toomai was hanging eight feet up in the air, and he wished very much that he were eight feet underground.

"He is Toomai, my son, Sahib," said Big Toomai, scowling. "He is a very bad boy, and he will end in a jail, Sahib."

"Of that I have my doubts," said Petersen Sahib. "A boy who can face a full Keddah at his age does not end in jails. See, little one, here are four annas to spend in sweetmeats because thou hast a little head under that great thatch of hair. In time thou mayest become a hunter too." Big Toomai scowled more than ever. "Remember, though, that Keddahs are not good for children to play in," Petersen Sahib went on.

"Must I never go there, Sahib?" asked Little Toomai with a big gasp.

"Yes." Petersen Sahib smiled again. "When thou hast seen the elephants dance. That is the proper time. Come to me when thou hast seen the elephants dance, and then I will let thee go into all the Keddahs."

There was another roar of laughter, for that is an old joke among elephant-catchers, and it means just never. There are great cleared flat places hidden away in the forests that are called elephants' ball-rooms, but even these are only found by accident, and no man has ever seen the elephants dance. When a driver boasts of his skill and bravery the other drivers say, "And when didst thou see the elephants dance?"

Kala Nag put Little Toomai down, and he bowed to the earth again and went away with his father, and gave the silver four-anna piece to his mother, who was nursing his baby brother, and they all were put up on Kala Nag's back, and the line of grunting, squealing elephants rolled down the hill path to the plains. It was a very lively march on account of the new elephants, who gave trouble at every ford, and needed coaxing or beating every other minute.

Big Toomai prodded Kala Nag spitefully, for he was very angry, but Little Toomai was too happy to speak. Petersen Sahib had noticed him, and given him money, so he felt as a private soldier would feel if he had been called out of the ranks and praised by his commander-in-chief.

"What did Petersen Sahib mean by the elephant dance?" he said, at last, softly to his mother.

Big Toomai heard him and grunted. "That thou shouldst never be one of these hill buffaloes of trackers. That was what he meant. Oh, you in front, what is blocking the way?"

An Assamese driver, two or three elephants ahead, turned round angrily, crying: "Bring up Kala Nag, and knock this youngster of mine into good behavior. Why should Petersen Sahib have chosen me to go down with you donkeys of the rice fields? Lay your beast alongside, Toomai, and let him prod with his tusks. By all the Gods of the Hills, these new elephants are possessed, or else they can smell their companions in the jungle." Kala Nag hit the new elephant in the ribs and knocked the wind out of him, as Big Toomai said, "We have swept the hills of wild elephants at the last catch. It is only your carelessness in driving. Must I keep order along the whole line?"

"Hear him!" said the other driver. "We have swept the hills! Ho! Ho! You are very wise, you plains people. Anyone but a mud-head who never saw the jungle would know that they know that the drives are ended for the season. Therefore all the wild elephants to-night will--but why should I waste wisdom on a river-turtle?"

Lesson 19
1. Finish reading the chapter.

2. The father is from the plains of India and looks down on the people from the jungle. How does that affect how he treats his son? (Answers)

"What will they do?" Little Toomai called out.

"Ohe, little one. Art thou there? Well, I will tell thee, for thou hast a cool head. They will dance, and it behooves thy father, who has swept all the hills of all the elephants, to double-chain his pickets to-night."

"What talk is this?" said Big Toomai. "For forty years, father and son, we have tended elephants, and we have never heard such moonshine about dances."

"Yes; but a plainsman who lives in a hut knows only the four walls of his hut. Well, leave thy elephants unshackled tonight and see what comes. As for their dancing, I have seen the place where--Bapree-bap! How many windings has the Dihang River? Here is another ford, and we must swim the calves. Stop still, you behind there."

And in this way, talking and wrangling and splashing through the rivers, they made their first march to a sort of receiving camp for the new elephants. But they lost their tempers long before they got there.

Then the elephants were chained by their hind legs to their big stumps of pickets, and extra ropes were fitted to the new elephants, and the fodder was piled before them, and the hill drivers went back to Petersen Sahib through the afternoon light, telling the plains drivers to be extra careful that night, and laughing when the plains drivers asked the reason.

Little Toomai attended to Kala Nag's supper, and as evening fell, wandered through the camp, unspeakably happy, in search of a tom-tom. When an Indian child's heart is full, he does not run about and make a noise in an irregular fashion. He sits down to a sort of revel all by himself. And Little Toomai had been spoken to by Petersen Sahib! If he had not found what he wanted, I believe he would have been ill. But the sweetmeat seller in the camp lent him a little tom-tom--a drum beaten with the flat of the hand--and he sat down, cross-legged, before Kala Nag as the stars began to come out, the tom-tom in his lap, and he thumped and he thumped and he thumped, and the more he thought of the great honor that had been done to him, the more he thumped, all alone among the elephant fodder. There was no tune and no words, but the thumping made him happy.

The new elephants strained at their ropes, and squealed and trumpeted from time to time, and he could hear his mother in the camp hut putting his small brother to sleep with an old, old song about the great God Shiv, who once told all the animals what they should eat. It is a very soothing lullaby, and the first verse says:

Shiv, who poured the harvest and made the winds to blow, Sitting at the doorways of a day of long ago, Gave to each his portion, food and toil and fate, From the King upon the guddee to the Beggar at the gate. All things made he--Shiva the Preserver. Mahadeo! Mahadeo! He made all-- Thorn for the camel, fodder for the kine, And mother's heart for sleepy head, O little son of mine!

Little Toomai came in with a joyous tunk-a-tunk at the end of each verse, till he felt sleepy and stretched himself on the fodder at Kala Nag's side. At last the elephants began to lie down one after another as is their custom, till only Kala Nag at the right of the line was left standing up; and he rocked slowly from side to side, his ears put forward to listen to the night wind as it blew very slowly across the hills. The air was full of all the night noises that, taken together, make one big silence--the click of one bamboo stem against the other, the rustle of something alive in the undergrowth, the scratch and squawk of a half-waked bird (birds are awake in the night much more often than we imagine), and the fall of water ever so far away. Little Toomai slept for some time, and when he waked it was brilliant moonlight, and Kala Nag was still standing up with his ears cocked. Little Toomai turned, rustling in the fodder, and watched the curve of his big back against half the stars in heaven, and while he watched he heard, so far away that it sounded no more than a pinhole of noise pricked through the stillness, the "hoot-toot" of a wild elephant.

All the elephants in the lines jumped up as if they had been shot, and their grunts at last waked the sleeping mahouts, and they came out and drove in the picket pegs with big mallets, and tightened this rope and knotted that till all was quiet. One new elephant had nearly grubbed up his picket, and Big Toomai took off Kala Nag's leg chain and shackled that elephant fore-foot to hind-foot, but slipped a loop of grass string round Kala Nag's leg, and told him to remember that he was tied fast. He knew that he and his father and his grandfather had done the very same thing hundreds of times before. Kala Nag did not answer to the order by gurgling, as he usually did. He stood still, looking out across the moonlight, his head a little raised and his ears spread like fans, up to the great folds of the Garo hills.

"Tend to him if he grows restless in the night," said Big Toomai to Little Toomai, and he went into the hut and slept. Little Toomai was just going to sleep, too, when he heard the coir string snap with a little "tang," and Kala Nag rolled out of his pickets as slowly and as silently as a cloud rolls out of the mouth of a valley. Little Toomai pattered after him, barefooted, down the road in the moonlight, calling under his breath, "Kala Nag! Kala Nag! Take me with you, O Kala Nag!" The elephant turned, without a sound, took three strides back to the boy in the moonlight, put down his trunk, swung him up to his neck, and almost before Little Toomai had settled his knees, slipped into the forest.

There was one blast of furious trumpeting from the lines, and then the silence shut down on everything, and Kala Nag began to move. Sometimes a tuft of high grass washed along his sides as a wave washes along the sides of a ship, and sometimes a cluster of wild-pepper vines would scrape along his back, or a bamboo would creak where his shoulder touched it. But between those times he moved absolutely without any sound, drifting through the thick Garo forest as though it had been smoke. He was going uphill, but though Little Toomai watched the stars in the rifts of the trees, he could not tell in what direction.

Then Kala Nag reached the crest of the ascent and stopped for a minute, and Little Toomai could see the tops of the trees lying all speckled and furry under the moonlight for miles and miles, and the blue-white mist over the river in the hollow. Toomai leaned forward and looked, and he felt that the forest was awake below him--awake and alive and crowded. A big brown fruit-eating bat brushed past his ear; a porcupine's quills rattled in the thicket; and in the darkness between the tree stems he heard a hog-bear digging hard in the moist warm earth, and snuffing as it digged.

Then the branches closed over his head again, and Kala Nag began to go down into the valley--not quietly this time, but as a runaway gun goes down a steep bank--in one rush. The huge limbs moved as steadily as pistons, eight feet to each stride, and the wrinkled skin of the elbow points rustled. The undergrowth on either side of him ripped with a noise like torn canvas, and the saplings that he heaved away right and left with his shoulders sprang back again and banged him on the flank, and great trails of creepers, all matted together, hung from his tusks as he threw his head from side to side and plowed out his pathway. Then Little Toomai laid himself down close to the great neck lest a swinging bough should sweep him to the ground, and he wished that he were back in the lines again.

The grass began to get squashy, and Kala Nag's feet sucked and squelched as he put them down, and the night mist at the bottom of the valley chilled Little Toomai. There was a splash and a trample, and the rush of running water, and Kala Nag strode through the bed of a river, feeling his way at each step. Above the noise of the water, as it swirled round the elephant's legs, Little Toomai could hear more splashing and some trumpeting both upstream and down--great grunts and angry snortings, and all the mist about him seemed to be full of rolling, wavy shadows.

"Ai!" he said, half aloud, his teeth chattering. "The elephant-folk are out tonight. It is the dance, then!"

Kala Nag swashed out of the water, blew his trunk clear, and began another climb. But this time he was not alone, and he had not to make his path. That was made already, six feet wide, in front of him, where the bent jungle-grass was trying to recover itself and stand up. Many elephants must have gone that way only a few minutes before. Little Toomai looked back, and behind him a great wild tusker with his little pig's eyes glowing like hot coals was just lifting himself out of the misty river. Then the trees closed up again, and they went on and up, with trumpetings and crashings, and the sound of breaking branches on every side of them.

At last Kala Nag stood still between two tree-trunks at the very top of the hill. They were part of a circle of trees that grew round an irregular space of some three or four acres, and in all that space, as Little Toomai could see, the ground had been trampled down as hard as a brick floor. Some trees grew in the center of the clearing, but their bark was rubbed away, and the white wood beneath showed all shiny and polished in the patches of moonlight. There were creepers hanging from the upper branches, and the bells of the flowers of the creepers, great waxy white things like convolvuluses, hung down fast asleep. But within the limits of the clearing there was not a single blade of green--nothing but the trampled earth.

The moonlight showed it all iron gray, except where some elephants stood upon it, and their shadows were inky black. Little Toomai looked, holding his breath, with his eyes starting out of his head, and as he looked, more and more and more elephants swung out into the open from between the tree trunks. Little Toomai could only count up to ten, and he counted again and again on his fingers till he lost count of the tens, and his head began to swim. Outside the clearing he could hear them crashing in the undergrowth as they worked their way up the hillside, but as soon as they were within the circle of the tree trunks they moved like ghosts.

There were white-tusked wild males, with fallen leaves and nuts and twigs lying in the wrinkles of their necks and the folds of their ears; fat, slow-footed she-elephants, with restless, little pinky black calves only three or four feet high running under their stomachs; young elephants with their tusks just beginning to show, and very proud of them; lanky, scraggy old-maid elephants, with their hollow anxious faces, and trunks like rough bark; savage old bull elephants, scarred from shoulder to flank with great weals and cuts of bygone fights, and the caked dirt of their solitary mud baths dropping from their shoulders; and there was one with a broken tusk and the marks of the full-stroke, the terrible drawing scrape, of a tiger's claws on his side.

They were standing head to head, or walking to and fro across the ground in couples, or rocking and swaying all by themselves--scores and scores of elephants.

Toomai knew that so long as he lay still on Kala Nag's neck nothing would happen to him, for even in the rush and scramble of a Keddah drive a wild elephant does not reach up with his trunk and drag a man off the neck of a tame elephant. And these elephants were not thinking of men that night. Once they started and put their ears forward when they heard the chinking of a leg iron in the forest, but it was Pudmini, Petersen Sahib's pet elephant, her chain snapped short off, grunting, snuffling up the hillside. She must have broken her pickets and come straight from Petersen Sahib's camp; and Little Toomai saw another elephant, one that he did not know, with deep rope galls on his back and breast. He, too, must have run away from some camp in the hills about.

At last there was no sound of any more elephants moving in the forest, and Kala Nag rolled out from his station between the trees and went into the middle of the crowd, clucking and gurgling, and all the elephants began to talk in their own tongue, and to move about.

Still lying down, Little Toomai looked down upon scores and scores of broad backs, and wagging ears, and tossing trunks, and little rolling eyes. He heard the click of tusks as they crossed other tusks by accident, and the dry rustle of trunks twined together, and the chafing of enormous sides and shoulders in the crowd, and the incessant flick and hissh of the great tails. Then a cloud came over the moon, and he sat in black darkness. But the quiet, steady hustling and pushing and gurgling went on just the same. He knew that there were elephants all round Kala Nag, and that there was no chance of backing him out of the assembly; so he set his teeth and shivered. In a Keddah at least there was torchlight and shouting, but here he was all alone in the dark, and once a trunk came up and touched him on the knee.

Then an elephant trumpeted, and they all took it up for five or ten terrible seconds. The dew from the trees above spattered down like rain on the unseen backs, and a dull booming noise began, not very loud at first, and Little Toomai could not tell what it was. But it grew and grew, and Kala Nag lifted up one forefoot and then the other, and brought them down on the ground--one-two, one-two, as steadily as trip-hammers. The elephants were stamping all together now, and it sounded like a war drum beaten at the mouth of a cave. The dew fell from the trees till there was no more left to fall, and the booming went on, and the ground rocked and shivered, and Little Toomai put his hands up to his ears to shut out the sound. But it was all one gigantic jar that ran through him--this stamp of hundreds of heavy feet on the raw earth. Once or twice he could feel Kala Nag and all the others surge forward a few strides, and the thumping would change to the crushing sound of juicy green things being bruised, but in a minute or two the boom of feet on hard earth began again. A tree was creaking and groaning somewhere near him. He put out his arm and felt the bark, but Kala Nag moved forward, still tramping, and he could not tell where he was in the clearing. There was no sound from the elephants, except once, when two or three little calves squeaked together. Then he heard a thump and a shuffle, and the booming went on. It must have lasted fully two hours, and Little Toomai ached in every nerve, but he knew by the smell of the night air that the dawn was coming.

The morning broke in one sheet of pale yellow behind the green hills, and the booming stopped with the first ray, as though the light had been an order. Before Little Toomai had got the ringing out of his head, before even he had shifted his position, there was not an elephant in sight except Kala Nag, Pudmini, and the elephant with the rope-galls, and there was neither sign nor rustle nor whisper down the hillsides to show where the others had gone.

Little Toomai stared again and again. The clearing, as he remembered it, had grown in the night. More trees stood in the middle of it, but the undergrowth and the jungle grass at the sides had been rolled back. Little Toomai stared once more. Now he understood the trampling. The elephants had stamped out more room--had stamped the thick grass and juicy cane to trash, the trash into slivers, the slivers into tiny fibers, and the fibers into hard earth.

"Wah!" said Little Toomai, and his eyes were very heavy. "Kala Nag, my lord, let us keep by Pudmini and go to Petersen Sahib's camp, or I shall drop from thy neck."

The third elephant watched the two go away, snorted, wheeled round, and took his own path. He may have belonged to some little native king's establishment, fifty or sixty or a hundred miles away.

Two hours later, as Petersen Sahib was eating early breakfast, his elephants, who had been double chained that night, began to trumpet, and Pudmini, mired to the shoulders, with Kala Nag, very footsore, shambled into the camp. Little Toomai's face was gray and pinched, and his hair was full of leaves and drenched with dew, but he tried to salute Petersen Sahib, and cried faintly: "The dance--the elephant dance! I have seen it, and--I die!" As Kala Nag sat down, he slid off his neck in a dead faint.

But, since native children have no nerves worth speaking of, in two hours he was lying very contentedly in Petersen Sahib's hammock with Petersen Sahib's shooting-coat under his head, and a glass of warm milk, a little brandy, with a dash of quinine, inside of him, and while the old hairy, scarred hunters of the jungles sat three deep before him, looking at him as though he were a spirit, he told his tale in short words, as a child will, and wound up with:

"Now, if I lie in one word, send men to see, and they will find that the elephant folk have trampled down more room in their dance-room, and they will find ten and ten, and many times ten, tracks leading to that dance-room. They made more room with their feet. I have seen it. Kala Nag took me, and I saw. Also Kala Nag is very leg-weary!"

Little Toomai lay back and slept all through the long afternoon and into the twilight, and while he slept Petersen Sahib and Machua Appa followed the track of the two elephants for fifteen miles across the hills. Petersen Sahib had spent eighteen years in catching elephants, and he had only once before found such a dance-place. Machua Appa had no need to look twice at the clearing to see what had been done there, or to scratch with his toe in the packed, rammed earth.

"The child speaks truth," said he. "All this was done last night, and I have counted seventy tracks crossing the river. See, Sahib, where Pudmini's leg-iron cut the bark of that tree! Yes; she was there too."

They looked at one another and up and down, and they wondered. For the ways of elephants are beyond the wit of any man, black or white, to fathom.

"Forty years and five," said Machua Appa, "have I followed my lord, the elephant, but never have I heard that any child of man had seen what this child has seen. By all the Gods of the Hills, it is-- what can we say?" and he shook his head.

When they got back to camp it was time for the evening meal. Petersen Sahib ate alone in his tent, but he gave orders that the camp should have two sheep and some fowls, as well as a double ration of flour and rice and salt, for he knew that there would be a feast.

Big Toomai had come up hotfoot from the camp in the plains to search for his son and his elephant, and now that he had found them he looked at them as though he were afraid of them both. And there was a feast by the blazing campfires in front of the lines of picketed elephants, and Little Toomai was the hero of it all. And the big brown elephant catchers, the trackers and drivers and ropers, and the men who know all the secrets of breaking the wildest elephants, passed him from one to the other, and they marked his forehead with blood from the breast of a newly killed jungle-cock, to show that he was a forester, initiated and free of all the jungles.

And at last, when the flames died down, and the red light of the logs made the elephants look as though they had been dipped in blood too, Machua Appa, the head of all the drivers of all the Keddahs--Machua Appa, Petersen Sahib's other self, who had never seen a made road in forty years: Machua Appa, who was so great that he had no other name than Machua Appa,--leaped to his feet, with Little Toomai held high in the air above his head, and shouted: "Listen, my brothers. Listen, too, you my lords in the lines there, for I, Machua Appa, am speaking! This little one shall no more be called Little Toomai, but Toomai of the Elephants, as his great-grandfather was called before him. What never man has seen he has seen through the long night, and the favor of the elephant-folk and of the Gods of the Jungles is with him. He shall become a great tracker. He shall become greater than I, even I, Machua Appa! He shall follow the new trail, and the stale trail, and the mixed trail, with a clear eye! He shall take no harm in the Keddah when he runs under their bellies to rope the wild tuskers; and if he slips before the feet of the charging bull elephant, the bull elephant shall know who he is and shall not crush him. Aihai! my lords in the chains,"--he whirled up the line of pickets--"here is the little one that has seen your dances in your hidden places,--the sight that never man saw! Give him honor, my lords! Salaam karo, my children. Make your salute to Toomai of the Elephants! Gunga Pershad, ahaa! Hira Guj, Birchi Guj, Kuttar Guj, ahaa! Pudmini,--thou hast seen him at the dance, and thou too, Kala Nag, my pearl among elephants!-- ahaa! Together! To Toomai of the Elephants. Barrao!"

And at that last wild yell the whole line flung up their trunks till the tips touched their foreheads, and broke out into the full salute--the crashing trumpet-peal that only the Viceroy of India hears, the Salaamut of the Keddah.

But it was all for the sake of Little Toomai, who had seen what never man had seen before--the dance of the elephants at night and alone in the heart of the Garo hills!

Lesson 20

1. Introduction: "The narrator is a human who overhears the animals talking. It is a very interesting and humorous way of presenting the story."
   (from classical-childrens-books.com/jungle-book-unit-study.html)
2. Read the first part of "Her Majesty's Servants."
3. What can you tell someone about what you've read so far?

You can work it out by Fractions or by simple Rule of Three, But the way of Tweedle-dum is not the way of Tweedle-dee. You can twist it, you can turn it, you can plait it till you drop, But the way of Pilly Winky's not the way of Winkie Pop!

It had been raining heavily for one whole month--raining on a camp of thirty thousand men and thousands of camels, elephants, horses, bullocks, and mules all gathered together at a place called Rawal Pindi, to be reviewed by the Viceroy of India. He was receiving a visit from the Amir of Afghanistan--a wild king of a very wild country. The Amir had brought with him for a bodyguard eight hundred men and horses who had never seen a camp or a locomotive before in their lives-- savage men and savage horses from somewhere at the back of Central Asia. Every night a mob of these horses would be sure to break their heel ropes and stampede up and down the camp through the mud in the dark, or the camels would break loose and run about and fall over the ropes of the tents, and you can imagine how pleasant that was for men trying to go to sleep. My tent lay far away from the camel lines, and I thought it was safe. But one night a man popped his head in and shouted, "Get out, quick! They're coming! My tent's gone!"

I knew who "they" were, so I put on my boots and waterproof and scuttled out into the slush. Little Vixen, my fox terrier, went out through the other side; and then there was a roaring and a grunting and bubbling, and I saw the tent cave in, as the pole snapped, and begin to dance about like a mad ghost. A camel had blundered into it, and wet and angry as I was, I could not help laughing. Then I ran on, because I did not know how many camels might have got loose, and before long I was out of sight of the camp, plowing my way through the mud.

At last I fell over the tail-end of a gun, and by that knew I was somewhere near the artillery lines where the cannon were stacked at night. As I did not want to plowter about any more in the drizzle and the dark, I put my waterproof over the muzzle of one gun, and made a sort of wigwam with two or three rammers that I found, and lay along the tail of another gun, wondering where Vixen had got to, and where I might be.

Just as I was getting ready to go to sleep I heard a jingle of harness and a grunt, and a mule passed me shaking his wet ears. He belonged to a screw-gun battery, for I could hear the rattle of the straps and rings and chains and things on his saddle pad. The screw-guns are tiny little cannon made in two pieces, that are screwed together when the time comes to use them. They are taken up mountains, anywhere that a mule can find a road, and they are very useful for fighting in rocky country.

Behind the mule there was a camel, with his big soft feet squelching and slipping in the mud, and his neck bobbing to and fro like a strayed hen's. Luckily, I knew enough of beast language--not wild-beast language, but camp-beast language, of course--from the natives to know what he was saying.

He must have been the one that flopped into my tent, for he called to the mule, "What shall I do? Where shall I go? I have fought with a white thing that waved, and it took a stick and hit me on the neck." (That was my broken tent pole, and I was very glad to know it.) "Shall we run on?"

"Oh, it was you," said the mule, "you and your friends, that have been disturbing the camp? All right. You'll be beaten for this in the morning. But I may as well give you something on account now."

I heard the harness jingle as the mule backed and caught the camel two kicks in the ribs that rang like a drum. "Another time," he said, "you'll know better than to run through a mule battery at night, shouting 'Thieves and fire!' Sit down, and keep your silly neck quiet."
The camel doubled up camel-fashion, like a two-foot rule, and sat down whimpering. There was a regular beat of hoofs in the darkness, and a big troop-horse cantered up as steadily as though he were on parade, jumped a gun tail, and landed close to the mule.

"It's disgraceful," he said, blowing out his nostrils. "Those camels have racketed through our lines again--the third time this week. How's a horse to keep his condition if he isn't allowed to sleep. Who's here?"

"I'm the breech-piece mule of number two gun of the First Screw Battery," said the mule, "and the other's one of your friends. He's waked me up too. Who are you?"

"Number Fifteen, E troop, Ninth Lancers--Dick Cunliffe's horse. Stand over a little, there."

"Oh, beg your pardon," said the mule. "It's too dark to see much. Aren't these camels too sickening for anything? I walked out of my lines to get a little peace and quiet here."

"My lords," said the camel humbly, "we dreamed bad dreams in the night, and we were very much afraid. I am only a baggage camel of the 39th Native Infantry, and I am not as brave as you are, my lords."

"Then why didn't you stay and carry baggage for the 39th Native Infantry, instead of running all round the camp?" said the mule.

"They were such very bad dreams," said the camel. "I am sorry. Listen! What is that? Shall we run on again?"

"Sit down," said the mule, "or you'll snap your long stick-legs between the guns." He cocked one ear and listened. "Bullocks!" he said. "Gun bullocks. On my word, you and your friends have waked the camp very thoroughly. It takes a good deal of prodding to put up a gun-bullock."

I heard a chain dragging along the ground, and a yoke of the great sulky white bullocks that drag the heavy siege guns when the elephants won't go any nearer to the firing, came shouldering along together. And almost stepping on the chain was another battery mule, calling wildly for "Billy."

"That's one of our recruits," said the old mule to the troop horse. "He's calling for me. Here, youngster, stop squealing. The dark never hurt anybody yet."

The gun-bullocks lay down together and began chewing the cud, but the young mule huddled close to Billy.

"Things!" he said. "Fearful and horrible, Billy! They came into our lines while we were asleep. D'you think they'll kill us?"

"I've a very great mind to give you a number-one kicking," said Billy. "The idea of a fourteen-hand mule with your training disgracing the battery before this gentleman!"

"Gently, gently!" said the troop-horse. "Remember they are always like this to begin with. The first time I ever saw a man (it was in Australia when I was a three-year-old) I ran for half a day, and if I'd seen a camel, I should have been running still."

Nearly all our horses for the English cavalry are brought to India from Australia, and are broken in by the troopers themselves.

"True enough," said Billy. "Stop shaking, youngster. The first time they put the full harness with all its chains on my back I stood on my forelegs and kicked every bit of it off. I hadn't learned the real science of kicking then, but the battery said they had never seen anything like it."

"But this wasn't harness or anything that jingled," said the young mule. "You know I don't mind that now, Billy. It was Things like trees, and they fell up and down the lines and bubbled; and my head-rope broke, and I couldn't find my driver, and I couldn't find you, Billy, so I ran off with-- with these gentlemen."

"H'm!" said Billy. "As soon as I heard the camels were loose I came away on my own account. When a battery--a screw-gun mule calls gun-bullocks gentlemen, he must be very badly shaken up. Who are you fellows on the ground there?"

The gun bullocks rolled their cuds, and answered both together: "The seventh yoke of the first gun of the Big Gun Battery. We were asleep when the camels came, but when we were trampled on we got up and walked away. It is better to lie quiet in the mud than to be disturbed on good bedding. We told your friend here that there was nothing to be afraid of, but he knew so much that he thought otherwise. Wah!"

They went on chewing.

"That comes of being afraid," said Billy. "You get laughed at by gun-bullocks. I hope you like it, young un."

The young mule's teeth snapped, and I heard him say something about not being afraid of any beefy old bullock in the world. But the bullocks only clicked their horns together and went on chewing.

"Now, don't be angry after you've been afraid. That's the worst kind of cowardice," said the troop-horse. "Anybody can be forgiven for being scared in the night, I think, if they see things they don't understand. We've broken out of our pickets, again and again, four hundred and fifty of us, just because a new recruit got to telling tales of whip snakes at home in Australia till we were scared to death of the loose ends of our head-ropes."

"That's all very well in camp," said Billy. "I'm not above stampeding myself, for the fun of the thing, when I haven't been out for a day or two. But what do you do on active service?"

"Oh, that's quite another set of new shoes," said the troop horse. "Dick Cunliffe's on my back then, and drives his knees into me, and all I have to do is to watch where I am putting my feet, and to keep my hind legs well under me, and be bridle-wise."

"What's bridle-wise?" said the young mule.

"By the Blue Gums of the Back Blocks," snorted the troop-horse, "do you mean to say that you aren't taught to be bridle-wise in your business? How can you do anything, unless you can spin round at once when the rein is pressed on your neck? It means life or death to your man, and of course that's life and death to you. Get round with your hind legs under you the instant you feel the rein on your neck. If you haven't room to swing round, rear up a little and come round on your hind legs. That's being bridle-wise."

"We aren't taught that way," said Billy the mule stiffly. "We're taught to obey the man at our head: step off when he says so, and step in when he says so. I suppose it comes to the same thing. Now, with all this fine fancy business and rearing, which must be very bad for your hocks, what do you do?"

"That depends," said the troop-horse. "Generally I have to go in among a lot of yelling, hairy men with knives--long shiny knives, worse than the farrier's knives--and I have to take care that Dick's boot is just touching the next man's boot without crushing it. I can see Dick's lance to the right of my right eye, and I know I'm safe. I shouldn't care to be the man or horse that stood up to Dick and me when we're in a hurry."

"Don't the knives hurt?" said the young mule.

"Well, I got one cut across the chest once, but that wasn't Dick's fault--"

"A lot I should have cared whose fault it was, if it hurt!" said the young mule.

"You must," said the troop horse. "If you don't trust your man, you may as well run away at once. That's what some of our horses do, and I don't blame them. As I was saying, it wasn't Dick's fault. The man was lying on the ground, and I stretched myself not to tread on him, and he slashed up at me. Next time I have to go over a man lying down I shall step on him--hard."

"H'm!" said Billy. "It sounds very foolish. Knives are dirty things at any time. The proper thing to do is to climb up a mountain with a well-balanced saddle, hang on by all four feet and your ears too, and creep and crawl and wriggle along, till you come out hundreds of feet above anyone else on a ledge where there's just room enough for your hoofs. Then you stand still and keep quiet-- never ask a man to hold your head, young un--keep quiet while the guns are being put together, and then you watch the little poppy shells drop down into the tree-tops ever so far below."
"Don't you ever trip?" said the troop-horse.

"They say that when a mule trips you can split a hen's ear," said Billy. "Now and again perhaps a badly packed saddle will upset a mule, but it's very seldom. I wish I could show you our business. It's beautiful. Why, it took me three years to find out what the men were driving at. The science of the thing is never to show up against the sky line, because, if you do, you may get fired at. Remember that, young un. Always keep hidden as much as possible, even if you have to go a mile out of your way. I lead the battery when it comes to that sort of climbing."

"Fired at without the chance of running into the people who are firing!" said the troop-horse, thinking hard. "I couldn't stand that. I should want to charge--with Dick."

"Oh, no, you wouldn't. You know that as soon as the guns are in position they'll do all the charging. That's scientific and neat. But knives--pah!"

The baggage-camel had been bobbing his head to and fro for some time past, anxious to get a word in edgewise. Then I heard him say, as he cleared his throat, nervously:

"I--I--I have fought a little, but not in that climbing way or that running way."

"No. Now you mention it," said Billy, "you don't look as though you were made for climbing or running--much. Well, how was it, old Hay-bales?"

"The proper way," said the camel. "We all sat down--"

"Oh, my crupper and breastplate!" said the troop-horse under his breath. "Sat down!"

"We sat down--a hundred of us," the camel went on, "in a big square, and the men piled our packs and saddles, outside the square, and they fired over our backs, the men did, on all sides of the square."

"What sort of men? Any men that came along?" said the troop-horse. "They teach us in riding school to lie down and let our masters fire across us, but Dick Cunliffe is the only man I'd trust to do that. It tickles my girths, and, besides, I can't see with my head on the ground."

"What does it matter who fires across you?" said the camel. "There are plenty of men and plenty of other camels close by, and a great many clouds of smoke. I am not frightened then. I sit still and wait."

"And yet," said Billy, "you dream bad dreams and upset the camp at night. Well, well! Before I'd lie down, not to speak of sitting down, and let a man fire across me, my heels and his head would have something to say to each other. Did you ever hear anything so awful as that?"

There was a long silence, and then one of the gun bullocks lifted up his big head and said, "This is very foolish indeed. There is only one way of fighting."

"Oh, go on," said Billy. "Please don't mind me. I suppose you fellows fight standing on your tails?"

"Only one way," said the two together. (They must have been twins.) "This is that way. To put all twenty yoke of us to the big gun as soon as Two Tails trumpets." ("Two Tails" is camp slang for the elephant.)

"What does Two Tails trumpet for?" said the young mule.

"To show that he is not going any nearer to the smoke on the other side. Two Tails is a great coward. Then we tug the big gun all together--Heya--Hullah! Heeyah! Hullah! We do not climb like cats nor run like calves. We go across the level plain, twenty yoke of us, till we are unyoked again, and we graze while the big guns talk across the plain to some town with mud walls, and pieces of the wall fall out, and the dust goes up as though many cattle were coming home."

"Oh! And you choose that time for grazing?" said the young mule.

"That time or any other. Eating is always good. We eat till we are yoked up again and tug the gun back to where Two Tails is waiting for it. Sometimes there are big guns in the city that speak back, and some of us are killed, and then there is all the more grazing for those that are left. This is Fate. None the less, Two Tails is a great coward. That is the proper way to fight. We are brothers from Hapur. Our father was a sacred bull of Shiva. We have spoken."

"Well, I've certainly learned something tonight," said the troop-horse. "Do you gentlemen of the screw-gun battery feel inclined to eat when you are being fired at with big guns, and Two Tails is behind you?"

"About as much as we feel inclined to sit down and let men sprawl all over us, or run into people with knives. I never heard such stuff. A mountain ledge, a well-balanced load, a driver you can trust to let you pick your own way, and I'm your mule. But--the other things--no!" said Billy, with a stamp of his foot.

"Of course," said the troop horse, "everyone is not made in the same way, and I can quite see that your family, on your father's side, would fail to understand a great many things."

"Never you mind my family on my father's side," said Billy angrily, for every mule hates to be reminded that his father was a donkey. "My father was a Southern gentleman, and he could pull down and bite and kick into rags every horse he came across. Remember that, you big brown Brumby!"

Lesson 21

1. Finish the chapter.
2. What does the elephant mean when it says he can *"see inside your head?"*
3. How does that help or hurt the elephant?
4. What makes the animals obey their masters and go to war?
5. What makes the humans obey their leaders and go to war?

Brumby means wild horse without any breeding. Imagine the feelings of Sunol if a car-horse called her a "skate," and you can imagine how the Australian horse felt. I saw the white of his eye glitter in the dark.

"See here, you son of an imported Malaga jackass," he said between his teeth, "I'd have you know that I'm related on my mother's side to Carbine, winner of the Melbourne Cup, and where I come from we aren't accustomed to being ridden over roughshod by any parrot-mouthed, pig-headed mule in a pop-gun pea-shooter battery. Are you ready?"

"On your hind legs!" squealed Billy. They both reared up facing each other, and I was expecting a furious fight, when a gurgly, rumbly voice, called out of the darkness to the right--"Children, what are you fighting about there? Be quiet."

Both beasts dropped down with a snort of disgust, for neither horse nor mule can bear to listen to an elephant's voice.

"It's Two Tails!" said the troop-horse. "I can't stand him. A tail at each end isn't fair!"

"My feelings exactly," said Billy, crowding into the troop-horse for company. "We're very alike in some things."

"I suppose we've inherited them from our mothers," said the troop horse. "It's not worth quarreling about. Hi! Two Tails, are you tied up?"

"Yes," said Two Tails, with a laugh all up his trunk. "I'm picketed for the night. I've heard what you fellows have been saying. But don't be afraid. I'm not coming over."

The bullocks and the camel said, half aloud, "Afraid of Two Tails--what nonsense!" And the bullocks went on, "We are sorry that you heard, but it is true. Two Tails, why are you afraid of the guns when they fire?"

"Well," said Two Tails, rubbing one hind leg against the other, exactly like a little boy saying a poem, "I don't quite know whether you'd understand."

"We don't, but we have to pull the guns," said the bullocks.

"I know it, and I know you are a good deal braver than you think you are. But it's different with me. My battery captain called me a Pachydermatous Anachronism the other day."

"That's another way of fighting, I suppose?" said Billy, who was recovering his spirits.

"You don't know what that means, of course, but I do. It means betwixt and between, and that is just where I am. I can see inside my head what will happen when a shell bursts, and you bullocks can't."

"I can," said the troop-horse. "At least a little bit. I try not to think about it."

"I can see more than you, and I do think about it. I know there's a great deal of me to take care of, and I know that nobody knows how to cure me when I'm sick. All they can do is to stop my driver's pay till I get well, and I can't trust my driver."

"Ah!" said the troop horse. "That explains it. I can trust Dick."

"You could put a whole regiment of Dicks on my back without making me feel any better. I know just enough to be uncomfortable, and not enough to go on in spite of it."

"We do not understand," said the bullocks.

"I know you don't. I'm not talking to you. You don't know what blood is."

"We do," said the bullocks. "It is red stuff that soaks into the ground and smells."

The troop-horse gave a kick and a bound and a snort.

"Don't talk of it," he said. "I can smell it now, just thinking of it. It makes me want to run--when I haven't Dick on my back."

"But it is not here," said the camel and the bullocks. "Why are you so stupid?"

"It's vile stuff," said Billy. "I don't want to run, but I don't want to talk about it."

"There you are!" said Two Tails, waving his tail to explain.

"Surely. Yes, we have been here all night," said the bullocks.

Two Tails stamped his foot till the iron ring on it jingled. "Oh, I'm not talking to you. You can't see inside your heads."

"No. We see out of our four eyes," said the bullocks. "We see straight in front of us."

"If I could do that and nothing else, you wouldn't be needed to pull the big guns at all. If I was like my captain--he can see things inside his head before the firing begins, and he shakes all over, but he knows too much to run away--if I was like him I could pull the guns. But if I were as wise as all that I should never be here. I should be a king in the forest, as I used to be, sleeping half the day and bathing when I liked. I haven't had a good bath for a month."

"That's all very fine," said Billy. "But giving a thing a long name doesn't make it any better."

"H'sh!" said the troop horse. "I think I understand what Two Tails means."

"You'll understand better in a minute," said Two Tails angrily. "Now you just explain to me why you don't like this!"

He began trumpeting furiously at the top of his trumpet.

"Stop that!" said Billy and the troop horse together, and I could hear them stamp and shiver. An elephant's trumpeting is always nasty, especially on a dark night.

"I shan't stop," said Two Tails. "Won't you explain that, please? Hhrrmph! Rrrt! Rrrmph! Rrrhha!" Then he stopped suddenly, and I heard a little whimper in the dark, and knew that Vixen had found me at last. She knew as well as I did that if there is one thing in the world the elephant is more afraid of than another it is a little barking dog. So she stopped to bully Two Tails in his pickets, and yapped round his big feet. Two Tails shuffled and squeaked. "Go away, little dog!" he said. "Don't snuff at my ankles, or I'll kick at you. Good little dog--nice little doggie, then! Go home, you yelping little beast! Oh, why doesn't someone take her away? She'll bite me in a minute."

"Seems to me," said Billy to the troop horse, "that our friend Two Tails is afraid of most things. Now, if I had a full meal for every dog I've kicked across the parade-ground I should be as fat as Two Tails nearly."

I whistled, and Vixen ran up to me, muddy all over, and licked my nose, and told me a long tale about hunting for me all through the camp. I never let her know that I understood beast talk, or she would have taken all sorts of liberties. So I buttoned her into the breast of my overcoat, and Two Tails shuffled and stamped and growled to himself.

"Extraordinary! Most extraordinary!" he said. "It runs in our family. Now, where has that nasty little beast gone to?"

I heard him feeling about with his trunk.

"We all seem to be affected in various ways," he went on, blowing his nose. "Now, you gentlemen were alarmed, I believe, when I trumpeted."

"Not alarmed, exactly," said the troop-horse, "but it made me feel as though I had hornets where my saddle ought to be. Don't begin again."

"I'm frightened of a little dog, and the camel here is frightened by bad dreams in the night."

"It is very lucky for us that we haven't all got to fight in the same way," said the troop-horse.

"What I want to know," said the young mule, who had been quiet for a long time--"what I want to know is, why we have to fight at all."

"Because we're told to," said the troop-horse, with a snort of contempt.

"Orders," said Billy the mule, and his teeth snapped.

"Hukm hai!" (It is an order!), said the camel with a gurgle, and Two Tails and the bullocks repeated, "Hukm hai!"

"Yes, but who gives the orders?" said the recruit-mule.

"The man who walks at your head--Or sits on your back--Or holds the nose rope--Or twists your tail," said Billy and the troop-horse and the camel and the bullocks one after the other.

"But who gives them the orders?"

"Now you want to know too much, young un," said Billy, "and that is one way of getting kicked. All you have to do is to obey the man at your head and ask no questions."

"He's quite right," said Two Tails. "I can't always obey, because I'm betwixt and between. But Billy's right. Obey the man next to you who gives the order, or you'll stop all the battery, besides getting a thrashing."

The gun-bullocks got up to go. "Morning is coming," they said. "We will go back to our lines. It is true that we only see out of our eyes, and we are not very clever. But still, we are the only people to-night who have not been afraid. Good-night, you brave people."

Nobody answered, and the troop-horse said, to change the conversation, "Where's that little dog? A dog means a man somewhere about."

"Here I am," yapped Vixen, "under the gun tail with my man. You big, blundering beast of a camel you, you upset our tent. My man's very angry."

"Phew!" said the bullocks. "He must be white!"

"Of course he is," said Vixen. "Do you suppose I'm looked after by a black bullock-driver?"
"Huah! Ouach! Ugh!" said the bullocks. "Let us get away quickly."

They plunged forward in the mud, and managed somehow to run their yoke on the pole of an ammunition wagon, where it jammed.

"Now you have done it," said Billy calmly. "Don't struggle. You're hung up till daylight. What on earth's the matter?"

The bullocks went off into the long hissing snorts that Indian cattle give, and pushed and crowded and slued and stamped and slipped and nearly fell down in the mud, grunting savagely.

"You'll break your necks in a minute," said the troop-horse. "What's the matter with white men? I live with 'em."

"They--eat--us! Pull!" said the near bullock. The yoke snapped with a twang, and they lumbered off together.

I never knew before what made Indian cattle so scared of Englishmen. We eat beef--a thing that no cattle-driver touches--and of course the cattle do not like it.

"May I be flogged with my own pad-chains! Who'd have thought of two big lumps like those losing their heads?" said Billy.

"Never mind. I'm going to look at this man. Most of the white men, I know, have things in their pockets," said the troop-horse.

"I'll leave you, then. I can't say I'm over-fond of 'em myself. Besides, white men who haven't a place to sleep in are more than likely to be thieves, and I've a good deal of Government property on my back. Come along, young un, and we'll go back to our lines. Good-night, Australia! See you on parade to-morrow, I suppose. Good-night, old Hay-bale!--try to control your feelings, won't you? Good-night, Two Tails! If you pass us on the ground tomorrow, don't trumpet. It spoils our formation."

Billy the Mule stumped off with the swaggering limp of an old campaigner, as the troop-horse's head came nuzzling into my breast, and I gave him biscuits, while Vixen, who is a most conceited little dog, told him fibs about the scores of horses that she and I kept.

"I'm coming to the parade to-morrow in my dog-cart," she said. "Where will you be?"

"On the left hand of the second squadron. I set the time for all my troop, little lady," he said politely. "Now I must go back to Dick. My tail's all muddy, and he'll have two hours' hard work dressing me for parade."

The big parade of all the thirty thousand men was held that afternoon, and Vixen and I had a good place close to the Viceroy and the Amir of Afghanistan, with high, big black hat of astrakhan wool and the great diamond star in the center. The first part of the review was all sunshine, and the regiments went by in wave upon wave of legs all moving together, and guns all in a line, till our eyes grew dizzy. Then the cavalry came up, to the beautiful cavalry canter of "Bonnie Dundee," and Vixen cocked her ear where she sat on the dog-cart. The second squadron of the Lancers shot by, and there was the troop-horse, with his tail like spun silk, his head pulled into his breast, one ear forward and one back, setting the time for all his squadron, his legs going as smoothly as waltz music. Then the big guns came by, and I saw Two Tails and two other elephants harnessed in line to a forty-pounder siege gun, while twenty yoke of oxen walked behind. The seventh pair had a new yoke, and they looked rather stiff and tired. Last came the screw guns, and Billy the mule carried himself as though he commanded all the troops, and his harness was oiled and polished till it winked. I gave a cheer all by myself for Billy the mule, but he never looked right or left.

The rain began to fall again, and for a while it was too misty to see what the troops were doing. They had made a big half circle across the plain, and were spreading out into a line. That line grew and grew and grew till it was three-quarters of a mile long from wing to wing--one solid wall of men, horses, and guns. Then it came on straight toward the Viceroy and the Amir, and as it got nearer the ground began to shake, like the deck of a steamer when the engines are going fast.

Unless you have been there you cannot imagine what a frightening effect this steady come-down of troops has on the spectators, even when they know it is only a review. I looked at the Amir. Up till then he had not shown the shadow of a sign of astonishment or anything else. But now his eyes began to get bigger and bigger, and he picked up the reins on his horse's neck and looked behind him. For a minute it seemed as though he were going to draw his sword and slash his way out through the English men and women in the carriages at the back. Then the advance stopped dead, the ground stood still, the whole line saluted, and thirty bands began to play all together. That was the end of the review, and the regiments went off to their camps in the rain, and an infantry band struck up with--

The animals went in two by two, Hurrah!
The animals went in two by two,
The elephant and the battery mul',
and they all got into the Ark
For to get out of the rain!

Then I heard an old grizzled, long-haired Central Asian chief, who had come down with the Amir, asking questions of a native officer.

"Now," said he, "in what manner was this wonderful thing done?"

And the officer answered, "An order was given, and they obeyed."

"But are the beasts as wise as the men?" said the chief.

"They obey, as the men do. Mule, horse, elephant, or bullock, he obeys his driver, and the driver his sergeant, and the sergeant his lieutenant, and the lieutenant his captain, and the captain his major, and the major his colonel, and the colonel his brigadier commanding three regiments, and the brigadier the general, who obeys the Viceroy, who is the servant of the Empress. Thus it is done."

"Would it were so in Afghanistan!" said the chief, "for there we obey only our own wills."

"And for that reason," said the native officer, twirling his mustache, "your Amir whom you do not obey must come here and take orders from our Viceroy."

Lesson 22

1. Write a paragraph responding to the following question. Make sure to start with a sentence that gives your introduction. You shouldn't just start with your answer. We should know that you are talking about *The Jungle Book*, and we should understand what the question was. Explain the answer you have chosen and give examples from the book. (examples, plural, more than one) Finish with a concluding sentence.
   - What do you think Kipling believes about which is more important to a person, who your parents are (your heredity and genes) or the environment you are brought up in?

Lesson 23

1. Read Kipling's famous poem "If."
2. Who is this written to and from? (Answers)
3. What do you think the poem is saying?
4. What is your favorite part?

> If you can keep your head when all about you
>   Are losing theirs and blaming it on you,
> If you can trust yourself when all men doubt you,
>   But make allowance for their doubting too;
> If you can wait and not be tired by waiting,
>   Or being lied about, don't deal in lies,
> Or being hated, don't give way to hating,
>   And yet don't look too good, nor talk too wise:
>
> If you can dream—and not make dreams your master;
>   If you can think—and not make thoughts your aim;

If you can meet with Triumph and Disaster
    And treat those two impostors just the same;
If you can bear to hear the truth you've spoken
    Twisted by knaves to make a trap for fools,
Or watch the things you gave your life to, broken,
    And stoop and build 'em up with worn-out tools:

If you can make one heap of all your winnings
    And risk it on one turn of pitch-and-toss,
And lose, and start again at your beginnings
    And never breathe a word about your loss;
If you can force your heart and nerve and sinew
    To serve your turn long after they are gone,
And so hold on when there is nothing in you
    Except the Will which says to them: 'Hold on!'

If you can talk with crowds and keep your virtue,
    Or walk with Kings—nor lose the common touch,
If neither foes nor loving friends can hurt you,
    If all men count with you, but none too much;
If you can fill the unforgiving minute
    With sixty seconds' worth of distance run,
Yours is the Earth and everything that's in it,
    And—which is more—you'll be a Man, my son!

After you've answered the questions for today, read the excerpts below from an analysis of the poem. Do you think she's right?

(below are excerpts from http://groundreport.com/poetry-analysis-of-if-by-rudyard-kipling/ by Angel Sharum)

"The first section of the poem, in my opinion, is about being true to one's self. Know the value of your self worth, but don't become conceited....

The second section is about overcoming obstacles that get in your path, whether by others, or of your own making....

I believe the most important lesson in the third section is to never give up!...

The last section has two important lessons. First, that we are all equal. The second lesson I take from this section, is to never waste time. Make every minute of every day count!"

Lesson 24

1. The new book you will be reading is a **satire** or uses **satire**. (pronounced sat – tire): **The use of humor, irony, exaggeration, or ridicule to expose and criticize people's stupidity or vices, particularly in the context of contemporary politics and other topical issues.**

2. An example is Dr. Seuss's *Butter Battle Book* which is a satire about nuclear proliferation during the cold war (Russia and America getting more and more and bigger and bigger nuclear bombs). If you can, borrow it from the library or read it online. You might even be able to find the cartoon version of it online. Explain to a parent why it is a satire.

3. Following are two examples of satire. The first is just funny. What does the artist think of the French hairstyles of the time period? How is humor used to make a point?

4. This second one is a political cartoon. It's called "White Man's Burden." It depicts white leaders, but they are the burdens being carried by the non-white men. The satire is the irony in the contradiction between the title and who is actually burdened.

THE WHITE (?) MAN'S BURDEN.

Lesson 25

1. Read the satire examples that follow.
2. Explain to someone why the examples are satirical.

> "If this is going to be a Christian nation that doesn't help the poor, either we have to pretend that Jesus was just as selfish as we are, or we've got to acknowledge that He commanded us to love the poor and serve the needy without condition and then admit that we just don't want to do it." (Stephen Colbert)

The Adventures of Huckleberry Finn was written shortly after the Civil War, in which slavery was one of the key issues. While Mark Twain's father had slaves throughout his childhood, Twain did not believe that slavery was right in any way. Through the character of Jim, and the major moral dilemma that followed Huck throughout the novel, Twain mocks slavery and makes a strong statement about the way people treated slaves. Miss Watson is revered as a good Christian woman, who had strong values, but she is a slave owner in the story. She owns a slave called Jim, who runs away upon hearing that Miss Watson might sell him to New Orleans.
(from http://classic-literature.yoexpert.com/read-and-study-books/what-are-some-examples-of-satire-in-%22the-adventure-644.html)

A great example of irony in literature comes from The Gift of the Magi by O. Henry. It is a story of two people, much in love, who are very poor and want to give a Christmas gift to one another. She is very proud of her long, beautiful hair and he is equally proud of his pocket watch. The irony comes in to play when she cuts and sells her hair to buy him a chain for his watch, and he sells the watch to buy her combs for her hair.

Sarcasm is a sharp or cutting statement like a taunt or jibe, meant to really drive a point home. It can be meant to give pain and can include irony. On the other hand, sometimes you can make a point and still be funny.

Oscar Wilde wrote, "I am not young enough to know everything."
(above excerpts from http://examples.yourdictionary.com/satire-examples.html)

Jonathan Swift's *Gulliver Travels* is one of the finest satirical works in English Literature. Swift relentlessly satirizes politics, religion, and Western Culture. During Swift's times, two rival political parties, the Whigs and the Tories, dominated the English political scene. Similarly, "The Kingdom of Lilliput" is dominated by two parties distinguished by the size of the heels of their boots. By the trivial disputes between the two Lilliputian parties, Swift satirizes the minor disputes of the two English parties of his period. (http://literarydevices.net/satire/)

3. Read this portion of an article from satirewire.com.
4. What makes this article a satire? What is the humor element of it? What is the point of it? (Answers)
5. Write in your notebook a definition of satire.

From the article:

HIGH SCHOOL STUDENTS DEMAND WARS
IN EASIER-TO-FIND COUNTRIES
"How Come No One Fights in Big Famous Nations Anymore?" They Ask

A delegation of American high school students today demanded the United States stop waging war in obscure nations such as Afghanistan, Kuwait, and Bosnia-Herzegovina, and instead attack places they've actually heard of, such as France, Australia, and Austria, unless, they said, those last two are the same country.

"People claim we don't know as much geography as our parents and grandparents, but it's so not our fault," Josh Beldoni, a senior at Fischer High School in Los Angeles, told the Senate Armed Services Committee. "Back then they only had wars in, like, Germany and England, but we're supposed to know about places like Somalia and Massachusetts."

"Macedonia," corrected committee Chairman Carl Levin of Michigan.

"See?" said Beldoni.

Beldoni's frustration was shared by nearly three dozen students at the hearing, who blamed the U.S. military for making them look bad.

"I totally support our soldiers and all that, but I am seriously failing both geography and social studies because I keep getting asked to find Croatia or Yemvrekia, or whatever bizarre-o country we send troops to," said Amelia Nash, a junior at Clark High School in Orlando, Fla. "Can't we fight in, like, Italy? It's boot-shaped."
(from http://www.satirewire.com/news/jan02/geography.shtml)

Lesson 26

1. Look at this cartoon.
2. Make observations:
    - what characters are in the cartoon, who do they represent
    - what objects are in the cartoon, what do they represent
    - what can you read in the cartoon
3. Write the title of the cartoon, what you think the point is, and how the cartoonist used satire (how humor was used to get the point across). (Answers)

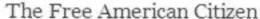

The Free American Citizen

Lesson 27

1. Look at this cartoon. (TR is Theodore, or Teddy, Roosevelt.)
2. Make observations:
    *   what characters are in the cartoon, who do they represent
    *   what objects are in the cartoon, what do they represent
    *   what can you read in the cartoon (spelling reform, old dictionary)
3. Write the title of the cartoon, what you think the point is, and how the cartoonist used satire (how humor was used to get the point across). (Answers)

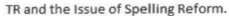

TR and the Issue of Spelling Reform.

Lesson 28

1. Look at this cartoon.
2. Make observations:
    - what characters are in the cartoon, who do they represent (TR is at the window. Trusts were huge corporations who tried to get to monopolies, owning everything in one area so that they could charge as much as they wanted.)
    - what objects are in the cartoon, what do they represent
    - what can you read in the cartoon (the trusts, Cortelyou–the secretary of the treasury)
3. Write the title of the cartoon, what you think the point is, and how the cartoonist used satire (how humor was used to get the point across). (Answers)

TR and the Trusts

Lesson 29

1. Read about some themes of the book *Gulliver's Travels*. Themes are what a book is *really* about, not just what is happening in the plot. Be on the lookout for these ideas as you read. As you are reading the book, note passages (chapter numbers and where in chapter) that show the themes.

   (excerpts from http://www.brighthubeducation.com/homework-help-literature/86333-three-main-themes-in-gullivers-travels/)

Individual verses the Community

Several of the societies that Gulliver visits show different structures than the traditional Western family model...The Lilliputians raise their children in a common setting instead of in family units.

Despite [the] different models, two truths emerge: there is no perfect social structure, and there is always tension between the individual's needs and the goals of the community. The Lilliputians are even sillier than the British and French were in their territorial disputes before and during the time when Swift was alive....

The ideal path, for Swift, is a medium path between the needs of the individual and the goals of the community. An individual willing to sacrifice for the greater good will mesh well with a society willing to give that individual a reasonable degree of autonomy and opportunity.

Power verses Ethics

In Lilliput, Gulliver has unlimited power but places himself in the service of the monarch; he drags the navy of rival Blefuscu out to sea. However, when he urinates in the queen's chamber to put out a palace fire, he is accused of treason -- a sign of how contrary to human nature it can seem to subjugate power to ethics at times....

Leaders who claim the high moral ground [have] a hard time proving their claims. Look at the egg dispute between Lilliput and Blefuscu -- this centers on a matter of religious interpretation that has driven the nations apart.

2. Read this summary of chapter 1: The author gives some account of himself and family. His first inducements to travel. He is shipwrecked, and swims for his life. Gets safe on shore in the country of Lilliput; is made a prisoner, and carried up the country.

Lesson 30

1. Read chapter 1 of *Gulliver's Travels*. This book is in two parts and each part starts over at chapter 1.
2. As Gulliver meets new characters in his travels, list them. As the main character travels to new settings, list them. Write a few words about each character and setting

as you list them. Create a page where you will write the book title, author and the themes you are going to be looking for: individual, community, power and ethics. Use that page to take your notes about the themes. Include page numbers when you take notes about themes.

3. Each time you read a chapter, tell someone about it.

PART I. *A VOYAGE TO LILLIPUT*
CHAPTER I.

My father had a small estate in Nottinghamshire; I was the third of five sons. He sent me to Emmanuel College in Cambridge at fourteen years old, where I resided three years, and applied myself close to my studies; but the charge of maintaining me, although I had a very scanty allowance, being too great for a narrow fortune, I was bound apprentice to Mr. James Bates, an eminent surgeon in London, with whom I continued four years; and my father now and then sending me small sums of money, I laid them out in learning navigation, and other parts of the mathematics useful to those who intend to travel, as I always believed it would be, some time or other, my fortune to do. When I left Mr. Bates, I went down to my father, where, by the assistance of him, and my uncle John and some other relations, I got forty pounds, and a promise of thirty pounds a year, to maintain me at Leyden. There I studied physic two years and seven months, knowing it would be useful in long voyages.

Soon after my return from Leyden, I was recommended by my good master, Mr. Bates, to be surgeon to the "Swallow," Captain Abraham Pannell, commander; with whom I continued three years and a half, making a voyage or two into the Levant, and some other parts. When I came back I resolved to settle in London; to which Mr. Bates, my master, encouraged me, and by him I was recommended to several patients. I took part of a small house in the Old Jewry; and, being advised to alter my condition, I married Mrs. Mary Burton, second daughter to Mr. Edmund Burton, hosier in Newgate Street, with whom I received four hundred pounds for a portion.

But my good master, Bates, dying in two years after, and I having few friends, my business began to fail; for my conscience would not suffer me to imitate the bad practice of too many among my brethren. Having, therefore, consulted with my wife, and some of my acquaintance, I determined to go again to sea. I was surgeon successively in two ships, and made several voyages, for six years, to the East and West Indies, by which I got some addition to my fortune. My hours of leisure I spent in reading the best authors, ancient and modern, being always provided with a good number of books; and, when I was ashore, in observing the manners and dispositions of the people, as well as learning their language, wherein I had a great facility, by the strength of my memory.

The last of these voyages not proving very fortunate, I grew weary of the sea, and intended to stay at home with my wife and family. I removed from the Old Jewry to Fetter Lane, and from thence to Wapping, hoping to get business among the sailors; but it would not turn to account. After three years' expectation that things would mend, I accepted an advantageous offer from Captain William

Prichard, master of the "Antelope," who was making a voyage to the South Sea. We set sail from Bristol, May 4, 1699; and our voyage at first was very prosperous.

It would not be proper, for some reasons, to trouble the reader with the particulars of our adventures in those seas. Let it suffice to inform him, that, in our passage from thence to the East Indies, we were driven by a violent storm, to the northwest of Van Diemen's Land.

By an observation, we found ourselves in the latitude of 30 degrees and 2 minutes south. Twelve of our crew were dead by immoderate labor and ill food; the rest were in a very weak condition.

On the fifth of November, which was the beginning of summer in those parts, the weather being very hazy, the seamen spied a rock within half a cable's length of the ship; but the wind was so strong, that we were driven directly upon it, and immediately split. Six of the crew, of whom I was one, having let down the boat into the sea, made a shift to get clear of the ship and the rock. We rowed, by my computation, about three leagues, till we were able to work no longer, being already spent with labor, while we were in the ship. We, therefore, trusted ourselves to the mercy of the waves; and, in about half an hour, the boat was overset by a sudden flurry from the north. What became of my companions in the boat, as well as those who escaped on the rock, or were left in the vessel, I cannot tell, but conclude they were all lost.

For my own part, I swam as fortune directed me, and was pushed forward by wind and tide. I often let my legs drop, and could feel no bottom; but, when I was almost gone, and able to struggle no longer, I found myself within my depth; and, by this time, the storm was much abated.

The declivity was so small that I walked near a mile before I got to the shore, which I conjectured was about eight o'clock in the evening. I then advanced forward near half a mile, but could not discover any sign of houses or inhabitants; at least, I was in so weak a condition, that I did not observe them. I was extremely tired, and with that, and the heat of the weather, and about half a pint of brandy that I drank as I left the ship, I found myself much inclined to sleep. I lay down on the grass, which was very short and soft, where I slept sounder than ever I remembered to have done in my life, and, as I reckoned, about nine hours; for, when I awaked, it was just daylight. I attempted to rise, but was not able to stir: for as I happened to lie on my back, I found my arms and legs were strongly fastened on each side to the ground; and my hair, which was long and thick, tied down in the same manner. I likewise felt several slender ligatures across my body, from my arm-pits to my thighs. I could only look upwards, the sun began to grow hot, and the light offended my eyes.

I heard a confused noise about me; but, in the posture I lay, could see nothing except the sky. In a little time, I felt something alive moving on my left leg, which, advancing gently forward over my breast, came almost up to my chin; when, bending my eyes downward, as much as I could, I perceived it to be a human creature, not six inches high, with a bow and arrow in his hands, and a quiver at his back. In the meantime I felt at least forty more of the same kind (as I conjectured) following the first.

114

I was in the utmost astonishment, and roared so loud that they all ran back in a fright; and some of them, as I was afterwards told, were hurt with the falls they got by leaping from my sides upon the ground. However, they soon returned, and one of them, who ventured so far as to get a full sight of my face, lifting up his hands and eyes by way of admiration, cried out in a shrill, but distinct voice— *Hekinah degul!* the others repeated the same words several times, but I then knew not what they meant.

I lay all this while, as the reader may believe, in great uneasiness. At length, struggling to get loose, I had the fortune to break the strings, and wrench out the pegs, that fastened my left arm to the ground; for by lifting it up to my face, I discovered the methods they had taken to bind me, and, at the same time, with a violent pull, which gave me excessive pain, I a little loosened the strings that tied down my hair on the left side, so that I was just able to turn my head about two inches.

But the creatures ran off a second time, before I could seize them; whereupon there was a great shout in a very shrill accent, and after it ceased, I heard one of them cry aloud, *Tolgo phonac*; when, in an instant, I felt above an hundred arrows discharged on my left hand, which pricked me like so many needles; and, besides, they shot another flight into the air, as we do bombs in Europe, whereof many, I suppose, fell on my body (though I felt them not), and some on my face, which I immediately covered with my left hand.

When this shower of arrows was over, I fell a-groaning with grief and pain, and then striving again to get loose, they discharged another volley larger than the first, and some of them attempted with spears to stick me in the sides; but by good luck I had on me a buff jerkin, which they could not pierce. I thought it the most prudent method to lie still, and my design was to continue so till night, when, my left hand being already loose, I could easily free myself; and as for the inhabitants, I had reason to believe I might be a match for the greatest army they could bring against me, if they were all of the same size with him that I saw.

But fortune disposed otherwise of me. When the people observed I was quiet, they discharged no more arrows: but, by the noise I heard, I knew their numbers increased; and about four yards from me, over against my right ear, I heard a knocking for above an hour, like that of people at work; when, turning my head that way, as well as the pegs and strings would permit me, I saw a stage erected, about a foot and a half from the ground, capable of holding four of the inhabitants, with two or three ladders to mount it; from whence one of them, who seemed to be a person of quality, made me a long speech, whereof I understood not one syllable.

But I should have mentioned, that before the principal person began his oration, he cried out three times, *Langro debul san* (these words, and the former, were afterwards repeated, and explained to me). Whereupon immediately about fifty of the inhabitants came and cut the strings that fastened the left side of my head, which gave me the liberty of turning it to the right, and of observing the person and gesture of him that was to speak. He appeared to be of a middle age, and taller than any of the other three who attended him, whereof one was a page that held up his train, and seemed to be somewhat longer than my middle finger; the other two stood one on each side, to support him.

He acted every part of an orator, and I could observe many periods of threatenings, and others of promises, pity, and kindness.

I answered in a few words, but in the most submissive manner, lifting up my left hand, and both my eyes, to the sun, as calling him for a witness: and, being almost famished with hunger, having not eaten a morsel for some hours before I left the ship, I found the demands of nature so strong upon me, that I could not forbear showing my impatience (perhaps against the strict rules of decency) by putting my finger frequently to my mouth, to signify that I wanted food. The *hurgo* (for so they call a great lord, as I afterwards learned) understood me very well. He descended from the stage, and commanded that several ladders should be applied to my sides; on which above a hundred of the inhabitants mounted, and walked towards my mouth, laden with baskets full of meat, which had been provided and sent thither by the king's orders, upon the first intelligence he received of me.

I observed there was the flesh of several animals, but could not distinguish them by the taste. There were shoulders, legs, and loins, shaped like those of mutton, and very well dressed, but smaller than the wings of a lark. I ate them by two or three at a mouthful, and took three loaves at a time, about the bigness of musket bullets. They supplied me as they could, showing a thousand marks of wonder and astonishment at my bulk and appetite. I then made another sign that I wanted drink.

They found by my eating that a small quantity would not suffice me; and being a most ingenious people, they slung up with great dexterity, one of their largest hogsheads, then rolled it towards my hand, and beat out the top: I drank it off at a draught; which I might well do, for it did not hold half a pint, and tasted like a small wine of Burgundy, but much more delicious. They brought me a second hogshead, which I drank in the same manner, and made signs for more; but they had none to give me.

When I had performed these wonders, they shouted for joy, and danced upon my breast, repeating, several times, as they did at first, *Hekinah degul*. They made me a sign, that I should throw down the two hogsheads, but first warning the people below to stand out of the way, crying aloud, *Borach nevola*; and, when they saw the vessels in the air, there was an universal shout of *Hekinah degul*. I confess, I was often tempted, while they were passing backwards and forwards on my body, to seize forty or fifty of the first that came in my reach, and dash them against the ground. But the remembrance of what I had felt, which probably might not be the worst they could do, and the promise of honor I made them—for so I interpreted my submissive behavior—soon drove out those imaginations. Besides, I now considered myself as bound, by the laws of hospitality, to a people who had treated me with so much expense and magnificence. However, in my thoughts I could not sufficiently wonder at the intrepidity of these diminutive mortals, who durst venture to mount and walk upon my body, while one of my hands was at liberty, without trembling at the very sight of so prodigious a creature, as I must appear to them.

After some time, when they observed that I made no more demands for meat, there appeared before me a person of high rank from his imperial majesty. His excellency, having mounted on the small of my right leg, advanced forwards up to my face, with about a dozen of his retinue: and, producing his credentials under the signet-royal, which he applied close to my eyes, spoke about ten minutes, without any signs of anger, but with a kind of determinate resolution, often pointing forwards, which, as I afterwards found, was towards the capital city, about half a mile distant, whither it was agreed by his majesty in council that I must be conveyed. I answered in few words, but to no purpose, and made a sign with my hand that was loose, putting it to the other (but over his excellency's head, for fear of hurting him or his train) and then to my own head and body, to signify that I desired my liberty.

It appeared that he understood me well enough, for he shook his head by way of disapprobation, and held his hand in a posture to show that I must be carried as a prisoner. However, he made other signs, to let me understand that I should have meat and drink enough, and very good treatment. Whereupon I once more thought of attempting to break my bonds; but again, when I felt the smart of their arrows upon my face and hands, which were all in blisters, and many of the darts still sticking in them, and observing, likewise, that the number of my enemies increased, I gave tokens to let them know, that they might do with me what they pleased. Upon this the *hurgo* and his train withdrew, with much civility, and cheerful countenances.

Soon after, I heard a general shout, with frequent repetitions of the words, *Peplom selan*, and I felt great numbers of people on my left side, relaxing the cords to such a degree, that I was able to turn upon my right, and to get a little ease. But, before this, they had daubed my face and both my hands with a sort of ointment very pleasant to the smell, which, in a few minutes, removed all the smart of their arrows. These circumstances, added to the refreshment I had received by their victuals and drink, which were very nourishing, disposed me to sleep. I slept about eight hours, as I was afterwards assured; and it was no wonder, for the physicians, by the emperor's order, had mingled a sleepy potion in the hogsheads of wine.

It seems that, upon the first moment I was discovered sleeping on the ground after my landing, the emperor had early notice of it, by an express; and determined in council, that I should be tied in the manner I have related (which was done in the night, while I slept), that plenty of meat and drink should be sent to me, and a machine prepared to carry me to the capital city.

This resolution, perhaps, may appear very bold and dangerous, and I am confident would not be imitated by any prince in Europe, on the like occasion. However, in my opinion, it was extremely prudent, as well as generous; for, supposing these people had endeavored to kill me with their spears and arrows, while I was asleep, I should certainly have awaked with the first sense of smart, which might so far have roused my rage and strength, as to have enabled me to break the strings wherewith I was tied; after which, as they were not able to make resistance, so they could expect no mercy.

These people are most excellent mathematicians, and arrived to a great perfection in mechanics, by the countenance and encouragement of the emperor, who is a renowned patron of learning. The prince hath several machines fixed on wheels for the carriage of trees, and other great weights. He often builds his largest men of war, whereof some are nine feet long, in the woods where the timber grows, and has them carried on these engines three or four hundred yards to the sea. Five hundred carpenters and engineers were immediately set to work, to prepare the greatest engine they had. It was a frame of wood, raised three inches from the ground, about seven feet long and four wide, moving upon twenty-two wheels. The shout I heard was upon the arrival of this engine, which, it seems, set out in four hours after my landing. It was brought parallel to me, as I lay. But the principal difficulty was, to raise and place me in this vehicle.

Eighty poles, each of one foot high, were erected for this purpose, and very strong cords, of the bigness of packthread, were fastened by hooks to many bandages, which the workmen had girt round my neck, my hands, my body, and my legs. Nine hundred of the strongest men were employed to draw up these cords by many pulleys fastened on the poles; and thus, in less than three hours, I was raised and slung into the engine, and tied fast.

All this I was told; for, while the whole operation was performing, I lay in a profound sleep, by the force of that soporiferous medicine infused into my liquor. Fifteen hundred of the emperor's largest horses, each about four inches and a half high, were employed to draw me towards the metropolis, which, as I said, was half a mile distant.

About four hours after we began our journey, I awaked, by a very ridiculous accident; for, the carriage being stopt a while, to adjust something that was out of order, two or three of the young natives had the curiosity to see how I looked, when I was asleep. They climbed up into the engine, and advancing very softly to my face, one of them, an officer in the guards, put the sharp end of his half-pike a good way up into my left nostril, which tickled my nose like a straw, and made me sneeze violently; whereupon they stole off, unperceived, and it was three weeks before I knew the cause of my awaking so suddenly.

We made a long march the remaining part of the day, and rested at night with five hundred guards on each side of me, half with torches, and half with bows and arrows, ready to shoot me, if I should offer to stir. The next morning, at sunrise, we continued our march, and arrived within two hundred yards of the city gates about noon. The emperor, and all his court, came out to meet us; but his great officers would by no means suffer his majesty to endanger his person, by mounting on my body.

At the place where the carriage stopt, there stood an ancient temple, esteemed to be the largest in the whole kingdom, which, having been polluted some years before by an unnatural murder, was, according to the zeal of those people, looked upon as profane, and therefore had been applied to common use, and all the ornaments and furniture carried away. In this edifice it was determined I should lodge. The great gate, fronting to the north, was about four feet high, and almost two feet wide, through which I could easily creep. On each side of the gate was a small window, not above six inches from the ground; into that on the left side the king's smith conveyed four score and eleven chains, like those that hang to a lady's watch in Europe, and almost as large, which were locked to my left leg with six-and-thirty padlocks.

Over against this temple, on the other side of the great highway, at twenty feet distance, there was a turret at least five feet high. Here the emperor ascended, with many principal lords of his court, to have an opportunity of viewing me, as I was told, for I could not see them. It was reckoned that above an hundred thousand inhabitants came out of the town upon the same errand; and, in spite of my guards, I believe there could not be fewer than ten thousand, at several times, who mounted my body, by the help of ladders. But a proclamation was soon issued, to forbid it, upon pain of death. When the workmen found it was impossible for me to break loose, they cut all the strings that bound me; whereupon I rose up, with as melancholy a disposition as ever I had in my life. But the noise and astonishment of the people, at seeing me rise and walk, are not to be expressed. The chains that held my left leg were about two yards long, and gave me not only the liberty of walking backwards and forwards in a semi-circle, but, being fixed within four inches of the gate, allowed me to creep in, and lie at my full length in the temple.

Lesson 31

1. *Gulliver's Travels* Read this summary of chapter 2: The emperor of Lilliput, attended by several of the nobility, comes to see the author in his confinement. The emperor's person and habit described. Learned men appointed to teach the author their language. He gains favour by his mild disposition. His pockets are searched, and his sword and pistols taken from him.
2. Read chapter 2.

CHAPTER II.

When I found myself on my feet, I looked about me, and must confess I never beheld a more entertaining prospect. The country around, appeared like a continued garden, and the enclosed fields, which were generally forty feet square, resembled so many beds of flowers. These fields were intermingled with woods of half a stang, and the tallest trees, as I could judge, appeared to be seven feet high. I viewed the town on my left hand, which looked like the painted scene of a city in a theatre.

The emperor was already descended from the tower, and advancing on horseback towards me, which had like to have cost him dear; for the beast, though very well trained, yet wholly unused to such a sight, which appeared as if a mountain moved before him, reared up on his hind feet. But that prince, who is an excellent horseman, kept his seat, till his attendants ran in and held the bridle, while his majesty had time to dismount.

When he alighted, he surveyed me round with great admiration, but kept without the length of my chain. He ordered his cooks and butlers, who were already prepared, to give me victuals and drink, which they pushed forward in a sort of vehicles upon wheels, till I could reach them. I took these vehicles, and soon emptied them all; twenty of them were filled with meat; each afforded me two or three good mouthfuls. The empress and young princes of the blood of both sexes, attended by many ladies, sat at some distance in their chairs; but upon the accident that happened to the emperor's horse, they alighted, and came near his person, which I am now going to describe. He is taller, by almost the breadth of my nail, than any of his court, which alone is enough to strike an awe into the beholders. His features are strong and masculine, with an Austrian lip and arched nose, his complexion olive, his countenance erect, his body and limbs well proportioned, all his motions graceful, and his deportment majestic. He was then past his prime, being twenty-eight years and three-quarters old, of which he had reigned about seven in great felicity, and generally victorious. For the better convenience of beholding him, I lay on my side, so that my face was parallel to his, and he stood but three yards off. However, I have had him since many times in my hand, and therefore cannot be deceived in the description.

His dress was very plain and simple, and the fashion of it between the Asiatic and the European; but he had on his head a light helmet of gold, adorned with jewels, and a plume an the crest. He held his sword drawn in his hand, to defend himself, if I should happen to break loose; it was almost three inches long; the hilt and scabbard were gold, enriched with diamonds. His voice was shrill, but very clear and articulate, and I could distinctly hear it, when I stood up.

The ladies and courtiers were all most magnificently clad; so that the spot they stood upon seemed to resemble a petticoat spread on the ground, embroidered with figures of gold and silver. His imperial majesty spoke often to me, and I returned answers, but neither of us could understand a syllable. There were several of his priests and lawyers present (as I conjectured by their habits), who were commanded to address themselves to me; and I spoke to them in as many languages as I had the least smattering of, which were, High and Low Dutch, Latin, French, Spanish, Italian, and Lingua Franca; but all to no purpose.

After about two hours the court retired, and I was left with a strong guard, to prevent the impertinence, and probably the malice of the rabble, who were very impatient to crowd about me as near as they durst; and some of them had the impudence to shoot their arrows at me, as I sat on the ground by the door of my house, whereof one very narrowly missed my left eye. But the colonel ordered six of the ring-leaders to be seized, and thought no punishment so proper as to deliver them bound into my hands; which some of his soldiers accordingly did, pushing them forwards with the butt-ends of their pikes into my reach. I took them all on my right hand, put five of them into my coat-pocket; and as to the sixth, I made a countenance as if I would eat him alive. The poor man squalled terribly, and the colonel and his officers were in much pain, especially when they saw me take out my penknife; but I soon put them out of fear, for, looking mildly, and immediately cutting the strings he was bound with, I set him gently on the ground, and away he ran. I treated the rest in the same manner, taking them one by one out of my pocket; and I observed both the soldiers and people were highly delighted at this mark of my clemency, which was represented very much to my advantage at court.

Towards night, I got with some difficulty into my house, where I lay on the ground, and continued to do so about a fortnight, during which time the emperor gave orders to have a bed prepared for me. Six hundred beds, of the common measure, were brought in carriages and worked up in my house; an hundred and fifty of their beds, sewn together, made up the breadth and length; and these were four double, which, however, kept me but very indifferently from the hardness of the floor, which was of smooth stone. By the same computation, they provided me with sheets, blankets, and coverlets, which were tolerable enough for one who had been so long inured to hardships as I.

As the news of my arrival spread through the kingdom, it brought prodigious numbers of rich, idle, and curious people to see me; so that the villages were almost emptied; and great neglect of tillage and household affairs must have ensued, if his imperial majesty had not provided, by several proclamations and orders of state, against this inconvenience. He directed that those who had already beheld me should return home, and not presume to come within fifty yards of my house without license from court; whereby the secretaries of state got considerable fees.

In the meantime, the emperor held frequent councils, to debate what course should be taken with me; and I was afterwards assured by a particular friend, a person of great quality, who was as much in the secret as any, that the court was under many difficulties concerning me. They apprehended my breaking loose; that my diet would be very expensive, and might cause a famine. Sometimes they determined to starve me, or at least to shoot me in the face and hands with poisoned arrows, which would soon despatch me: but again they considered that the stench of so large a carcase might produce a plague in the metropolis, and probably spread through the whole kingdom.

In the midst of these consultations, several officers of the army went to the door of the great council-chamber, and two of them being admitted, gave an account of my behavior to the six criminals above-mentioned, which made so favorable an impression in the breast of his majesty, and the whole board, in my behalf, that an imperial commission was issued out, obliging all the villages nine hundred yards round the city to deliver in, every morning, six beeves, forty sheep, and other victuals, for my sustenance; together with a proportionable quantity of bread and wine, and other liquors; for the due payment of which his majesty gave assignments upon his treasury. For this prince lives chiefly upon his own demesnes, seldom, except upon great occasions, raising any subsidies upon his subjects, who are bound to attend him in his wars at their own expense. An establishment was also made of six hundred persons, to be my domestics, who had board-wages allowed for their maintenance, and tents built for them very conveniently on each side of my door. It was likewise ordered that three hundred tailors should make me a suit of clothes, after the fashion of the country; that six of his majesty's greatest scholars should be employed to instruct me in their language; and lastly, that the emperor's horses, and those of the nobility and troops of guards, should be frequently exercised in my sight, to accustom themselves to me.

All these orders were duly put in execution, and in about three weeks I made a great progress in learning their language; during which time the emperor frequently honored me with his visits, and was pleased to assist my masters in teaching me. We began already to converse together in some sort; and the first words I learnt were to express my desire that he would please give me my liberty, which I every day repeated on my knees. His answer, as I could apprehend it, was, that this must be a work of time, not to be thought on without the advice of his council, and that first I must *lumos kelmin pesso desmar lon emposo*; that is, swear a peace with him and his kingdom. However, that I should be used with all kindness; and he advised me to acquire, by my patience and discreet behavior, the good opinion of himself and his subjects.

He desired I would not take it ill, if he gave orders to certain proper officers to search me; for probably I might carry about me several weapons which must needs be dangerous things, if they answered the bulk of so prodigious a person. I said his majesty should be satisfied, for I was ready to strip myself and turn up my pockets before him. This I delivered, part in words, and part in signs. He replied, that by the laws of the kingdom, I must be searched by two of his officers; that he knew this could not be done without my consent and assistance; that he had so good an opinion of my generosity and justice, as to trust their persons in my hands; that whatever they took from me should be returned when I left the country, or paid for at the rate which I should set upon them. I took up the two officers in my hands, put them first into my coat-pockets, and then into every other pocket about me, except my two fobs and another secret pocket, which I had no mind should be searched, wherein I had some little necessaries that were of no consequence to any but myself. In one of my fobs there was a silver watch, and in the other a small quantity of gold in a purse.

These gentlemen having pen, ink, and paper about them, made an exact inventory of everything they saw; and, when they had done, desired I would set them down, that they might deliver it to the emperor. This inventory I afterwards translated into English, and is word for word as follows:—

Imprimis, In the right coat-pocket of the great man-mountain (for so I interpret the words *quinbus flestrin*), after the strictest search, we found only one great piece of coarse cloth, large enough to be a foot-cloth for your majesty's chief room of state. In the left pocket, we saw a huge silver chest, with a cover of the same metal, which we the searchers were not able to lift. We desired it should be opened, and one of us stepping into it, found himself up to the mid-leg in a sort of dust, some part whereof flying up to our faces, set us both a sneezing for several times together. In his right waistcoat pocket we found a prodigious number of white thin substances folded one over another, about the bigness of three men, tied with a strong cable, and marked with black figures; which we humbly conceive to be writings, every letter almost half as large as the palm of our hands. In the left, there was a sort of engine, from the back of which were extended twenty long poles, resembling the palisadoes before your majesty's court; wherewith we conjecture the man-mountain combs his head, for we did not always trouble him with questions, because we found it a great difficulty to make him understand us. In the large pocket on the right side of his middle cover (so I translate the word *ranfu-lo*, by which they meant my breeches), we saw a hollow pillar of iron, about the length of a man, fastened to a strong piece of timber, larger than the pillar; and upon one side of the pillar were huge pieces of iron sticking out, cut into strange figures, which we know not what to make of. In the left pocket, another engine of the same kind. In the smaller pocket on the right side were several round flat pieces of white and red metal, of different bulk; some of the white, which seemed to be silver, were so large and so heavy, that my comrade and I could hardly lift them. In the left pocket, were two black pillars irregularly shaped; we could not without difficulty reach the top of them, as we stood at the bottom of his pocket. One of them was covered, and seemed all of a piece;

but at the upper end of the other, there appeared a white and round substance, about twice the bigness of our heads. Within each of these was enclosed a prodigious plate of steel, which, by our orders, we obliged him to show us, because we apprehended they might be dangerous engines. He took them out of their cases, and told us that in his own country his practice was to shave his beard with one of these, and to cut his meat with the other. There were two pockets which we could not enter: these he called his fobs. Out of the right fob hung a great silver chain, with a wonderful kind of engine at the bottom. We directed him to draw out whatever was at the end of that chain, which appeared to be a globe, half silver, and half of some transparent metal; for on the transparent side we saw certain strange figures, circularly drawn, and thought we could touch them till we found our fingers stopped by that lucid substance. He put this engine to our ears, which made an incessant noise, like that of a water-mill; and we conjecture it is either some unknown animal, or the god that he worships; but we are more inclined to the latter opinion, because he assured us (if we understood him right, for he expressed himself very imperfectly), that he seldom did anything without consulting it. He called it his oracle, and said it pointed out the time for every action of his life. From the left fob he took out a net almost large enough for a fisherman, but contrived to open and shut like a purse, and served him for the same use; we found therein several massy pieces of yellow metal, which, if they be real gold, must be of immense value.

Having thus, in obedience to your majesty's commands, diligently searched all his pockets, we observed a girdle about his waist, made of the hide of some prodigious animal, from which, on the left side, hung a sword of the length of five men; and on the right, a bag or pouch, divided into two cells, each cell capable of holding three of your majesty's subjects. In one of these cells were several globes, or balls, of a most ponderous metal, about the bigness of our heads, and required a strong hand to lift them; the other cell contained a heap of certain black grains, but of no great bulk or weight, for we could hold about fifty of them in the palms of our hands.

This is an exact inventory of what we found about the body of the man-mountain, who used us with great civility and due respect to your majesty's commission. Signed and sealed, on the fourth day of the eighty-ninth moon of your majesty's auspicious reign.
CLEFRIN FRELOC.
MARSI FRELOC.

When this inventory was read over to the emperor, he directed me, although in very gentle terms, to deliver up the several particulars.

He first called for my scimitar, which I took out, scabbard and all. In the meantime, he ordered three thousand of his choicest troops (who then attended him) to surround me at a distance, with their bows and arrows just ready to discharge; but I did not observe it, for mine eyes were wholly fixed upon his majesty. He then desired me to draw my scimitar, which, although it had got some rust by the sea-water, was in most parts exceedingly bright. I did so, and immediately all the troops gave a shout between terror and surprise; for the sun shone clear, and the reflection dazzled their eyes, as I waved the scimitar to and fro in my hand. His majesty, who is a most magnanimous prince, was less daunted than I could expect; he ordered me to return it into the scabbard, and cast it on the ground as gently as I could, about six feet from the end of my chain.

The next thing he demanded was one of the hollow iron pillars, by which he meant my pocket-pistols. I drew it out, and at his desire, as well as I could, expressed to him the use of it; and charging it only with powder, which, by the closeness of my pouch, happened to escape wetting in the sea (an inconvenience against which all prudent mariners take special care to provide), I first cautioned the emperor not to be afraid, and then let it off in the air.

The astonishment here was much greater than at the sight of my scimitar. Hundreds fell down as if they had been struck dead; and even the emperor, although he stood his ground, could not recover himself in some time I delivered up both my pistols, in the same manner as I had done my scimitar, and then my pouch of powder and bullets, begging him that the former might be kept from fire, for it would kindle with the smallest spark, and blow up his imperial palace into the air.

I likewise delivered up my watch, which the emperor was very curious to see, and commanded two of his tallest yeomen of the guards to bear it on a pole upon their shoulders, as draymen in England do a barrel of ale. He was amazed at the continual noise it made and the motion of the minute-hand, which he could easily discern; for their sight is much more acute than ours. He asked the opinions of his learned men about it, which were various and remote, as the reader may well imagine without my repeating; although, indeed, I could not very perfectly understand them.

I then gave up my silver and copper money, my purse, with nine large pieces of gold, and some smaller ones; my knife and razor, my comb and silver snuffbox, my handkerchief and journal-book. My scimitar, pistols, and pouch were conveyed in carriages to his majesty's stores; but the rest of my goods were returned to me.

I had, as I before observed, one private pocket, which escaped their search, wherein there was a pair of spectacles (which I sometimes use for the weakness of mine eyes), a pocket perspective, and some other little conveniences; which, being of no consequence to the emperor, I did not think myself bound in honor to discover; and I apprehended they might be lost or spoiled if I ventured them out of my possession.

Lesson 32

1. *Gulliver's Travels* Read this summary of chapter 3: The author diverts the emperor, and his nobility of both sexes, in a very uncommon manner. The diversions of the court of Lilliput described. The author has his liberty granted him upon certain conditions.

2. Read chapter 3.

3. Reread the last sentence in chapter 3. What does the sentence say, in your own words? What does it mean? (helps: ingenuity mean clever or inventive; prudent means practical in decision making about the future; economy in this sense means careful management of resources)

CHAPTER III.

My gentleness and good behavior had gained so far on the emperor and his court, and indeed upon the army and people in general, that I began to conceive hopes of getting my liberty in a short time, I took all possible methods to cultivate this favorable disposition. The natives came by degrees to be less apprehensive of any danger from me. I would sometimes lie down, and let five or six of them dance on my hand, and at last the boys and girls would venture to come and play at hide and seek in my hair. I had now made a good progress in understanding and speaking their language.

The emperor had a mind, one day, to entertain me with one of the country shows, wherein they exceed all nations I have known, both for dexterity and magnificence. I was diverted with none so much as that of the rope-dancers, performed upon a slender white thread, extended about two feet, and twelve inches from the ground. Upon which I shall desire liberty, with the reader's patience, to enlarge a little.

This diversion is only practised by those persons who are candidates for great employments and high favor at court. They are trained in this art from their youth, and are not always of noble birth or liberal education. When a great office is vacant, either by death or disgrace (which often happens) five or six of those candidates petition the emperor to entertain his majesty, and the court, with a dance on the rope, and whoever jumps the highest, without falling, succeeds in the office. Very often the chief ministers themselves are commanded to show their skill, and to convince the emperor that they have not lost their faculty. Flimnap, the treasurer, is allowed to cut a caper on the straight rope, at least an inch higher than any lord in the whole empire. I have seen him do the summersault several times together upon a trencher, fixed on a rope, which is no thicker than a common packthread in England. My friend Reldresal, principal secretary for private affairs, is, in my opinion, if I am not partial, the second after the treasurer; the rest of the great officers are much upon a par.

These diversions are often attended with fatal accidents, whereof great numbers are on record. I myself have seen two or three candidates break a limb. But the danger is much greater when the ministers themselves are commanded to show their dexterity! for, by contending to excel themselves and their fellows, they strain so far that there is hardly one of them who hath not received a fall, and some of them two or three. I was assured that a year or two before my arrival, Flimnap would have infallibly broke his neck if one of the king's cushions, that accidentally lay on the ground, had not weakened the force of his fall.

There is likewise another diversion, which is only shown before the emperor and empress and first minister, upon particular occasions. The emperor lays on the table three fine silken threads, of six inches long; one is purple, the other yellow, and the third white. These threads are proposed as prizes for those persons whom the emperor hath a mind to distinguish by a peculiar mark of his favor. The ceremony is performed in his majesty's great chamber of state, where the candidates are to undergo a trial of dexterity very different from the former, and such as I have not observed the least resemblance of in any other country of the old or new world.

The emperor holds a stick in his hands, both ends parallel to the horizon, while the candidates, advancing one by one, sometimes leap over the stick, sometimes creep under it, backwards and forwards several times, according as the stick is advanced or depressed. Sometimes the emperor holds one end of the stick, and his first minister the other: sometimes the minister has it entirely to himself. Whoever performs his part with most agility, and holds out the longest in leaping and creeping, is rewarded with the blue-colored silk; the yellow is given to the next, and the green to the third, which they all wear girt twice about the middle; and you see few great persons round about this court who are not adorned with one of these girdles.

The horses of the army, and those of the royal stables, having been daily led before me, were no longer shy, but would come up to my very feet without starting. The riders would leap them over my hand as I held it on the ground; and one of the emperor's huntsmen, upon a large courser, took my foot, shoe and all, which was indeed a prodigious leap.

I had the good fortune to divert the emperor one day after a very extraordinary manner. I desired he would order several sticks of two feet high, and the thickness of an ordinary cane, to be brought me; whereupon his majesty commanded the master of his woods to give directions accordingly; and the next morning six wood-men arrived with as many carriages, drawn by eight horses to each. I took nine of these sticks, and fixing them firmly in the ground in a quadrangular figure, two feet and a half square, I took four other sticks and tied them parallel at each corner, about two feet from the ground; then I fastened my handkerchief to the nine sticks that stood erect, and extended it on all sides, till it was as tight as the top of a drum; and the four parallel sticks, rising about five inches higher than the handkerchief, served as ledges on each side.

When I had finished my work, I desired the emperor to let a troop of his best horse, twenty-four in number, come and exercise upon this plain. His majesty approved of the proposal, and I took them up one by one in my hands, ready mounted and armed, with the proper officers to exercise them. As soon as they got into order, they divided into two parties, performed mock skirmishes, discharged blunt arrows, drew their swords, fled and pursued, attacked and retired, and, in short, discovered the best military discipline I ever beheld. The parallel sticks secured them and their horses from falling over the stage: and the emperor was so much delighted that he ordered this entertainment to be repeated several days, and once was pleased to be lifted up and give the word of command; and, with great difficulty, persuaded even the empress herself to let me hold her in her close chair within two yards of the stage, from whence she was able to take a full view of the whole performance.

It was my good fortune that no ill accident happened in these entertainments; only once a fiery horse, that belonged to one of the captains, pawing with his hoof, struck a hole in my handkerchief, and his foot slipping, he overthrew his rider and himself; but I immediately relieved them both, and covering the hole with one hand, I set down the troop with the other, in the same manner as I took them up. The horse that fell was strained in the left shoulder, but the rider got no hurt, and I repaired my handkerchief as well as I could; however, I would not trust to the strength of it any more in such dangerous enterprises.

About two or three days before I was set at liberty, as I was entertaining the court with feats of this kind, there arrived an express to inform his majesty that some of his subjects riding near the place where I was first taken up, had seen a great black substance lying on the ground, very oddly shaped, extending its edges round as wide as his majesty's bed-chamber, and rising up in the middle as high as a man; that it was no living creature, as they had at first apprehended, for it lay on the grass without motion; and some of them had walked round it several times; that, by mounting upon each other's shoulders, they had got to the top, which was flat and even, and, stamping upon it, they found it was hollow within; that they humbly conceived it might be something belonging to the man-mountain; and if his majesty pleased, they would undertake to bring it with only five horses.

I presently knew what they meant, and was glad at heart to receive this intelligence. It seems, upon my first reaching the shore after our shipwreck, I was in such confusion that, before I came to the place where I went to sleep, my hat, which I had fastened with a string to my head while I was rowing, and had stuck on all the time I was swimming, fell off after I came to land; the string, as I conjecture, breaking by some accident which I never observed, but thought my hat had been lost at sea. I intreated his imperial majesty to give orders it might be brought to me as soon as possible, describing to him the use and nature of it; and the next day the wagoners arrived with it, but not in a very good condition; they had bored two holes in the brim, within an inch and a half of the edge, and fastened two hooks in the holes; these hooks were tied by a long cord to the harness; and thus my hat was dragged along for above half an English mile; but the ground in that country being extremely smooth and level, it received less damage than I expected.

Two days after this adventure, the emperor, having ordered that part of the army which quarters in and about his metropolis to be in readiness, took a fancy of diverting himself in a very singular manner. He desired I would stand like a colossus, with my legs as far asunder as I conveniently could. He then commanded his general (who was an old, experienced leader and a great patron of mine) to draw up the troops in close order and march under me; the foot by twenty-four abreast and the horse by sixteen, with drums beating, colors flying, and pikes advanced. This body consisted of three thousand foot and a thousand horse.

I had sent so many memorials and petitions for my liberty, that his majesty at length mentioned the matter, first in the cabinet, and then in full council; where it was opposed by none, except Skyrris Bolgolam who was pleased, without any provocation, to be my mortal enemy. But it was carried against him by the whole board, and confirmed by the emperor. That minister was *galbet*, or admiral of the realm, very much in his master's confidence, and a person well versed in affairs, but of a morose and sour complexion. However, he was at length persuaded to comply; but prevailed, that the articles and conditions upon which I should be set free, and to which I must swear, should be drawn up by himself.

These articles were brought to me by Skyrris Bolgolam in person, attended by two under-secretaries, and several persons of distinction. After they were read, I was demanded to swear to the performance of them, first in the manner of my own country, and afterwards in the method prescribed by their laws; which was, to hold my right foot in my left hand, and to place the middle finger of my right hand on the crown of my head, and my thumb on the tip of my right ear.

But because the reader may be curious to have some idea of the style and manner of expression peculiar to that people, as well as to know the articles upon which I recovered my liberty, I have made a translation of the whole instrument, word for word, as near as I was able, which I here offer to the public.

Golbasto Momaren Evlame Gurdilo Shefin Mully Ully Gue, Most Mighty Emperor of Lilliput, delight and terror of the universe, whose dominions extend five thousand *blustrugs* (about twelve miles in circumference) to the extremities of the globe; monarch of all monarchs, taller than the sons of men; whose feet press down to the centre, and whose head strikes against the sun; at whose nod the princes of the earth shake their knees; pleasant as the spring, comfortable as the summer, fruitful as autumn, dreadful as winter. His most sublime majesty proposeth to the man-mountain, lately arrived at our celestial dominions, the following articles, which by a solemn oath he shall be obliged to perform.

First. The man-mountain shall not depart from our dominions without our license under our great seal.

Second. He shall not presume to come into our metropolis, without our express order, at which time the inhabitants shall have two hours warning to keep within doors.

Third. The said man-mountain shall confine his walks to our principal high roads, and not offer to walk or lie down in a meadow or field of corn.

Fourth. As he walks the said roads, he shall take the utmost care not to trample upon the bodies of any of our loving subjects, their horses or carriages, nor take any of our subjects into his hands without their own consent.

Fifth. If an express requires extraordinary despatch, the man-mountain shall be obliged to carry in his pocket the messenger and horse a six-days' journey once in every moon, and return the said messenger back (if so required) safe to our imperial presence.

Sixth. He shall be our ally against our enemies in the island of Blefuscu, and do his utmost to destroy their fleet, which is now preparing to invade us.

Seventh. That the said man-mountain shall at his times of leisure be aiding and assisting to our workmen, in helping to raise certain great stones, towards covering the wall of the principal park, and other our royal buildings.

Eighth. That the said man-mountain shall, in two moons time, deliver in an exact survey of the circumference of our dominions, by a computation of his own paces round the coast.

Lastly. That upon his solemn oath to observe all the above articles, the said man-mountain shall have a daily allowance of meat and drink sufficient for the support of 1724 of our subjects, with free access to our royal person, and other marks of our favor. Given at our palace at Belfaborac, the twelfth day of the ninety-first moon of our reign.

I swore and subscribed to the articles with great cheerfulness and content, although some of them were not so honorable as I could have wished; which proceeded wholly from the malice of Skyrris Bolgolam, the high admiral; whereupon my chains were immediately unlocked, and I was at full liberty. The emperor himself in person did me the honor to be by at the whole ceremony. I made my acknowledgments, by prostrating myself at his majesty's feet: but he commanded me to rise; and after many gracious expressions, which, to avoid the censure of vanity, I shall not repeat, he added, that he hoped I should prove a useful servant, and well deserve all the favors he had already conferred upon me, or might do for the future.

The reader may please to observe, that, in the last article for the recovery of my liberty, the emperor stipulates to allow me a quantity of meat and drink sufficient for the support of 1724 Lilliputians. Some time after, asking a friend at court, how they came to fix on that determinate number, he told me, that his majesty's mathematicians having taken the height of my body by the help of a quadrant, and finding it to exceed theirs in the proportion of twelve to one, they concluded, from the similarity of their bodies, that mine must contain at least 1724 of theirs, and consequently would require as much food as was necessary to support that number of Lilliputians. By which the reader may conceive an idea of the ingenuity of that people, as well as the prudent and exact economy of so great a prince.

Lesson 33

1. *Gulliver's Travels* Read this summary of chapter 4: Mildendo, the metropolis of Lilliput, described, together with the emperor's palace. A conversation between the author and a principal secretary, concerning the affairs of that empire. The author's offers to serve the emperor in his wars.
2. Read chapter 4.
3. Remember to be taking notes on characters, settings and themes.

CHAPTER IV.

The first request I made, after I had obtained my liberty, was, that I might have license to see Milendo, the metropolis; which the emperor easily granted me, but with a special charge to do no hurt, either to the inhabitants or their houses. The people had notice, by proclamation, of my design to visit the town.

The wall, which encompassed it, is two feet and a half high, and at least eleven inches broad, so that a coach and horses may be driven very safely round it; and it is flanked with strong towers at ten feet distance. I stept over the great western gate, and passed very gently, and sideling, through the two principal streets, only in my short waistcoat, for fear of damaging the roofs and eaves of the houses with the skirts of my coat. I walked with the utmost circumspection, to avoid treading on any stragglers who might remain in the streets; although the orders were very strict, that all people should keep in their houses at their own peril. The garret-windows and tops of houses were so crowded with spectators, that I thought in all my travels I had not seen a more populous place.

The city is an exact square, each side of the wall being five hundred feet long. The two great streets, which run across and divide it into four quarters, are five feet wide. The lanes and alleys, which I could not enter, but only viewed them as I passed, are from twelve to eighteen inches. The town is capable of holding five hundred thousand souls; the houses are from three to five stories; the shops and markets well provided.

The emperor's palace is in the centre of the city, where the two great streets meet. It is enclosed by a wall of two foot high, and twenty foot distant from the buildings. I had his majesty's permission to step over this wall; and the space being so wide between that and the palace, I could easily view it on every side.

The outward court is a square of forty feet, and includes two other courts; in the inmost are the royal apartments, which I was very desirous to see, but found it extremely difficult; for the great gates from one square into another were but eighteen inches high, and seven inches wide. Now the buildings of the outer court were at least five feet high, and it was impossible for me to stride over them without infinite damage to the pile, though the walls were strongly built of hewn stone, and four inches thick.

At the same time, the emperor had a great desire that I should see the magnificence of his palace; but this I was not able to do till three days after, which I spent in cutting down, with my knife, some of the largest trees in the royal park, about an hundred yards distance from the city. Of these trees I made two stools, each about three feet high, and strong enough to bear my weight.

The people having received notice a second time, I went again through the city to the palace, with my two stools in my hands. When I came to the side of the outer court, I stood upon one stool, and took the other in my hand; this I lifted over the roof, and gently set it down on the space between the first and second court, which was eight feet wide. I then stept over the building very conveniently, from one stool to the other, and drew up the first after me with a hooked stick. By this contrivance I got into the inmost court; and, lying down upon my side, I applied my face to the windows of the middle stories, which were left open on purpose, and discovered the most splendid apartments that can be imagined. There I saw the empress and the young princes in their several lodgings, with their chief attendants about them. Her imperial majesty was pleased to smile very graciously upon me, and gave me out of the window her hand to kiss.

But I shall not anticipate the reader with farther descriptions of this kind, because I reserve them for a greater work, which is now almost ready for the press, containing a general description of this empire, from its first erection, through a long series of princes, with a particular account of their wars and politics, laws, learning, and religion, their plants and animals, their peculiar manners and customs, with other matters very curious and useful; my chief design, at present, being only to relate such events and transactions as happened to the public, or to myself, during a residence of about nine months in that empire.

One morning, about a fortnight after I had obtained my liberty, Reldresal, principal secretary (as they style him) for private affairs, came to my house, attended only by one servant. He ordered his coach to wait at a distance, and desired I would give him an hour's audience; which I readily consented to, on account of his quality and personal merits, as well as of the many good offices he had done me during my solicitations at court. I offered to lie down, that he might the more conveniently reach my ear; but he chose rather to let me hold him in my hand during our conversation.

He began with compliments on my liberty; said he might pretend to some merit in it. But however, added, that if it had not been for the present situation of things at court, perhaps I might not have obtained it so soon. For, said he, as flourishing a condition as we may appear to be in to foreigners, we labor under two mighty evils: a violent faction at home, and the danger of an invasion, by a most potent enemy, from abroad. As to the first, you are to understand, that, for above seventy moons past, there have been two struggling parties in this empire, under the names of *Tramecksan* and *Slamecksan*, from the high and low heels of their shoes, by which they distinguish themselves. It is alleged, indeed, that the high heels are most agreeable to our ancient constitution; but, however this may be, his majesty hath determined to make use only of low heels in the administration of the government, and all offices in the gift of the crown, as you cannot but observe: and particularly, that his majesty's imperial heels are lower, at least by a *drurr*, than any of his court (*drurr* is a measure about the fourteenth part of an inch). The animosities between these two parties run so high, that they will neither eat nor drink nor talk with each other. We compute the *Tramecksan*, or high heels, to exceed us in number; but the power is wholly on our side. We apprehend his imperial highness, the heir to the crown, to have some tendency towards the high heels; at least, we can plainly discover that one of his heels is higher than the other, which gives him a hobble in his gait. Now, in the midst of these intestine disquiets, we are threatened with an invasion from the island of Blefuscu, which is the other great empire of the universe, almost as large and powerful as this of his majesty. For, as to what we have heard you affirm, that there are other kingdoms and states in the world, inhabited by human creatures as large as yourself, our philosophers are in much doubt, and would rather conjecture that you dropped from the moon or one of the stars, because it is certain, that an hundred mortals of your bulk would, in a short time, destroy all the fruits and cattle of his majesty's dominions. Besides, our histories of six thousand moons make no mention of any other regions than the two great empires of Lilliput and Blefuscu. Which two mighty powers have, as I was going to tell you, been engaged in a most obstinate war for six-and-thirty moons past. It began upon the following occasion: It is allowed on all hands, that the primitive way of breaking eggs, before we eat them, was upon the larger end; but his present majesty's grandfather, while he was a boy, going to eat an egg, and breaking it according to the ancient practice, happened to cut one of his fingers. Whereupon the emperor, his father, published an edict, commanding all his subjects, upon great penalties, to break the smaller end of their eggs. The people so highly resented this law, that our histories tell us, there have been six rebellions raised on that account, wherein one emperor lost his life, and another his crown. These civil commotions were constantly fomented by the monarchs of Blefuscu; and when they were quelled, the exiles always fled for refuge to that empire. It is computed, that eleven thousand persons have, at several times, suffered death, rather than submit to break their eggs at the smaller end. Many hundred large volumes have been published upon this controversy, but the books of the Big-endians have been long forbidden, and the whole party rendered incapable, by law, of holding employments.

During the course of these troubles, the Emperors of Blefuscu did frequently expostulate, by their ambassadors, accusing us of making a schism in religion, by offending against a fundamental doctrine of our great prophet Lustrog, in the fifty-fourth chapter of the Blundecral (which is their Alcoran) This, however, is thought to be a mere strain upon the text; for the words are these: That all true believers break their eggs at the convenient end. And which is the convenient end, seems, in my humble opinion, to be left to every man's conscience, or, at least, in the power of the chief magistrate to determine. Now, the Big-endian exiles have found so much credit in the emperor of Blefuscu's court, and so much private assistance and encouragement from their party here at home, that a bloody war hath been carried on between the two empires of six-and-thirty moons, with various success; during which time we have lost forty capital ships, and a much greater number of smaller vessels, together with thirty thousand of our best seamen and soldiers; and the damage received by the enemy is reckoned to be somewhat greater than ours. However, they have now equipped a numerous fleet, and are just preparing to make a descent upon us; and his imperial majesty, placing great confidence in your valor and strength, hath commanded me to lay this account of his affairs before you.

I desired the secretary to present my humble duty to the emperor, and to let him know that I thought it would not become me, who was a foreigner, to interfere with parties; but I was ready, with the hazard of my life, to defend his person and state against all invaders.

Lesson 34

1. *Gulliver's Travels* Read this summary of chapter 5: The author, by an extraordinary stratagem, prevents an invasion. A high title of honour is conferred upon him. Ambassadors arrive from the emperor of Blefuscu, and sue for peace. The empress's apartment on fire by an accident; the author instrumental in saving the rest of the palace.
2. Read chapter 5.

CHAPTER V.

The empire of Blefuscu is an island, situate to the north northeast of Lilliput, from whence it is parted only by a channel of eight hundred yards wide. I had not yet seen it; and upon this notice of an intended invasion, I avoided appearing on that side of the coast, for fear of being discovered by some of the enemy's ships, who had received no intelligence of me, all intercourse between the two empires having been strictly forbidden during the war, upon the pain of death, and an embargo laid by our emperor upon all vessels whatsoever.

I communicated to his majesty a project I had formed, of seizing the enemy's whole fleet; which, as our scouts assured us, lay at anchor in the harbor, ready to sail with the first fair wind. I consulted the most experienced seamen upon the depth of the channel, which they had often plumbed; who told me, that in the middle, at high water, it was seventy *glumgluffs* deep, which is about six feet of European measure; and the rest of it fifty *glumgluffs* at most. I walked towards the northeast coast, over against Blefuscu; where, lying down behind a hillock, I took out my small perspective glass, and viewed the enemy's fleet at anchor, consisting of about fifty men-of-war, and a great number of transports; I then came back to my house, and gave orders (for which I had a warrant) for a great quantity of the strongest cable and bars of iron. The cable was about as thick as packthread, and the bars of the length and size of a knitting needle. I trebled the cable, to make it stronger; and, for the same reason, I twisted three of the iron bars together, bending the extremities into a hook.

Having thus fixed fifty hooks to as many cables, I went back to the northeast coast, and putting off my coat, shoes, and stockings, walked into the sea in my leathern jerkin, about half an hour before high-water. I waded with what haste I could, and swam in the middle about thirty yards, till I felt ground; I arrived at the fleet in less than half an hour. The enemy were so frightened, when they saw me, that they leaped out of their ships, and swam to shore, where there could not be fewer than thirty thousand souls: I then took my tackling, and fastening a hook to the hole at the prow of each, I tied all the cords together at the end.

While I was thus employed, the enemy discharged several thousand arrows, many of which stuck in my hands and face; and, besides the excessive smart, gave me much disturbance in my work. My greatest apprehension was for mine eyes, which I should have infallibly lost, if I had not suddenly thought of an expedient. I kept, among other little necessaries, a pair of spectacles, in a private pocket, which, as I observed before, had escaped the emperor's searchers. These I took out, and fastened as strongly as I could upon my nose, and thus armed, went on boldly with my work, in spite of the enemy's arrows, many of which struck against the glasses of my spectacles, but without any other effect, farther than a little to discompose them. I had now fastened all the hooks, and, taking the knot in my hand, began to pull: but not a ship would stir, for they were all too fast held by their anchors; so that the boldest part of my enterprise remained. I therefore let go the cord, and, leaving the hooks fixed to the ships, I resolutely cut with my knife the cables that fastened the anchors, receiving above two hundred shots in my face and hands; then I took up the knotted end of the cables, to which my hooks were tied, and, with great ease, drew fifty of the enemy's largest men-of-war after me.

The Blefuscudians, who had not the least imagination of what I intended, were at first confounded with astonishment. They had seen me cut the cables, and thought my design was only to let the ships run adrift, or fall foul on each other: but when they perceived the whole fleet moving in order, and saw me pulling at the end, they set up such a scream of grief and despair as it is almost impossible to describe or conceive. When I had got out of danger, I stopped awhile to pick out the arrows that stuck in my hands and face: and rubbed on some of the same ointment that was given me at my first arrival, as I have formerly mentioned. I then took off my spectacles, and waiting about an hour, till the tide was a little fallen, I waded through the middle with my cargo, and arrived safe at the royal port of Lilliput.

The emperor and his whole court stood on the shore, expecting the issue of this great adventure. They saw the ships move forward in a large half-moon, but could not discern me, who was up to my breast in water. When I advanced to the middle of the channel, they were yet more in pain, because I was under water to my neck. The emperor concluded me to be drowned, and that the enemy's fleet was approaching in an hostile manner: but he was soon eased of his fears; for the channel growing shallower every step I made, I came in a short time within hearing; and holding up the end of the cable, by which the fleet was fastened, I cried in a loud voice, Long live the most puissant emperor of Lilliput! This great prince received me at my landing, with all possible encomiums, and created me a *nardac* upon the spot, which is the highest title of honor among them. His majesty desired I would take some other opportunity of bringing all the rest of his enemy's ships into his ports. And so immeasurable is the ambition of princes, that he seemed to think of nothing less than reducing the whole empire of Blefuscu into a province, and governing it by viceroy; of destroying the Big-endian exiles, and compelling that people to break the smaller end of their eggs, by which he would remain the sole monarch of the whole world. But I endeavored to divert him from this design, by many arguments, drawn from the topics of policy, as well as justice. And I plainly protested, that I would never be an instrument of bringing a free and brave people into slavery. And when the matter was debated in council, the wisest part of the ministry were of my opinion.

This open, bold declaration of mine was so opposite to the schemes and politics of his imperial majesty, that he could never forgive me; he mentioned it, in a very artful manner, at council, where, I was told, that some of the wisest appeared, at least by their silence, to be of my opinion; but others, who were my secret enemies, could not forbear some expressions, which by a side-wind reflected on me. And, from this time began an intrigue between his majesty and a junto of ministers maliciously bent against me, which broke out in less than two months, and had like to have ended in my utter destruction. Of so little weight are the greatest services to princes, when put into the balance with a refusal to gratify their passions.

About three weeks after this exploit, there arrived a solemn embassy from Blefuscu, with humble offers of peace; which was soon concluded, upon conditions very advantageous to our emperor, wherewith I shall not trouble the reader. There were six ambassadors, with a train of about five hundred persons; and their entry was very magnificent, suitable to the grandeur of their master, and the importance of their business. When their treaty was finished, wherein I did them several good offices, by the credit I now had, or at least appeared to have at court, their excellencies, who were privately told how much I had been their friend, made me a visit in form. They began with many compliments upon my valor and generosity, invited me to that kingdom, in the emperor their master's name, and desired me to show some proofs of my prodigious strength, of which they had heard so many wonders; wherein I readily obliged them, but shall not trouble the reader with the particulars.

When I had for some time entertained their Excellencies, to their infinite satisfaction and surprise, I desired they would do me the honor to present my most humble respects to the emperor their master, the renown of whose virtues had so justly filled the whole world with admiration, and whose royal person I resolved to attend, before I returned to my own country. Accordingly, the next time I had the honor to see our emperor, I desired his general license to wait on the Blefuscudian monarch, which he was pleased to grant me, as I could plainly perceive, in a very cold manner; but could not guess the reason, till I had a whisper from a certain person, that Flimnap and Bolgolam had represented my intercourse with those ambassadors as a mark of disaffection, from which, I am sure, my heart was wholly free. And this was the first time I began to conceive some imperfect idea of courts and ministers.

It is to be observed, that these ambassadors spoke to me by an interpreter, the languages of both empires differing as much from each other as any two in Europe, and each nation priding itself upon the antiquity, beauty, and energy of its own tongue, with an avowed contempt for that of its neighbor; yet our emperor, standing upon the advantage he had got by the seizure of their fleet, obliged them to deliver their credentials, and make their speech in the Lilliputian tongue.

And it must be confessed, that, from the great intercourse of trade and commerce between both realms; from the continual reception of exiles, which is mutual among them; and from the custom in each empire, to send their young nobility, and richer gentry, to the other, in order to polish themselves, by seeing the world, and understanding men and manners; there are few persons of distinction, or merchants, or, seamen, who dwell in the maritime parts, but what can hold conversation in both tongues, as I found some weeks after, when I went to pay my respects to the Emperor of Blefuscu, which, in the midst of great misfortunes, through the malice of my enemies, proved a very happy adventure to me, as I shall relate in its proper place.

The reader may remember, that when I signed those articles, upon which I recovered my liberty, there were some which I disliked, upon account of their being too servile; neither could anything but an extreme necessity have forced me to submit. But, being now a *nardac* of the highest rank in that empire, such offices were looked upon as below my dignity, and the emperor, to do him justice, never once mentioned them to me. However, it was not long before I had an opportunity of doing his majesty, at least as I then thought, a most signal service. I was alarmed at midnight with the cries of many hundred people at my door, by which, being suddenly awaked, I was in some kind of terror. I heard the word *burglum* repeated incessantly.

Several of the emperor's court, making their way through the crowd, entreated me to come immediately to the palace, where her imperial majesty's apartment was on fire, by the carelessness of a maid of honor, who fell asleep while she was reading a romance. I got up in an instant; and orders being given to clear the way before me, and it being likewise a moonshine night, I made a shift to get to the palace, without trampling on any of the people. I found they had already applied ladders to the walls of the apartment, and were well provided with buckets, but the water was at some distance. These buckets were about the size of a large thimble, and the poor people supplied me with them as fast as they could; but the flame was so violent that they did little good. I might easily have stifled it with my coat, which I unfortunately left behind me for haste, and came away only in my leathern jerkin. The case seemed wholly desperate and deplorable, and this magnificent palace would have infallibly been burnt down to the ground, if, by a presence of mind unusual to me, I had not suddenly thought of an expedient by which in three minutes the fire was wholly extinguished, and the rest of that noble pile, which had cost so many ages in erecting, preserved from destruction.

It was now daylight, and I returned to my house, without waiting to congratulate with the emperor; because, although I had done a very eminent piece of service, yet I could not tell how his majesty might resent the manner by which I had performed it: for, by the fundamental laws of the realm, it is capital in any man, of what quality soever, to even touch the empress or the royal princesses without invitation. But I was a little comforted by a message from his majesty, that he would give orders to the grand justiciary for passing my pardon in form, which, however, I could not obtain. And I was privately assured that the empress, conceiving the greatest abhorrence of me, and, in the presence of her chief confidants, could not forbear vowing revenge.

Lesson 35

1. *Gulliver's Travels* Read this summary of chapter 6: Of the inhabitants of Lilliput; their learning, laws, and customs; the manner of educating their children. The author's way of living in that country. His vindication of a great lady.
2. Read chapter 6.

CHAPTER VI.

Although I intend to leave the description of this empire to a particular treatise, yet, in the meantime, I am content to gratify the curious reader with some general ideas. As the common size of the natives is somewhat under six inches high, so there is an exact proportion in all other animals, as well as plants and trees: for instance, the tallest horses and oxen are between four and five inches in height, the sheep an inch and a half, more or less; their geese about the bigness of a sparrow, and so the several gradations downwards, till you come to the smallest, which, to my sight, were almost invisible; but nature hath adapted the eyes of the Lilliputians to all objects proper for their view; they see with great exactness, but at no great distance. And, to show the sharpness of their sight, towards objects that are near, I have been much pleased with observing a cook pulling a lark, which was not so large as a common fly; and a young girl threading an invisible needle with invisible silk. Their tallest trees are about seven feet high; I mean some of those in the great royal park, the tops whereof I could but just reach with my fist clenched. The other vegetables are in the same proportion; but this I leave to the reader's imagination.

I shall say but little at present of their learning, which, for many ages, hath flourished in all its branches among them: but their manner of writing is very peculiar, being neither from the left to the right like the Europeans; nor from the right to the left, like the Arabians; nor from up to down, like the Chinese, but aslant, from one corner of the paper to the other, like ladies in England.

They bury their dead with their heads directly downwards, because they hold an opinion, that in eleven thousand moons they are all to rise again, in which period the earth (which they conceive to be flat) will turn upside down, and by this means they shall, at the resurrection, be found ready, standing on their feet. The learned among them confess the absurdity of this doctrine, but the practice still continues, in compliance to the vulgar.

There are some laws and customs in this empire very peculiar; and, if they were not so directly contrary to those of my own dear country, I should be tempted to say a little in their justification. It is only to be wished they were as well executed. The first I shall mention relates to informers. All crimes against the state are punished here with the utmost severity; but, if the person accused maketh his innocence plainly to appear upon his trial, the accuser is immediately put to an ignominious death; and, out of his goods, or lands, the innocent person is quadruply recompensed for the loss of his time, for the danger he underwent, for the hardship of his imprisonment, and for all the charges he hath been at in making his defence, or, it that fund be deficient, it is largely supplied by the crown. The emperor also confers on him some public mark of his favor, and proclamation is made of his innocence through the whole city.

They look upon fraud as a greater crime than theft, and therefore seldom fail to punish it with death; for they allege, that care and vigilance, with a very common understanding, may preserve a man's goods from thieves, but honesty has no fence against superior cunning; and, since it is necessary that there should be a perpetual intercourse of buying and selling, and dealing upon credit, where fraud is permitted and connived at, or hath no law to punish it, the honest dealer is always undone, and the knave gets the advantage. I remember, when I was once interceding with the king for a criminal, who had wronged his master of a great sum of money, which he had received by order, and run away with, and happening to tell his majesty, by way of extenuation, that it was only a breach of trust, the emperor thought it monstrous in me, to offer as a defence the greatest aggravation of the crime; and, truly, I had little to say in return, farther than the common answer, that different nations had different customs; for, I confess, I was heartily ashamed.

Although we usually call reward and punishment the two hinges upon which all government turns, yet I could never observe this maxim to be put in practice by any nation except that of Lilliput. Whoever can there bring sufficient proof that he hath strictly observed the laws of his country for seventy-three moons, hath a claim to certain privileges, according to his quality and condition of life, with a proportionable sum of out of a fund appropriated for that use; he likewise acquires the title of *snillpall*, or *legal*, which is added to his name, but doth not descend to his posterity. And these people thought it a prodigious defect of policy among us, when I told them that our laws were enforced only by penalties, without any mention of reward. It is upon this account that the image of Justice, in their courts of judicature, is formed with six eyes, two before, as many behind, and on each side one, to signify circumspection, with a bag of gold open in her right hand, and a sword sheath in her left, to show she was more disposed to reward than to punish.

In choosing persons for all employments, they have more regard to good morals than to great abilities; for, since government is necessary to mankind, they believe that the common size of human understanding is fitted to some station or other, and that Providence never intended to make the management of public affairs a mystery, to be comprehended only by a few persons of sublime genius, of which there seldom are three born in an age; but they suppose truth, justice, temperance, and the like, to be in every man's power, the practice of which virtues, assisted by experience, and a good intention, would qualify any man for the service of his country, except where a course of study is required. But they thought the want of moral virtues was so far from being supplied by superior endowments of the mind, that employments could never be put into such dangerous hands as those of persons so qualified; and at least, that the mistakes committed by ignorance, in a virtuous disposition, would never be of such fatal consequences to the public weal as the practices of a man whose inclinations led him to be corrupt, and who had great abilities to manage, to multiply, and defend his corruptions.

In like manner, the disbelief of a Divine Providence renders a man incapable of holding any public station; for, since kings avow themselves to be the deputies of Providence, the Lilliputians think nothing can be more absurd than for a prince to employ such men as disown the authority under which he acts.

In relating these and the following laws, I would only be understood to mean the original institutions, and not the most scandalous corruptions into which these people are fallen, by the degenerate nature of man. For, as to that infamous practice of acquiring great employments by dancing on the ropes, or badges of favor and distinction by leaping over sticks, and creeping under them, the reader is to observe, that they were first introduced by the grandfather of the emperor, now reigning, and grew to the present height by the gradual increase of party and faction.

Ingratitude is, among them, a capital crime, as we read it to have been in some other countries; for they reason thus, that whoever makes ill returns to his benefactor, must needs be a common enemy to the rest of mankind, from whom he hath received no obligation, and therefore such a man is not fit to live.

Their notions relating to the duties of parents and children differ extremely from ours. Their opinion is, that parents are the last of all others to be trusted with the education of their own children; and, therefore, they have, in every town, public nurseries, where all parents, except cottagers and laborers, are obliged to send their infants of both sexes to be reared and educated, when they come to the age of twenty moons, at which time they are supposed to have some rudiments of docility. These schools are of several kinds, suited to different qualities, and to both sexes. They have certain professors, well skilled in preparing children for such a condition of life as befits the rank of their parents, and their own capacities as well as inclinations. I shall first say something of the male nurseries, and then of the female.

The nurseries for males of noble or eminent birth are provided with grave and learned professors, and their several deputies. The clothes and food of the children are plain and simple. They are bred up in the principles of honor, justice, courage, modesty, clemency, religion, and love of their country; they are always employed in some business, except in the times of eating and sleeping, which are very short, and two hours for diversions, consisting of bodily exercises. They are dressed by men till four years of age, and then are obliged to dress themselves, although their quality be ever so great; and the women attendants, who are aged proportionably to ours at fifty, perform only the most menial offices. They are never suffered to converse with servants, but go together in smaller or greater numbers to take their diversions, and always in the presence of a professor, or one of his deputies; whereby they avoid those early bad impressions of folly and vice, to which our children are subject. Their parents are suffered to see them only twice a year; the visit to last but an hour; they are allowed to kiss the child at meeting and parting; but a professor, who always stands by on those occasions, will not suffer them to whisper, or use any fondling expressions, or bring any presents of toys, sweetmeats, and the like.

The pension from each family, for the education and entertainment of a child, upon failure of due payment, is levied by the emperor's officers.

The nurseries for children of ordinary gentlemen, merchants, traders, and handicrafts, are managed proportionally after the same manner; only those designed for trades are put out apprentices at eleven years old, whereas those persons of quality continue in their exercises till fifteen, which answers to twenty-one with us; but the confinement is gradually lessened for the last three years.

In the female nurseries, the young girls of quality are educated much like the males, only they are dressed by orderly servants of their own sex; but always in the presence of a professor or deputy, till they come to dress themselves, which is at five years old. And if it be found that these nurses ever presume to entertain the girls with frightful or foolish stories, or the common follies practised by the chambermaids among us, they are publicly whipped thrice about the city, imprisoned for a year, and banished for life to the most desolate part of the country. Thus, the young ladies there are as much ashamed of being cowards and fools as the men, and despise all personal ornaments beyond decency and cleanliness: neither did I perceive any difference in their education, made by their difference of sex, only that the exercises of the women were not altogether so robust, and that some rules were given them relating to domestic life, and a smaller compass of learning was enjoined them: for their maxim is that, among people of quality, a wife should be always a reasonable and agreeable companion, because she cannot always be young. When the girls are twelve years old, which among them is the marriageable age, their parents or guardians take them home, with great expressions of gratitude to the professors, and seldom without tears of the young lady and her companions.

In the nurseries of females of the meaner sort, the children are instructed in all kinds of works proper for their sex and their several degrees; those intended for apprentices are dismissed at seven years old, the rest are kept to eleven.

The meaner families who have children at these nurseries are obliged, besides their annual pension, which is as low as possible, to return to the steward of the nursery a small monthly share of their gettings, to be a portion for the child; and, therefore, all parents are limited in their expenses by the law. For the Lilliputians think nothing can be more unjust than for people to leave the burden of supporting their children on the public. As to persons of quality, they give security to appropriate a certain sum for each child, suitable to their condition; and these funds are always managed with good husbandry and the most exact justice.

The cottagers and laborers keep their children at home, their business being only to till and cultivate the earth, and therefore their education is of little consequence to the public; but the old and diseased among them are supported by hospitals; for begging is a trade unknown in this empire.

And here it may perhaps divert the curious reader to give some account of my domestic, and my manner of living in this country, during a residence of nine months and thirteen days. Having a head for mechanics, and being likewise forced by necessity, I had made for myself a table and chair, convenient enough, out of the largest trees in the royal park. Two hundred sempstresses were employed to make me shirts, and linen for my bed and table, all of the strongest and coarsest kind they could get; which, however, they were forced to quilt together in several folds, for the thickest was some degrees finer than lawn. Their linen is usually three inches wide, and three feet make a piece.

The sempstresses took my measure as I lay on the ground, one standing at my neck, and another at my mid-leg, with a strong cord extended that each held by the end, while a third measured the length of the cord with a rule of an inch long. Then they measured my right thumb, and desired no more; for, by a mathematical computation, that twice round the thumb is once round the wrist, and so on to the neck and the waist, and by the help of my old shirt, which I displayed on the ground before them for a pattern, they fitted me exactly. Three hundred tailors were employed in the same manner to make me clothes; but they had another contrivance for taking my measure. I kneeled down, and they raised a ladder from the ground to my neck; upon this ladder one of them mounted, and let fall a plumb-line from my collar to the floor, which just answered the length of my coat; but my waist and arms I measured myself. When my clothes were finished, which was done in my house (for the largest of theirs would not have been able to hold them), they looked like the patchwork made by the ladies in England, only that mine were all of a color.

I had three hundred cooks to dress my victuals, in little convenient huts built about my house, where they and their families lived, and prepared me two dishes a-piece. I took up twenty waiters in my hand, and placed them on the table; an hundred more attended below on the ground, some with dishes of meat, and some with barrels of wine and other liquors, flung on their shoulders; all of which the waiters above drew up, as I wanted, in a very ingenious manner, by certain cords, as we draw the bucket up a well in Europe. A dish of their meat was a good mouthful, and a barrel of their liquor a reasonable draught. Their mutton yields to ours, but their beef is excellent, I have had a sirloin so large that I have been forced to make three bites of it; but this is rare. My servants were astonished to see me eat it, bones and all, as in our country we do the leg of a lark. Their geese and turkeys I usually eat at a mouthful, and I must confess they far exceed ours. Of their smaller fowl, I could take up twenty or thirty at the end of my knife.

One day his imperial majesty, being informed of my way of living, desired that himself and his royal consort, with the young princes of the blood of both sexes, might have the happiness, as he was pleased to call it, of dining with me. They came accordingly, and I placed them in chairs of state upon my table, just over against me, with their guards about them. Flimnap, the lord high treasurer, attended there likewise, with his white staff; and I observed he often looked on me with a sour countenance, which I would not seem to regard, but eat more than usual, in honor to my dear country, as well as to fill the court with admiration. I have some private reasons to believe that this visit from his majesty gave Flimnap an opportunity of doing me ill offices to his master. That minister had always been my secret enemy, though he outwardly caressed me more than was usual to the moroseness of his nature. He represented to the emperor the low condition of his treasury; that he was forced to take up money at a great discount; that exchequer bills would not circulate under nine per cent, below par; that I had cost his majesty above a million and a half of *sprugs* (their greatest gold coin, about the bigness of a spangle); and, upon the whole, that it would be advisable in the emperor to take the first fair occasion of dismissing me.

Lesson 36

1. *Gulliver's Travels* Read this summary of chapter 7: The author, being informed of a design to accuse him of high-treason, makes his escape to Blefuscu. His reception there.
2. Read chapter 7.

CHAPTER VII.

Before I proceed to give an account of my leaving this kingdom, it may be proper to inform the reader of a private intrigue which had been for two months forming against me.

I had been hitherto all my life a stranger to courts, for which I was unqualified by the meanness of my condition. I had indeed heard and read enough of the dispositions of great princes and ministers, but never expected to have found such terrible effects of them in so remote a country, governed, as I thought, by very different maxims from those in Europe.

When I was just preparing to pay my attendance on the emperor of Blefuscu, a considerable person at court (to whom I had been very serviceable, at a time when he lay under the highest displeasure of his imperial majesty) came to my house very privately at night, in a close chair, and without sending his name, desired admittance. The chairmen were dismissed; I put the chair, with his lordship in it, into my coat-pocket; and, giving orders to a trusty servant to say I was indisposed and gone to sleep, I fastened the door of my house, placed the chair on the table, according to my usual custom, and sat down by it. After the common salutations were over, observing his lordship's countenance full of concern, and inquiring into the reason, he desired I would hear him with patience, in a matter that highly concerned my honor and my life. His speech was to the following effect, for I took notes of it as soon as he left me:—

You are to know, said he, that several committees of council have been lately called in the most private manner on your account; and it is but two days since his majesty came to a full resolution. You are very sensible that Skyrris Bolgolam (*galbet* or high-admiral) hath been your mortal enemy almost ever since your arrival: his original reasons I know not; but his hatred is increased since your great success against Blefuscu, by which his glory, as admiral, is much obscured. This lord, in conjunction with Flimnap the high treasurer, whose enmity against you is notorious, Limtoc the general, Lalcon the chamberlain, and Balmuff the grand justiciary, have prepared articles of impeachment against you, for treason, and other capital crimes.

This preface made me so impatient, being conscious of my own merits and innocence, that I was going to interrupt; when he entreated me to be silent, and thus proceeded.

Out of gratitude for the favors you have done for me, I procured information of the whole proceedings, and a copy of the articles; wherein I venture my head for your service.

ARTICLES OF IMPEACHMENT AGAINST QUINBUS FLESTRIN, THE MAN-MOUNTAIN.

ARTICLE I.
Whereas, by a statute made in the reign of his Imperial Majesty Calin Deffar Plune, it is enacted, That whoever shall lay hands upon the empress, or upon any of the royal children, shall be liable to the pains and penalties of high treason. Notwithstanding, the said Quinbus Flestrin, in open breach of the said law, under color of extinguishing the fire kindled in the apartment of his Majesty's most dear imperial consort, did maliciously, and traitorously, pull her by the arms, and lift her high in the air in both his hands, against the statute in that case provided, &c., against the duty, &c.

ARTICLE II.
That the said Quinbus Flestrin, having brought the imperial fleet of Blefuscu into the royal port, and being afterwards commanded by his imperial majesty to seize all the other ships of the said empire of Blefuscu, and reduce that empire to a province, to be governed by a viceroy from hence, and to destroy and put to death, not only all the Big-endian exiles, but likewise all the people of that empire who would not immediately forsake the Big-endian heresy. He, the said Flestrin, like a false traitor against his most auspicious, serene, imperial majesty, did petition to be excused from the said service, upon pretence of unwillingness to force the consciences or destroy the liberties and lives of an innocent people.

ARTICLE III.
That, whereas certain ambassadors arrived from the court of Blefuscu, to sue for peace in his majesty's court; he, the said Flestrin, did, like a false traitor, aid, abet, comfort, and divert the said ambassadors, although he knew them to be servants to a prince who was lately an open enemy to his imperial majesty, and in open war against his said majesty.

ARTICLE IV.
That the said Quinbus Flestrin, contrary to the duty of a faithful subject, is now preparing to make a voyage to the court and empire of Blefuscu, for which he hath received only verbal license from his imperial majesty; and under color of the said license, doth falsely and traitorously intend to take the said voyage, and thereby to aid, comfort, and abet the emperor of Blefuscu, so late an enemy, and in open war with his imperial majesty aforesaid.

There are some other articles, but these are the most important, of which I have read you an abstract. In the several debates upon this impeachment, it must be confessed that his majesty gave many marks of his great lenity, often urging the services you had done him, and endeavoring to extenuate your crimes. The treasurer and admiral insisted that you should be put to the most painful and ignominious death, by setting fire on your house at night; and the general was to attend, with twenty thousand men armed with poisoned arrows, to shoot you on the face and hands. Some of your servants were to have private orders to strew a poisonous juice on your shirts and sheets, which would soon make you tear your own flesh, and die in the utmost torture. The general came into the same opinion; so that for a long time there was a majority against you: but his majesty resolving, if possible, to spare your life, at last brought off the chamberlain.

Upon this incident, Reldresal, principal secretary for private affairs, who always approved himself your true friend, was commanded by the emperor to deliver his opinion, which he accordingly did; and therein justified the good thoughts you have of him. He allowed your crimes to be great, but that still there was room for mercy, the most commendable virtue in a prince, and for which his majesty was so justly celebrated. He said, the friendship between you and him was so well known to the world, that perhaps the most honorable board might think him partial; however, in obedience to the command he had received, he would freely offer his sentiments; that if his majesty, in consideration of your services, and pursuant to his own merciful disposition, would please to spare your life, and only give orders to put out both your eyes, he humbly conceived that, by this expedient, justice might in some measure be satisfied, and all the world would applaud the lenity of the emperor, as well as the fair and generous proceedings of those who have the honor to be his counsellors: that the loss of your eyes would be no impediment to your bodily strength, by which you might still be useful to his majesty: that blindness is an addition to courage, by concealing dangers from us: that the fear you had for your eyes was the greatest difficulty in bringing over the enemy's fleet: and it would be sufficient for you to see by the eyes of the ministers, since the greatest princes do no more.

This proposal was received with the utmost disapprobation by the whole board. Bolgolam, the admiral, could not preserve his temper, but rising up in fury, said he wondered how the secretary durst presume to give his opinion for preserving the life of a traitor: that the services you had performed were, by all true reasons of state, the great aggravation of your crimes: that you, who extinguished the fire in that unprincipled manner, might at another time inundate and drown the whole palace; and the same strength, which enabled you to bring over the enemy's fleet, might serve, upon the first discontent, to carry it back: that he had good reasons to think you were a Big-endian in your heart; and, as treason begins in the heart, before it appears in overt acts, so he accused you as a traitor on that account, and therefore insisted you should be put to death.

The treasurer was of the same opinion. He showed to what straits his majesty's revenue was reduced, by the charge of maintaining you, which would soon grow insupportable. That the secretary's expedient of putting out your eyes was so far from being a remedy against this evil, that it would probably increase it, as is manifest from the common practice of blinding some sort of fowls, after which they fed the faster, and grew sooner fat. That his sacred majesty, and the council, who are your judges, were to their own consciences fully convinced of your guilt, which was a sufficient argument to condemn you to death without the formal proofs required by the strict letter of the law.

But his imperial majesty, fully determined against capital punishment, was graciously pleaded to say, that since the council thought the loss of your eyes too easy a censure, some other might be inflicted hereafter. And your friend, the secretary, humbly desiring to be heard again, in answer to what the treasurer had objected concerning the great charge his majesty was at in maintaining you, said that his excellency, who had the sole disposal of the emperor's revenue, might easily provide against that evil, by gradually lessening your establishment; by which, for want of sufficient food, you would grow weak and faint, and lose your appetite, and consume in a few months; neither would the stench of your carcase be then so dangerous when it should become more than half diminished; and, immediately upon your death, five or six thousand of his majesty's subjects might in two or three days cut your flesh from your bones, take it away by cart-loads, and bury it in distant parts, to prevent infection, leaving the skeleton as a monument of admiration to posterity.

Thus, by the great friendship of the secretary, the whole affair was compromised. It was strictly enjoined that the project of starving you by degrees should be kept a secret, but the sentence of putting out your eyes was entered on the books, none dissenting except Bolgolam, the admiral, who, being a creature of the empress, was perpetually instigated by her majesty to insist upon your death, she having borne perpetual malice against you, on account of that illegal method you took to remove her and her children the night of the fire.

In three days, your friend the secretary will be directed to come to your house and read before you the articles of impeachment; and then to signify the great lenity and favor of his majesty and council, whereby you are only condemned to the loss of your eyes, which his majesty doth not question you will gratefully and humbly submit to; and twenty of his majesty's surgeons will attend, in order to see the operation well performed, by discharging very sharp-pointed arrows into the balls of your eyes as you lie on the ground.

I leave to your prudence what measures you will take; and, to avoid suspicion, I must immediately return, in as private a manner as I came.

His lordship did so, and I remained alone, under many doubts and perplexities of mind.

It was a custom, introduced by this prince and his ministry (very different, as I have been assured, from the practices of former times), that after the court had decreed any cruel execution either to gratify the monarch's resentment or the malice of a favorite, the emperor always made a speech to his whole council, expressing his great lenity and tenderness, as qualities known and confessed by all the world. This speech was immediately published through the kingdom; nor did anything terrify the people so much as those encomiums on his majesty's mercy; because it was observed that, the more these praises were enlarged and insisted on, the more inhuman was the punishment, and the sufferer more innocent. Yet, as to myself, I must confess, having never been designed for a courtier, either by my birth or education, I was so ill a judge of things that I could not discover the lenity and favor of this sentence, but conceived it (perhaps erroneously) rather to be rigorous than gentle, I sometimes thought of standing my trial; for although I could not deny the facts alleged in the several articles, yet I hoped they would admit of some extenuation. But having in my life perused many state-trials, which I ever observed to terminate as the judges thought fit to direct, I durst not rely on so dangerous a decision, in so critical a juncture, and against such powerful enemies. Once I was strongly bent upon resistance, for, while I had liberty, the whole strength of that empire could hardly subdue me, and I might easily with stones pelt the metropolis to pieces; but I soon rejected that project with horror, by remembering the oath I had made to the emperor, the favors I received from him, and the high title of *nardac* he conferred upon me. Neither had I so soon learned the gratitude of courtiers as to persuade myself that his majesty's present seventies acquitted me of all past obligations.

At last I fixed upon a resolution, for which it is probable I may incur some censure, and not unjustly; for I confess I owe the preserving mine eyes, and consequently my liberty, to my own great rashness and want of experience; because if I had then known the nature of princes and ministers, which I have since observed in many other courts, and their methods of treating criminals less obnoxious than myself, I should with great alacrity and readiness have submitted to so easy a punishment. But, hurried on by the precipitancy of youth, and having his imperial majesty's license to pay my attendance upon the emperor of Blefuscu, I took this opportunity, before the three days were elapsed, to send a letter to my friend the secretary, signifying my resolution of setting out that morning for Blefuscu pursuant to the leave I had got; and, without waiting for an answer, I went to that side of the island where our fleet lay. I seized a large man-of-war, tied a cable to the prow, and lifting up the anchors, I stript myself, put my clothes (together with my coverlet, which I carried under my arm) into the vessel, and drawing it after me, between wading and swimming arrived at the royal port of Blefuscu, where the people had long expected me; they lent me two guides to direct me to the capital city, which is of the same name. I held them in my hands until I came within two hundred yards of the gate, and desired them to signify my arrival to one of the secretaries, and let him know I there waited his majesty's command. I had an answer in about an hour, that his majesty, attended by the royal family and great officers of the court, was coming out to receive me. I advanced a hundred yards. The emperor and his train alighted from their horses, the empress and ladies from their coaches, and I did not perceive they were in any fright or concern. I lay on the ground to kiss his majesty's and the empress's hand.

I told his majesty that I was come, according to my promise, and with the license of the emperor, my master, to have the honor of seeing so mighty a monarch, and to offer him any service in my power consistent with my duty to my own prince, not mentioning a word of my disgrace, because I had hitherto no regular information of it, and might suppose myself wholly ignorant of any such design; neither could I reasonably conceive that the emperor would discover the secret while I was out of his power, wherein however it soon appeared I was deceived.

I shall not trouble the reader with the particular account of my reception at this court, which was suitable to the generosity of so great a prince; nor of the difficulties I was in for want of a house and bed, being forced to lie on the ground, wrapped up in my coverlet.

Lesson 37

1. *Gulliver's Travels* Read this summary of chapter 8: The author, by a lucky accident, finds means to leave Blefuscu; and, after some difficulties, returns safe to his native country.
2. Read chapter 8.
3. Answer these questions about part 1:

- Who do the soldiers think has sent the giant?

- Evaluate the emperor as a ruler. Whose advice does he rely on?

- Why are Bigenders the enemies of the Lilliputans? What is the origin of their feud? How is that an example of satire?

CHAPTER VIII.

Three days after my arrival, walking out of curiosity to the northeast coast of the island, I observed, about half a league off in the sea, somewhat that looked like a boat overturned. I pulled off my shoes and stockings, and wading two or three hundred yards, I found the object to approach nearer by force of the tide; and then plainly saw it to be a real boat, which I supposed might by some tempest have been driven from a ship: whereupon I returned immediately towards the city, and desired his imperial majesty to lend me twenty of the tallest vessels he had left after the loss of his fleet, and three thousand seamen under the command of his vice-admiral. This fleet sailed round, while I went back the shortest way to the coast, where I first discovered the boat. I found the tide had driven it still nearer. The seamen were all provided with cordage, which I had beforehand twisted to a sufficient strength. When the ships came up, I stripped myself, and waded till I came within a hundred yards of the boat, after which I was forced to swim till I got up to it. The seamen threw me the end of the cord, which I fastened to a hole in the forepart of the boat, and the other end to a man-of-war. But I found all my labor to little purpose; for, being out of my depth, I was not able to work. In this necessity, I was forced to swim behind, and push the boat forwards as often as I could with one of my hands, and, the tide favoring me, I advanced so far, that I could just hold up my chin and feel the ground. I rested two or three minutes, and then gave the boat another shove, and so on till the sea was no higher than my arm-pits; and now, the most laborious part being over, I took out my other cables, which were stowed in one of the ships, and fastened them first to the boat, and then to nine of the vessels which attended me; the wind being favorable, the seamen towed, and I shoved, till we arrived within forty yards of the shore, and waiting till the tide was out, I got dry to the boat, and, by the assistance of two thousand men, with ropes and engines, I made a shift to turn it on its bottom, and found it was but little damaged.

I shall not trouble the reader with the difficulties I was under, by the help of certain paddles, which cost me ten days making, to get my boat to the royal port of Blefuscu, where a mighty concourse of people appeared upon my arrival, full of wonder at the sight of so prodigious a vessel. I told the emperor that my good fortune had thrown this boat in my way, to carry me to some place from whence I might return into my native country, and begged his majesty's orders for getting materials to fit it up, together with his license to depart, which, after some kind expostulation, he was pleased to grant.

I did very much wonder, in all this time, not to have heard of any express relating to me from our emperor to the court of Blefuscu. But I was afterwards given privately to understand that his imperial majesty, never imagining I had the least notice of his designs, believed I was only gone to Blefuscu in performance of my promise according to the license he had given me, which was well known at our court, and would return in a few days when the ceremony was ended. But he was at last in pain at my long absence; and, after consulting with the treasurer and the rest of that cabal, a person of quality was despatched with the copy of the articles against me. This envoy had instructions to represent to the monarch of Blefuscu the great lenity of his master, who was content to punish me no farther than the loss of mine eyes; that I had fled from justice, and, if I did not return in two hours, I should be deprived of my title of *nardac* and declared a traitor. The envoy farther added that, in order to maintain the peace and amity between both empires, his master expected that his brother of Blefuscu would give orders to have me sent back to Lilliput, bound hand and foot, to be punished as a traitor.

The emperor of Blefuscu, having taken three days to consult, returned an answer consisting of many civilities and excuses. He said that, as for sending me bound, his brother knew it was impossible. That, although I had deprived him of his fleet, yet he owed great obligations to me for many good offices I had done him in making the peace. That, however, both their majesties would soon be made easy; for I had found a prodigious vessel on the shore, able to carry me on the sea, which he had given orders to fit up with my own assistance and direction; and he hoped in a few weeks both empires would be freed from so insupportable an incumbrance.

With this answer the envoy returned to Lilliput, and the monarch of Blefuscu related to me all that had passed; offering me at the same time (but under the strictest confidence) his gracious protection if I would continue in his service; wherein, although I believed him sincere, yet I resolved never more to put any confidence in princes or ministers where I could possibly avoid it; and, therefore, with all due acknowledgments for his favorable intentions, I humbly begged to be excused. I told him that, since fortune, whether good or evil, had thrown a vessel in my way, I was resolved to venture myself in the ocean, rather than be an occasion of difference between two such mighty monarchs. Neither did I find the emperor at all displeased; and I discovered, by a certain accident, that he was very glad of my resolution, and so were most of his ministers.

These considerations moved me to hasten my departure somewhat sooner than I intended; to which the court, impatient to have me gone, very readily contributed. Five hundred workmen were employed to make two sails to my boat, according to my directions, by quilting thirteen folds of their strongest linen together. I was at the pains of making ropes and cables, by twisting ten, twenty, or thirty of the thickest and strongest of theirs. A great stone, that I happened to find after a long search by the sea-shore, served me for an anchor. I had the tallow of three hundred cows for greasing my boat, and other uses. I was at incredible pains in cutting down some of the largest timber-trees for oars and masts, wherein I was, however, much assisted by his majesty's ship-carpenters, who helped me in smoothing them after I had done the rough work.

In about a month, when all was prepared, I sent to receive his majesty's commands, and to take my leave. The emperor and royal family came out of the palace. I lay down on my face to kiss his hand, which he very graciously gave me; so did the empress and young princes of the blood. His majesty presented me with fifty purses of two hundred *sprugs* a-piece, together with his picture at full length, which I put immediately into one of my gloves, to keep it from being hurt. The ceremonies at my departure were too many to trouble the reader with at this time.

I stored the boat with the carcases of a hundred oxen, and three hundred sheep, with bread and drink proportionable, and as much meat ready dressed as four hundred cooks could provide. I took with me six cows and two bulls alive, with as many ewes and lambs, intending to carry them into my own country, and propagate the breed. And to feed them on board, I had a good bundle of hay and a bag of corn. I would gladly have taken a dozen of the natives, but this was a thing the emperor would by no means permit; and, besides a diligent search into my pockets, his majesty engaged my honor not to carry away any of his subjects, although with their own consent and desire.

Having thus prepared all things as well as I was able, I set sail on the twenty-fourth day of September, 1701, at six in the morning; and, when I had gone about four leagues to the northward, the wind being at southeast, at six in the evening I descried a small island about half a league to the northwest I advanced forward, and cast anchor on the lee side of the island, which seemed to be uninhabited. I then took some refreshment, and went to my rest. I slept well, and, as I conjecture, at least six hours, for I found the day broke two hours after I awaked. It was a clear night. I ate my breakfast before the sun was up; and heaving anchor, the wind being favorable, I steered the same course that I had done the day before, wherein I was directed by my pocket-compass. My intention was to reach, if possible, one of those islands, which, I had reason to believe, lay to the northeast of Van Diemen's Land. I discovered nothing all that day; but upon the next, about three o'clock in the afternoon, when I had, by my computation, made twenty-four leagues from Blefuscu, I descried a sail steering to the southeast: my course was due east. I hailed her, but could get no answer; yet I found I gained upon her, for the wind slackened. I made all the sail I could, and in half-an-hour she spied me, then hung out her ancient, and discharged a gun.

It is not easy to express the joy I was in, upon the unexpected hope of once more seeing my beloved country, and the dear pledges I left in it. The ship slackened her sails, and I came up with her, between five and six in the evening, September twenty-sixth; but my heart leaped within me to see her English colors.

I put my cows and sheep into my coat-pockets, and got on board with all my little cargo of provisions. The vessel was an English merchantman returning from Japan by the North and South Seas; the captain, Mr. John Biddle, of Deptford, a very civil man and an excellent sailor. We were now in the latitude of 30 degrees south. There were about fifty men in the ship; and here I met an old comrade of mine, one Peter Williams, who gave me a good character to the captain. This gentleman treated me with kindness, and desired I would let him know what place I came from last, and whither I was bound; which I did in few words, but he thought I was raving, and that the dangers I had underwent had disturbed my head; whereupon I took my black cattle and sheep out of my pocket, which, after great astonishment, clearly convinced him of my veracity. I then showed him the gold given me by the emperor of Blefuscu, together with his majesty's picture at full length, and some other rareties of that country. I gave him two purses of two hundred *sprugs* each, and promised, when we arrived in England, to make him a present of a cow and a sheep.

I shall not trouble the reader with a particular account of this voyage, which was very prosperous for the most part. We arrived in the Downs on the thirteenth of April, 1702. I had only one misfortune, that the rats on board carried away one of my sheep; I found her bones in a hole, picked clean from the flesh. I got the rest of my cattle safe ashore, and set them a-grazing in a bowling-green at Greenwich, where the fineness of the grass made them feed very heartily, though I had always feared the contrary: neither could I possibly have preserved them in so long a voyage, if the captain had not allowed me some of his best biscuits, which, rubbed to powder, and mingled with water, was their constant food. The short time I continued in England, I made a considerable profit by showing my cattle to many persons of quality and others: and before I began my second voyage I sold them for six hundred pounds.

Since my last return, I find the breed is considerably increased, especially the sheep, which I hope will prove much to the advantage of the woollen manufacture, by the fineness of the fleeces.

I stayed but two months with my wife and family; for my insatiable desire of seeing foreign countries would suffer me to continue no longer. I left fifteen hundred pounds with my wife and fixed her in a good house at Redriff. My remaining stock I carried with me, part in money, and part in goods, in hopes to improve my fortune. My eldest uncle, John, had left me an estate in land, near Epping, of about thirty pounds a year; and I had a long lease of the "Black Bull," in Fetter Lane, which yielded me as much more: so that I was not in any danger of leaving my family upon the parish. My son Johnny, named so after his uncle, was at the grammar-school, and a towardly child. My daughter Betty (who is now well married, and has children), was then at her needlework. I took leave of my wife and boy and girl, with tears on both sides, and went on board the "Adventure," a merchant ship of three hundred tons, bound for Surat, Captain John Nicholas, of Liverpool, commander. But my account of this voyage must be referred to the second part of my travels.

THE END OF THE FIRST PART.

Lesson 38

1. *Gulliver's Travels* Read this summary of chapter 1 of part 2: A great storm described; the long boat sent to fetch water; the author goes with it to discover the country. He is left on shore, is seized by one of the natives, and carried to a farmer's house. His reception, with several accidents that happened there. A description of the inhabitants.
2. Read chapter 1 of part 2.
3. Remember to take notes. Include page numbers when you take notes about the themes: individual, community, power and ethics.
4. Also remember to tell someone about each chapter you read.

TRAVELS PART II. *A VOYAGE TO BROBDINGNAG*
CHAPTER I.

Having been condemned by nature and fortune to an active and restless life, in two months after my return I again left my native country, and took shipping in the Downs on the twentieth day of June, 1702, in the "Adventure," Captain John Nicholas, a Cornish man, commander, bound for Surat. We had a very prosperous gale till we arrived at the Cape of Good Hope, where we landed for fresh water; but, discovering a leak, we unshipped our goods and wintered there: for, the captain falling sick of an ague, we could not leave the Cape till the end of March. We then set sail, and had a good voyage till we passed the Straits of Madagascar; but having got northward of that island, and to about five degrees south latitude, the winds, which in those seas are observed to blow a constant equal gale, between the north and west, from the beginning of December to the beginning of May, on the nineteenth of April began to blow with much greater violence and more westerly than usual, continuing so for twenty days together, during which time we were driven a little to the east of the Molucca Islands, and about three degrees northward of the line, as our captain found by an observation he took the second of May, at which time the wind ceased and it was a perfect calm; whereat I was not a little rejoiced. But, he, being a man well experienced in the navigation of those seas, bid us all prepare against a storm, which accordingly happened the day following: for the southern wind, called the southern monsoon, began to set in, and soon it was a fierce storm.

Finding it was like to overblow, we took in our sprit-sail, and stood by to hand the foresail; but making foul weather, we looked the guns were all fast, and handed the mizzen.

The ship lay very broad off, so we thought it better spooning before the sea, than trying, or hulling. We reefed the foresail and set him, we hauled aft the foresheet: the helm was hard-a-weather. The ship wore bravely. We belayed the fore down-haul; but the sail was split, and we hauled down the yard, and got the sail into the ship, and unbound all the things clear of it. It was a very fierce storm; the sea broke strange and dangerous. We hauled off the laniard of the whipstaff, and helped the man at the helm. We could not get down our topmast, but let all stand, because she scudded before the sea very well, and we knew that the topmast being aloft, the ship was the wholesomer, and made better way through the sea, seeing we had sea-room. When the storm was over, we set foresail and mainsail, and brought the ship to. Then we set the mizzen, main-top-sail, and the fore-top-sail. Our course was east north east, the wind was at southwest. We got the starboard tacks aboard, we cast off our weather braces and lifts; we set in the lee braces, and hauled forward by the weather bowlings, and hauled them tight and belayed them, and hauled over the mizzen tack to wind-ward and kept her full and by, as near as she could lie.

During this storm, which was followed by a strong wind, west southwest, we were carried, by my computation, about five hundred leagues to the east, so that the oldest sailor on board could not tell in what part of the world we were. Our provisions held out well, our ship was staunch, and our crew all in good health; but we lay in the utmost distress for water. We thought it best to hold on the same course, rather than turn more northerly, which might have brought us to the northwest parts of Great Tartary, and into the Frozen Sea.

On the sixteenth day of June, 1703, a boy on the topmast discovered land. On the seventeenth, we came in full view of a great island or continent (for we knew not which), on the south side whereof was a small neck of land, jutting out into the sea, and a creek too shallow to hold a ship of above one hundred tons. We cast anchor within a league of this creek, and our captain sent a dozen of his men well armed in the long-boat, with vessels for water, if any could be found. I desired his leave to go with them, that I might see the country, and make what discoveries I could.

When we came to land, we saw no river or spring, nor any sign of inhabitants. Our men therefore wandered on the shore to find out some fresh water near the sea, and I walked alone about a mile on the other side, where I observed the country all barren and rocky. I now began to be weary, and seeing nothing to entertain my curiosity, I returned gently down toward the creek; and the sea being full in my view, I saw our men already got into the boat, and rowing for life to the ship. I was going to holla after them, although it had been to little purpose, when I observed a huge creature walking after them in the sea, as fast as he could; he waded not much deeper than his knees, and took prodigious strides; but our men had the start of him about half a league, and the sea thereabouts being full of pointed rocks, the monster was not able to overtake the boat. This I was afterwards told, for I durst not stay to see the issue of the adventure; but ran as fast as I could the way I first went, and then climbed up a steep hill, which gave me some prospect of the country. I found it fully cultivated; but that which first surprised me was the length of the grass, which, in those grounds that seemed to be kept for hay, was about twenty feet high.

I fell into a high road, for so I took it to be, though it served to the inhabitants only as a footpath through a field of barley. Here I walked on for some time, but could see little on either side, it being now near harvest, and the corn rising at least forty feet. I was an hour walking to the end of this field, which was fenced in with a hedge of at least one hundred and twenty feet high, and the trees so lofty that I could make no computation of their altitude. There was a stile to pass from this field into the next. It had four steps, and a stone to cross over when you came to the uppermost. It was impossible for me to climb this stile because every step was six feet high, and the upper stone above twenty.

I was endeavoring to find some gap in the hedge, when I discovered one of the inhabitants in the next field, advancing towards the stile, of the same size with him whom I saw in the sea pursuing our boat. He appeared as tall as an ordinary spire steeple, and took about ten yards at every stride, as near as I could guess. I was struck with the utmost fear and astonishment, and ran to hide myself in the corn, from whence I saw him at the top of the stile, looking back into the next field on the right hand, and heard him call in a voice many degrees louder than a speaking trumpet; but the noise was so high in the air that at first I certainly thought it was thunder. Whereupon seven monsters, like himself, came towards him with reaping-hooks in their hands, each hook about the largeness of six scythes. These people were not so well clad as the first, whose servants or laborers they seemed to be; for, upon some words he spoke, they went to reap the corn in the field where I lay. I kept from them at as great a distance as I could, but was forced to move, with extreme difficulty, for the stalks of the corn were sometimes not above a foot distance, so that I could hardly squeeze my body betwixt them. However, I made a shift to go forward till I came to a part of the field where the corn had been laid by the rain and wind. Here it was impossible for me to advance a step; for the stalks were so interwoven that I could not creep through, and the beards of the fallen ears so strong and pointed that they pierced through my clothes into my flesh. At the same time I heard the reapers not above a hundred yards behind me.

Being quite dispirited with toil, and wholly overcome by grief and despair, I lay down between two ridges, and heartily wished I might there end my days. I bemoaned my desolate widow and fatherless children. I lamented my own folly and wilfulness in attempting a second voyage against the advice of all my friends and relations. In this terrible agitation of mind, I could not forbear thinking of Lilliput, whose inhabitants looked upon me as the greatest prodigy that ever appeared in the world; where I was able to draw an imperial fleet in my hand, and perform those other actions which will be recorded forever in the chronicles of that empire, while posterity shall hardly believe them, although attested by millions. I reflected what a mortification it must prove to me to appear as inconsiderable in this nation as one single Lilliputian would be among us. But this I conceived was to be among the least of my misfortunes: for, as human creatures are observed to be more savage and cruel in proportion to their bulk, what could I expect but to be a morsel in the mouth of the first among these enormous barbarians that should happen to seize me? Undoubtedly philosophers are in the right when they tell us that nothing is great or little otherwise than by comparison. It might have pleased fortune to let the Lilliputians find some nation where the people were as diminutive with respect to them as they were to me. And who knows but that even this prodigious race of mortals might be equally overmatched in some distant part of the world, whereof we have yet no discovery?

Scared and confounded as I was, I could not forbear going on with these reflections, when one of the reapers, approaching within ten yards of the ridge where I lay, made me apprehend that with the next step I should be squashed to death under his foot, or cut in two with his reaping-hook. And, therefore, when he was again about to move, I screamed as loud as fear could make me. Whereupon the huge creature trod short, and looking round about under him for some time, at last espied me as I lay on the ground. He considered awhile, with the caution of one who endeavors to lay hold on a small dangerous animal in such a manner that it shall not be able either to scratch or to bite him, as I myself have sometimes done with a weasel in England.

At length he ventured to take me up between his forefinger and thumb, and brought me within three yards of his eyes, that he might behold my shape more perfectly. I guessed his meaning, and my good fortune gave me so much presence of mind that I resolved not to struggle in the least as he held me in the air, above sixty feet from the ground, although he grievously pinched my sides, for fear I should slip through his fingers. All I ventured was to raise my eyes towards the sun, and place my hands together in a supplicating posture, and to speak some words in an humble melancholy tone, suitable to the condition I then was in. For I apprehended every moment that he would dash me against the ground, as we usually do any little hateful animal which we have a mind to destroy. But my good star would have it that he appeared pleased with my voice and gestures, and began to look upon me as a curiosity, much wondering to hear me pronounce articulate words, although he could not understand them. In the meantime I was not able to forbear groaning and shedding tears, and turning my head towards my sides; letting him know, as well as I could, how cruelly I was hurt by the pressure of his thumb and finger. He seemed to apprehend my meaning; for, lifting up the lappet of his coat, he put me gently into it, and immediately ran along with me to his master, who was a substantial farmer, and the same person I had first seen in the field.

The farmer, having (as I suppose by their talk) received such an account of me as his servant could give him, took a piece of a small straw, about the size of a walking-staff, and therewith lifted up the lappets of my coat, which it seems he thought to be some kind of covering that nature had given me. He blew my hair aside, to take a better view of my face. He called his hinds about him, and asked them (as I afterwards learned) whether they had ever seen in the fields any little creature that resembled me. He then placed me softly on the ground upon all fours, but I got immediately up, and walked slowly backwards and forwards to let those people see that I had no intent to run away. They all sat down in a circle about me, the better to observe my motions. I pulled off my hat, and made a low bow towards the farmer. I fell on my knees, and lifted up my hands and eyes, and spoke several words as loud as I could: I took a purse of gold out of my pocket, and humbly presented it to him. He received it on the palm of his hand, then applied it close to his eye to see what it was, and afterwards turned it several times with the point of a pin (which he took out of his sleeve), but could make nothing of it. Whereupon I made a sign that he should place his hand on the ground. I then took the purse, and opening it, poured all the gold into his palm. There were six Spanish pieces, of four pistoles each, besides twenty or thirty smaller coins. I saw him wet the tip of his little finger upon his tongue, and take up one of my largest pieces, and then another, but he seemed to be wholly ignorant what they were. He made me a sign to put them again into my purse, and the purse again into my pocket, which, after offering it to him several times, I thought it best to do.

The farmer by this time was convinced I must be a rational creature. He spoke often to me, but the sound of his voice pierced my ears like that of a water-mill, yet his words were articulate enough. I answered as loud as I could in several languages, and he often laid his ear within two yards of me; but all in vain, for we were wholly unintelligible to each other. He then sent his servants to their work, and taking his handkerchief out of his pocket, he doubled and spread it on his left hand, which he placed flat on the ground, with the palm upwards, making me a sign to step into it, as I could easily do, for it was not above a foot in thickness.

I thought it my part to obey, and, for fear of falling, laid myself at full length upon the handkerchief, with the remainder of which he lapped me up to the head for farther security, and in this manner carried me home to his house. There he called his wife, and showed me to her; but she screamed and ran back, as women in England do at the sight of a toad or a spider. However, when she had awhile seen my behavior, and how well I observed the signs her husband made, she was soon reconciled, and by degrees grew extremely tender of me.

It was about twelve at noon, and a servant brought in dinner. It was only one substantial dish of meat (fit for the plain condition of an husbandman) in a dish of about four-and-twenty feet diameter.

The company were the farmer and his wife, three children, and an old grandmother. When they were sat down, the farmer placed me at some distance from him on the table, which was thirty feet high from the floor. I was in a terrible fright, and kept as far as I could from the edge for fear of falling. The wife minced a bit of meat, then crumbled some bread on a trencher, and placed it before me. I made her a low bow, took out my knife and fork, and fell to eat, which gave them exceeding delight.

The mistress sent her maid for a small dram cup, which held about three gallons, and filled it with drink: I took up the vessel with much difficulty in both hands, and in a most respectful manner drank to her ladyship's health, expressing the words as loud as I could in English, which made the company laugh so heartily that I was almost deafened by the noise. This liquor tasted like a small cider, and was not unpleasant. Then the master made me a sign to come to his trencher-side; but as I walked on the table, being in great surprise all the time, as the indulgent reader will easily conceive and excuse, I happened to stumble against a crust, and fell flat on my face, but received no hurt. I got up immediately, and observing the good people to be in much concern, I took my hat (which I held under my arm out of good manners), and, waving it over my head, made three huzzas, to show that I had got no mischief by my fall.

But advancing forwards towards my master (as I shall henceforth call him), his youngest son, who sat next him, an arch boy of about ten years old, took me up by the legs, and held me so high in the air, that I trembled in every limb; but his father snatched me from him, and at the same time gave him such a box in the left ear as would have felled an European troop of horse to the earth, ordering him to be taken from the table. But being afraid the boy might owe me a spite, and well remembering how mischievous all children among us naturally are to sparrows, rabbits, young kittens, and puppy dogs, I fell on my knees, and, pointing to the boy, made my master to understand as well as I could, that I desired his son might be pardoned. The father complied, and the lad took his seat again; whereupon I went to him and kissed his hand, which my master took, and made him stroke me gently with it.

In the midst of dinner, my mistress's favorite cat leapt into her lap. I heard a noise behind me like that of a dozen stocking-weavers at work; and, turning my head, I found it proceeded from the purring of that animal, who seemed to be three times larger than an ox, as I computed by the view of her head and one of her paws, while her mistress was feeding and stroking her. The fierceness of this creature's countenance altogether discomposed me, though I stood at the further end of the table, above fifty feet off, and although my mistress held her fast, for fear she might give a spring and seize me in her talons.

But it happened there was no danger; for the cat took not the least notice of me, when my master placed me within three yards of her. And as I have been always told, and found true by experience in my travels, that flying or discovering fear before a fierce animal is a certain way to make it pursue or attack you, so I resolved in this dangerous juncture to show no manner of concern. I walked with intrepidity five or six times before the very head of the cat, and came within half a yard of her; whereupon she drew herself back, as if she were more afraid of me. I had less apprehension concerning the dogs, whereof three or four came into the room, as it is usual in farmers' houses; one of which was a mastiff equal in bulk to four elephants, and a greyhound somewhat taller than the mastiff, but not so large.

When dinner was almost done, the nurse came in with a child of a year old in her arms, who immediately spied me, and began a squall that you might have heard from London Bridge to Chelsea, after the usual oratory of infants, to get me for a plaything. The mother out of pure indulgence took me up, and put me towards the child, who presently seized me by the middle and got my head in its mouth, where I roared so loud that the urchin was frighted, and let me drop, and I should infallibly have broke my neck if the mother had not held her apron under me. The nurse, to quiet her babe, made use of a rattle, which was a kind of hollow vessel filled with great stones, and fastened by a cable to the child's waist. As she sat down close to the table on which I stood, her appearance astonished me not a little. This made me reflect upon the fair skins of our English ladies, who appear so beautiful to us, only because they are of our own size, and their defects not to be seen but through a magnifying glass, where we find by experiment that the smoothest and whitest skins look rough, and coarse and ill-colored.

I remember, when I was at Lilliput, the complexions of those diminutive people appeared to me the fairest in the world; and talking upon this subject with a person of learning there, who was an intimate friend of mine, he said that my face appeared much fairer and smoother when he looked on me from the ground than it did upon a nearer view, when I took him up in my hand and brought him close, which he confessed was at first a very shocking sight. He said he could discover great holes in my skin; that the stumps of my beard were ten times stronger than the bristles of a boar, and my complexion made up of several colors altogether disagreeable: although I must beg leave to say for myself that I am as fair as most of my sex and country, and very little sunburnt by my travels. On the other side, discoursing of the ladies of that emperor's court, he used to tell me one had freckles, another too wide a mouth, a third too large a nose, nothing of which I was able to distinguish. I confess this reflection was obvious enough; which, however, I could not forbear, lest the reader might think those vast creatures were actually deformed: for I must do them justice to say they are a comely race of people; and particularly the features of my master's countenance, although he were but a farmer, when I beheld him from the height of sixty feet, appeared very well proportioned.

When dinner was done my master went out to his labors, and, as I could discover by his voice and gestures, gave his wife a strict charge to take care of me. I was very much tired and disposed to sleep, which, my mistress perceiving, she put me on her own bed, and covered me with a clean white handkerchief, but larger and coarser than the mainsail of a man-of-war.

I slept about two hours, and dreamed I was at home with my wife and children, which aggravated my sorrows when I awaked and found myself alone in a vast room, between two and three hundred feet wide, and above two hundred high, lying in a bed twenty yards wide. My mistress was gone about her household affairs, and had locked me in. The bed was eight yards from the floor.

Presently two rats crept up the curtains, and ran smelling backwards and forwards on my bed. One of them came almost up to my face; whereupon I rose in a fright, and drew out my hanger to defend myself. The horrible animals had the boldness to attack me both sides, and one of them held his forefeet at my collar; but I killed him before he could do me any mischief. He fell down at my feet; and the other, seeing the fate of his comrade, made his escape, but not without one good wound on the back, which I gave him as he fled, and made the blood run trickling from him. After this exploit I walked gently to and fro on the bed to recover my breath and loss of spirits. These creatures were of the size of a large mastiff, but infinitely more nimble and fierce; so that, if I had taken off my belt before I went to sleep, I must infallibly have been torn to pieces and devoured. I measured the tail of the dead rat, and found it to be two yards long wanting an inch; but it went against my stomach to draw the carcass off the bed, where it still lay bleeding. I observed it had yet some life; but, with a strong slash across the neck, I thoroughly despatched it.

I hope the gentle reader will excuse me for dwelling on these and the like particulars, which, however insignificant they may appear to grovelling vulgar minds, yet will certainly help a philosopher to enlarge his thoughts and imagination, and apply them to the benefit of public as well as private life, which was my sole design in presenting this and other accounts of my travels to the world; wherein I have been chiefly studious of truth, without affecting any ornaments of teaming or style. But the whole scene of this voyage made so strong an impression on my mind, and is so deeply memory, that in committing it to paper I did not omit one material circumstance. However, upon a strict review, I blotted out several passages of less moment which were in my first copy, for fear of being censured as tedious and trifling, whereof travellers are often, perhaps not without justice, accused.

Lesson 39

1. *Gulliver's Travels* Read this summary of chapter 2: A description of the farmer's daughter. The author carried to a market-town, and then to the metropolis. The particulars of his journey
2. Read chapter 2.

CHAPTER II.

My mistress had a daughter of nine years old, a child of toward parts for her age, very dexterous at her needle, and skilful in dressing her baby. Her mother and she contrived to fit up the baby's cradle for me against night. The cradle was put into a small drawer cabinet, and the drawer placed upon a hanging shelf for fear of the rats. This was my bed all the time I stayed with these people, though made more convenient by degrees, as I began to learn their language and make my wants known. She made me seven shirts, and some other linen, of as fine cloth as could be got, which indeed was coarser than sackcloth; and these she constantly washed for me with her own hands. She was likewise my school-mistress, to teach me the language. When I pointed to anything, she told me the name of it in her own tongue, so that in a few days I was able to call for whatever I had a mind to. She was very good-natured, and not above forty feet high, being little for her age. She gave me the name of Grildrig, which the family took up, and afterwards the whole kingdom. The word imports what the Latins call *nanunculus*, the Italians *homunceletino*, and the English *mannikin*. To her I chiefly owe my preservation in that country. We never parted while I was there; I called her my Glumdalclitch, or little nurse; and should be guilty of great ingratitude if I omitted this honorable mention of her care and affection towards me, which I heartily wish it lay in my power to requite as she deserves.

It now began to be known and talked of in the neighborhood, that my master had found a strange animal in the field, about the bigness of a *splacnuck*, but exactly shaped in every part like a human creature; which it likewise imitated in all its actions, seemed to speak in a little language of its own, had already learned several words of theirs, went erect upon two legs, was tame and gentle, would come when it was called, do whatever it was bid, had the finest limbs in the world, and a complexion fairer than a nobleman's daughter of three years old. Another farmer, who lived hard by, and was a particular friend of my master, came on a visit on purpose to inquire into the truth of this story. I was immediately produced and placed upon a table, where I walked as I was commanded, drew my hanger, put it up again, made my reverence to my master's guest, asked him in his own language how he did, and told him *he was welcome*, just as my little nurse had instructed me. This man, who was old and dim-sighted, put on his spectacles to behold me better, at which I could not forbear laughing very heartily, for his eyes appeared like the full moon shining into a chamber at two windows. Our people, who discovered the cause of my mirth, bore me company in laughing, at which the old fellow was fool enough to be angry and out of countenance. He had the character of a great miser; and, to my misfortune, he well deserved it by the cursed advice he gave my master, to show me as a sight upon a market-day in the next town, which was half an hour's riding, about two-and-twenty miles from our house. I guessed there was some mischief contriving, when I observed my master and his friend whispering long together, sometimes pointing at me; and my fears made me fancy that I overheard and understood some of their words.

But the next morning, Glumdalclitch, my little nurse, told me the whole matter, which she had cunningly picked out from her mother. The poor girl laid me on her bosom, and fell a-weeping with shame and grief. She apprehended some mischief would happen to me from rude vulgar folks, who might squeeze me to death, or break one of my limbs by taking me in their hands. She had also observed how modest I was in my nature, how nicely I regarded my honor, and what an indignity conceive it to be exposed for money, as a public spectacle, to the meanest of the people. She said her papa and mamma had promised that Grildrig should be hers, but now she found they meant to serve her as they did last year when they pretended to give her a lamb, and yet as soon as it was fat sold it to a butcher. For my own part I may truly affirm that I was less concerned than my nurse. I had a strong hope, which left me, that I should one day recover my liberty; to the ignominy of being carried about for a monster, I considered myself to be a perfect stranger in the country, and that such a misfortune could never be charged upon me as a reproach if ever I should return to England; since the king of Great Britain himself, in my condition, must have undergone the same distress.

My master, pursuant to the advice of his friend, carried me in a box the next market-day, to the neighboring town, and took along with him his little daughter, my nurse, upon a pillion behind him. The box was close on every side, with a little door for me to go in and out, and a few gimlet holes to let in air. The girl had been so careful as to put the quilt of her baby's bed into it, for me to lie down on. However, I was terribly shaken and discomposed in this journey, though it were but of half an hour. For the horse went about forty feet at every step, and trotted so high that the agitation was equal to the rising and falling of a ship in a great storm, but much more frequent; our journey was somewhat farther than from London to St. Alban's. My master alighted at an inn which he used to frequent; and after consulting a while with the innkeeper and making some necessary preparations, he hired the *grultrud*, or crier, to give notice through the town, of a strange creature to be seen at the sign of the Green Eagle, not so big as a *splacnuck* (an animal in that country, very finely shaped, about six feet long), and in every part of the body resembling a human creature, could speak several words, and perform a hundred diverting tricks.

I was placed upon a table in the largest room of the inn, which might be near three hundred feet square. My little nurse stood on a low stool close to the table, to take care of me, and direct what I should do. My master, to avoid a crowd, would suffer only thirty people at a time to see me. I walked about on the table as the girl commanded. She asked me questions, as far as she knew my understanding of the language reached, and I answered them as loud as I could. I turned about several times to the company, paid my humble respects, said they were welcome, and used some other speeches I had been taught. I took a thimble filled with liquor, which Glumdalclitch had given me for a cup, and drank their health. I drew out my hanger, and flourished with it, after the manner of fencers in England. My nurse gave me part of a straw, which I exercised as a pike, having learnt the art in my youth. I was that day shown to twelve sets of company, and as often forced to act over again the same fopperies, till I was half dead with weariness and vexation. For those who had seen me made such wonderful reports, that the people were ready to break down the doors to come in.

My master, for his own interest, would not suffer any one to touch me except my nurse, and, to prevent danger, benches were set round the table at such a distance as to put me out of everybody's reach. However, an unlucky school-boy aimed a hazel-nut directly at my head, which very narrowly missed me: otherwise, it came with so much violence, that it would have infallibly knocked out my brains, for it was almost as large as a small pumpion, but I had the satisfaction to see the young rogue well beaten, and turned out of the room.

My master gave public notice that he would show me again the next market-day, and in the meantime he prepared a more convenient vehicle for me, which he had reason enough to do; for I was so tired with my first journey, and with entertaining company for eight hours together, that I could hardly stand upon my legs or speak a word. It was at least three days before I recovered my strength; and that I might have no rest at home, all the neighboring gentleman, from a hundred miles round, hearing of my fame, came to see me at my master's own house. There could not be fewer than thirty persons with their wives and children (for the country was very populous); and my master demanded the rate of a full room whenever he showed me at home, although it were only to a single family; so that for some time I had but little ease every day of the week (except Wednesday which is their Sabbath), although I was not carried to the town.

My master, finding how profitable I was like to be, resolved to carry me to the most considerable cities of the kingdom. Having, therefore, provided himself with all things necessary for a long journey, and settled his affairs at home, he took leave of his wife, and upon the seventeenth of August, 1703, about two months after my arrival, we set out for the metropolis, situated the middle of that empire, and about three thousand miles distance from our house. My master made his daughter Glumdalclitch ride behind him. She carried me on her lap, in a box tied about her waist. The girl had lined it on all sides with the softest cloth she could get, well quilted underneath, furnished it with her baby's bed, provided me with linen and other necessaries, and made everything as conveniently as she could. We had no other company but a boy of the house, who rode after us with the luggage.

My master's design was to show me in all the towns by the way, and to step out of the road for fifty or a hundred miles, to any village, or person of quality's house, where he might expect custom. We made easy journeys of not above seven or eight score miles a day; for Glumdalclitch, on purpose to spare me, complained she was tired with the trotting of the horse. She often took me out of my box at my own desire, to give me air and show me the country, but always held me fast by a leading-string. We passed over five or six rivers, many degrees broader and deeper than the Nile or the Ganges; and there was hardly a rivulet so small as the Thames at London Bridge. We were ten weeks in our journey, and I was shown in eighteen large towns, besides many villages and private families.

On the twenty-sixth of October we arrived at the metropolis, called in their language, *Lorbrulgrud*, or Pride of the Universe. My master took a lodging in the principal street of the city, not far from the royal palace, and put out bills in the usual form, containing an exact description of my person and parts. He hired a large room between three and four hundred feet wide. He provided a table sixty feet in diameter, upon which I was to act my part, and palisadoed it round three feet from the edge, and as many high, to prevent my falling over. I was shown ten times a day, to the wonder and satisfaction of all people. I could now speak the language tolerably well, and perfectly understood every word that was spoken to me. Besides, I had learned their alphabet, and could make a shift to explain a sentence here and there; for Glumdalclitch had been my instructor while we were at home, and at leisure hours during our journey. She carried a little book in her pocket, not much larger than a Sanson's Atlas; it was a common treatise for the use of young girls, giving a short account of their religion; out of this she taught me my letters, and interpreted the words.

Lesson 40

1. *Gulliver's Travels* Read this summary of chapter 3: The author sent for to court. The queen buys him of his master the farmer, and presents him to the king. He disputes with his majesty's great scholars. An apartment at court provided for the author. He is in high favour with the queen. He stands up for the honor of his own country. His quarrels with the queen's dwarf.
2. Read chapter 3.

CHAPTER III.

The frequent labors I underwent every day, made in a few weeks a very considerable change in my health; the more my master got by me, the more insatiable he grew. I had quite lost my stomach, and was almost reduced to a skeleton. The farmer observed it, and, concluding I must soon die, resolved to make as good a hand of me as he could. While he was thus reasoning and resolving with himself, a *slardral*, or gentleman-usher, came from court, commanding my master to carry me immediately thither, for the diversion of the queen and her ladies. Some of the latter had already been to see me, and reported strange things of my beauty, behavior, and good sense. Her majesty, and those who attended her, were beyond measure delighted with my demeanor. I fell on my knees and begged the honor of kissing her imperial foot; but this gracious princess held out her little finger towards me, after I was set on a table, which I embraced in both my arms, and put the tip of it with the utmost respect to my lip.

She made me some general questions about my country, and my travels, which I answered as distinctly, and in as few words, as I could. She asked whether I would be content to live at court. I bowed down to the board of the table, and humbly answered that I was my master's slave; but if I were at my own disposal, I should be proud to devote my life to her majesty's service. She then asked my master whether he were willing to sell me at a good price. He, who apprehended I could not live a month, was ready enough to part with me, and demanded a thousand pieces of gold, which were ordered him on the spot, each piece being the bigness of eight hundred moidores; but, for the proportion of all things between that country and Europe, and the high price of gold among them, was hardly so great a sum as a thousand guineas would be in England. I then said to the queen, since I was now her majesty's most humble creature and vassal, I must beg the favor, that Glumdalclitch, who had always attended me with so much care and kindness, and understood to do it so well, might be admitted into her service, and continue to be my nurse and instructor.

Her majesty agreed to my petition, and easily got the farmer's consent, who was glad enough to have his daughter preferred at court, and the poor girl herself was not able to hide her joy. My late master withdrew, bidding me farewell, and saying he had left me in good service, to which I replied not a word, only making him a slight bow.

The queen observed my coldness, and, when the farmer was gone out of the apartment, asked me the reason. I made bold to tell her majesty that I owed no other obligation to my late master, than his not dashing out the brains of a poor harmless creature, found by chance in his field; which obligation was amply recompensed by the gain he had made in showing me through half the kingdom, and the price he had now sold me for. That the life I had since led was laborious enough to kill an animal of ten times my strength. That my health was much impaired by the continual drudgery of entertaining the rabble every hour of the day, and that, if my master had not thought my life in danger, her majesty would not have got so cheap a bargain. But as I was out of all fear of being ill-treated under the protection of so great and good an empress, the ornament of nature, the darling of the world, the delight of her subjects, the phoenix of the creation; so, I hoped my late master's apprehensions would appear to be groundless, for I already found my spirits to revive, by the influence of her most august presence.

This was the sum of my speech, delivered with great improprieties and hesitation; the latter part was altogether framed in the style peculiar to that people, whereof I learned some phrases from Glumdalclitch, while she was carrying me to court.

The queen, giving great allowance for my defectiveness in speaking, was, however, surprised at so much wit and good sense in so diminutive an animal.

She took me in her own hand, and carried me to the king, who was then retired to his cabinet. His majesty, a prince of much gravity and austere countenance, not well observing my shape at first view, asked the queen, after a cold manner, how long it was since she grew fond of a *splacnuck*; for such it seems he took me to be, as I lay upon my breast in her majesty's right hand. But this princess, who hath an infinite deal of wit and humor, set me gently on my feet upon the scrutoire, and commanded me to give his majesty an account of myself, which I did in a very few words; and Glumdalclitch, who attended at the cabinet-door, and could not endure I should be out of her sight, being admitted, confirmed all that had passed from my arrival at her father's house.

The king, although he be as learned a person as any in his dominions, had been educated in the study of philosophy, and particularly mathematics; yet, when he observed my shape exactly, and saw me walk erect, before I began to speak, conceived I might be a piece of clockwork (which is in that country arrived to a very great perfection) contrived by some ingenious artist. But when he heard my voice, and found what I delivered to be regular and rational, he could not conceal his astonishment. He was by no means satisfied with the relation I gave him of the manner I came into his kingdom, but thought it a story concerted between Glumdalclitch and her father, who had taught me a set of words, to make me sell at a better price. Upon this imagination he put several other questions to me, and still received rational answers, no otherwise defective than by a foreign accent, and an imperfect knowledge in the language, with some rustic phrases, which I had learned at the farmer's house, and did not suit the polite style of a court.

His majesty sent for three great scholars, who were then in their weekly waiting according to the custom in that country. These gentlemen, after they had a while examined my shape with much nicety, were of different opinions concerning me. They all agreed that I could not be produced according to the regular laws of nature, because I was not framed with a capacity of preserving my life, either by swiftness or climbing of trees, or digging holes in the earth. They observed by my teeth, which they viewed with great exactness, that I was a carnivorous animal; yet most quadrupeds being an overmatch for me, and field-mice, with some others, too nimble, they could not imagine how I should be able to support myself, unless I fed upon snails and other insects, which they offered, by many learned arguments, to evince that I could not possibly do. They would not allow me to be a dwarf, because my littleness was beyond all degrees of comparison; for the queen's favorite dwarf, the smallest ever known in that kingdom, was nearly thirty feet high. After much debate, they concluded unanimously that I was only *relplum scalcath*, which is interpreted literally, *lusus naturae*; a determination exactly agreeable to the modern philosophy of Europe: whose professors, disdaining the old evasion of occult causes, whereby the followers of Aristotle endeavored in vain to disguise their ignorance, have invented this wonderful solution of all difficulties, to the unspeakable advancement of human knowledge.

After this decisive conclusion, I entreated to be heard a word or two. I applied myself to the king, and assured his majesty that I came from a country which abounded with several millions of both sexes, and of my own stature; where the animals, trees, and houses were all in proportion, and where, by consequence, I might be as able to defend myself, and to find sustenance, as any of his majesty's subjects could do here; which I took for a full answer to those gentlemen's arguments. To this they only replied with a smile of contempt, saying, that the farmer had instructed me very well in my lesson. The king, who had a much better understanding, dismissing his learned men, sent for the farmer, who, by good fortune, was not yet gone out of town; having therefore first examined him privately, and then confronted him with me and the young girl, his majesty began to think that what we had told him might possibly be true. He desired the queen to order that a particular care should be taken of me, and was of opinion that Glumdalclitch should still continue in her office of tending me, because he observed that we had a great affection for each other. A convenient apartment was provided for her at court; she had a sort of governess appointed to take care of her education, a maid to dress her, and two other servants for menial offices; but the care of me was wholly appropriated to herself. The queen commanded her own cabinet-maker to contrive a box, that might serve me for a bed-chamber, after the model that Glumdalclitch and I should agree upon. This man was a most ingenious artist, and, according to my directions, in three weeks finished to me a wooden chamber of sixteen feet square and twelve high, with sash-windows, a door, and two closets, like a London bed-chamber. The board that made the ceiling was to be lifted up and down by two hinges, to put in a bed ready furnished by her majesty's upholsterer, which Glumdalclitch took out every day to air, made it with her own hands, and, letting it down at night, locked up the roof over me. A nice workman, who was famous for little curiosities, undertook to make me two chairs, with backs and frames, of a substance not unlike ivory, and two tables, with a cabinet to put my things in. The room was quilted on all sides, as well as the floor and the ceiling, to prevent any accident from the carelessness of those who carried me, and to break the force of a jolt when I went in a coach. I desired a lock for my door, to prevent rats and mice from coming in: the smith, after several attempts, made the smallest that ever was seen among them; for I have known a larger at the gate of a gentleman's house in England. I made a shift to keep the key in a pocket of my own, fearing Glumdalclitch might lose it. The queen likewise ordered the thinnest silks that could be gotten to make me clothes, not much thicker than an English blanket, very cumbersome, till I was accustomed to them. They were after the fashion of the kingdom, partly resembling the Persian, and partly the Chinese, and are a very grave and decent habit.

The queen became so fond of my company that she could not dine without me. I had a table placed upon the same at which her Majesty ate, just at her left elbow, and a chair to sit on. Glumdalclitch stood on a stool on the floor, near my table, to assist and take care of me. I had an entire set of silver dishes and plates, and other necessaries, which, in proportion to those of the queen, were not much bigger than what I have seen in a London toy-shop for the furniture of a baby-house: these my little nurse kept in her pocket in a silver box, and gave me at meals as I wanted them, always cleaning them herself. No person dined with the queen but the two princesses royal the elder sixteen years old, and the younger at that time thirteen and a month. Her majesty used to put a bit of meat upon one of my dishes, out of which I carved for myself: and her diversion was to see me eat in miniature; for the queen (who had, indeed, but a weak stomach) took up at one mouthful as much as a dozen English farmers could eat at a meal, which to me was for some time a very nauseous sight. She would craunch the wing of a lark, bones and all, between her teeth, although it were nine times as large as that of a full-grown turkey; and put a bit of bread in her mouth as big as two twelve-penny loaves. She drank out of a golden cup, above a hogshead at a draught. Her knives were twice as long as a scythe, set straight upon the handle. The spoons, forks, and other instruments, were all in the same proportion. I remember when Glumdalclitch carried me, out of curiosity, to see some of the tables at court, where ten or a dozen of these enormous knives and forks were lifted up together, I thought I had never till then beheld so terrible a sight.

It is the custom that every Wednesday (which, as I have before observed, is their Sabbath) the king and queen, with the royal issue of both sexes dine together in the apartment of his majesty, to whom I was now become a great favorite; and, at these times, my little chair and table were placed at his left hand, before one of the salt-cellars. This prince took a pleasure in conversing with me, inquiring into the manners, religion, taws, government, and learning of Europe; wherein I gave him the best account I was able. His apprehension was so clear, and his judgment so exact, that he made very wise reflections and observations upon all I said. But I confess that after I had been a little too copious in talking of my own beloved country, of our trade, and wars by sea and land, of our schisms in religion, and parties in the state; the prejudices of his education prevailed so far that he could not forbear taking me up in his right hand, and, stroking me gently with the other, after a hearty fit of laughing, asked me, whether I was a whig or a tory? Then turning to his first minister, who waited behind him with a white staff, near as tall as the mainmast of the "Royal Sovereign,"he observed how contemptible a thing was human grandeur, which could be mimicked by such diminutive insects as I: and yet, says he, I dare engage these creatures have their titles and distinctions of honor; they contrive little nests and burrows, that they call houses and cities; they make a figure in dress and equipage; they love, they fight, they dispute, they cheat, they betray. And thus he continued on, while my color came and went several times with indignation, to hear our noble country, the mistress of arts and arms, the scourge of France, the arbitress of Europe, the seat of virtue, piety, honor, and truth, the pride and envy of the world, so contemptuously treated. But, as I was not in a condition to resent injuries, so upon mature thoughts, I began to doubt whether I was injured or no. For, after having been accustomed, several months, to the sight and converse of this people, and observed every object upon which I cast mine eyes to be of proportionable magnitude, the horror I had at first conceived from their bulk and aspect was so far worn off, that, if I had then beheld a company of English lords and ladies in their finery, and birthday clothes, acting their several parts in the most courtly manner of strutting and bowing and prating, to say the truth, I should have been strongly tempted to laugh as much at them as the king and his grandees did at me. Neither, indeed, could I forbear smiling at myself, when the queen used to place me upon her hand towards a looking-glass, by which both our persons appeared before me in full view together; and there could nothing be more ridiculous than the comparison; so that I really began to imagine myself dwindled many degrees below my usual size.

Nothing angered and mortified me so much, as the queen's dwarf, who being of the lowest stature that ever in that country (for I verily think he was not full thirty feet high) became so insolent at seeing a creature so much beneath him, that he would always affect to swagger, and look big, as he passed by me in the queen's ante-chamber, while I was standing on some table, talking with the lords or ladies of the court, and he seldom failed of a smart word or two upon my littleness; against which I could only revenge myself, by calling him brother, challenging him to wrestle, and such repartees as are usual in the mouths of court pages. One day, at dinner, this malicious little cub was so nettled with something I had said to him, that, raising himself upon the frame of her majesty's chair, he took me up, as I was sitting down, not thinking any harm; and let me drop into a large silver bowl of cream, and then ran away as fast as he could. I fell over head and ears, and, if I had not been a good swimmer, it might have gone very hard with me; for Glumdalclitch, in that instant, happened to be at the other end of the room, and the queen was in such a fright, that she wanted presence of mind to assist me. But my little nurse ran to my relief, and took me out, after I had swallowed above a quart of cream. I was put to bed; however, I received no other damage than the loss of a suit of clothes, which was utterly spoiled. The dwarf was soundly whipped, and, as a farther punishment, forced to drink up the bowl of cream into which he had thrown me; neither was he ever restored to favor; for, soon after, the queen bestowed him on a lady of high quality, so that I saw him no more, to my very great satisfaction; for I could not tell to what extremity such a malicious urchin might have carried his resentment.

He had before served me a scurvy trick, which set the queen a-laughing, although, at the same time she was heartily vexed, and would have immediately cashiered him, if I had not been so generous as to intercede. Her majesty had taken a marrow-bone upon her plate and, after knocking out the marrow, placed the bone on the dish erect, as it stood before. The dwarf watching his opportunity, while Glumdalclitch was gone to the sideboard, mounted upon the stool she stood on to take care of me at meals, took me up in both hands, and, squeezing my legs together, wedged them into the marrow-bone above my waist, where I stuck for some time, and made a very ridiculous figure, I believe it was near a minute before any one knew what was became of me; for I thought it below me to cry out. But, as princes seldom get their meat hot, my legs were not scalded, only my stockings and breeches in a sad condition. The dwarf, at my entreaty, had no other punishment than a sound whipping.

I was frequently rallied by the queen upon account of my fearfulness; and she used to ask me, whether the people of my country were as great cowards as myself? The occasion was this; the kingdom is much pestered with flies in summer; and these odious insects, each of them as big as a Dunstable lark, hardly gave me any rest, while I sat at dinner, with their continual humming and buzzing about my ears. They would sometimes alight upon my victuals. Sometimes they would fix upon my nose or forehead, where they stung me to the quick, and I had much ado to defend myself against these detestable animals, and could not forbear starting when they came on my face. It was the common practice of the dwarf, to catch a number of these insects in his hand, as school-boys do among us, and let them out suddenly under my nose, on purpose to frighten me, and divert the queen. My remedy was, to cut them in pieces with my knife, as they flew in the air, wherein my dexterity was much admired.

I remember, one morning, when Glumdalclitch had set me in my box upon a window, as she usually did in fair days, to give me air (for I durst not venture to let the box be hung on a nail out of the window, as we do with cages in England) after I had lifted up one of my sashes, and sat down at my table to eat a piece of sweet-cake for my breakfast, above twenty wasps, allured by the smell, came flying into the room, humming louder than the drones of as many bag-pipes. Some of them seized my cake, and carried it piece-meal away; others flew about my head and face, confounding me with the noise, and putting me in the utmost terror of their stings. However, I had the courage to rise and draw my hanger, and attack them in the air. I despatched four of them, but the rest got away, and I presently shut my window. These creatures were as large as partridges; I took out their stings, found them an inch and a half long, and as sharp as needles. I carefully preserved them all, and having since shown them, with some other curiosities, in several parts of Europe, upon my return to England, I gave three of them to Gresham College, and kept the fourth for myself.

Lesson 41

1. *Gulliver's Travels* Read the summary of chapter 4.

2. Chapter 4: The country described. A proposal for correcting modern maps. The king's palace; and some account of the metropolis. The author's way of travelling. The chief temple described.

3. Read chapter 4.

CHAPTER IV

I now intend to give the reader a short description of this country, as far as I travelled in it, which was not above two thousand miles round Lorbrulgrud, the metropolis. For the queen, whom I always attended, never went farther when she accompanied the king in his progresses, and there staid till his majesty returned from viewing his frontiers. The whole extent of this prince's dominions reacheth about six thousand miles in length, and from three to five in breadth. From whence I cannot but conclude, that our geographers of Europe are in a great error, by supposing nothing but sea between Japan and California; for it was ever my opinion, that there must be a balance of earth to counterpoise the great continent of Tartary; and therefore they ought to correct their maps and charts, by joining this vast tract of land to the northwest parts of America, wherein I shall be ready to lend them my assistance.

The kingdom is a peninsula, terminated to the northeast by a ridge of mountains, thirty miles high, which are altogether impassable, by reason of the volcanoes upon the tops: neither do the most learned know what sort of mortals inhabit beyond those mountains, or whether they be inhabited at all. On the three other sides it is bounded by the ocean. There is not one sea-port in the whole kingdom, and those parts of the coasts into which the rivers issue, are so full of pointed rocks, and the sea generally so rough, that there is no venturing with the smallest of their boats; so that these people are wholly excluded from any commerce with the rest of the world.

But the large rivers are full of vessels, and abound with excellent fish, for they seldom get any from the sea, because the sea-fish are of the same size with those in Europe, and consequently not worth catching, whereby it is manifest, that nature, in the production of plants and animals of so extraordinary a bulk, is wholly confined to this continent, of which I leave the reasons to be determined by philosophers. However, now and then, they take a whale, that happens to be dashed against the rocks, which the common people feed on heartily. These whales I have known so large, that a man could hardly carry one upon his shoulders; and sometimes, for curiosity, they are brought in hampers to Lorbrulgrud: I saw one of them in a dish at the king's table, which passed for a rarity, but I did not observe he was fond of it; for I think indeed the bigness disgusted him, although I have seen one somewhat larger in Greenland.

The country is well inhabited, for it contains fifty-one cities, near a hundred walled towns, and a great number of villages. To satisfy my curious reader, it may be sufficient to describe Lorbrulgrud. This city stands upon almost two equal parts on each side the river that passes through. It contains above eighty thousand houses, and about six hundred thousand inhabitants. It is in length three *glomglungs* (which make about fifty-four English miles) and two and a half in breadth, as I measured it myself in the royal map made by the king's order, which was laid on the ground on purpose for me, and extended a hundred feet: I paced the diameter and circumference several times barefoot, and, computing by the scale, measured it pretty exactly.

The king's palace is no regular edifice, but a heap of buildings, about seven miles round: the chief rooms are generally two hundred and forty feet high, and broad and long in proportion. A coach was allowed to Glumdalclitch and me, wherein her governess frequently took her out to see the town, or go among the shops; and I was always of the party, carried in my box; although the girl, at my own desire, would often take me out, and hold me in her hand, that I might more conveniently view the houses and the people as we passed along the streets, I reckoned our coach to be about the square of Westminster-hall, but not altogether so high: however, I cannot be very exact.

Besides the large box in which I was usually carried, the queen ordered a smaller one to be made for me, of about twelve feet square and ten high, for the convenience of travelling, because the other was somewhat too large for Glumdalclitch's lap, and cumbersome in the coach. It was made by the same artist, whom I directed in the whole contrivance. This travelling closet was an exact square, with a window in the middle of three of the squares, and each window was latticed with iron wire on the outside, to prevent accidents in long journeys. On the fourth side, which had no window, two strong staples were fixed, through which the person who carried me, when I had a mind to be on horseback, put a leathern belt, and buckled it about his waist. This was always the office of some grave, trusty servant, in whom I could confide, whether I attended the king and queen in their progresses, or were disposed to see the gardens, or pay a visit to some great lady or minister of state in the court; for I soon began to be known and esteemed among the greatest officers, I suppose more on account of their majesties' favor than any merit of my own.

In journeys, when I was weary of the coach, a servant on horseback would buckle on my box, and place it upon a cushion before him; and there I had a full prospect of the country on three sides from my three windows. I had in this closet a field-bed, and a hammock hung from the ceiling, two chairs and a table, neatly screwed to the floor, to prevent being tossed about by the agitation of the horse or the coach. And having been long used to sea voyages, those motions, although sometimes very violent, did not much discompose me.

Whenever I had a mind to see the town, it was always in my travelling closet, which Glumdalclitch held in her lap, in a kind of open sedan, after the fashion of the country, borne by four men, and attended by two others in the queen's livery. The people, who had often heard of me, were very curious to crowd about the sedan, and the girl was complaisant enough to make the bearers stop, and to take me in her hand, that I might be more conveniently seen.

I was very desirous to see the chief temple, and particularly the tower belonging to it, which is reckoned the highest in the kingdom. Accordingly, one day my nurse carried me thither, but I must truly say I came back disappointed; for the height is not above three thousand feet, reckoning from the ground to the highest pinnacle top; which, allowing for the difference between the size of those people and us in Europe, is no great matter for admiration, nor at all equal in proportion (if I rightly remember) to Salisbury steeple. But, not to detract from a nation, to which during my life I shall acknowledge myself extremely obliged, it must be allowed that whatever this famous tower wants in height is amply made up in beauty and strength. For the walls are nearly a hundred feet thick, built of hewn stone, whereof each is about forty feet square, and adorned on all sides with statues of gods and emperors, cut in marble larger than life, placed in their several niches. I measured a little finger which had fallen down from one of these statues, and lay unperceived among some rubbish, and found it exactly four feet and an inch in length. Glumdalclitch wrapped it up in her handkerchief and carried it home in her pocket, to keep among other trinkets, of which the girl was very fond, as children at her age usually are.

The king's kitchen is indeed a noble building, vaulted at top, and about six hundred feet high. The great oven is not so wide by ten paces as the cupola at St. Paul's, for I measured the latter on purpose after my return. But if I should describe the kitchen-grate, the prodigious pots and kettles, the joints of meat turning on the spits, with many other particulars, perhaps I should be hardly believed; at least, a severe critic would be apt to think I enlarged a little, as travellers are often suspected to do. To avoid which censure, I fear I have run too much into the other extreme; and that if this treatise should happen to be translated into the language of Brobdingnag (which is the general name of that kingdom) and transmitted thither, the king and his people would have reason to complain that I had done them an injury, by a false and diminutive representation.

His majesty seldom keeps above six hundred horses in his stables: they are generally from fifty-four to sixty feet high. But when he goes abroad on solemn days, he is attended for state by a militia guard of five hundred horse, which indeed I thought was the most splendid sight that could be ever beheld, till I saw part of his army in battalia, whereof I shall find another occasion to speak.

Lesson 42

1. *Gulliver's Travels* Read the summary of chapters 5.

2. Chapter 5: Several adventures that happened to the author. The execution of a criminal. The author shows his skill in navigation.

3. Read chapter 5 of *Gulliver's Travels.*

Vocabulary

1. Find a word in your reading today that you don't understand and try to figure out its meaning from the sentence.

2. Look up the definition and rewrite the sentence adding in the meaning. For instance, "I am *flabbergasted* at what just happened, *completely shocked.*" The end of the sentence explains flabbergasted.

CHAPTER V.

I should have lived happily enough in that country, if my littleness had not exposed me to several ridiculous and troublesome accidents, some of which I shall venture to relate. Glumdalclitch often carried me into the gardens of the court in my smaller box, and would sometimes take me out of it, and hold me in her hand, or set me down to walk. I remember, before the dwarf left the queen, he followed us one day into those gardens, and my nurse having set me down, he and I being close together, near some dwarf apple-trees, I must needs show my wit by a silly allusion between him and the trees, which happens to hold in their language, as it doth in ours. Whereupon the malicious rogue, watching his opportunity, when I was walking under one of them, shook it directly over my head; by which a dozen apples, each of them near as large as a Bristol barrel, came tumbling about my ears; one of them hit me on the back as I chanced to stoop, and knocked me down flat on my face; but I received no other hurt; and the dwarf was pardoned at my desire, because I had given the provocation.

Another day, Glumdalclitch left me on a smooth grass-plot to divert myself, while she walked at some distance with her governess. In the meantime there suddenly fell such a violent shower of hail, that I was immediately, by the force of it, struck to the ground; and when I was down, the hail stones gave me such cruel bangs all over the body as if I had been pelted with tennis-balls, however, I made a shift to creep on all fours, and shelter myself by lying flat on my face on the lee-side of a border of lemon-thyme, but so bruised from head to foot that I could not go abroad in ten days. Neither is this at all to be wondered at, because nature, in that country, observing the same proportion through all her operations, a hail-stone is near eighteen hundred times as large as one in Europe, which I can assert upon experience, having been so curious to weigh and measure them.

But a more dangerous accident happened to me in the same garden, when my little nurse, believing she had put me in a secure place, which I often entreated her to do, that I might enjoy my own thoughts, and having left my box at home, to avoid the trouble of carrying it, went to another part of the garden with governess and some ladies of her acquaintance, she was absent and out of hearing, a small white belonging to one of the chief gardeners, having got by accident into the garden, happened to place where I lay: the dog, following the scent, came directly up, and taking me in his mouth, ran straight to his master, wagging his tail, and set me gently on the ground. By good fortune, he had been so well taught, that I was carried between his teeth without the least hurt, or even tearing my clothes. But the poor gardener, who knew me well, and had a great kindness for me, was in a terrible fright: he gently took me up in both his hands, and asked me how I did; but I was so amazed and out of breath, that I could not speak a word. In a few minutes I came to myself, and he carried me safe to my little nurse, who by this time had returned to the place where she left me, and was in cruel agonies when I did not appear nor answer when she called. She severely reprimanded the gardener on account of his dog, but the thing was bushed up and never known at court; for the girl was afraid of the queen's anger, and truly, as to myself, I thought it would not be for my reputation that such a story should go about.

This accident absolutely determined Glumdalclitch never to trust me abroad for the future out of her sight. I had been long afraid of this resolution, and therefore concealed from her some little unlucky adventures that happened in those times when I was left by myself. Once a kite, hovering over the garden, made a stoop at me; and if I had not resolutely drawn my hanger, and run under a thick espalier, he would have certainly carried me away in his talons. Another time, walking to the top of a fresh mole-hill, I fell to my neck in the hole through which that animal had cast up the earth. I likewise broke my right shin against the shell of a snail, which I happened to stumble over as I was walking alone and thinking on poor England.

I cannot tell whether I were more pleased or mortified to observe in those solitary walks that the smaller birds did not appear to be at all afraid of me, but would hop about within a yard's distance, looking for worms and other food, with as much indifference and security as if no creature at all were near them. I remember a thrush had the confidence to snatch out of my hand with his bill a piece of cake that Glumdalclitch had just given me for my breakfast.

When I attempted to catch any of these birds they would boldly turn against me, endeavoring to pick my fingers, which I durst not venture within their reach; and then they would hop back unconcerned to hunt for worms and snails as they did before. But one day I took a thick cudgel, and threw it with all my strength so luckily at a linnet that I knocked him down, and seizing him by the neck with both my hands ran with him in triumph to my nurse. However, the bird, who had only been stunned, recovering himself, gave me so many boxes with his wings on both sides of my head and body, though I held him at arm's length and was out of the reach of his claws, that I was twenty times thinking of letting him go. But I was soon relieved by one of our servants, who wrung off the bird's neck, and I had him next day for dinner by the queen's command. This linnet, as near as I can remember, seemed to be somewhat larger than an English swan.

The queen, who often used to hear me talk of my sea-voyages, and took all occasions to divert me when I was melancholy, asked me, whether I understood how to handle a sail or an oar, and whether a little exercise of rowing might not be convenient for my health. I answered, that I understood both very well; for, although nay proper employment had been to be surgeon or doctor to the ship, yet often, upon a pinch, I was forced to work like a common mariner. But I could not see how this could be done in their country, where the smallest wherry was equal to a first-rate man-of-war among us, and such a boat as I could manage would never live in any of their rivers.

Her majesty said, if I could contrive a boat, her own joiner should make it, and she would provide a place for me to sail in. The fellow was an ingenious workman, and, by my instructions, in ten days finished a pleasure-boat, with all its tackling, able conveniently to hold eight Europeans. When it was finished, the queen was so delighted that she ran with it in her lap to the king, who ordered it to be put in a cistern full of water, with me in it, by way of trial; where I could not manage my two sculls, or little oars, for want of room.

But the queen had before contrived another project. She ordered the joiner to make a wooden trough of three hundred feet long, fifty broad, and eight deep; which, being well pitched, to prevent leaking, was placed on the floor along the wall in an outer room of the palace. It had a cock near the bottom to let out the water, when it began to grow stale; and two servants could easily fill it in half-an-hour. Here I often used to row for my own diversion, as well as that of the queen and her ladies, who thought themselves well entertained with my skill and agility. Sometimes I would put up my sail, and then my business was only to steer, while the ladies gave me a gale with their fans; and when they were weary, some of their pages would blow my sail forward with their breath, while I showed my art by steering starboard or larboard, as I pleased. When I had done, Glumdalclitch always carried back my boat, into her closet, and hung it on a nail to dry.

In this exercise I once met an accident, which had like to have cost me my life; for one of the pages having put my boat into the trough, the governess, who attended Glumdalclitch, very officiously lifted me up to place me in the boat, but I happened to slip through her fingers, and should infallibly have fallen down forty feet upon the floor, if, by the luckiest chance in the world, I had not been stopped by a corking-pin that stuck in the good gentlewoman's stomacher; the head of the pin passed between my shirt and the waistband of my breeches, and thus I held by the middle in the air, till Glumdalclitch ran to my relief.

Another time, one of the servants, whose office it was to fill my trough every third day with fresh water, was so careless as to let a huge frog (not perceiving it) slip out of his pail. The frog lay concealed till I was put into my boat, but then seeing a resting-place, climbed up, and made it lean so much on one side that I was forced to balance it with all my weight on the other to prevent overturning. When the frog was got in, it hopped at once half the length of the boat, and then over my head backwards and forwards. The largeness of its features made it appear the most deformed animal that can be conceived. However, I desired Glumdalclitch to let me deal with it alone. I banged it a good while with one of my sculls, and at last forced it to leap out of the boat.

But the greatest danger I ever underwent in that kingdom was from a monkey, who belonged to one of the clerks of the kitchen. Glumdalclitch had locked the up in her closet, while she went somewhere upon business or a visit. The weather being very warm the closet window was left open, as well as the windows and the door of my bigger box, in which I usually lived, because of its largeness and conveniency. As I sat quietly meditating at my table, I heard something bounce in at the closet window, and skip about from one side to the other; whereat, although I was much alarmed, yet I ventured to look out, but not stirring from my seat; and then I saw this frolicsome animal frisking and leaping up and down, till at last he came to my box, which he seemed to view with great pleasure and curiosity, peeping in at the door and every window.

I retreated to the farther corner of my room or box; but the monkey looking in at every side, put me into such a fright that I wanted presence of mind to conceal myself under the bed, as I might easily have done. After some time spent in peeping, grinning, and chattering, he at last espied me, and reaching one of his paws in at the door, as a cat does when she plays with a mouse, although I often shifted place to avoid him, he at length seized the lappet of my coat (which, being made of that country silk, was very thick and strong), and dragged me out. He took me out in his right fore-foot, and held me as a nurse does a child, just as I have seen the same sort of creature do with a kitten in Europe: and, when I offered to struggle, he squeezed me so hard that I thought it more prudent to submit. I have good reason to believe that he took me for a young one of his own species, by his often stroking my face very gently with his other paw.

In these diversions he was interrupted by a noise at the closet door, as if somebody were opening it; whereupon he suddenly leaped up to the window, at which he had come in, and thence upon the leads and gutters walking upon three legs, and holding me in the fourth, till he clambered up to a roof that was next to ours. I heard Glumdalclitch give a shriek at the moment he was carrying me out. The poor girl was almost distracted. That quarter of the palace was all in an uproar; the servants ran for ladders; the monkey was seen by hundreds in the court, sitting upon the ridge of a building, holding me like a baby in one of his fore-paws: whereat many of the rabble below could not forbear laughing; neither do I think they justly ought to be blamed, for without question, the sight was ridiculous enough to everybody but myself. Some of the people threw up stones, hoping to drive the monkey down; but this was strictly forbidden, or else very probably my brains had been dashed out.

The ladders were now applied, and mounted by several men, which the monkey observing, and finding himself almost encompassed, not being able to make speed enough with his three legs, let me drop on a ridge tile, and made his escape. Here I sat for some time, five hundred yards from the ground, expecting every moment to be blown down by the wind, or to fall by my own giddiness, and come tumbling over and over from the ridge to the eaves; but an honest lad, one of my nurse's footmen, climbed up, and putting me into his breeches-pocket, brought me down safe.

I was so weak and bruised in the sides with the squeezes given me by this odious animal, that I was forced to keep my bed a fortnight. The king, queen, and all the court, sent every day to inquire after my health, and her majesty made me several visits during my sickness. The monkey was killed, and an order made that no such animal should be kept about the palace.

When I attended the king, after my recovery, to return him thanks for his favors, he was pleased to rally me a good deal upon this adventure. He asked me what my thoughts and speculations were while I lay in the monkey's paw. He desired to know what I would have done upon such an occasion in my own country. I told his majesty that in Europe we had no monkeys, except such as were brought for curiosities from other places, and so small, that I could deal with a dozen of them together if they presumed to attack me. And as for that monstrous animal with whom I was so lately engaged (it was, indeed, as large as an elephant) if my fears had suffered me to think so far as to make use of my hanger (looking fiercely, and clapping my hand upon the hilt, as I spoke) when he poked his paw into my chamber, perhaps I should have given him such a wound as would have made him glad to withdraw it with more haste than he put it in. This I delivered in a firm tone, like a person who was jealous lest his courage should be called in question.

However, my speech produced nothing else besides a loud laughter, which all the respect due to his majesty from those about him could not make them contain. This made me reflect how vain an attempt it is for a man to endeavor to do himself honor among those who are out of all degree of equality or comparison with him. And yet I have seen the moral of my own behavior very frequent in England since my return, where a little contemptible varlet, without the least title to birth, person, wit, or common-sense, shall presume to look with importance, and put himself upon a foot with the greatest persons of the kingdom.

I was every day furnishing the court with some ridiculous story; and Glumdalclitch, although she loved me to excess, yet was arch enough to inform the queen whenever I committed any folly that she thought would be diverting to her majesty. The girl, who had been out of order, was carried by her governess to take the air about an hour's distance, or thirty miles from town. They alighted out of the coach near a small footpath in a field, and, Glumdalclitch setting down my travelling-box, I went out of it to walk. There was a pool of mud in the path, and I must needs try my activity by attempting to leap over it. I took a run, but unfortunately jumped short, and found myself just in the middle up to my knees. I waded through with some difficulty, and one of the footmen wiped me as clean as he could with his handkerchief, for I was filthily bemired; and my nurse confined me to my box till we returned home, when the queen was soon informed of what had passed, and the footman spread it about the court; so that all the mirth for some days was at my expense.

Lesson 43

1. *Gulliver's Travels* Read the summary of chapter 6: Several contrivances of the author to please the king and queen. He shows his skill in music. The king inquires into the state of England, which the author relates to him. The king's observations thereon.
2. Read chapter 6.

CHAPTER VI.

I used to attend the king's levee once or twice a week, and had often seen him under the barber's hand, which indeed was at first very terrible to behold; for the razor was almost twice as long as an ordinary scythe. His majesty, according to the custom of the country, was only shaved twice a week. I once prevailed on the barber to give me some of the suds or lather, out of which I picked forty or fifty of the strongest stumps of hair, I then took a piece of fine wood and cut it like the back of a comb, making several holes in it at equal distance with as small a needle as I could get from Glumdalclitch. I fixed in the stumps so artificially, scraping and sloping them with my knife towards the points, that I made a very tolerable comb; which was a seasonable supply, my own being so much broken in the teeth that it was almost useless: neither did I know any artist in that country so nice and exact as would undertake to make me another.

And this puts me in mind of an amusement wherein I spent many of my leisure hours. I desired the queen's woman to save for me the combings of her majesty's hair, whereof in time I got a good quantity; and consulting with my friend the cabinet-maker, who had received general orders to do little jobs for me, I directed him to make two chair-frames, no larger than those I had in my box, and then to bore little holes with a fine awl round those parts where I designed the backs and seats; through these holes I wove the strongest hairs I could pick out, just after the manner of cane chairs in England. When they were finished I made a present of them to her majesty, who kept them in her cabinet, and used to shew them for curiosities, as indeed they were the wonder of every one that beheld them. Of these hairs (as I had always a mechanical genius) I likewise made a neat little purse, about five feet long, with her majesty's name deciphered in gold letters, which I gave to Glumdalclitch, by the queen's consent. To say the truth, it was more for show than use, being not of strength to bear the weight of the larger coins, and therefore she kept nothing in it, but some little coins that girls are fond of.

The king, who delighted in music, had frequent concerts at court, to which I was sometimes carried, and set in my box on a table to hear them; but the noise was so great that I could hardly distinguish the tunes. I am confident that all the drums and trumpets of a royal army beating and sounding together just at your ears, could not equal it. My practice was to have my box removed from the place where the performers sat, as far as I could, then to shut the doors and windows of it, and draw the window-curtains, after which I found their music not disagreeable.

I had learnt in my youth to play a little upon the spinet. Glumdalclitch kept one in her chamber, and a master attended twice a week to teach her. I called it a spinet, because it somewhat resembled that instrument, and was played upon in the same manner.

A fancy came into my head that I would entertain the king and queen with an English tune upon this instrument. But this appeared extremely difficult; for the spinet was nearly sixty feet long, each key being almost a foot wide, so that with my arms extended I could not reach to above five keys, and to press them down required a good smart stroke with my fist, which would be too great a labor, and to no purpose. The method I contrived was this: I prepared two round sticks, about the bigness of common cudgels; they were thicker at one end than the other, and I covered the thicker ends with a piece of mouse's skin, that by rapping on them I might neither damage the tops of the keys nor interrupt the sound. Before the spinet a bench was placed about four feet below the keys, and I was put upon the bench. I ran sideling upon it that way and this as fast as I could, banging the proper keys with my two sticks, and made a shift to play a jig to the great satisfaction of both their majesties; but it was the most violent exercise I ever underwent, and yet I could not strike above sixteen keys, nor consequently play the bass and treble together as other artists do, which was a great disadvantage to my performance.

The king, who, as I before observed, was a prince of excellent understanding, would frequently order that I should be brought in my box, and set upon the table in his closet. He would then command me to bring one of my chairs out of the box, and sit down within three yards distance upon the top of the cabinet, which brought me almost to a level with his face. In this manner I had several conversations with him. I one day took the freedom to tell his majesty that the contempt he discovered towards Europe and the rest of the world did not seem answerable to those excellent qualities of mind that he was master of; that reason did not extend itself with the bulk of the body; on the contrary, we observed in our country that the tallest persons were usually least provided with it. That, among other animals, bees and ants had the reputation of more industry, art, and sagacity than many of the larger kinds; and that, as inconsiderable as he took me to be, I hoped I might live to do his majesty some signal service. The king heard me with attention, and began to conceive a much better opinion of me than he had ever before. He desired I would give him as exact an account of the government of England as I possibly could because, as fond as princes commonly are of their own customs (for he conjectured of other monarchs by my former discourses), he should be glad to hear of anything that might deserve imitation.

Imagine with thyself, courteous reader, how often I then wished for the tongue of Demosthenes or Cicero, that might have enabled me to celebrate the praise of my own dear native country, in a style equal to its merits and felicity.

I began my discourse by informing his majesty that our dominions consisted of two islands, which composed three mighty kingdoms, under one sovereign, besides our plantations in America. I dwelt long upon the fertility of our soil and the temperature of our climate. I then spoke at large upon the constitution of an English parliament, partly made up of an illustrious body, called the House of Peers, persons of the noblest blood and of the most ancient and ample patrimonies. I described that extraordinary care always taken of their education in arts and arms, to qualify them for being counsellors both to the king and kingdom; to have a share in the legislature; to be members of the highest court of judicature, from whence there could be no appeal; and to be champions always ready for the defence of their prince and country, by their valor, conduct, and fidelity. That these were the ornament and bulwark of the kingdom, worthy followers of their most renowned ancestors, whose honor had been the reward of their virtue, from which their posterity were never once known to degenerate. To these were joined several holy persons, as part of that assembly, under the title of bishops, whose peculiar business it is to take care of religion, and those who instruct the people therein. These were searched and sought out through the whole nation, by the prince and his wisest counsellors, among such of the priesthood as were most deservedly distinguished by the sanctity of their lives and the depth of their erudition, who were indeed the spiritual fathers of the clergy and the people.

That the other part of the parliament consisted of an assembly, called the House of Commons, who were all principal gentlemen, *freely* picked and culled out by the people themselves, for their great abilities and love of their country, to represent the wisdom of the whole nation. And that these two bodies made up the most august assembly in Europe, to whom, in conjunction with the prince, the whole legislature is committed.

I then descended to the courts of justice, over which the judges, those venerable sages and interpreters of the law, presided, for determining the disputed rights and properties of men, as well as for the punishment of vice and protection of innocence. I mentioned the prudent management of our treasury, the valor and achievements of our forces by sea and land. I computed the number of our people, by reckoning how many millions there might be of each religious sect or political party among us. I did not omit even our sports and pastimes, or any other particular, which I thought might redound to the honor of my country. And I finished all with a brief historical account of affairs and events in England for about a hundred years past.
This conversation was not ended under five audiences, each of several hours; and the king heard the whole with great attention, frequently taking notes of what I spoke, as well as memorandums of what questions he intended to ask me.

When I had put an end to these long discourses, his majesty, in a sixth audience, consulting his notes, proposed many doubts, queries, and objections, upon every article. He asked what methods were used to cultivate the minds and bodies of our young nobility, and in what kind of business they commonly spent the first and teachable part of their lives? What course was taken to supply that assembly when any noble family became extinct? What qualifications were necessary in those who are to be created new lords; whether the humor of the prince, a sum of money to a court lady as a prime minister, or a design of strengthening a party opposite to the public interest, ever happened to be motives in those advancements? What share of knowledge these lords had in the laws of their country, and how they came by it, so as to enable them to decide the properties of their fellow-subjects in the last resort? Whether they were always so free from avarice, partialities, or want, that a bribe or some other sinister view could have no place among them? Whether those holy lords I spoke of were always promoted to that rank upon account of their knowledge in religious matters and the sanctity of their lives; had never been compilers with the times while they were common priests, or slavish prostitute chaplains to some noblemen, whose opinions they continued servilely to follow, after they were admitted into that assembly?

He then desired to know what arts were practised in electing those whom I called commoners; whether a stranger, with a strong purse, might not influence the vulgar voters to choose him before their own landlord, or the most considerable gentleman in the neighborhood? How it came to pass that people were so violently bent upon getting into this assembly, which I allowed to be a great trouble and expense, often to the ruin of their families, without any salary or pension: because this appeared such an exalted strain of virtue and public spirit, that his majesty seemed to doubt it might possibly not be always sincere; and he desired to know whether such zealous gentlemen could have any views of refunding themselves for the charges and trouble they were at, by sacrificing the public good to the designs of a weak and vicious prince, in conjunction with a corrupted ministry? He multiplied his questions, and sifted me thoroughly upon every part of this head, proposing numberless inquiries and objections, which I think it not prudent or convenient to repeat.

Upon what I said in relation to our courts of justice, his majesty desired to be satisfied in several points; and this I was the better able to do, having been formerly almost ruined by a long suit in chancery, which was decreed for me with costs. He asked what time was usually spent in determining between right and wrong, and what degree of expense? Whether advocates and orators had liberty to plead in causes, manifestly known to be unjust, vexatious, or oppressive? Whether party in religion or politics was observed to be of any weight in the scale of justice? Whether those pleading orators were persons educated in the general knowledge of equity, or only in provincial, national, and other local customs? Whether they, or their judges, had any part in penning those laws which they assumed the liberty of interpreting and glossing upon at their pleasure? Whether they had ever, at different times, pleaded for or against the same cause, and cited precedents to prove contrary opinions? Whether they were a rich or a poor corporation? Whether they received any pecuniary reward for pleading or delivering their opinions? And, particularly, whether they were admitted as members in the lower senate?

He fell next upon the management of our treasury, and said he thought my memory had failed me, because I computed our taxes at about five or six millions a year, and, when I came to mention the issues, he found they sometimes amounted to more than double; for the notes he had taken were very particular in this point, because he hoped, as he told me, that the knowledge of our conduct might be useful to him, and he could not be deceived in his calculations. But if what I told him were true, he was still at a loss how a kingdom could run out of its estate like a private person. He asked me who were our creditors, and where we found to pay them. He wondered to hear me talk of such chargeable and expensive wars; that certainly we must be a quarrelsome people, or live among very bad neighbors and that our generals must needs be richer than our kings. He asked what business we had out of our own islands, unless upon the score of trade or treaty, or to defend the coasts with our fleet. Above all, he was amazed to hear me talk of a mercenary standing army in the midst of peace and among a free people. He said if we were governed by our own consent, in the persons of our representatives, he could not imagine of whom we were afraid, or against whom we were to fight; and would hear my opinion, whether a private man's house might not better be defended by himself, his children, and family, than by half-a-dozen rascals, picked up at a venture in the streets for small wages, who might get a hundred times more by cutting their throats?

He laughed at my odd kind of arithmetic (as he was pleased to call it), in reckoning the numbers of our people by a computation drawn from the several sects among us, in religion and politics. He said, he knew no reason why those who entertain opinions prejudicial to the public should be obliged to change, or should not be obliged to conceal them. And as it was tyranny in any government to require the first, so it was weakness not to enforce the second: for a man may be allowed to keep poisons in his closet, but not to vend them about for cordials.

He observed, that among the diversions of our nobility and gentry, I had mentioned gaming: he desired to know at what age this entertainment was usually taken up, and when it was laid down; how much of their time it employed: whether it ever went so high as to affect their fortunes: whether mean, vicious people, by their dexterity in that art, might not arrive at great riches, and sometimes keep our very nobles in dependence, as well as habituate them to vile companions, wholly take them from the improvement of their minds, and force them, by the losses they received, to learn and practise that infamous dexterity upon others?

He was perfectly astonished with the historical account I gave him of our affairs during the last century, protesting it was only a heap of conspiracies, rebellions, murders, massacres, revolutions, banishments, the very worst effects that avarice, faction, hypocrisy, perfidiousness, cruelty, rage, madness, hatred, envy, lust, malice, and ambition, could produce.

His majesty, in another audience, was at the pains to recapitulate the sum of all I had spoken; compared the questions he made with the answers I had given; then taking me into his hands, and stroking me gently, delivered himself in these words which I shall never forget, nor the manner he spoke them in: "My little friend Grildrig, you have made a most admirable panegyric upon your country; you have clearly proved that ignorance, idleness, and vice are the proper ingredients for qualifying a legislator; that laws are best explained, interpreted, and applied by those whose interest and abilities lie in perverting, confounding, and eluding them. I observe among you some lines of an institution, which in its original might have been tolerable, but these half erased, and the rest wholly blurred and blotted by corruptions. It doth not appear, from all you have said, how any one perfection is required towards the procurement of any one station among you; much less that men are ennobled on account of their virtue, that priests are advanced for their piety or learning, soldiers for their conduct or valor, judges for their integrity, senators for the love of their country, or counsellors for their wisdom. As for yourself, continued the king, who have spent the greatest part of your life in travelling, I am well disposed to hope you may hitherto have escaped many vices of your country. But by what I have gathered from your own relation, and the answers I have with much pains wrung and extorted from you, I cannot but conclude the bulk of your natives to be the most pernicious race of little odious vermin that nature ever suffered to crawl upon the surface of the earth."

Lesson 44

1. *Gulliver's Travels* Read the summary of chapter 7: The author's love of his country. He makes a proposal of much advantage to the king, which is rejected. The king's great ignorance in politics. The learning of that country very imperfect and confined. The laws, and military affairs, and parties in the state.

2. Read chapter 7.

CHAPTER VII

Nothing but an extreme love of truth could have hindered me from concealing this part of my story. It was in vain to discover my resentments, which were always turned into ridicule; and I was forced to rest with patience, while my noble and beloved country was so injuriously treated. I am as heartily sorry as any of my readers can possibly be, that such an occasion was given: but this prince happened to be so curious and inquisitive upon every particular, that it could not consist either with gratitude or good manners, to refuse giving him what satisfaction I was able. Yet this much I may be allowed to say, in my own vindication, that I artfully eluded many of his questions, and gave to every point a more favorable turn, by many degrees, than the strictness of truth would allow. For I have always borne that laudable partiality to my own country, which Dionysius Halicarnassensis with so much justice, recommends to an historian: I would hide the frailties and deformities of my political mother, and place her virtues and beauties in the most advantageous light. This was my sincere endeavor, in those many discourses I had with that monarch, although it unfortunately failed of success.

But great allowances should be given to a king who lives wholly secluded from the rest of the world, and must therefore be altogether unacquainted with the manners and customs that most prevail in other nations: the want of which knowledge will ever produce many prejudices, and a certain narrowness of thinking, from which we and the politer countries of Europe are wholly exempted. And it would be hard indeed, if so remote a prince's notions of virtue and vice were to be offered as a standard for all mankind.

To confirm what I have now said, and farther to show the miserable effects of a confined education, I shall here insert a passage which will hardly obtain belief. In hopes to ingratiate myself farther into his majesty's favor, I told him of an invention discovered between three and four hundred years ago, to make a certain powder into a heap, on which the smallest spark of fire falling would kindle the whole in a moment, although it were as big as a mountain, and make it all fly up in the air together with a noise and agitation greater than thunder. That a proper quantity of this powder rammed into a hollow tube of brass or iron, according to its bigness, would drive a ball of iron or lead with such violence and speed as nothing was able to sustain its force. That the largest balls thus discharged would not only destroy whole ranks of an army at once, but batter the strongest walls to the ground, sink down ships with a thousand men in each to the bottom of the sea; and, when linked together by a chain, would cut through masts and rigging, divide hundreds of bodies in the middle, and lay all waste before them. That we often put this powder into large hollow balls of iron, and discharged them by an engine into some city we were besieging, which would rip up the pavements, tear the houses to pieces, burst and throw splinters on every side, dashing out the brains of all who came near. That I knew the ingredients very well, which were cheap and common; I understood the manner of compounding them, and could direct his workman how to make those tubes of a size proportionable to all other things in his majesty's kingdom, and the largest need not to be above a hundred feet long; twenty or thirty of which tubes, charged with the proper quantity of powder and balls, would batter down the walls of the strongest town in his dominions in a few hours, or destroy the whole metropolis if ever it should pretend to dispute his absolute commands. This I humbly offered to his majesty as a small tribute of acknowledgment, in return for so many marks that I had received of his royal favor and protection.

The king was struck with horror at the description I had given him of those terrible engines, and the proposal I had made. He was amazed, how so impotent and grovelling an insect as I (these were his expressions), could entertain such inhuman ideas, and in so familiar a manner, as to appear wholly unmoved at all the scenes of blood and desolation, which I had painted, as the common effects of those destructive machines, whereof, he said, some evil genius, enemy to mankind, must have been the first contriver. As for himself, he protested, that although few things delighted him so much as new discoveries in art or in nature, yet he would rather lose half his kingdom than be privy to such a secret, which he commanded me, as I valued my life, never to mention any more.
A strange effect of narrow principles and short views! that a prince possessed of every quality which procures veneration, love, and esteem; of strong parts, great wisdom, and profound learning, endowed with admirable talents for government, and almost adored by his subjects, should, from a nice unnecessary scruple, whereof in Europe we can have no conception, let slip an opportunity put into his hands, that would have made him absolute master of the lives, the liberties, and the fortunes of his people. Neither do I say this with the least intention to detract from the many virtues of that excellent king, whose character I am sensible will on this account be very much lessened in the opinion of an English reader; but I take this defect among them to have arisen from their ignorance, by not having hitherto reduced politics into a science, as the more acute wits of Europe have done. For I remember very well, in a discourse one day with the king, when I happened to say there were several thousand books among us, written upon the art of government, it gave him (directly contrary to my intention) a very mean opinion of our understandings. He professed both to abominate and despise all mystery, refinement, and intrigue, either in a prince or a minister. He could not tell what I meant by secrets of state, where an enemy or some rival nation were not in the case. He confined the knowledge of governing within very narrow bounds, to common sense and reason, to justice and lenity, to the speedy determination of civil and criminal causes, with some other obvious topics, which are not worth considering. And he gave it for his opinion, that whoever could make two ears of corn, or two blades of grass to grow upon a spot of ground, where only one grew before, would

deserve better of mankind, and do more essential service to his country, than the whole race of politicians put together.

The learning of this people is very defective, consisting only in morality, history, poetry, and mathematics, wherein they must be allowed to excel. But the last of these is wholly applied to what may be useful in life, to the improvement of agriculture, and all mechanical arts; so that among us it would be little esteemed. And as to ideas, entities, abstractions, and transcendentals, I could never drive the least conception into their heads.

No law of that country must exceed in words the number of letters in their alphabet, which consists only in two-and-twenty. But indeed few of them extend even to that length. They are expressed in the most plain and simple terms, wherein those people are not mercurial enough to discover above one interpretation; and to write a comment upon any law is a capital crime. As to the decision of civil causes, or proceedings against criminals, their precedents are so few, that they have little reason to boast of any extraordinary skill in either.

They have had the art of printing, as well as the Chinese, time out of mind: but their libraries are not very large; for that of the king, which is reckoned the largest, doth not amount to above a thousand volumes, placed in a gallery of twelve hundred feet long, from whence I had liberty to borrow what books I pleased. The queen's joiner had contrived in one of Glumdalclitch's rooms, a kind of wooden machine, five-and-twenty feet high, formed like a standing ladder; the steps were each fifty feet long: it was indeed a movable pair of stairs, the lowest end placed at ten feet distance from the wall of the chamber. The book I had a mind to read was put up leaning against the wall: I first mounted to the upper step of the ladder, and turning my face towards the book began at the top of the page, and so walking to the right and left about eight or ten paces, according to the length of the lines, till I had gotten a little below the level of mine eyes, and then descending gradually, till I came to the bottom: after which I mounted again, and began the other page in the same manner, and so turned over the leaf, which I could easily do with both my hands, for it was as thick and stiff as a paste-board, and in the largest folios not above eighteen or twenty feet long.

Their style is clear, masculine, and smooth, but not florid; for they avoid nothing more than multiplying unnecessary words, or using various expressions. I have perused many of their books, especially those in history and morality. Among the rest, I was much diverted with a little old treatise, which always lay in Glumdalclitch's bed-chamber, and belonged to her governess, a grave elderly gentlewoman, who dealt in writings of morality and devotion. The book treats of the weakness of human kind, and is in little esteem, except among the women and the vulgar. However, I was curious to see what an author of that country could say upon such a subject.

This writer went through all the usual topics of European moralists, showing how diminutive, contemptible, and helpless an animal was man in his own nature; how unable to defend himself from inclemencies of the air, or the fury of wild beasts; how much he was excelled by one creature in strength, by another in speed, by a third in foresight, by a fourth in industry. He added, that nature was degenerated in these latter declining ages of the world, and could now produce only small births, in comparison to those in ancient times. He said, it was very reasonable to think, not only that the species of men were originally much larger, but also, that there must have been giants in former ages; which as it is asserted by history and tradition, so it hath been confirmed by huge bones and skulls, casually dug up in several parts of the kingdom, far exceeding the common dwindled race of man in our days. He argued, that the very laws of nature absolutely required we should have been made in the beginning of a size more large and robust, not so liable to destruction, from every little accident, of a tile falling from a house, or a stone cast from the hand of a boy, or being drowned in a little brook. From this way of reasoning the author drew several moral applications, useful in the conduct of life, but needless here to repeat. For my own part, I could not avoid reflecting, how universally this talent was spread, of drawing lectures in morality, or, indeed, rather matter of discontent and repining, from the quarrels we raise with nature. And I believe, upon a strict inquiry, those quarrels might be shown as ill-grounded among us as they are among that people.

As to their military affairs, they boast that the king's army consists of a hundred and seventy-six thousand foot, and thirty-two thousand horse: if that may be called an army which is made up of tradesmen in the several cities, and farmers in the country, whose commanders are only the nobility and gentry, without pay or reward. They are indeed perfect enough in their exercises, and under very good discipline, wherein I saw no great merit; for how should it be otherwise, where every farmer is under the command of his own landlord, and every citizen under that of the principal men in his own city, chosen after the manner of Venice, by ballot?

I have often seen the militia of Lorbrulgrud drawn out to exercise in a great field, near the city, of twenty miles square. They were in all not above twenty-five thousand foot, and six thousand horse: but it was impossible for me to compute their number, considering the space of ground they took up. A cavalier, mounted on a large steed, might be about ninety feet high. I have seen this whole body of horse, upon a word of command, draw their swords at once, and brandish them in the air. Imagination can figure nothing so grand, so surprising, and so astonishing! it looked as if ten thousand flashes of lightning were darting at the same time from every quarter of the sky.

I was curious to know how this prince, to whose dominions there is no access from any other country, came to think of armies, or to teach his people the practice of military discipline. But I was soon informed, both by conversation and reading their histories: for in the course of many ages, they have been troubled with the same disease to which the whole race of mankind is subject; the nobility often contending for power, the people for liberty, and the king for absolute dominion. All which, however, happily tempered by the laws of that kingdom, have been sometimes violated by each of the three parties, and have more than once occasioned civil wars, the last whereof was happily put an end to by this prince's grandfather, in a general composition; and the militia, then settled with common consent, hath been ever since kept in the strictest duty.

Lesson 45

1. *Gulliver's Travels* Read the summary of chapter 8: The king and queen make a progress to the frontiers. The author attends them. The manner in which he leaves the country very particularly related. He returns to England.
2. Read chapter 8 of *Gulliver's Travels.* (This is the end of part 2.)
3. Answer these questions about part 2:

   - What is unusual about the land of the Brobdingnags?

   - What do you notice about the ruler of the Brobdingnags?

   - How do the Brobdingnags govern themselves?

   - What do you notice about the place of science and education in the land of the Brobdingnags?

Vocabulary

1. Review your vocabulary from Lesson 18.

CHAPTER VIII

I had always a strong impulse that I should sometime recover my liberty, though it was impossible to conjecture by what means, or to form any project with the least hope of succeeding. The ship in which I sailed was the first ever known to be driven within sight of the coast; and the king had given strict orders, that if at any time another appeared, it should be taken ashore, and with all its crew and passengers brought in a tumbrel to Lorbrulgrud. I was treated with much kindness: I was the favorite of a great king and queen, and the delight of the whole court; but it was upon such a footing as ill became the dignity of human kind. I could never forget those domestic pledges I had left behind me. I wanted to be among people with whom I could converse upon even terms, and walk about the streets and fields, without being afraid of being trod to death like a frog or a young puppy. But my deliverance came sooner than I expected, and in a manner not very common: the whole story and circumstances of which I shall faithfully relate.

I had now been two years in this country; and about the beginning of the third, Glumdalclitch and I attended the king and queen in a progress to the south coast of the kingdom. I was carried, as usual, in my travelling-box, which, as I have already described, was a very convenient closet of twelve feet wide. And I had ordered a hammock to be fixed by silken ropes from the four corners at the top, to break the jolts, when a servant carried me before him on horseback, as I sometimes desired, and would often sleep in my hammock while we were upon the road. On the roof of my closet, not directly over the middle of the hammock, I ordered the joiner to cut out a hole of a foot square, to give me air in hot weather as I slept, which hole I shut at pleasure with a board that drew backwards and forwards through a groove.

When we came to our journey's end, the king thought proper to pass a few days at a palace he hath near Flanflasnic, a city within eighteen English of the sea-side Glumdalclitch and I were much fatigued, I had gotten a small cold, but the poor girl was so ill as to be confined to her chamber. I longed to see the ocean, which must be the only scene of my escape, if ever it should happen I pretended to be worse than I really was, and desired leave to take the fresh air of the sea with a page, whom I was very fond of, and who had sometimes been trusted with me. I shall never forget with what unwillingness Glumdalclitch consented, nor the strict charge she gave the page to be careful of me, bursting at the same time into a flood of tears, as if she had some foreboding of what was to happen.

The boy took me out in my box about half-an-hour's walk from the palace towards the rocks on the sea-shore. I ordered him to set me down, and lifting up one of my sashes, cast many a wistful melancholy look towards the sea. I found myself not very well, and told the page that I had a mind to take a nap in my hammock, which I hoped would do me good. I got in, and the boy shut the window close down to keep out the cold. I soon fell asleep, and all I can conjecture is, that while I slept, the page, thinking no danger could happen, went among the rocks to look for birds' eggs, having before observed him from my windows searching about, and picking up one or two in the clefts. Be that as it will, I found myself suddenly awaked with a violent pull upon the ring, which was fastened at the top of my box for the conveniency of carriage. I felt my box raised very high in the air, and then borne forward with prodigious speed. The first jolt had like to have shaken me out of my hammock, but afterwards the motion was easy enough. I called out several times, as loud as I could raise my voice, but all to no purpose. I looked towards my windows, and could see nothing but the clouds and sky. I heard a noise just over my head like the clapping of wings, and then began to perceive the woful condition I was in, that some eagle had got the ring of my box in his beak, with an intent to let it fall on a rock like a tortoise in a shell, and then pick out my body and devour it; for the sagacity and smell of this bird enabled him to discover his quarry at a great distance, though better concealed than I could be within a two-inch board.

In a little time I observed the noise and flutter of wings to increase very fast, and my box was tossed up and down like a sign in a windy day. I heard several bangs or buffets, as I thought, given to the eagle (for such I am certain it must have been, that held the ring of my box in his beak), and then all on a sudden felt myself falling perpendicularly down for above a minute, but with such incredible swiftness, that I almost lost my breath. My fall was stopped by a terrible squash, that sounded louder to my ears than the cataract of Niagara; after which I was quite in the dark for another minute, and then my box began to rise so high that I could see light from the tops of the windows. I now perceived I was fallen into the sea. My box, by the weight of my body, the goods that were in, and the broad plates of iron fixed for strength at the four corners of the top and bottom, floated about five feet deep in the water. I did then, and do now suppose, that the eagle which flew away with my box was pursued by two or three others, and forced to let me drop while he defended himself against the rest, who hoped to share in the prey. The plates of iron fastened at the bottom of the box (for those were the strongest) preserved the balance while it fell, and hindered it from being broken on the surface of the water. Every joint of it was well grooved, and the door did not move on hinges, but up and down like a sash, which kept my closet so tight that very little water came in. I got with much difficulty out of my hammock, having first ventured to draw back my slip-board on the roof already mentioned, contrived on purpose to let in air, for want of which I found myself almost stifled.

How often did I then wish myself with my dear Glumdalchtch, from whom one single hour had so far divided me. And I may say with truth that in the midst of my own misfortunes I could not forbear lamenting my poor nurse, the grief she would suffer for my loss, the displeasure of the queen, and the ruin of her fortune. Perhaps many travellers have not been under greater difficulties and distress than I was at juncture, expecting every moment to see my box dashed to pieces, or at least overset by the first violent blast or rising wave. A breach in one single pane of glass would have been immediate death; nor could anything have preserved the windows but the strong lattice-wires placed on the outside against accidents in travelling. I saw the water ooze in at several crannies, although the leaks were not considerable, and I endeavored to stop them as well as I could, I was not able to lift up the roof of my closet, which otherwise I certainly should have done, and sat on the top of it, where I might at least preserve myself some hours longer, than by being shut up (as I may call it) in the hold. Or, if I escaped these dangers for a day or two, what could I expect but a miserable death of cold and hunger? I was four hours under these circumstances, expecting, and indeed wishing, every moment to be my last.

I have already told the reader that there were two strong staples fixed upon that side of my box which had no window, and into which the servant who used to carry me on horseback would put a leathern belt, and buckle it about his waist. Being in this disconsolate state, I heard, or at least thought I heard, some kind of grating noise on that side of my box where the staples were fixed, and soon after I began to fancy that the box was pulled or towed along in the sea, for I now and then felt a sort of tugging which made the waves rise near the tops of my windows, leaving me almost in the dark. This gave me some faint hopes of relief, although I was not able to imagine how it could be brought about. I ventured to unscrew one of my chairs, which were always fastened to the floor, and having made a hard shift to screw it down again directly under the slipping board that I had lately opened, I mounted on the chair, and putting my mouth as near as I could to the hole, I called for help in a loud voice and in all the languages I understood. I then fastened my handkerchief to a stick I usually carried, and thrusting it up the hole, waved it several times in the air, that if any boat or ship were near, the seamen might conjecture some unhappy mortal to be shut up in the box. I found no effect from all I could do, but plainly perceived my closet to be moved along; and in the space of an hour or better, that side of the box where the staples were and had no window struck against something that was hard. I apprehended it to be a rock, and found myself tossed more than ever. I plainly heard a noise upon the cover of my closet like that of a cable, and the grating of it as it passed through the ring. I then found myself hoisted up by degrees, at least three feet higher than I was before. Whereupon I again thrust up my stick and handkerchief, calling for help till I was almost hoarse. In return to which I heard a great shout repeated three times, giving me such transports of joy as are not to be conceived but by those who feel them. I now heard a trampling over my head, and somebody calling through the hole with a loud voice in the English tongue. "If there be anybody below, let them speak." I answered I was an Englishman, drawn by ill fortune into the greatest calamity that ever any creature underwent, and begged by all that was moving to be delivered out of the dungeon I was in. The voice replied I was safe, for my box was fastened to their ship; and the carpenter should immediately come and saw a hole in the cover, large enough to pull me out. I answered that was needless, and would take up too much time, for there was no more to be done, but let one of the crew put his finger into the ring, and take the box out of the sea into the ship, and so into the captain's cabin. Some of them upon hearing me talk so wildly thought I was mad; others laughed; for indeed it never came into my head that I was now got among people of my own stature and strength. The carpenter came, and in a few minutes sawed a passage about four feet square, then let down a small ladder upon which I mounted, and from thence was taken into the ship in a very weak condition.

The sailors were all in amazement, and asked me a thousand questions, which I had no inclination to answer. I was equally confounded at the sight of so many pygmies, for such I took them to be, after having so long accustomed mine eyes to the monstrous objects I had left. But the captain, Mr. Thomas Wilcocks, an honest, worthy Shropshire man, observing I was ready to faint, took me into his cabin, gave me a cordial to comfort me, and made me turn in upon his own bed, advising me to take a little rest, of which I had great need. Before I went to sleep, I gave him to understand that I had some valuable furniture in my box, too good to be lost; a fine hammock, a handsome two chairs, a table, and a cabinet. That my closet was hung on all sides, or rather quilted, with silk and cotton: that if he would let one of the crew bring my closet into his cabin, I would open it there before him, and show him my goods. The captain, hearing me utter these absurdities, concluded I was raving: however (I suppose to pacify me), he promised to give orders as I desired, and going upon deck, sent some of his men down into my closet, from whence (as I afterwards found) they drew up all my goods, and stripped off the quilting; but the chairs, cabinet, and bedstead, being screwed to the floor, were much damaged by the ignorance of the seamen, who tore them up by force. Then they knocked off some of the boards for the use of the ship, and when they had got all they had a mind for, let the hull drop into the sea, which, by reason of so many breaches made in the bottom and sides, sunk to rights. And indeed I was glad not to have been a spectator of the havoc they made; because I am confident it would have sensibly touched me, by bringing former passages into my mind, which I had rather forgotten.

I slept some hours, but was perpetually disturbed with dreams of the place I had left, and the dangers I had escaped. However, upon waking, I found myself much recovered. It was now about eight o'clock at night, and the captain ordered supper immediately, thinking I had already fasted too long. He entertained me with great kindness, observing me not to look wildly, or talk inconsistently; and when we were left alone, desired I would give him a relation of my travels, and by what accident I came to be set adrift in that monstrous wooden chest.

He said that about twelve o'clock at noon, as he was looking through his glass, he spied it at a distance, and thought it was a sail, which he had a mind to make, being not much out of his course, in hopes of buying some biscuit, his own beginning to fall short. That upon coming nearer and finding his error, he sent out his long-boat to discover what it was; that his men came back in a fright, swearing they had seen a swimming-house. That he laughed at their folly, and went himself in the boat, ordering his men to take a strong cable along with them. That the weather being calm, he rowed round me several times, observed my windows and wire-lattices that defenced them. That he discovered two staples upon one side, which was all of boards, without any passage for light. He then commanded his men to row up to that side, and fastening a cable to one of the staples, ordered them to tow my chest (as they called it) towards the ship. When it was there, he gave directions to fasten another cable to the ring fixed in the cover, and to raise up my chest with pulleys, which all the sailors were not able to do above two or three feet. He said they saw my stick and handkerchief thrust out of the hole, and concluded that some unhappy man must be shut up in the cavity. I asked whether he or the crew had seen any prodigious birds in the air about the time he first discovered me? to which he answered, that, discoursing this matter with the sailors while I was asleep, one of them said he had observed three eagles flying towards the north, but remarked nothing of their being larger than the usual size, which I suppose must be imputed to the great height they were at; and he could not guess the reason of my question. I then asked the captain how far he reckoned we might be from land?

He said, by the best computation he could make, we were at least a hundred leagues. I assured him that he must be mistaken by almost half, for I had not left the country from whence I came above two hours before I dropt into the sea. Whereupon he began again to think that my brain was disturbed, of which he gave me a hint, and advised me to go to bed in a cabin he had provided. I assured him I was well refreshed with his good entertainment and company, and as much in my senses as ever I was in my life.

He then grew serious, and desired to ask me freely whether I were not troubled in mind by the consciousness of some enormous crime, for which I was punished by the command of some prince, by exposing me in that chest, as great criminals in other countries have been forced to sea in a leaky vessel without provisions; for although he should be sorry to have taken so ill a man into his ship, yet he would engage his word to set me safe ashore in the first port where we arrived. He added that his suspicions were much increased by some very absurd speeches I had delivered, at first to his sailors, and afterwards to himself, in relation to my closet chest, as well as by my odd looks and behavior while I was at supper.

I begged his patience to hear me tell my story, which I faithfully did, from the last time I left England to the moment he first discovered me. And as truth always forceth its way into rational minds, so this honest worthy gentleman, who had some tincture of learning and very good sense, was immediately convinced of my candor and veracity. But, farther to confirm all I had said, I entreated him to give order that my cabinet should be brought, of which I had the key in my pocket (for he had already informed me how seamen disposed of my closet). I opened it in his own presence, and showed him the small collection of rarities I made in the country from whence I had been so strangely delivered. There was the comb I had contrived out of the stumps of the king's beard. There was a collection of needles and pins, from a foot to half a yard long; four wasps' stings, like joiners' tacks; some combings of the queen's hair; a gold ring, which one day she made me a present of in a most obliging manner, taking it from her little finger and throwing it over my head like a collar. I desired the captain would please to accept this ring in return of his civilities, which he absolutely refused. Lastly I desired him to see the breeches I had then on, which were made of a mouse's skin.

I could force nothing upon him but a footman's tooth, which I observed him to examine with great curiosity, and found he had a fancy for it. He received it with abundance of thanks, more than such a trifle could deserve. It was drawn by an unskilful surgeon, in a mistake, from one of Glumdalclitch's men, who was affected with the toothache, but it was as sound as any in his head. I got it cleaned, and put it in my cabinet. It was about a foot long, and four inches in diameter.

The captain was very well satisfied with this plain relation I had given him, and said he hoped when we returned to England I would oblige the world by putting it on paper, and making it public. My answer was, that I thought we were already overstocked with books of travels; that nothing could now pass which was not extraordinary; wherein I doubted some authors less consulted truth than their own vanity, or interest, or the diversion of ignorant readers, that my story could contain little besides common events, without those ornamental descriptions of strange plants, trees, birds, and other animals; or of the barbarous customs and idolatry of savage people, with which most writers abound. However, I thanked him for his good opinion, and promised to take the matter into my thoughts.

He said he wondered at one thing very much, which was, to hear me speak so loud, asking me whether the king or queen of that country were thick of hearing. I told him it was what I had been used to for above two years past, and that I wondered as much at the voices of him and his men, who seemed to me only to whisper, and yet I could hear them well enough. But when I spoke in that country, it was like a man talking in the street to another looking out from the top of a steeple, unless when I was placed on a table, or held in any person's hand. I told him I had likewise observed another thing, that when I first got into the ship, and the sailors stood all about me, I thought they were the most contemptible little creatures I had ever beheld. For indeed, while I was in that prince's country, I could never endure to look in a glass, after my eyes had been accustomed to such prodigious objects, because the comparison gave me so despicable a conceit of myself. The captain said that while we were at supper he observed me to look at everything with a sort of wonder, and that I often seemed hardly able to contain my laughter, which he knew not well how to take, but imputed it to some disorder in my brain. I answered, it was very true, and I wondered how I could forbear, when I saw his dishes of the size of a silver threepence, a leg of pork hardly a mouthful, a cup not so big as a nut-shell, and so I went on, describing the rest of his household stuff and provisions after the same manner. For although the queen had ordered a little equipage of all things necessary for me, while I was in her service, yet my ideas were wholly taken up with what I saw on every side of me, and I winked at my own littleness, as people do at their own faults. The captain understood my raillery very well, and merrily replied that he did not observe my stomach so good, although I had fasted all day; and, continuing in his mirth, protested he would have gladly given a hundred pounds to have seen my closet in the eagle's bill, and afterwards in its fall from so great a height into the sea; which would certainly have been a most astonishing object, worthy to have the description of it transmitted to future ages: and the comparison of Phaeton was so obvious, that he could not forbear applying it, although I did not much admire the conceit.

The captain having been at Tonquin, was, in his return to England, driven northeastward, to the latitude of 44 degrees, and of longitude 143. But meeting a trade-wind two days after I came on board him, we sailed southward a long time, and, coasting New Holland, kept our course west-south-west, and then south-south-west, till we doubled the Cape of Good Hope. Our voyage was very prosperous, but I shall not trouble the reader with a journal of it. The captain called in at one or two ports, and sent in his long-boat for provisions and fresh water, but I never went out of the ship till we came into the Downs, which was on the third day of June, 1706, about nine months after my escape. I offered to leave pay goods in security for payment of my freight, but the captain protested he would not receive one farthing. We took a kind leave of each other, and I made him promise he would come to see me at my house in Redriff. I hired a horse and guide for five shillings, which I borrowed of the captain.

As I was on the road, observing the littleness of the houses—the trees, the cattle, and the people, I began to think myself in Lilliput. I was afraid of trampling on every traveller I met, and often called aloud to have them stand out of the way, so that I had like to have gotten one or two broken heads for my impertinence.

When I came to my own house, for which I was forced to inquire, one of the servants opened the door, I bent down to go in (like a goose under a gate), for fear of striking my head. My wife ran out to embrace me, but I stooped lower than her knees, thinking she could otherwise never be able to reach my mouth. My daughter kneeled to ask my blessing, but I could not see her till she arose, having been so long used to stand with my head and eyes erect to above sixty feet; and then I went to take her up with one hand by the waist. I looked down upon the servants, and one or two friends who were in the house, as if they had been pygmies, and I a giant. I told my wife she had been too thrifty, for I found she had starved herself and her daughter to nothing. In short, I behaved myself so unaccountably, that they were all of the captain's opinion when he first saw me, and concluded I had lost my wits. This I mention as an instance of the great power of habit and prejudice.

In a little time, I and my family and friends came to a right understanding: but my wife protested I should never go to sea any more; although my evil destiny so ordered, that she had not power to hinder me, as the reader may know hereafter. In the meantime I here conclude the second part of my unfortunate voyages.

THE END

Lesson 46

1. The main idea of a paragraph is the point it is trying to make, the overall idea. It is supported by the details of the paragraph. Even if the details are important, they aren't the main idea; they tell us more about the main idea. Often we can find the main idea stated in the first sentence. Sometimes, though, it is implied and not explicitly stated.
2. Read these two selections and state the main idea of each. (Answers)

A thunderbolt overthrows, breaks, and rends bodies that do not permit electricity to circulate freely. It shatters rocks and throws the fragments great distances; it unroofs our dwellings; it splits the trunks of trees and divides the wood into little shreds; it overthrows walls, or even wrenches them from their foundations. In penetrating the ground, it melts the sand on its way and makes irregular

glass tubes. It reddens, melts, and vaporizes metallic substances that give free passage to the electric current, such as metal chains, the iron wire of bells, the gilding of frames. Its preference, in short, is for objects made of metal. There are instances of persons left uninjured while the lightning consumed the various metallic objects worn or carried by them, such as gold-lace, metal buttons, and coins. It sets fire to piles of combustible matter like bundles of straw and stacks of dried fodder.
(from *The Story Book of Science*)

Often when it rains, a particular dreariness descends upon the earth. Most people hide out in their houses sending forlorn glances out the window. Animals scamper off to nooks and crannies, poking their heads out to timidly sniff the air for signs of dry weather. Despite the pellets of water cascading from the sky, an occasional brave soul will venture out for a jog in the drizzle or a bird will chirp merrily in a mud puddle, dismissing the downpour. Some people call these adventurers crazy, but others celebrate the willingness of these individuals to embrace negativity and turn it into something positive.
(from http://testprep.about.com/od/readingtesttips/l/Finding_Main_Idea_2.doc.pdf)

Lesson 47

1. What is the main idea of each selection? (Answers)

Now there are two distinct kinds of electricity, which are present in equal quantities in all bodies. As long as they are united, nothing betrays their presence; it is as if they did not exist. But, once separated, they seek each other across all obstacles, attract each other, and rush toward each other with an explosion and a flash of light. Then all is in complete repose until these two electric principles are again separated. The two electricities, therefore, supplement and neutralize each other; that is to say, they form something invisible, inoffensive, inert, that is found everywhere and is called neutral electricity. To electrify a body is to decompose its neutral electricity, to disunite the two principles which, when mixed remain inert, but, separated from each other, manifest their wonderful properties and their violent tendency to recombination. Rubbing is one way of effecting the separation of the two electric principles, but it is far from being the only one. Every radical change in the inmost nature of a body also causes a manifestation of the two electricities.
(from *The Story Book of Science*)

Slowly, over the past several decades, technology, in all its various forms, has been creeping into the educational institutions of the United States and is now a pervasive presence. Computers are present in most classrooms; second grade students use digital cameras for science projects; teachers use document cameras for lectures; and students of all ages research on the Internet via smartphones, smartpads and laptops. While advocates have cheered and opponents have grumbled, technology has made its way into classrooms across the U. S. and knowledge of its applications has become a prerequisite for a modern education. Some people, however, do not accept this stance wholeheartedly. Opponents of the massive influx of technology into school systems state that the results of the technology have, thus far, not proven to be sufficient grounds for accepting it and its shortcomings. Despite their good intentions, these critics of technology integration are mistaken, and about twenty years behind the times.

(from http://testprep.about.com/od/readingtesttips/l/Finding_Main_Idea_2.doc.pdf)

Lesson 48

1. Complete the reading and find the main ideas.
2. What's the main idea of paragraphs 2, 3, 4. (Answers)
3. What's the main idea of the whole thing? (Answers)

The more you know about plants and foods, the healthier you will be. Some foods can provide you with essential vitamins to keep you healthy, but some foods can make you sick. It is very important to know how to distinguish between the two. You also need to learn how to keep foods safe and prevent them from spoiling. There's so much to learn.

There is a lot to learn about plants people eat, such as how to grow them and how to prepare them for eating. Scientists can learn how to keep them safe to eat. Sometimes people who don't know something can make a mistake. For example, some mushrooms are poisonous, and people need to know which those are so they don't eat them. People need to know about plants in order to stay healthy.

If you don't know about foods and plants, you can make a big mistake. You need to know which plants are safe to eat. At one time, people feared the tomato, because they believed it to be poisonous. They thought it was dangerous because it grows on a vine that looks like a poisonous plant called nightshade. Therefore, in the early 1800s, people in the United States were afraid to eat it. It took several years before the tomato was accepted as a food in the United States. Today, it is a big part of the American diet. It's found in things like soup and ketchup.

Any food can become a source of sickness if it's not stored safely. Tomatoes can be dangerous if they rot, and so can most other foods if they are not stored properly. One way to store food safely is to dry it. Before people invented cans, they used to dry food to store it for long periods of time. For example, they would dry tomatoes in the sun. Today, people still eat sun-dried tomatoes.

Some plants actually help keep people safe, for example, cloves. No one really knows how people figured that out, but it was most likely from someone trying to use cloves to flavor their food. Cloves have a nice, spicy taste.

The clove plant was first found on islands sometimes called the Spice Islands. A tree grows there; it's a tree that makes cloves. These cloves actually are buds from that tree. The people on the islands picked the buds; the buds were pink when people picked them, and then they dried and turned dark. When they were dried, people put them with food, and they made the food taste great. Probably, the people found that they also helped to preserve foods. Cloves help meat and other foods keep from spoiling.

Today we know why cloves help food stay safe. Scientists have studied cloves and have discovered that cloves contain a kind of oil in them called eugenol. That oil is an antiseptic. Antiseptic is a word with two important parts. The prefix anti means against, and the root sepsis means poisoning. In other words, eugenol helps prevent poisoning. It's a good thing we have scientists to help us stay safe.

Scientists are people who have careers learning about plants and food. They study the history of plants, and they observe them in order to learn how to make them grow better. They study how to keep them safe, which in turn helps people live healthier lives.
(Reading from Center for Urban Education)

Lesson 49
1. Complete the reading and find the main ideas.
2. What's the main idea of the 2nd, 3rd and 4th paragraphs? (Answers)
3. What's the main idea of the whole story? (Answers)

This is an old American fable. It's not certain who first told it, but it teaches a lesson of importance.

Badger always had a good day—he never complained and always turned a problem into an opportunity. He liked living on the high, dry plains where he had many ground squirrels and prairie dogs as his neighbors. He probably enjoyed their company much more than they did his. If anyone had asked them, they would have said that they wished Badger were somewhere else. He was always disturbing their tranquil community with his daily digging.

Badger wanted to be helpful, and he was—he enabled his neighbors to construct safe homes. They lived in burrows, which are homes under the ground, and creating them is a challenge. Usually the soil is hard and difficult to move, especially below the topsoil. They made their tunnels where he had dug, they were able to dig easily because he had made the soil soft.

Badger was lonely because the other animals never stopped to be with him. They would run and stay inside their burrows shouting, "Watch out, boring Badger is coming." Badger would try to follow them into their homes for companionship, but the other animals just ignored him.

So Badger just dug and dug all day every day. "I'm designed for digging," he said to himself. He had a powerful body: short, stout legs, and big feet, which had long, strong claws. When he started to dig, he could make the dirt fly.

Badger enjoyed digging so much that he dug countless holes of his own, just for the fun it gave him and how it helped others. More than one fox and coyote had made his home in a hole dug by Badger. They never did take the trouble to thank him though. Instead, they often laughed about his odd way of having fun and commented that Benny must be a stupid fellow.

If they really thought that, they were wrong as well as ungrateful. He was slow and clumsy at everything except digging. He was too heavy and squat to be quick on his feet in order to chase and catch his faster neighbors. That was not because he was not smart. His wits were sharp, he knew he was designed to dig.

Usually, nobody saw Badger until night. He rarely left his den in the daytime, except to sun himself. Then not many noticed him because of camouflage. He did not hide when anyone surprised him while taking sunbath, but he had a trick of lying flat in the grass without moving, and his striped body blended with the vegetation. So, it took a sharp eye to spy him when he lay low in that fashion.

Sleeping, with his long fur on end, he looked too comfortable to disturb. At least, that was what the ground squirrels thought. And if one of those busy little fellows ever paused to stare at Benny when he was napping in the sunshine, Badger just had to turn his head toward the onlooker. That was sure to make him run away.

One day there was a great wind, a tornado with tremendous force. It blew all the trees away and even removed bushes and grass. The animals all hid in their burrows. When it was calm again, they came out. They said to themselves, it's a good thing we have our holes to keep us safe. Then they said, "What a difference it makes to have holes for homes. We should thank Badger for doing all that digging."

He was glad the animals thanked him, they now realized that his help to build their homes had safeguarded them. He would keep digging so that every day was a good one and everyone would have a safe home.
(Reading from Center for Urban Education)

Lesson 50

1. Read "Jim Wolf and the Cats" by Mark Twain.

IT was back in those far-distant days—1848 or '49—that Jim Wolf came to us. He was from a hamlet thirty or forty miles back in the country, and he brought all his native sweetnesses and gentlenesses and simplicities with him. He was approaching seventeen, a grave and slender lad, trustful, honest, honorable, a creature to love and cling to. And he was incredibly bashful. He was with us a good while, but he could never conquer that peculiarity; he could not be at ease in the presence of any woman, not even in my good and gentle mother's; and as to speaking to any girl, it was wholly impossible. He sat perfectly still, one day—there were ladies chatting in the room— while a wasp up his leg stabbed him cruelly a dozen times; and all the sign he gave was a slight wince for each stab and the tear of torture in his eye. He was too bashful to move.

It is to this kind that untoward things happen. My sister gave a "candy-pull" on a winter's night. I was too young to be of the company, and Jim was too diffident. I was sent up to bed early, and Jim followed of his own motion. His room was in the new part of the house and his window looked out on the roof of the L annex. That roof was six inches deep in snow, and the snow had an ice crust upon it which was as slick as glass. Out of the comb of the roof projected a short chimney, a common resort for sentimental cats on light nights—and this was a moonlight night. Down at the eaves, below the chimney, a canopy of dead vines spread away to some posts, making a cozy shelter, and after an hour or two the rollicking crowd of young ladies and gentlemen grouped themselves in its shade, with their saucers of liquid and piping-hot candy disposed about them on the frozen ground to cool. There was joyous chaffing and joking and laughter—peal upon peal of it.

About this time a couple of old, disreputable tomcats got up on the chimney and started a heated argument about something; also about this time I gave up trying to get to sleep and went visiting to Jim's room. He was awake and fuming about the cats and their intolerable yowling. I asked him, mockingly, why he didn't climb out and drive them away. He was nettled, and said overboldly that for two cents he would.

It was a rash remark and was probably repented of before it was fairly out of his mouth. But it was too late—he was committed. I knew him; and I knew he would rather break his neck than back down, if I egged him on judiciously.

"Oh, of course you would! Who's doubting it?"

It galled him, and he burst out, with sharp irritation, "Maybe you doubt it!"

"I? Oh no! I shouldn't think of such a thing. You are always doing wonderful things, with your mouth."

He was in a passion now. He snatched on his yarn socks and began to raise the window, saying in a voice quivering with anger:

"You think I dasn't—you do! Think what you blame please. I don't care what you think. I'll show you!"

The window made him rage; it wouldn't stay up.

I said, "Never mind, I'll hold it."

Indeed, I would have done anything to help. I was only a boy and was already in a radiant heaven of anticipation. He climbed carefully out, clung to the window sill until his feet were safely placed, then began to pick his perilous way on all-fours along the glassy comb, a foot and a hand on each side of it. I believe I enjoy it now as much as I did then; yet it is nearly fifty years ago. The frosty breeze flapped his short shirt about his lean legs; the crystal roof shone like polished marble in the intense glory of the moon; the unconscious cats sat erect upon the chimney, alertly watching each other, lashing their tails and pouring out their hollow grievances; and slowly and cautiously Jim crept on, flapping as he went, the gay and frolicsome young creatures under the vine canopy unaware, and outraging these solemnities with their misplaced laughter. Every time Jim slipped I had a hope; but always on he crept and disappointed it. At last he was within reaching distance. He paused, raised himself carefully up, measured his distance deliberately, then made a frantic grab at the nearest cat—and missed it. Of course he lost his balance. His heels flew up, he struck on his back, and like a rocket he darted down the roof feet first, crashed through the dead vines, and landed in a sitting position in fourteen saucers of red-hot candy, in the midst of all that party—and dressed as he was—this lad who could not look a girl in the face with his clothes on. There was a wild scramble and a storm of shrieks, and Jim fled up the stairs, dripping broken crockery all the way.

Lesson 51

1. Your next book is by author, Booth Tarkington. He is a Pulitzer Prize winning author. He was born in 1869 in Indiana. His mother was a lawyer and his father, a judge. He attended Princeton University and knew right away that he wanted to be an author. He wrote short stories growing up. It wasn't until he was 30 years old that he finally had a book accepted by a publisher. Several of his works (he wrote plays and novels) were turned into movies. He didn't have children but the book you are going to read was based on his childhood memories and his nephews.

2. The book you are going to read next takes place around 1900 in the mid-west, similar to where Booth grew up. Read this brief history of the time and place where Booth grew up.

    - "The ratification of the 15th Amendment by Indiana was not followed by an immediate change in the Indiana Constitution. Blacks were still excluded from voting in the state and, in addition, free Blacks were not allowed to enter the state. During the next two decades, Blacks were gradually granted the standing of full citizen. The laws made to restrict Blacks within Indiana were eventually eliminated and they were allowed to take part in the making of contracts. In education there was to be a fair distribution of public funds between white and colored schools. In 1881, Blacks gained full equality in voting and the only remaining discrimination in the Indiana constitution at the time was the clause that prevented Blacks from taking part in the state militia."

      (from http://centerforhistory.org/learn-history/indiana-history/the-development-of-modern-indiana-1865-1900#Reconstruction_Governors_in_Indiana)

3. What events or beliefs of the time do you think would influence his actions and thoughts?

4. You will come across prejudice that was common then. We've edited it somewhat.

Lesson 52

1. Read chapter 1 of *Penrod* by Booth Tarkington.
2. Reread the first sentence.
3. Write definitions of **morose** and **wistful**. Look them up if you can't.
4. What do you know about Penrod so far, after reading chapter 1?
5. Make a list of characters as you read. Write them down on the page with a couple spaces between each. Write in a few words about each character. You don't have to write in full sentences. Just take some notes. Who are they? What are they like?

Chapter I. A Boy and His Dog

Penrod sat morosely upon the back fence and gazed with envy at Duke, his wistful dog.

A bitter soul dominated the various curved and angular surfaces known by a careless world as the face of Penrod Schofield. Except in solitude, that face was almost always cryptic and emotionless; for Penrod had come into his twelfth year wearing an expression carefully trained to be inscrutable. Since the world was sure to misunderstand everything, mere defensive instinct prompted him to give it as little as possible to lay hold upon. Nothing is more impenetrable than the face of a boy who has learned this, and Penrod's was habitually as fathomless as the depth of his hatred this morning for the literary activities of Mrs. Lora Rewbush--an almost universally respected fellow citizen, a lady of charitable and poetic inclinations, and one of his own mother's most intimate friends.

Mrs. Lora Rewbush had written something which she called "The Children's Pageant of the Table Round," and it was to be performed in public that very afternoon at the Women's Arts and Guild Hall for the benefit of the Coloured Infants' Betterment Society. And if any flavour of sweetness remained in the nature of Penrod Schofield after the dismal trials of the school-week just past, that problematic, infinitesimal remnant was made pungent acid by the imminence of his destiny to form a prominent feature of the spectacle, and to declaim the loathsome sentiments of a character named upon the programme the Child Sir Lancelot.

After each rehearsal he had plotted escape, and only ten days earlier there had been a glimmer of light: Mrs. Lora Rewbush caught a very bad cold, and it was hoped it might develop into pneumonia; but she recovered so quickly that not even a rehearsal of the Children's Pageant was postponed. Darkness closed in. Penrod had rather vaguely debated plans for a self-mutilation such as would make his appearance as the Child Sir Lancelot inexpedient on public grounds; it was a heroic and attractive thought, but the results of some extremely sketchy preliminary experiments caused him to abandon it.

There was no escape; and at last his hour was hard upon him. Therefore he brooded on the fence and gazed with envy at his wistful Duke.

The dog's name was undescriptive of his person, which was obviously the result of a singular series of mesalliances. He wore a grizzled moustache and indefinite whiskers; he was small and shabby, and looked like an old postman. Penrod envied Duke because he was sure Duke would never be compelled to be a Child Sir Lancelot. He thought [he would like to be] a dog free and unshackled to go or come as the wind listeth.

There was a long soliloquy upon the fence, a plaintive monologue without words: the boy's thoughts were adjectives, but they were expressed by a running film of pictures in his mind's eye, morbidly prophetic of the hideosities before him. Finally he spoke aloud, with such spleen that Duke rose from his haunches and lifted one ear in keen anxiety.

"'I hight Sir Lancelot du Lake, the Child, Gentul-hearted, meek, and mild. What though I'm *but* a littul child, Gentul-hearted, meek, and----' *oof*!"

All of this except "oof" was a quotation from the Child Sir Lancelot, as conceived by Mrs. Lora Rewbush. Choking upon it, Penrod slid down from the fence, and with slow and thoughtful steps entered a one-storied wing of the stable, consisting of a single apartment, floored with cement and used as a storeroom for broken bric-a-brac, old paint-buckets, decayed garden-hose, worn-out carpets, dead furniture, and other condemned odds and ends not yet considered hopeless enough to be given away. In one corner stood a large box, a part of the building itself: it was eight feet high and open at the top, and it had been constructed as a sawdust magazine from which was drawn material for the horse's bed in a stall on the other side of the partition. The big box, so high and towerlike, so commodious, so suggestive, had ceased to fulfil its legitimate function; though, providentially, it had been at least half full of sawdust when the horse died. Two years had gone by since that passing; an interregnum in transportation during which Penrod's father was "thinking" (he explained sometimes) of an automobile. Meanwhile, the gifted and generous sawdust-box had served brilliantly in war and peace: it was Penrod's stronghold.

There was a partially defaced sign upon the front wall of the box; the donjon-keep had known mercantile impulses:

The O. K. RaBiT Co. PENROD ScHoFiELD AND CO. iNQuiRE FOR PRicEs

This was a venture of the preceding vacation, and had netted, at one time, an accrued and owed profit of $1.38. Prospects had been brightest on the very eve of cataclysm. The storeroom was locked and guarded, but twenty-seven rabbits and Belgian hares, old and young, had perished here on a single night--through no human agency, but in a foray of cats, the besiegers treacherously tunnelling up through the sawdust from the small aperture which opened into the stall beyond the partition. Commerce has its martyrs.

Penrod climbed upon a barrel, stood on tiptoe, grasped the rim of the box; then, using a knot-hole as a stirrup, threw one leg over the top, drew himself up, and dropped within. Standing upon the packed sawdust, he was just tall enough to see over the top.

Duke had not followed him into the storeroom, but remained near the open doorway in a concave and pessimistic attitude. Penrod felt in a dark corner of the box and laid hands upon a simple apparatus consisting of an old bushel-basket with a few yards of clothes-line tied to each of its handles. He passed the ends of the lines over a big spool, which revolved upon an axle of wire suspended from a beam overhead, and, with the aid of this improvised pulley, lowered the empty basket until it came to rest in an upright position upon the floor of the storeroom at the foot of the sawdust-box.

"Eleva-ter!" shouted Penrod. "Ting-ting!"

Duke, old and intelligently apprehensive, approached slowly, in a semicircular manner, deprecatingly, but with courtesy. He pawed the basket delicately; then, as if that were all his master had expected of him, uttered one bright bark, sat down, and looked up triumphantly. His hypocrisy was shallow: many a horrible quarter of an hour had taught him his duty in this matter.

"El-e-*vay*-ter!" shouted Penrod sternly. "You want me to come down there to you?"

Duke looked suddenly haggard. He pawed the basket feebly again and, upon another outburst from on high, prostrated himself flat. Again threatened, he gave a superb impersonation of a worm.

"You get in that el-e-*vay*-ter!"

Reckless with despair, Duke jumped into the basket, landing in a dishevelled posture, which he did not alter until he had been drawn up and poured out upon the floor of sawdust with the box. There, shuddering, he lay in doughnut shape and presently slumbered.

It was dark in the box, a condition that might have been remedied by sliding back a small wooden panel on runners, which would have let in ample light from the alley; but Penrod Schofield had more interesting means of illumination. He knelt, and from a former soap-box, in a corner, took a lantern, without a chimney, and a large oil-can, the leak in the latter being so nearly imperceptible that its banishment from household use had seemed to Penrod as inexplicable as it was providential.

He shook the lantern near his ear: nothing splashed; there was no sound but a dry clinking. But there was plenty of kerosene in the can; and he filled the lantern, striking a match to illumine the operation. Then he lit the lantern and hung it upon a nail against the wall. The sawdust floor was slightly impregnated with oil, and the open flame quivered in suggestive proximity to the side of the box; however, some rather deep charrings of the plank against which the lantern hung offered evidence that the arrangement was by no means a new one, and indicated at least a possibility of no fatality occurring this time.

Next, Penrod turned up the surface of the sawdust in another corner of the floor, and drew forth a cigar-box in which were half a dozen cigarettes, made of hayseed and thick brown wrapping paper, a lead-pencil, an eraser, and a small note-book, the cover of which was labelled in his own handwriting:

"English Grammar. Penrod Schofield. Room 6, Ward School Nomber Seventh."

The first page of this book was purely academic; but the study of English undefiled terminated with a slight jar at the top of the second: "Nor must an adverb be used to modif----"

Immediately followed: "HARoLD RAMoREZ THE RoADAGENT OR WiLD LiFE AMoNG THE ROCKY MTS."

And the subsequent entries in the book appeared to have little concern with Room 6, Ward School Nomber Seventh.

Lesson 53

1. Read chapters 2 and 3 of *Penrod*.
2. Add what you can to your character notes.

Chapter II. Romance

The author of "Harold Ramorez," etc., lit one of the hayseed cigarettes, seated himself comfortably, with his back against the wall and his right shoulder just under the lantern, elevated his knees to support the note-book, turned to a blank page, and wrote, slowly and earnestly: "CHAPITER THE SIXTH"

He took a knife from his pocket, and, broodingly, his eyes upon the inward embryos of vision, sharpened his pencil. After that, he extended a foot and meditatively rubbed Duke's back with the side of his shoe. Creation, with Penrod, did not leap, full-armed, from the brain; but finally he began to produce. He wrote very slowly at first, and then with increasing rapidity; faster and faster, gathering momentum and growing more and more fevered as he sped, till at last the true fire came, without which no lamp of real literature may be made to burn.

Mr. Wilson reched for his gun but our hero had him covred and soon said Well I guess you don't come any of that on me my freind.

Well what makes you so sure about it sneered the other bitting his lip so savageley that the blood ran. You are nothing but a common Roadagent any way and I do not propose to be bafled by such, Ramorez laughed at this and kep Mr. Wilson covred by his ottomatick

Soon the two men were struggling together in the death-roes but soon Mr Wilson got him bound and gaged his mouth and went away for awhile leavin our hero, it was dark and he writhd at his bonds writhing on the floor wile the rats came out of their holes and bit him and vernim got all over him from the floor of that helish spot but soon he managed to push the gag out of his mouth with the end of his toungeu and got all his bonds off

Soon Mr Wilson came back to tant him with his helpless condition flowed by his gang of detectives and they said Oh look at Ramorez sneering at his plight and tanted him with his helpless condition because Ramorez had put the bonds back sos he would look the same but could throw them off him when he wanted to Just look at him now sneered they. To hear him talk you would thought he was hot stuff and they said Look at him now, him that was going to do so much, Oh I would not like to be in his fix

Soon Harold got mad at this and jumped up with blasing eyes throwin off his bonds like they were air Ha Ha sneered he I guess you better not talk so much next time. Soon there flowed another awful struggle and siezin his ottomatick back from Mr Wilson he shot two of the detectives through the heart Bing Bing went the ottomatick and two more went to meet their Maker only two detectives left now and so he stabbed one and the scondrel went to meet his Maker for now our hero was fighting for his very life. It was dark in there now for night had falen and a terrible view met the eye Blood was just all over everything and the rats were eatin the dead men.

Soon our hero manged to get his back to the wall for he was fighting for his very life now and shot Mr Wilson through the abodmen Oh said Mr Wilson you---- ---- ---- (The dashes are Penrod's.) Mr Wilson stagerd back vile oaths soilin his lips for he was in pain Why you---- ----you sneered he I will get you yet---- ----you Harold Ramorez

The remainin scondrel had an ax which he came near our heros head with but missed him and ramand stuck in the wall Our heros amunition was exhaused what was he to do, the remanin scondrel would soon get his ax lose so our hero sprung forward and bit him till his teeth met in the flech for now our hero was fighting for his very life. At this the remanin scondrel also cursed and swore vile oaths. Oh sneered he---- ---- ----you Harold Ramorez what did you bite me for Yes sneered Mr Wilson also and he has shot me in the abdomen too the----

Soon they were both cursin and reviln him together Why you---- ---- ---- ---- ----sneered they what did you want to injure us for----you Harold Ramorez you have not got any sence and you think you are so much but you are no better than anybody else and you are a---- ---- ---- ---- ---- ----
Soon our hero could stand this no longer. If you could learn to act like gentlmen said he I would not do any more to you now and your low vile exppresions have not got any effect on me only to injure your own self when you go to meet your Maker Oh I guess you have had enogh for one day and I think you have learned a lesson and will not soon atemp to beard Harold Ramorez again so with a tantig laugh he cooly lit a cigarrete and takin the keys of the cell from Mr Wilson poket went on out

Soon Mr Wilson and the wonded detective manged to bind up their wonds and got up off the floor---- ----it I will have that dasstads life now sneered they if we have to swing for it---- ---- ---- ----him he shall not eccape us again the low down---- ---- ---- ---- ---- Chapter seventh
A mule train of heavily laden burros laden with gold from the mines was to be seen wondering among the highest clifts and gorgs of the Rocky Mts and a tall man with a long silken mustash and a cartigde belt could be heard cursin vile oaths because he well knew this was the lair of Harold Ramorez Why---- ---- ----you you---- ---- ---- ---- mules you sneered he because the poor mules were not able to go any quicker ---- you I will show you Why---- ---- ---- ---- ---- ----it sneered he his oaths growing viler and viler I will whip you---- ---- ---- ---- ---- ---- ----you sos you will not be able to walk for a week---- ----you you mean old---- ---- ---- ---- ---- ---- ---- ---- ----mules you
Scarcly had the vile words left his lips when----

"Penrod!"

It was his mother's voice, calling from the back porch.

Simultaneously, the noon whistles began to blow, far and near; and the romancer in the sawdust-box, summoned prosaically from steep mountain passes above the clouds, paused with stubby pencil halfway from lip to knee. His eyes were shining: there was a rapt sweetness in his gaze. As he wrote, his burden had grown lighter; thoughts of Mrs. Lora Rewbush had almost left him; and in particular as he recounted (even by the chaste dash) the annoyed expressions of Mr. Wilson, the wounded detective, and the silken moustached mule-driver, he had felt mysteriously relieved concerning the Child Sir Lancelot. Altogether he looked a better and a brighter boy.

"Pen-rod!"

The rapt look faded slowly. He sighed, but moved not.

"Penrod! We're having lunch early just on your account, so you'll have plenty of time to be dressed for the pageant. Hurry!"

There was silence in Penrod's aerie.

"Pen-rod!"

Mrs. Schofields voice sounded nearer, indicating a threatened approach. Penrod bestirred himself: he blew out the lantern, and shouted plaintively:

"Well, ain't I coming fast's I can?"

"Do hurry," returned the voice, withdrawing; and the kitchen door could be heard to close.

Languidly, Penrod proceeded to set his house in order.

Replacing his manuscript and pencil in the cigar-box, he carefully buried the box in the sawdust, put the lantern and oil-can back in the soap-box, adjusted the elevator for the reception of Duke, and, in no uncertain tone, invited the devoted animal to enter.

Duke stretched himself amiably, affecting not to hear; and when this pretence became so obvious that even a dog could keep it up no longer, sat down in a corner, facing it, his back to his master, and his head perpendicular, nose upward, supported by the convergence of the two walls. This, from a dog, is the last word, the comble of the immutable. Penrod commanded, stormed, tried gentleness; persuaded with honeyed words and pictured rewards. Duke's eyes looked backward; otherwise he moved not. Time elapsed. Penrod stooped to flattery, finally to insincere caresses; then, losing patience spouted sudden threats.

Duke remained immovable, frozen fast to his great gesture of implacable despair.

A footstep sounded on the threshold of the store-room.

"Penrod, come down from that box this instant!"

"Ma'am?"

"Are you up in that sawdust-box again?" As Mrs. Schofield had just heard her son's voice issue from the box, and also, as she knew he was there anyhow, her question must have been put for oratorical purposes only. "Because if you are," she continued promptly, "I'm going to ask your papa not to let you play there any----"

Penrod's forehead, his eyes, the tops of his ears, and most of his hair, became visible to her at the top of the box. "I ain't playing!" he said indignantly.

"Well, what are you doing?"

"Just coming down," he replied, in a grieved but patient tone.

"Then why don't you come?"

"I got Duke here. I got to get him down, haven't I? You don't suppose I want to leave a poor dog in here to starve, do you?"

"Well, hand him down over the side to me. Let me----"

"I'll get him down all right," said Penrod. "I got him up here, and I guess I can get him down!"

"Well then, do it!"

"I will if you'll let me alone. If you'll go on back to the house I promise to be there inside of two minutes. Honest!"

He put extreme urgency into this, and his mother turned toward the house. "If you're not there in two minutes----"

"I will be!"

After her departure, Penrod expended some finalities of eloquence upon Duke, then disgustedly gathered him up in his arms, dumped him into the basket and, shouting sternly, "All in for the ground floor--step back there, madam--all ready, Jim!" lowered dog and basket to the floor of the storeroom. Duke sprang out in tumultuous relief, and bestowed frantic affection upon his master as the latter slid down from the box.

Penrod dusted himself sketchily, experiencing a sense of satisfaction, dulled by the overhanging afternoon, perhaps, but perceptible: he had the feeling of one who has been true to a cause. The operation of the elevator was unsinful and, save for the shock to Duke's nervous system, it was harmless; but Penrod could not possibly have brought himself to exhibit it in the presence of his mother or any other grown person in the world. The reasons for secrecy were undefined; at least, Penrod did not define them.

Chapter III. The Costume

After lunch his mother and his sister Margaret, a pretty girl of nineteen, dressed him for the sacrifice. They stood him near his mother's bedroom window and did what they would to him.

During the earlier anguishes of the process he was mute, exceeding the pathos of the stricken calf in the shambles; but a student of eyes might have perceived in his soul the premonitory symptoms of a sinister uprising. At a rehearsal (in citizens' clothes) attended by mothers and grown-up sisters, Mrs. Lora Rewbush had announced that she wished the costuming to be "as medieval and artistic as possible." Otherwise, and as to details, she said, she would leave the costumes entirely to the good taste of the children's parents. Mrs. Schofield and Margaret were no archeologists, but they knew that their taste was as good as that of other mothers and sisters concerned; so with perfect confidence they had planned and executed a costume for Penrod; and the only misgiving they felt was connected with the tractability of the Child Sir Lancelot himself.

Stripped to his underwear, he had been made to wash himself vehemently; then they began by shrouding his legs in a pair of silk stockings, once blue but now mostly whitish. Upon Penrod they visibly surpassed mere ampleness; but they were long, and it required only a rather loose imagination to assume that they were tights.

The upper part of his body was next concealed from view by a garment so peculiar that its description becomes difficult. In 1886, Mrs. Schofield, then unmarried, had worn at her "coming-out party" a dress of vivid salmon silk which had been remodelled after her marriage to accord with various epochs of fashion until a final, unskilful campaign at a dye-house had left it in a condition certain to attract much attention to the wearer. Mrs. Schofield had considered giving it to Della, the cook; but had decided not to do so, because you never could tell how Della was going to take things, and cooks were scarce.

It may have been the word "medieval" (in Mrs. Lora Rewbush's rich phrase) which had inspired the idea for a last conspicuous usefulness; at all events, the bodice of that once salmon dress, somewhat modified and moderated, now took a position, for its farewell appearance in society, upon the back, breast, and arms of the Child Sir Lancelot.

The area thus costumed ceased at the waist, leaving a Jaeger-like and unmedieval gap thence to the tops of the stockings. The inventive genius of woman triumphantly bridged it, but in a manner which imposes upon history almost insuperable delicacies of narration. Penrod's father was an old-fashioned man: the twentieth century had failed to shake his faith in red flannel for cold weather; and it was while Mrs. Schofield was putting away her husband's winter underwear that she perceived how hopelessly one of the elder specimens had dwindled; and simultaneously she received the inspiration which resulted in a pair of trunks for the Child Sir Lancelot, and added an earnest bit of colour, as well as a genuine touch of the Middle Ages, to his costume. Reversed, fore to aft, with the greater part of the legs cut off, and strips of silver braid covering the seams, this garment, she felt, was not traceable to its original source.

When it had been placed upon Penrod, the stockings were attached to it by a system of safety-pins, not very perceptible at a distance. Next, after being severely warned against stooping, Penrod got his feet into the slippers he wore to dancing-school--"patent-leather pumps" now decorated with large pink rosettes.

"If I can't stoop," he began, smolderingly, "I'd like to know how'm I goin' to kneel in the pag----"

"You must manage!" This, uttered through pins, was evidently thought to be sufficient.

They fastened some ruching about his slender neck, pinned ribbons at random all over him, and then Margaret thickly powdered his hair.

"Oh, yes, that's all right," she said, replying to a question put by her mother. "They always powdered their hair in Colonial times."

"It doesn't seem right to me--exactly," objected Mrs. Schofield, gently. "Sir Lancelot must have been ever so long before Colonial times."

"That doesn't matter," Margaret reassured her. "Nobody'll know the difference--Mrs. Lora Rewbush least of all. I don't think she knows a thing about it, though, of course, she does write splendidly and the words of the pageant are just beautiful. Stand still, Penrod!" (The author of "Harold Ramorez" had moved convulsively.) "Besides, powdered hair's always becoming. Look at him. You'd hardly know it was Penrod!"

The pride and admiration with which she pronounced this undeniable truth might have been thought tactless, but Penrod, not analytical, found his spirits somewhat elevated. No mirror was in his range of vision and, though he had submitted to cursory measurements of his person a week earlier, he had no previous acquaintance with the costume. He began to form a not unpleasing mental picture of his appearance, something somewhere between the portraits of George Washington and a vivid memory of Miss Julia Marlowe at a matinee of "Twelfth Night."

He was additionally cheered by a sword which had been borrowed from a neighbor, who was a Knight of Pythias. Finally there was a mantle, an old golf cape of Margaret's. Fluffy polka-dots of white cotton had been sewed to it generously; also it was ornamented with a large cross of red flannel, suggested by the picture of a Crusader in a newspaper advertisement. The mantle was fastened to Penrod's shoulder (that is, to the shoulder of Mrs. Schofield's ex-bodice) by means of large safety- pins, and arranged to hang down behind him, touching his heels, but obscuring nowise the glory of his facade. Then, at last, he was allowed to step before a mirror.

It was a full-length glass, and the worst immediately happened. It might have been a little less violent, perhaps, if Penrod's expectations had not been so richly and poetically idealized; but as things were, the revolt was volcanic.

Victor Hugo's account of the fight with the devil-fish, in "Toilers of the Sea," encourages a belief that, had Hugo lived and increased in power, he might have been equal to a proper recital of the half hour which followed Penrod's first sight of himself as the Child Sir Lancelot. But Mr. Wilson himself, dastard but eloquent foe of Harold Ramorez, could not have expressed, with all the vile dashes at his command, the sentiments which animated Penrod's bosom when the instantaneous and unalterable conviction descended upon him that he was intended by his loved ones to make a public spectacle of himself in his sister's stockings and part of an old dress of his mother's.

To him these familiar things were not disguised at all; there seemed no possibility that the whole world would not know them at a glance. The stockings were worse than the bodice. He had been assured that these could not be recognized, but, seeing them in the mirror, he was sure that no human eye could fail at first glance to detect the difference between himself and the former purposes of these stockings. Fold, wrinkle, and void shrieked their history with a hundred tongues, invoking earthquake, eclipse, and blue ruin. The frantic youth's final submission was obtained only after a painful telephonic conversation between himself and his father, the latter having been called up and upon, by the exhausted Mrs. Schofield, to subjugate his offspring by wire.

The two ladies made all possible haste, after this, to deliver Penrod into the hands of Mrs. Lora Rewbush; nevertheless, they found opportunity to exchange earnest congratulations upon his not having recognized the humble but serviceable paternal garment now brilliant about the Lancelotish middle. Altogether, they felt that the costume was a success. Penrod looked like nothing ever remotely imagined by Sir Thomas Malory or Alfred Tennyson;--for that matter, he looked like nothing ever before seen on earth; but as Mrs. Schofield and Margaret took their places in the audience at the Women's Arts and Guild Hall, the anxiety they felt concerning Penrod's elocutionary and gesticular powers, so soon to be put to public test, was pleasantly tempered by their satisfaction that, owing to their efforts, his outward appearance would be a credit to the family.

Lesson 54

1. Read chapters 4 and 5 of *Penrod*.
2. What embarrassment did Penrod suffer in chapter 4?
3. What does the last sentence in chapter 4 mean? What did he do?
   "And now, in this extremity, when all seemed lost indeed, particularly including honour, the dilating eye of the outlaw fell upon the blue overalls which the janitor had left hanging upon a peg. Inspiration and action were almost simultaneous." (Answers)

Chapter IV. Desperation

The Child Sir Lancelot found himself in a large anteroom behind the stage--a room crowded with excited children, all about equally medieval and artistic. Penrod was less conspicuous than he thought himself, but he was so preoccupied with his own shame, steeling his nerves to meet the first inevitable taunting reference to his sister's stockings, that he failed to perceive there were others present in much of his own unmanned condition. Retiring to a corner, immediately upon his entrance, he managed to unfasten the mantle at the shoulders, and, drawing it round him, pinned it again at his throat so that it concealed the rest of his costume. This permitted a temporary relief, but increased his horror of the moment when, in pursuance of the action of the "pageant," the sheltering garment must be cast aside.

Some of the other child knights were also keeping their mantles close about them. A few of the envied opulent swung brilliant fabrics from their shoulders, airily, showing off hired splendours from a professional costumer's stock, while one or two were insulting examples of parental indulgence, particularly little Maurice Levy, the Child Sir Galahad. This shrinking person went clamorously about, making it known everywhere that the best tailor in town had been dazzled by a great sum into constructing his costume. It consisted of blue velvet knickerbockers, a white satin waistcoat, and a beautifully cut little swallow-tailed coat with pearl buttons. The medieval and artistic triumph was completed by a mantle of yellow velvet, and little white boots, sporting gold tassels.

All this radiance paused in a brilliant career and addressed the Child Sir Lancelot, gathering an immediately formed semicircular audience of little girls. Woman was ever the trailer of magnificence.

"What you got on?" inquired Mr. Levy, after dispensing information. "What you got on under that ole golf cape?"

Penrod looked upon him coldly. At other times his questioner would have approached him with deference, even with apprehension. But to-day the Child Sir Galahad was somewhat intoxicated with the power of his own beauty.

"What you got on?" he repeated.

"Oh, nothin'," said Penrod, with an indifference assumed at great cost to his nervous system.

The elate Maurice was inspired to set up as a wit. "Then you're nakid!" he shouted exultantly. "Penrod Schofield says he hasn't got nothin' on under that ole golf cape! He's nakid! He's nakid."

The indelicate little girls giggled delightedly, and a javelin pierced the inwards of Penrod when he saw that the Child Elaine, amber-curled and beautiful Marjorie Jones, lifted golden laughter to the horrid jest.

Other boys and girls came flocking to the uproar. "He's nakid, he's nakid!" shrieked the Child Sir Galahad. "Penrod Schofield's nakid! He's na-a-a-kid!"

"Hush, hush!" said Mrs. Lora Rewbush, pushing her way into the group. "Remember, we are all little knights and ladies to-day. Little knights and ladies of the Table Round would not make so much noise. Now children, we must begin to take our places on the stage. Is everybody here?"

Penrod made his escape under cover of this diversion: he slid behind Mrs. Lora Rewbush, and being near a door, opened it unnoticed and went out quickly, closing it behind him. He found himself in a narrow and vacant hallway which led to a door marked "Janitor's Room."

Burning with outrage, heart-sick at the sweet, cold-blooded laughter of Marjorie Jones, Penrod rested his elbows upon a window-sill and speculated upon the effects of a leap from the second story. One of the reasons he gave it up was his desire to live on Maurice Levy's account: already he was forming educational plans for the Child Sir Galahad.

A stout man in blue overalls passed through the hallway muttering to himself petulantly. "I reckon they'll find that hall hot enough now!" he said, conveying to Penrod an impression that some too feminine women had sent him upon an unreasonable errand to the furnace. He went into the Janitor's Room and, emerging a moment later, minus the overalls, passed Penrod again with a bass rumble--"Dern 'em!" it seemed he said-- and made a gloomy exit by the door at the upper end of the hallway.

The conglomerate and delicate rustle of a large, mannerly audience was heard as the janitor opened and closed the door; and stage-fright seized the boy. The orchestra began an overture, and, at that, Penrod, trembling violently, tiptoed down the hall into the Janitor's Room. It was a cul-de-sac: There was no outlet save by the way he had come.

Despairingly he doffed his mantle and looked down upon himself for a last sickening assurance that the stockings were as obviously and disgracefully Margaret's as they had seemed in the mirror at home. For a moment he was encouraged: perhaps he was no worse than some of the other boys. Then he noticed that a safety-pin had opened; one of those connecting the stockings with his trunks. He sat down to fasten it and his eye fell for the first time with particular attention upon the trunks. Until this instant he had been preoccupied with the stockings.

Slowly recognition dawned in his eyes.

The Schofields' house stood on a corner at the intersection of two main-travelled streets; the fence was low, and the publicity obtained by the washable portion of the family apparel, on Mondays, had often been painful to Penrod; for boys have a peculiar sensitiveness in these matters. A plain, matter-of-fact washerwoman' employed by Mrs. Schofield, never left anything to the imagination of the passer-by; and of all her calm display the scarlet flaunting of his father's winter wear had most abashed Penrod. One day Marjorie Jones, all gold and starch, had passed when the dreadful things were on the line: Penrod had hidden himself, shuddering. The whole town, he was convinced, knew these garments intimately and derisively.

And now, as he sat in the janitor's chair, the horrible and paralyzing recognition came. He had not an instant's doubt that every fellow actor, as well as every soul in the audience, would recognize what his mother and sister had put upon him. For as the awful truth became plain to himself it seemed blazoned to the world; and far, far louder than the stockings, the trunks did fairly bellow the grisly secret: whose they were and what they were!

Most people have suffered in a dream the experience of finding themselves very inadequately clad in the midst of a crowd of well-dressed people, and such dreamers' sensations are comparable to Penrod's, though faintly, because Penrod was awake and in much too full possession of the most active capacities for anguish.

A human male whose dress has been damaged, or reveals some vital lack, suffers from a hideous and shameful loneliness which makes every second absolutely unbearable until he is again as others of his sex and species; and there is no act or sin whatever too desperate for him in his struggle to attain that condition. Also, there is absolutely no embarrassment possible to a woman which is comparable to that of a man under corresponding circumstances and in this a boy is a man. Gazing upon the ghastly trunks, the stricken Penrod felt that he was a degree worse then nude; and a great horror of himself filled his soul.

"Penrod Schofield!"

The door into the hallway opened, and a voice demanded him. He could not be seen from the hallway, but the hue and the cry was up; and he knew he must be taken. It was only a question of seconds. He huddled in his chair.

"Penrod Schofield!" cried Mrs. Lora Rewbush angrily.

The distracted boy rose and, as he did so, a long pin sank deep into his back. He extracted it frenziedly, which brought to his ears a protracted and sonorous ripping, too easily located by a final gesture of horror.

"Penrod Schofield!" Mrs. Lora Rewbush had come out into the hallway.

And now, in this extremity, when all seemed lost indeed, particularly including honour, the dilating eye of the outlaw fell upon the blue overalls which the janitor had left hanging upon a peg.

Inspiration and action were almost simultaneous.

Chapter V. The Pageant of the Table Round

"Penrod!" Mrs. Lora Rewbush stood in the doorway, indignantly gazing upon a Child Sir Lancelot mantled to the heels. "Do you know that you have kept an audience of five hundred people waiting for ten minutes?" She, also, detained the five hundred while she spake further.

"Well," said Penrod contentedly, as he followed her toward the buzzing stage, "I was just sitting there thinking."

Two minutes later the curtain rose on a medieval castle hall richly done in the new stage-craft made in Germany and consisting of pink and blue cheesecloth. The Child King Arthur and the Child Queen Guinevere were disclosed upon thrones, with the Child Elaine and many other celebrities in attendance; while about fifteen Child Knights were seated at a dining-room table round, which was covered with a large Oriental rug, and displayed (for the knights' refreshment) a banquet service of silver loving-cups and trophies, borrowed from the Country Club and some local automobile manufacturers.

In addition to this splendour, potted plants and palms have seldom been more lavishly used in any castle on the stage or off.

The footlights were aided by a "spot-light" from the rear of the hall; and the children were revealed in a blaze of glory.

A hushed, multitudinous "O-oh" of admiration came from the decorous and delighted audience. Then the children sang feebly:

"Chuldrun of the Tabul Round, Lit-tul knights and ladies we. Let our voy-siz all resound Faith and hope and charitee!"

The Child King Arthur rose, extended his sceptre with the decisive gesture of a semaphore, and spake:

"Each littul knight and lady born Has noble deeds to perform In thee child-world of shivullree, No matter how small his share may be. Let each advance and tell in turn What claim has each to knighthood earn."

The Child Sir Mordred, the villain of this piece, rose in his place at the table round, and piped the only lines ever written by Mrs. Lora Rewbush which Penrod Schofield could have pronounced without loathing. Georgie Bassett, a really angelic boy, had been selected for the role of Mordred. His perfect conduct had earned for him the sardonic sobriquet, "The Little Gentleman," among his boy acquaintances. (Naturally he had no friends.) Hence the other boys supposed that he had been selected for the wicked Mordred as a reward of virtue. He declaimed serenely:

"I hight Sir Mordred the Child, and I teach Lessons of selfishest evil, and reach Out into darkness. Thoughtless, unkind, And ruthless is Mordred, and unrefined."

The Child Mordred was properly rebuked and denied the accolade, though, like the others, he seemed to have assumed the title already. He made a plotter's exit. Whereupon Maurice Levy rose, bowed, announced that he highted the Child Sir Galahad, and continued with perfect sang-froid:

"I am the purest of the pure. I have but kindest thoughts each day. I give my riches to the poor, And follow in the Master's way."

This elicited tokens of approval from the Child King Arthur, and he bade Maurice "stand forth" and come near the throne, a command obeyed with the easy grace of conscious merit.

It was Penrod's turn. He stepped back from his chair, the table between him and the audience, and began in a high, breathless monotone:

"I hight Sir Lancelot du Lake, the Child, Gentul-hearted, meek, and mild. What though I'm but a littul child, Gentul-heartud, meek, and mild, I do my share though but--though but----"

Penrod paused and gulped. The voice of Mrs. Lora Rewbush was heard from the wings, prompting irritably, and the Child Sir Lancelot repeated:

"I do my share though but--though but a tot, I pray you knight Sir Lancelot!"

This also met the royal favour, and Penrod was bidden to join Sir Galahad at the throne. As he crossed the stage, Mrs. Schofield whispered to Margaret:

"That boy! He's unpinned his mantle and fixed it to cover his whole costume. After we worked so hard to make it becoming!"

"Never mind; he'll have to take the cape off in a minute," returned Margaret. She leaned forward suddenly, narrowing her eyes to see better. "What is that thing hanging about his left ankle?" she whispered uneasily. "How queer! He must have got tangled in something."

"Where?" asked Mrs. Schofield, in alarm.

"His left foot. It makes him stumble. Don't you see? It looks--it looks like an elephant's foot!"

The Child Sir Lancelot and the Child Sir Galahad clasped hands before their Child King. Penrod was conscious of a great uplift; in a moment he would have to throw aside his mantle, but even so he was protected and sheltered in the human garment of a man. His stage-fright had passed, for the audience was but an indistinguishable blur of darkness beyond the dazzling lights. His most repulsive speech (that in which he proclaimed himself a "tot") was over and done with; and now at last the small, moist hand of the Child Sir Galahad lay within his own. Craftily his brown fingers stole from Maurice's palm to the wrist. The two boys declaimed in concert:

"We are two chuldrun of the Tabul Round Strewing kindness all a-round. With love and good deeds striving ever for the best, May our littul efforts e'er be blest. Two littul hearts we offer. See United in love, faith, hope, and char--ow!"

The conclusion of the duet was marred. The Child Sir Galahad suddenly stiffened, and, uttering an irrepressible shriek of anguish, gave a brief exhibition of the contortionist's art. ("He's twistin' my wrist! Dern you, leggo!")

The voice of Mrs. Lora Rewbush was again heard from the wings; it sounded bloodthirsty. Penrod released his victim; and the Child King Arthur, somewhat disconcerted, extended his sceptre and, with the assistance of the enraged prompter, said:

"Sweet child-friends of the Tabul Round, In brotherly love and kindness abound, Sir Lancelot, you have spoken well, Sir Galahad, too, as clear as bell. So now pray doff your mantles gay. You shall be knighted this very day."

And Penrod doffed his mantle.

Simultaneously, a thick and vasty gasp came from the audience, as from five hundred bathers in a wholly unexpected surf. This gasp was punctuated irregularly, over the auditorium, by imperfectly subdued screams both of dismay and incredulous joy, and by two dismal shrieks. Altogether it was an extraordinary sound, a sound never to be forgotten by any one who heard it. It was almost as unforgettable as the sight which caused it; the word "sight" being here used in its vernacular sense, for Penrod, standing unmantled and revealed in all the medieval and artistic glory of the janitor's blue overalls, falls within its meaning.

The janitor was a heavy man, and his overalls, upon Penrod, were merely oceanic. The boy was at once swaddled and lost within their blue gulfs and vast saggings; and the left leg, too hastily rolled up, had descended with a distinctively elephantine effect, as Margaret had observed. Certainly, the Child Sir Lancelot was at least a sight.

It is probable that a great many in that hall must have had, even then, a consciousness that they were looking on at History in the Making. A supreme act is recognizable at sight: it bears the birthmark of immortality. But Penrod, that marvellous boy, had begun to declaim, even with the gesture of flinging off his mantle for the accolade:

"I first, the Child Sir Lancelot du Lake, Will volunteer to knighthood take, And kneeling here before your throne I vow to----"

He finished his speech unheard. The audience had recovered breath, but had lost self-control, and there ensued something later described by a participant as a sort of cultured riot.

The actors in the "pageant" were not so dumfounded by Penrod's costume as might have been expected. A few precocious geniuses perceived that the overalls were the Child Lancelot's own comment on maternal intentions; and these were profoundly impressed: they regarded him with the grisly admiration of young and ambitious criminals for a jail-mate about to be distinguished by hanging. But most of the children simply took it to be the case (a little strange, but not startling) that Penrod's mother had dressed him like that--which is pathetic. They tried to go on with the "pageant."

They made a brief, manful effort. But the irrepressible outbursts from the audience bewildered them; every time Sir Lancelot du Lake the Child opened his mouth, the great, shadowy house fell into an uproar, and the children into confusion. Strong women and brave girls in the audience went out into the lobby, shrieking and clinging to one another. Others remained, rocking in their seats, helpless and spent. The neighbourhood of Mrs. Schofield and Margaret became, tactfully, a desert. Friends of the author went behind the scenes and encountered a hitherto unknown phase of Mrs. Lora Rewbush; they said, afterward, that she hardly seemed to know what she was doing. She begged to be left alone somewhere with Penrod Schofield, for just a little while.

They led her away.

Lesson 55

1. Read chapters 6 and 7 in *Penrod.*
2. Add notes to your character page. Have you learned anything more about Penrod?

Chapter VI. Evening

The sun was setting behind the back fence (though at a considerable distance) as Penrod Schofield approached that fence and looked thoughtfully up at the top of it, apparently having in mind some purpose to climb up and sit there. Debating this, he passed his fingers gently up and down the backs of his legs; and then something seemed to decide him not to sit anywhere. He leaned against the fence, sighed profoundly, and gazed at Duke, his wistful dog.

The sigh was reminiscent: episodes of simple pathos were passing before his inward eye. About the most painful was the vision of lovely Marjorie Jones, weeping with rage as the Child Sir Lancelot was dragged, insatiate, from the prostrate and howling Child Sir Galahad, after an onslaught delivered the precise instant the curtain began to fall upon the demoralized "pageant." And then--oh, pangs! oh, woman!--she slapped at the ruffian's cheek, as he was led past her by a resentful janitor; and turning, flung her arms round the Child Sir Galahad's neck.

"Penrod Schofield, don't you dare ever speak to me again as long as you live!" Maurice's little white boots and gold tassels had done their work.

At home the late Child Sir Lancelot was consigned to a locked clothes-closet pending the arrival of his father. Mr. Schofield came and, shortly after, there was put into practice an old patriarchal custom. It is a custom of inconceivable antiquity: probably primordial, certainly prehistoric, but still in vogue in some remaining citadels of the ancient simplicities of the Republic.

And now, therefore, in the dusk, Penrod leaned against the fence and sighed.

His case is comparable to that of an adult who could have survived a similar experience. Looking back to the sawdust-box, fancy pictures this comparable adult a serious and inventive writer engaged in congenial literary activities in a private retreat. We see this period marked by the creation of some of the most virile passages of a Work dealing exclusively in red corpuscles and huge primal impulses. We see this thoughtful man dragged from his calm seclusion to a horrifying publicity; forced to adopt the stage and, himself a writer, compelled to exploit the repulsive sentiments of an author not only personally distasteful to him but whose whole method and school in belles lettres he despises.

We see him reduced by desperation and modesty to stealing a pair of overalls. We conceive him to have ruined, then, his own reputation, and to have utterly disgraced his family; next, to have engaged in the duello and to have been spurned by his lady-love, thus lost to him (according to her own declaration) forever. Finally, we must behold: imprisonment by the authorities; the third degree and flagellation.

We conceive our man decided that his career had been perhaps too eventful. Yet Penrod had condensed all of it into eight hours.

It appears that he had at least some shadowy perception of a recent fulness of life, for, as he leaned against the fence, gazing upon his wistful Duke, he sighed again and murmured aloud:

"Well, hasn't this been a day!"

But in a little while a star came out, freshly lighted, from the highest part of the sky, and Penrod, looking up, noticed it casually and a little drowsily. He yawned. Then he sighed once more, but not reminiscently: evening had come; the day was over. It was a sigh of pure ennui.

Chapter VII. Evils of Drink

Next day, Penrod acquired a dime by a simple and antique process which was without doubt sometimes practised by the boys of Babylon. When the teacher of his class in Sunday-school requested the weekly contribution, Penrod, fumbling honestly (at first) in the wrong pockets, managed to look so embarrassed that the gentle lady told him not to mind, and said she was often forgetful herself. She was so sweet about it that, looking into the future, Penrod began to feel confident of a small but regular income.

At the close of the afternoon services he did not go home, but proceeded to squander the funds just withheld from China upon an orgy of the most pungently forbidden description. In a Drug Emporium, near the church, he purchased a five-cent sack of candy consisting for the most part of the heavily flavoured hoofs of horned cattle, but undeniably substantial, and so generously capable of resisting solution that the purchaser must needs be avaricious beyond reason who did not realize his money's worth.

Equipped with this collation, Penrod contributed his remaining nickel to a picture show, countenanced upon the seventh day by the legal but not the moral authorities. Here, in cozy darkness, he placidly insulted his liver with jaw-breaker upon jaw-breaker from the paper sack, and in a surfeit of content watched the silent actors on the screen.

One film made a lasting impression upon him. It depicted with relentless pathos the drunkard's progress; beginning with his conversion to beer in the company of loose travelling men; pursuing him through an inexplicable lapse into evening clothes and the society of some remarkably painful ladies, next, exhibiting the effects of alcohol on the victim's domestic disposition, the unfortunate man was seen in the act of striking his wife and, subsequently, his pleading baby daughter with an abnormally heavy walking-stick. Their flight--through the snow--to seek the protection of a relative was shown, and finally, the drunkard's picturesque behaviour at the portals of a madhouse.

So fascinated was Penrod that he postponed his departure until this film came round again, by which time he had finished his unnatural repast and almost, but not quite, decided against following the profession of a drunkard when he grew up.

Emerging, satiated, from the theatre, a public timepiece before a jeweller's shop confronted him with an unexpected dial and imminent perplexities. How was he to explain at home these hours of dalliance? There was a steadfast rule that he return direct from Sunday-school; and Sunday rules were important, because on that day there was his father, always at home and at hand, perilously ready for action. One of the hardest conditions of boyhood is the almost continuous strain put upon the powers of invention by the constant and harassing necessity for explanations of every natural act.

Proceeding homeward through the deepening twilight as rapidly as possible, at a gait half skip and half canter, Penrod made up his mind in what manner he would account for his long delay, and, as he drew nearer, rehearsed in words the opening passage of his defence.

"Now see here," he determined to begin; "I do not wished to be blamed for things I couldn't help, nor any other boy. I was going along the street by a cottage and a lady put her head out of the window and said her husband was drunk and whipping her and her little girl, and she asked me wouldn't I come in and help hold him. So I went in and tried to get hold of this drunken lady's husband where he was whipping their baby daughter, but he wouldn't pay any attention, and I told her I ought to be getting home, but she kep' on askin' me to stay----"

At this point he reached the corner of his own yard, where a coincidence not only checked the rehearsal of his eloquence but happily obviated all occasion for it. A cab from the station drew up in front of the gate, and there descended a troubled lady in black and a fragile little girl about three. Mrs. Schofield rushed from the house and enfolded both in hospitable arms.

They were Penrod's Aunt Clara and cousin, also Clara, from Dayton, Illinois, and in the flurry of their arrival everybody forgot to put Penrod to the question. It is doubtful, however, if he felt any relief; there may have been even a slight, unconscious disappointment not altogether dissimilar to that of an actor deprived of a good part.

In the course of some really necessary preparations for dinner he stepped from the bathroom into the pink-and-white bedchamber of his sister, and addressed her rather thickly through a towel.

"When'd mamma find out Aunt Clara and Cousin Clara were coming?"

"Not till she saw them from the window. She just happened to look out as they drove up. Aunt Clara telegraphed this morning, but it wasn't delivered."

"How long they goin' to stay?"

"I don't know."

Penrod ceased to rub his shining face, and thoughtfully tossed the towel through the bathroom door. "Uncle John won't try to make 'em come back home, I guess, will he?" (Uncle John was Aunt Clara's husband, a successful manufacturer of stoves, and his lifelong regret was that he had not entered the Baptist ministry.) "He'll let 'em stay here quietly, won't he?"

"What are you talking about?" demanded Margaret, turning from her mirror. "Uncle John sent them here. Why shouldn't he let them stay?"

Penrod looked crestfallen. "Then he hasn't taken to drink?"

"Certainly not!" She emphasized the denial with a pretty peal of soprano laughter.

"Then why," asked her brother gloomily, "why did Aunt Clara look so worried when she got here?"

"Good gracious! Don't people worry about anything except somebody's drinking? Where did you get such an idea?"

"Well," he persisted, "you don't know it ain't that."

She laughed again, wholeheartedly. "Poor Uncle John! He won't even allow grape juice or ginger ale in his house. They came because they were afraid little Clara might catch the measles. She's very delicate, and there's such an epidemic of measles among the children over in Dayton the schools had to be closed. Uncle John got so worried that last night he dreamed about it; and this morning he couldn't stand it any longer and packed them off over here, though he thinks its wicked to travel on Sunday. And Aunt Clara was worried when she got here because they'd forgotten to check her trunk and it will have to be sent by express. Now what in the name of the common sense put it into your head that Uncle John had taken to----"

"Oh, nothing." He turned lifelessly away and went downstairs, a new-born hope dying in his bosom. Life seems so needlessly dull sometimes.

Lesson 56

1. Read chapters 8 and 9 of *Penrod.*
2. Take notes on characters.
3. Be on the lookout for words you don't know. Write down at least one along with the definition of the word.

Chapter VIII. School

Next morning, when he had once more resumed the dreadful burden of education, it seemed infinitely duller. And yet what pleasanter sight is there than a schoolroom well filled with children of those sprouting years just before the 'teens? The casual visitor, gazing from the teacher's platform upon these busy little heads, needs only a blunted memory to experience the most agreeable and exhilarating sensations. Still, for the greater part, the children are unconscious of the happiness of their condition; for nothing is more pathetically true than that we "never know when we are well off." The boys in a public school are less aware of their happy state than are the girls; and of all the boys in his room, probably Penrod himself had the least appreciation of his felicity.

He sat staring at an open page of a textbook, but not studying; not even reading; not even thinking. Nor was he lost in a reverie: his mind's eye was shut, as his physical eye might well have been, for the optic nerve, flaccid with ennui, conveyed nothing whatever of the printed page upon which the orb of vision was partially focused. Penrod was doing something very unusual and rare, something almost never accomplished except by a boy in school on a spring day: he was doing really nothing at all. He was merely a state of being.

From the street a sound stole in through the open window, and abhorring Nature began to fill the vacuum called Penrod Schofield; for the sound was the spring song of a mouth-organ, coming down the sidewalk. The windows were intentionally above the level of the eyes of the seated pupils; but the picture of the musician was plain to Penrod, painted for him by a quality in the runs and trills, partaking of the oboe, of the calliope, and of cats in anguish; an excruciating sweetness. The music came down the street and passed beneath the window, accompanied by the care-free shuffling of a pair of old shoes scuffing syncopations on the cement sidewalk. It passed into the distance; became faint and blurred; was gone. Emotion stirred in Penrod a great and poignant desire, but (perhaps fortunately) no fairy godmother made her appearance.

Roused from perfect apathy, the boy cast about the schoolroom an eye wearied to nausea by the perpetual vision of the neat teacher upon the platform, the backs of the heads of the pupils in front of him, and the monotonous stretches of blackboard threateningly defaced by arithmetical formulae and other insignia of torture. Above the blackboard, the walls of the high room were of white plaster--white with the qualified whiteness of old snow in a soft coal town. This dismal expanse was broken by four lithographic portraits, votive offerings of a thoughtful publisher. The portraits were of good and great men, kind men; men who loved children. Their faces were noble and benevolent. But the lithographs offered the only rest for the eyes of children fatigued by the everlasting sameness of the schoolroom. Long day after long day, interminable week in and interminable week out, vast month on vast month, the pupils sat with those four portraits beaming kindness down upon them. The faces became permanent in the consciousness of the children; they became an obsession--in and out of school the children were never free of them. The four faces haunted the minds of children falling asleep; they hung upon the minds of children waking at night; they rose forebodingly in the minds of children waking in the morning; they became monstrously alive in the minds of children lying sick of fever. Never, while the children of that schoolroom lived, would they be able to forget one detail of the four lithographs: the hand of Longfellow was fixed, for them, forever, in his beard. And by a simple and unconscious association of ideas, Penrod Schofield was accumulating an antipathy for the gentle Longfellow and for James Russell Lowell and for Oliver Wendell Holmes and for John Greenleaf Whittier, which would never permit him to peruse a work of one of those great New Englanders without a feeling of personal resentment.

His eyes fell slowly and inimically from the brow of Whittier to the braid of reddish hair belonging to Victorine Riordan, the little octoroon girl who sat directly in front of him. Victorine's back was as familiar to Penrod as the necktie of Oliver Wendell Holmes. So was her gayly coloured plaid waist. He hated the waist as he hated Victorine herself, without knowing why. Enforced companionship in large quantities and on an equal basis between the sexes appears to sterilize the affections, and schoolroom romances are few.

Victorine's hair was thick, and the brickish glints in it were beautiful, but Penrod was very tired of it. A tiny knot of green ribbon finished off the braid and kept it from unravelling; and beneath the ribbon there was a final wisp of hair which was just long enough to repose upon Penrod's desk when Victorine leaned back in her seat. It was there now. Thoughtfully, he took the braid between thumb and forefinger, and, without disturbing Victorine, dipped the end of it and the green ribbon into the inkwell of his desk. He brought hair and ribbon forth dripping purple ink, and partially dried them on a blotter, though, a moment later when Victorine leaned forward, they were still able to add a few picturesque touches to the plaid waist.

Rudolph Krauss, across the aisle from Penrod, watched the operation with protuberant eyes, fascinated. Inspired to imitation, he took a piece of chalk from his pocket and wrote "RATS" across the shoulder-blades of the boy in front of him, then looked across appealingly to Penrod for tokens of congratulation. Penrod yawned. It may not be denied that at times he appeared to be a very self-centred boy.

Chapter IX. Soaring

Half the members of the class passed out to a recitation-room, the empurpled Victorine among them, and Miss Spence started the remaining half through the ordeal of trial by mathematics. Several boys and girls were sent to the blackboard, and Penrod, spared for the moment, followed their operations a little while with his eyes, but not with his mind; then, sinking deeper in his seat, limply abandoned the effort. His eyes remained open, but saw nothing; the routine of the arithmetic lesson reached his ears in familiar, meaningless sounds, but he heard nothing; and yet, this time, he was profoundly occupied. He had drifted away from the painful land of facts, and floated now in a new sea of fancy which he had just discovered.

Maturity forgets the marvellous realness of a boy's day-dreams, how colourful they glow, rosy and living, and how opaque the curtain closing down between the dreamer and the actual world. That curtain is almost sound-proof, too, and causes more throat-trouble among parents than is suspected.

The nervous monotony of the schoolroom inspires a sometimes unbearable longing for something astonishing to happen, and as every boy's fundamental desire is to do something astonishing himself, so as to be the centre of all human interest and awe, it was natural that Penrod should discover in fancy the delightful secret of self-levitation. He found, in this curious series of imaginings, during the lesson in arithmetic, that the atmosphere may be navigated as by a swimmer under water, but with infinitely greater ease and with perfect comfort in breathing. In his mind he extended his arms gracefully, at a level with his shoulders, and delicately paddled the air with his hands, which at once caused him to be drawn up out of his seat and elevated gently to a position about midway between the floor and the ceiling, where he came to an equilibrium and floated; a sensation not the less exquisite because of the screams of his fellow pupils, appalled by the miracle. Miss Spence herself was amazed and frightened, but he only smiled down carelessly upon her when she commanded him to return to earth; and then, when she climbed upon a desk to pull him down, he quietly paddled himself a little higher, leaving his toes just out of her reach. Next, he swam through a few slow somersaults to show his mastery of the new art, and, with the shouting of the dumfounded scholars ringing in his ears, turned on his side and floated swiftly out of the window, immediately rising above the housetops, while people in the street below him shrieked, and a trolley car stopped dead in wonder.

With almost no exertion he paddled himself, many yards at a stroke, to the girls' private school where Marjorie Jones was a pupil--Marjorie Jones of the amber curls and the golden voice! Long before the "Pageant of the Table Round," she had offered Penrod a hundred proofs that she considered him wholly undesirable and ineligible. At the Friday Afternoon Dancing Class she consistently incited and led the laughter at him whenever Professor Bartet singled him out for admonition in matters of feet and decorum. And but yesterday she had chid him for his slavish lack of memory in daring to offer her a greeting on the way to Sunday-school. "Well! I expect you must forgot I told you never to speak to me again! If I was a boy, I'd be too proud to come hanging around people that don't speak to me, even if I was the Worst Boy in Town!" So she flouted him. But now, as he floated in through the window of her classroom and swam gently along the ceiling like an escaped toy balloon, she fell upon her knees beside her little desk, and, lifting up her arms toward him, cried with love and admiration:

"Oh, Penrod!"

He negligently kicked a globe from the high chandelier, and, smiling coldly, floated out through the hall to the front steps of the school, while Marjorie followed, imploring him to grant her one kind look.

In the street an enormous crowd had gathered, headed by Miss Spence and a brass band; and a cheer from a hundred thousand throats shook the very ground as Penrod swam overhead. Marjorie knelt upon the steps and watched adoringly while Penrod took the drum-major's baton and, performing sinuous evolutions above the crowd, led the band. Then he threw the baton so high that it disappeared from sight; but he went swiftly after it, a double delight, for he had not only the delicious sensation of rocketing safely up and up into the blue sky, but also that of standing in the crowd below, watching and admiring himself as he dwindled to a speck, disappeared and then, emerging from a cloud, came speeding down, with the baton in his hand, to the level of the treetops, where he beat time for the band and the vast throng and Marjorie Jones, who all united in the "Star-spangled Banner" in honour of his aerial achievements. It was a great moment.

It was a great moment, but something seemed to threaten it. The face of Miss Spence looking up from the crowd grew too vivid--unpleasantly vivid. She was beckoning him and shouting, "Come down, Penrod Schofield! Penrod Schofield, come down here!"

He could hear her above the band and the singing of the multitude; she seemed intent on spoiling everything. Marjorie Jones was weeping to show how sorry she was that she had formerly slighted him, and throwing kisses to prove that she loved him; but Miss Spence kept jumping between him and Marjorie, incessantly calling his name.

He grew more and more irritated with her; he was the most important person in the world and was engaged in proving it to Marjorie Jones and the whole city, and yet Miss Spence seemed to feel she still had the right to order him about as she did in the old days when he was an ordinary schoolboy.

He was furious; he was sure she wanted him to do something disagreeable. It seemed to him that she had screamed "Penrod Schofield!" thousands of times.

From the beginning of his aerial experiments in his own schoolroom, he had not opened his lips, knowing somehow that one of the requirements for air floating is perfect silence on the part of the floater; but, finally, irritated beyond measure by Miss Spence's clamorous insistence, he was unable to restrain an indignant rebuke and immediately came to earth with a frightful bump.

Miss Spence--in the flesh--had directed toward the physical body of the absent Penrod an inquiry as to the fractional consequences of dividing seventeen apples, fairly, among three boys, and she was surprised and displeased to receive no answer although to the best of her knowledge and belief, he was looking fixedly at her. She repeated her question crisply, without visible effect; then summoned him by name with increasing asperity. Twice she called him, while all his fellow pupils turned to stare at the gazing boy. She advanced a step from the platform.

"Penrod Schofield!"

"Oh, my goodness!" he shouted suddenly. "Can't you keep still a minute?"

Lesson 57

1. Read chapters 10 and 11 of *Penrod.*
2. Take notes on characters. What are you learning about Penrod? others?
3. What does this sentence mean? "Nothing is more treacherous than the human mind; nothing else so loves to play the Iscariot." (hint: Iscariot refers to Judas Iscariot, the man who betrayed Jesus) (Answers)

Chapter X. Uncle John
Miss Spence gasped. So did the pupils.

The whole room filled with a swelling conglomerate "O-O-O-O-H!"

As for Penrod himself, the walls reeled with the shock. He sat with his mouth open, a mere lump of stupefaction. For the appalling words that he had hurled at the teacher were as inexplicable to him as to any other who heard them.

Nothing is more treacherous than the human mind; nothing else so loves to play the Iscariot. Even when patiently bullied into a semblance of order and training, it may prove but a base and shifty servant. And Penrod's mind was not his servant; it was a master, with the April wind's whims; and it had just played him a diabolical trick. The very jolt with which he came back to the schoolroom in the midst of his fancied flight jarred his day-dream utterly out of him; and he sat, open-mouthed in horror at what he had said.

The unanimous gasp of awe was protracted. Miss Spence, however, finally recovered her breath, and, returning deliberately to the platform, faced the school. "And then for a little while," as pathetic stories sometimes recount, "everything was very still." It was so still, in fact, that Penrod's newborn notoriety could almost be heard growing. This grisly silence was at last broken by the teacher.

"Penrod Schofield, stand up!"

The miserable child obeyed.

"What did you mean by speaking to me in that way?"

He hung his head, raked the floor with the side of his shoe, swayed, swallowed, looked suddenly at his hands with the air of never having seen them before, then clasped them behind him. The school shivered in ecstatic horror, every fascinated eye upon him; yet there was not a soul in the room but was profoundly grateful to him for the sensation--including the offended teacher herself. Unhappily, all this gratitude was unconscious and altogether different from the kind which, results in testimonials and loving-cups. On the contrary!

"Penrod Schofield!"

He gulped.

"Answer me at once! Why did you speak to me like that?"

"I was----" He choked, unable to continue.

"Speak out!"

"I was just--thinking," he managed to stammer.

"That will not do," she returned sharply. "I wish to know immediately why you spoke as you did."

The stricken Penrod answered helplessly:

"Because I was just thinking."

Upon the very rack he could have offered no ampler truthful explanation. It was all he knew about it.

"Thinking what?"

"Just thinking."

Miss Spence's expression gave evidence that her power of self-restraint was undergoing a remarkable test. However, after taking counsel with herself, she commanded:

"Come here!"

He shuffled forward, and she placed a chair upon the platform near her own.

"Sit there!"

Then (but not at all as if nothing had happened), she continued the lesson in arithmetic. Spiritually the children may have learned a lesson in very small fractions indeed as they gazed at the fragment of sin before them on the stool of penitence. They all stared at him attentively with hard and passionately interested eyes, in which there was never one trace of pity. It cannot be said with precision that he writhed; his movement was more a slow, continuous squirm, effected with a ghastly assumption of languid indifference; while his gaze, in the effort to escape the marble-hearted glare of his schoolmates, affixed itself with apparent permanence to the waistcoat button of James Russell Lowell just above the "U" in "Russell."

Classes came and classes went, grilling him with eyes. Newcomers received the story of the crime in darkling whispers; and the outcast sat and sat and sat, and squirmed and squirmed and squirmed. (He did one or two things with his spine which a professional contortionist would have observed with real interest.) And all this while of freezing suspense was but the criminal's detention awaiting trial. A known punishment may be anticipated with some measure of equanimity; at least, the prisoner may prepare himself to undergo it; but the unknown looms more monstrous for every attempt to guess it. Penrod's crime was unique; there were no rules to aid him in estimating the vengeance to fall upon him for it. What seemed most probable was that he would be expelled from the schools in the presence of his family, the mayor, and council, and afterward whipped by his father upon the State House steps, with the entire city as audience by invitation of the authorities.

Noon came. The rows of children filed out, every head turning for a last unpleasingly speculative look at the outlaw. Then Miss Spence closed the door into the cloakroom and that into the big hall, and came and sat at her desk, near Penrod. The tramping of feet outside, the shrill calls and shouting and the changing voices of the older boys ceased to be heard--and there was silence. Penrod, still affecting to be occupied with Lowell, was conscious that Miss Spence looked at him intently.

"Penrod," she said gravely, "what excuse have you to offer before I report your case to the principal?"
The word "principal" struck him to the vitals. Grand Inquisitor, Grand Khan, Sultan, Emperor, Tsar, Caesar Augustus--these are comparable. He stopped squirming instantly, and sat rigid.

"I want an answer. Why did you shout those words at me?"

"Well," he murmured, "I was just--thinking."

"Thinking what?" she asked sharply.

"I don't know."

"That won't do!"

He took his left ankle in his right hand and regarded it helplessly.

"That won't do, Penrod Schofield," she repeated severely. "If that is all the excuse you have to offer I shall report your case this instant!"

And she rose with fatal intent.

But Penrod was one of those whom the precipice inspires. "Well, I have got an excuse."

"Well"--she paused impatiently--"what is it?"

He had not an idea, but he felt one coming, and replied automatically, in a plaintive tone:

"I guess anybody that had been through what I had to go through, last night, would think they had an excuse."

Miss Spence resumed her seat, though with the air of being ready to leap from it instantly.

"What has last night to do with your insolence to me this morning?"

"Well, I guess you'd see," he returned, emphasizing the plaintive note, "if you knew what I know."

"Now, Penrod," she said, in a kinder voice, "I have a high regard for your mother and father, and it would hurt me to distress them, but you must either tell me what was the matter with you or I'll have to take you to Mrs. Houston."

"Well, ain't I going to?" he cried, spurred by the dread name. "It's because I didn't sleep last night."

"Were you ill?" The question was put with some dryness.

He felt the dryness. "No'm; I wasn't."

"Then if someone in your family was so ill that even you were kept up all night, how does it happen they let you come to school this morning?"

"It wasn't illness," he returned, shaking his head mournfully. "It was lots worse'n anybody's being sick. It was--it was--well, it was jest awful."

"What was?" He remarked with anxiety the incredulity in her tone.

"It was about Aunt Clara," he said.

"Your Aunt Clara!" she repeated. "Do you mean your mother's sister who married Mr. Farry of Dayton, Illinois?"

"Yes--Uncle John," returned Penrod sorrowfully. "The trouble was about him."

Miss Spence frowned a frown which he rightly interpreted as one of continued suspicion. "She and I were in school together," she said. "I used to know her very well, and I've always heard her married life was entirely happy. I don't----"

"Yes, it was," he interrupted, "until last year when Uncle John took to running with travelling men----"

"What?"

"Yes'm." He nodded solemnly. "That was what started it. At first he was a good, kind husband, but these travelling men would coax him into a saloon on his way home from work, and they got him to drinking beer and then ales, wines, liquors, and cigars----"

"Penrod!"

"Ma'am?"

"I'm not inquiring into your Aunt Clara's private affairs; I'm asking you if you have anything to say which would palliate----"

"That's what I'm tryin' to tell you about, Miss Spence," he pleaded,--"if you'd jest only let me. When Aunt Clara and her little baby daughter got to our house last night----"

"You say Mrs. Farry is visiting your mother?"

"Yes'm--not just visiting--you see, she had to come. Well of course, little baby Clara, she was so bruised up and mauled, where he'd been hittin' her with his cane----"
"You mean that your uncle had done such a thing as that!" exclaimed Miss Spence, suddenly disarmed by this scandal.

"Yes'm, and mamma and Margaret had to sit up all night nursin' little Clara--and Aunt Clara was in such a state somebody had to keep talkin' to her, and there wasn't anybody but me to do it, so I----"

"But where was your father?" she cried.

"Ma'am?"

"Where was your father while----"

"Oh--papa?" Penrod paused, reflected; then brightened. "Why, he was down at the train, waitin' to see if Uncle John would try to follow 'em and make 'em come home so's he could persecute 'em some more. I wanted to do that, but they said if he did come I mightn't be strong enough to hold him and----" The brave lad paused again, modestly. Miss Spence's expression was encouraging. Her eyes were wide with astonishment, and there may have been in them, also, the mingled beginnings of admiration and self-reproach. Penrod, warming to his work, felt safer every moment.

"And so," he continued, "I had to sit up with Aunt Clara. She had some pretty big bruises, too, and I had to----"

"But why didn't they send for a doctor?" However, this question was only a flicker of dying incredulity.

"Oh, they didn't want any doctor," exclaimed the inspired realist promptly. "They don't want anybody to hear about it because Uncle John might reform--and then where'd he be if everybody knew he'd been a drunkard and whipped his wife and baby daughter?"

"Oh!" said Miss Spence.

"You see, he used to be upright as anybody," he went on explanatively. "It all begun----"

"Began, Penrod."

"Yes'm. It all commenced from the first day he let those travelling men coax him into the saloon." Penrod narrated the downfall of his Uncle John at length. In detail he was nothing short of plethoric; and incident followed incident, sketched with such vividness, such abundance of colour, and such verisimilitude to a drunkard's life as a drunkard's life should be, that had Miss Spence possessed the rather chilling attributes of William J. Burns himself, the last trace of skepticism must have vanished from her mind. Besides, there are two things that will be believed of any man whatsoever, and one of them is that he has taken to drink. And in every sense it was a moving picture which, with simple but eloquent words, the virtuous Penrod set before his teacher.

His eloquence increased with what it fed on; and as with the eloquence so with self-reproach in the gentle bosom of the teacher. She cleared her throat with difficulty once or twice, during his description of his ministering night with Aunt Clara. "And I said to her, 'Why, Aunt Clara, what's the use of takin' on so about it?' And I said, 'Now, Aunt Clara, all the crying in the world can't make things any better.' And then she'd just keep catchin' hold of me, and sob and kind of holler, and I'd say, 'Don't cry, Aunt Clara--please don't cry.'"

Then, under the influence of some fragmentary survivals of the respectable portion of his Sunday adventures, his theme became more exalted; and, only partially misquoting a phrase from a psalm, he related how he had made it of comfort to Aunt Clara, and how he had besought her to seek Higher guidance in her trouble.

The surprising thing about a structure such as Penrod was erecting is that the taller it becomes the more ornamentation it will stand. Gifted boys have this faculty of building magnificence upon cobwebs--and Penrod was gifted. Under the spell of his really great performance, Miss Spence gazed more and more sweetly upon the prodigy of spiritual beauty and goodness before her, until at last, when Penrod came to the explanation of his "just thinking," she was forced to turn her head away.

"You mean, dear," she said gently, "that you were all worn out and hardly knew what you were saying?"

"Yes'm."

"And you were thinking about all those dreadful things so hard that you forgot where you were?"

"I was thinking," he said simply, "how to save Uncle John."

And the end of it for this mighty boy was that the teacher kissed him!

Chapter XI. Fidelity of a Little Dog

The returning students, that afternoon, observed that Penrod's desk was vacant--and nothing could have been more impressive than that sinister mere emptiness. The accepted theory was that Penrod had been arrested. How breathtaking, then, the sensation when, at the beginning of the second hour, he strolled--in with inimitable carelessness and, rubbing his eyes, somewhat noticeably in the manner of one who has snatched an hour of much needed sleep, took his place as if nothing in particular had happened. This, at first supposed to be a superhuman exhibition of sheer audacity, became but the more dumfounding when Miss Spence--looking up from her desk--greeted him with a pleasant little nod. Even after school, Penrod gave numerous maddened investigators no relief. All he would consent to say was:

"Oh, I just talked to her."

A mystification not entirely unconnected with the one thus produced was manifested at his own family. dinner-table the following evening. Aunt Clara had been out rather late, and came to the table after the rest were seated. She wore a puzzled expression.

"Do you ever see Mary Spence nowadays?" she inquired, as she unfolded her napkin, addressing Mrs. Schofield. Penrod abruptly set down his soup-spoon and gazed at his aunt with flattering attention.

"Yes; sometimes," said Mrs. Schofield. "She's Penrod's teacher."

"Is she?" said Mrs. Farry. "Do you--" She paused. "Do people think her a little--queer, these days?"

"Why, no," returned her sister. "What makes you say that?"

"She has acquired a very odd manner," said Mrs. Farry decidedly. "At least, she seemed odd to me. I met her at the corner just before I got to the house, a few minutes ago, and after we'd said howdy-do to each other, she kept hold of my hand and looked as though she was going to cry. She seemed to be trying to say something, and choking----"

"But I don't think that's so very queer, Clara. She knew you in school, didn't she?"

"Yes, but----"

"And she hadn't seen you for so many years, I think it's perfectly natural she----"

"Wait! She stood there squeezing my hand, and struggling to get her voice--and I got really embarrassed--and then finally she said, in a kind of tearful whisper, 'Be of good cheer--this trial will pass!'"

"How queer!" exclaimed Margaret.

Penrod sighed, and returned somewhat absently to his soup.

"Well, I don't know," said Mrs. Schofield thoughtfully. "Of course she's heard about the outbreak of measles in Dayton, since they had to close the schools, and she knows you live there----"

"But doesn't it seem a very exaggerated way," suggested Margaret, "to talk about measles?"

"Wait!" begged Aunt Clara. "After she said that, she said something even queerer, and then put her handkerchief to her eyes and hurried away."

Penrod laid down his spoon again and moved his chair slightly back from the table. A spirit of prophecy was upon him: he knew that someone was going to ask a question which he felt might better remain unspoken.

"What was the other thing she said?" Mr. Schofield inquired, thus immediately fulfilling his son's premonition.

"She said," returned Mrs. Farry slowly, looking about the table, "she said, 'I know that Penrod is a great, great comfort to you!'"

There was a general exclamation of surprise. It was a singular thing, and in no manner may it be considered complimentary to Penrod, that this speech of Miss Spence's should have immediately confirmed Mrs. Farry's doubts about her in the minds of all his family.

Mr. Schofield shook his head pityingly.

"I'm afraid she's a goner," he went so far as to say.

"Of all the weird ideas!" cried Margaret.

"I never heard anything like it in my life!" Mrs. Schofield exclaimed. "Was that all she said?"

"Every word!"

Penrod again resumed attention to his soup. His mother looked at him curiously, and then, struck by a sudden thought, gathered the glances of the adults of the table by a significant movement of the head, and, by another, conveyed an admonition to drop the subject until later. Miss Spence was Penrod's teacher: it was better, for many reasons, not to discuss the subject of her queerness before him. This was Mrs. Schofield's thought at the time. Later she had another, and it kept her awake.

The next afternoon, Mr. Schofield, returning at five o'clock from the cares of the day, found the house deserted, and sat down to read his evening paper in what appeared to be an uninhabited apartment known to its own world as the "drawing-room." A sneeze, unexpected both to him and the owner, informed him of the presence of another person.

"Where are you, Penrod?" the parent asked, looking about.

"Here," said Penrod meekly.

Stooping, Mr. Schofield discovered his son squatting under the piano, near an open window--his wistful Duke lying beside him.

"What are you doing there?"

"Me?"

"Why under the piano?"

"Well," the boy returned, with grave sweetness, "I was just kind of sitting here--thinking."

"All right." Mr. Schofield, rather touched, returned to the digestion of a murder, his back once more to the piano; and Penrod silently drew from beneath his jacket (where he had slipped it simultaneously with the sneeze) a paper-backed volume entitled: "Slimsy, the Sioux City Squealer, or, 'Not Guilty, Your Honor.'"

In this manner the reading-club continued in peace, absorbed, contented, the world well forgot-- until a sudden, violently irritated slam-bang of the front door startled the members; and Mrs. Schofield burst into the room and threw herself into a chair, moaning.

"What's the matter, mamma?" asked her husband laying aside his paper.

"Henry Passloe Schofield," returned the lady, "I don't know what is to be done with that boy; I do not!"

"You mean Penrod?"

"Who else could I mean?" She sat up, exasperated, to stare at him. "Henry Passloe Schofield, you've got to take this matter in your hands--it's beyond me!"

"Well, what has he----"

"Last night I got to thinking," she began rapidly, "about what Clara told us--thank Heaven she and Margaret and little Clara have gone to tea at Cousin Charlotte's!--but they'll be home soon--about what she said about Miss Spence----"

"You mean about Penrod's being a comfort?"

"Yes, and I kept thinking and thinking and thinking about it till I couldn't stand it any----"

"By george!" shouted Mr. Schofield startlingly, stooping to look under the piano. A statement that he had suddenly remembered his son's presence would be lacking in accuracy, for the highly sensitized Penrod was, in fact, no longer present. No more was Duke, his faithful dog.

"What's the matter?"

"Nothing," he returned, striding to the open window and looking out. "Go on."

"Oh," she moaned, "it must be kept from Clara--and I'll never hold up my head again if John Farry ever hears of it!"

"Hears of what?"

"Well, I just couldn't stand it, I got so curious; and I thought of course if Miss Spence had become a little unbalanced it was my duty to know it, as Penrod's mother and she his teacher; so I thought I would just call on her at her apartment after school and have a chat and see and I did and--oh--"

"Well?"

"I've just come from there, and she told me--she told me! Oh, I've never known anything like this!"

"What did she tell you?"

Mrs. Schofield, making a great effort, managed to assume a temporary appearance of calm. "Henry," she said solemnly, "bear this in mind: whatever you do to Penrod, it must be done in some place when Clara won't hear it. But the first thing to do is to find him."

Within view of the window from which Mr. Schofield was gazing was the closed door of the storeroom in the stable, and just outside this door Duke was performing a most engaging trick.

His young master had taught Duke to "sit up and beg" when he wanted anything, and if that didn't get it, to "speak." Duke was facing the closed door and sitting up and begging, and now he also spoke--in a loud, clear bark.

There was an open transom over the door, and from this descended--hurled by an unseen agency-- a can half filled with old paint.

It caught the small besieger of the door on his thoroughly surprised right ear, encouraged him to some remarkable acrobatics, and turned large portions of him a dull blue. Allowing only a moment to perplexity, and deciding, after a single and evidently unappetizing experiment, not to cleanse himself of paint, the loyal animal resumed his quaint, upright posture.

Mr. Schofield seated himself on the window-sill, whence he could keep in view that pathetic picture of unrequited love.

"Go on with your story, mamma," he said. "I think I can find Penrod when we want him."

And a few minutes later he added, "And I think I know the place to do it in."

Again the faithful voice of Duke was heard, pleading outside the bolted door.

Lesson 58

1. Read chapters 12 and 13 of *Penrod*.
2. Be on the lookout for words you don't know. Write down at least one along with the definition of the word.

Chapter XII. Miss Rennsdale Accepts

"One-two-three; one-two-three--glide!" said Professor Bartet, emphasizing his instructions by a brisk collision of his palms at "glide." "One-two-three; one-two-three--glide!"

The school week was over, at last, but Penrod's troubles were not.

Round and round the ballroom went the seventeen struggling little couples of the Friday Afternoon Dancing Class. Round and round went their reflections with them, swimming rhythmically in the polished, dark floor--white and blue and pink for the girls; black, with dabs of white, for the white-collared, white-gloved boys; and sparks and slivers of high light everywhere as the glistening pumps flickered along the surface like a school of flying fish. Every small pink face--with one exception--was painstaking and set for duty. It was a conscientious little merry-go-round.

"One-two-three; one-two-three--glide! One-two-three; one-two-three--glide! One-two-th--Ha! Mister Penrod Schofield, you lose the step. Your left foot! No, no! This is the left! See--like me! Now again! One-two-three; one-two-three--glide! Better! Much better! Again! One-two-three; one-two-three--gl--Stop! Mr. Penrod Schofield, this dancing class is provided by the kind parents of the pupilses as much to learn the mannerss of good societies as to dance. You think you shall ever see a gentleman in good societies to tickle his partner in the dance till she say Ouch? Never! I assure you it is not done. Again! Now then! Piano, please! One-two-three; one-two-three--glide! Mr. Penrod Schofield, your right foot--your right foot! No, no! Stop!"

The merry-go-round came to a standstill.

"Mr. Penrod Schofield and partner"--Professor Bartet wiped his brow--"will you kindly observe me? One-two-three--glide! So! Now then--no; you will please keep your places, ladies and gentlemen. Mr. Penrod Schofield, I would puttickly like your attention, this is for you!"

"Pickin' on me again!" murmured the smouldering Penrod to his small, unsympathetic partner. "Can't let me alone a minute!"

"Mister Georgie Bassett, please step to the centre," said the professor.

Mr. Bassett complied with modest alacrity.

"Teacher's pet!" whispered Penrod hoarsely. He had nothing but contempt for Georgie Bassett. The parents, guardians, aunts, uncles, cousins, governesses, housemaids, cooks, chauffeurs and coachmen, appertaining to the members of the dancing class, all dwelt in the same part of town and shared certain communal theories; and among the most firmly established was that which maintained Georgie Bassett to be the Best Boy in Town. Contrariwise, the unfortunate Penrod, largely because of his recent dazzling but disastrous attempts to control forces far beyond him, had been given a clear title as the Worst Boy in Town. (Population, 135,000.) To precisely what degree his reputation was the product of his own energies cannot be calculated. It was Marjorie Jones who first applied the description, in its definite simplicity, the day after the "pageant," and, possibly, her frequent and effusive repetitions of it, even upon wholly irrelevant occasions, had something to do with its prompt and quite perfect acceptance by the community.

"Miss Rennsdale will please do me the fafer to be Mr. Georgie Bassett's partner for one moment," said Professor Bartet. "Mr. Penrod Schofield will please give his attention. Miss Rennsdale and Mister Bassett, obliche me, if you please. Others please watch. Piano, please! Now then!"

Miss Rennsdale, aged eight--the youngest lady in the class-- and Mr. Georgie Bassett one-two-three--glided with consummate technique for the better education of Penrod Schofield. It is possible that amber-curled, beautiful Marjorie felt that she, rather than Miss Rennsdale, might have been selected as the example of perfection--or perhaps her remark was only woman.

"Stopping everybody for that boy!" said Marjorie.

Penrod, across the circle from her, heard distinctly--nay, he was obviously intended to hear; but over a scorched heart he preserved a stoic front. Whereupon Marjorie whispered derisively in the ear of her partner, Maurice Levy, who wore a pearl pin in his tie.

"Again, please, everybody--ladies and gentlemen!" cried Professor Bartet. "Mister Penrod Schofield, if you please, pay puttickly attention! Piano, please! Now then!"

The lesson proceeded. At the close of the hour Professor Bartet stepped to the centre of the room and clapped his hands for attention.

"Ladies and gentlemen, if you please to seat yourselves quietly," he said; "I speak to you now about to-morrow. As you all know--Mister Penrod Schofield, I am not sticking up in a tree outside that window! If you do me the fafer to examine I am here, insides of the room. Now then! Piano, pl--no, I do not wish the piano! As you all know, this is the last lesson of the season until next October. Tomorrow is our special afternoon; beginning three o'clock, we dance the cotillon. But this afternoon comes the test of mannerss. You must see if each know how to make a little formal call like a grown-up people in good societies. You have had good, perfect instruction; let us see if we know how to perform like societies ladies and gentlemen twenty-six years of age.

"Now, when you're dismissed each lady will go to her home and prepare to receive a call. The gentlemen will allow the ladies time to reach their houses and to prepare to receive callers; then each gentleman will call upon a lady and beg the pleasure to engage her for a partner in the cotillon to-morrow. You all know the correct, proper form for these calls, because didn't I work teaching you last lesson till I thought I would drop dead? Yes! Now each gentleman, if he reach a lady's house behind some-other gentleman, then he must go somewhere else to a lady's house, and keep calling until he secures a partner; so, as there are the same number of both, everybody shall have a partner.

"Now please all remember that if in case--Mister Penrod Schofield, when you make your call on a lady I beg you to please remember that gentlemen in good societies do not scratch the back in societies as you appear to attempt; so please allow the hands to rest carelessly in the lap. Now please all remember that if in case--Mister Penrod Schofield, if you please! Gentlemen in societies do not scratch the back by causing frictions between it and the back of your chair, either! Nobody else is itching here! I do not itch! I cannot talk if you must itch! In the name of Heaven, why must you always itch? What was I saying? Where ah! the cotillon--yes! For the cotillon it is important nobody shall fail to be here tomorrow; but if any one should be so very ill he cannot possible come he must write a very polite note of regrets in the form of good societies to his engaged partner to excuse himself--and he must give the reason.

"I do not think anybody is going to be that sick to-morrow--no; and I will find out and report to parents if anybody would try it and not be. But it is important for the cotillon that we have an even number of so many couples, and if it should happen that someone comes and her partner has sent her a polite note that he has genuine reasons why he cannot come, the note must be handed at once to me, so that I arrange some other partner. Is all understood? Yes. The gentlemen will remember now to allow the ladies plenty of time to reach their houses and prepare to receive calls. Ladies and gentlemen, I thank you for your polite attention."

It was nine blocks to the house of Marjorie Jones; but Penrod did it in less than seven minutes from a flying start--such was his haste to lay himself and his hand for the cotillon at the feet of one who had so recently spoken unamiably of him in public. He had not yet learned that the only safe male rebuke to a scornful female is to stay away from her--especially if that is what she desires. However, he did not wish to rebuke her; simply and ardently he wished to dance the cotillon with her. Resentment was swallowed up in hope.

The fact that Miss Jones' feeling for him bore a striking resemblance to that of Simon Legree for Uncle Tom, deterred him not at all. Naturally, he was not wholly unconscious that when he should lay his hand for the cotillon at her feet it would be her inward desire to step on it; but he believed that if he were first in the field Marjorie would have to accept. These things are governed by law.

It was his fond intention to reach her house even in advance of herself, and with grave misgiving he beheld a large automobile at rest before the sainted gate. Forthwith, a sinking feeling became a portent inside him as little Maurice Levy emerged from the front door of the house.

"'Lo, Penrod!" said Maurice airily.

"What you doin' in there?" inquired Penrod.
"In where?"

"In Marjorie's."

"Well, what shouldn't I be doin' in Marjorie's?" Mr. Levy returned indignantly. "I was inviting her for my partner in the cotillon--what you s'pose?"

"You haven't got any right to!" Penrod protested hotly. "You can't do it yet."

"I did do it yet!" said Maurice.

"You can't!" insisted Penrod. "You got to allow them time first. He said the ladies had to be allowed time to prepare."

"Well, ain't she had time to prepare?"

"When?" Penrod demanded, stepping close to his rival threateningly. "I'd like to know when----"

"When?" echoed the other with shrill triumph. "When? Why, in mamma's sixty-horse powder limousine automobile, what Marjorie came home with me in! I guess that's when!"

An impulse in the direction of violence became visible upon the countenance of Penrod.

"I expect you need some wiping down," he began dangerously. "I'll give you sumpthing to remem----"

"Oh, you will!" Maurice cried with astonishing truculence, contorting himself into what he may have considered a posture of defense. "Let's see you try it, you--you itcher!"

For the moment, defiance from such a source was dumfounding. Then, luckily, Penrod recollected something and glanced at the automobile.

Perceiving therein not only the alert chauffeur but the magnificent outlines of Mrs. Levy, his enemy's mother, he manoeuvred his lifted hand so that it seemed he had but meant to scratch his ear.

"Well, I guess I better be goin'," he said casually. "See you tomorrow!"

Maurice mounted to the lap of luxury, and Penrod strolled away with an assumption of careless ease which was put to a severe strain when, from the rear window of the car, a sudden protuberance in the nature of a small, dark, curly head shrieked scornfully:

"Go on--you big stiff!"

The cotillon loomed dismally before Penrod now; but it was his duty to secure a partner and he set about it with a dreary heart. The delay occasioned by his fruitless attempt on Marjorie and the altercation with his enemy at her gate had allowed other ladies ample time to prepare for callers-- and to receive them. Sadly he went from house to house, finding that he had been preceded in one after the other. Altogether his hand for the cotillon was declined eleven times that afternoon on the legitimate ground of previous engagement. This, with Marjorie, scored off all except five of the seventeen possible partners; and four of the five were also sealed away from him, as he learned in chance encounters with other boys upon the street.

One lady alone remained; he bowed to the inevitable and entered this lorn damsel's gate at twilight with an air of great discouragement. The lorn damsel was Miss Rennsdale, aged eight.

We are apt to forget that there are actually times of life when too much youth is a handicap. Miss Rennsdale was beautiful; she danced like a premiere; she had every charm but age. On that account alone had she been allowed so much time to prepare to receive callers that it was only by the most manful efforts she could keep her lip from trembling.

A decorous maid conducted the long-belated applicant to her where she sat upon a sofa beside a nursery governess. The decorous maid announced him composedly as he made his entrance.

"Mr. Penrod Schofield!"

Miss Rennsdale suddenly burst into loud sobs.

"Oh!" she wailed. "I just knew it would be him!"

The decorous maid's composure vanished at once--likewise her decorum. She clapped her hand over her mouth and fled, uttering sounds. The governess, however, set herself to comfort her heartbroken charge, and presently succeeded in restoring Miss Rennsdale to a semblance of that poise with which a lady receives callers and accepts invitations to dance cotillons. But she continued to sob at intervals.

Feeling himself at perhaps a disadvantage, Penrod made offer of his hand for the morrow with a little embarrassment. Following the form prescribed by Professor Bartet, he advanced several paces toward the stricken lady and bowed formally.

"I hope," he said by rote, "you're well, and your parents also in good health. May I have the pleasure of dancing the cotillon as your partner t'-morrow afternoon?"

The wet eyes of Miss Rennsdale searched his countenance without pleasure, and a shudder wrung her small shoulders; but the governess whispered to her instructively, and she made a great effort.

"I thu-thank you fu-for your polite invu-invu-invutation; and I ac----" Thus far she progressed when emotion overcame her again. She beat frantically upon the sofa with fists and heels. "Oh, I did want it to be Georgie Bassett!"

"No, no, no!" said the governess, and whispered urgently, whereupon Miss Rennsdale was able to complete her acceptance.

"And I ac-accept wu-with pu-pleasure!" she moaned, and immediately, uttering a loud yell, flung herself face downward upon the sofa, clutching her governess convulsively.

Somewhat disconcerted, Penrod bowed again.

"I thank you for your polite acceptance," he murmured hurriedly; "and I trust--I trust--I forget. Oh, yes--I trust we shall have a most enjoyable occasion. Pray present my compliments to your parents; and I must now wish you a very good afternoon."

Concluding these courtly demonstrations with another bow he withdrew in fair order, though thrown into partial confusion in the hall by a final wail from his crushed hostess:

"Oh! Why couldn't it be anybody but him!"

Chapter XIII. The Smallpox Medicine

Next morning Penrod woke in profound depression of spirit, the cotillon ominous before him. He pictured Marjorie Jones and Maurice, graceful and light-hearted, flitting by him fairylike, loosing silvery laughter upon him as he engaged in the struggle to keep step with a partner about four years and two feet his junior. It was hard enough for Penrod to keep step with a girl of his size.

The foreboding vision remained with him, increasing in vividness, throughout the forenoon. He found himself unable to fix his mind upon anything else, and, having bent his gloomy footsteps toward the sawdust-box, after breakfast, presently descended therefrom, abandoning Harold Ramorez where he had left him the preceding Saturday. Then, as he sat communing silently with wistful Duke, in the storeroom, coquettish fortune looked his way.

It was the habit of Penrod's mother not to throw away anything whatsoever until years of storage conclusively proved there would never be a use for it; but a recent house-cleaning had ejected upon the back porch a great quantity of bottles and other paraphernalia of medicine, left over from illnesses in the family during a period of several years. This debris Della, the cook, had collected in a large market basket, adding to it some bottles of flavouring extracts that had proved unpopular in the household; also, old catsup bottles; a jar or two of preserves gone bad; various rejected dental liquids--and other things. And she carried the basket out to the storeroom in the stable.

Penrod was at first unaware of what lay before him. Chin on palms, he sat upon the iron rim of a former aquarium and stared morbidly through the open door at the checkered departing back of Della. It was another who saw treasure in the basket she had left.

Mr. Samuel Williams, aged eleven, and congenial to Penrod in years, sex, and disposition, appeared in the doorway, shaking into foam a black liquid within a pint bottle, stoppered by a thumb.

"Yay, Penrod!" the visitor gave greeting.

"Yay," said Penrod with slight enthusiasm. "What you got?"

"Lickrish water."

"Drinkin's!" demanded Penrod promptly. This is equivalent to the cry of "Biters" when an apple is shown, and establishes unquestionable title.

"Down to there!" stipulated Sam, removing his thumb to affix it firmly as a mark upon the side of the bottle a check upon gormandizing that remained carefully in place while Penrod drank.

This rite concluded, the visitor's eye fell upon the basket deposited by Della. He emitted tokens of pleasure.

"Looky! Looky! Looky there! That ain't any good pile o' stuff--oh, no!"

"What for?"

"Drug store!" shouted Sam. "We'll be partners----"

"Or else," Penrod suggested, "I'll run the drug store and you be a customer----"

"No! Partners!" insisted Sam with such conviction that his host yielded; and within ten minutes the drug store was doing a heavy business with imaginary patrons. Improvising counters with boards and boxes, and setting forth a very druggish-looking stock from the basket, each of the partners found occupation to his taste--Penrod as salesman and Sam as prescription clerk.

"Here you are, madam!" said Penrod briskly, offering a vial of Sam's mixing to an invisible matron. "This will cure your husband in a few minutes. Here's the camphor, mister. Call again! Fifty cents' worth of pills? Yes, madam. There you are! Hurry up with that dose for the lady, Bill!"

"I'll 'tend to it soon's I get time, Jim," replied the prescription clerk. "I'm busy fixin' the smallpox medicine for the sick policeman downtown."

Penrod stopped sales to watch this operation. Sam had found an empty pint bottle and, with the pursed lips and measuring eye of a great chemist, was engaged in filling it from other bottles.

First, he poured into it some of the syrup from the condemned preserves; and a quantity of extinct hair oil; next the remaining contents of a dozen small vials cryptically labelled with physicians' prescriptions; then some remnants of catsup and essence of beef and what was left in several bottles of mouthwash; after that a quantity of rejected flavouring extract--topping off by shaking into the mouth of the bottle various powders from small pink papers, relics of Mr. Schofield's influenza of the preceding winter.

Sam examined the combination with concern, appearing unsatisfied. "We got to make that smallpox medicine good and strong!" he remarked; and, his artistic sense growing more powerful than his appetite, he poured about a quarter of the licorice water into the smallpox medicine.

"What you doin'?" protested Penrod. "What you want to waste that lickrish water for? We ought to keep it to drink when we're tired."

"I guess I got a right to use my own lickrish water any way I want to," replied the prescription clerk. "I tell you, you can't get smallpox medicine too strong. Look at her now!" He held the bottle up admiringly. "She's as black as lickrish. I bet you she's strong all right!"

"I wonder how she tastes?" said Penrod thoughtfully.

"Don't smell so awful much," observed Sam, sniffing the bottle--"a good deal, though!"

"I wonder if it'd make us sick to drink it?" said Penrod.

Sam looked at the bottle thoughtfully; then his eye, wandering, fell upon Duke, placidly curled up near the door, and lighted with the advent of an idea new to him, but old, old in the world--older than Egypt!

"Let's give Duke some!" he cried.

That was the spark. They acted immediately; and a minute later Duke, released from custody with a competent potion of the smallpox medicine inside him, settled conclusively their doubts concerning its effect. The patient animal, accustomed to expect the worst at all times, walked out of the door, shaking his head with an air of considerable annoyance, opening and closing his mouth with singular energy--and so repeatedly that they began to count the number of times he did it. Sam thought it was thirty-nine times, but Penrod had counted forty-one before other and more striking symptoms appeared.

All things come from Mother Earth and must return--Duke restored much at this time. Afterward, he ate heartily of grass; and then, over his shoulder, he bent upon his master one inscrutable look and departed feebly to the front yard.

The two boys had watched the process with warm interest. "I told you she was strong!" said Mr. Williams proudly.

"Yes, sir--she is!" Penrod was generous enough to admit. "I expect she's strong enough----" He paused in thought, and added:

"We haven't got a horse any more."

"I bet you she'd fix him if you had!" said Sam. And it may be that this was no idle boast.

The pharmaceutical game was not resumed; the experiment upon Duke had made the drug store commonplace and stimulated the appetite for stronger meat. Lounging in the doorway, the near-vivisectionists sipped licorice water alternately and conversed.

"I bet some of our smallpox medicine would fix ole P'fessor Bartet all right!" quoth Penrod. "I wish he'd come along and ask us for some."

"We could tell him it was lickrish water," added Sam, liking the idea. "The two bottles look almost the same."

"Then we wouldn't have to go to his ole cotillon this afternoon," Penrod sighed. "There wouldn't be any!"

"Who's your partner, Pen?"

"Who's yours?"

"Who's yours? I just ast you."

"Oh, she's all right!" And Penrod smiled boastfully.

"I bet you wanted to dance with Marjorie!" said his friend.

"Me? I wouldn't dance with that girl if she begged me to! I wouldn't dance with her to save her from drowning! I wouldn't da----"

"Oh, no--you wouldn't!" interrupted Mr. Williams skeptically.

Penrod changed his tone and became persuasive.

"Looky here, Sam," he said confidentially. "I've got 'a mighty nice partner, but my mother don't like her mother; and so I've been thinking I better not dance with her. I'll tell you what I'll do; I've got a mighty good sling in the house, and I'll give it to you if you'll change partners."

"You want to change and you don't even know who mine is!" said Sam, and he made the simple though precocious deduction: "Yours must be a lala! Well, I invited Mabel Rorebeck, and she wouldn't let me change if I wanted to. Mabel Rorebeck'd rather dance with me," he continued serenely, "than anybody; and she said she was awful afraid you'd ast her. But I ain't goin' to dance with Mabel after all, because this morning she sent me a note about her uncle died last night--and P'fessor Bartet'll have to find me a partner after I get there. Anyway I bet you haven't got any sling--and I bet your partner's Baby Rennsdale!"

"What if she is?" said Penrod. "She's good enough for me!" This speech held not so much modesty in solution as intended praise of the lady. Taken literally, however, it was an understatement of the facts and wholly insincere.

"Yay!" jeered Mr. Williams, upon whom his friend's hypocrisy was quite wasted. "How can your mother not like her mother? Baby Rennsdale hasn't got any mother! You and her'll be a sight!"

That was Penrod's own conviction; and with this corroboration of it he grew so spiritless that he could offer no retort. He slid to a despondent sitting posture upon the door sill and gazed wretchedly upon the ground, while his companion went to replenish the licorice water at the hydrant-- enfeebling the potency of the liquor no doubt, but making up for that in quantity.

"Your mother goin' with you to the cotillon?" asked Sam when he returned.

"No. She's goin' to meet me there. She's goin' somewhere first."

"So's mine," said Sam. "I'll come by for you."

"All right."

"I better go before long. Noon whistles been blowin'."

"All right," Penrod repeated dully.

Sam turned to go, but paused. A new straw hat was peregrinating along the fence near the two boys. This hat belonged to someone passing upon the sidewalk of the cross- street; and the someone was Maurice Levy. Even as they stared, he halted and regarded them over the fence with two small, dark eyes.

Fate had brought about this moment and this confrontation.

Lesson 59
1. Read chapters 14 and 15 of *Penrod.*
2. Chapter 14's title doesn't refer to a law document. Here's a definition of constitution from dictionary.com: "the physical character of the body as to strength, health, etc."
3. Tell someone about *Penrod.* What's happening in the book?

Chapter XIV. Maurice Levy's Constitution
"Lo, Sam!" said Maurice cautiously. "What you doin'?"

Penrod at that instant had a singular experience--an intellectual shock like a flash of fire in the brain. Sitting in darkness, a great light flooded him with wild brilliance. He gasped!

"What you doin'?" repeated Mr. Levy.

Penrod sprang to his feet, seized the licorice bottle, shook it with stoppering thumb, and took a long drink with histrionic unction.

"What you doin'?" asked Maurice for the third time, Sam Williams not having decided upon a reply.

It was Penrod who answered.

"Drinkin' lickrish water," he said simply, and wiped his mouth with such delicious enjoyment that Sam's jaded thirst was instantly stimulated. He took the bottle eagerly from Penrod.

"A-a-h!" exclaimed Penrod, smacking his lips. "That was a good un!"

The eyes above the fence glistened.

"Ask him if he don't want some," Penrod whispered urgently. "Quit drinkin' it! It's no good any more. Ask him!"

"What for?" demanded the practical Sam.

"Go on and ask him!" whispered Penrod fiercely.

"Say, M'rice!" Sam called, waving the bottle. "Want some?"

"Bring it here!" Mr. Levy requested.

"Come on over and get some," returned Sam, being prompted.

"I can't. Penrod Schofield's after me."

"No, I'm not," said Penrod reassuringly. "I won't touch you, M'rice. I made up with you yesterday afternoon--don't you remember? You're all right with me, M'rice."

Maurice looked undecided. But Penrod had the delectable bottle again, and tilting it above his lips, affected to let the cool liquid purl enrichingly into him, while with his right hand he stroked his middle facade ineffably. Maurice's mouth watered.

"Here!" cried Sam, stirred again by the superb manifestations of his friend. "Gimme that!"

Penrod brought the bottle down, surprisingly full after so much gusto, but withheld it from Sam; and the two scuffled for its possession. Nothing in the world could have so worked upon the desire of the yearning observer beyond the fence.

"Honest, Penrod--you ain't goin' to touch me if I come in your yard?" he called. "Honest?"

"Cross my heart!" answered Penrod, holding the bottle away from Sam. "And we'll let you drink all you want."

Maurice hastily climbed the fence, and while he was thus occupied Mr. Samuel Williams received a great enlightenment. With startling rapidity Penrod, standing just outside the storeroom door, extended his arm within the room, deposited the licorice water upon the counter of the drug store, seized in its stead the bottle of smallpox medicine, and extended it cordially toward the advancing Maurice.

Genius is like that--great, simple, broad strokes!

Dazzled, Mr. Samuel Williams leaned against the wall. He had the sensations of one who comes suddenly into the presence of a chef-d'oeuvre. Perhaps his first coherent thought was that almost universal one on such huge occasions: "Why couldn't I have done that!"

Sam might have been even more dazzled had he guessed that he figured not altogether as a spectator in the sweeping and magnificent conception of the new Talleyrand. Sam had no partner for the cotillon. If Maurice was to be absent from that festivity--as it began to seem he might be-- Penrod needed a male friend to take care of Miss Rennsdale and he believed he saw his way to compel Mr. Williams to be that male friend. For this he relied largely upon the prospective conduct of Miss Rennsdale when he should get the matter before her--he was inclined to believe she would favour the exchange. As for Talleyrand Penrod himself, he was going to dance that cotillon with Marjorie Jones!

"You can have all you can drink at one pull, M'rice," said Penrod kindly.

"You said I could have all I want!" protested Maurice, reaching for the bottle.

"No, I didn't," returned Penrod quickly, holding it away from the eager hand.

"He did, too! Didn't he, Sam?"

Sam could not reply; his eyes, fixed upon the bottle, protruded strangely.

"You heard him--didn't you, Sam?"

"Well, if I did say it I didn't mean it!" said Penrod hastily, quoting from one of the authorities. "Looky here, M'rice," he continued, assuming a more placative and reasoning tone, "that wouldn't be fair to us. I guess we want some of our own lickrish water, don't we? The bottle ain't much over two-thirds full anyway. What I meant was, you can have all you can drink at one pull."

"How do you mean?"

"Why, this way: you can gulp all you want, so long as you keep swallering; but you can't take the bottle out of your mouth and commence again. Soon's you quit swallering it's Sam's turn."

"No; you can have next, Penrod," said Sam.

"Well, anyway, I mean M'rice has to give the bottle up the minute he stops swallering."

Craft appeared upon the face of Maurice, like a poster pasted on a wall.

"I can drink so long I don't stop swallering?"

"Yes; that's it."

"All right!" he cried. "Gimme the bottle!"

And Penrod placed it in his hand.

"You promise to let me drink until I quit swallering?" Maurice insisted.

"Yes!" said both boys together.

With that, Maurice placed the bottle to his lips and began to drink. Penrod and Sam leaned forward in breathless excitement. They had feared Maurice might smell the contents of the bottle; but that danger was past--this was the crucial moment. Their fondest hope was that he would make his first swallow a voracious one--it was impossible to imagine a second. They expected one big, gulping swallow and then an explosion, with fountain effects.

Little they knew the mettle of their man! Maurice swallowed once; he swallowed twice--and thrice--and he continued to swallow! No Adam's apple was sculptured on that juvenile throat, but the internal progress of the liquid was not a whit the less visible. His eyes gleamed with cunning and malicious triumph, sidewise, at the stunned conspirators; he was fulfilling the conditions of the draught, not once breaking the thread of that marvelous swallering.
His audience stood petrified. Already Maurice had swallowed more than they had given Duke and still the liquor receded in the uplifted bottle! And now the clear glass gleamed above the dark contents full half the vessel's length--and Maurice went on drinking! Slowly the clear glass increased in its dimensions--slowly the dark diminished.

Sam Williams made a horrified movement to check him--but Maurice protested passionately with his disengaged arm, and made vehement vocal noises remindful of the contract; whereupon Sam desisted and watched the continuing performance in a state of grisly fascination.

Maurice drank it all! He drained the last drop and threw the bottle in the air, uttering loud ejaculations of triumph and satisfaction.

"Hah!" he cried, blowing out his cheeks, inflating his chest, squaring his shoulders, patting his stomach, and wiping his mouth contentedly. "Hah! Aha! Waha! Wafwah! But that was good!"

The two boys stood looking at him in stupor.

"Well, I gotta say this," said Maurice graciously: "You stuck to your bargain all right and treated me fair."

Stricken with a sudden horrible suspicion, Penrod entered the storeroom in one stride and lifted the bottle of licorice water to his nose--then to his lips. It was weak, but good; he had made no mistake. And Maurice had really drained--to the dregs--the bottle of old hair tonics, dead catsups, syrups of undesirable preserves, condemned extracts of vanilla and lemon, decayed chocolate, ex-essence of beef, mixed dental preparations, aromatic spirits of ammonia, spirits of nitre, alcohol, arnica, quinine, ipecac, sal volatile, nux vomica and licorice water--with traces of arsenic, belladonna and strychnine.

Penrod put the licorice water out of sight and turned to face the others. Maurice was seating himself on a box just outside the door and had taken a package of cigarettes from his pocket.

"Nobody can see me from here, can they?" he said, striking a match. "You fellers smoke?"

"No," said Sam, staring at him haggardly.

"No," said Penrod in a whisper.

Maurice lit his cigarette and puffed showily.

"Well, sir," he remarked, "you fellers are certainly square--I gotta say that much. Honest, Penrod, I thought you was after me! I did think so," he added sunnily; "but now I guess you like me, or else you wouldn't of stuck to it about lettin' me drink it all if I kept on swallering."

He chatted on with complete geniality, smoking his cigarette in content. And as he ran from one topic to another his hearers stared at him in a kind of torpor. Never once did they exchange a glance with each other; their eyes were frozen to Maurice. The cheerful conversationalist made it evident that he was not without gratitude.

"Well," he said as he finished his cigarette and rose to go, "you fellers have treated me nice and some day you come over to my yard; I'd like to run with you fellers. You're the kind of fellers I like."

Penrod's jaw fell; Sam's mouth had been open all the time. Neither spoke.

"I gotta go," observed Maurice, consulting a handsome watch. "Gotta get dressed for the cotillon right after lunch. Come on, Sam. Don't you have to go, too?"

Sam nodded dazedly.

"Well, good-bye, Penrod," said Maurice cordially. "I'm glad you like me all right. Come on, Sam."

Penrod leaned against the doorpost and with fixed and glazing eyes watched the departure of his two visitors. Maurice was talking volubly, with much gesticulation, as they went; but Sam walked mechanically and in silence, staring at his brisk companion and keeping at a little distance from him.

They passed from sight, Maurice still conversing gayly--and Penrod slowly betook himself into the house, his head bowed upon his chest.

Some three hours later, Mr. Samuel Williams, waxen clean and in sweet raiment, made his reappearance in Penrod's yard, yodelling a code-signal to summon forth his friend. He yodelled loud, long, and frequently, finally securing a faint response from the upper air.

"Where are you?" shouted Mr. Williams, his roving glance searching ambient heights. Another low-spirited yodel reaching his ear, he perceived the head and shoulders of his friend projecting above the roofridge of the stable. The rest of Penrod's body was concealed from view, reposing upon the opposite slant of the gable and precariously secured by the crooking of his elbows over the ridge.

"Yay! What you doin' up there?"

"Nothin'."

"You better be careful!" Sam called. "You'll slide off and fall down in the alley if you don't look out. I come pert' near it last time we was up there. Come on down! Ain't you goin' to the cotillon?"
Penrod made no reply. Sam came nearer.

"Say," he called up in a guarded voice, "I went to our telephone a while ago and ast him how he was feelin', and he said he felt fine!"

"So did I," said Penrod. "He told me he felt bully!"

Sam thrust his hands in his pockets and brooded. The opening of the kitchen door caused a diversion. It was Della.

"Mister Penrod," she bellowed forthwith, "come ahn down fr'm up there! Y'r mamma's at the dancin' class waitin' fer ye, an' she's telephoned me they're goin' to begin--an' what's the matter with ye? Come ahn down fr'm up there!"

"Come on!" urged Sam. "We'll be late. There go Maurice and Marjorie now."

A glittering car spun by, disclosing briefly a genre picture of Marjorie Jones in pink, supporting a monstrous sheaf of American Beauty roses. Maurice, sitting shining and joyous beside her, saw both boys and waved them a hearty greeting as the car turned the corner.

Penrod uttered some muffled words and then waved both arms--either in response or as an expression of his condition of mind; it may have been a gesture of despair. How much intention there was in this act--obviously so rash, considering the position he occupied--it is impossible to say. Undeniably there must remain a suspicion of deliberate purpose.

Della screamed and Sam shouted. Penrod had disappeared from view.

The delayed dance was about to begin a most uneven cotillon when Samuel Williams arrived.

Mrs. Schofield hurriedly left the ballroom; while Miss Rennsdale, flushing with sudden happiness, curtsied profoundly to Professor Bartet and obtained his attention.

"I have told you fifty times," he informed her passionately ere she spoke, "I cannot make no such changes. If your partner comes you have to dance with him. You are going to drive me crazy, sure! What is it? What now? What you want?"

The damsel curtsied again and handed him the following communication, addressed to herself:

"Dear madam Please excuse me from dancing the cotilon with you this afternoon as I have fell off the barn.

"Sincerly yours,
"Penrod Schofield"

Chapter XV. The Two Families
Penrod entered the schoolroom, Monday picturesquely leaning upon a man's cane shortened to support a cripple approaching the age of twelve. He arrived about twenty minutes late, limping deeply, his brave young mouth drawn with pain, and the sensation he created must have been a solace to him; the only possible criticism of this entrance being that it was just a shade too heroic.

251

Perhaps for that reason it failed to stagger Miss Spence, a woman so saturated with suspicion that she penalized Penrod for tardiness as promptly and as coldly as if he had been a mere, ordinary, unmutilated boy. Nor would she entertain any discussion of the justice of her ruling. It seemed, almost, that she feared to argue with him.

However, the distinction of cane and limp remained to him, consolations which he protracted far into the week--until Thursday evening, in fact, when Mr. Schofield, observing from a window his son's pursuit of Duke round and round the backyard, confiscated the cane, with the promise that it should not remain idle if he saw Penrod limping again. Thus, succeeding a depressing Friday, another Saturday brought the necessity for new inventions.

It was a scented morning in apple-blossom time. At about ten of the clock Penrod emerged hastily from the kitchen door. His pockets bulged abnormally; so did his checks, and he swallowed with difficulty. A threatening mop, wielded by a cooklike arm in a checkered sleeve, followed him through the doorway, and he was preceded by a small, hurried, wistful dog with a warm doughnut in his mouth. The kitchen door slammed petulantly, enclosing the sore voice of Della, whereupon Penrod and Duke seated themselves upon the pleasant sward and immediately consumed the spoils of their raid.

From the cross-street which formed the side boundary of the Schofields' ample yard came a jingle of harness and the cadenced clatter of a pair of trotting horses, and Penrod, looking up, beheld the passing of a fat acquaintance, torpid amid the conservative splendours of a rather old-fashioned victoria. This was Roderick Magsworth Bitts, Junior, a fellow sufferer at the Friday Afternoon Dancing Class, but otherwise not often a companion: a home-sheltered lad, tutored privately and preserved against the coarsening influences of rude comradeship and miscellaneous information. Heavily overgrown in all physical dimensions, virtuous, and placid, this cloistered mutton was wholly uninteresting to Penrod Schofield. Nevertheless, Roderick Magsworth Bitts, Junior, was a personage on account of the importance of the Magsworth Bitts family; and it was Penrod's destiny to increase Roderick's celebrity far, far beyond its present aristocratic limitations.

The Magsworth Bittses were important because they were impressive; there was no other reason. And they were impressive because they believed themselves important. The adults of the family were impregnably formal; they dressed with reticent elegance, and wore the same nose and the same expression--an expression which indicated that they knew something exquisite and sacred which other people could never know. Other people, in their presence, were apt to feel mysteriously ignoble and to become secretly uneasy about ancestors, gloves, and pronunciation. The Magsworth Bitts manner was withholding and reserved, though sometimes gracious, granting small smiles as great favours and giving off a chilling kind of preciousness. Naturally, when any citizen of the community did anything unconventional or improper, or made a mistake, or had a relative who went wrong, that citizen's first and worst fear was that the Magsworth Bittses would hear of it. In fact, this painful family had for years terrorized the community, though the community had never realized that it was terrorized, and invariably spoke of the family as the "most charming circle in town." By common consent, Mrs. Roderick Magsworth Bitts officiated as the supreme model as well as critic-in-chief of morals and deportment for all the unlucky people prosperous enough to be elevated to her acquaintance.

Magsworth was the important part of the name. Mrs. Roderick Magsworth Bitts was a Magsworth born, herself, and the Magsworth crest decorated not only Mrs. Magsworth Bitts' note-paper but was on the china, on the table linen, on the chimney-pieces, on the opaque glass of the front door, on the victoria, and on the harness, though omitted from the garden-hose and the lawn-mower.

Naturally, no sensible person dreamed of connecting that illustrious crest with the unfortunate and notorious Rena Magsworth whose name had grown week by week into larger and larger type upon the front pages of newspapers, owing to the gradually increasing public and official belief that she had poisoned a family of eight. However, the statement that no sensible person could have connected the Magsworth Bitts family with the arsenical Rena takes no account of Penrod Schofield.

Penrod never missed a murder, a hanging or an electrocution in the newspapers; he knew almost as much about Rena Magsworth as her jurymen did, though they sat in a court-room two hundred miles away, and he had it in mind--so frank he was--to ask Roderick Magsworth Bitts, Junior, if the murderess happened to be a relative.

The present encounter, being merely one of apathetic greeting, did not afford the opportunity. Penrod took off his cap, and Roderick, seated between his mother and one of his grown-up sisters, nodded sluggishly, but neither Mrs. Magsworth Bitts nor her daughter acknowledged the salutation of the boy in the yard. They disapproved of him as a person of little consequence, and that little, bad. Snubbed, Penrod thoughtfully restored his cap to his head. A boy can be cut as effectually as a man, and this one was chilled to a low temperature. He wondered if they despised him because they had seen a last fragment of doughnut in his hand; then he thought that perhaps it was Duke who had disgraced him. Duke was certainly no fashionable looking dog.

The resilient spirits of youth, however, presently revived, and discovering a spider upon one knee and a beetle simultaneously upon the other, Penrod forgot Mrs. Roderick Magsworth Bitts in the course of some experiments infringing upon the domain of Doctor Carrel. Penrod's efforts--with the aid of a pin--to effect a transference of living organism were unsuccessful; but he convinced himself forever that a spider cannot walk with a beetle's legs. Della then enhanced zoological interest by depositing upon the back porch a large rat-trap from the cellar, the prison of four live rats awaiting execution.

Penrod at once took possession, retiring to the empty stable, where he installed the rats in a small wooden box with a sheet of broken window-glass--held down by a brickbat--over the top. Thus the symptoms of their agitation, when the box was shaken or hammered upon, could be studied at leisure. Altogether this Saturday was starting splendidly.

After a time, the student's attention was withdrawn from his specimens by a peculiar smell, which, being followed up by a system of selective sniffing, proved to be an emanation leaking into the stable from the alley. He opened the back door.

Across the alley was a cottage which a thrifty neighbour had built on the rear line of his lot and rented it out; and the fact that a family was now in process of "moving in" was manifested by the presence of a thin mule and a ramshackle wagon, the latter laden with the semblance of a stove and a few other unpretentious household articles.

A very small Black boy stood near the mule. In his hand was a rusty chain, and at the end of the chain the delighted Penrod perceived the source of the special smell he was tracing--a large raccoon. Duke, who had shown not the slightest interest in the rats, set up a frantic barking and simulated a ravening assault upon the strange animal. It was only a bit of acting, however, for Duke was an old dog, had suffered much, and desired no unnecessary sorrow, wherefore he confined his demonstrations to alarums and excursions, and presently sat down at a distance and expressed himself by intermittent threatenings in a quavering falsetto.

"What's that 'coon's name?" asked Penrod, intending no discourtesy.

"Aim gommo mame," said the small boy.

"What?"

"Aim gommo mame."

"What?"

The small boy looked annoyed.

"Aim gommo mame, I hell you," he said impatiently.

Penrod conceived that insult was intended.

"What's the matter of you?" he demanded advancing. "You get fresh with me, and I'll----"

"Hyuh, white boy!" A youth of Penrod's own age appeared in the doorway of the cottage. "You let 'at brothuh mine alone. He ain' do nothin' to you."

"Well, why can't he answer?"

"He can't. He can't talk no better'n what he was talkin'. He tongue-tie'."

"Oh," said Penrod, mollified. Then, obeying an impulse so universally aroused in the human breast under like circumstances that it has become a quip, he turned to the afflicted one.

"Talk some more," he begged eagerly.

"I hoe you ackoom aim gommo mame," was the prompt response, in which a slight ostentation was manifest. Unmistakable tokens of vanity had appeared upon the small countenance.

"What's he mean?" asked Penrod, enchanted.

"He say he tole you 'at 'coon ain' got no name."

"What's your name?"

"I'm name Herman."

"What's his name?" Penrod pointed to the tongue-tied boy.

"Verman."

"What!"

"Verman. Was three us boys in ow fam'ly. Ol'est one name Sherman. 'N'en come me; I'm Herman. 'N'en come him; he Verman. Sherman dead. Verman, he de littles' one."

"You goin' to live here?"

"Umhuh. Done move in f'm way outen on a fahm."

He pointed to the north with his right hand, and Penrod's eyes opened wide as they followed the gesture. Herman had no forefinger on that hand.

"Look there!" exclaimed Penrod. "You haven't got any finger!"

"I mum map," said Verman, with egregious pride.

"He done 'at," interpreted Herman, chuckling. "Yessuh; done chop 'er spang off, long 'go. He's a playin' wif a ax an' I lay my finguh on de do'-sill an' I say, 'Verman, chop 'er off!' So Verman he chop 'er right spang off up to de roots! Yessuh."

"What for?"

"Jes' fo' nothin'."

"He hoe me hoo," remarked Verman.

"Yessuh, I tole him to," said Herman, "an' he chop 'er off, an' ey ain't airy oth' one evuh grown on wheres de ole one use to grow. Nosuh!"

"But what'd you tell him to do it for?"

"Nothin'. I 'es' said it 'at way--an' he jes' chop er off!"

Both brothers looked pleased and proud. Penrod's profound interest was flatteringly visible, a tribute to their unusualness.

"Hem bow goy," suggested Verman eagerly.

"Aw ri'," said Herman. "Ow sistuh Queenie, she a growed-up woman; she got a goituh."

"Got a what?"

"Goituh. Swellin' on her neck--grea' big swellin'. She heppin' mammy move in now. You look in de front-room winduh wheres she sweepin'; you kin see it on her."

Penrod looked in the window and was rewarded by a fine view of Queenie's goitre. He had never before seen one, and only the lure of further conversation on the part of Verman brought him from the window.

"Verman say tell you 'bout pappy," explained Herman. "Mammy an' Queenie move in town an' go git de house all fix up befo' pappy git out."

"Out of where?"

"Jail. Pappy cut a man, an' de police done kep' him in jail evuh sense Chris'mus-time; but dey goin' tuhn him loose ag'in nex' week."

"What'd he cut the other man with?"

"Wif a pitchfawk."

Penrod began to feel that a lifetime spent with this fascinating family were all too short. The brothers, glowing with amiability, were as enraptured as he. For the first time in their lives they moved in the rich glamour of sensationalism. Herman was prodigal of gesture with his right hand; and Verman, chuckling with delight, talked fluently, though somewhat consciously. They cheerfully agreed to keep the raccoon--already beginning to be mentioned as "our 'coon" by Penrod--in Mr. Schofield's empty stable, and, when the animal had been chained to the wall near the box of rats and supplied with a pan of fair water, they assented to their new friend's suggestion (inspired by a fine sense of the artistic harmonies) that the heretofore nameless pet be christened Sherman, in honour of their deceased relative.

At this juncture was heard from the front yard the sound of that yodelling which is the peculiar accomplishment of those whose voices have not "changed." Penrod yodelled a response; and Mr. Samuel Williams appeared, a large bundle under his arm.

"Yay, Penrod!" was his greeting, casual enough from without; but, having entered, he stopped short and emitted a prodigious whistle. "Ya-a-ay!" he then shouted. "Look at the 'coon!"

"I guess you better say, 'Look at the 'coon!'" Penrod returned proudly. "They's a good deal more'n him to look at, too. Talk some, Verman." Verman complied.

Sam was warmly interested. "What'd you say his name was?" he asked.

"Verman."

"How d'you spell it?"

"V-e-r-m-a-n," replied Penrod, having previously received this information from Herman.

"Oh!" said Sam.

"Point to sumpthing, Herman," Penrod commanded, and Sam's excitement, when Herman pointed was sufficient to the occasion.

Penrod, the discoverer, continued his exploitation of the manifold wonders of the Sherman, Herman, and Verman collection. With the air of a proprietor he escorted Sam into the alley for a good look at Queenie (who seemed not to care for her increasing celebrity) and proceeded to a dramatic climax--the recital of the episode of the pitchfork and its consequences.

The cumulative effect was enormous, and could have but one possible result. The normal boy is always at least one half Barnum.

"Let's get up a show!"

Penrod and Sam both claimed to have said it first, a question left unsettled in the ecstasies of hurried preparation. The bundle under Sam's arm, brought with no definite purpose, proved to have been an inspiration. It consisted of broad sheets of light yellow wrapping-paper, discarded by Sam's mother in her spring house-cleaning. There were half-filled cans and buckets of paint in the storeroom adjoining the carriage-house, and presently the side wall of the stable flamed information upon the passer-by from a great and spreading poster.

"Publicity," primal requisite of all theatrical and amphitheatrical enterprise thus provided, subsequent arrangements proceeded with a fury of energy which transformed the empty hay- loft. True, it is impossible to say just what the hay-loft was transformed into, but history warrantably clings to the statement that it was transformed. Duke and Sherman were secured to the rear wall at a considerable distance from each other, after an exhibition of reluctance on the part of Duke, during which he displayed a nervous energy and agility almost miraculous in so small and middle-aged a dog. Benches were improvised for spectators; the rats were brought up; finally the rafters, corn-crib, and hay-chute were ornamented with flags and strips of bunting from Sam Williams' attic, Sam returning from the excursion wearing an old silk hat, and accompanied (on account of a rope) by a fine dachshund encountered on the highway. In the matter of personal decoration paint was generously used: an interpretation of the spiral, inclining to whites and greens, becoming brilliantly effective upon the dark facial backgrounds of Herman and Verman; while the countenances of Sam and Penrod were each supplied with the black moustache and imperial, lacking which, no professional showman can be esteemed conscientious.

It was regretfully decided, in council, that no attempt be made to add Queenie to the list of exhibits, her brothers warmly declining to act as ambassadors in that cause. They were certain Queenie would not like the idea, they said, and Herman picturesquely described her activity on occasions when she had been annoyed by too much attention to her appearance. However, Penrod's disappointment was alleviated by an inspiration which came to him in a moment of pondering upon the dachshund, and the entire party went forth to add an enriching line to the poster.

They found a group of seven, including two adults, already gathered in the street to read and admire this work.

SCHoFiELD & WiLLiAMS BiG SHOW ADMiSSioN 1 CENT oR 20 PiNS MUSUEM oF CURioSiTES Now GoiNG oN SHERMAN HERMAN & VERMAN THiER FATHERS iN JAiL STABED A MAN WiTH A PiTCHFORK SHERMAN THE WiLD ANIMAL CAPTURED iN AFRiCA HERMAN THE ONE FiNGERED TATOOD WILD MAN VERMAN THE SAVAGE TATOOD WILD BoY TALKS ONLY iN HiS NAiTiVE LANGUAGS. Do NoT FAIL TO SEE DUKE THE INDiAN DOG ALSO THE MiCHiGAN TRAiNED RATS

A heated argument took place between Sam and Penrod, the point at issue being settled, finally, by the drawing of straws; whereupon Penrod, with pardonable self-importance--in the presence of an audience now increased to nine--slowly painted the words inspired by the dachshund:

IMPoRTENT Do NoT MISS THE SoUTH AMERiCAN DoG PART ALLIGATOR.

Lesson 60
1. Read chapters 16 and 17 of *Penrod*.
2. What do you think is going to happen in the book?

Chapter XVI. The New Star

Sam, Penrod, Herman, and Verman withdrew in considerable state from non-paying view, and, repairing to the hay-loft, declared the exhibition open to the public. Oral proclamation was made by Sam, and then the loitering multitude was enticed by the seductive strains of a band; the two partners performing upon combs and paper, Herman and Verman upon tin pans with sticks.

The effect was immediate. Visitors appeared upon the stairway and sought admission. Herman and Verman took position among the exhibits, near the wall; Sam stood at the entrance, officiating as barker and ticket-seller; while Penrod, with debonair suavity, acted as curator, master of ceremonies, and lecturer. He greeted the first to enter with a courtly bow. They consisted of Miss Rennsdale and her nursery governess, and they paid spot cash for their admission.

"Walk in, lay-deeze, walk right in--pray do not obstruck the passageway," said Penrod, in a remarkable voice. "Pray be seated; there is room for each and all."

Miss Rennsdale and governess were followed by Mr. Georgie Bassett and baby sister (which proves the perfection of Georgie's character) and six or seven other neighbourhood children--a most satisfactory audience, although, subsequent to Miss Rennsdale and governess, admission was wholly by pin.

"Gen-til-mun and lay-deeze," shouted Penrod, "I will first call your at-tain-shon to our genuine South American dog, part alligator!" He pointed to the dachshund, and added, in his ordinary tone, "That's him." Straightway reassuming the character of showman, he bellowed: "Next, you see Duke, the genuine, full-blooded Indian dog from the far Western Plains and Rocky Mountains. Next, the trained Michigan rats, captured way up there, and trained to jump and run all around the box at the--at the--at the slightest pre-text!" He paused, partly to take breath and partly to enjoy his own surprised discovery that this phrase was in his vocabulary.

"At the slightest pre-text!" he repeated, and continued, suiting the action to the word: "I will now hammer upon the box and each and all may see these genuine full-blooded Michigan rats perform at the slightest pre-text! There! (That's all they do now, but I and Sam are goin' to train 'em lots more before this afternoon.) gen-til-mun and lay-deeze I will kindly now call your at-tain-shon to Sherman, the wild animal from Africa, costing the lives of the wild trapper and many of his companions. Next, let me kindly interodoos Herman and Verman. Their father got mad and stuck his pitchfork right inside of another man, exactly as promised upon the advertisements outside the big tent, and got put in jail. Look at them well, gen-til-mun and lay-deeze, there is no extra charge, and re-mem-bur you are each and all now looking at two wild, tattooed men which the father of is in jail. Point, Herman. Each and all will have a chance to see. Point to sumpthing else, Herman. This is the only genuine one-fingered tattooed wild man. Last on the programme, gen-til-mun and lay-deeze, we have Verman, the savage tattooed wild boy, that can't speak only his native foreign languages. Talk some, Verman."

Verman obliged and made an instantaneous hit. He was encored rapturously, again and again; and, thrilling with the unique pleasure of being appreciated and misunderstood at the same time, would have talked all day but too gladly. Sam Williams, however, with a true showman's foresight, whispered to Penrod, who rang down on the monologue.

"Gen-til-mun and lay-deeze, this closes our pufformance. Pray pass out quietly and with as little jostling as possible. As soon as you are all out there's goin' to be a new pufformance, and each and all are welcome at the same and simple price of admission. Pray pass out quietly and with as little jostling as possible. Re-mem-bur the price is only one cent, the tenth part of a dime, or twenty pins, no bent ones taken. Pray pass out quietly and with as little jostling as possible. The Schofield and Williams Military Band will play before each pufformance, and each and all are welcome for the same and simple price of admission. Pray pass out quietly and with as little jostling as possible."

Forthwith, the Schofield and Williams Military Band began a second overture, in which something vaguely like a tune was at times distinguishable; and all of the first audience returned, most of them having occupied the interval in hasty excursions for more pins; Miss Rennsdale and governess, however, again paying coin of the Republic and receiving deference and the best seats accordingly. And when a third performance found all of the same inveterate patrons once more crowding the auditorium, and seven recruits added, the pleasurable excitement of the partners in their venture will be understood by any one who has seen a metropolitan manager strolling about the foyer of his theatre some evening during the earlier stages of an assured "phenomenal run."

From the first, there was no question which feature of the entertainment was the attraction extraordinary: Verman--Verman, the savage tattooed wild boy, speaking only his native foreign languages--Verman was a triumph! Beaming, wreathed in smiles, melodious, incredibly fluent, he had but to open his lips and a dead hush fell upon the audience. Breathless, they leaned forward, hanging upon his every semi-syllable, and, when Penrod checked the flow, burst into thunders of applause, which Verman received with happy laughter.

Alas! he delayed not o'er long to display all the egregiousness of a new star; but for a time there was no caprice of his too eccentric to be forgiven. During Penrod's lecture upon the other curios, the tattooed wild boy continually stamped his foot, grinned, and gesticulated, tapping his tiny chest, and pointing to himself as it were to say: "Wait for Me! I am the Big Show." So soon they learn; so soon they learn! And (again alas!) this spoiled darling of public favour, like many another, was fated to know, in good time, the fickleness of that favour.

But during all the morning performances he was the idol of his audience and looked it! The climax of his popularity came during the fifth overture of the Schofield and Williams Military Band, when the music was quite drowned in the agitated clamours of Miss Rennsdale, who was endeavouring to ascend the stairs in spite of the physical dissuasion of her governess.

"I won't go home to lunch!" screamed Miss Rennsdale, her voice accompanied by a sound of ripping. "I will hear the tattooed wild boy talk some more! It's lovely--I will hear him talk! I will! I will! I want to listen to Verman-- I want to--I want to----"

Wailing, she was borne away--of her sex not the first to be fascinated by obscurity, nor the last to champion its eloquence.

Verman was almost unendurable after this, but, like many, many other managers, Schofield and Williams restrained their choler, and even laughed fulsomely when their principal attraction essayed the role of a comedian in private, and capered and squawked in sheer, fatuous vanity.

The first performance of the afternoon rivalled the successes of the morning, and although Miss Rennsdale was detained at home, thus drying up the single source of cash income developed before lunch, Maurice Levy appeared, escorting Marjorie Jones, and paid coin for two admissions, dropping the money into Sam's hand with a careless--nay, a contemptuous--gesture. At sight of Marjorie, Penrod Schofield flushed under his new moustache (repainted since noon) and lectured as he had never lectured before. A new grace invested his every gesture; a new sonorousness rang in his voice; a simple and manly pomposity marked his very walk as he passed from curio to curio. And when he fearlessly handled the box of rats and hammered upon it with cool insouciance, he beheld--for the first time in his life--a purl of admiration eddying in Marjorie's lovely eye, a certain softening of that eye. And then Verman spake and Penrod was forgotten. Marjorie's eye rested upon him no more.

A heavily equipped chauffeur ascended the stairway, bearing the message that Mrs. Levy awaited her son and his lady. Thereupon, having devoured the last sound permitted (by the managers) to issue from Verman, Mr. Levy and Miss Jones departed to a real matinee at a real theatre, the limpid eyes of Marjorie looking back softly over her shoulder--but only at the tattooed wild boy. Nearly always it is woman who puts the irony into life.

After this, perhaps because of sated curiosity, perhaps on account of a pin famine, the attendance began to languish. Only four responded to the next call of the band; the four dwindled to three; finally the entertainment was given for one blase auditor, and Schofield and Williams looked depressed. Then followed an interval when the band played in vain.

About three o'clock Schofield and Williams were gloomily discussing various unpromising devices for startling the public into a renewal of interest, when another patron unexpectedly appeared and paid a cent for his admission. News of the Big Show and Museum of Curiosities had at last penetrated the far, cold spaces of interstellar niceness, for this new patron consisted of no less than Roderick Magsworth Bitts, Junior, escaped in a white "sailor suit" from the Manor during a period of severe maternal and tutorial preoccupation.

He seated himself without parley, and the pufformance was offered for his entertainment with admirable conscientiousness. True to the Lady Clara caste and training, Roderick's pale, fat face expressed nothing except an impervious superiority and, as he sat, cold and unimpressed upon the front bench, like a large, white lump, it must be said that he made a discouraging audience "to play to." He was not, however, unresponsive--far from it. He offered comment very chilling to the warm grandiloquence of the orator.

"That's my uncle Ethelbert's dachshund," he remarked, at the beginning of the lecture. "You better take him back if you don't want to get arrested." And when Penrod, rather uneasily ignoring the interruption, proceeded to the exploitation of the genuine, full-blooded Indian dog, Duke, "Why don't you try to give that old dog away?" asked Roderick. "You couldn't sell him."

"My papa would buy me a lots better 'coon than that," was the information volunteered a little later, "only I wouldn't want the nasty old thing."

Herman of the missing finger obtained no greater indulgence. "Pooh!" said Roderick. "We have two fox-terriers in our stables that took prizes at the kennel show, and their tails were bit off. There's a man that always bites fox-terriers' tails off."

"Oh, my gosh, what a lie!" exclaimed Sam Williams ignorantly.

"Go on with the show whether he likes it or not, Penrod. He's paid his money."

Verman, confident in his own singular powers, chuckled openly at the failure of the other attractions to charm the frosty visitor, and, when his turn came, poured forth a torrent of conversation which was straightway damned.

"Rotten," said Mr. Bitts languidly. "Anybody could talk like that. I could do it if I wanted to."

Verman paused suddenly.

"Yes, you could!" exclaimed Penrod, stung. "Let's hear you do it, then."

"Yessir!" the other partner shouted. "Let's just hear you do it!"

"I said I could if I wanted to," responded Roderick. "I didn't say I would."

"Yay! Knows he can't!" sneered Sam.

"I can, too, if I try."

"Well, let's hear you try!"

So challenged, the visitor did try, but, in the absence of an impartial jury, his effort was considered so pronounced a failure that he was howled down, derided, and mocked with great clamours.

"Anyway," said Roderick, when things had quieted down, "if I couldn't get up a better show than this I'd sell out and leave town."

Not having enough presence of mind to inquire what he would sell out, his adversaries replied with mere formless yells of scorn.

"I could get up a better show than this with my left hand," Roderick asserted.

"Well, what would you have in your ole show?" asked Penrod, condescending to language.

"That's all right, what I'd have. I'd have enough!"

"You couldn't get Herman and Verman in your ole show."

"No, and I wouldn't want 'em, either!"

"Well, what would you have?" insisted Penrod derisively. "You'd have to have sumpthing--you couldn't be a show yourself!"

"How do you know?" This was but meandering while waiting for ideas, and evoked another yell.

"You think you could be a show all by yourself?" demanded Penrod.

"How do you know I couldn't?"

Two white boys and two black boys shrieked their scorn of the boaster.

"I could, too!" Roderick raised his voice to a sudden howl, obtaining a hearing.

"Well, why don't you tell us how?"

"Well, I know how, all right," said Roderick. "If anybody asks you, you can just tell him I know how, all right."

"Why, you can't do anything," Sam began argumentatively. "You talk about being a show all by yourself; what could you try to do? Show us sumpthing you can do."

"I didn't say I was going to do anything," returned the badgered one, still evading.

"Well, then, how'd you be a show?" Penrod demanded. "We got a show here, even if Herman didn't point or Verman didn't talk. Their father stabbed a man with a pitchfork, I guess, didn't he?"

"How do I know?"

"Well, I guess he's in jail, ain't he?"

"Well, what if their father is in jail? I didn't say he wasn't, did I?"

"Well, your father ain't in jail, is he?"

"Well, I never said he was, did I?"

"Well, then," continued Penrod, "how could you be a----" He stopped abruptly, staring at Roderick, the birth of an idea plainly visible in his altered expression. He had suddenly remembered his intention to ask Roderick Magsworth Bitts, Junior, about Rena Magsworth, and this recollection collided in his mind with the irritation produced by Roderick's claiming some mysterious attainment which would warrant his setting up as a show in his single person. Penrod's whole manner changed instantly.

"Roddy," he asked, almost overwhelmed by a prescience of something vast and magnificent, "Roddy, are you any relation of Rena Magsworth?"

Roderick had never heard of Rena Magsworth, although a concentration of the sentence yesterday pronounced upon her had burned, black and horrific, upon the face of every newspaper in the country. He was not allowed to read the journals of the day and his family's indignation over the sacrilegious coincidence of the name had not been expressed in his presence. But he saw that it was an awesome name to Penrod Schofield and Samuel Williams. Even Herman and Verman, though lacking many educational advantages on account of a long residence in the country, were informed on the subject of Rena Magsworth through hearsay, and they joined in the portentous silence.

"Roddy," repeated Penrod, "honest, is Rena Magsworth some relation of yours?"

There is no obsession more dangerous to its victims than a conviction especially an inherited one--of superiority: this world is so full of Missourians. And from his earliest years Roderick Magsworth Bitts, Junior, had been trained to believe in the importance of the Magsworth family. At every meal he absorbed a sense of Magsworth greatness, and yet, in his infrequent meetings with persons of his own age and sex, he was treated as negligible. Now, dimly, he perceived that there was a Magsworth claim of some sort which was impressive, even to boys. Magsworth blood was the essential of all true distinction in the world, he knew. Consequently, having been driven into a cul-de-sac, as a result of flagrant and unfounded boasting, he was ready to take advantage of what appeared to be a triumphal way out.

"Roddy," said Penrod again, with solemnity, "is Rena Magsworth some relation of yours?"

"Is she, Roddy?" asked Sam, almost hoarsely.

"She's my aunt!" shouted Roddy.

Silence followed. Sam and Penrod, spellbound, gazed upon Roderick Magsworth Bitts, Junior. So did Herman and Verman. Roddy's staggering lie had changed the face of things utterly. No one questioned it; no one realized that it was much too good to be true.

"Roddy," said Penrod, in a voice tremulous with hope, "Roddy, will you join our show?"

Roddy joined.

Even he could see that the offer implied his being starred as the paramount attraction of a new order of things. It was obvious that he had swelled out suddenly, in the estimation of the other boys, to that importance which he had been taught to believe his native gift and natural right. The sensation was pleasant. He had often been treated with effusion by grown- up callers and by acquaintances of his mothers and sisters; he had heard ladies speak of him as "charming" and "that delightful child," and little girls had sometimes shown him deference, but until this moment no boy had ever allowed him, for one moment, to presume even to equality. Now, in a trice, he was not only admitted to comradeship, but patently valued as something rare and sacred to be acclaimed and pedestalled. In fact, the very first thing that Schofield and Williams did was to find a box for him to stand upon.

The misgivings roused in Roderick's bosom by the subsequent activities of the firm were not bothersome enough to make him forego his prominence as Exhibit A. He was not a "quick-minded" boy, and it was long (and much happened) before he thoroughly comprehended the causes of his new celebrity. He had a shadowy feeling that if the affair came to be heard of at home it might not be liked, but, intoxicated by the glamour and bustle which surround a public character, he made no protest. On the contrary, he entered whole-heartedly into the preparations for the new show. Assuming, with Sam's assistance, a blue moustache and "side-burns," he helped in the painting of a new poster, which, supplanting the old one on the wall of the stable facing the cross-street, screamed bloody murder at the passers in that rather populous thoroughfare.

SCHoFiELD & WiLLiAMS
NEW BiG SHoW
RoDERiCK MAGSWoRTH BiTTS JR
ONLY LiViNG NEPHEW
oF
RENA MAGSWORTH
THE FAMOS
MUDERESS GoiNG To BE HUNG
NEXT JULY KiLED EiGHT PEOPLE
PUT ARSiNECK iN THiER MiLK ALSO
SHERMAN HERMAN AND VERMAN
THE MiCHiGAN RATS DOG PART
ALLiGATOR DUKE THE GENUiNE
InDiAN DoG ADMISSioN 1 CENT oR
20 PINS SAME AS BEFORE Do NoT

MISS THIS CHANSE TO SEE RoDERICK
ONLY LiViNG NEPHEW oF RENA
MAGSWORTH THE GREAT FAMOS
MUDERESS
GoiNG To BE
HUNG

Chapter XVII. Retiring from the Show Business

Megaphones were constructed out of heavy wrapping-paper, and Penrod, Sam, and Herman set out in different directions, delivering vocally the inflammatory proclamation of the poster to a large section of the residential quarter, and leaving Roderick Magsworth Bitts, Junior, with Verman in the loft, shielded from all deadhead eyes. Upon the return of the heralds, the Schofield and Williams Military Band played deafeningly, and an awakened public once more thronged to fill the coffers of the firm.

Prosperity smiled again. The very first audience after the acquisition of Roderick was larger than the largest of the morning. Master Bitts--the only exhibit placed upon a box--was a supercurio. All eyes fastened upon him and remained, hungrily feasting, throughout Penrod's luminous oration.

But the glory of one light must ever be the dimming of another. We dwell in a vale of seesaws-- and cobwebs spin fastest upon laurel. Verman, the tattooed wild boy, speaking only in his native foreign languages, Verman the gay, Verman the caperer, capered no more; he chuckled no more, he beckoned no more, nor tapped his chest, nor wreathed his idolatrous face in smiles. Gone, all gone, were his little artifices for attracting the general attention to himself; gone was every engaging mannerism which had endeared him to the mercurial public. He squatted against the wall and glowered at the new sensation. It was the old story--the old, old story of too much temperament: Verman was suffering from artistic jealousy.

The second audience contained a cash-paying adult, a spectacled young man whose poignant attention was very flattering. He remained after the lecture, and put a few questions to Roddy, which were answered rather confusedly upon promptings from Penrod. The young man went away without having stated the object of his interrogations, but it became quite plain, later in the day. This same object caused the spectacled young man to make several brief but stimulating calls directly after leaving the Schofield and Williams Big Show, and the consequences thereof loitered not by the wayside.

The Big Show was at high tide. Not only was the auditorium filled and throbbing; there was an indubitable line--by no means wholly juvenile--waiting for admission to the next pufformance. A group stood in the street examining the poster earnestly as it glowed in the long, slanting rays of the westward sun, and people in automobiles and other vehicles had halted wheel in the street to read the message so piquantly given to the world. These were the conditions when a crested victoria arrived at a gallop, and a large, chastely magnificent and highly flushed woman descended, and progressed across the yard with an air of violence.

At sight of her, the adults of the waiting line hastily disappeared, and most of the pausing vehicles moved instantly on their way. She was followed by a stricken man in livery.

The stairs to the auditorium were narrow and steep; Mrs. Roderick Magsworth Bitts was of a stout favour; and the voice of Penrod was audible during the ascent.

"Re-mem-bur, gentilmun and lay-deeze, each and all are now gazing upon Roderick Magsworth Bitts, Junior, the only living nephew of the great Rena Magsworth. She stuck ars'nic in the milk of eight separate and distinck people to put in their coffee and each and all of 'em died. The great ars'nic murderess, Rena Magsworth, gentilmun and lay-deeze, and Roddy's her only living nephew. She's a relation of all the Bitts family, but he's her one and only living nephew. Re-mem-bur! Next July she's goin' to be hung, and, each and all, you now see before you----"

Penrod paused abruptly, seeing something before himself--the august and awful presence which filled the entryway. And his words (it should be related) froze upon his lips.

Before herself, Mrs. Roderick Magsworth Bitts saw her son--her scion--wearing a moustache and sideburns of blue, and perched upon a box flanked by Sherman and Verman, the Michigan rats, the Indian dog Duke, Herman, and the dog part alligator.

Roddy, also, saw something before himself. It needed no prophet to read the countenance of the dread apparition in the entryway. His mouth opened--remained open--then filled to capacity with a calamitous sound of grief not unmingled with apprehension.

Penrod's reason staggered under the crisis. For a horrible moment he saw Mrs. Roderick Magsworth Bitts approaching like some fatal mountain in avalanche. She seemed to grow larger and redder; lightnings played about her head; he had a vague consciousness of the audience spraying out in flight, of the squealings, tramplings and dispersals of a stricken field. The mountain was close upon him----

He stood by the open mouth of the hay-chute which went through the floor to the manger below. Penrod also went through the floor. He propelled himself into the chute and shot down, but not quite to the manger, for Mr. Samuel Williams had thoughtfully stepped into the chute a moment in advance of his partner. Penrod lit upon Sam.

Catastrophic noises resounded in the loft; volcanoes seemed to romp upon the stairway.

There ensued a period when only a shrill keening marked the passing of Roderick as he was borne to the tumbril. Then all was silence.

. . . Sunset, striking through a western window, rouged the walls of the Schofields' library, where gathered a joint family council and court martial of four--Mrs. Schofield, Mr. Schofield, and Mr. and Mrs. Williams, parents of Samuel of that ilk. Mr. Williams read aloud a conspicuous passage from the last edition of the evening paper:

267

"Prominent people here believed close relations of woman sentenced to hang. Angry denial by Mrs. R. Magsworth Bitts. Relationship admitted by younger member of family. His statement confirmed by boy-friends----"

"Don't!" said Mrs. Williams, addressing her husband vehemently. "We've all read it a dozen times. We've got plenty of trouble on our hands without hearing that again!"

Singularly enough, Mrs. Williams did not look troubled; she looked as if she were trying to look troubled. Mrs. Schofield wore a similar expression. So did Mr. Schofield. So did Mr. Williams.

"What did she say when she called you up?" Mrs. Schofield inquired breathlessly of Mrs. Williams.

"She could hardly speak at first, and then when she did talk, she talked so fast I couldn't understand most of it, and----"

"It was just the same when she tried to talk to me," said Mrs. Schofield, nodding.

"I never did hear any one in such a state before," continued Mrs. Williams. "So furious----"

"Quite justly, of course," said Mrs. Schofield.

"Of course. And she said Penrod and Sam had enticed Roderick away from home--usually he's not allowed to go outside the yard except with his tutor or a servant--and had told him to say that horrible creature was his aunt----"

"How in the world do you suppose Sam and Penrod ever thought of such a thing as that!" exclaimed Mrs. Schofield. "It must have been made up just for their 'show.' Della says there were just streams going in and out all day. Of course it wouldn't have happened, but this was the day Margaret and I spend every month in the country with Aunt Sarah, and I didn't dream----"

"She said one thing I thought rather tactless," interrupted Mrs. Williams. "Of course we must allow for her being dreadfully excited and wrought up, but I do think it wasn't quite delicate in her, and she's usually the very soul of delicacy. She said that Roderick had never been allowed to associate with--common boys----"

"Meaning Sam and Penrod," said Mrs. Schofield. "Yes, she said that to me, too."

"She said that the most awful thing about it," Mrs. Williams went on, "was that, though she's going to prosecute the newspapers, many people would always believe the story, and----"

"Yes, I imagine they will," said Mrs. Schofield musingly. "Of course you and I and everybody who really knows the Bitts and Magsworth families understand the perfect absurdity of it; but I suppose there are ever so many who'll believe it, no matter what the Bittses and Magsworths say."

"Hundreds and hundreds!" said Mrs. Williams. "I'm afraid it will be a great come-down for them."

"I'm afraid so," said Mrs. Schofield gently. "A very great one--yes, a very, very great one."

"Well," observed Mrs. Williams, after a thoughtful pause, "there's only one thing to be done, and I suppose it had better be done right away."

She glanced toward the two gentlemen.

"Certainly," Mr. Schofield agreed. "But where are they?"

"Have you looked in the stable?" asked his wife.

"I searched it. They've probably started for the far West."

"Did you look in the sawdust-box?"

"No, I didn't."

"Then that's where they are."

Thus, in the early twilight, the now historic stable was approached by two fathers charged to do the only thing to be done. They entered the storeroom.

"Penrod!" said Mr. Schofield.

"Sam!" said Mr. Williams.

Nothing disturbed the twilight hush.

But by means of a ladder, brought from the carriage-house, Mr. Schofield mounted to the top of the sawdust-box. He looked within, and discerned the dim outlines of three quiet figures, the third being that of a small dog.

The two boys rose, upon command, descended the ladder after Mr. Schofield, bringing Duke with them, and stood before the authors of their being, who bent upon them sinister and threatening brows. With hanging heads and despondent countenances, each still ornamented with a moustache and an imperial, Penrod and Sam awaited sentence.

This is a boy's lot: anything he does, anything whatever, may afterward turn out to have been a crime--he never knows.

And punishment and clemency are alike inexplicable.

Mr. Williams took his son by the ear.

"You march home!" he commanded.

Sam marched, not looking back, and his father followed the small figure implacably.

"You goin' to whip me?" quavered Penrod, alone with Justice.

"Wash your face at that hydrant," said his father sternly.

About fifteen minutes later, Penrod, hurriedly entering the corner drug store, two blocks distant, was astonished to perceive a familiar form at the soda counter.

"Yay, Penrod," said Sam Williams. "Want some sody? Come on. He didn't lick me. He didn't do anything to me at all. He gave me a quarter."

"So'd mine," said Penrod.

Lesson 61
1. Read chapters 18 and 19 of *Penrod*.
2. Find a word in your reading that you don't know.
3. Write the word and the definition underneath the sentence.
4. Tell someone about the story so far.

Chapter XVIII. Music
Boyhood is the longest time in life for a boy. The last term of the school-year is made of decades, not of weeks, and living through them is like waiting for the millennium. But they do pass, somehow, and at last there came a day when Penrod was one of a group that capered out from the gravelled yard of "Ward School, Nomber Seventh," carolling a leave-taking of the institution, of their instructress, and not even forgetting Mr. Capps, the janitor.

"Good-bye, teacher! Good-bye, school!
Good-bye, Cappsie, dern ole fool!"

Penrod sang the loudest. For every boy, there is an age when he "finds his voice." Penrod's had not "changed," but he had found it. Inevitably that thing had come upon his family and the neighbours; and his father, a somewhat dyspeptic man, quoted frequently the expressive words of the "Lady of Shalott," but there were others whose sufferings were as poignant.

Vacation-time warmed the young of the world to pleasant languor; and a morning came that was like a brightly coloured picture in a child's fairy story. Miss Margaret Schofield, reclining in a hammock upon the front porch, was beautiful in the eyes of a newly made senior, well favoured and in fair raiment, beside her. A guitar rested lightly upon his knee, and he was trying to play--a matter of some difficulty, as the floor of the porch also seemed inclined to be musical. From directly under his feet came a voice of song, shrill, loud, incredibly piercing and incredibly flat, dwelling upon each syllable with incomprehensible reluctance to leave it.

"I have lands and earthly pow-wur. I'd give all for a now-wur, Whi-ilst setting at my-y-y dear old mother's knee-ee, So-o-o rem-mem-bur whilst you're young----"

Miss Schofield stamped heartily upon the musical floor.

"It's Penrod," she explained. "The lattice at the end of the porch is loose, and he crawls under and comes out all bugs. He's been having a dreadful singing fit lately--running away to picture shows and vaudeville, I suppose."

Mr. Robert Williams looked upon her yearningly. He touched a thrilling chord on his guitar and leaned nearer. "But you said you have missed me," he began. I----"

The voice of Penrod drowned all other sounds.

"So-o-o rem-mem-bur, whi-i-ilst you're young, That the day-a-ys to you will come, When you're o-o-old and only in the way, Do not scoff at them bee-cause----"

"Penrod!" Miss Schofield stamped again.

"You did say you'd missed me," said Mr. Robert Williams, seizing hurriedly upon the silence. "Didn't you say----"

A livelier tune rose upward.

"Oh, you talk about your fascinating beauties, Of your dem-O-zells, your belles, But the littil dame I met, while in the city, She's par excellaws the queen of all the swells. She's sweeter far----"

Margaret rose and jumped up and down repeatedly in a well-calculated area, whereupon the voice of Penrod cried chokedly, "Quit that!" and there were subterranean coughings and sneezings.

"You want to choke a person to death?" he inquired severely, appearing at the end of the porch, a cobweb upon his brow. And, continuing, he put into practice a newly acquired phrase, "You better learn to be more considerick of other people's comfort."

271

Slowly and grievedly he withdrew, passed to the sunny side of the house, reclined in the warm grass beside his wistful Duke, and presently sang again.

"She's sweeter far than the flower I named her after, And the memery of her smile it haunts me yet! When in after years the moon is soffly beamun' And at eve I smell the smell of mignonette I will re-call that----"

"Pen-rod!"

Mr. Schofield appeared at an open window upstairs, a book in his hand.

"Stop it!" he commanded. "Can't I stay home with a headache one morning from the office without having to listen to--I never did hear such squawking!" He retired from the window, having too impulsively called upon his Maker. Penrod, shocked and injured, entered the house, but presently his voice was again audible as far as the front porch. He was holding converse with his mother, somewhere in the interior.

"Well, what of it? Sam Williams told me his mother said if Bob ever did think of getting married to Margaret, his mother said she'd like to know what in the name o' goodness they expect to----"

Bang! Margaret thought it better to close the front door.

The next minute Penrod opened it. "I suppose you want the whole family to get a sunstroke," he said reprovingly. "Keepin' every breath of air out o' the house on a day like this!"

And he sat down implacably in the doorway.

The serious poetry of all languages has omitted the little brother; and yet he is one of the great trials of love--the immemorial burden of courtship. Tragedy should have found place for him, but he has been left to the haphazard vignettist of Grub Street. He is the grave and real menace of lovers; his head is sacred and terrible, his power illimitable. There is one way--only one--to deal with him; but Robert Williams, having a brother of Penrod's age, understood that way.

Robert had one dollar in the world. He gave it to Penrod immediately.

Enslaved forever, the new Rockefeller rose and went forth upon the highway, an overflowing heart bursting the floodgates of song.

"In her eyes the light of love was soffly gleamun', So sweetlay, So neatlay. On the banks the moon's soff light was brightly streamun', Words of love I then spoke to her. She was purest of the pew-er:

'Littil sweetheart, do not sigh, Do not weep and do not cry. I will build a littil cottige just for yew-ew-ew and I.'"

In fairness, it must be called to mind that boys older than Penrod have these wellings of pent melody; a wife can never tell when she is to undergo a musical morning, and even the golden wedding brings her no security, a man of ninety is liable to bust-loose in song, any time.

Invalids murmured pitifully as Penrod came within hearing; and people trying to think cursed the day that they were born, when he went shrilling by. His hands in his pockets, his shining face uplifted to the sky of June, he passed down the street, singing his way into the heart's deepest hatred of all who heard him.

"One evuning I was sturow-ling Midst the city of the dead, I viewed where all a-round me Their peace-full graves was spread. But that which touched me mostlay----"

He had reached his journey's end, a junk-dealer's shop wherein lay the long-desired treasure of his soul--an accordion which might have possessed a high quality of interest for an antiquarian, being unquestionably a ruin, beautiful in decay, and quite beyond the sacrilegious reach of the restorer. But it was still able to disgorge sounds--loud, strange, compelling sounds, which could be heard for a remarkable distance in all directions; and it had one rich calf-like tone that had gone to Penrod's heart. He obtained the instrument for twenty-two cents, a price long since agreed upon with the junk-dealer, who falsely claimed a loss of profit, Shylock that he was! He had found the wreck in an alley.

With this purchase suspended from his shoulder by a faded green cord, Penrod set out in a somewhat homeward direction, but not by the route he had just travelled, though his motive for the change was not humanitarian. It was his desire to display himself thus troubadouring to the gaze of Marjorie Jones. Heralding his advance by continuous experiments in the music of the future, he pranced upon his blithesome way, the faithful Duke at his heels. (It was easier for Duke than it would have been for a younger dog, because, with advancing age, he had begun to grow a little deaf.)

Turning the corner nearest to the glamoured mansion of the Joneses, the boy jongleur came suddenly face to face with Marjorie, and, in the delicious surprise of the encounter, ceased to play, his hands, in agitation, falling from the instrument.

Bareheaded, the sunshine glorious upon her amber curls, Marjorie was strolling hand-in-hand with her baby brother, Mitchell, four years old. She wore pink that day--unforgettable pink, with a broad, black patent-leather belt, shimmering reflections dancing upon its surface. How beautiful she was! How sacred the sweet little baby brother, whose privilege it was to cling to that small hand, delicately powdered with freckles.

"Hello, Marjorie," said Penrod, affecting carelessness.

"Hello!" said Marjorie, with unexpected cordiality. She bent over her baby brother with motherly affections. "Say 'howdy' to the gentymuns, Mitchy-Mitch," she urged sweetly, turning him to face Penrod.

"Won't!" said Mitchy-Mitch, and, to emphasize his refusal, kicked the gentymuns upon the shin.

Penrod's feelings underwent instant change, and in the sole occupation of disliking Mitchy-Mitch, he wasted precious seconds which might have been better employed in philosophic consideration of the startling example, just afforded, of how a given law operates throughout the universe in precisely the same manner perpetually. Mr. Robert Williams would have understood this, easily.

"Oh, oh!" Marjorie cried, and put Mitchy-Mitch behind her with too much sweetness. "Maurice Levy's gone to Atlantic City with his mamma," she remarked conversationally, as if the kicking incident were quite closed.

"That's nothin'," returned Penrod, keeping his eye uneasily upon Mitchy-Mitch. "I know plenty people been better places than that--Chicago and everywhere."

There was unconscious ingratitude in his low rating of Atlantic City, for it was largely to the attractions of that resort he owed Miss Jones' present attitude of friendliness.

Of course, too, she was curious about the accordion. It would be dastardly to hint that she had noticed a paper bag which bulged the pocket of Penrod's coat, and yet this bag was undeniably conspicuous--"and children are very like grown people sometimes!"

Penrod brought forth the bag, purchased on the way at a drug store, and till this moment unopened, which expresses in a word the depth of his sentiment for Marjorie. It contained an abundant fifteen-cents' worth of lemon drops, jaw-breakers, licorice sticks, cinnamon drops, and shopworn choclate creams.

"Take all you want," he said, with off-hand generosity.

"Why, Penrod Schofield," exclaimed the wholly thawed damsel, "you nice boy!"

"Oh, that's nothin'," he returned airily. "I got a good deal of money, nowadays."

"Where from?"

"Oh--just around." With a cautious gesture he offered a jaw-breaker to Mitchy-Mitch, who snatched it indignantly and set about its absorption without delay.

"Can you play on that?" asked Marjorie, with some difficulty, her cheeks being rather too hilly for conversation.

"Want to hear me?"

She nodded, her eyes sweet with anticipation.

This was what he had come for. He threw back his head, lifted his eyes dreamily, as he had seen real musicians lift theirs, and distended the accordion preparing to produce the wonderful calf-like noise which was the instrument's great charm.

But the distention evoked a long wail which was at once drowned in another one.

"Ow! Owowaoh! Wowohah! Waowwow!" shrieked Mitchy-Mitch and the accordion together.

Mitchy-Mitch, to emphasize his disapproval of the accordion, opening his mouth still wider, lost therefrom the jaw-breaker, which rolled in the dust. Weeping, he stooped to retrieve it, and Marjorie, to prevent him, hastily set her foot upon it. Penrod offered another jaw-breaker; but Mitchy-Mitch struck it from his hand, desiring the former, which had convinced him of its sweetness.

Marjorie moved inadvertently; whereupon Mitchy-Mitch pounced upon the remains of his jaw-breaker and restored them, with accretions, to his mouth. His sister, uttering a cry of horror, sprang to the rescue, assisted by Penrod, whom she prevailed upon to hold Mitchy-Mitch's mouth open while she excavated. This operation being completed, and Penrod's right thumb severely bitten, Mitchy-Mitch closed his eyes tightly, stamped, squealed, bellowed, wrung his hands, and then, unexpectedly, kicked Penrod again.

Penrod put a hand in his pocket and drew forth a copper two-cent piece, large, round, and fairly bright.

He gave it to Mitchy-Mitch.

Mitchy-Mitch immediately stopped crying and gazed upon his benefactor with the eyes of a dog.

This world!

Thereafter did Penrod--with complete approval from Mitchy-Mitch--play the accordion for his lady to his heart's content, and hers. Never had he so won upon her; never had she let him feel so close to her before. They strolled up and down upon the sidewalk, eating, one thought between them, and soon she had learned to play the accordion almost as well as he. So passed a happy hour, which the Good King Rene of Anjou would have envied them, while Mitchy-Mitch made friends with Duke, romped about his sister and her swain, and clung to the hand of the latter, at intervals, with fondest affection and trust.

The noon whistles failed to disturb this little Arcady; only the sound of Mrs. Jones' voice for the third time summoning Marjorie and Mitchy-Mitch to lunch--sent Penrod on his way.

"I could come back this afternoon, I guess," he said, in parting.

"I'm not goin' to be here. I'm goin' to Baby Rennsdale's party."

Penrod looked blank, as she intended he should. Having thus satisfied herself, she added:

"There aren't goin' to be any boys there."

He was instantly radiant again.

"Marjorie----"

"Hum?"

"Do you wish I was goin' to be there?"

She looked shy, and turned away her head.

"Marjorie Jones!" (This was a voice from home.) "How many more times shall I have to call you?"

Marjorie moved away, her face still hidden from Penrod.

"Do you?" he urged.

At the gate, she turned quickly toward him, and said over her shoulder, all in a breath: "Yes! Come again to-morrow morning and I'll be on the corner. Bring your 'cordion!"

And she ran into the house, Mitchy-Mitch waving a loving hand to the boy on the sidewalk until the front door closed.

Chapter XIX. The Inner Boy

Penrod went home in splendour, pretending that he and Duke were a long procession; and he made enough noise to render the auricular part of the illusion perfect. His own family were already at the lunch-table when he arrived, and the parade halted only at the door of the dining-room.

"Oh something!" shouted Mr. Schofield, clasping his bilious brow with both hands. "Stop that noise! Isn't it awful enough for you to sing? Sit down! Not with that thing on! Take that green rope off your shoulder! Now take that thing out of the dining-room and throw it in the ash-can! Where did you get it?"

"Where did I get what, papa?" asked Penrod meekly, depositing the accordion in the hall just outside the dining-room door.

"That da--that third-hand concertina."

"It's a 'cordian," said Penrod, taking his place at the table, and noticing that both Margaret and Mr. Robert Williams (who happened to be a guest) were growing red.

"I don't care what you call it," said Mr. Schofield irritably. "I want to know where you got it."

Penrod's eyes met Margaret's: hers had a strained expression.

She very slightly shook her head. Penrod sent Mr. Williams a grateful look, and might have been startled if he could have seen himself in a mirror at that moment; for he regarded Mitchy-Mitch with concealed but vigorous aversion and the resemblance would have horrified him.

"A man gave it to me," he answered gently, and was rewarded by the visibly regained ease of his patron's manner, while Margaret leaned back in her chair and looked at her brother with real devotion.

"I should think he'd have been glad to," said Mr. Schofield. "Who was he?"

"Sir?" In spite of the candy which he had consumed in company with Marjorie and Mitchy-Mitch, Penrod had begun to eat lobster croquettes earnestly.

"Who was he?"

"Who do you mean, papa?"

"The man that gave you that ghastly Thing!"

"Yessir. A man gave it to me."

"I say, Who was he?" shouted Mr. Schofield.

"Well, I was just walking along, and the man came up to me--it was right down in front of Colgate's, where most of the paint's rubbed off the fence----"

"Penrod!" The father used his most dangerous tone.

"Sir?"

"Who was the man that gave you the concertina?"

"I don't know. I was walking along----"

"You never saw him before?"

"No, sir. I was just walk----"

"That will do," said Mr. Schofield, rising. "I suppose every family has its secret enemies and this was one of ours. I must ask to be excused!"

With that, he went out crossly, stopping in the hall a moment before passing beyond hearing. And, after lunch, Penrod sought in vain for his accordion; he even searched the library where his father sat reading, though, upon inquiry, Penrod explained that he was looking for a misplaced schoolbook. He thought he ought to study a little every day, he said, even during vacation-time. Much pleased, Mr. Schofield rose and joined the search, finding the missing work on mathematics with singular ease--which cost him precisely the price of the book the following September.

Penrod departed to study in the backyard. There, after a cautious survey of the neighbourhood, he managed to dislodge the iron cover of the cistern, and dropped the arithmetic within. A fine splash rewarded his listening ear. Thus assured that when he looked for that book again no one would find it for him, he replaced the cover, and betook himself pensively to the highway, discouraging Duke from following by repeated volleys of stones, some imaginary and others all too real.

Distant strains of brazen horns and the throbbing of drums were borne to him upon the kind breeze, reminding him that the world was made for joy, and that the Barzee and Potter Dog and Pony Show was exhibiting in a banlieue not far away. So, thither he bent his steps--the plentiful funds in his pocket burning hot holes all the way. He had paid twenty-two cents for the accordion, and fifteen for candy; he had bought the mercenary heart of Mitchy-Mitch for two: it certainly follows that there remained to him of his dollar, sixty-one cents--a fair fortune, and most unusual.

Arrived upon the populous and festive scene of the Dog and Pony Show, he first turned his attention to the brightly decorated booths which surrounded the tent. The cries of the peanut vendors, of the popcorn men, of the toy-balloon sellers, the stirring music of the band, playing before the performance to attract a crowd, the shouting of excited children and the barking of the dogs within the tent, all sounded exhilaratingly in Penrod's ears and set his blood a-tingle. Nevertheless, he did not squander his money or fling it to the winds in one grand splurge. Instead, he began cautiously with the purchase of an extraordinarily large pickle, which he obtained from an aged woman for his odd cent, too obvious a bargain to be missed. At an adjacent stand he bought a glass of raspberry lemonade (so alleged) and sipped it as he ate the pickle. He left nothing of either.

Next, he entered a small restaurant-tent and for a modest nickel was supplied with a fork and a box of sardines, previously opened, it is true, but more than half full. He consumed the sardines utterly, but left the tin box and the fork, after which he indulged in an inexpensive half-pint of lukewarm cider, at one of the open booths. Mug in hand, a gentle glow radiating toward his surface from various centres of activity deep inside him, he paused for breath--and the cool, sweet cadences of the watermelon man fell delectably upon his ear:

"Ice-cole water-melon; ice-cole water-melon; the biggest slice of ice-cole, ripe, red, ice-cole, rich an' rare; the biggest slice of ice-cole watermelon ever cut by the hand of man! Buy our ice-cole water-melon?"

Penrod, having drained the last drop of cider, complied with the watermelon man's luscious entreaty, and received a round slice of the fruit, magnificent in circumference and something over an inch in thickness. Leaving only the really dangerous part of the rind behind him, he wandered away from the vicinity of the watermelon man and supplied himself with a bag of peanuts, which, with the expenditure of a dime for admission, left a quarter still warm in his pocket. However, he managed to "break" the coin at a stand inside the tent, where a large, oblong paper box of popcorn was handed him, with twenty cents change. The box was too large to go into his pocket, but, having seated himself among some wistful Polack children, he placed it in his lap and devoured the contents at leisure during the performance. The popcorn was heavily larded with partially boiled molasses, and Penrod sandwiched mouthfuls of peanuts with gobs of this mass until the peanuts were all gone. After that, he ate with less avidity; a sense almost of satiety beginning to manifest itself to him, and it was not until the close of the performance that he disposed of the last morsel.

He descended a little heavily to the outflowing crowd in the arena, and bought a caterwauling toy balloon, but showed no great enthusiasm in manipulating it. Near the exit, as he came out, was a hot-waffle stand which he had overlooked, and a sense of duty obliged him to consume the three waffles, thickly powdered with sugar, which the waffle man cooked for him upon command.

They left a hottish taste in his mouth; they had not been quite up to his anticipation, indeed, and it was with a sense of relief that he turned to the "hokey-pokey" cart which stood close at hand, laden with square slabs of "Neapolitan ice-cream" wrapped in paper. He thought the ice-cream would be cooling, but somehow it fell short of the desired effect, and left a peculiar savour in his throat.

He walked away, too languid to blow his balloon, and passed a fresh-taffy booth with strange indifference. A bare-armed man was manipulating the taffy over a hook, pulling a great white mass to the desired stage of "candying," but Penrod did not pause to watch the operation; in fact, he averted his eyes (which were slightly glazed) in passing. He did not analyze his motives: simply, he was conscious that he preferred not to look at the mass of taffy.

For some reason, he put a considerable distance between himself and the taffy-stand, but before long halted in the presence of a red-faced man who flourished a long fork over a small cooking apparatus and shouted jovially: "Winnies! Here's your hot winnies! Hot winny-wurst! Food for the over-worked brain, nourishing for the weak stummick, entertaining for the tired business man! Here's your hot winnies, three for a nickel, a half-a-dime, the twentieth-pot-of- a-dollah!"

This, above all nectar and ambrosia, was the favourite dish of Penrod Schofield. Nothing inside him now craved it--on the contrary! But memory is the great hypnotist; his mind argued against his inwards that opportunity knocked at his door: "winny-wurst" was rigidly forbidden by the home authorities. Besides, there was a last nickel in his pocket; and nature protested against its survival. Also, the redfaced man had himself proclaimed his wares nourishing for the weak stummick.

Penrod placed the nickel in the red hand of the red-faced man. He ate two of the three greasy, cigarlike shapes cordially pressed upon him in return. The first bite convinced him that he had made a mistake; these winnies seemed of a very inferior flavour, almost unpleasant, in fact. But he felt obliged to conceal his poor opinion of them, for fear of offending the red-faced man. He ate without haste or eagerness--so slowly, indeed, that he began to think the redfaced man might dislike him, as a deterrent of trade. Perhaps Penrod's mind was not working well, for he failed to remember that no law compelled him to remain under the eye of the red-faced man, but the virulent repulsion excited by his attempt to take a bite of the third sausage inspired him with at least an excuse for postponement.

"Mighty good," he murmured feebly, placing the sausage in the pocket of his jacket with a shaking hand. "Guess I'll save this one to eat at home, after--after dinner."

He moved sluggishly away, wishing he had not thought of dinner. A side-show, undiscovered until now, failed to arouse his interest, not even exciting a wish that he had known of its existence when he had money. For a time he stared without attraction; the weather-worn colours conveying no meaning to comprehension at a huge canvas poster depicting the chief his torpid eye. Then, little by little, the poster became more vivid to his consciousness. There was a greenish-tinted person in the tent, it seemed, who thrived upon a reptilian diet.

Suddenly, Penrod decided that it was time to go home.

Lesson 62

1. Read chapters 20 and 21 of *Penrod*.
2. Write about Rupe Collins on your character sheet.

Chapter XX. Brothers of Angels

"Indeed, doctor," said Mrs. Schofield, with agitation and profound conviction, just after eight o'clock that evening, "I shall always believe in mustard plasters--mustard plasters and hot--water bags. If it hadn't been for them I don't believed he'd have lived till you got here--I do not!"

"Margaret," called Mr. Schofield from the open door of a bedroom, "Margaret, where did you put that aromatic ammonia? Where's Margaret?"

But he had to find the aromatic spirits of ammonia himself, for Margaret was not in the house. She stood in the shadow beneath a maple tree near the street corner, a guitar-case in her hand; and she scanned with anxiety a briskly approaching figure. The arc light, swinging above, revealed this figure as that of him she awaited. He was passing toward the gate without seeing her, when she arrested him with a fateful whisper.

"Bob!"

Mr. Robert Williams swung about hastily. "Why, Margaret!"

"Here, take your guitar," she whispered hurriedly. "I was afraid if father happened to find it he'd break it all to pieces!"

"What for?" asked the startled Robert.

"Because I'm sure he knows it's yours."

"But what----"

"Oh, Bob," she moaned, "I was waiting here to tell you. I was so afraid you'd try to come in----"

"Try!" exclaimed the unfortunate young man, quite dumfounded. "Try to come----"

"Yes, before I warned you. I've been waiting here to tell you, Bob, you mustn't come near the house if I were you I'd stay away from even this neighbourhood--far away! For a while I don't think it would be actually safe for----"

"Margaret, will you please----"

"It's all on account of that dollar you gave Penrod this morning," she walled. "First, he bought that horrible concertina that made papa so furious "But Penrod didn't tell that I----"

"Oh, wait!" she cried lamentably. "Listen! He didn't tell at lunch, but he got home about dinner-time in the most--well! I've seen pale people before, but nothing like Penrod. Nobody could imagine it--not unless they'd seen him! And he looked, so strange, and kept making such unnatural faces, and at first all he would say was that he'd eaten a little piece of apple and thought it must have some microbes on it. But he got sicker and sicker, and we put him to bed--and then we all thought he was going to die--and, of course, no little piece of apple would have--well, and he kept getting worse and then he said he'd had a dollar. He said he'd spent it for the concertina, and watermelon, and chocolate-creams, and licorice sticks, and lemon-drops, and peanuts, and jaw-breakers, and sardines, and raspberry lemonade, and pickles, and popcorn, and ice-cream, and cider, and sausage--there was sausage in his pocket, and mamma says his jacket is ruined--and cinnamon drops--and waffles--and he ate four or five lobster croquettes at lunch--and papa said, 'Who gave you that dollar?' Only he didn't say 'who'--he said something horrible, Bob! And Penrod thought he was going to die, and he said you gave it to him, and oh! it was just pitiful to hear the poor child, Bob, because he thought he was dying, you see, and he blamed you for the whole thing. He said if you'd only let him alone and not given it to him, he'd have grown up to be a good man--and now he couldn't! I never heard anything so heart-rending--he was so weak he could hardly whisper, but he kept trying to talk, telling us over and over it was all your fault."

In the darkness Mr. Williams' facial expression could not be seen, but his voice sounded hopeful.

"Is he--is he still in a great deal of pain?"

"They say the crisis is past," said Margaret, "but the doctor's still up there. He said it was the acutest case of indigestion he had ever treated in the whole course of his professional practice."

"Of course I didn't know what he'd do with the dollar," said Robert.

She did not reply.

He began plaintively, "Margaret, you don't----"

"I've never seen papa and mamma so upset about anything," she said, rather primly.

"You mean they're upset about me?"

"We are all very much upset," returned Margaret, more starch in her tone as she remembered not only Penrod's sufferings but a duty she had vowed herself to perform.

"Margaret! You don't----"

"Robert," she said firmly and, also, with a rhetorical complexity which breeds a suspicion of pre-rehearsal--"Robert, for the present I can only look at it in one way: when you gave that money to Penrod you put into the hands of an unthinking little child a weapon which might be, and, indeed was, the means of his undoing. Boys are not respon----"

"But you saw me give him the dollar, and you didn't----"

"Robert!" she checked him with increasing severity. "I am only a woman and not accustomed to thinking everything out on the spur of the moment; but I cannot change my mind. Not now, at least."

"And you think I'd better not come in to-night?"

"To-night!" she gasped. "Not for weeks! Papa would----"

"But Margaret," he urged plaintively, "how can you blame me for----"

"I have not used the word 'blame,'" she interrupted. "But I must insist that for your carelessness to--to wreak such havoc--cannot fail to--to lessen my confidence in your powers of judgment. I cannot change my convictions in this matter--not to-night--and I cannot remain here another instant. The poor child may need me. Robert, good-night."

With chill dignity she withdrew, entered the house, and returned to the sick-room, leaving the young man in outer darkness to brood upon his crime--and upon Penrod.

That sincere invalid became convalescent upon the third day; and a week elapsed, then, before he found an opportunity to leave the house unaccompanied--save by Duke. But at last he set forth and approached the Jones neighbourhood in high spirits, pleasantly conscious of his pallor, hollow cheeks, and other perquisites of illness provocative of interest.

One thought troubled him a little because it gave him a sense of inferiority to a rival. He believed, against his will, that Maurice Levy could have successfully eaten chocolate-creams, licorice sticks, lemon-drops, jaw-breakers, peanuts, waffles, lobster croquettes, sardines, cinnamon-drops, watermelon, pickles, popcorn, ice-cream and sausage with raspberry lemonade and cider. Penrod had admitted to himself that Maurice could do it and afterward attend to business, or pleasure, without the slightest discomfort; and this was probably no more than a fair estimate of one of the great constitutions of all time. As a digester, Maurice Levy would have disappointed a Borgia.

Fortunately, Maurice was still at Atlantic City--and now the convalescent's heart leaped. In the distance he saw Marjorie coming--in pink again, with a ravishing little parasol over her head. And alone! No Mitchy-Mitch was to mar this meeting.

Penrod increased the feebleness of his steps, now and then leaning upon the fence as if for support.

"How do you do, Marjorie?" he said, in his best sick-room voice, as she came near.

To his pained amazement, she proceeded on her way, her nose at a celebrated elevation--an icy nose.

She cut him dead.

He threw his invalid's airs to the winds, and hastened after her.

"Marjorie," he pleaded, "what's the matter? Are you mad? Honest, that day you said to come back next morning, and you'd be on the corner, I was sick. Honest, I was awful sick, Marjorie! I had to have the doctor----"

"Doctor!" She whirled upon him, her lovely eyes blazing.

"I guess we've had to have the doctor enough at our house, thanks to you, Mister Penrod Schofield. Papa says you haven't got near sense enough to come in out of the rain, after what you did to poor little Mitchy-Mitch----"

"What?"

"Yes, and he's sick in bed yet!" Marjorie went on, with unabated fury. "And papa says if he ever catches you in this part of town----"

"What'd I do to Mitchy-Mitch?" gasped Penrod.

"You know well enough what you did to Mitchy-Mitch!" she cried. "You gave him that great, big, nasty two-cent piece!"

"Well, what of it?"

"Mitchy-Mitch swallowed it!"

"What!"

"And papa says if he ever just lays eyes on you, once, in this neighbourhood----"

But Penrod had started for home.

In his embittered heart there was increasing a critical disapproval of the Creator's methods. When He made pretty girls, thought Penrod, why couldn't He have left out their little brothers!

Chapter XXI. Rupe Collins

For several days after this, Penrod thought of growing up to be a monk, and engaged in good works so far as to carry some kittens (that otherwise would have been drowned) and a pair of Margaret's outworn dancing-slippers to a poor, ungrateful old man sojourning in a shed up the alley. And although Mr. Robert Williams, after a very short interval, began to leave his guitar on the front porch again, exactly as if he thought nothing had happened, Penrod, with his younger vision of a father's mood, remained coldly distant from the Jones neighbourhood. With his own family his manner was gentle, proud and sad, but not for long enough to frighten them. The change came with mystifying abruptness at the end of the week.

It was Duke who brought it about.

Duke could chase a much bigger dog out of the Schofields' yard and far down the street. This might be thought to indicate unusual valour on the part of Duke and cowardice on that of the bigger dogs whom he undoubtedly put to rout. On the contrary, all such flights were founded in mere superstition, for dogs are even more superstitious than boys; and the most firmly established of all dog superstitions is that any dog--be he the smallest and feeblest in the world--can whip any trespasser whatsoever.

A rat-terrier believes that on his home grounds he can whip an elephant. It follows, of course, that a big dog, away from his own home, will run from a little dog in the little dog's neighbourhood. Otherwise, the big dog must face a charge of inconsistency, and dogs are as consistent as they are superstitious. A dog believes in war, but he is convinced that there are times when it is moral to run; and the thoughtful physiognomist, seeing a big dog fleeing out of a little dog's yard, must observe that the expression of the big dog's face is more conscientious than alarmed: it is the expression of a person performing a duty to himself.

Penrod understood these matters perfectly; he knew that the gaunt brown hound Duke chased up the alley had fled only out of deference to a custom, yet Penrod could not refrain from bragging of Duke to the hound's owner, a fat-faced stranger of twelve or thirteen, who had wandered into the neighbourhood.

"You better keep that ole yellow dog o' yours back," said Penrod ominously, as he climbed the fence. "You better catch him and hold him till I get mine inside the yard again. Duke's chewed up some pretty bad bulldogs around here."

The fat-faced boy gave Penrod a fishy stare. "You'd oughta learn him not to do that," he said. "It'll make him sick."

"What will?"

The stranger laughed raspingly and gazed up the alley, where the hound, having come to a halt, now coolly sat down, and, with an expression of roguish benevolence, patronizingly watched the tempered fury of Duke, whose assaults and barkings were becoming perfunctory.

"What'll make Duke sick?" Penrod demanded.

"Eatin' dead bulldogs people leave around here."

This was not improvisation but formula, adapted from other occasions to the present encounter; nevertheless, it was new to Penrod, and he was so taken with it that resentment lost itself in admiration. Hastily committing the gem to memory for use upon a dog-owning friend, he inquired in a sociable tone:

"What's your dog's name?"

"Dan. You better call your ole pup, 'cause Dan eats live dogs."

Dan's actions poorly supported his master's assertion, for, upon Duke's ceasing to bark, Dan rose and showed the most courteous interest in making the little, old dog's acquaintance. Dan had a great deal of manner, and it became plain that Duke was impressed favourably in spite of former prejudice, so that presently the two trotted amicably back to their masters and sat down with the harmonious but indifferent air of having known each other intimately for years.

They were received without comment, though both boys looked at them reflectively for a time. It was Penrod who spoke first.

"What number you go to?" (In an "oral lesson in English," Penrod had been instructed to put this question in another form: "May I ask which of our public schools you attend?")

"Me? What number do I go to?" said the stranger, contemptuously. "I don't go to no number in vacation!"

"I mean when it ain't."

"Third," returned the fat-faced boy. "I got 'em all scared in that school."

"What of?" innocently asked Penrod, to whom "the Third"--in a distant part of town--was undiscovered country.

"What of? I guess you'd soon see what of, if you ever was in that school about one day. You'd be lucky if you got out alive!"

"Are the teachers mean?"

The other boy frowned with bitter scorn. "Teachers! Teachers don't order me around, I can tell you! They're mighty careful how they try to run over Rupe Collins."

"Who's Rupe Collins?"

"Who is he?" echoed the fat-faced boy incredulously. "Say, ain't you got any sense?"

"What?"

"Say, wouldn't you be just as happy if you had some sense?"

"Ye-es." Penrod's answer, like the look he lifted to the impressive stranger, was meek and placative. "Rupe Collins is the principal at your school, guess."

The other yelled with jeering laughter, and mocked Penrod's manner and voice. "Rupe Collins is the principal at your school, I guess!" He laughed harshly again, then suddenly showed truculence. "Say, 'bo, whyn't you learn enough to go in the house when it rains? What's the matter of you, anyhow?"

"Well," urged Penrod timidly, "nobody ever told me who Rupe Collins is: I got a right to think he's the principal, haven't I?"

The fat-faced boy shook his head disgustedly. "Honest, you make me sick!"

Penrod's expression became one of despair. "Well, who is he?" he cried.

"'Who is he?'" mocked the other, with a scorn that withered. "'Who is he?' Me!"

"Oh!" Penrod was humiliated but relieved: he felt that he had proved himself criminally ignorant, yet a peril seemed to have passed. "Rupe Collins is your name, then, I guess. I kind of thought it was, all the time."

The fat-faced boy still appeared embittered, burlesquing this speech in a hateful falsetto. "'Rupe Collins is your name, then, I guess!' Oh, you 'kind of thought it was, all the time,' did you?" Suddenly concentrating his brow into a histrionic scowl he thrust his face within an inch of Penrod's. "Yes, sonny, Rupe Collins is my name, and you better look out what you say when he's around or you'll get in big trouble! You understand that, 'Bo?"

Penrod was cowed but fascinated: he felt that there was something dangerous and dashing about this newcomer.

"Yes," he said, feebly, drawing back. "My name's Penrod Schofield."

"Then I reckon your father and mother ain't got good sense," said Mr. Collins promptly, this also being formula.

"Why?"

"Cause if they had they'd of give you a good name!" And the agreeable youth instantly rewarded himself for the wit with another yell of rasping laughter, after which he pointed suddenly at Penrod's right hand.

"Where'd you get that wart on your finger?" he demanded severely.

"Which finger?" asked the mystified Penrod, extending his hand.

"The middle one."

"Where?"

"There!" exclaimed Rupe Collins, seizing and vigorously twisting the wartless finger naively offered for his inspection.

"Quit!" shouted Penrod in agony. "Quee-yut!"

"Say your prayers!" commanded Rupe, and continued to twist the luckless finger until Penrod writhed to his knees.

"Ow!" The victim, released, looked grievously upon the still painful finger.

At this Rupe's scornful expression altered to one of contrition. "Well, I declare!" he exclaimed remorsefully. "I didn't s'pose it would hurt. Turn about's fair play; so now you do that to me."

He extended the middle finger of his left hand and Penrod promptly seized it, but did not twist it, for he was instantly swung round with his back to his amiable new acquaintance: Rupe's right hand operated upon the back of Penrod's slender neck; Rupe's knee tortured the small of Penrod's back.

"Ow!" Penrod bent far forward involuntarily and went to his knees again.

"Lick dirt," commanded Rupe, forcing the captive's face to the sidewalk; and the suffering Penrod completed this ceremony.

Mr. Collins evinced satisfaction by means of his horse laugh.

"You'd last jest about one day up at the Third!" he said. "You'd come runnin' home, yellin' 'Mom-muh, Mom-muh,' before recess was over!"

"No, I wouldn't," Penrod protested rather weakly, dusting his knees.

"You would, too!"

"No, I w----

"Looky here," said the fat-faced boy, darkly, "what you mean, counterdicking me?"

He advanced a step and Penrod hastily qualified his contradiction.

"I mean, I don't think I would. I----"

"You better look out!" Rupe moved closer, and unexpectedly grasped the back of Penrod's neck again. "Say, 'I would run home yellin' "Mom-muh!"

"Ow! I would run home yellin' 'Mom-muh.'"

"There!" said Rupe, giving the helpless nape a final squeeze. "That's the way we do up at the Third."

Penrod rubbed his neck and asked meekly:

"Can you do that to any boy up at the Third?"

"See here now," said Rupe, in the tone of one goaded beyond all endurance, "You say if I can! You better say it quick, or----"

"I knew you could," Penrod interposed hastily, with the pathetic semblance of a laugh. "I only said that in fun."

"In 'fun'!" repeated Rupe stormily. "You better look out how you----"

"Well, I said I wasn't in earnest!" Penrod retreated a few steps. "I knew you could, all the time. I expect I could do it to some of the boys up at the Third, myself. Couldn't I?"

"No, you couldn't."

"Well, there must be some boy up there that I could----"

"No, they ain't! You better----"

"I expect not, then," said Penrod, quickly.

"You better 'expect not.' Didn't I tell you once you'd never get back alive if you ever tried to come up around the Third? You want me to show you how we do up there, 'bo?"

He began a slow and deadly advance, whereupon Penrod timidly offered a diversion:

"Say, Rupe, I got a box of rats in our stable under a glass cover, so you can watch 'em jump around when you hammer on the box. Come on and look at 'em."

"All right," said the fat-faced boy, slightly mollified. "We'll let Dan kill 'em."

"No, sir! I'm goin' to keep 'em. They're kind of pets; I've had 'em all summer--I got names for em, and----"

"Looky here, 'bo. Did you hear me say we'll let 'Dan kill 'em?"

"Yes, but I won't----"

"What won't you?" Rupe became sinister immediately. "It seems to me you're gettin' pretty fresh around here."

"Well, I don't want----"

Mr. Collins once more brought into play the dreadful eye-to- eye scowl as practised "up at the Third," and, sometimes, also by young leading men upon the stage. Frowning appallingly, and thrusting forward his underlip, he placed his nose almost in contact with the nose of Penrod, whose eyes naturally became crossed.

"Dan kills the rats. See?" hissed the fat-faced boy, maintaining the horrible juxtaposition.

"Well, all right," said Penrod, swallowing. "I don't want 'em much." And when the pose had been relaxed, he stared at his new friend for a moment, almost with reverence. Then he brightened.

"Come on, Rupe!" he cried enthusiastically, as he climbed the fence. "We'll give our dogs a little live meat--'bo!"

Lesson 63

1. Read chapters 22 and 23 of *Penrod.*
2. What is the first paragraph of chapter 23 talking about? (Answers)
3. What is the "expurgator" in the first sentence of paragraph 2? What does that tell you about the fight? (Answers)

Chapter XXII. The Imitator

At the dinner-table, that evening, Penrod Surprised his family by remarking, in a voice they had never heard him attempt--a law- giving voice of intentional gruffness:

"Any man that's makin' a hunderd dollars a month is makin' good money."

"What?" asked Mr. Schofield, staring, for the previous conversation had concerned the illness of an infant relative in Council Bluffs.

"Any man that's makin' a hunderd dollars a month is makin' good money."

"What is he talking about!" Margaret appealed to the invisible.

"Well," said Penrod, frowning, "that's what foremen at the ladder works get."

"How in the world do you know?" asked his mother.

"Well, I know it! A hunderd dollars a month is good money, I tell you!"

"Well, what of it?" said the father, impatiently.

"Nothin'. I only said it was good money."

Mr. Schofield shook his head, dismissing the subject; and here he made a mistake: he should have followed up his son's singular contribution to the conversation. That would have revealed the fact that there was a certain Rupe Collins whose father was a foreman at the ladder works. All clues are important when a boy makes his first remark in a new key.

"'Good money'?" repeated Margaret, curiously. "What is 'good' money?"

Penrod turned upon her a stern glance. "Say, wouldn't you be just as happy if you had some sense?"

"Penrod!" shouted his father. But Penrod's mother gazed with dismay at her son: he had never before spoken like that to his sister.

Mrs. Schofield might have been more dismayed than she was, if she had realized that it was the beginning of an epoch. After dinner, Penrod was slightly scalded in the back as the result of telling Della, the cook, that there was a wart on the middle finger of her right hand. Della thus proving poor material for his new manner to work upon, he approached Duke, in the backyard, and, bending double, seized the lowly animal by the forepaws.

"I let you know my name's Penrod Schofield," hissed the boy. He protruded his underlip ferociously, scowled, and thrust forward his head until his nose touched the dog's. "And you better look out when Penrod Schofield's around, or you'll get in big trouble! You understan' that, 'Bo?"

The next day, and the next, the increasing change in Penrod puzzled and distressed his family, who had no idea of its source.

How might they guess that hero-worship takes such forms? They were vaguely conscious that a rather shabby boy, not of the neighbourhood, came to "play" with Penrod several times; but they failed to connect this circumstance with the peculiar behaviour of the son of the house, whose ideals (his father remarked) seemed to have suddenly become identical with those of Gyp the Blood.

Meanwhile, for Penrod himself, "life had taken on new meaning, new richness." He had become a fighting man--in conversation at least. "Do you want to know how I do when they try to slip up on me from behind?" he asked Della. And he enacted for her unappreciative eye a scene of fistic manoeuvres wherein he held an imaginary antagonist helpless in a net of stratagems.

Frequently, when he was alone, he would outwit, and pummel this same enemy, and, after a cunning feint, land a dolorous stroke full upon a face of air. "There! I guess you'll know better next time. That's the way we do up at the Third!"

Sometimes, in solitary pantomime, he encountered more than one opponent at a time, for numbers were apt to come upon him treacherously, especially at a little after his rising hour, when he might be caught at a disadvantage--perhaps standing on one leg to encase the other in his knickerbockers. Like lightning, he would hurl the trapping garment from him, and, ducking and pivoting, deal great sweeping blows among the circle of sneaking devils. (That was how he broke the clock in his bedroom.) And while these battles were occupying his attention, it was a waste of voice to call him to breakfast, though if his mother, losing patience, came to his room, she would find him seated on the bed pulling at a stocking. "Well, ain't I coming fast as I can?"

At the table and about the house generally he was bumptious, loud with fatuous misinformation, and assumed a domineering tone, which neither satire nor reproof seemed able to reduce: but it was among his own intimates that his new superiority was most outrageous. He twisted the fingers and squeezed the necks of all the boys of the neighbourhood, meeting their indignation with a hoarse and rasping laugh he had acquired after short practice in the stable, where he jeered and taunted the lawn-mower, the garden-scythe and the wheelbarrow quite out of countenance.

Likewise he bragged to the other boys by the hour, Rupe Collins being the chief subject of encomium--next to Penrod himself. "That's the way we do up at the Third," became staple explanation of violence, for Penrod, like Tartarin, was plastic in the hands of his own imagination, and at times convinced himself that he really was one of those dark and murderous spirits exclusively of whom "the Third" was composed--according to Rupe Collins.

Then, when Penrod had exhausted himself repeating to nausea accounts of the prowess of himself and his great friend, he would turn to two other subjects for vainglory. These were his father and Duke.

Mothers must accept the fact that between babyhood and manhood their sons do not boast of them. The boy, with boys, is a Choctaw; and either the influence or the protection of women is shameful. "Your mother won't let you," is an insult. But, "My father won't let me," is a dignified explanation and cannot be hooted. A boy is ruined among his fellows if he talks much of his mother or sisters; and he must recognize it as his duty to offer at least the appearance of persecution to all things ranked as female, such as cats and every species of fowl. But he must champion his father and his dog, and, ever, ready to pit either against any challenger, must picture both as ravening for battle and absolutely unconquerable.

Penrod, of course, had always talked by the code, but, under the new stimulus, Duke was represented virtually as a cross between Bob, Son of Battle, and a South American vampire; and this in spite of the fact that Duke himself often sat close by, a living lie, with the hope of peace in his heart. As for Penrod's father, that gladiator was painted as of sentiments and dimensions suitable to a super-demon composed of equal parts of Goliath, Jack Johnson and the Emperor Nero.

Even Penrod's walk was affected; he adopted a gait which was a kind of taunting swagger; and, when he passed other children on the street, he practised the habit of feinting a blow; then, as the victim dodged, he rasped the triumphant horse laugh which he gradually mastered to horrible perfection. He did this to Marjorie Jones--ay! this was their next meeting, and such is Eros, young! What was even worse, in Marjorie's opinion, he went on his way without explanation, and left her standing on the corner talking about it, long after he was out of hearing.

Within five days from his first encounter with Rupe Collins, Penrod had become unbearable. He even almost alienated Sam Williams, who for a time submitted to finger twisting and neck squeezing and the new style of conversation, but finally declared that Penrod made him "sick." He made the statement with fervour, one sultry afternoon, in Mr. Schofield's stable, in the presence of Herman and Verman.

"You better look out, 'bo," said Penrod, threateningly. "I'll show you a little how we do up at the Third."

"Up at the Third!" Sam repeated with scorn. "You haven't ever been up there."

"I haven't?" cried Penrod. "I haven't?"

"No, you haven't!"

"Looky here!" Penrod, darkly argumentative, prepared to perform the eye-to-eye business. "When haven't I been up there?"

"You haven't never been up there!" In spite of Penrod's closely approaching nose Sam maintained his ground, and appealed for confirmation. "Has he, Herman?"

"I don' reckon so," said Herman, laughing.

293

"What!" Penrod transferred his nose to the immediate vicinity of Herman's nose. "You don't reckon so, 'bo, don't you? You better look out how you reckon around here! You understan' that, 'Bo?"

Herman bore the eye-to-eye very well; indeed, it seemed to please him, for he continued to laugh while Verman chuckled delightedly. The brothers had been in the country picking berries for a week, and it happened that this was their first experience of the new manifestation of Penrod.

"Haven't I been up at the Third?" the sinister Penrod demanded.

"I don' reckon so. How come you ast me?"

"Didn't you just hear me say I been up there?"

"Well," said Herman mischievously, "hearin' ain't believin'!"

Penrod clutched him by the back of the neck, but Herman, laughing loudly, ducked and released himself at once, retreating to the wall.

"You take that back!" Penrod shouted, striking out wildly.

"Don' git mad," begged the small boy, while a number of blows falling upon his warding arms failed to abate his amusement, and a sound one upon the cheek only made him laugh the more unrestrainedly. He behaved exactly as if Penrod were tickling him, and his brother, Verman, rolled with joy in a wheelbarrow. Penrod pummelled till he was tired, and produced no greater effect.

"There!" he panted, desisting finally. "Now I reckon you know whether I been up there or not!"

Herman rubbed his smitten cheek. "Pow!" he exclaimed. "Pow-ee! You cert'ny did lan' me good one nat time! Oo-ee! she hurt!"

"You'll get hurt worse'n that," Penrod assured him, "if you stay around here much. Rupe Collins is comin' this afternoon, he said. We're goin' to make some policemen's billies out of the rake handle."

"You go' spoil new rake you' pa bought?"

"What do we care? I and Rupe got to have billies, haven't we?"

"How you make 'em?"

"Melt lead and pour in a hole we're goin' to make in the end of 'em. Then we're goin' to carry 'em in our pockets, and if anybody says anything to us--oh, oh! look out! They won't get a crack on the head--oh, no!"

"When's Rupe Collins coming?" Sam Williams inquired rather uneasily. He had heard a great deal too much of this personage, but as yet the pleasure of actual acquaintance had been denied him.

"He's liable to be here any time," answered Penrod. "You better look out. You'll be lucky if you get home alive, if you stay till he comes."

"I ain't afraid of him," Sam returned, conventionally.

"You are, too!" (There was some truth in the retort.) "There ain't any boy in this part of town but me that wouldn't be afraid of him. You'd be afraid to talk to him. You wouldn't get a word out of your mouth before old Rupie'd have you where you'd wished you never come around him, lettin' on like you was so much! You wouldn't run home yellin' 'Mom-muh' or nothin'! Oh, no!"

"Who Rupe Collins?" asked Herman.

"'Who Rupe Collins?'" Penrod mocked, and used his rasping laugh, but, instead of showing fright, Herman appeared to think he was meant to laugh, too; and so he did, echoed by Verman. "You just hang around here a little while longer," Penrod added, grimly, "and you'll find out who Rupe Collins is, and I pity you when you do!"

"What he go' do?"

"You'll see; that's all! You just wait and----"

At this moment a brown hound ran into the stable through the alley door, wagged a greeting to Penrod, and fraternized with Duke. The fat-faced boy appeared upon the threshold and gazed coldly about the little company in the carriage-house, whereupon the brothers, ceasing from merriment, were instantly impassive, and Sam Williams moved a little nearer the door leading into the yard.

Obviously, Sam regarded the newcomer as a redoubtable if not ominous figure. He was a head taller than either Sam or Penrod; head and shoulders taller than Herman, who was short for his age; and Verman could hardly be used for purposes of comparison at all, being a mere squat brown spot, not yet quite nine years on this planet. And to Sam's mind, the aspect of Mr. Collins realized Penrod's portentous foreshadowings. Upon the fat face there was an expression of truculent intolerance which had been cultivated by careful habit to such perfection that Sam's heart sank at sight of it. A somewhat enfeebled twin to this expression had of late often decorated the visage of Penrod, and appeared upon that ingenuous surface now, as he advanced to welcome the eminent visitor.

The host swaggered toward the door with a great deal of shoulder movement, carelessly feinting a slap at Verman in passing, and creating by various means the atmosphere of a man who has contemptuously amused himself with underlings while awaiting an equal.

"Hello, 'bo!" Penrod said in the deepest voice possible to him.

"Who you callin' 'bo?" was the ungracious response, accompanied by immediate action of a similar nature. Rupe held Penrod's head in the crook of an elbow and massaged his temples with a hard-pressing knuckle.

"I was only in fun, Rupie," pleaded the sufferer, and then, being set free, "Come here, Sam," he said.

"What for?"

Penrod laughed pityingly. "Pshaw, I ain't goin' to hurt you. Come on." Sam, maintaining his position near the other door, Penrod went to him and caught him round the neck.

"Watch me, Rupie!" Penrod called, and performed upon Sam the knuckle operation which he had himself just undergone, Sam submitting mechanically, his eyes fixed with increasing uneasiness upon Rupe Collins. Sam had a premonition that something even more painful than Penrod's knuckle was going to be inflicted upon him.

"That don' hurt," said Penrod, pushing him away.

"Yes, it does, too!" Sam rubbed his temple.

"Puh! It didn't hurt me, did it, Rupie? Come on in, Rupe: show this baby where he's got a wart on his finger."

"You showed me that trick," Sam objected. "You already did that to me. You tried it twice this afternoon and I don't know how many times before, only you weren't strong enough after the first time. Anyway, I know what it is, and I don't----"

"Come on, Rupe," said Penrod. "Make the baby lick dirt."

At this bidding, Rupe approached, while Sam, still protesting, moved to the threshold of the outer door; but Penrod seized him by the shoulders and swung him indoors with a shout.

"Little baby wants to run home to its Mom-muh! Here he is, Rupie."

Thereupon was Penrod's treachery to an old comrade properly rewarded, for as the two struggled, Rupe caught each by the back of the neck, simultaneously, and, with creditable impartiality, forced both boys to their knees.

"Lick dirt!" he commanded, forcing them still forward, until their faces were close to the stable floor.

At this moment he received a real surprise. With a loud whack something struck the back of his head, and, turning, he beheld Verman in the act of lifting a piece of lath to strike again.

"Em moys ome!" said Verman, the Giant Killer.

"He tongue-tie'," Herman explained. "He say, let 'em boys alone."

Rupe addressed his host briefly:

"Chase them out o' here!"

"I mine my own biznuss," said Herman. "You let 'em boys alone."

Rupe strode across the still prostrate Sam, stepped upon Penrod, and, equipping his countenance with the terrifying scowl and protruded jaw, lowered his head to the level of Herman's.

"You'll be lucky if you leave here alive!" And he leaned forward till his nose was within less than an inch of Herman's nose.

It could be felt that something awful was about to happen, and Penrod, as he rose from the floor, suffered an unexpected twinge of apprehension and remorse: he hoped that Rupe wouldn't really hurt Herman. A sudden dislike of Rupe and Rupe's ways rose within him, as he looked at the big boy overwhelming the little boy with that ferocious scowl. Penrod, all at once, felt sorry about something indefinable; and, with equal vagueness, he felt foolish. "Come on, Rupe," he suggested, feebly, "let Herman go, and let's us make our billies out of the rake handle."

The rake handle, however, was not available, if Rupe had inclined to favour the suggestion. Verman had discarded his lath for the rake, which he was at this moment lifting in the air.

"You," the fat-faced boy said venomously to Herman, "I'm agoin' to----"

But he had allowed his nose to remain too long near Herman's.

Penrod's familiar nose had been as close with only a ticklish spinal effect upon the boy. The result produced by the glare of Rupe's unfamiliar eyes, and by the dreadfully suggestive proximity of Rupe's unfamiliar nose, was altogether different.

Penrod and Sam heard Rupe suddenly squawk and bellow; saw him writhe and twist and fling out his arms like flails, though without removing his face from its juxtaposition; indeed, for a moment, the two heads seemed even closer.

Then they separated--and battle was on!

Chapter XXIII. Troops in Action

How neat and pure is the task of the chronicler who has the tale to tell of a "good rousing fight" between boys or men who fight in the "good old English way," according to a model set for fights in books long before Tom Brown went to Rugby. There are seconds and rounds and rules of fair-play, and always there is great good feeling in the end--though sometimes, to vary the model, "the Butcher" defeats the hero--and the chronicler who stencils this fine old pattern on his page is certain of applause as the stirrer of "red blood." There is no surer recipe.

But when Herman and Verman set to 't the record must be no more than a few fragments left by the expurgator. It has been perhaps sufficiently suggested that the altercation in Mr. Schofield's stable opened with mayhem in respect to the aggressor's nose. Expressing vocally his indignation and the extremity of his pained surprise, Mr. Collins stepped backward, holding his left hand over his nose, and striking at Herman with his right. Then Verman hit him with the rake.

Verman struck from behind. He struck as hard as he could. And he struck with the tines down--For, in his simple, direct African way he wished to kill his enemy, and he wished to kill him as soon as possible. That was his single, earnest purpose.

On this account, Rupe Collins was peculiarly unfortunate. He was plucky and he enjoyed conflict, but neither his ambitions nor his anticipations had ever included murder. He had not learned that an habitually aggressive person runs the danger of colliding with beings for whom theories about "hitting below the belt" have not yet made their appearance.

The rake glanced from the back of Rupe's head to his shoulder, but it felled him. Both darkies jumped full upon him instantly, and the three rolled and twisted upon the stable-floor, unloosing upon the air sincere maledictions closely connected with complaints of cruel and unusual treatment; while certain expressions of feeling presently emanating from Herman and Verman indicated that Rupe Collins, in this extremity, was proving himself not too slavishly addicted to fighting by rule. Dan and Duke, mistaking all for mirth, barked gayly.

From the panting, pounding, yelling heap issued words and phrases hitherto quite unknown to Penrod and Sam; also, a hoarse repetition in the voice of Rupe concerning his ear left it not to be doubted that additional mayhem was taking place. Appalled, the two spectators retreated to the doorway nearest the yard, where they stood dumbly watching the cataclysm.

The struggle increased in primitive simplicity: time and again the howling Rupe got to his knees only to go down again as the earnest brothers, in their own way, assisted him to a more reclining position. Primal forces operated here, and Sam and Penrod had no more thought of interfering than they would have thought of interfering with an earthquake.

At last, out of the ruck rose Verman, disfigured and maniacal. With a wild eye he looked about him for his trusty rake; but Penrod, in horror, had long since thrown the rake out into the yard. Naturally, it had not seemed necessary to remove the lawn-mower.

The frantic eye of Verman fell upon the lawn-mower, and instantly he leaped to its handle. Shrilling a wordless war-cry, he charged, propelling the whirling, deafening knives straight upon the prone legs of Rupe Collins. The lawn-mower was sincerely intended to pass longitudinally over the body of Mr. Collins from heel to head; and it was the time for a death-song. Black Valkyrie hovered in the shrieking air.

"Cut his gizzud out!" shrieked Herman, urging on the whirling knives.

They touched and lacerated the shin of Rupe, as, with the supreme agony of effort a creature in mortal peril puts forth before succumbing, he tore himself free of Herman and got upon his feet.

Herman was up as quickly. He leaped to the wall and seized the garden-scythe that hung there.

"I'm go to cut you' gizzud out," he announced definitely, "an' eat it!"

Rupe Collins had never run from anybody (except his father) in his life; he was not a coward; but the present situation was very, very unusual. He was already in a badly dismantled condition, and yet Herman and Verman seemed discontented with their work: Verman was swinging the grass-cutter about for a new charge, apparently still wishing to mow him, and Herman had made a quite plausible statement about what he intended to do with the scythe.

Rupe paused but for an extremely condensed survey of the horrible advance of the brothers, and then, uttering a blood-curdled scream of fear, ran out of the stable and up the alley at a speed he had never before attained, so that even Dan had hard work to keep within barking distance. And a 'cross-shoulder glance, at the corner, revealing Verman and Herman in pursuit, the latter waving his scythe overhead, Mr. Collins slackened not his gait, but, rather, out of great anguish, increased it; the while a rapidly developing purpose became firm in his mind--and ever after so remained--not only to refrain from visiting that neighbourhood again, but never by any chance to come within a mile of it.

From the alley door, Penrod and Sam watched the flight, and were without words. When the pursuit rounded the corner, the two looked wanly at each other, but neither spoke until the return of the brothers from the chase.

Herman and Verman came back, laughing and chuckling.

"Hiyi!" cackled Herman to Verman, as they came, "See 'at ole boy run!"

"Who-ee!" Verman shouted in ecstasy.

"Nev' did see boy run so fas'!" Herman continued, tossing the scythe into the wheelbarrow. "I bet he home in bed by viss time!"

Verman roared with delight, appearing to be wholly unconscious that the lids of his right eye were swollen shut and that his attire, not too finical before the struggle, now entitled him to unquestioned rank as a sansculotte. Herman was a similar ruin, and gave as little heed to his condition.

Penrod looked dazedly from Herman to Verman and back again. So did Sam Williams.

"Herman," said Penrod, in a weak voice, "you wouldn't honest of cut his gizzard out, would you?"

"Who? Me? I don' know. He mighty mean ole boy!" Herman shook his head gravely, and then, observing that Verman was again convulsed with unctuous merriment, joined laughter with his brother. "Sho'! I guess I uz dess talkin' whens I said 'at! Reckon he thought I meant it, f'm de way he tuck an' run. Hiyi! Reckon he thought ole Herman bad man! No, suh! I uz dess talkin', 'cause I nev' would cut nobody! I ain' tryin' git in no jail--no, suh!"

Penrod looked at the scythe: he looked at Herman. He looked at the lawn-mower, and he looked at Verman. Then he looked out in the yard at the rake. So did Sam Williams.

"Come on, Verman," said Herman. "We ain' go' 'at stove-wood f' supper yit."

Giggling reminiscently, the brothers disappeared leaving silence behind them in the carriage-house. Penrod and Sam retired slowly into the shadowy interior, each glancing, now and then, with a preoccupied air, at the open, empty doorway where the late afternoon sunshine was growing ruddy. At intervals one or the other scraped the floor reflectively with the side of his shoe. Finally, still without either having made any effort at conversation, they went out into the yard and stood, continuing their silence.

"Well," said Sam, at last, "I guess it's time I better be gettin' home. So long, Penrod!"

"So long, Sam," said Penrod, feebly.

With a solemn gaze he watched his friend out of sight. Then he went slowly into the house, and after an interval occupied in a unique manner, appeared in the library, holding a pair of brilliantly gleaming shoes in his hand.

Mr. Schofield, reading the evening paper, glanced frowningly over it at his offspring.

"Look, papa," said Penrod. "I found your shoes where you'd taken 'em off in your room, to put on your slippers, and they were all dusty. So I took 'em out on the back porch and gave 'em a good blacking. They shine up fine, don't they?"

"Well, I'll be d-dud-dummed!" said the startled Mr. Schofield.

Penrod was zigzagging back to normal.

Lesson 64

1. Read chapters 24 and 25 of *Penrod.*

2. Tell someone what happened in these chapters.

Chapter XXIV. "Little Gentleman"

The midsummer sun was stinging hot outside the little barber-shop next to the corner drug store and Penrod, undergoing a toilette preliminary to his very slowly approaching twelfth birthday, was adhesive enough to retain upon his face much hair as it fell from the shears. There is a mystery here: the tonsorial processes are not unagreeable to manhood; in truth, they are soothing; but the hairs detached from a boy's head get into his eyes, his ears, his nose, his mouth, and down his neck, and he does everywhere itch excruciatingly. Wherefore he blinks, winks, weeps, twitches, condenses his countenance, and squirms; and perchance the barber's scissors clip more than intended--belike an outlying flange of ear.

"Um--muh--ow!" said Penrod, this thing having happened.

"D' I touch y' up a little?" inquired the barber, smiling falsely.

"Ooh--uh!" The boy in the chair offered inarticulate protest, as the wound was rubbed with alum.

"That don't hurt!" said the barber. "You will get it, though, if you don't sit stiller," he continued, nipping in the bud any attempt on the part of his patient to think that he already had "it."

"Pfuff!" said Penrod, meaning no disrespect, but endeavoring to dislodge a temporary moustache from his lip.

"You ought to see how still that little Georgie Bassett sits," the barber went on, reprovingly. "I hear everybody says he's the best boy in town."

"Pfuff! Phirr!" There was a touch of intentional contempt in this.

"I haven't heard nobody around the neighbourhood makin' no such remarks," added the barber, "about nobody of the name of Penrod Schofield."

"Well," said Penrod, clearing his mouth after a struggle, "who wants 'em to? Ouch!"

"I hear they call Georgie Bassett the 'little gentleman,'" ventured the barber, provocatively, meeting with instant success.

"They better not call me that," returned Penrod truculently. "I'd like to hear anybody try. Just once, that's all! I bet they'd never try it ag----ouch!"

"Why? What'd you do to 'em?"

"It's all right what I'd do! I bet they wouldn't want to call me that again long as they lived!"

"What'd you do if it was a little girl? You wouldn't hit her, would you?"

"Well, I'd---- Ouch!"

"You wouldn't hit a little girl, would you?" the barber persisted, gathering into his powerful fingers a mop of hair from the top of Penrod's head and pulling that suffering head into an unnatural position. "Doesn't the Bible say it ain't never right to hit the weak sex?"

"Ow! Say, look out!"

"So you'd go and punch a pore, weak, little girl, would you?" said the barber, reprovingly.

"Well, who said I'd hit her?" demanded the chivalrous Penrod. "I bet I'd fix her though, all right. She'd see!"

"You wouldn't call her names, would you?"

"No, I wouldn't! What hurt is it to call anybody names?"

"Is that so!" exclaimed the barber. "Then you was intending what I heard you hollering at Fisher's grocery delivery wagon driver fer a favour, the other day when I was goin' by your house, was you? I reckon I better tell him, because he says to me after-werds if he ever lays eyes on you when you ain't in your own yard, he's goin' to do a whole lot o' things you ain't goin' to like! Yessir, that's what he says to me!"

"He better catch me first, I guess, before he talks so much."

"Well," resumed the barber, "that ain't sayin' what you'd do if a young lady ever walked up and called you a little gentleman. I want to hear what you'd do to her. I guess I know, though--come to think of it."

"What?" demanded Penrod.

"You'd sick that pore ole dog of yours on her cat, if she had one, I expect," guessed the barber derisively.

"No, I would not!"

"Well, what would you do?"

"I'd do enough. Don't worry about that!"

"Well, suppose it was a boy, then: what'd you do if a boy come up to you and says, 'Hello, little gentleman'?"

"He'd be lucky," said Penrod, with a sinister frown, "if he got home alive."

"Suppose it was a boy twice your size?"

"Just let him try," said Penrod ominously. "You just let him try. He'd never see daylight again; that's all!"

The barber dug ten active fingers into the helpless scalp before him and did his best to displace it, while the anguished Penrod, becoming instantly a seething crucible of emotion, misdirected his natural resentment into maddened brooding upon what he would do to a boy "twice his size" who should dare to call him "little gentleman." The barber shook him as his father had never shaken him; the barber buffeted him, rocked him frantically to and fro; the barber seemed to be trying to wring his neck; and Penrod saw himself in staggering zigzag pictures, destroying large, screaming, fragmentary boys who had insulted him.

The torture stopped suddenly; and clenched, weeping eyes began to see again, while the barber applied cooling lotions which made Penrod smell like a housemaid's ideal.

"Now what," asked the barber, combing the reeking locks gently, "what would it make you so mad fer, to have somebody call you a little gentleman? It's a kind of compliment, as it were, you might say. What would you want to hit anybody fer that fer?"

To the mind of Penrod, this question was without meaning or reasonableness. It was within neither his power nor his desire to analyze the process by which the phrase had become offensive to him, and was now rapidly assuming the proportions of an outrage. He knew only that his gorge rose at the thought of it.

"You just let 'em try it!" he said threateningly, as he slid down from the chair. And as he went out of the door, after further conversation on the same subject, he called back those warning words once more: "Just let 'em try it! Just once-- that's all I ask 'em to. They'll find out what they get!"

The barber chuckled. Then a fly lit on the barber's nose and he slapped at it, and the slap missed the fly but did not miss the nose. The barber was irritated. At this moment his birdlike eye gleamed a gleam as it fell upon customers approaching: the prettiest little girl in the world, leading by the hand her baby brother, Mitchy-Mitch, coming to have Mitchy-Mitch's hair clipped, against the heat. It was a hot day and idle, with little to feed the mind--and the barber was a mischievous man with an irritated nose. He did his worst.

Meanwhile, the brooding Penrod pursued his homeward way; no great distance, but long enough for several one-sided conflicts with malign insulters made of thin air. "You better not call me that!" he muttered. "You just try it, and you'll get what other people got when they tried it. You better not ack fresh with me! Oh, you will, will you?" He delivered a vicious kick full upon the shins of an iron fence-post, which suffered little, though Penrod instantly regretted his indiscretion. "Oof!" he grunted, hopping; and went on after bestowing a look of awful hostility upon the fence-post. "I guess you'll know better next time," he said, in parting, to this antagonist. "You just let me catch you around here again and I'll----" His voice sank to inarticulate but ominous murmurings. He was in a dangerous mood.

Nearing home, however, his belligerent spirit was diverted to happier interests by the discovery that some workmen had left a caldron of tar in the cross-street, close by his father's stable. He tested it, but found it inedible. Also, as a substitute for professional chewing-gum it was unsatisfactory, being insufficiently boiled down and too thin, though of a pleasant, lukewarm temperature. But it had an excess of one quality--it was sticky. It was the stickiest tar Penrod had ever used for any purposes whatsoever, and nothing upon which he wiped his hands served to rid them of it; neither his polka-dotted shirt waist nor his knickerbockers; neither the fence, nor even Duke, who came unthinkingly wagging out to greet him, and retired wiser.

Nevertheless, tar is tar. Much can be done with it, no matter what its condition; so Penrod lingered by the caldron, though from a neighbouring yard could be heard the voices of comrades, including that of Sam Williams. On the ground about the caldron were scattered chips and sticks and bits of wood to the number of a great multitude. Penrod mixed quantities of this refuse into the tar, and interested himself in seeing how much of it he could keep moving in slow swirls upon the ebon surface.

Other surprises were arranged for the absent workmen. The caldron was almost full, and the surface of the tar near the rim.

Penrod endeavoured to ascertain how many pebbles and brickbats, dropped in, would cause an overflow. Labouring heartily to this end, he had almost accomplished it, when he received the suggestion for an experiment on a much larger scale. Embedded at the corner of a grassplot across the street was a whitewashed stone, the size of a small watermelon and serving no purpose whatever save the questionable one of decoration. It was easily pried up with a stick; though getting it to the caldron tested the full strength of the ardent labourer. Instructed to perform such a task, he would have sincerely maintained its impossibility but now, as it was unbidden, and promised rather destructive results, he set about it with unconquerable energy, feeling certain that he would be rewarded with a mighty splash. Perspiring, grunting vehemently, his back aching and all muscles strained, he progressed in short stages until the big stone lay at the base of the caldron. He rested a moment, panting, then lifted the stone, and was bending his shoulders for the heave that would lift it over the rim, when a sweet, taunting voice, close behind him, startled him cruelly.

"How do you do, little gentleman!"

Penrod squawked, dropped the stone, and shouted, "Shut up, you dern fool!" purely from instinct, even before his about-face made him aware who had so spitefully addressed him.

It was Marjorie Jones. Always dainty, and prettily dressed, she was in speckless and starchy white to-day, and a refreshing picture she made, with the new-shorn and powerfully scented Mitchy-Mitch clinging to her hand. They had stolen up behind the toiler, and now stood laughing together in sweet merriment. Since the passing of Penrod's Rupe Collins period he had experienced some severe qualms at the recollection of his last meeting with Marjorie and his Apache behaviour; in truth, his heart instantly became as wax at sight of her, and he would have offered her fair speech; but, alas! in Marjorie's wonderful eyes there shone a consciousness of new powers for his undoing, and she denied him opportunity.

"Oh, oh!" she cried, mocking his pained outcry. "What a way for a little gentleman to talk! Little gentleman don't say wicked----"

"Marjorie!" Penrod, enraged and dismayed, felt himself stung beyond all endurance. Insult from her was bitterer to endure than from any other. "Don't you call me that again!"

"Why not, little gentleman?"

He stamped his foot. "You better stop!"

Marjorie sent into his furious face her lovely, spiteful laughter.

"Little gentleman, little gentleman, little gentleman!" she said deliberately. "How's the little gentleman, this afternoon? Hello, little gentleman!"

Penrod, quite beside himself, danced eccentrically. "Dry up!" he howled. "Dry up, dry up, dry up, dry up!"

Mitchy-Mitch shouted with delight and applied a finger to the side of the caldron--a finger immediately snatched away and wiped upon a handkerchief by his fastidious sister.

"'Ittle gellamun!" said Mitchy-Mitch.

"You better look out!" Penrod whirled upon this small offender with grim satisfaction. Here was at least something male that could without dishonour be held responsible. "You say that again, and I'll give you the worst----"

"You will not!" snapped Marjorie, instantly vitriolic. "He'll say just whatever he wants to, and he'll say it just as much as he wants to. Say it again, Mitchy-Mitch!"

"'Ittle gellamun!" said Mitchy-Mitch promptly.

"Ow-yah!" Penrod's tone-production was becoming affected by his mental condition. "You say that again, and I'll----"

"Go on, Mitchy-Mitch," cried Marjorie. "He can't do a thing. He don't dare! Say it some more, Mitchy-Mitch--say it a whole lot!"

Mitchy-Mitch, his small, fat face shining with confidence in his immunity, complied.

"'Ittle gellamun!" he squeaked malevolently. "'Ittle gellamun! 'Ittle gellamun! 'Ittle gellamun!"

The desperate Penrod bent over the whitewashed rock, lifted it, and then--outdoing Porthos, John Ridd, and Ursus in one miraculous burst of strength--heaved it into the air.

Marjorie screamed.

But it was too late. The big stone descended into the precise midst of the caldron and Penrod got his mighty splash. It was far, far beyond his expectations.

Spontaneously there were grand and awful effects--volcanic spectacles of nightmare and eruption. A black sheet of eccentric shape rose out of the caldron and descended upon the three children, who had no time to evade it.

After it fell, Mitchy-Mitch, who stood nearest the caldron, was the thickest, though there was enough for all. Br'er Rabbit would have fled from any of them.

Chapter XXV. Tar

When Marjorie and Mitchy-Mitch got their breath, they used it vocally; and seldom have more penetrating sounds issued from human throats. Coincidentally, Marjorie, quite baresark, laid hands upon the largest stick within reach and fell upon Penrod with blind fury. He had the presence of mind to flee, and they went round and round the caldron, while Mitchy-Mitch feebly endeavoured to follow--his appearance, in this pursuit, being pathetically like that of a bug fished out of an ink-well, alive but discouraged.

Attracted by the riot, Samuel Williams made his appearance, vaulting a fence, and was immediately followed by Maurice Levy and Georgie Bassett. They stared incredulously at the extraordinary spectacle before them.

"Little gen-til-mun!" shrieked Marjorie, with a wild stroke that landed full upon Penrod's tarry cap. "Oooch!" bleated Penrod.

"It's Penrod!" shouted Sam Williams, recognizing him by the voice. For an instant he had been in some doubt.

"Penrod Schofield!" exclaimed Georgie Bassett. "What does this mean?" That was Georgie's style, and had helped to win him his title.

Marjorie leaned, panting, upon her stick. "I cu-called--uh--him--oh!" she sobbed--"I called him a lul-little--oh--gentleman! And oh--lul-look!--oh! lul-look at my du-dress! Lul-look at Mu-mitchy--oh--Mitch--oh!"

Unexpectedly, she smote again--with results--and then, seizing the indistinguishable hand of Mitchy-Mitch, she ran wailing homeward down the street.

"'Little gentleman'?" said Georgie Bassett, with some evidences of disturbed complacency. "Why, that's what they call me!"

"Yes, and you are one, too!" shouted the maddened Penrod. "But you better not let anybody call me that! I've stood enough around here for one day, and you can't run over me, Georgie Bassett. Just you put that in your gizzard and smoke it!"

"Anybody has a perfect right," said Georgie, with, dignity, "to call a person a little gentleman. There's lots of names nobody ought to call, but this one's a nice----"

"You better look out!"

Unavenged bruises were distributed all over Penrod, both upon his body and upon his spirit. Driven by subtle forces, he had dipped his hands in catastrophe and disaster: it was not for a Georgie Bassett to beard him. Penrod was about to run amuck.

"I haven't called you a little gentleman, yet," said Georgie. "I only said it. Anybody's got a right to say it."

"Not around me! You just try it again and----"

"I shall say it," returned Georgie, "all I please. Anybody in this town has a right to say 'little gentleman'----"

Bellowing insanely, Penrod plunged his right hand into the caldron, rushed upon Georgie and made awful work of his hair and features.

Alas, it was but the beginning! Sam Williams and Maurice Levy screamed with delight, and, simultaneously infected, danced about the struggling pair, shouting frantically:
"Little gentleman! Little gentleman! Sick him, Georgie! Sick him, little gentleman! Little gentleman! Little gentleman!"

The infuriated outlaw turned upon them with blows and more tar, which gave Georgie Bassett his opportunity and later seriously impaired the purity of his fame. Feeling himself hopelessly tarred, he dipped both hands repeatedly into the caldron and applied his gatherings to Penrod. It was bringing coals to Newcastle, but it helped to assuage the just wrath of Georgie.

307

The four boys gave a fine imitation of the Laocoon group complicated by an extra figure frantic splutterings and chokings, strange cries and stranger words issued from this tangle; hands dipped lavishly into the inexhaustible reservoir of tar, with more and more picturesque results. The caldron had been elevated upon bricks and was not perfectly balanced; and under a heavy impact of the struggling group it lurched and went partly over, pouring forth a Stygian tide which formed a deep pool in the gutter.

It was the fate of Master Roderick Bitts, that exclusive and immaculate person, to make his appearance upon the chaotic scene at this juncture. All in the cool of a white "sailor suit," he turned aside from the path of duty--which led straight to the house of a maiden aunt--and paused to hop with joy upon the sidewalk. A repeated epithet continuously half panted, half squawked, somewhere in the nest of gladiators, caught his ear, and he took it up excitedly, not knowing why.

"Little gentleman!" shouted Roderick, jumping up and down in childish glee. "Little gentleman! Little gentleman! Lit----"

A frightful figure tore itself free from the group, encircled this innocent bystander with a black arm, and hurled him headlong. Full length and flat on his face went Roderick into the Stygian pool. The frightful figure was Penrod.

Instantly, the pack flung themselves upon him again, and, carrying them with him, he went over upon Roderick, who from that instant was as active a belligerent as any there.

Thus began the Great Tar Fight, the origin of which proved, afterward, so difficult for parents to trace, owing to the opposing accounts of the combatants. Marjorie said Penrod began it; Penrod said Mitchy-Mitch began it; Sam Williams said Georgie Bassett began it; Georgie and Maurice Levy said Penrod began it; Roderick Bitts, who had not recognized his first assailant, said Sam Williams began it.

Nobody thought of accusing the barber. But the barber did not begin it; it was the fly on the barber's nose that began it--though, of course, something else began the fly. Somehow, we never manage to hang the real offender.

The end came only with the arrival of Penrod's mother, who had been having a painful conversation by telephone with Mrs. Jones, the mother of Marjorie, and came forth to seek an errant son. It is a mystery how she was able to pick out her own, for by the time she got there his voice was too hoarse to be recognizable. Mr. Schofield's version of things was that Penrod was insane. "He's a stark, raving lunatic!" declared the father, descending to the library from a before-dinner interview with the outlaw, that evening. "I'd send him to military school, but I don't believe they'd take him. Do you know why he says all that awfulness happened?"

"When Margaret and I were trying to scrub him," responded Mrs. Schofield wearily, "he said 'everybody' had been calling him names."

"'Names!'" snorted her husband. "'Little gentleman!' That's the vile epithet they called him! And because of it he wrecks the peace of six homes!"

"Sh! Yes; he told us about it," said Mrs. Schofield, moaning. "He told us several hundred times, I should guess, though I didn't count. He's got it fixed in his head, and we couldn't get it out. All we could do was to put him in the closet. He'd have gone out again after those boys if we hadn't. I don't know what to make of him!"

"He's a mystery to me!" said her husband. "And he refuses to explain why he objects to being called 'little gentleman.' Says he'd do the same thing--and worse--if anybody dared to call him that again. He said if the President of the United States called him that he'd try to whip him. How long did you have him locked up in the closet?"

"Sh!" said Mrs. Schofield warningly. "About two hours; but I don't think it softened his spirit at all, because when I took him to the barber's to get his hair clipped again, on account of the tar in it, Sammy Williams and Maurice Levy were there for the same reason, and they just whispered 'little gentleman,' so low you could hardly hear them--and Penrod began fighting with them right before me, and it was really all the barber and I could do to drag him away from them. The barber was very kind about it, but Penrod----"

"I tell you he's a lunatic!" Mr. Schofield would have said the same thing of a Frenchman infuriated by the epithet "camel." The philosophy of insult needs expounding.

"Sh!" said Mrs. Schofield. "It does seem a kind of frenzy."

"Why on earth should any sane person mind being called----"

"Sh!" said Mrs. Schofield. "It's beyond me!"

"What are you sh-ing me for?" demanded Mr. Schofield explosively.

"Sh!" said Mrs. Schofield. "It's Mr. Kinosling, the new rector of Saint Joseph's."

"Where?"

"Sh! On the front porch with Margaret; he's going to stay for dinner. I do hope----"

"Bachelor, isn't he?"

"Yes."

"Our old minister was speaking of him the other day," said Mr. Schofield, "and he didn't seem so terribly impressed."

"Sh! Yes; about thirty, and of course so superior to most of Margaret's friends--boys home from college. She thinks she likes young Robert Williams, I know--but he laughs so much! Of course there isn't any comparison. Mr. Kinosling talks so intellectually; it's a good thing for Margaret to hear that kind of thing, for a change and, of course, he's very spiritual. He seems very much interested in her." She paused to muse. "I think Margaret likes him; he's so different, too. It's the third time he's dropped in this week, and I----"

"Well," said Mr. Schofield grimly, "if you and Margaret want him to come again, you'd better not let him see Penrod."

"But he's asked to see him; he seems interested in meeting all the family. And Penrod nearly always behaves fairly well at table." She paused, and then put to her husband a question referring to his interview with Penrod upstairs. "Did you--did you--do it?"

"No," he answered gloomily. "No, I didn't, but----" He was interrupted by a violent crash of china and metal in the kitchen, a shriek from Della, and the outrageous voice of Penrod. The well-informed Della, ill-inspired to set up for a wit, had ventured to address the scion of the house roguishly as "little gentleman," and Penrod, by means of the rapid elevation of his right foot, had removed from her supporting hands a laden tray. Both parents, started for the kitchen, Mr. Schofield completing his interrupted sentence on the way.

"But I will, now!"

The rite thus promised was hastily but accurately performed in that apartment most distant from the front porch; and, twenty minutes later, Penrod descended to dinner. The Rev. Mr. Kinosling had asked for the pleasure of meeting him, and it had been decided that the only course possible was to cover up the scandal for the present, and to offer an undisturbed and smiling family surface to the gaze of the visitor.

Scorched but not bowed, the smouldering Penrod was led forward for the social formulae simultaneously with the somewhat bleak departure of Robert Williams, who took his guitar with him, this time, and went in forlorn unconsciousness of the powerful forces already set in secret motion to be his allies.

The punishment just undergone had but made the haughty and unyielding soul of Penrod more stalwart in revolt; he was unconquered. Every time the one intolerable insult had been offered him, his resentment had become the hotter, his vengeance the more instant and furious. And, still burning with outrage, but upheld by the conviction of right, he was determined to continue to the last drop of his blood the defense of his honour, whenever it should be assailed, no matter how mighty or august the powers that attacked it. In all ways, he was a very sore boy.

During the brief ceremony of presentation, his usually inscrutable countenance wore an expression interpreted by his father as one of insane obstinacy, while Mrs. Schofield found it an incentive to inward prayer. The fine graciousness of Mr. Kinosling, however, was unimpaired by the glare of virulent suspicion given him by this little brother: Mr. Kinosling mistook it for a natural curiosity concerning one who might possibly become, in time, a member of the family. He patted Penrod upon the head, which was, for many reasons, in no condition to be patted with any pleasure to the patter. Penrod felt himself in the presence of a new enemy.

"How do you do, my little lad," said Mr. Kinosling. "I trust we shall become fast friends."

To the ear of his little lad, it seemed he said, "A trost we shall bick-home fawst frainds." Mr. Kinosling's pronunciation was, in fact, slightly precious; and, the little lad, simply mistaking it for some cryptic form of mockery of himself, assumed a manner and expression which argued so ill for the proposed friendship that Mrs. Schofield hastily interposed the suggestion of dinner, and the small procession went in to the dining-room.

"It has been a delicious day," said Mr. Kinosling, presently; "warm but balmy." With a benevolent smile he addressed Penrod, who sat opposite him. "I suppose, little gentleman, you have been indulging in the usual outdoor sports of vacation?"

Penrod laid down his fork and glared, open-mouthed at Mr. Kinosling.

"You'll have another slice of breast of the chicken?" Mr. Schofield inquired, loudly and quickly.

"A lovely day!" exclaimed Margaret, with equal promptitude and emphasis. "Lovely, oh, lovely! Lovely!"

"Beautiful, beautiful, beautiful!" said Mrs. Schofield, and after a glance at Penrod which confirmed her impression that he intended to say something, she continued, "Yes, beautiful, beautiful, beautiful, beautiful, beautiful beautiful!"

Penrod closed his mouth and sank back in his chair--and his relatives took breath.

Mr. Kinosling looked pleased. This responsive family, with its ready enthusiasm, made the kind of audience he liked. He passed a delicate white hand gracefully over his tall, pale forehead, and smiled indulgently.

"Youth relaxes in summer," he said. "Boyhood is the age of relaxation; one is playful, light, free, unfettered. One runs and leaps and enjoys one's self with one's companions. It is good for the little lads to play with their friends; they jostle, push, and wrestle, and simulate little, happy struggles with one another in harmless conflict. The young muscles are toughening. It is good. Boyish chivalry develops, enlarges, expands. The young learn quickly, intuitively, spontaneously. They perceive the obligations of noblesse oblige. They begin to comprehend the necessity of caste and its requirements. They learn what birth means--ah,--that is, they learn what it means to be well born. They learn courtesy in their games; they learn politeness, consideration for one another in their pastimes, amusements, lighter occupations. I make it my pleasure to join them often, for I sympathize with them in all their wholesome joys as well as in their little bothers and perplexities. I understand them, you see; and let me tell you it is no easy matter to understand the little lads and lassies." He sent to each listener his beaming glance, and, permitting it to come to rest upon Penrod, inquired:

"And what do you say to that, little gentleman?"

Mr. Schofield uttered a stentorian cough. "More? You'd better have some more chicken! More! Do!"

"More chicken!" urged Margaret simultaneously. "Do please! Please! More! Do! More!"

"Beautiful, beautiful," began Mrs. Schofield. "Beautiful, beautiful, beautiful, beautiful----"

It is not known in what light Mr. Kinosling viewed the expression of Penrod's face. Perhaps he mistook it for awe; perhaps he received no impression at all of its extraordinary quality. He was a rather self-engrossed young man, just then engaged in a double occupation, for he not only talked, but supplied from his own consciousness a critical though favourable auditor as well, which of course kept him quite busy. Besides, it is oftener than is expected the case that extremely peculiar expressions upon the countenances of boys are entirely overlooked, and suggest nothing to the minds of people staring straight at them. Certainly Penrod's expression--which, to the perception of his family, was perfectly horrible--caused not the faintest perturbation in the breast of Mr. Kinosling.

Mr. Kinosling waived the chicken, and continued to talk. "Yes, I think I may claim to understand boys," he said, smiling thoughtfully. "One has been a boy one's self. Ah, it is not all playtime! I hope our young scholar here does not overwork himself at his Latin, at his classics, as I did, so that at the age of eight years I was compelled to wear glasses. He must be careful not to strain the little eyes at his scholar's tasks, not to let the little shoulders grow round over his scholar's desk. Youth is golden; we should keep it golden, bright, glistening. Youth should frolic, should be sprightly; it should play its cricket, its tennis, its hand-ball. It should run and leap; it should laugh, should sing madrigals and glees, carol with the lark, ring out in chanties, folk-songs, ballads, roundelays----"

He talked on. At any instant Mr. Schofield held himself ready to cough vehemently and shout, "More chicken," to drown out Penrod in case the fatal words again fell from those eloquent lips; and Mrs. Schofield and Margaret kept themselves prepared at all times to assist him. So passed a threatening meal, which Mrs. Schofield hurried, by every means with decency, to its conclusion. She felt that somehow they would all be safer out in the dark of the front porch, and led the way thither as soon as possible.

"No cigar, I thank you." Mr. Kinosling, establishing himself in a wicker chair beside Margaret, waved away her father's proffer. "I do not smoke. I have never tasted tobacco in any form." Mrs. Schofield was confirmed in her opinion that this would be an ideal son-in-law. Mr. Schofield was not so sure.

"No," said Mr. Kinosling. "No tobacco for me. No cigar, no pipe, no cigarette, no cheroot. For me, a book--a volume of poems, perhaps. Verses, rhymes, lines metrical and cadenced--those are my dissipation. Tennyson by preference: 'Maud,' or 'Idylls of the King'--poetry of the sound Victorian days; there is none later. Or Longfellow will rest me in a tired hour. Yes; for me, a book, a volume in the hand, held lightly between the fingers."

Mr. Kinosling looked pleasantly at his fingers as he spoke, waving his hand in a curving gesture which brought it into the light of a window faintly illuminated from the interior of the house. Then he passed those graceful fingers over his hair, and turned toward Penrod, who was perched upon the railing in a dark corner.

"The evening is touched with a slight coolness," said Mr. Kinosling. "Perhaps I may request the little gentleman----"

"B'gr-r-ruff!" coughed Mr. Schofield. "You'd better change your mind about a cigar."

"No, I thank you. I was about to request the lit----"

"Do try one," Margaret urged. "I'm sure papa's are nice ones. Do try----"

"No, I thank you. I remarked a slight coolness in the air, and my hat is in the hallway. I was about to request----"

"I'll get it for you," said Penrod suddenly.

"If you will be so good," said Mr. Kinosling. "It is a black bowler hat, little gentleman, and placed upon a table in the hall."

"I know where it is." Penrod entered the door, and a feeling of relief, mutually experienced, carried from one to another of his three relatives their interchanged congratulations that he had recovered his sanity.

"'The day is done, and the darkness,'" began Mr. Kinosling--and recited that poem entire. He followed it with "The Children's Hour," and after a pause, at the close, to allow his listeners time for a little reflection upon his rendition, he passed his hand again over his head, and called, in the direction of the doorway:

"I believe I will take my hat now, little gentleman."

313

"Here it is," said Penrod, unexpectedly climbing over the porch railing, in the other direction. His mother and father and Margaret had supposed him to be standing in the hallway out of deference, and because he thought it tactful not to interrupt the recitations. All of them remembered, later, that this supposed thoughtfulness on his part struck them as unnatural.

"Very good, little gentleman!" said Mr. Kinosling, and being somewhat chilled, placed the hat firmly upon his head, pulling it down as far as it would go. It had a pleasant warmth, which he noticed at once. The next instant, he noticed something else, a peculiar sensation of the scalp--a sensation which he was quite unable to define. He lifted his hand to take the hat off, and entered upon a strange experience: his hat seemed to have decided to remain where it was.

"Do you like Tennyson as much as Longfellow, Mr. Kinosling?" inquired Margaret.

"I--ah--I cannot say," he returned absently. "I--ah--each has his own--ugh! flavour and savour, each his--ah--ah----"

Struck by a strangeness in his tone, she peered at him curiously through the dusk. His outlines were indistinct, but she made out that his arms were, uplifted in a singular gesture. He seemed to be wrenching at his head.

"Is--is anything the matter?" she asked anxiously. "Mr. Kinosling, are you ill?"

"Not at--ugh!--all," he replied, in the same odd tone. "I--ah--I believe--ugh!"

He dropped his hands from his hat, and rose. His manner was slightly agitated. "I fear I may have taken a trifling--ah--cold. I should--ah--perhaps be--ah--better at home. I will--ah--say good-night."

At the steps, he instinctively lifted his hand to remove his hat, but did not do so, and, saying "Goodnight," again in a frigid voice, departed with visible stiffness from that house, to return no more.

"Well, of all----!" cried Mrs. Schofield, astounded. "What was the matter? He just went--like that!" She made a flurried gesture. "In heaven's name, Margaret, what did you say to him?"

"I!" exclaimed Margaret indignantly. "Nothing! He just went!"

"Why, he didn't even take off his hat when he said good- night!" said Mrs. Schofield.

Margaret, who had crossed to the doorway, caught the ghost of a whisper behind her, where stood Penrod.

"You bet he didn't!"

He knew not that he was overheard.

A frightful suspicion flashed through Margaret's mind--a suspicion that Mr. Kinosling's hat would have to be either boiled off or shaved off. With growing horror she recalled Penrod's long absence when he went to bring the hat.

"Penrod," she cried, "let me see your hands!"

She had toiled at those hands herself late that afternoon, nearly scalding her own, but at last achieving a lily purity.

"Let me see your hands!"

She seized them.

Again they were tarred!

Lesson 65

1. Read chapters 26 and 27 of *Penrod*.
2. The dialect is hard to read sometimes. "uh" at the end of a word is the sound "er." Reading it out loud will help you figure out what they are saying.
3. Irony — when the opposite is true of what seems should be. What's the irony in the ending of chapter 27? (Answers)

Chapter XXVI. The Quiet Afternoon

Perhaps middle-aged people might discern Nature's real intentions in the matter of pain if they would examine a boy's punishments and sorrows, for he prolongs neither beyond their actual duration. With a boy, trouble must be of Homeric dimensions to last overnight. To him, every next day is really a new day. Thus, Penrod woke, next morning, with neither the unspared rod, nor Mr. Kinosling in his mind. Tar, itself, so far as his consideration of it went, might have been an undiscovered substance. His mood was cheerful and mercantile; some process having worked mysteriously within him, during the night, to the result that his first waking thought was of profits connected with the sale of old iron--or perhaps a ragman had passed the house, just before he woke.

By ten o'clock he had formed a partnership with the indeed amiable Sam, and the firm of Schofield and Williams plunged headlong into commerce. Heavy dealings in rags, paper, old iron and lead gave the firm a balance of twenty-two cents on the evening of the third day; but a venture in glassware, following, proved disappointing on account of the scepticism of all the druggists in that part of town, even after seven laborious hours had been spent in cleansing a wheelbarrow-load of old medicine bottles with hydrant water and ashes. Likewise, the partners were disheartened by their failure to dispose of a crop of "greens," although they had uprooted specimens of that decorative and unappreciated flower, the dandelion, with such persistence and energy that the Schofields' and Williams' lawns looked curiously haggard for the rest of that summer.

The fit passed: business languished; became extinct. The dog-days had set in.

One August afternoon was so hot that even boys sought indoor shade. In the dimness of the vacant carriage-house of the stable, lounged Masters Penrod Schofield, Samuel Williams, Maurice Levy, Georgie Bassett, and Herman. They sat still and talked. It is a hot day, in rare truth, when boys devote themselves principally to conversation, and this day was that hot.

Their elders should beware such days. Peril hovers near when the fierceness of weather forces inaction and boys in groups are quiet. The more closely volcanoes, Western rivers, nitroglycerin, and boys are pent, the deadlier is their action at the point of outbreak. Thus, parents and guardians should look for outrages of the most singular violence and of the most peculiar nature during the confining weather of February and August.

The thing which befell upon this broiling afternoon began to brew and stew peacefully enough. All was innocence and languor; no one could have foretold the eruption.

They were upon their great theme: "When I get to be a man!" Being human, though boys, they considered their present estate too commonplace to be dwelt upon. So, when the old men gather, they say: "When I was a boy!" It really is the land of nowadays that we never discover.

"When I'm a man," said Sam Williams, "I'm goin' to hire me a couple of waiters to swing me in a hammock and keep pourin' ice-water on me all day out o' those waterin'-cans they sprinkle flowers from. I'll hire you for one of 'em, Herman."

"No; you ain' goin' to," said Herman promptly. "You ain' no flowuh. But nev' min' nat, anyway. Ain' nobody goin' haih me whens I'm a man. Goin' be my own boss. I'm go' be a rai'road man!"

"You mean like a superintendent, or sumpthing like that, and sell tickets?" asked Penrod.

"Sup'in--nev' min' nat! Sell ticket? No suh! Go' be a po'tuh! My uncle a po'tuh right now. Solid gole buttons--oh, oh!"

"Generals get a lot more buttons than porters," said Penrod. "Generals----"
"Po'tuhs make the bes' l'vin'," Herman interrupted. "My uncle spen' mo' money 'n any white man n'is town."

"Well, I rather be a general," said Penrod, "or a senator, or sumpthing like that."

"Senators live in Warshington," Maurice Levy contributed the information. "I been there. Warshington ain't so much; Niag'ra Falls is a hundred times as good as Warshington. So's 'Tlantic City, I was there, too. I been everywhere there is. I----"

"Well, anyway," said Sam Williams, raising his voice in order to obtain the floor, "anyway, I'm goin' to lay in a hammock all day, and have ice-water sprinkled on top o' me, and I'm goin' to lay there all night, too, and the next day. I'm goin' to lay there a couple o' years, maybe."

"I bet you don't!" exclaimed Maurice. "What'd you do in winter?"

"What?"

"What you goin' to do when it's winter, out in a hammock with water sprinkled on top o' you all day? I bet you----"

"I'd stay right there," Sam declared, with strong conviction, blinking as he looked out through the open doors at the dazzling lawn and trees, trembling in the heat. "They couldn't sprinkle too much for me!"

"It'd make icicles all over you, and----"

"I wish it would," said Sam. "I'd eat 'em up."

"And it'd snow on you----"

"Yay! I'd swaller it as fast as it'd come down. I wish I had a barrel o' snow right now. I wish this whole barn was full of it. I wish they wasn't anything in the whole world except just good ole snow."

Penrod and Herman rose and went out to the hydrant, where they drank long and ardently. Sam was still talking about snow when they returned.

"No, I wouldn't just roll in it. I'd stick it all round inside my clo'es, and fill my hat. No, I'd freeze a big pile of it all hard, and I'd roll her out flat and then I'd carry her down to some ole tailor's and have him make me a suit out of her, and----"

"Can't you keep still about your ole snow?" demanded Penrod petulantly. "Makes me so thirsty I can't keep still, and I've drunk so much now I bet I bust. That ole hydrant water's mighty near hot anyway."
"I'm goin' to have a big store, when I grow up," volunteered Maurice.

"Candy store?" asked Penrod.

"No, sir! I'll have candy in it, but not to eat, so much. It's goin' to be a deportment store: ladies' clothes, gentlemen's clothes, neckties, china goods, leather goods, nice lines in woollings and lace goods----"

"Yay! I wouldn't give a five-for-a-cent marble for your whole store," said Sam. "Would you, Penrod?"

"Not for ten of 'em; not for a million of 'em! I'm goin' to have----"

"Wait!" clamoured Maurice. "You'd be foolish, because they'd be a toy deportment in my store where they'd be a hunderd marbles! So, how much would you think your five-for-a-cent marble counts for? And when I'm keepin' my store I'm goin' to get married."

"Yay!" shrieked Sam derisively. "Married! Listen!" Penrod and Herman joined in the howl of contempt.

"Certumly I'll get married," asserted Maurice stoutly. "I'll get married to Marjorie Jones. She likes me awful good, and I'm her beau."

"What makes you think so?" inquired Penrod in a cryptic voice.

"Because she's my beau, too," came the prompt answer. "I'm her beau because she's my beau; I guess that's plenty reason! I'll get married to her as soon as I get my store running nice."

Penrod looked upon him darkly, but, for the moment, held his peace.

"Married!" jeered Sam Williams. "Married to Marjorie Jones! You're the only boy I ever heard say he was going to get married. I wouldn't get married for--why, I wouldn't for--for----" Unable to think of any inducement the mere mention of which would not be ridiculously incommensurate, he proceeded: "I wouldn't do it! What you want to get married for? What do married people do, except just come home tired, and worry around and kind of scold? You better not do it, M'rice; you'll be mighty sorry."

"Everybody gets married," stated Maurice, holding his ground.

"They gotta."

"I'll bet I don't!" Sam returned hotly. "They better catch me before they tell me I have to. Anyway, I bet nobody has to get married unless they want to."
"They do, too," insisted Maurice. "They gotta!"

"Who told you?"

"Look at what my own papa told me!" cried Maurice, heated with argument. "Didn't he tell me your papa had to marry your mamma, or else he never'd got to handle a cent of her money? Certumly, people gotta marry. Everybody. You don't know anybody over twenty years old that isn't married--except maybe teachers."

"Look at policemen!" shouted Sam triumphantly. 'You don't s'pose anybody can make policemen get married, I reckon, do you?"

"Well, policemen, maybe," Maurice was forced to admit. "Policemen and teachers don't, but everybody else gotta."

"Well, I'll be a policeman," said Sam. "then I guess they won't come around tellin' me I have to get married. What you goin' to be, Penrod?"

"Chief police," said the laconic Penrod.

"What you?" Sam inquired of quiet Georgie Bassett.

"I am going to be," said Georgie, consciously, "a minister."

This announcement created a sensation so profound that it was followed by silence. Herman was the first to speak.

"You mean preachuh?" he asked incredulously. "You go' preach?"

"Yes," answered Georgie, looking like Saint Cecilia at the organ.

Herman was impressed. "You know all 'at preachuh talk?"

"I'm going to learn it," said Georgie simply.

"How loud kin you holler?" asked Herman doubtfully.

"He can't holler at all," Penrod interposed with scorn. "He hollers like a girl. He's the poorest hollerer in town!"

Herman shook his head. Evidently he thought Georgie's chance of being ordained very slender. Nevertheless, a final question put to the candidate by the expert seemed to admit one ray of hope.

"How good kin you clim a pole?"

"He can't climb one at all," Penrod answered for Georgie. "Over at Sam's turning-pole you ought to see him try to----"

"Preachers don't have to climb poles," Georgie said with dignity.

"Good ones do," declared Herman. "Bes' one ev' I hear, he clim up an' down same as a circus man. One n'em big 'vivals outen whens we livin' on a fahm, preachuh clim big pole right in a middle o' the church, what was to hol' roof up. He clim way high up, an' holler: 'Goin' to heavum, goin' to heavum, goin' to heavum now. Hallelujah, praise my Lawd!' An' he slide down little, an' holler: 'Devil's got a hol' o' my coat-tails; devil tryin' to drag me down! Sinnuhs, take wawnun! Devil got a hol' o' my coat-tails; I'm a-goin' to hell, oh Lawd!' Nex', he clim up little mo', an' yell an' holler: 'Done shuck ole devil loose; goin' straight to heavum agin! Goin' to heavum, goin' to heavum, my Lawd!' Nex', he slide down some mo' an' holler, 'Leggo my coat-tails, ole devil! Goin' to hell agin, sinnuhs! Goin' straight to hell, my Lawd!' An' he clim an' he slide, an' he slide, an' he clim, an' all time holler: 'Now 'm a-goin' to heavum; now 'm a-goin' to hell! Goin' to heavum, heavum, heavum, my Lawd!' Las' he slide all a-way down, jes' a-squallin' an' a-kickin' an' a-rarin' up an' squealin', 'Goin' to hell. Goin' to hell! Ole Satum got my soul! Goin' to hell! Goin' to hell! Goin' to hell, hell, hell!'"

Herman possessed that extraordinary facility for vivid acting which is the great native gift of his race, and he enchained his listeners. They sat fascinated and spellbound.

"Herman, tell that again!" said Penrod, breathlessly.

Herman, nothing loath, accepted the encore and repeated the Miltonic episode, expanding it somewhat, and dwelling with a fine art upon those portions of the narrative which he perceived to be most exciting to his audience. Plainly, they thrilled less to Paradise gained than to its losing, and the dreadful climax of the descent into the Pit was the greatest treat of all.

The effect was immense and instant. Penrod sprang to his feet.

"Georgie Bassett couldn't do that to save his life," he declared. "I'm goin' to be a preacher! I'd be all right for one, wouldn't I, Herman?"

"So am I!" Sam Williams echoed loudly. "I guess I can do it if you can. I'd be better'n Penrod, wouldn't I, Herman?"

"I am, too!" Maurice shouted. "I got a stronger voice than anybody here, and I'd like to know what--"

The three clamoured together indistinguishably, each asserting his qualifications for the ministry according to Herman's theory, which had been accepted by these sudden converts without question.

"Listen to me!" Maurice bellowed, proving his claim to at least the voice by drowning the others. "Maybe I can't climb a pole so good, but who can holler louder'n this? Listen to me-e-e!"

"Shut up!" cried Penrod, irritated. "Go to heaven; go to hell!"

"Oo-o-oh!" exclaimed Georgie Bassett, profoundly shocked.

Sam and Maurice, awed by Penrod's daring, ceased from turmoil, staring wide-eyed.

"You cursed and swore!" said Georgie.

"I did not!" cried Penrod, hotly. "That isn't swearing."

"You said, 'Go to a big H'!" said Georgie.

"I did not! I said, 'Go to heaven,' before I said a big H. That isn't swearing, is it, Herman? It's almost what the preacher said, ain't it, Herman? It ain't swearing now, any more--not if you put 'go to heaven' with it, is it, Herman? You can say it all you want to, long as you say 'go to heaven' first, can't you, Herman? Anybody can say it if the preacher says it, can't they, Herman? I guess I know when I ain't swearing, don't I, Herman?"

Judge Herman ruled for the defendant, and Penrod was considered to have carried his point. With fine consistency, the conclave established that it was proper for the general public to "say it," provided "go to heaven" should in all cases precede it. This prefix was pronounced a perfect disinfectant, removing all odour of impiety or insult; and, with the exception of Georgie Bassett (who maintained that the minister's words were "going" and "gone," not "go"), all the boys proceeded to exercise their new privilege so lavishly that they tired of it.

But there was no diminution of evangelical ardour; again were heard the clamours of dispute as to which was the best qualified for the ministry, each of the claimants appealing passionately to Herman, who, pleased but confused, appeared to be incapable of arriving at a decision.

During a pause, Georgie Bassett asserted his prior rights. "Who said it first, I'd like to know?" he demanded. "I was going to be a minister from long back of to-day, I guess. And I guess I said I was going to be a minister right to-day before any of you said anything at all. Didn't I, Herman? You heard me, didn't you, Herman? That's the very thing started you talking about it, wasn't it, Herman?"

"You' right," said Herman. "You the firs' one to say it."

Penrod, Sam, and Maurice immediately lost faith in Herman.

"What if you did say it first?" Penrod shouted. "You couldn't be a minister if you were a hunderd years old!"

"I bet his mother wouldn't let him be one," said Sam. "She never lets him do anything."

"She would, too," retorted Georgie. "Ever since I was little, she----"

"He's too sissy to be a preacher!" cried Maurice. "Listen at his squeaky voice!"

"I'm going to be a better minister," shouted Georgie, "than all three of you put together. I could do it with my left hand!"

The three laughed bitingly in chorus. They jeered, derided, scoffed, and raised an uproar which would have had its effect upon much stronger nerves than Georgie's. For a time he contained his rising choler and chanted monotonously, over and over: "I could! I could, too! I could! I could, too!" But their tumult wore upon him, and he decided to avail himself of the recent decision whereby a big H was rendered innocuous and unprofane. Having used the expression once, he found it comforting, and substituted it for: "I could! I could, too!"

But it relieved him only temporarily. His tormentors were unaffected by it and increased their howlings, until at last Georgie lost his head altogether. Badgered beyond bearing, his eyes shining with a wild light, he broke through the besieging trio, hurling little Maurice from his path with a frantic hand.

"I'll show you!" he cried, in this sudden frenzy. "You give me a chance, and I'll prove it right now!"

"That's talkin' business!" shouted Penrod. "Everybody keep still a minute. Everybody!"

He took command of the situation at once, displaying a fine capacity for organization and system. It needed only a few minutes to set order in the place of confusion and to determine, with the full concurrence of all parties, the conditions under which Georgie Bassett was to defend his claim by undergoing what may be perhaps intelligibly defined as the Herman test. Georgie declared he could do it easily. He was in a state of great excitement and in no condition to think calmly or, probably, he would not have made the attempt at all. Certainly he was overconfident.

Chapter XXVII. Conclusion of the Quiet Afternoon

It was during the discussion of the details of this enterprise that Georgie's mother, a short distance down the street, received a few female callers, who came by appointment to drink a glass of iced tea with her, and to meet the Rev. Mr. Kinosling. Mr. Kinosling was proving almost formidably interesting to the women and girls of his own and other flocks. What favour of his fellow clergymen a slight precociousness of manner and pronunciation cost him was more than balanced by the visible ecstasies of ladies. They blossomed at his touch.

He had just entered Mrs. Bassett's front door, when the son of the house, followed by an intent and earnest company of four, opened the alley gate and came into the yard. The unconscious Mrs. Bassett was about to have her first experience of a fatal coincidence. It was her first, because she was the mother of a boy so well behaved that he had become a proverb of transcendency. Fatal coincidences were plentiful in the Schofield and Williams families, and would have been familiar to Mrs. Bassett had Georgie been permitted greater intimacy with Penrod and Sam.

Mr. Kinosling sipped his iced tea and looked about him approvingly. Seven ladies leaned forward, for it was to be seen that he meant to speak.

"This cool room is a relief," he said, waving a graceful hand in a neatly limited gesture, which everybody's eyes followed, his own included. "It is a relief and a retreat. The windows open, the blinds closed--that is as it should be. It is a retreat, a fastness, a bastion against the heat's assault. For me, a quiet room--a quiet room and a book, a volume in the hand, held lightly between the fingers. A volume of poems, lines metrical and cadenced; something by a sound Victorian. We have no later poets."

"Swinburne?" suggested Miss Beam, an eager spinster. "Swinburne, Mr. Kinosling? Ah, Swinburne!"

"Not Swinburne," said Mr. Kinosling chastely. "No."

That concluded all the remarks about Swinburne.

Miss Beam retired in confusion behind another lady.

"I do not observe your manly little son," Mr. Kinosling addressed his hostess.

"He's out playing in the yard," Mrs. Bassett returned. "I heard his voice just now, I think."

"Everywhere I hear wonderful report of him," said Mr. Kinosling. "I may say that I understand boys, and I feel that he is a rare, a fine, a pure, a lofty spirit. I say spirit, for spirit is the word I hear spoken of him."

A chorus of enthusiastic approbation affirmed the accuracy of this proclamation, and Mrs. Bassett flushed with pleasure. Georgie's spiritual perfection was demonstrated by instances of it, related by the visitors; his piety was cited, and wonderful things he had said were quoted.

"Not all boys are pure, of fine spirit, of high mind," said Mr. Kinosling, and continued with true feeling: "You have a neighbour, dear Mrs. Bassett, whose household I indeed really feel it quite impossible to visit until such time when better, firmer, stronger handed, more determined discipline shall prevail. I find Mr. and Mrs. Schofield and their daughter charming----"

Three or four ladies said "Oh!" and spoke a name simultaneously. It was as if they had said, "Oh, the bubonic plague!"

"Oh! Penrod Schofield!"

"Georgie does not play with him," said Mrs. Bassett quickly-- "that is, he avoids him as much as he can without hurting Penrod's feelings. Georgie is very sensitive to giving pain. I suppose a mother should not tell these things, and I know people who talk about their own children are dreadful bores, but it was only last Thursday night that Georgie looked up in my face so sweetly, after he had said his prayers and his little cheeks flushed, as he said: "Mamma, I think it would be right for me to go more with Penrod. I think it would make him a better boy."

A sibilance went about the room. "Sweet! How sweet! The sweet little soul! Ah, sweet!"

"And that very afternoon," continued Mrs. Bassett, "he had come home in a dreadful state. Penrod had thrown tar all over him."

"Your son has a forgiving spirit!" said Mr. Kinosling with vehemence. "A too forgiving spirit, perhaps." He set down his glass. "No more, I thank you. No more cake, I thank you. Was it not Cardinal Newman who said----"

He was interrupted by the sounds of an altercation just outside the closed blinds of the window nearest him.

"Let him pick his tree!" It was the voice of Samuel Williams. "Didn't we come over here to give him one of his own trees? Give him a fair show, can't you?"

"The little lads!" Mr. Kinosling smiled. "They have their games, their outdoor sports, their pastimes. The young muscles are toughening. The sun will not harm them. They grow; they expand; they learn. They learn fair play, honour, courtesy, from one another, as pebbles grow round in the brook. They learn more from themselves than from us. They take shape, form, outline. Let them."

"Mr. Kinosling!" Another spinster--undeterred by what had happened to Miss Beam--leaned fair forward, her face shining and ardent. "Mr. Kinosling, there's a question I do wish to ask you."

"My dear Miss Cosslit," Mr. Kinosling responded, again waving his hand and watching it, "I am entirely at your disposal."

"Was Joan of Arc," she asked fervently, "inspired by spirits?"

He smiled indulgently. "Yes--and no," he said. "One must give both answers. One must give the answer, yes; one must give the answer, no."

"Oh, thank you!" said Miss Cosslit, blushing.

"She's one of my great enthusiasms, you know."

"And I have a question, too," urged Mrs. Lora Rewbush, after a moment's hasty concentration. "I've never been able to settle it for myself, but now----"

"Yes?" said Mr. Kinosling encouragingly.

"Is--ah--is--oh, yes: Is Sanskrit a more difficult language than Spanish, Mr. Kinosling?"

"It depends upon the student," replied the oracle smiling. "One must not look for linguists everywhere. In my own especial case--if one may cite one's self as an example--I found no great, no insurmountable difficulty in mastering, in conquering either."

"And may I ask one?" ventured Mrs. Bassett. "Do you think it is right to wear egrets?"

"There are marks of quality, of caste, of social distinction," Mr. Kinosling began, "which must be permitted, allowed, though perhaps regulated. Social distinction, one observes, almost invariably implies spiritual distinction as well. Distinction of circumstances is accompanied by mental distinction. Distinction is hereditary; it descends from father to son, and if there is one thing more true than 'Like father, like son,' it is--" he bowed gallantly to Mrs. Bassett--"it is, 'Like mother, like son.' What these good ladies have said this afternoon of your----"

This was the fatal instant. There smote upon all ears the voice of Georgie, painfully shrill and penetrating--fraught with protest and protracted, strain. His plain words consisted of the newly sanctioned and disinfected curse with a big H.

With an ejaculation of horror, Mrs. Bassett sprang to the window and threw open the blinds.

Georgie's back was disclosed to the view of the tea-party. He was endeavouring to ascend a maple tree about twelve feet from the window. Embracing the trunk with arms and legs, he had managed to squirm to a point above the heads of Penrod and Herman, who stood close by, watching him earnestly--Penrod being obviously in charge of the performance. Across the yard were Sam Williams and Maurice Levy, acting as a jury on the question of voice-power, and it was to a complaint of theirs that Georgie had just replied.

"That's right, Georgie," said Penrod encouragingly. "They can, too, hear you. Let her go!"

"Going to heaven!" shrieked Georgie, squirming up another inch. "Going to heaven, heaven, heaven!"

His mother's frenzied attempts to attract his attention failed utterly. Georgie was using the full power of his lungs, deafening his own ears to all other sounds. Mrs. Bassett called in vain; while the tea-party stood petrified in a cluster about the window.

"Going to heaven!" Georgie bellowed. "Going to heaven! Going to heaven, my Lord! Going to heaven, heaven, heaven!"

He tried to climb higher, but began to slip downward, his exertions causing damage to his apparel. A button flew into the air, and his knickerbockers and his waistband severed relations.

325

"Devil's got my coat-tails, sinners! Old devil's got my coat-tails!" he announced appropriately. Then he began to slide.

He relaxed his clasp of the tree and slid to the ground.

"Going to hell!" shrieked Georgie, reaching a high pitch of enthusiasm in this great climax. "Going to hell! Going to hell! I'm gone to hell, hell, hell!"

With a loud scream, Mrs. Bassett threw herself out of the window, alighting by some miracle upon her feet with ankles unsprained.

Mr. Kinosling, feeling that his presence as spiritual adviser was demanded in the yard, followed with greater dignity through the front door. At the corner of the house a small departing figure collided with him violently. It was Penrod, tactfully withdrawing from what promised to be a family scene of unusual painfulness.

Mr. Kinosling seized him by the shoulders and, giving way to emotion, shook him viciously.

"You horrible boy!" exclaimed Mr. Kinosling. "You ruffianly creature! Do you know what's going to happen to you when you grow up? Do you realize what you're going to be!"

With flashing eyes, the indignant boy made know his unshaken purpose. He shouted the reply:

"A minister!"

Lesson 66
1. Read chapters 28 and 29 of *Penrod.*
2. Why is being twelve so great?

Chapter XXVIII. Twelve
This busy globe which spawns us is as incapable of flattery and as intent upon its own affair, whatever that is, as a gyroscope; it keeps steadily whirling along its lawful track, and, thus far seeming to hold a right of way, spins doggedly on, with no perceptible diminution of speed to mark the most gigantic human events--it did not pause to pant and recuperate even when what seemed to Penrod its principal purpose was accomplished, and an enormous shadow, vanishing westward over its surface, marked the dawn of his twelfth birthday.

To be twelve is an attainment worth the struggle. A boy, just twelve, is like a Frenchman just elected to the Academy.

Distinction and honour wait upon him. Younger boys show deference to a person of twelve: his experience is guaranteed, his judgment, therefore, mellow; consequently, his influence is profound. Eleven is not quite satisfactory: it is only an approach. Eleven has the disadvantage of six, of nineteen, of forty-four, and of sixty-nine. But, like twelve, seven is an honourable age, and the ambition to attain it is laudable. People look forward to being seven. Similarly, twenty is worthy, and so, arbitrarily, is twenty-one; forty-five has great solidity; seventy is most commendable and each year thereafter an increasing honour. Thirteen is embarrassed by the beginnings of a new colthood; the child becomes a youth. But twelve is the very top of boyhood.

Dressing, that morning, Penrod felt that the world was changed from the world of yesterday. For one thing, he seemed to own more of it; this day was his day. And it was a day worth owning; the midsummer sunshine, pouring gold through his window, came from a cool sky, and a breeze moved pleasantly in his hair as he leaned from the sill to watch the tribe of clattering blackbirds take wing, following their leader from the trees in the yard to the day's work in the open country. The blackbirds were his, as the sunshine and the breeze were his, for they all belonged to the day which was his birthday and therefore most surely his. Pride suffused him: he was twelve!

His father and his mother and Margaret seemed to understand the difference between to-day and yesterday. They were at the table when he descended, and they gave him a greeting which of itself marked the milestone. Habitually, his entrance into a room where his elders sat brought a cloud of apprehension: they were prone to look up in pathetic expectancy, as if their thought was, "What new awfulness is he going to start now?" But this morning they laughed; his mother rose and kissed him twelve times, so did Margaret; and his father shouted, "Well, well! How's the man?"

Then his mother gave him a Bible and "The Vicar of Wakefield"; Margaret gave him a pair of silver-mounted hair brushes; and his father gave him a "Pocket Atlas" and a small compass.

"And now, Penrod," said his mother, after breakfast, "I'm going to take you out in the country to pay your birthday respects to Aunt Sarah Crim."

Aunt Sarah Crim, Penrod's great-aunt, was his oldest living relative. She was ninety, and when Mrs. Schofield and Penrod alighted from a carriage at her gate they found her digging with a spade in the garden.

"I'm glad you brought him," she said, desisting from labour. "Jinny's baking a cake I'm going to send for his birthday party. Bring him in the house. I've got something for him."
She led the way to her "sitting-room," which had a pleasant smell, unlike any other smell, and, opening the drawer of a shining old what-not, took therefrom a boy's "sling-shot," made of a forked stick, two strips of rubber and a bit of leather.

"This isn't for you," she said, placing it in Penrod's eager hand. "No. It would break all to pieces the first time you tried to shoot it, because it is thirty-five years old. I want to send it back to your father. I think it's time. You give it to him from me, and tell him I say I believe I can trust him with it now. I took it away from him thirty-five years ago, one day after he'd killed my best hen with it, accidentally, and broken a glass pitcher on the back porch with it--accidentally. He doesn't look like a person who's ever done things of that sort, and I suppose he's forgotten it so well that he believes he never did, but if you give it to him from me I think he'll remember. You look like him, Penrod. He was anything but a handsome boy."

After this final bit of reminiscence--probably designed to be repeated to Mr. Schofield--she disappeared in the direction of the kitchen, and returned with a pitcher of lemonade and a blue china dish sweetly freighted with flat ginger cookies of a composition that was her own secret. Then, having set this collation before her guests, she presented Penrod with a superb, intricate, and very modern machine of destructive capacities almost limitless. She called it a pocket-knife.

"I suppose you'll do something horrible with it," she said, composedly. "I hear you do that with everything, anyhow, so you might as well do it with this, and have more fun out of it. They tell me you're the Worst Boy in Town."

"Oh, Aunt Sarah!" Mrs. Schofield lifted a protesting hand.

"Nonsense!" said Mrs. Crim.

"But on his birthday!"

"That's the time to say it. Penrod, aren't you the Worst Boy in Town?"

Penrod, gazing fondly upon his knife and eating cookies rapidly, answered as a matter of course, and absently, "Yes'm."

"Certainly!" said Mrs. Crim. "Once you accept a thing about yourself as established and settled, it's all right. Nobody minds. Boys are just people, really."

"No, no!" Mrs. Schofield cried, involuntarily.

"Yes, they are," returned Aunt Sarah. "Only they're not quite so awful, because they haven't learned to cover themselves all over with little pretences. When Penrod grows up he'll be just the same as he is now, except that whenever he does what he wants to do he'll tell himself and other people a little story about it to make his reason for doing it seem nice and pretty and noble."
"No, I won't!" said Penrod suddenly.

"There's one cookie left," observed Aunt Sarah. "Are you going to eat it?"

"Well," said her great-nephew, thoughtfully, "I guess I better."

"Why?" asked the old lady. "Why do you guess you'd 'better'?"

"Well," said Penrod, with a full mouth, "it might get all dried up if nobody took it, and get thrown out and wasted."

"You're beginning finely," Mrs. Crim remarked. "A year ago you'd have taken the cookie without the same sense of thrift."

"Ma'am?"

"Nothing. I see that you're twelve years old, that's all. There are more cookies, Penrod." She went away, returning with a fresh supply and the observation, "Of course, you'll be sick before the day's over; you might as well get a good start."

Mrs. Schofield looked thoughtful. "Aunt Sarah," she ventured, "don't you really think we improve as we get older?"

"Meaning," said the old lady, "that Penrod hasn't much chance to escape the penitentiary if he doesn't? Well, we do learn to restrain ourselves in some things; and there are people who really want someone else to take the last cookie, though they aren't very common. But it's all right, the world seems to be getting on." She gazed whimsically upon her great-nephew and added, "Of course, when you watch a boy and think about him, it doesn't seem to be getting on very fast."

Penrod moved uneasily in his chair; he was conscious that he was her topic but unable to make out whether or not her observations were complimentary; he inclined to think they were not. Mrs. Crim settled the question for him.

"I suppose Penrod is regarded as the neighbourhood curse?"

"Oh, no," cried Mrs. Schofield. "He----"

"I dare say the neighbours are right," continued the old lady placidly. "He's had to repeat the history of the race and go through all the stages from the primordial to barbarism. You don't expect boys to be civilized, do you?"

"Well, I----"

"You might as well expect eggs to crow. No; you've got to take boys as they are, and learn to know them as they are."

"Naturally, Aunt Sarah," said Mrs. Schofield, "I know Penrod."

Aunt Sarah laughed heartily. "Do you think his father knows him, too?"

"Of course, men are different," Mrs. Schofield returned, apologetically. "But a mother knows----"

"Penrod," said Aunt Sarah, solemnly, "does your father understand you?"

"Ma'am?"

"About as much as he'd understand Sitting Bull!" she laughed.

"And I'll tell you what your mother thinks you are, Penrod. Her real belief is that you're a novice in a convent."

"Ma'am?"

"Aunt Sarah!"

"I know she thinks that, because whenever you don't behave like a novice she's disappointed in you. And your father really believes that you're a decorous, well-trained young business man, and whenever you don't live up to that standard you get on his nerves and he thinks you need a walloping. I'm sure a day very seldom passes without their both saying they don't know what on earth to do with you. Does whipping do you any good, Penrod?"

"Ma'am?"

"Go on and finish the lemonade; there's about glassful left. Oh, take it, take it; and don't say why! Of course you're a little pig."

Penrod laughed gratefully, his eyes fixed upon her over the rim of his uptilted glass.

"Fill yourself up uncomfortably," said the old lady. "You're twelve years old, and you ought to be happy--if you aren't anything else. It's taken over nineteen hundred years of Christianity and some hundreds of thousands of years of other things to produce you, and there you sit!"

"Ma'am?"

"It'll be your turn to struggle and muss things up, for the betterment of posterity, soon enough," said Aunt Sarah Crim. "Drink your lemonade!"

Chapter XXIX. Fanchon

"Aunt Sarah's a funny old lady," Penrod observed, on the way back to the town. "What's she want me to give papa this old sling for? Last thing she said was to be sure not to forget to give it to him. He don't want it; and she said, herself, it ain't any good. She's older than you or papa, isn't she?"

"About fifty years older," answered Mrs. Schofield, turning upon him a stare of perplexity. "Don't cut into the leather with your new knife, dear; the livery man might ask us to pay if---- No. I wouldn't scrape the paint off, either--nor whittle your shoe with it. Couldn't you put it up until we get home?"

"We goin' straight home?"

"No. We're going to stop at Mrs. Gelbraith's and ask a strange little girl to come to your party, this afternoon."

"Who?"

"Her name is Fanchon. She's Mrs. Gelbraith's little niece."

"What makes her so queer?"

"I didn't say she's queer."

"You said----"

"No; I mean that she is a stranger. She lives in New York and has come to visit here."

"What's she live in New York for?"

"Because her parents live there. You must be very nice to her, Penrod; she has been very carefully brought up. Besides, she doesn't know the children here, and you must help to keep her from feeling lonely at your party."

"Yes'm."

When they reached Mrs. Gelbraith's, Penrod sat patiently humped upon a gilt chair during the lengthy exchange of greetings between his mother. and Mrs. Gelbraith. That is one of the things a boy must learn to bear: when his mother meets a compeer there is always a long and dreary wait for him, while the two appear to be using strange symbols of speech, talking for the greater part, it seems to him, simultaneously, and employing a wholly incomprehensible system of emphasis at other times not in vogue. Penrod twisted his legs, his cap and his nose.

"Here she is!" Mrs. Gelbraith cried, unexpectedly, and a dark-haired, demure person entered the room wearing a look of gracious social expectancy. In years she was eleven, in manner about sixty-five, and evidently had lived much at court. She performed a curtsey in acknowledgment of Mrs. Schofield's greeting, and bestowed her hand upon Penrod, who had entertained no hope of such an honour, showed his surprise that it should come to him, and was plainly unable to decide what to do about it.

"Fanchon, dear," said Mrs. Gelbraith, "take Penrod out in the yard for a while, and play."

"Let go the little girl's hand, Penrod," Mrs. Schofield laughed, as the children turned toward the door.

Penrod hastily dropped the small hand, and exclaiming, with simple honesty, "Why, I don't want it!" followed Fanchon out into the sunshiny yard, where they came to a halt and surveyed each other.

Penrod stared awkwardly at Fanchon, no other occupation suggesting itself to him, while Fanchon, with the utmost coolness, made a very thorough visual examination of Penrod, favouring him with an estimating scrutiny which lasted until he literally wiggled. Finally, she spoke.

"Where do you buy your ties?" she asked.

"What?"

"Where do you buy your neckties? Papa gets his at Skoone's. You ought to get yours there. I'm sure the one you're wearing isn't from Skoone's."

"Skoone's?" Penrod repeated. "Skoone's?"

"On Fifth Avenue," said Fanchon. "It's a very smart shop, the men say."

"Men?" echoed Penrod, in a hazy whisper. "Men?"

"Where do your people go in summer?" inquired the lady. "We go to Long Shore, but so many middle-class people have begun coming there, mamma thinks of leaving. The middle classes are simply awful, don't you think?"

"What?"

"They're so boorjaw. You speak French, of course?"

"Me?"

"We ran over to Paris last year. It's lovely, don't you think? Don't you love the Rue de la Paix?"

Penrod wandered in a labyrinth. This girl seemed to be talking, but her words were dumfounding, and of course there was no way for him to know that he was really listening to her mother. It was his first meeting with one of those grown-up little girls, wonderful product of the winter apartment and summer hotel; and Fanchon, an only child, was a star of the brand. He began to feel resentful.

"I suppose," she went on, "I'll find everything here fearfully Western. Some nice people called yesterday, though. Do you know the Magsworth Bittses? Auntie says they're charming. Will Roddy be at your party?"

332

"I guess he will," returned Penrod, finding this intelligible. "The mutt!"

"Really!" Fanchon exclaimed airily. "Aren't you great pals with him?"

"What's 'pals'?"

"Good heavens! Don't you know what it means to say you're 'great pals' with any one? You are an odd child!"

It was too much.

"Oh, Bugs!" said Penrod.

This bit of ruffianism had a curious effect. Fanchon looked upon him with sudden favour.

"I like you, Penrod!" she said, in an odd way, and, whatever else there may have been in her manner, there certainly was no shyness.

"Oh, Bugs!" This repetition may have lacked gallantry, but it was uttered in no very decided tone. Penrod was shaken.

"Yes, I do!" She stepped closer to him, smiling. "Your hair is ever so pretty."

Sailors' parrots swear like mariners, they say; and gay mothers ought to realize that all children are imitative, for, as the precocious Fanchon leaned toward Penrod, the manner in which she looked into his eyes might have made a thoughtful observer wonder where she had learned her pretty ways.

Penrod was even more confused than he had been by her previous mysteries: but his confusion was of a distinctly pleasant and alluring nature: he wanted more of it. Looking intentionally into another person's eyes is an act unknown to childhood; and Penrod's discovery that it could be done was sensational. He had never thought of looking into the eyes of Marjorie Jones.

Despite all anguish, contumely, tar, and Maurice Levy, he still secretly thought of Marjorie, with pathetic constancy, as his "beau"--though that is not how he would have spelled it. Marjorie was beautiful; her curls were long and the colour of amber; her nose was straight and her freckles were honest; she was much prettier than this accomplished visitor. But beauty is not all.

"I do!" breathed Fanchon, softly.

She seemed to him a fairy creature from some rosier world than this. So humble is the human heart, it glorifies and makes glamorous almost any poor thing that says to it: "I like you!"

Penrod was enslaved. He swallowed, coughed, scratched the back of his neck, and said, disjointedly:

"Well--I don't care if you want to. I just as soon."

"We'll dance together," said Fanchon, "at your party."

"I guess so. I just as soon."

"Don't you want to, Penrod?"

"Well, I'm willing to."

"No. Say you want to!"

"Well----"

He used his toe as a gimlet, boring into the ground, his wide open eyes staring with intense vacancy at a button on his sleeve.

His mother appeared upon the porch in departure, calling farewells over her shoulder to Mrs. Gelbraith, who stood in the doorway.

"Say it!" whispered Fanchon.

"Well, I just as soon."

She seemed satisfied.

Lesson 67

1. Read chapters 30 and 31 of *Penrod.*
2. What would he remember most about his twelfth birthday?

Chapter XXX. The Birthday Party

A dancing floor had been laid upon a platform in the yard, when Mrs. Schofield and her son arrived at their own abode; and a white and scarlet striped canopy was in process of erection overhead, to shelter the dancers from the sun. Workmen were busy everywhere under the direction of Margaret, and the smitten heart of Penrod began to beat rapidly. All this was for him; he was Twelve!

After lunch, he underwent an elaborate toilette and murmured not. For the first time in his life he knew the wish to be sand-papered, waxed, and polished to the highest possible degree. And when the operation was over, he stood before the mirror in new bloom, feeling encouraged to hope that his resemblance to his father was not so strong as Aunt Sarah seemed to think.

The white gloves upon his hands had a pleasant smell, he found; and, as he came down the stairs, he had great content in the twinkling of his new dancing slippers. He stepped twice on each step, the better to enjoy their effect and at the same time he deeply inhaled the odour of the gloves. In spite of everything, Penrod had his social capacities. Already it is to be perceived that there were in him the makings of a cotillon leader.

Then came from the yard a sound of tuning instruments, squeak of fiddle, croon of 'cello, a falling triangle ringing and tinkling to the floor; and he turned pale.

Chosen guests began to arrive, while Penrod, suffering from stage-fright and perspiration, stood beside his mother, in the "drawing-room," to receive them. He greeted unfamiliar acquaintances and intimate fellow-criminals with the same frigidity, murmuring: "'M glad to see y'," to all alike, largely increasing the embarrassment which always prevails at the beginning of children's festivities. His unnatural pomp and circumstance had so thoroughly upset him, in truth, that Marjorie Jones received a distinct shock, now to be related. Doctor Thrope, the kind old clergyman who had baptized Penrod, came in for a moment to congratulate the boy, and had just moved away when it was Marjorie's turn, in the line of children, to speak to Penrod. She gave him what she considered a forgiving look, and, because of the occasion, addressed him in a perfectly courteous manner.

"I wish you many happy returns of the day, Penrod."

"Thank you, sir!" he returned, following Dr. Thrope with a glassy stare in which there was absolutely no recognition of Marjorie. Then he greeted Maurice Levy, who was next to Marjorie: "'M glad to see y'!"

Dumfounded, Marjorie turned aside, and stood near, observing Penrod with gravity. It was the first great surprise of her life. Customarily, she had seemed to place his character somewhere between that of the professional rioter and that of the orang-outang; nevertheless, her manner at times just hinted a consciousness that this Caliban was her property. Wherefore, she stared at him incredulously as his head bobbed up and down, in the dancing-school bow, greeting his guests. Then she heard an adult voice, near her, exclaim:

"What an exquisite child!"

Mariorie galanced up--a little consciously, though she was used to it--naturally curious to ascertain who was speaking of her. It was Sam Williams' mother addressing Mrs. Bassett, both being present to help Mrs. Schofield make the festivities festive.

"Exquisite!"

Here was a second heavy surprise for Marjorie: they were not looking at her. They were looking with beaming approval at a girl she had never seen; a dark and modish stranger of singularly composed and yet modest aspect. Her downcast eyes, becoming in one thus entering a crowded room, were all that produced the effect of modesty, counteracting something about her which might have seemed too assured. She was very slender, very dainty, and her apparel was disheartening to the other girls; it was of a knowing picturesqueness wholly unfamiliar to them. There was a delicate trace of powder upon the lobe of Fanchon's left ear, and the outlines of her eyelids, if very closely scrutinized, would have revealed successful experimentation with a burnt match.

Marjorie's lovely eyes dilated: she learned the meaning of hatred at first sight. Observing the stranger with instinctive suspicion, all at once she seemed, to herself, awkward. Poor Marjorie underwent that experience which hearty, healthy, little girls and big girls undergo at one time or another--from heels to head she felt herself, somehow, too thick.

Fanchon leaned close to Penrod and whispered in his ear:

"Don't you forget!"

Penrod blushed.

Marjorie saw the blush. Her lovely eyes opened even wider, and in them there began to grow a light. It was the light of indignation;--at least, people whose eyes glow with that light always call it indignation.

Roderick Magsworth Bitts, Junior, approached Fanchon, when she had made her courtesy to Mrs. Schofield. Fanchon whispered in Roderick's ear also.

"Your hair is pretty, Roddy! Don't forget what you said yesterday!"

Roderick likewise blushed.

Maurice Levy, captivated by the newcomer's appearance, pressed close to Roderick.

"Give us an intaduction, Roddy?"

Roddy being either reluctant or unable to perform the rite, Fanchon took matters into her own hands, and was presently favourably impressed with Maurice, receiving the information that his tie had been brought to him by his papa from Skoone's, whereupon she privately informed him that she liked wavy hair, and arranged to dance with him. Fanchon also thought sandy hair attractive, Sam Williams discovered, a few minutes later, and so catholic was her taste that a ring of boys quite encircled her before the musicians in the yard struck up their thrilling march, and Mrs. Schofield brought Penrod to escort the lady from out-of-town to the dancing pavilion.

Headed by this pair, the children sought partners and paraded solemnly out of the front door and round a corner of the house. There they found the gay marquee; the small orchestra seated on the lawn at one side of it, and a punch bowl of lemonade inviting attention, under a tree. Decorously the small couples stepped upon the platform, one after another, and began to dance.

"It's not much like a children's party in our day," Mrs. Williams said to Penrod's mother. "We'd have been playing 'Quaker-meeting,' 'Clap-in, Clap-out,' or 'Going to Jerusalem,' I suppose."

"Yes, or 'Post-office' and 'Drop-the-handkerchief,'" said Mrs. Schofield. "Things change so quickly. Imagine asking little Fanchon Gelbraith to play 'London Bridge'! Penrod seems to be having a difficult time with her, poor boy; he wasn't a shining light in the dancing class."

However, Penrod's difficulty was not precisely of the kind his mother supposed. Fanchon was showing him a new step, which she taught her next partner in turn, continuing instructions during the dancing. The children crowded the floor, and in the kaleidoscopic jumble of bobbing heads and intermingling figures her extremely different style of motion was unobserved by the older people, who looked on, nodding time benevolently.

Fanchon fascinated girls as well as boys. Many of the former eagerly sought her acquaintance and thronged about her between the dances, when, accepting the deference due a cosmopolitan and an oracle of the mode, she gave demonstrations of the new step to succeeding groups, professing astonishment to find it unknown: it had been "all the go," she explained, at the Long Shore Casino for fully two seasons. She pronounced "slow" a "Fancy Dance" executed during an intermission by Baby Rennsdale and Georgie Bassett, giving it as her opinion that Miss Rennsdale and Mr. Bassett were "dead ones"; and she expressed surprise that the punch bowl contained lemonade and not champagne.

The dancing continued, the new step gaining instantly in popularity, fresh couples adventuring with every number. The word "step" is somewhat misleading, nothing done with the feet being vital to the evolutions introduced by Fanchon. Fanchon's dance came from the Orient by a roundabout way; pausing in Spain, taking on a Gallic frankness in gallantry at the Bal Bullier in Paris, combining with a relative from the South Seas encountered in San Francisco, flavouring itself with a carefree abandon in New Orleans, and, accumulating, too, something inexpressible from Mexico and South America, it kept, throughout its travels, to the underworld, or to circles where nature is extremely frank and rank, until at last it reached the dives of New York, when it immediately broke out in what is called civilized society. Thereafter it spread, in variously modified forms--some of them

337

disinfected--to watering-places, and thence, carried by hundreds of older male and female Fanchons, over the country, being eagerly adopted everywhere and made wholly pure and respectable by the supreme moral axiom that anything is all right if enough people do it. Everybody was doing it.

Not quite everybody. It was perhaps some test of this dance that earth could furnish no more grotesque sight than that of children doing it.

Earth, assisted by Fanchon, was furnishing this sight at Penrod's party. By the time ice-cream and cake arrived, about half the guests had either been initiated into the mysteries by Fanchon or were learning by imitation, and the education of the other half was resumed with the dancing, when the attendant ladies, unconscious of what was happening, withdrew into the house for tea.

"That orchestra's a dead one," Fanchon remarked to Penrod. "We ought to liven them up a little!"

. She approached the musicians.

"Don't you know," she asked the leader, "the Slingo Sligo Slide?"

The leader giggled, nodded, rapped with his bow upon his violin; and Penrod, following Fanchon back upon the dancing floor, blindly brushed with his elbow a solitary little figure standing aloof on the lawn at the edge of the platform.

It was Marjorie.

In no mood to approve of anything introduced by Fanchon, she had scornfully refused, from the first, to dance the new "step," and, because of its bonfire popularity, found herself neglected in a society where she had reigned as beauty and belle. Faithless Penrod, dazed by the sweeping Fanchon, had utterly forgotten the amber curls; he had not once asked Marjorie to dance. All afternoon the light of indignation had been growing brighter in her eyes, though Maurice Levy's defection to the lady from New York had not fanned this flame. From the moment Fanchon had whispered familiarly in Penrod's ear, and Penrod had blushed, Marjorie had been occupied exclusively with resentment against that guilty pair. It seemed to her that Penrod had no right to allow a strange girl to whisper in his ear; that his blushing, when the strange girl did it, was atrocious; and that the strange girl, herself, ought to be arrested.

Forgotten by the merrymakers, Marjorie stood alone upon the lawn, clenching her small fists, watching the new dance at its high tide, and hating it with a hatred that made every inch of her tremble. And, perhaps because jealousy is a great awakener of the virtues, she had a perception of something in it worse than lack of dignity--something vaguely but outrageously reprehensible. Finally, when Penrod brushed by her, touched her with his elbow, and, did not even see her, Marjorie's state of mind (not unmingled with emotion!) became dangerous. In fact, a trained nurse, chancing to observe her at this juncture, would probably have advised that she be taken home and put to bed. Marjorie was on the verge of hysterics.

She saw Fanchon and Penrod assume the double embrace required by the dance; the "Slingo Sligo Slide" burst from the orchestra; and all the little couples began to bob and dip and sway.

Marjorie made a scene. She sprang upon the platform and stamped her foot.

"Penrod Schofield!" she shouted. "You behave yourself!"

The remarkable girl took Penrod by the ear. By his ear she swung him away from Fanchon and faced him toward the lawn.

"You march straight out of here!" she commanded.

Penrod marched.

He was stunned; obeyed automatically, without question, and had very little realization of what was happening to him. Altogether, and without reason, he was in precisely the condition of an elderly spouse detected in flagrant misbehaviour. Marjorie, similarly, was in precisely the condition of the party who detects such misbehaviour. It may be added that she had acted with a promptness, a decision and a disregard of social consequences all to be commended to the attention of ladies in like predicament.

"You ought to be ashamed of yourself!" she raged, when they reached the lawn. "Aren't you ashamed of yourself?"

"What for?" he inquired, helplessly.

"You be quiet!"

"But what'd I do, Marjorie? I haven't done anything to you," he pleaded. "I haven't even seen you, all aftern----"

"You be quiet!" she cried, tears filling her eyes. "Keep still! You ugly boy! Shut up!"

She slapped him.

He should have understood from this how much she cared for him. But he rubbed his cheek and declared ruefully:

"I'll never speak to you again!"

"You will, too!" she sobbed, passionately.

"I will not!"

He turned to leave her, but paused.

His mother, his sister Margaret, and their grownup friends had finished their tea and were approaching from the house. Other parents and guardians were with them, coming for their children; and there were carriages and automobiles waiting in the street. But the "Slingo Slide" went on, regardless.

The group of grown-up people hesitated and came to a halt, gazing at the pavilion.

"What are they doing?" gasped Mrs. Williams, blushing deeply. "What is it? What is it?"

"What is it?" Mrs. Gelbraith echoed in a frightened whisper. "What----"

"They're Tangoing!" cried Margaret Schofield. "Or Bunny Hugging or Grizzly Bearing, or----"

"They're only Turkey Trotting," said Robert Williams.

With fearful outcries the mothers, aunts, and sisters rushed upon the pavilion.

"Of course it was dreadful," said Mrs. Schofield, an hour later, rendering her lord an account of the day, "but it was every bit the fault of that one extraordinary child. And of all the quiet, demur little things--that is, I mean, when she first came. We all spoke of how exquisite she seemed--so well trained, so finished! Eleven years old! I never saw anything like her in my life!"

"I suppose it's the New Child," her husband grunted.

"And to think of her saying there ought to have been champagne in the lemonade!"

"Probably she'd forgotten to bring her pocket flask," he suggested musingly.

"But aren't you proud of Penrod?" cried Penrod's mother. "It was just as I told you: he was standing clear outside the pavilion----"

"I never thought to see the day! And Penrod was the only boy not doing it, the only one to refuse? All the others were----"

"Every one!" she returned triumphantly. "Even Georgie Bassett!"

"Well," said Mr. Schofield, patting her on the shoulder. "I guess we can hold up our heads at last."

Chapter XXXI. Over the Fence

Penrod was out in the yard, staring at the empty marquee. The sun was on the horizon line, so far behind the back fence, and a western window of the house blazed in gold unbearable to the eye: his day was nearly over. He sighed, and took from the inside pocket of his new jacket the "sling-shot" aunt Sarah Crim had given him that morning.

He snapped the rubbers absently. They held fast; and his next impulse was entirely irresistible. He found a shapely stone, fitted it to the leather, and drew back the ancient catapult for a shot. A sparrow hopped upon a branch between him and the house, and he aimed at the sparrow, but the reflection from the dazzling window struck in his eyes as he loosed the leather.

He missed the sparrow, but not the window. There was a loud crash, and to his horror he caught a glimpse of his father, stricken in mid-shaving, ducking a shower of broken glass, glittering razor flourishing wildly. Words crashed with the glass, stentorian words, fragmentary but collossal.

Penrod stood petrified, a broken sling in his hand. He could hear his parent's booming descent of the back stairs, instant and furious; and then, red-hot above white lather, Mr. Schofield burst out of the kitchen door and hurtled forth upon his son.

"What do you mean?" he demanded, shaking Penrod by the shoulder. "Ten minutes ago, for the very first time in our lives, your mother and I were saying we were proud of you, and here you go and throw a rock at me through the window when I'm shaving for dinner!"

"I didn't!" Penrod quavered. "I was shooting at a sparrow, and the sun got in his eyes, and the sling broke----"

"What sling?"

"This'n."

"Where'd you get that devilish thing? Don't you know I've forbidden you a thousand times----"

"It ain't mine," said Penrod. "It's yours."

"What?"

"Yes, sir," said the boy meekly. "Aunt Sarah Crim gave it to me this morning and told me to give it back to you. She said she took it away from you thirty-five years ago. You killed her hen, she said. She told me some more to tell you, but I've forgotten."

"Oh!" said Mr. Schofield.

He took the broken sling in his hand, looked at it long and thoughtfully--and he looked longer, and quite as thoughtfully, at Penrod. Then he turned away, and walked toward the house.

"I'm sorry, papa," said Penrod.

Mr. Schofield coughed, and, as he reached the door, called back, but without turning his head.

"Never mind, little boy. A broken window isn't much harm."

When he had gone in, Penrod wandered down the yard to the back fence, climbed upon it, and sat in reverie there.

A slight figure appeared, likewise upon a fence, beyond two neighbouring yards.

"Yay, Penrod!" called comrade Sam Williams.

"Yay!" returned Penrod, mechanically.

"I caught Billy Blue Hill!" shouted Sam, describing retribution in a manner perfectly clear to his friend. "You were mighty lucky to get out of it."

"I know that!"

"You wouldn't of, if it hadn't been for Marjorie."

"Well, don't I know that?" Penrod shouted, with heat.

"Well, so long!" called Sam, dropping from his fence; and the friendly voice came then, more faintly, "Many happy returns of the day, Penrod!"

And now, a plaintive little whine sounded from below Penrod's feet, and, looking down, he saw that Duke, his wistful, old, scraggly dog sat in the grass, gazing seekingly up at him.

The last shaft of sunshine of that day fell graciously and like a blessing upon the boy sitting on the fence. Years afterward, a quiet sunset would recall to him sometimes the gentle evening of his twelfth birthday, and bring him the picture of his boy self, sitting in rosy light upon the fence, gazing pensively down upon his wistful, scraggly, little old dog, Duke. But something else, surpassing, he would remember of that hour, for, in the side street, close by, a pink skirt flickered from behind a shade tree to the shelter of the fence, there was a gleam of amber curls, and Penrod started, as something like a tiny white wing fluttered by his head, and there came to his ears the sound of a light laugh and of light footsteps departing, the laughter tremulous, the footsteps fleet.

In the grass, between Duke's forepaws, there lay a white note, folded in the shape of a cocked hat, and the sun sent forth a final amazing glory as Penrod opened it and read: "Your my bow."

THE END

Lesson 68

Vocabulary: Choose the definition that best matches the word. Write the numbers and letters of the matches on a separate piece of paper. (Answers)

1. reverberating
A. echoing
B. interruption
C. make or become wider
D. eagerness, interest in

2. flecked
A. to be full of
B. a collection of different items
C. set apart as holy
D. marked or dotted with color

3. knoll
A. small hill
B. knobby
C. excited, disorderly
D. lots of plant leaves together

4. cumulative
A. knobby
B. bring under control
C. rut or trench
D. increasing

5. teeming
A. interruption
B. to be full of
C. rut or trench
D. set apart as holy

6. keen
A. eagerness, interest in
B. set apart as holy
C. lots of plant leaves together
D. make or become wider

7. interposed
A. interruption
B. lots of plant leaves together
C. rut or trench
D. knobby

8. furrows
A. echoing
B. rut or trench
C. lots of plant leaves together
D. adult male singing voice

9. tumultuous
A. excited, disorderly
B. understand
C. path of a flying object
D. echoing

10. fathom
A. eagerness, interest in
B. understand
C. echoing
D. knobby

11. gnarled
A. adult male singing voice
C. excited, disorderly
B. knobby
D. lots of plant leaves together

12. baritone
A. marked or dotted with color
C. lots of plant leaves together
B. adult male singing voice
D. rut or trench

13. foliage
A. a collection of different items
C. excited, disorderly
B. echoing
D. lots of plant leaves together

14. dilating
A. lots of plant leaves together
C. make or become wider
B. understand
D. a collection of different items

15. trajectory
A. a collection of different items
C. understand
B. increasing
D. path of a flying object

16. sanctify
A. echoing
C. make or become wider
B. interruption
D. set apart as holy

17. subdue
A. adult male singing voice
C. a collection of different items
B. bring under control
D. set apart as holy

18. miscellany
A. to be full of
C. a collection of different items
B. increasing
D. eagerness, interest in

Lesson 69

1. Read the first part of "How Santa Claus Found the Poor-House" by Sophie Swett.

HELIOGABALUS was shoveling snow. The snow was very deep, and the path from the front door to the road was a long one, and the shovel was almost as big as Heliogabalus.

But Gobaly—as everybody called him, for short—didn't give up easily. You might have known that he wouldn't give up easily by one glance at his sturdy little figure, at his bright, wide-open eyes, his firm mouth, and his square, prominent chin; even the little, turned-up end of his nose looked resolute.

Besides, Mrs. Pynchum had told him to shovel out the path; and she had a switch behind the wood-shed door, to say nothing of her slipper.

Mrs. Pynchum kept the poor-farm, and Gobaly was "town's poor." The boys sometimes called him that, when he went to coast on Three-Pine Hill or to see the skating on the mill-pound; and sometimes, too, they made fun of his clothes. But it was only the boys who were a great deal bigger than he who dared to make fun of Gobaly, and some of them even ran when he doubled up his fists. But Methuselah! I don't know what would have become of Methuselah if he had not had Gobaly to defend him. For he was a delicate little fellow; "spindlin' and good for nothin'," Mrs. Pynchum called him; and he had come to her in a basket—in other words, Methuselah was a foundling.

Mrs. Pynchum "didn't think much of children who came in a basket from no body knew where. It didn't seem to be long to Poplarville to support him, since he didn't belong to anybody that ever lived there, and his keep and his medicine cost more than he would ever be worth to anybody."

Gobaly's mother died in the poor-house, and left him there, a baby; she had always lived in the town, and so had his father, so of course Gobaly had a perfect right there; and old Dr. Barnacle, who was very learned, had said of him that he was an uncommonly fine baby, and had named him Heliogabalus.

Besides, he was strong and willing, and did a great deal of work. Mrs. Pynchum "could put up with Gobaly." But. Methuselah, she said, was "a thorn in her side." And now, after being a trial all his life, he had a hip disease, which the doctor feared was incurable, and which made him more troublesome still!

But, after all, Mrs. Pynchum wasn't quite so bad as one would have thought from her talk. She must have had a soft spot somewhere in her heart, for she put plums in Methuselah's porridge, now that he was ill, and once she had let Gobaly leave his wood-chopping to draw him out on his sled.

I suppose there is a soft spot in everybody's heart, only sometimes it isn't very easy to find it; and Mrs. Pynchum might not have been so cross if she had led an easier life. There were a good many queer people in the poor-house, "flighty in their heads and wearin' in their ways," she said, and sometimes they must have been trying to the patience.

Once in a great while, indeed, Mrs. Pynchum was good-natured, and then, sometimes for a whole evening, the poor-house would seem like home. All those who lived there would then sit around the fire and roast apples; and Mrs. Pynchum would even unlock the closet under the back stairs, where there was a great bag full of nuts that Sandy Gooding and Gobaly had gathered; and Uncle Sim Perkins would tell stories.

But it happened very unfortunately that Mrs. Pynchum never had one of her good-natured days on Thanksgiving, or Christmas, or any holiday. She was sure to say on those days that she was "all tried to pieces." And everybody was frightened and unhappy when Mrs. Pynchum was "all tried to pieces," and so that was the reason why Gobaly's heart sank as he remembered, while he was shoveling the path through the snow, that the next day was Christmas.

Some people from the village went by with a Christmas-tree, which they had cut down in the woods just beyond the poorhouse; there were children in the party, and they called to Gobaly and wished him a merry Christmas, and asked him if they were going to have a Christmas-tree at his house, and expressed great surprise that he wasn't going to hang up his stocking. Then one of the children suddenly exclaimed:

"Why, that's the poor-house! It's never Christmas there!"

Poor Gobaly's heart sank still more as he caught these words, and somehow he felt very tired, and minded the cold, as he had not thought of minding it a moment before, and the snow-bank looked as if he never could shovel through it. For though Gobaly was stout-hearted, he didn't like to be reminded that he was "town's poor," and that Christmas was nothing to him.

Just then he caught sight of Methuselah's little pinched face pressed against the window-pane. Methuselah always had, even when he was a baby, a worn and pallid face, like a little old man, and that was why they called him Methuselah. It was cold in the front room but Methuselah had wrapped himself in a piece of an old quilt and stolen into the back room and to the window, where he could see Gobaly shoveling the snow.

Methuselah never was quite happy when Gobaly was out of his sight.

Gobaly went up to the window.

"To-morrow's Christmas, 'Thusely!" he said.

"Is it? Do you s'pose she knows it? She'll be 'all tried to pieces,' won't she?"
("She" always meant Mrs. Pynchum in the poor-house; nobody there ever spoke of her in any other way.)

Gobaly was sadly afraid that she would, but he said, cheerfully:

"May be she won't. May be she'll let me take you out on my sled; and one Christmas there was turkey and plum-pudding."

"Must have been a good many Christmases ago; I can't remember it!" said Methuselah. "Some folks have 'em every Christmas, Uncle Sim says, but perhaps it isn't true. Gobaly, do you believe there really is any Santa Claus, such as Uncle Sim tells about, or did he make it all up? To be sure, he showed me a picture of him."

"I know there is," said Gobaly firmly, "because I've seen presents that he brought to boys and girls in the village."

"Then why don't he ever come here and bring us some?" said Methuselah, as if a new idea had suddenly struck him. "Do you s'pose it's because we're worse than any other boys in the world? She says we are, sometimes. Or may be he's too proud to stop at the poor-house."

"Perhaps he can't find the way," said Gobaly. "'Cause it's a pretty crooked road, you know. Or may be he wouldn't think it was worth the while to come so far out of the village just for us; he wouldn't be going to Squire Thorndike's, because there aren't any children there, and there aren't any other houses on this road."

"I wish we lived where there was a truly Christmas, like places where Uncle Sim has been; don't you, Gobaly? May be he makes them all up, though; it seems if they must be too good to be true."

"I shouldn't wonder if you got lots of plums in your porridge to-morrow and perhaps a piece of mince-pie. And I'll ask her to let me take you up to ThreePine Hill on the sled."

Gobaly always showed the bright side of things to Methuselah and he had become so accustomed to looking for a bright side that he could find one when you wouldn't have thought there was any there.

And whenever he found a very big lump in his throat he swallowed it for Methuselah's sake, and pretended that he didn't see anything in the world to cry about.

He had to go back to his shoveling then, but after he had started he turned back to say:

"When I'm a man, you shall have Christmases, 'Thusely!"

It was in that way that Gobaly often comforted Methuselah. It never seemed to occur to either of them that 'Thusely might possibly grow to be a man too.

Gobaly went to work at the snow again as if it were not a bit bigger than he was, and he soon had a rampart piled up on each side of the path so high that he thought it must look like the Chinese Wall which Uncle Sim was always telling of.

As he was digging the very last shovelful of snow out of the path, he heard the jingle of sleighbells, and saw the butcher's wagon, set upon runners and drawn by a very frisky horse, going in the direction of the village. The butcher's boy and three of his comrades occupied the seat, and as many more boys were wedged in among the joints of meat and heaps of poultry in the back of the wagon. They were evidently combining pleasure with business in the liveliest manner.

Coming in the other direction, from the village, was a large Newfoundland dog with a basket in his mouth. Gobaly liked dogs, and he was sure that he was acquainted with everyone in the village. As he was on intimate terms with every big one, he knew that this must be a stranger.

The butcher's boy was driving recklessly, and seemed to think it would be fun to make a sudden turn into the drifts through which the dog was bounding. The horse, taken by surprise and somewhat frightened, made a sudden plunge; and though Gobaly could not quite see how it happened, it seemed that before the dog had time to get out of the way, the sled had gone over him, and he lay helpless and howling upon the snow!

The boys either found it impossible to stop their horse, or were too frightened to investigate the extent of the mischief they had done, for they went careering on, and left the poor dog to his fate.

Gobaly was at his side in a moment, patting his shaggy black head, calling him "poor doggie" and "good doggie," and trying to discover how badly he was hurt. He came to the conclusion, after a thorough examination, that his leg was either broken or badly sprained,—and Gobaly was a judge of such things. He had once doctored a rooster's lame leg, and though the rooster was never again able to mount a fence, and crowed with diminished energy, he was still able to cheer his heart by fighting the three other roosters all at once, and was likely to escape the dinner-pot for a long time to come, though his gait was no longer lordly. Gobaly had also successfully treated a kitten with a sprained ankle—to say nothing of one whose tail the gobbler had nipped off. And he had seen the doctor in the village set a puppy's leg, and had carefully watched the operation.

He helped the dog along toward the house—and it was well that he was a strong and sturdy little fellow or he could not have done it—and managed at last to get the poor creature, unobserved, into the wood-shed. He was very much afraid that Mrs. Pynchum, if she should see him, would order him to leave the dog in the road, and he knew it would not do to carry him in beside the kitchen fire, as he wanted to, for Mrs. Pynchum never wanted "a dirty dog in her clean house."

Lesson 70

1. Read to the end of "How Santa Claus Found the Poor-House" by Sophie Swett.

Gobaly found it hard to decide whether the bone was broken or only out of place, but he made a sort of a splint, such as he had seen the doctor use upon the puppy's leg, and then wound soft cloths, wet with liniment, about it, and the dog certainly seemed relieved, and licked Gobaly's hand, and looked at him with grateful eyes.

He ventured into the house after a while, and beckoned to Methuselah to come out to the woodshed.

Methuselah was convinced that Santa Claus had sent the dog to them as a Christmas present, and his delight was unbounded.

"Of course, Santa Claus must have sent him, or why would he have come down this lonely road all by himself? And you will cure him" (Methuselah thought there was little that Gobaly couldn't do if he tried), "and perhaps she will let us keep him!"

But a sudden recollection had struck Gobaly. The dog had been carrying a basket in his mouth; there might be something in it that would tell where he came from.

Though the dog's appearance was mysterious, Gobaly was not so ready as Methuselah to accept the Santa Claus theory.

He ran out and found the basket, half buried in the snow, where it had fallen from the dog's mouth. There were several letters and papers in it addressed to "Dr. Carruthers, care of Richard Thorndike, Esq."

Dr. Carruthers was the famous New York physician who was visiting Squire Thorndike! Gobaly had heard the people in the village talking about him. The dog probably belonged to him, and had been sent to the post-office for his letters.

Although he had not really believed that Santa Claus sent the dog, Gobaly did feel a pang of disappointment that they must part with him so soon. But then Mrs. Pynchum would probably not have allowed them to keep him, anyhow, and she might have had him shot because his leg was hurt. That thought consoled Gobaly, and having obtained Mrs. Pynchum's permission to carry him to his master,—which was readily given, since it was the easiest way to get rid of the dog,—he put a very large box, with a bed in it made of straw and soft cloth, upon his sled, and then lifted the dog gently into the box. The dog whined with pain when he was moved, but still licked Gobaly's hand, as if he understood that he was his friend and did not mean to hurt him.

Methuselah stood in the shed door, and looked after them, weeping, sadly making up his mind that Santa Claus was proud and would never come to the poor-house.

Gobaly had never been even inside Squire Thorndike's gate before, and he went up to one of the back doors with fear and trembling; the servants at Squire Thorndike's were said to be "stuck-up," and they might not be very civil to "town's poor." But at the sight of the dog they raised a great cry, and at once ushered Gobaly into the presence of Squire Thorndike and Dr. Carruthers, that he might tell them all he knew about the accident.

Dr. Carruthers was a big, jolly-looking man, with white hair and a long white beard, just like pictures of Santa Claus. Gobaly was sure that Methuselah would think he was Santa Claus if he could see him. He evidently felt very sorry about the dog's accident, and pitied him and petted him as if he were a baby; Gobaly, who had never had so much petting in his whole life, thought the dog ought to forget all about his leg.

And then he suddenly turned to Gobaly and asked him who set the leg.

Gobaly answered, modestly, that he "fixed it as well as he could because there wasn't anybody else around."

"How did you know how?" asked the doctor. And Gobaly related his experiences with the rooster and the kitten and the puppy. Dr. Carruthers looked at him steadily out of a pair of eyes that were very sharp, although very kind. Then he turned to Squire Thorndike and said "an uncommon boy." Squire Thorndike answered, and they talked together in a low tone, casting an occasional glance at Gobaly.

How Gobaly's ears did burn! He wondered what Squire Thorndike knew about him, and he thought of every prank he ever had played in his life. Gobaly was an unusually good boy, but he had played a few pranks,—being a boy,— and he thought they were a great deal worse than they really were, because Mrs. Pynchum said so. And he imagined that Dr. Carruthers was hearing all about them, and would presently turn round and say that such a bad boy had no right to touch his dog, and that such conduct was just what he should expect of "town's poor." But instead of that, after several minutes' conversation with Squire Thorndike, he turned to Gobaly, and said:

"I want an office-boy, and I think you are just the boy to suit me. How would you like to come and live with me, and perhaps, one of these days, be a doctor yourself."

Gobaly caught his breath.

To go away from Mrs. Pynchum; not to be "town's poor" any more; to learn to be a doctor! He had said once in Mrs. Pynchum's hearing that he wanted to be a doctor when he grew up, and she had said, sneeringly, that "town's poor weren't very likely to get a chance to learn to be doctors."

And now the chance had come to him!

Gobaly thought it seemed too much like heaven to be anything that could happen to a mortal boy!

"Well, would you like to go?" asked the doctor again, as Gobaly could find no words to answer.

"Would I, sir? Wouldn't I!" said Gobaly, with a radiant face.

"Well, then, I will make an arrangement with the selectmen—which I have no doubt it will be easy to do—and will take you home with me to-morrow night," said the good doctor.

But the brightness had suddenly faded from Gobaly's face. He stood with his hands thrust into his trousers pockets, gazing irresolutely at the carpet. But it was not the carpet that Gobaly saw; it might as well have been the yellow paint of the poor-house floors for all that he noticed of its luxurious pile and beautiful colors. It was 'Thusely's pale, pinched little face that he saw! It had risen before him even while the doctor was speaking. If he went away, who would take care of 'Thusely? And 'Thusely's heart would be broken.

"I can't go, sir; I forgot. No—no—I can't go!" said Gobaly.

Oh, what a lump there was in his throat!

He had swallowed many a lump for 'Thusely's sake, but that was the very biggest one!

And then he turned and ran out of the house, without any ceremony. He knew it was rude, but that lump wouldn't stay down, and though he might be called "town's poor," he wasn't going to be called a cry-baby!

And home he ran, as fast as his legs would carry him.

That night something very unusual happened. Mrs. Pynchum went to the village to a Christmas festival. She went before dark, and the spirits of everybody in the poor-house rose as soon as she was out of sight. Mr. Pynchum piled great logs upon the fire-place, till there was such a roaring fire as had not been seen there for many a long day; and he told Joe Golightly and Gobaly to go down cellar and bring up as many apples as they wanted to, and he found the key of the closet where the bag of nuts was kept! And Sandy Gooding brought out some fine pop-corn that he had saved up; and Joe Golightly brought out his violin, which, though some of its strings were broken and its voice was a little cracked and wheezy, could yet cheer one up wonderfully with "Bonnie Dundee" and "The Campbells are Coming." Everybody was merry,—although there was no Christmas-tree, and nobody had a present except 'Thusely, who had a big red peppermint-drop that Gobaly bought him with a penny hoarded for six weeks—and it would have been a very pleasant evening if there had not been one great drawback. Mrs. Pynchum had a way of pouncing upon people when they least expected her. If a window rattled or a mouse stirred in the wall, a hush fell upon the mirth, and everybody shrank with dread. It would be so like Mrs. Pynchum to suspect that they were having a good time, and turn back to put a stop to it before she had fairly reached the festival!

Just as they had poured out a popperful of corn,—popped out so big and white that it would do you good to see it,—and Uncle Sim was clearing his throat to begin a story, there came a loud knock at the door. Everybody jumped. Mr. Pynchum and Sandy began to cram the apples into their pockets, and thrust the corn popper into the closet, and Joe hid his violin under his coat-tails. It took them all fully two minutes to remember that Mrs. Pynchum never knocked.

Mr. Pynchum sat down again, and said, in a tone of surprise, as if he had not been in the least agitated:

"What is the matter with you all? Gobaly, open the door."

Gobaly opened the door, and who should be there but Squire Thorndike and the city doctor!

The moment 'Thusely saw Dr. Carruthers he called out "Santa Claus!" And the big doctor laughed, and took a great package of candy out of his pocket and gave it to 'Thusely.

After that it was of no use for Gobaly to whisper, "The dog gentleman!" in 'Thusely's ear; he couldn't think it was anybody but Santa Claus.

"I'm so glad you've come!" he said, confidentially. "And you look just like your picture. And I don't see why you never came before, for you don't seem proud. And we aren't such very bad boys; anyway, Gobaly isn't. Don't you believe what Mrs. Pynchum tells you!—Will you?"

The doctor laughed, and said he was getting to be an old fellow, and the snow was deep, and it was hard for him to get about; but he was sorry he hadn't come before, for he thought they did look like good boys. Then he asked Methuselah about his lameness and the pain in his side, and said he ought to be sent to a certain hospital in New York, where he might be cured. And then he asked if he had no relatives or friends.

"I've got Gobaly," said 'Thusely.

The doctor turned and looked sharply at Gobaly. "Is he the reason why you wouldn't go with me?" he asked.

"He's such a little chap, and I'm all he's got," said Gobaly.

The doctor took out his handkerchief and said it was bad weather for colds.
"Suppose I take him, too?" said he.

This time the lump in his throat fairly got the better of Gobaly!

But 'Thusely clapped his hands for joy. He didn't understand what was to happen, only that Santa Claus was to take him somewhere with Gobaly; and one thing that 'Thusely was sure of was that he wanted to go wherever Gobaly went. And he kept saying:

"I told you that Santa Claus sent the dog,—now, didn't I, Gobaly?"

Methuselah went to the hospital and was cured, and Gobaly—well, if I should tell you his name, you might say that you had heard of him as a famous surgeon-doctor. I think it is probable that he could now make a lame rooster or a kitten with a sprained ankle just as good as new, and I am sure he wouldn't be above trying; for he has a heart big enough to sympathize with any creature that suffers.

There is at least one person in the world who will agree with me, and that is a gentleman who was once a miserable little cripple in a poor-house, and was called Methuselah.

Lesson 71

1. Read this introduction to *Black Beauty*.

   - *"Black Beauty* is a novel told in the first person (or "first horse") as an autobiographical memoir told by a highbred horse named Black Beauty-beginning with his carefree days as a colt on an English farm, to his difficult life pulling cabs in London, to his happy retirement in the country."
   (from http://etc.usf.edu/lit2go/125/black-beauty/)

2. *Black Beauty* was written by Anna Sewell in 1877 in England. She wrote it to teach others to show kindness to horses. She grew up in a Quaker home where she was taught to love all of God's creation, including the creatures. Her family also introduced her to writing as her mother authored stories for children and Anna helped edit them. *Black Beauty* was the only book that Anna ever wrote, and she died just a year after it was published.

3. The horses in the book are based on Anna's family's horses. The book served its purpose and brought about changes in the treatment of horses. In Anna's day horses were used by the rich for the carriages and horses were hurt just to make them have what was considered a more regal appearance. Other horses worked for the poor in the coal mines and other industries where some horses worked until they died of exhaustion.

Vocabulary

1. Review your vocabulary on Lesson 10.

Lesson 72

1. You are going to start reading *Black Beauty* by Anna Sewell. Today you will read the first three chapters.

2. Create a *Black Beauty* page to write about the character "I." Who is the character? What does the character look like and act like? How do others act towards the character?

01 My Early Home

The first place that I can well remember was a large pleasant meadow with a pond of clear water in it. Some shady trees leaned over it, and rushes and water-lilies grew at the deep end. Over the hedge on one side we looked into a plowed field, and on the other we looked over a gate at our master's house, which stood by the roadside; at the top of the meadow was a grove of fir trees, and at the bottom a running brook overhung by a steep bank.

While I was young I lived upon my mother's milk, as I could not eat grass. In the daytime I ran by her side, and at night I lay down close by her. When it was hot we used to stand by the pond in the shade of the trees, and when it was cold we had a nice warm shed near the grove.

As soon as I was old enough to eat grass my mother used to go out to work in the daytime, and come back in the evening.

There were six young colts in the meadow besides me; they were older than I was; some were nearly as large as grown-up horses. I used to run with them, and had great fun; we used to gallop all together round and round the field as hard as we could go. Sometimes we had rather rough play, for they would frequently bite and kick as well as gallop.

One day, when there was a good deal of kicking, my mother whinnied to me to come to her, and then she said:

"I wish you to pay attention to what I am going to say to you. The colts who live here are very good colts, but they are cart-horse colts, and of course they have not learned manners. You have been well-bred and well-born; your father has a great name in these parts, and your grandfather won the cup two years at the Newmarket races; your grandmother had the sweetest temper of any horse I ever knew, and I think you have never seen me kick or bite. I hope you will grow up gentle and good, and never learn bad ways; do your work with a good will, lift your feet up well when you trot, and never bite or kick even in play."

I have never forgotten my mother's advice; I knew she was a wise old horse, and our master thought a great deal of her. Her name was Duchess, but he often called her Pet.

Our master was a good, kind man. He gave us good food, good lodging, and kind words; he spoke as kindly to us as he did to his little children. We were all fond of him, and my mother loved him very much. When she saw him at the gate she would neigh with joy, and trot up to him. He would pat and stroke her and say, "Well, old Pet, and how is your little Darkie?" I was a dull black, so he called me Darkie; then he would give me a piece of bread, which was very good, and sometimes he brought a carrot for my mother. All the horses would come to him, but I think we were his favorites. My mother always took him to the town on a market day in a light gig.

There was a plowboy, Dick, who sometimes came into our field to pluck blackberries from the hedge. When he had eaten all he wanted he would have what he called fun with the colts, throwing stones and sticks at them to make them gallop. We did not much mind him, for we could gallop off; but sometimes a stone would hit and hurt us.

One day he was at this game, and did not know that the master was in the next field; but he was there, watching what was going on; over the hedge he jumped in a snap, and catching Dick by the arm, he gave him such a box on the ear as made him roar with the pain and surprise. As soon as we saw the master we trotted up nearer to see what went on.
"Bad boy!" he said, "bad boy! to chase the colts. This is not the first time, nor the second, but it shall be the last. There-take your money and go home; I shall not want you on my farm again." So

we never saw Dick any more. Old Daniel, the man who looked after the horses, was just as gentle as our master, so we were well off.

02 The Hunt

Before I was two years old a circumstance happened which I have never forgotten. It was early in the spring; there had been a little frost in the night, and a light mist still hung over the woods and meadows. I and the other colts were feeding at the lower part of the field when we heard, quite in the distance, what sounded like the cry of dogs. The oldest of the colts raised his head, pricked his ears, and said, "There are the hounds!" and immediately cantered off, followed by the rest of us to the upper part of the field, where we could look over the hedge and see several fields beyond. My mother and an old riding horse of our master's were also standing near, and seemed to know all about it.

"They have found a hare," said my mother, "and if they come this way we shall see the hunt."

And soon the dogs were all tearing down the field of young wheat next to ours. I never heard such a noise as they made. They did not bark, nor howl, nor whine, but kept on a "yo! yo, o, o! yo! yo, o, o!" at the top of their voices. After them came a number of men on horseback, some of them in green coats, all galloping as fast as they could. The old horse snorted and looked eagerly after them, and we young colts wanted to be galloping with them, but they were soon away into the fields lower down; here it seemed as if they had come to a stand; the dogs left off barking, and ran about every way with their noses to the ground.

"They have lost the scent," said the old horse; "perhaps the hare will get off."

"What hare?" I said.

"Oh! I don't know what hare; likely enough it may be one of our own hares out of the woods; any hare they can find will do for the dogs and men to run after;" and before long the dogs began their "yo! yo, o, o!" again, and back they came altogether at full speed, making straight for our meadow at the part where the high bank and hedge overhang the brook.

"Now we shall see the hare," said my mother; and just then a hare wild with fright rushed by and made for the woods. On came the dogs; they burst over the bank, leaped the stream, and came dashing across the field followed by the huntsmen. Six or eight men leaped their horses clean over, close upon the dogs. The hare tried to get through the fence; it was too thick, and she turned sharp round to make for the road, but it was too late; the dogs were upon her with their wild cries; we heard one shriek, and that was the end of her. One of the huntsmen rode up and whipped off the dogs, who would soon have torn her to pieces. He held her up by the leg torn and bleeding, and all the gentlemen seemed well pleased.

As for me, I was so astonished that I did not at first see what was going on by the brook; but when I did look there was a sad sight; two fine horses were down, one was struggling in the stream, and the other was groaning on the grass. One of the riders was getting out of the water covered with mud, the other lay quite still.

"His neck is broke," said my mother.

"And serve him right, too," said one of the colts.

I thought the same, but my mother did not join with us.

"Well, no," she said, "you must not say that; but though I am an old horse, and have seen and heard a great deal, I never yet could make out why men are so fond of this sport; they often hurt themselves, often spoil good horses, and tear up the fields, and all for a hare or a fox, or a stag, that they could get more easily some other way; but we are only horses, and don't know."

While my mother was saying this we stood and looked on. Many of the riders had gone to the young man; but my master, who had been watching what was going on, was the first to raise him. His head fell back and his arms hung down, and every one looked very serious. There was no noise now; even the dogs were quiet, and seemed to know that something was wrong. They carried him to our master's house. I heard afterward that it was young George Gordon, the squire's only son, a fine, tall young man, and the pride of his family.

There was now riding off in all directions to the doctor's, to the farrier's, and no doubt to Squire Gordon's, to let him know about his son. When Mr. Bond, the farrier, came to look at the black horse that lay groaning on the grass, he felt him all over, and shook his head; one of his legs was broken. Then some one ran to our master's house and came back with a gun; presently there was a loud bang and a dreadful shriek, and then all was still; the black horse moved no more.

My mother seemed much troubled; she said she had known that horse for years, and that his name was "Rob Roy"; he was a good horse, and there was no vice in him. She never would go to that part of the field afterward.

Not many days after we heard the church-bell tolling for a long time, and looking over the gate we saw a long, strange black coach that was covered with black cloth and was drawn by black horses; after that came another and another and another, and all were black, while the bell kept tolling, tolling. They were carrying young Gordon to the churchyard to bury him. He would never ride again. What they did with Rob Roy I never knew; but 'twas all for one little hare.

03 My Breaking In

I was now beginning to grow handsome; my coat had grown fine and soft, and was bright black. I had one white foot and a pretty white star on my forehead. I was thought very handsome; my master would not sell me till I was four years old; he said lads ought not to work like men, and colts ought not to work like horses till they were quite grown up.

When I was four years old Squire Gordon came to look at me. He examined my eyes, my mouth, and my legs; he felt them all down; and then I had to walk and trot and gallop before him. He seemed to like me, and said, "When he has been well broken in he will do very well." My master said he would break me in himself, as he should not like me to be frightened or hurt, and he lost no time about it, for the next day he began.

Every one may not know what breaking in is, therefore I will describe it. It means to teach a horse to wear a saddle and bridle, and to carry on his back a man, woman or child; to go just the way they wish, and to go quietly. Besides this he has to learn to wear a collar, a crupper, and a breeching, and to stand still while they are put on; then to have a cart or a chaise fixed behind, so that he cannot walk or trot without dragging it after him; and he must go fast or slow, just as his driver wishes. He must never start at what he sees, nor speak to other horses, nor bite, nor kick, nor have any will of his own; but always do his master's will, even though he may be very tired or hungry; but the worst of all is, when his harness is once on, he may neither jump for joy nor lie down for weariness. So you see this breaking in is a great thing.

I had of course long been used to a halter and a headstall, and to be led about in the fields and lanes quietly, but now I was to have a bit and bridle; my master gave me some oats as usual, and after a good deal of coaxing he got the bit into my mouth, and the bridle fixed, but it was a nasty thing! Those who have never had a bit in their mouths cannot think how bad it feels; a great piece of cold hard steel as thick as a man's finger to be pushed into one's mouth, between one's teeth, and over one's tongue, with the ends coming out at the corner of your mouth, and held fast there by straps over your head, under your throat, round your nose, and under your chin; so that no way in the world can you get rid of the nasty hard thing; it is very bad! yes, very bad! at least I thought so; but I knew my mother always wore one when she went out, and all horses did when they were grown up; and so, what with the nice oats, and what with my master's pats, kind words, and gentle ways, I got to wear my bit and bridle.

Next came the saddle, but that was not half so bad; my master put it on my back very gently, while old Daniel held my head; he then made the girths fast under my body, patting and talking to me all the time; then I had a few oats, then a little leading about; and this he did every day till I began to look for the oats and the saddle. At length, one morning, my master got on my back and rode me round the meadow on the soft grass. It certainly did feel queer; but I must say I felt rather proud to carry my master, and as he continued to ride me a little every day I soon became accustomed to it.

The next unpleasant business was putting on the iron shoes; that too was very hard at first. My master went with me to the smith's forge, to see that I was not hurt or got any fright. The blacksmith took my feet in his hand, one after the other, and cut away some of the hoof. It did not pain me, so I stood still on three legs till he had done them all. Then he took a piece of iron the shape of my foot, and clapped it on, and drove some nails through the shoe quite into my hoof, so that the shoe was firmly on. My feet felt very stiff and heavy, but in time I got used to it.

And now having got so far, my master went on to break me to harness; there were more new things to wear. First, a stiff heavy collar just on my neck, and a bridle with great side-pieces against my eyes called blinkers, and blinkers indeed they were, for I could not see on either side, but only straight in front of me; next, there was a small saddle with a nasty stiff strap that went right under my tail; that was the crupper. I hated the crupper; to have my long tail doubled up and poked through that strap was almost as bad as the bit. I never felt more like kicking, but of course I could not kick such a good master, and so in time I got used to everything, and could do my work as well as my mother.

I must not forget to mention one part of my training, which I have always considered a very great advantage. My master sent me for a fortnight to a neighboring farmer's, who had a meadow which was skirted on one side by the railway. Here were some sheep and cows, and I was turned in among them.

I shall never forget the first train that ran by. I was feeding quietly near the pales which separated the meadow from the railway, when I heard a strange sound at a distance, and before I knew whence it came – with a rush and a clatter, and a puffing out of smoke – a long black train of something flew by, and was gone almost before I could draw my breath. I turned and galloped to the further side of the meadow as fast as I could go, and there I stood snorting with astonishment and fear. In the course of the day many other trains went by, some more slowly; these drew up at the station close by, and sometimes made an awful shriek and groan before they stopped. I thought it very dreadful, but the cows went on eating very quietly, and hardly raised their heads as the black frightful thing came puffing and grinding past.

For the first few days I could not feed in peace; but as I found that this terrible creature never came into the field, or did me any harm, I began to disregard it, and very soon I cared as little about the passing of a train as the cows and sheep did.

Since then I have seen many horses much alarmed and restive at the sight or sound of a steam engine; but thanks to my good master's care, I am as fearless at railway stations as in my own stable.

Now if any one wants to break in a young horse well, that is the way.

My master often drove me in double harness with my mother, because she was steady and could teach me how to go better than a strange horse. She told me the better I behaved the better I should be treated, and that it was wisest always to do my best to please my master; "but," said she, "there are a great many kinds of men; there are good thoughtful men like our master, that any horse may be proud to serve; and there are bad, cruel men, who never ought to have a horse or dog to call their own. Besides, there are a great many foolish men, vain, ignorant, and careless, who never trouble themselves to think; these spoil more horses than all, just for want of sense; they don't mean it, but they do it for all that. I hope you will fall into good hands; but a horse never knows who may buy him, or who may drive him; it is all a chance for us; but still I say, do your best wherever it is, and keep up your good name."

Lesson 73

1. Read chapters 4, 5 and 6.
2. On your *Black Beauty* page write about the setting of the beginning of the book. Describe it.

04 Birtwick Park

At this time I used to stand in the stable and my coat was brushed every day till it shone like a rook's wing. It was early in May, when there came a man from Squire Gordon's, who took me away to the hall. My master said, "Good-by, Darkie; be a good horse, and always do your best." I could not say "good-by", so I put my nose into his hand; he patted me kindly, and I left my first home. As I lived some years with Squire Gordon, I may as well tell something about the place.

Squire Gordon's park skirted the village of Birtwick. It was entered by a large iron gate, at which stood the first lodge, and then you trotted along on a smooth road between clumps of large old trees; then another lodge and another gate, which brought you to the house and the gardens. Beyond this lay the home paddock, the old orchard, and the stables. There was accommodation for many horses and carriages; but I need only describe the stable into which I was taken; this was very roomy, with four good stalls; a large swinging window opened into the yard, which made it pleasant and airy.

The first stall was a large square one, shut in behind with a wooden gate; the others were common stalls, good stalls, but not nearly so large; it had a low rack for hay and a low manger for corn; it was called a loose box, because the horse that was put into it was not tied up, but left loose, to do as he liked. It is a great thing to have a loose box.

Into this fine box the groom put me; it was clean, sweet, and airy. I never was in a better box than that, and the sides were not so high but that I could see all that went on through the iron rails that were at the top.

He gave me some very nice oats, he patted me, spoke kindly, and then went away.

When I had eaten my corn I looked round. In the stall next to mine stood a little fat gray pony, with a thick mane and tail, a very pretty head, and a pert little nose.

I put my head up to the iron rails at the top of my box, and said, "How do you do? What is your name?"

He turned round as far as his halter would allow, held up his head, and said, "My name is Merrylegs. I am very handsome; I carry the young ladies on my back, and sometimes I take our mistress out in the low chair. They think a great deal of me, and so does James. Are you going to live next door to me in the box?"

I said, "Yes."

"Well, then," he said, "I hope you are good-tempered; I do not like any one next door who bites."

Just then a horse's head looked over from the stall beyond; the ears were laid back, and the eye looked rather ill-tempered. This was a tall chestnut mare, with a long handsome neck. She looked across to me and said:

"So it is you who have turned me out of my box; it is a very strange thing for a colt like you to come and turn a lady out of her own home."

"I beg your pardon," I said, "I have turned no one out; the man who brought me put me here, and I had nothing to do with it; and as to my being a colt, I am turned four years old and am a grown-up horse. I never had words yet with horse or mare, and it is my wish to live at peace."

"Well," she said, "we shall see. Of course, I do not want to have words with a young thing like you." I said no more.

In the afternoon, when she went out, Merrylegs told me all about it.

"The thing is this," said Merrylegs. "Ginger has a bad habit of biting and snapping; that is why they call her Ginger, and when she was in the loose box she used to snap very much. One day she bit James in the arm and made it bleed, and so Miss Flora and Miss Jessie, who are very fond of me, were afraid to come into the stable. They used to bring me nice things to eat, an apple or a carrot, or a piece of bread, but after Ginger stood in that box they dared not come, and I missed them very much. I hope they will now come again, if you do not bite or snap."

I told him I never bit anything but grass, hay, and corn, and could not think what pleasure Ginger found it.

"Well, I don't think she does find pleasure," says Merrylegs; "it is just a bad habit; she says no one was ever kind to her, and why should she not bite? Of course, it is a very bad habit; but I am sure, if all she says be true, she must have been very ill-used before she came here. John does all he can to please her, and James does all he can, and our master never uses a whip if a horse acts right; so I think she might be good-tempered here. You see," he said, with a wise look, "I am twelve years old; I know a great deal, and I can tell you there is not a better place for a horse all round the country than this. John is the best groom that ever was; he has been here fourteen years; and you never saw such a kind boy as James is; so that it is all Ginger's own fault that she did not stay in that box."

05 A Fair Start

The name of the coachman was John Manly; he had a wife and one little child, and they lived in the coachman's cottage, very near the stables.

The next morning he took me into the yard and gave me a good grooming, and just as I was going into my box, with my coat soft and bright, the squire came in to look at me, and seemed pleased. "John," he said, "I meant to have tried the new horse this morning, but I have other business. You may as well take him around after breakfast; go by the common and the Highwood, and back by the watermill and the river; that will show his paces."

"I will, sir," said John. After breakfast he came and fitted me with a bridle. He was very particular in letting out and taking in the straps, to fit my head comfortably; then he brought a saddle, but it was not broad enough for my back; he saw it in a minute and went for another, which fitted nicely. He rode me first slowly, then a trot, then a canter, and when we were on the common he gave me a light touch with his whip, and we had a splendid gallop.

"Ho, ho! my boy," he said, as he pulled me up, "you would like to follow the hounds, I think."

As we came back through the park we met the Squire and Mrs. Gordon walking; they stopped, and John jumped off.

"Well, John, how does he go?"

"First-rate, sir," answered John; "he is as fleet as a deer, and has a fine spirit too; but the lightest touch of the rein will guide him. Down at the end of the common we met one of those traveling carts hung all over with baskets, rugs, and such like; you know, sir, many horses will not pass those carts quietly; he just took a good look at it, and then went on as quiet and pleasant as could be. They were shooting rabbits near the Highwood, and a gun went off close by; he pulled up a little and looked, but did not stir a step to right or left. I just held the rein steady and did not hurry him, and it's my opinion he has not been frightened or ill-used while he was young."

"That's well," said the squire, "I will try him myself to-morrow."

The next day I was brought up for my master. I remembered my mother's counsel and my good old master's, and I tried to do exactly what he wanted me to do. I found he was a very good rider, and thoughtful for his horse too. When he came home the lady was at the hall door as he rode up.

"Well, my dear," she said, "how do you like him?"

"He is exactly what John said," he replied; "a pleasanter creature I never wish to mount. What shall we call him?"

"Would you like Ebony?" said she; "he is as black as ebony."

"No, not Ebony."

"Will you call him Blackbird, like your uncle's old horse?"

"No, he is far handsomer than old Blackbird ever was."

"Yes," she said, "he is really quite a beauty, and he has such a sweet, good-tempered face, and such a fine, intelligent eye – what do you say to calling him Black Beauty?"

"Black Beauty – why, yes, I think that is a very good name. If you like it shall be his name;" and so it was.

When John went into the stable he told James that master and mistress had chosen a good, sensible English name for me, that meant something; not like Marengo, or Pegasus, or Abdallah. They both laughed, and James said, "If it was not for bringing back the past, I should have named him Rob Roy, for I never saw two horses more alike."

"That's no wonder," said John; "didn't you know that Farmer Grey's old Duchess was the mother of them both?"

I had never heard that before; and so poor Rob Roy who was killed at that hunt was my brother! I did not wonder that my mother was so troubled. It seems that horses have no relations; at least they never know each other after they are sold.

John seemed very proud of me; he used to make my mane and tail almost as smooth as a lady's hair, and he would talk to me a great deal; of course I did not understand all he said, but I learned more and more to know what he meant, and what he wanted me to do. I grew very fond of him, he was so gentle and kind; he seemed to know just how a horse feels, and when he cleaned me he knew the tender places and the ticklish places; when he brushed my head he went as carefully over my eyes as if they were his own, and never stirred up any ill-temper.

James Howard, the stable boy, was just as gentle and pleasant in his way, so I thought myself well off. There was another man who helped in the yard, but he had very little to do with Ginger and me.

A few days after this I had to go out with Ginger in the carriage. I wondered how we should get on together; but except laying her ears back when I was led up to her, she behaved very well. She did her work honestly, and did her full share, and I never wish to have a better partner in double harness. When we came to a hill, instead of slackening her pace, she would throw her weight right into the collar, and pull away straight up. We had both the same sort of courage at our work, and John had oftener to hold us in than to urge us forward; he never had to use the whip with either of us; then our paces were much the same, and I found it very easy to keep step with her when trotting, which made it pleasant, and master always liked it when we kept step well, and so did John. After we had been out two or three times together we grew quite friendly and sociable, which made me feel very much at home.

As for Merrylegs, he and I soon became great friends; he was such a cheerful, plucky, good-tempered little fellow that he was a favorite with every one, and especially with Miss Jessie and Flora, who used to ride him about in the orchard, and have fine games with him and their little dog Frisky.

Our master had two other horses that stood in another stable. One was Justice, a roan cob, used for riding or for the luggage cart; the other was an old brown hunter, named Sir Oliver; he was past work now, but was a great favorite with the master, who gave him the run of the park; he sometimes did a little light carting on the estate, or carried one of the young ladies when they rode out with their father, for he was very gentle and could be trusted with a child as well as Merrylegs. The cob was a strong, well-made, good-tempered horse, and we sometimes had a little chat in the paddock, but of course I could not be so intimate with him as with Ginger, who stood in the same stable.
06 Liberty

I was quite happy in my new place, and if there was one thing that I missed it must not be thought I was discontented; all who had to do with me were good and I had a light airy stable and the best of food. What more could I want? Why, liberty! For three years and a half of my life I had had all the liberty I could wish for; but now, week after week, month after month, and no doubt year after year, I must stand up in a stable night and day except when I am wanted, and then I must be just as steady and quiet as any old horse who has worked twenty years. Straps here and straps there, a bit in my mouth, and blinkers over my eyes. Now, I am not complaining, for I know it must be so. I only mean to say that for a young horse full of strength and spirits, who has been used to some large field or plain where he can fling up his head and toss up his tail and gallop away at full speed, then round and back again with a snort to his companions – I say it is hard never to have a bit more liberty to do as you like. Sometimes, when I have had less exercise than usual, I have felt so full of life and spring that when John has taken me out to exercise I really could not keep quiet; do what I would, it seemed as if I must jump, or dance, or prance, and many a good shake I know I must have given him, especially at the first; but he was always good and patient.

"Steady, steady, my boy," he would say; "wait a bit, and we will have a good swing, and soon get the tickle out of your feet." Then as soon as we were out of the village, he would give me a few miles at a spanking trot, and then bring me back as fresh as before, only clear of the fidgets, as he called them. Spirited horses, when not enough exercised, are often called skittish, when it is only play; and some grooms will punish them, but our John did not; he knew it was only high spirits. Still, he had his own ways of making me understand by the tone of his voice or the touch of the rein. If he was very serious and quite determined, I always knew it by his voice, and that had more power with me than anything else, for I was very fond of him.

I ought to say that sometimes we had our liberty for a few hours; this used to be on fine Sundays in the summer-time. The carriage never went out on Sundays, because the church was not far off.

It was a great treat to us to be turned out into the home paddock or the old orchard; the grass was so cool and soft to our feet, the air so sweet, and the freedom to do as we liked was so pleasant-to gallop, to lie down, and roll over on our backs, or to nibble the sweet grass. Then it was a very good time for talking, as we stood together under the shade of the large chestnut tree.

Lesson 74
1. Read chapters 7, 8 and 9.
2. Start a plot page to record the plot, the action of the book. This is what you will be taking notes on while you read the book. Write down only major events that change the course of the story.

07 Ginger

One day when Ginger and I were standing alone in the shade, we had a great deal of talk; she wanted to know all about my bringing up and breaking in, and I told her.

"Well," said she, "if I had had your bringing up I might have had as good a temper as you, but now I don't believe I ever shall."

"Why not?" I said.

"Because it has been all so different with me," she replied. "I never had any one, horse or man, that was kind to me, or that I cared to please, for in the first place I was taken from my mother as soon as I was weaned, and put with a lot of other young colts; none of them cared for me, and I cared for none of them. There was no kind master like yours to look after me, and talk to me, and bring me nice things to eat. The man that had the care of us never gave me a kind word in my life. I do not mean that he ill-used me, but he did not care for us one bit further than to see that we had plenty to eat, and shelter in the winter. A footpath ran through our field, and very often the great boys passing through would fling stones to make us gallop. I was never hit, but one fine young colt was badly cut in the face, and I should think it would be a scar for life. We did not care for them, but of course it made us more wild, and we settled it in our minds that boys were our enemies. We had very good fun in the free meadows, galloping up and down and chasing each other round and round the field; then standing still under the shade of the trees. But when it came to breaking in, that was a bad time for me; several men came to catch me, and when at last they closed me in at one corner of the field, one caught me by the forelock, another caught me by the nose and held it so tight I could hardly draw my breath; then another took my under jaw in his hard hand and wrenched my mouth open, and so by force they got on the halter and the bar into my mouth; then one dragged me along by the halter, another flogging behind, and this was the first experience I had of men's kindness; it was all force. They did not give me a chance to know what they wanted. I was high bred and had a great deal of spirit, and was very wild, no doubt, and gave them, I dare say, plenty of trouble, but then it was dreadful to be shut up in a stall day after day instead of having my liberty, and I fretted and pined and wanted to get loose. You know yourself it's bad enough when you have a kind master and plenty of coaxing, but there was nothing of that sort for me.

"There was one – the old master, Mr. Ryder – who, I think, could soon have brought me round, and could have done anything with me; but he had given up all the hard part of the trade to his son and to another experienced man, and he only came at times to oversee. His son was a strong, tall, bold man; they called him Samson, and he used to boast that he had never found a horse that could throw him. There was no gentleness in him, as there was in his father, but only hardness, a hard voice, a hard eye, a hard hand; and I felt from the first that what he wanted was to wear all the spirit out of me, and just make me into a quiet, humble, obedient piece of horseflesh. 'Horseflesh'! Yes, that is all that he thought about," and Ginger stamped her foot as if the very thought of him made her angry. Then she went on:

"If I did not do exactly what he wanted he would get put out, and make me run round with that long rein in the training field till he had tired me out. I think he drank a good deal, and I am quite sure that the oftener he drank the worse it was for me. One day he had worked me hard in every way he could, and when I lay down I was tired, and miserable, and angry; it all seemed so hard. The next morning he came for me early, and ran me round again for a long time. I had scarcely had an hour's rest, when he came again for me with a saddle and bridle and a new kind of bit. I could never quite tell how it came about; he had only just mounted me on the training ground, when something I did put him out of temper, and he chucked me hard with the rein. The new bit was very painful, and I reared up suddenly, which angered him still more, and he began to flog me. I felt my whole spirit set against him, and I began to kick, and plunge, and rear as I had never done before, and we had a regular fight; for a long time he stuck to the saddle and punished me cruelly with his whip and spurs, but my blood was thoroughly up, and I cared for nothing he could do if only I could get him off. At last after a terrible struggle I threw him off backward. I heard him fall heavily on the turf, and without looking behind me, I galloped off to the other end of the field; there I turned round and saw my persecutor slowly rising from the ground and going into the stable. I stood under an oak tree and watched, but no one came to catch me. The time went on, and the sun was very hot; the flies swarmed round me and settled on my bleeding flanks where the spurs had dug in. I felt hungry, for I had not eaten since the early morning, but there was not enough grass in that meadow for a goose to live on. I wanted to lie down and rest, but with the saddle strapped tightly on there was no comfort, and there was not a drop of water to drink. The afternoon wore on, and the sun got low. I saw the other colts led in, and I knew they were having a good feed.

"At last, just as the sun went down, I saw the old master come out with a sieve in his hand. He was a very fine old gentleman with quite white hair, but his voice was what I should know him by among a thousand. It was not high, nor yet low, but full, and clear, and kind, and when he gave orders it was so steady and decided that every one knew, both horses and men, that he expected to be obeyed. He came quietly along, now and then shaking the oats about that he had in the sieve, and speaking cheerfully and gently to me: 'Come along, lassie, come along, lassie; come along, come along.' I stood still and let him come up; he held the oats to me, and I began to eat without fear; his voice took all my fear away. He stood by, patting and stroking me while I was eating, and seeing the clots of blood on my side he seemed very vexed. 'Poor lassie! it was a bad business, a bad business;' then he quietly took the rein and led me to the stable; just at the door stood Samson. I laid my ears back and snapped at him. 'Stand back,' said the master, 'and keep out of her way; you've done a bad day's work for this filly.' He growled out something about a vicious brute. 'Hark ye,' said the father, 'a bad-tempered man will never make a good-tempered horse. You've not learned your trade yet, Samson.' Then he led me into my box, took off the saddle and bridle with his own hands, and tied me up; then he called for a pail of warm water and a sponge, took off his coat, and while the stable-man held the pail, he sponged my sides a good while, so tenderly that I was sure he knew how sore and bruised they were. 'Whoa! my pretty one,' he said, 'stand still, stand still.' His very voice did me good, and the bathing was very comfortable. The skin was so broken at the corners of my mouth that I could not eat the hay, the stalks hurt me. He looked closely at it, shook his head, and told the man to fetch a good bran mash and put some meal into it. How good that mash was! and so soft and healing to my mouth. He stood by all the time I was eating, stroking me and talking to the man. 'If a high-mettled creature like this,' said he, 'can't be broken by fair means, she will never be good for anything.'

"After that he often came to see me, and when my mouth was healed the other breaker, Job, they called him, went on training me; he was steady and thoughtful, and I soon learned what he wanted."

08 Ginger's Story Continued

The next time that Ginger and I were together in the paddock she told me about her first place.

"After my breaking in," she said, "I was bought by a dealer to match another chestnut horse. For some weeks he drove us together, and then we were sold to a fashionable gentleman, and were sent up to London. I had been driven with a check-rein by the dealer, and I hated it worse than anything else; but in this place we were reined far tighter, the coachman and his master thinking we looked more stylish so. We were often driven about in the park and other fashionable places. You who never had a check-rein on don't know what it is, but I can tell you it is dreadful.

"I like to toss my head about and hold it as high as any horse; but fancy now yourself, if you tossed your head up high and were obliged to hold it there, and that for hours together, not able to move it at all, except with a jerk still higher, your neck aching till you did not know how to bear it. Besides that, to have two bits instead of one—and mine was a sharp one, it hurt my tongue and my jaw, and the blood from my tongue colored the froth that kept flying from my lips as I chafed and fretted at the bits and rein. It was worst when we had to stand by the hour waiting for our mistress at some grand party or entertainment, and if I fretted or stamped with impatience the whip was laid on. It was enough to drive one mad."

"Did not your master take any thought for you?" I said.

"No," said she, "he only cared to have a stylish turnout, as they call it; I think he knew very little about horses; he left that to his coachman, who told him I had an irritable temper! that I had not been well broken to the check-rein, but I should soon get used to it; but he was not the man to do it, for when I was in the stable, miserable and angry, instead of being smoothed and quieted by kindness, I got only a surly word or a blow. If he had been civil I would have tried to bear it. I was willing to work, and ready to work hard too; but to be tormented for nothing but their fancies angered me. What right had they to make me suffer like that? Besides the soreness in my mouth, and the pain in my neck, it always made my windpipe feel bad, and if I had stopped there long I know it would have spoiled my breathing; but I grew more and more restless and irritable, I could not help it; and I began to snap and kick when any one came to harness me; for this the groom beat me, and one day, as they had just buckled us into the carriage, and were straining my head up with that rein, I began to plunge and kick with all my might. I soon broke a lot of harness, and kicked myself clear; so that was an end of that place.

"After this I was sent to Tattersall's to be sold; of course I could not be warranted free from vice, so nothing was said about that. My handsome appearance and good paces soon brought a gentleman to bid for me, and I was bought by another dealer; he tried me in all kinds of ways and with different bits, and he soon found out what I could not bear. At last he drove me quite without a check-rein, and then sold me as a perfectly quiet horse to a gentleman in the country; he was a good master, and I was getting on very well, but his old groom left him and a new one came. This man was as hard-tempered and hard-handed as Samson; he always spoke in a rough, impatient voice, and if I did not move in the stall the moment he wanted me, he would hit me above the hocks with his stable broom or the fork, whichever he might have in his hand. Everything he did was rough, and I began to hate him; he wanted to make me afraid of him, but I was too high-mettled for that, and one day when he had aggravated me more than usual I bit him, which of course put him in a great rage, and he began to hit me about the head with a riding whip. After that he never dared to come into my stall again; either my heels or my teeth were ready for him, and he knew it. I was quite quiet with my master, but of course he listened to what the man said, and so I was sold again.

"The same dealer heard of me, and said he thought he knew one place where I should do well. ''Twas a pity,' he said, 'that such a fine horse should go to the bad, for want of a real good chance,' and the end of it was that I came here not long before you did; but I had then made up my mind that men were my natural enemies and that I must defend myself. Of course it is very different here, but who knows how long it will last? I wish I could think about things as you do; but I can't, after all I have gone through."

"Well," I said, "I think it would be a real shame if you were to bite or kick John or James."

"I don't mean to," she said, "while they are good to me. I did bite James once pretty sharp, but John said, 'Try her with kindness,' and instead of punishing me as I expected, James came to me with his arm bound up, and brought me a bran mash and stroked me; and I have never snapped at him since, and I won't either."

I was sorry for Ginger, but of course I knew very little then, and I thought most likely she made the worst of it; however, I found that as the weeks went on she grew much more gentle and cheerful, and had lost the watchful, defiant look that she used to turn on any strange person who came near her; and one day James said, "I do believe that mare is getting fond of me, she quite whinnied after me this morning when I had been rubbing her forehead."

"Ay, ay, Jim, 'tis ''he Birtwick balls'," said John, "she'll be as good as Black Beauty by and by; kindness is all the physic she wants, poor thing!" Master noticed the change, too, and one day when he got out of the carriage and came to speak to us, as he often did, he stroked her beautiful neck. "Well, my pretty one, well, how do things go with you now? You are a good bit happier than when you came to us, I think."

She put her nose up to him in a friendly, trustful way, while he rubbed it gently.

"We shall make a cure of her, John," he said.

"Yes, sir, she's wonderfully improved; she's not the same creature that she was; it's 'the Birtwick balls', sir," said John, laughing.

This was a little joke of John's; he used to say that a regular course of "the Birtwick horseballs" would cure almost any vicious horse; these balls, he said, were made up of patience and gentleness, firmness and petting, one pound of each to be mixed up with half a pint of common sense, and given to the horse every day.

09 Merrylegs

Mr. Blomefield, the vicar, had a large family of boys and girls; sometimes they used to come and play with Miss Jessie and Flora. One of the girls was as old as Miss Jessie; two of the boys were older, and there were several little ones. When they came there was plenty of work for Merrylegs, for nothing pleased them so much as getting on him by turns and riding him all about the orchard and the home paddock, and this they would do by the hour together.

One afternoon he had been out with them a long time, and when James brought him in and put on his halter he said:

"There, you rogue, mind how you behave yourself, or we shall get into trouble."

"What have you been doing, Merrylegs?" I asked.

"Oh!" said he, tossing his little head, "I have only been giving those young people a lesson; they did not know when they had had enough, nor when I had had enough, so I just pitched them off backward; that was the only thing they could understand."

"What!" said I, "you threw the children off? I thought you did know better than that! Did you throw Miss Jessie or Miss Flora?"

He looked very much offended, and said:

"Of course not; I would not do such a thing for the best oats that ever came into the stable; why, I am as careful of our young ladies as the master could be, and as for the little ones it is I who teach them to ride. When they seem frightened or a little unsteady on my back I go as smooth and as quiet as old pussy when she is after a bird; and when they are all right I go on again faster, you see, just to use them to it; so don't you trouble yourself preaching to me; I am the best friend and the best riding-master those children have. It is not them, it is the boys; boys," said he, shaking his mane, "are quite different; they must be broken in as we were broken in when we were colts, and just be taught what's what. The other children had ridden me about for nearly two hours, and then the boys thought it was their turn, and so it was, and I was quite agreeable. They rode me by turns, and I galloped them about, up and down the fields and all about the orchard, for a good hour. They had each cut a great hazel stick for a riding-whip, and laid it on a little too hard; but I took it in good part, till at last I thought we had had enough, so I stopped two or three times by way of a hint. Boys, you see, think a horse or pony is like a steam-engine or a thrashing-machine, and can go on as long and as fast as they please; they never think that a pony can get tired, or have any feelings; so as the one who was whipping me could not understand I just rose up on my hind legs and let him slip off behind – that was all. He mounted me again, and I did the same. Then the other boy got up, and as soon as he began to use his stick I laid him on the grass, and so on, till they were able to understand – that was all. They are not bad boys; they don't wish to be cruel. I like them very well; but you see I had to give them a lesson. When they brought me to James and told him I think he was very angry to see such big sticks. He said they were only fit for drovers or gypsies, and not for young gentlemen."

"If I had been you," said Ginger, "I would have given those boys a good kick, and that would have given them a lesson."

22222222222222

"No doubt you would," said Merrylegs; "but then I am not quite such a fool (begging your pardon) as to anger our master or make James ashamed of me. Besides, those children are under my charge when they are riding; I tell you they are intrusted to me. Why, only the other day I heard our master say to Mrs. Blomefield, 'My dear madam, you need not be anxious about the children; my old Merrylegs will take as much care of them as you or I could; I assure you I would not sell that pony for any money, he is so perfectly good-tempered and trustworthy;' and do you think I am such an ungrateful brute as to forget all the kind treatment I have had here for five years, and all the trust they place in me, and turn vicious because a couple of ignorant boys used me badly? No, no! you never had a good place where they were kind to you, and so you don't know, and I'm sorry for you; but I can tell you good places make good horses. I wouldn't vex our people for anything; I love them, I do," said Merrylegs, and he gave a low "ho, ho, ho!" through his nose, as he used to do in the morning when he heard James' footstep at the door.

"Besides," he went on, "if I took to kicking where should I be? Why, sold off in a jiffy, and no character, and I might find myself slaved about under a butcher's boy, or worked to death at some seaside place where no one cared for me, except to find out how fast I could go, or be flogged along in some cart with three or four great men in it going out for a Sunday spree, as I have often seen in the place I lived in before I came here; no," said he, shaking his head, "I hope I shall never come to that."

Lesson 75

1. Read chapters 10 and 11.
2. Take notes on any major events in the book.

10 A Talk in the Orchard

Ginger and I were not of the regular tall carriage horse breed, we had more of the racing blood in us. We stood about fifteen and a half hands high; we were therefore just as good for riding as we were for driving, and our master used to say that he disliked either horse or man that could do but one thing; and as he did not want to show off in London parks, he preferred a more active and useful kind of horse. As for us, our greatest pleasure was when we were saddled for a riding party; the master on Ginger, the mistress on me, and the young ladies on Sir Oliver and Merrylegs. It was so cheerful to be trotting and cantering all together that it always put us in high spirits. I had the best of it, for I always carried the mistress; her weight was little, her voice was sweet, and her hand was so light on the rein that I was guided almost without feeling it.

Oh! if people knew what a comfort to horses a light hand is, and how it keeps a good mouth and a good temper, they surely would not chuck, and drag, and pull at the rein as they often do. Our mouths are so tender that where they have not been spoiled or hardened with bad or ignorant treatment, they feel the slightest movement of the driver's hand, and we know in an instant what is required of us. My mouth has never been spoiled, and I believe that was why the mistress preferred me to Ginger, although her paces were certainly quite as good. She used often to envy me, and said

370

it was all the fault of breaking in, and the gag bit in London, that her mouth was not so perfect as mine; and then old Sir Oliver would say, "There, there! don't vex yourself; you have the greatest honor; a mare that can carry a tall man of our master's weight, with all your spring and sprightly action, does not need to hold her head down because she does not carry the lady; we horses must take things as they come, and always be contented and willing so long as we are kindly used."

I had often wondered how it was that Sir Oliver had such a very short tail; it really was only six or seven inches long, with a tassel of hair hanging from it; and on one of our holidays in the orchard I ventured to ask him by what accident it was that he had lost his tail. "Accident!" he snorted with a fierce look, "it was no accident! it was a cruel, shameful, cold-blooded act! When I was young I was taken to a place where these cruel things were done; I was tied up, and made fast so that I could not stir, and then they came and cut off my long and beautiful tail, through the flesh and through the bone, and took it away.

"How dreadful!" I exclaimed.

"Dreadful, ah! it was dreadful; but it was not only the pain, though that was terrible and lasted a long time; it was not only the indignity of having my best ornament taken from me, though that was bad; but it was this, how could I ever brush the flies off my sides and my hind legs any more? You who have tails just whisk the flies off without thinking about it, and you can't tell what a torment it is to have them settle upon you and sting and sting, and have nothing in the world to lash them off with. I tell you it is a lifelong wrong, and a lifelong loss; but thank heaven, they don't do it now."

"What did they do it for then?" said Ginger.

"For fashion!" said the old horse with a stamp of his foot; "for fashion! if you know what that means; there was not a well-bred young horse in my time that had not his tail docked in that shameful way, just as if the good God that made us did not know what we wanted and what looked best."

"I suppose it is fashion that makes them strap our heads up with those horrid bits that I was tortured with in London," said Ginger.

"Of course it is," said he; "to my mind, fashion is one of the wickedest things in the world. Now look, for instance, at the way they serve dogs, cutting off their tails to make them look plucky, and shearing up their pretty little ears to a point to make them both look sharp, forsooth. I had a dear friend once, a brown terrier; 'Skye' they called her. She was so fond of me that she never would sleep out of my stall; she made her bed under the manger, and there she had a litter of five as pretty little puppies as need be; none were drowned, for they were a valuable kind, and how pleased she was with them! and when they got their eyes open and crawled about, it was a real pretty sight; but one day the man came and took them all away; I thought he might be afraid I should tread upon them. But it was not so; in the evening poor Skye brought them back again, one by one in her mouth; not the happy little things that they were, but bleeding and crying pitifully; they had all had a piece of their tails cut off, and the soft flap of their pretty little ears was cut quite off. How their mother licked them, and how troubled she was, poor thing! I never forgot it. They healed in time, and they forgot the pain, but the nice soft flap, that of course was intended to protect the delicate part of their ears from dust and injury, was gone forever. Why don't they cut their own children's ears into points to make them look sharp? Why don't they cut the end off their noses to make them look plucky? One would be just as sensible as the other. What right have they to torment and disfigure God's creatures?"

Sir Oliver, though he was so gentle, was a fiery old fellow, and what he said was all so new to me, and so dreadful, that I found a bitter feeling toward men rise up in my mind that I never had before. Of course Ginger was very much excited; she flung up her head with flashing eyes and distended nostrils, declaring that men were both brutes and blockheads.

"Who talks about blockheads?" said Merrylegs, who just came up from the old apple-tree, where he had been rubbing himself against the low branch. "Who talks about blockheads? I believe that is a bad word."

"Bad words were made for bad things," said Ginger, and she told him what Sir Oliver had said.

"It is all true," said Merrylegs sadly, "and I've seen that about the dogs over and over again where I lived first; but we won't talk about it here. You know that master, and John and James are always good to us, and talking against men in such a place as this doesn't seem fair or grateful, and you know there are good masters and good grooms beside ours, though of course ours are the best."

This wise speech of good little Merrylegs, which we knew was quite true, cooled us all down, especially Sir Oliver, who was dearly fond of his master; and to turn the subject I said, "Can any one tell me the use of blinkers?"

"No!" said Sir Oliver shortly, "because they are no use."

"They are supposed," said Justice, the roan cob, in his calm way, "to prevent horses from shying and starting, and getting so frightened as to cause accidents."

"Then what is the reason they do not put them on riding horses; especially on ladies' horses?" said I.

"There is no reason at all," said he quietly, "except the fashion; they say that a horse would be so frightened to see the wheels of his own cart or carriage coming behind him that he would be sure to run away, although of course when he is ridden he sees them all about him if the streets are crowded. I admit they do sometimes come too close to be pleasant, but we don't run away; we are used to it, and understand it, and if we never had blinkers put on we should never want them; we should see what was there, and know what was what, and be much less frightened than by only seeing bits of things that we can't understand. Of course there may be some nervous horses who have been hurt or frightened when they were young, who may be the better for them; but as I never was nervous, I can't judge."

"I consider," said Sir Oliver, "that blinkers are dangerous things in the night; we horses can see much better in the dark than men can, and many an accident would never have happened if horses might have had the full use of their eyes. Some years ago, I remember, there was a hearse with two horses returning one dark night, and just by Farmer Sparrow's house, where the pond is close to the road, the wheels went too near the edge, and the hearse was overturned into the water; both the horses were drowned, and the driver hardly escaped. Of course after this accident a stout white rail was put up that might be easily seen, but if those horses had not been partly blinded, they would of themselves have kept further from the edge, and no accident would have happened. When our master's carriage was overturned, before you came here, it was said that if the lamp on the left side had not gone out, John would have seen the great hole that the road-makers had left; and so he might, but if old Colin had not had blinkers on he would have seen it, lamp or no lamp, for he was far too knowing an old horse to run into danger. As it was, he was very much hurt, the carriage was broken, and how John escaped nobody knew."

"I should say," said Ginger, curling her nostril, "that these men, who are so wise, had better give orders that in the future all foals should be born with their eyes set just in the middle of their foreheads, instead of on the side; they always think they can improve upon nature and mend what God has made."

Things were getting rather sore again, when Merrylegs held up his knowing little face and said, "I'll tell you a secret: I believe John does not approve of blinkers; I heard him talking with master about it one day. The master said that 'if horses had been used to them, it might be dangerous in some cases to leave them off'; and John said he thought it would be a good thing if all colts were broken in without blinkers, as was the case in some foreign countries. So let us cheer up, and have a run to the other end of the orchard; I believe the wind has blown down some apples, and we might just as well eat them as the slugs."

Merrylegs could not be resisted, so we broke off our long conversation, and got up our spirits by munching some very sweet apples which lay scattered on the grass.

11 Plain Speaking

The longer I lived at Birtwick the more proud and happy I felt at having such a place. Our master and mistress were respected and beloved by all who knew them; they were good and kind to everybody and everything; not only men and women, but horses and donkeys, dogs and cats, cattle and birds; there was no oppressed or ill-used creature that had not a friend in them, and their servants took the same tone. If any of the village children were known to treat any creature cruelly they soon heard about it from the Hall.

The squire and Farmer Grey had worked together, as they said, for more than twenty years to get check-reins on the cart-horses done away with, and in our parts you seldom saw them; and sometimes, if mistress met a heavily laden horse with his head strained up she would stop the carriage and get out, and reason with the driver in her sweet serious voice, and try to show him how foolish and cruel it was.

I don't think any man could withstand our mistress. I wish all ladies were like her. Our master, too, used to come down very heavy sometimes. I remember he was riding me toward home one morning when we saw a powerful man driving toward us in a light pony chaise, with a beautiful little bay pony, with slender legs and a high-bred sensitive head and face. Just as he came to the park gates the little thing turned toward them; the man, without word or warning, wrenched the creature's head round with such a force and suddenness that he nearly threw it on its haunches. Recovering itself it was going on, when he began to lash it furiously. The pony plunged forward, but the strong, heavy hand held the pretty creature back with force almost enough to break its jaw, while the whip still cut into him. It was a dreadful sight to me, for I knew what fearful pain it gave that delicate little mouth; but master gave me the word, and we were up with him in a second.

"Sawyer," he cried in a stern voice, "is that pony made of flesh and blood?"

"Flesh and blood and temper," he said; "he's too fond of his own will, and that won't suit me." He spoke as if he was in a strong passion. He was a builder who had often been to the park on business.

"And do you think," said master sternly, "that treatment like this will make him fond of your will?"

"He had no business to make that turn; his road was straight on!" said the man roughly.

"You have often driven that pony up to my place," said master; "it only shows the creature's memory and intelligence; how did he know that you were not going there again? But that has little to do with it. I must say, Mr. Sawyer, that a more unmanly, brutal treatment of a little pony it was never my painful lot to witness, and by giving way to such passion you injure your own character as much, nay more, than you injure your horse; and remember, we shall all have to be judged according to our works, whether they be toward man or toward beast."

Master rode me home slowly, and I could tell by his voice how the thing had grieved him. He was just as free to speak to gentlemen of his own rank as to those below him; for another day, when we were out, we met a Captain Langley, a friend of our master's; he was driving a splendid pair of grays in a kind of break. After a little conversation the captain said:

"What do you think of my new team, Mr. Douglas? You know, you are the judge of horses in these parts, and I should like your opinion."

The master backed me a little, so as to get a good view of them. "They are an uncommonly handsome pair," he said, "and if they are as good as they look I am sure you need not wish for anything better; but I see you still hold that pet scheme of yours for worrying your horses and lessening their power."

"What do you mean," said the other, "the check-reins? Oh, ah! I know that's a hobby of yours; well, the fact is, I like to see my horses hold their heads up."

"So do I," said master, "as well as any man, but I don't like to see them held up; that takes all the shine out of it. Now, you are a military man, Langley, and no doubt like to see your regiment look well on parade, 'heads up', and all that; but you would not take much credit for your drill if all your men had their heads tied to a backboard! It might not be much harm on parade, except to worry and fatigue them; but how would it be in a bayonet charge against the enemy, when they want the free use of every muscle, and all their strength thrown forward? I would not give much for their chance of victory. And it is just the same with horses: you fret and worry their tempers, and decrease their power; you will not let them throw their weight against their work, and so they have to do too much with their joints and muscles, and of course it wears them up faster. You may depend upon it, horses were intended to have their heads free, as free as men's are; and if we could act a little more according to common sense, and a good deal less according to fashion, we should find many things work easier; besides, you know as well as I that if a horse makes a false step, he has much less chance of recovering himself if his head and neck are fastened back. And now," said the master, laughing, "I have given my hobby a good trot out, can't you make up your mind to mount him, too, captain? Your example would go a long way."

"I believe you are right in theory," said the other, "and that's rather a hard hit about the soldiers; but – well – I'll think about it," and so they parted.

Lesson 76

1. Read chapters 12, 13, and 14.
2. Take notes on major events.

12 A Stormy Day

One day late in the autumn my master had a long journey to go on business. I was put into the dog-cart, and John went with his master. I always liked to go in the dog-cart, it was so light and the high wheels ran along so pleasantly. There had been a great deal of rain, and now the wind was very high and blew the dry leaves across the road in a shower. We went along merrily till we came to the toll-bar and the low wooden bridge. The river banks were rather high, and the bridge, instead of rising, went across just level, so that in the middle, if the river was full, the water would be nearly up to the woodwork and planks; but as there were good substantial rails on each side, people did not mind it.

The man at the gate said the river was rising fast, and he feared it would be a bad night. Many of the meadows were under water, and in one low part of the road the water was halfway up to my knees; the bottom was good, and master drove gently, so it was no matter.

When we got to the town of course I had a good bait, but as the master's business engaged him a long time we did not start for home till rather late in the afternoon. The wind was then much higher, and I heard the master say to John that he had never been out in such a storm; and so I thought, as we went along the skirts of a wood, where the great branches were swaying about like twigs, and the rushing sound was terrible.

"I wish we were well out of this wood," said my master.

"Yes, sir," said John, "it would be rather awkward if one of these branches came down upon us."

The words were scarcely out of his mouth when there was a groan, and a crack, and a splitting sound, and tearing, crashing down among the other trees came an oak, torn up by the roots, and it fell right across the road just before us. I will never say I was not frightened, for I was. I stopped still, and I believe I trembled; of course I did not turn round or run away; I was not brought up to that. John jumped out and was in a moment at my head.

"That was a very near touch," said my master. "What's to be done now?"

"Well, sir, we can't drive over that tree, nor yet get round it; there will be nothing for it, but to go back to the four crossways, and that will be a good six miles before we get round to the wooden bridge again; it will make us late, but the horse is fresh."

So back we went and round by the crossroads, but by the time we got to the bridge it was very nearly dark; we could just see that the water was over the middle of it; but as that happened sometimes when the floods were out, master did not stop. We were going along at a good pace, but the moment my feet touched the first part of the bridge I felt sure there was something wrong. I dare not go forward, and I made a dead stop. "Go on, Beauty," said my master, and he gave me a touch with the whip, but I dare not stir; he gave me a sharp cut; I jumped, but I dare not go forward.

"There's something wrong, sir," said John, and he sprang out of the dog-cart and came to my head and looked all about. He tried to lead me forward. "Come on, Beauty, what's the matter?" Of course I could not tell him, but I knew very well that the bridge was not safe.

Just then the man at the toll-gate on the other side ran out of the house, tossing a torch about like one mad.

"Hoy, hoy, hoy! halloo! stop!" he cried.

"What's the matter?" shouted my master.

"The bridge is broken in the middle, and part of it is carried away; if you come on you'll be into the river."

"Thank God!" said my master. "You Beauty!" said John, and took the bridle and gently turned me round to the right-hand road by the river side. The sun had set some time; the wind seemed to have lulled off after that furious blast which tore up the tree. It grew darker and darker, stiller and stiller. I trotted quietly along, the wheels hardly making a sound on the soft road. For a good while neither master nor John spoke, and then master began in a serious voice. I could not understand much of what they said, but I found they thought, if I had gone on as the master wanted me, most likely the bridge would have given way under us, and horse, chaise, master, and man would have fallen into the river; and as the current was flowing very strongly, and there was no light and no help at hand, it was more than likely we should all have been drowned. Master said, God had given men reason, by which they could find out things for themselves; but he had given animals knowledge which did not depend on reason, and which was much more prompt and perfect in its way, and by which they had often saved the lives of men. John had many stories to tell of dogs and horses, and the wonderful things they had done; he thought people did not value their animals half enough nor make friends of them as they ought to do. I am sure he makes friends of them if ever a man did.

At last we came to the park gates and found the gardener looking out for us. He said that mistress had been in a dreadful way ever since dark, fearing some accident had happened, and that she had sent James off on Justice, the roan cob, toward the wooden bridge to make inquiry after us.

We saw a light at the hall-door and at the upper windows, and as we came up mistress ran out, saying, "Are you really safe, my dear? Oh! I have been so anxious, fancying all sorts of things. Have you had no accident?"

"No, my dear; but if your Black Beauty had not been wiser than we were we should all have been carried down the river at the wooden bridge." I heard no more, as they went into the house, and John took me to the stable. Oh, what a good supper he gave me that night, a good bran mash and some crushed beans with my oats, and such a thick bed of straw! and I was glad of it, for I was tired.

13 The Devil's Trade Mark

One day when John and I had been out on some business of our master's, and were returning gently on a long, straight road, at some distance we saw a boy trying to leap a pony over a gate; the pony would not take the leap, and the boy cut him with the whip, but he only turned off on one side. He whipped him again, but the pony turned off on the other side. Then the boy got off and gave him a hard thrashing, and knocked him about the head; then he got up again and tried to make him leap the gate, kicking him all the time shamefully, but still the pony refused. When we were nearly at the spot the pony put down his head and threw up his heels, and sent the boy neatly over into a broad quickset hedge, and with the rein dangling from his head he set off home at a full gallop. John laughed out quite loud. "Served him right," he said.

"Oh, oh, oh!" cried the boy as he struggled about among the thorns; "I say, come and help me out."

"Thank ye," said John, "I think you are quite in the right place, and maybe a little scratching will teach you not to leap a pony over a gate that is too high for him," and so with that John rode off. "It may be," said he to himself, "that young fellow is a liar as well as a cruel one; we'll just go home by Farmer Bushby's, Beauty, and then if anybody wants to know you and I can tell 'em, ye see." So we turned off to the right, and soon came up to the stack-yard, and within sight of the house. The farmer was hurrying out into the road, and his wife was standing at the gate, looking very frightened.

"Have you seen my boy?" said Mr. Bushby as we came up; "he went out an hour ago on my black pony, and the creature is just come back without a rider."

"I should think, sir," said John, "he had better be without a rider, unless he can be ridden properly."

"What do you mean?" said the farmer.

"Well, sir, I saw your son whipping, and kicking, and knocking that good little pony about shamefully because he would not leap a gate that was too high for him. The pony behaved well, sir, and showed no vice; but at last he just threw up his heels and tipped the young gentleman into the thorn hedge. He wanted me to help him out, but I hope you will excuse me, sir, I did not feel inclined to do so. There's no bones broken, sir; he'll only get a few scratches. I love horses, and it riles me to see them badly used; it is a bad plan to aggravate an animal till he uses his heels; the first time is not always the last."

During this time the mother began to cry, "Oh, my poor Bill, I must go and meet him; he must be hurt."

"You had better go into the house, wife," said the farmer; "Bill wants a lesson about this, and I must see that he gets it; this is not the first time, nor the second, that he has ill-used that pony, and I shall stop it. I am much obliged to you, Manly. Good-evening."

So we went on, John chuckling all the way home; then he told James about it, who laughed and said, "Serve him right. I knew that boy at school; he took great airs on himself because he was a farmer's son; he used to swagger about and bully the little boys. Of course, we elder ones would not have any of that nonsense, and let him know that in the school and the playground farmers' sons and laborers' sons were all alike. I well remember one day, just before afternoon school, I found him at the large window catching flies and pulling off their wings. He did not see me and I gave him a box on the ears that laid him sprawling on the floor. Well, angry as I was, I was almost frightened, he roared and bellowed in such a style. The boys rushed in from the playground, and the master ran in from the road to see who was being murdered. Of course I said fair and square at once what I had done, and why; then I showed the master the flies, some crushed and some crawling about helpless, and I showed him the wings on the window sill. I never saw him so angry before; but as Bill was still howling and whining, like the coward that he was, he did not give him any more punishment of that kind, but set him up on a stool for the rest of the afternoon, and said that he should not go out to play for that week. Then he talked to all the boys very seriously about cruelty, and said how hard-hearted and cowardly it was to hurt the weak and the helpless; but what stuck in my mind was this, he said that cruelty was the devil's own trade-mark, and if we saw any one who took pleasure in cruelty we might know who he belonged to, for the devil was a murderer from the beginning, and a tormentor to the end. On the other hand, where we saw people who loved their neighbors, and were kind to man and beast, we might know that was God's mark."

"Your master never taught you a truer thing," said John; "there is no religion without love, and people may talk as much as they like about their religion, but if it does not teach them to be good and kind to man and beast it is all a sham – all a sham, James, and it won't stand when things come to be turned inside out."

14 James Howard

Early one morning in December John had just led me into my box after my daily exercise, and was strapping my cloth on and James was coming in from the corn chamber with some oats, when the master came into the stable. He looked rather serious, and held an open letter in his hand. John fastened the door of my box, touched his cap, and waited for orders.

"Good-morning, John," said the master. "I want to know if you have any complaint to make of James."

"Complaint, sir? No, sir."

"Is he industrious at his work and respectful to you?"

"Yes, sir, always."

"You never find he slights his work when your back is turned?"

"Never, sir."

"That's well; but I must put another question. Have you no reason to suspect, when he goes out with the horses to exercise them or to take a message, that he stops about talking to his acquaintances, or goes into houses where he has no business, leaving the horses outside?"

"No, sir, certainly not; and if anybody has been saying that about James, I don't believe it, and I don't mean to believe it unless I have it fairly proved before witnesses; it's not for me to say who has been trying to take away James' character, but I will say this, sir, that a steadier, pleasanter, honester, smarter young fellow I never had in this stable. I can trust his word and I can trust his work; he is gentle and clever with the horses, and I would rather have them in charge with him than with half the young fellows I know of in laced hats and liveries; and whoever wants a character of James Howard," said John, with a decided jerk of his head, "let them come to John Manly."

The master stood all this time grave and attentive, but as John finished his speech a broad smile spread over his face, and looking kindly across at James, who all this time had stood still at the door, he said, "James, my lad, set down the oats and come here; I am very glad to find that John's opinion of your character agrees so exactly with my own. John is a cautious man," he said, with a droll smile, "and it is not always easy to get his opinion about people, so I thought if I beat the bush on this side the birds would fly out, and I should learn what I wanted to know quickly; so now we will come to business. I have a letter from my brother-in-law, Sir Clifford Williams, of Clifford Hall. He wants me to find him a trustworthy young groom, about twenty or twenty-one, who knows his business. His old coachman, who has lived with him thirty years, is getting feeble, and he wants a man to work with him and get into his ways, who would be able, when the old man was pensioned off, to step into his place. He would have eighteen shillings a week at first, a stable suit, a driving suit, a bedroom over the coachhouse, and a boy under him. Sir Clifford is a good master, and if you could get the place it would be a good start for you. I don't want to part with you, and if you left us I know John would lose his right hand."

"That I should, sir," said John, "but I would not stand in his light for the world."

"How old are you, James?" said master.

"Nineteen next May, sir."

"That's young; what do you think, John?"

"Well, sir, it is young; but he is as steady as a man, and is strong, and well grown, and though he has not had much experience in driving, he has a light firm hand and a quick eye, and he is very careful, and I am quite sure no horse of his will be ruined for want of having his feet and shoes looked after."

"Your word will go the furthest, John," said the master, "for Sir Clifford adds in a postscript, 'If I could find a man trained by your John I should like him better than any other;' so, James, lad, think it over, talk to your mother at dinner-time, and then let me know what you wish."

In a few days after this conversation it was fully settled that James should go to Clifford Hall, in a month or six weeks, as it suited his master, and in the meantime he was to get all the practice in driving that could be given to him. I never knew the carriage to go out so often before; when the mistress did not go out the master drove himself in the two-wheeled chaise; but now, whether it was master or the young ladies, or only an errand, Ginger and I were put in the carriage and James drove us. At the first John rode with him on the box, telling him this and that, and after that James drove alone.

Then it was wonderful what a number of places the master would go to in the city on Saturday, and what queer streets we were driven through. He was sure to go to the railway station just as the train was coming in, and cabs and carriages, carts and omnibuses were all trying to get over the bridge together; that bridge wanted good horses and good drivers when the railway bell was ringing, for it was narrow, and there was a very sharp turn up to the station, where it would not have been at all difficult for people to run into each other, if they did not look sharp and keep their wits about them.

Lesson 77

1. Read chapters 15, 16, and 17.
2. Take notes on major events.

15 The Old Hostler

After this it was decided by my master and mistress to pay a visit to some friends who lived about forty-six miles from our home, and James was to drive them. The first day we traveled thirty-two miles. There were some long, heavy hills, but James drove so carefully and thoughtfully that we were not at all harassed. He never forgot to put on the brake as we went downhill, nor to take it off at the right place. He kept our feet on the smoothest part of the road, and if the uphill was very long, he set the carriage wheels a little across the road, so as not to run back, and gave us a breathing. All these little things help a horse very much, particularly if he gets kind words into the bargain.

We stopped once or twice on the road, and just as the sun was going down we reached the town where we were to spend the night. We stopped at the principal hotel, which was in the market-place; it was a very large one; we drove under an archway into a long yard, at the further end of which were the stables and coachhouses. Two hostlers came to take us out. The head hostler was a pleasant, active little man, with a crooked leg, and a yellow striped waistcoat. I never saw a man unbuckle harness so quickly as he did, and with a pat and a good word he led me to a long stable, with six or eight stalls in it, and two or three horses. The other man brought Ginger; James stood by while we were rubbed down and cleaned.

I never was cleaned so lightly and quickly as by that little old man. When he had done James stepped up and felt me over, as if he thought I could not be thoroughly done, but he found my coat as clean and smooth as silk.

"Well," he said, "I thought I was pretty quick, and our John quicker still, but you do beat all I ever saw for being quick and thorough at the same time."

"Practice makes perfect," said the crooked little hostler, "and 'twould be a pity if it didn't; forty years' practice, and not perfect! ha, ha! that would be a pity; and as to being quick, why, bless you!

381

that is only a matter of habit; if you get into the habit of being quick it is just as easy as being slow; easier, I should say; in fact it don't agree with my health to be hulking about over a job twice as long as it need take. Bless you! I couldn't whistle if I crawled over my work as some folks do! You see, I have been about horses ever since I was twelve years old, in hunting stables, and racing stables; and being small, ye see, I was jockey for several years; but at the Goodwood, ye see, the turf was very slippery and my poor Larkspur got a fall, and I broke my knee, and so of course I was of no more use there. But I could not live without horses, of course I couldn't, so I took to the hotels. And I can tell ye it is a downright pleasure to handle an animal like this, well-bred, well-mannered, well-cared-for; bless ye! I can tell how a horse is treated. Give me the handling of a horse for twenty minutes, and I'll tell you what sort of a groom he has had. Look at this one, pleasant, quiet, turns about just as you want him, holds up his feet to be cleaned out, or anything else you please to wish; then you'll find another fidgety, fretty, won't move the right way, or starts across the stall, tosses up his head as soon as you come near him, lays his ears, and seems afraid of you; or else squares about at you with his heels. Poor things! I know what sort of treatment they have had. If they are timid it makes them start or shy; if they are high-mettled it makes them vicious or dangerous; their tempers are mostly made when they are young. Bless you! they are like children, train 'em up in the way they should go, as the good book says, and when they are old they will not depart from it, if they have a chance."

"I like to hear you talk," said James, "that's the way we lay it down at home, at our master's."

"Who is your master, young man? if it be a proper question. I should judge he is a good one, from what I see."

"He is Squire Gordon, of Birtwick Park, the other side the Beacon Hills," said James.

"Ah! so, so, I have heard tell of him; fine judge of horses, ain't he? the best rider in the county."

"I believe he is," said James, "but he rides very little now, since the poor young master was killed."

"Ah! poor gentleman; I read all about it in the paper at the time. A fine horse killed, too, wasn't there?"

"Yes," said James; "he was a splendid creature, brother to this one, and just like him."

"Pity! pity!" said the old man; "'twas a bad place to leap, if I remember; a thin fence at top, a steep bank down to the stream, wasn't it? No chance for a horse to see where he is going. Now, I am for bold riding as much as any man, but still there are some leaps that only a very knowing old huntsman has any right to take. A man's life and a horse's life are worth more than a fox's tail; at least, I should say they ought to be."

During this time the other man had finished Ginger and had brought our corn, and James and the old man left the stable together.

16 The Fire

Later on in the evening a traveler's horse was brought in by the second hostler, and while he was cleaning him a young man with a pipe in his mouth lounged into the stable to gossip.

"I say, Towler," said the hostler, "just run up the ladder into the loft and put some hay down into this horse's rack, will you? only lay down your pipe."

"All right," said the other, and went up through the trapdoor; and I heard him step across the floor overhead and put down the hay. James came in to look at us the last thing, and then the door was locked.

I cannot say how long I had slept, nor what time in the night it was, but I woke up very uncomfortable, though I hardly knew why. I got up; the air seemed all thick and choking. I heard Ginger coughing and one of the other horses seemed very restless; it was quite dark, and I could see nothing, but the stable seemed full of smoke, and I hardly knew how to breathe.

The trapdoor had been left open, and I thought that was the place it came through. I listened, and heard a soft rushing sort of noise and a low crackling and snapping. I did not know what it was, but there was something in the sound so strange that it made me tremble all over. The other horses were all awake; some were pulling at their halters, others stamping.

At last I heard steps outside, and the hostler who had put up the traveler's horse burst into the stable with a lantern, and began to untie the horses, and try to lead them out; but he seemed in such a hurry and so frightened himself that he frightened me still more. The first horse would not go with him; he tried the second and third, and they too would not stir. He came to me next and tried to drag me out of the stall by force; of course that was no use. He tried us all by turns and then left the stable.

No doubt we were very foolish, but danger seemed to be all round, and there was nobody we knew to trust in, and all was strange and uncertain. The fresh air that had come in through the open door made it easier to breathe, but the rushing sound overhead grew louder, and as I looked upward through the bars of my empty rack I saw a red light flickering on the wall. Then I heard a cry of "Fire!" outside, and the old hostler quietly and quickly came in; he got one horse out, and went to another, but the flames were playing round the trapdoor, and the roaring overhead was dreadful.

The next thing I heard was James' voice, quiet and cheery, as it always was.

"Come, my beauties, it is time for us to be off, so wake up and come along." I stood nearest the door, so he came to me first, patting me as he came in.

"Come, Beauty, on with your bridle, my boy, we'll soon be out of this smother." It was on in no time; then he took the scarf off his neck, and tied it lightly over my eyes, and patting and coaxing he led me out of the stable. Safe in the yard, he slipped the scarf off my eyes, and shouted, "Here somebody! take this horse while I go back for the other."

A tall, broad man stepped forward and took me, and James darted back into the stable. I set up a shrill whinny as I saw him go. Ginger told me afterward that whinny was the best thing I could have done for her, for had she not heard me outside she would never have had courage to come out.

There was much confusion in the yard; the horses being got out of other stables, and the carriages and gigs being pulled out of houses and sheds, lest the flames should spread further. On the other side the yard windows were thrown up, and people were shouting all sorts of things; but I kept my eye fixed on the stable door, where the smoke poured out thicker than ever, and I could see flashes of red light; presently I heard above all the stir and din a loud, clear voice, which I knew was master's:

"James Howard! James Howard! Are you there?" There was no answer, but I heard a crash of something falling in the stable, and the next moment I gave a loud, joyful neigh, for I saw James coming through the smoke leading Ginger with him; she was coughing violently, and he was not able to speak.

"My brave lad!" said master, laying his hand on his shoulder, "are you hurt?"

James shook his head, for he could not yet speak.

"Ay," said the big man who held me; "he is a brave lad, and no mistake."

"And now," said master, "when you have got your breath, James, we'll get out of this place as quickly as we can," and we were moving toward the entry, when from the market-place there came a sound of galloping feet and loud rumbling wheels.

"'Tis the fire-engine! the fire-engine!" shouted two or three voices, "stand back, make way!" and clattering and thundering over the stones two horses dashed into the yard with a heavy engine behind them. The firemen leaped to the ground; there was no need to ask where the fire was -it was rolling up in a great blaze from the roof.

We got out as fast as we could into the broad quiet market-place; the stars were shining, and except the noise behind us, all was still. Master led the way to a large hotel on the other side, and as soon as the hostler came, he said, "James, I must now hasten to your mistress; I trust the horses entirely to you, order whatever you think is needed," and with that he was gone. The master did not run, but I never saw mortal man walk so fast as he did that night.

There was a dreadful sound before we got into our stalls – the shrieks of those poor horses that were left burning to death in the stable – it was very terrible! and made both Ginger and me feel very bad. We, however, were taken in and well done by.

The next morning the master came to see how we were and to speak to James. I did not hear much, for the hostler was rubbing me down, but I could see that James looked very happy, and I thought the master was proud of him. Our mistress had been so much alarmed in the night that the journey was put off till the afternoon, so James had the morning on hand, and went first to the inn to see about our harness and the carriage, and then to hear more about the fire. When he came back we heard him tell the hostler about it. At first no one could guess how the fire had been caused, but at last a man said he saw Dick Towler go into the stable with a pipe in his mouth, and when he came out he had not one, and went to the tap for another. Then the under hostler said he had asked Dick to go up the ladder to put down some hay, but told him to lay down his pipe first. Dick denied taking the pipe with him, but no one believed him. I remember our John Manly's rule, never to allow a pipe in the stable, and thought it ought to be the rule everywhere.

James said the roof and floor had all fallen in, and that only the black walls were standing; the two poor horses that could not be got out were buried under the burnt rafters and tiles.

17 John Manly's Talk

The rest of our journey was very easy, and a little after sunset we reached the house of my master's friend. We were taken into a clean, snug stable; there was a kind coachman, who made us very comfortable, and who seemed to think a good deal of James when he heard about the fire.

"There is one thing quite clear, young man," he said, "your horses know who they can trust; it is one of the hardest things in the world to get horses out of a stable when there is either fire or flood. I don't know why they won't come out, but they won't – not one in twenty."

We stopped two or three days at this place and then returned home. All went well on the journey; we were glad to be in our own stable again, and John was equally glad to see us.

Before he and James left us for the night James said, "I wonder who is coming in my place."

"Little Joe Green at the lodge," said John.

"Little Joe Green! why, he's a child!"

"He is fourteen and a half," said John.

"But he is such a little chap!"

"Yes, he is small, but he is quick and willing, and kind-hearted, too, and then he wishes very much to come, and his father would like it; and I know the master would like to give him the chance. He said if I thought he would not do he would look out for a bigger boy; but I said I was quite agreeable to try him for six weeks."

"Six weeks!" said James; "why, it will be six months before he can be of much use! It will make you a deal of work, John."

"Well," said John with a laugh, "work and I are very good friends; I never was afraid of work yet."

"You are a very good man," said James. "I wish I may ever be like you."

"I don't often speak of myself," said John, "but as you are going away from us out into the world to shift for yourself I'll just tell you how I look on these things. I was just as old as Joseph when my father and mother died of the fever within ten days of each other, and left me and my cripple sister Nelly alone in the world, without a relation that we could look to for help. I was a farmer's boy, not earning enough to keep myself, much less both of us, and she must have gone to the workhouse but for our mistress (Nelly calls her her angel, and she has good right to do so). She went and hired a room for her with old Widow Mallet, and she gave her knitting and needlework when she was able to do it; and when she was ill she sent her dinners and many nice, comfortable things, and was like a mother to her. Then the master he took me into the stable under old Norman, the coachman that was then. I had my food at the house and my bed in the loft, and a suit of clothes, and three shillings a week, so that I could help Nelly. Then there was Norman; he might have turned round and said at his age he could not be troubled with a raw boy from the plow-tail, but he was like a father to me, and took no end of pains with me. When the old man died some years after I stepped into his place, and now of course I have top wages, and can lay by for a rainy day or a sunny day, as it may happen, and Nelly is as happy as a bird. So you see, James, I am not the man that should turn up his nose at a little boy and vex a good, kind master. No, no! I shall miss you very much, James, but we shall pull through, and there's nothing like doing a kindness when 'tis put in your way, and I am glad I can do it."

"Then," said James, "you don't hold with that saying, 'Everybody look after himself, and take care of number one'?"

"No, indeed," said John, "where should I and Nelly have been if master and mistress and old Norman had only taken care of number one? Why, she in the workhouse and I hoeing turnips! Where would Black Beauty and Ginger have been if you had only thought of number one? why, roasted to death! No, Jim, no! that is a selfish, heathenish saying, whoever uses it; and any man who thinks he has nothing to do but take care of number one, why, it's a pity but what he had been drowned like a puppy or a kitten, before he got his eyes open; that's what I think," said John, with a very decided jerk of his head.

James laughed at this; but there was a thickness in his voice when he said, "You have been my best friend except my mother; I hope you won't forget me."

"No, lad, no!" said John, "and if ever I can do you a good turn I hope you won't forget me."

386

The next day Joe came to the stables to learn all he could before James left. He learned to sweep the stable, to bring in the straw and hay; he began to clean the harness, and helped to wash the carriage. As he was quite too short to do anything in the way of grooming Ginger and me, James taught him upon Merrylegs, for he was to have full charge of him, under John. He was a nice little bright fellow, and always came whistling to his work.

Merrylegs was a good deal put out at being "mauled about," as he said, "by a boy who knew nothing;" but toward the end of the second week he told me confidentially that he thought the boy would turn out well.

At last the day came when James had to leave us; cheerful as he always was, he looked quite down-hearted that morning.

"You see," he said to John, "I am leaving a great deal behind; my mother and Betsy, and you, and a good master and mistress, and then the horses, and my old Merrylegs. At the new place there will not be a soul that I shall know. If it were not that I shall get a higher place, and be able to help my mother better, I don't think I should have made up my mind to it; it is a real pinch, John."

"Ay, James, lad, so it is; but I should not think much of you if you could leave your home for the first time and not feel it. Cheer up, you'll make friends there; and if you get on well, as I am sure you will, it will be a fine thing for your mother, and she will be proud enough that you have got into such a good place as that."

So John cheered him up, but every one was sorry to lose James; as for Merrylegs, he pined after him for several days, and went quite off his appetite. So John took him out several mornings with a leading rein, when he exercised me, and, trotting and galloping by my side, got up the little fellow's spirits again, and he was soon all right.

Joe's father would often come in and give a little help, as he understood the work; and Joe took a great deal of pains to learn, and John was quite encouraged about him.

Lesson 78

1. Read chapters 18, 19, 20 and 21.
2. Take notes on major events.

18 Going for the Doctor

One night, a few days after James had left, I had eaten my hay and was lying down in my straw fast asleep, when I was suddenly roused by the stable bell ringing very loud. I heard the door of John's house open, and his feet running up to the hall. He was back again in no time; he unlocked the stable door, and came in, calling out, "Wake up, Beauty! You must go well now, if ever you did;" and almost before I could think he had got the saddle on my back and the bridle on my head. He just ran round for his coat, and then took me at a quick trot up to the hall door. The squire stood there, with a lamp in his hand.

"Now, John," he said, "ride for your life – that is, for your mistress' life; there is not a moment to lose. Give this note to Dr. White; give your horse a rest at the inn, and be back as soon as you can."

John said, "Yes, sir," and was on my back in a minute. The gardener who lived at the lodge had heard the bell ring, and was ready with the gate open, and away we went through the park, and through the village, and down the hill till we came to the toll-gate. John called very loud and thumped upon the door; the man was soon out and flung open the gate.

"Now," said John, "do you keep the gate open for the doctor; here's the money," and off he went again.

There was before us a long piece of level road by the river side; John said to me, "Now, Beauty, do your best," and so I did; I wanted no whip nor spur, and for two miles I galloped as fast as I could lay my feet to the ground; I don't believe that my old grandfather, who won the race at Newmarket, could have gone faster. When we came to the bridge John pulled me up a little and patted my neck. "Well done, Beauty! good old fellow," he said. He would have let me go slower, but my spirit was up, and I was off again as fast as before. The air was frosty, the moon was bright; it was very pleasant. We came through a village, then through a dark wood, then uphill, then downhill, till after eight miles' run we came to the town, through the streets and into the market-place. It was all quite still except the clatter of my feet on the stones – everybody was asleep. The church clock struck three as we drew up at Dr. White's door. John rang the bell twice, and then knocked at the door like thunder. A window was thrown up, and Dr. White, in his nightcap, put his head out and said, "What do you want?"

"Mrs. Gordon is very ill, sir; master wants you to go at once; he thinks she will die if you cannot get there. Here is a note."

"Wait," he said, "I will come."

He shut the window, and was soon at the door.

"The worst of it is," he said, "that my horse has been out all day and is quite done up; my son has just been sent for, and he has taken the other. What is to be done? Can I have your horse?"

"He has come at a gallop nearly all the way, sir, and I was to give him a rest here; but I think my master would not be against it, if you think fit, sir."

"All right," he said; "I will soon be ready."

John stood by me and stroked my neck; I was very hot. The doctor came out with his riding-whip.

"You need not take that, sir," said John; "Black Beauty will go till he drops. Take care of him, sir, if you can; I should not like any harm to come to him."

"No, no, John," said the doctor, "I hope not," and in a minute we had left John far behind.

I will not tell about our way back. The doctor was a heavier man than John, and not so good a rider; however, I did my very best. The man at the toll-gate had it open. When we came to the hill the doctor drew me up. "Now, my good fellow," he said, "take some breath." I was glad he did, for I was nearly spent, but that breathing helped me on, and soon we were in the park. Joe was at the lodge gate; my master was at the hall door, for he had heard us coming. He spoke not a word; the doctor went into the house with him, and Joe led me to the stable. I was glad to get home; my legs shook under me, and I could only stand and pant. I had not a dry hair on my body, the water ran down my legs, and I steamed all over, Joe used to say, like a pot on the fire. Poor Joe! he was young and small, and as yet he knew very little, and his father, who would have helped him, had been sent to the next village; but I am sure he did the very best he knew. He rubbed my legs and my chest, but he did not put my warm cloth on me; he thought I was so hot I should not like it. Then he gave me a pailful of water to drink; it was cold and very good, and I drank it all; then he gave me some hay and some corn, and thinking he had done right, he went away. Soon I began to shake and tremble, and turned deadly cold; my legs ached, my loins ached, and my chest ached, and I felt sore all over. Oh! how I wished for my warm, thick cloth, as I stood and trembled. I wished for John, but he had eight miles to walk, so I lay down in my straw and tried to go to sleep. After a long while I heard John at the door; I gave a low moan, for I was in great pain. He was at my side in a moment, stooping down by me. I could not tell him how I felt, but he seemed to know it all; he covered me up with two or three warm cloths, and then ran to the house for some hot water; he made me some warm gruel, which I drank, and then I think I went to sleep.

John seemed to be very much put out. I heard him say to himself over and over again, "Stupid boy! stupid boy! no cloth put on, and I dare say the water was cold, too; boys are no good;" but Joe was a good boy, after all.

I was now very ill; a strong inflammation had attacked my lungs, and I could not draw my breath without pain. John nursed me night and day; he would get up two or three times in the night to come to me. My master, too, often came to see me. "My poor Beauty," he said one day, "my good horse, you saved your mistress' life, Beauty; yes, you saved her life." I was very glad to hear that, for it seems the doctor had said if we had been a little longer it would have been too late. John told my master he never saw a horse go so fast in his life. It seemed as if the horse knew what was the matter. Of course I did, though John thought not; at least I knew as much as this-that John and I must go at the top of our speed, and that it was for the sake of the mistress.

19 Only Ignorance

I do not know how long I was ill. Mr. Bond, the horse-doctor, came every day. One day he bled me; John held a pail for the blood. I felt very faint after it and thought I should die, and I believe they all thought so too.

Ginger and Merrylegs had been moved into the other stable, so that I might be quiet, for the fever made me very quick of hearing; any little noise seemed quite loud, and I could tell every one's footstep going to and from the house. I knew all that was going on. One night John had to give me a draught; Thomas Green came in to help him. After I had taken it and John had made me as comfortable as he could, he said he should stay half an hour to see how the medicine settled. Thomas said he would stay with him, so they went and sat down on a bench that had been brought into Merrylegs' stall, and put down the lantern at their feet, that I might not be disturbed with the light.

For awhile both men sat silent, and then Tom Green said in a low voice:

"I wish, John, you'd say a bit of a kind word to Joe. The boy is quite broken-hearted; he can't eat his meals, and he can't smile. He says he knows it was all his fault, though he is sure he did the best he knew, and he says if Beauty dies no one will ever speak to him again. It goes to my heart to hear him. I think you might give him just a word; he is not a bad boy."

After a short pause John said slowly, "You must not be too hard upon me, Tom. I know he meant no harm, I never said he did; I know he is not a bad boy. But you see, I am sore myself; that horse is the pride of my heart, to say nothing of his being such a favorite with the master and mistress; and to think that his life may be flung away in this manner is more than I can bear. But if you think I am hard on the boy I will try to give him a good word to-morrow – that is, I mean if Beauty is better."

"Well, John, thank you. I knew you did not wish to be too hard, and I am glad you see it was only ignorance."

John's voice almost startled me as he answered:

"Only ignorance! only ignorance! how can you talk about only ignorance? Don't you know that it is the worst thing in the world, next to wickedness? – and which does the most mischief heaven only knows. If people can say, 'Oh! I did not know, I did not mean any harm,' they think it is all right. I suppose Martha Mulwash did not mean to kill that baby when she dosed it with Dalby and soothing syrups; but she did kill it, and was tried for manslaughter."

"And serve her right, too," said Tom. "A woman should not undertake to nurse a tender little child without knowing what is good and what is bad for it."

"Bill Starkey," continued John, "did not mean to frighten his brother into fits when he dressed up like a ghost and ran after him in the moonlight; but he did; and that bright, handsome little fellow, that might have been the pride of any mother's heart is just no better than an idiot, and never will be, if he lives to be eighty years old. You were a good deal cut up yourself, Tom, two weeks ago, when those young ladies left your hothouse door open, with a frosty east wind blowing right in; you said it killed a good many of your plants."

"A good many!" said Tom; "there was not one of the tender cuttings that was not nipped off. I shall have to strike all over again, and the worst of it is that I don't know where to go to get fresh ones. I was nearly mad when I came in and saw what was done."

"And yet," said John, "I am sure the young ladies did not mean it; it was only ignorance."

I heard no more of this conversation, for the medicine did well and sent me to sleep, and in the morning I felt much better; but I often thought of John's words when I came to know more of the world.

20 Joe Green

Joe Green went on very well; he learned quickly, and was so attentive and careful that John began to trust him in many things; but as I have said, he was small of his age, and it was seldom that he was allowed to exercise either Ginger or me; but it so happened one morning that John was out with Justice in the luggage cart, and the master wanted a note to be taken immediately to a gentleman's house, about three miles distant, and sent his orders for Joe to saddle me and take it, adding the caution that he was to ride steadily.

The note was delivered, and we were quietly returning when we came to the brick-field. Here we saw a cart heavily laden with bricks; the wheels had stuck fast in the stiff mud of some deep ruts, and the carter was shouting and flogging the two horses unmercifully. Joe pulled up. It was a sad sight. There were the two horses straining and struggling with all their might to drag the cart out, but they could not move it; the sweat streamed from their legs and flanks, their sides heaved, and every muscle was strained, while the man, fiercely pulling at the head of the fore horse, swore and lashed most brutally.

"Hold hard," said Joe; "don't go on flogging the horses like that; the wheels are so stuck that they cannot move the cart."

The man took no heed, but went on lashing.

"Stop! pray stop!" said Joe. "I'll help you to lighten the cart; they can't move it now."

"Mind your own business, you impudent young rascal, and I'll mind mine!" The man was in a towering passion and the worse for drink, and laid on the whip again. Joe turned my head, and the next moment we were going at a round gallop toward the house of the master brick-maker. I cannot say if John would have approved of our pace, but Joe and I were both of one mind, and so angry that we could not have gone slower.

The house stood close by the roadside. Joe knocked at the door, and shouted, "Halloo! Is Mr. Clay at home?" The door was opened, and Mr. Clay himself came out.

"Halloo, young man! You seem in a hurry; any orders from the squire this morning?"

"No, Mr. Clay, but there's a fellow in your brick-yard flogging two horses to death. I told him to stop, and he wouldn't; I said I'd help him to lighten the cart, and he wouldn't; so I have come to tell you. Pray, sir, go." Joe's voice shook with excitement.

"Thank ye, my lad," said the man, running in for his hat; then pausing for a moment, "Will you give evidence of what you saw if I should bring the fellow up before a magistrate?"

"That I will," said Joe, "and glad too." The man was gone, and we were on our way home at a smart trot.

"Why, what's the matter with you, Joe? You look angry all over," said John, as the boy flung himself from the saddle.

"I am angry all over, I can tell you," said the boy, and then in hurried, excited words he told all that had happened. Joe was usually such a quiet, gentle little fellow that it was wonderful to see him so roused.

"Right, Joe! you did right, my boy, whether the fellow gets a summons or not. Many folks would have ridden by and said it was not their business to interfere. Now I say that with cruelty and oppression it is everybody's business to interfere when they see it; you did right, my boy."

Joe was quite calm by this time, and proud that John approved of him, and cleaned out my feet and rubbed me down with a firmer hand than usual.

They were just going home to dinner when the footman came down to the stable to say that Joe was wanted directly in master's private room; there was a man brought up for ill-using horses, and Joe's evidence was wanted. The boy flushed up to his forehead, and his eyes sparkled. "They shall have it," said he.

"Put yourself a bit straight," said John. Joe gave a pull at his necktie and a twitch at his jacket, and was off in a moment. Our master being one of the county magistrates, cases were often brought to him to settle, or say what should be done. In the stable we heard no more for some time, as it was the men's dinner hour, but when Joe came next into the stable I saw he was in high spirits; he gave me a good-natured slap, and said, "We won't see such things done, will we, old fellow?" We heard afterward that he had given his evidence so clearly, and the horses were in such an exhausted state, bearing marks of such brutal usage, that the carter was committed to take his trial, and might possibly be sentenced to two or three months in prison.

It was wonderful what a change had come over Joe. John laughed, and said he had grown an inch taller in that week, and I believe he had. He was just as kind and gentle as before, but there was more purpose and determination in all that he did – as if he had jumped at once from a boy into a man.

21 The Parting

Now I had lived in this happy place three years, but sad changes were about to come over us. We heard from time to time that our mistress was ill. The doctor was often at the house, and the master looked grave and anxious. Then we heard that she must leave her home at once, and go to a warm country for two or three years. The news fell upon the household like the tolling of a deathbell. Everybody was sorry; but the master began directly to make arrangements for breaking up his establishment and leaving England. We used to hear it talked about in our stable; indeed, nothing else was talked about.

John went about his work silent and sad, and Joe scarcely whistled. There was a great deal of coming and going; Ginger and I had full work.

The first of the party who went were Miss Jessie and Flora, with their governess. They came to bid us good-by. They hugged poor Merrylegs like an old friend, and so indeed he was. Then we heard what had been arranged for us. Master had sold Ginger and me to his old friend, the Earl of W –, for he thought we should have a good place there. Merrylegs he had given to the vicar, who was wanting a pony for Mrs. Blomefield, but it was on the condition that he should never be sold, and that when he was past work he should be shot and buried.

Joe was engaged to take care of him and to help in the house, so I thought that Merrylegs was well off. John had the offer of several good places, but he said he should wait a little and look round.

The evening before they left the master came into the stable to give some directions, and to give his horses the last pat. He seemed very low-spirited; I knew that by his voice. I believe we horses can tell more by the voice than many men can.

"Have you decided what to do, John?" he said. "I find you have not accepted either of those offers."

"No, sir; I have made up my mind that if I could get a situation with some first-rate colt-breaker and horse-trainer, it would be the right thing for me. Many young animals are frightened and spoiled by wrong treatment, which need not be if the right man took them in hand. I always get on well with horses, and if I could help some of them to a fair start I should feel as if I was doing some good. What do you think of it, sir?"

"I don't know a man anywhere," said master, "that I should think so suitable for it as yourself. You understand horses, and somehow they understand you, and in time you might set up for yourself; I think you could not do better. If in any way I can help you, write to me. I shall speak to my agent in London, and leave your character with him."

Master gave John the name and address, and then he thanked him for his long and faithful service; but that was too much for John. "Pray, don't, sir, I can't bear it; you and my dear mistress have done so much for me that I could never repay it. But we shall never forget you, sir, and please God, we may some day see mistress back again like herself; we must keep up hope, sir." Master gave John his hand, but he did not speak, and they both left the stable.

The last sad day had come; the footman and the heavy luggage had gone off the day before, and there were only master and mistress and her maid. Ginger and I brought the carriage up to the hall door for the last time. The servants brought out cushions and rugs and many other things; and when all were arranged master came down the steps carrying the mistress in his arms (I was on the side next to the house, and could see all that went on); he placed her carefully in the carriage, while the house servants stood round crying.

"Good-by, again," he said; "we shall not forget any of you," and he got in. "Drive on, John."

Joe jumped up, and we trotted slowly through the park and through the village, where the people were standing at their doors to have a last look and to say, "God bless them."

When we reached the railway station I think mistress walked from the carriage to the waiting-room. I heard her say in her own sweet voice, "Good-by, John. God bless you." I felt the rein twitch, but John made no answer; perhaps he could not speak. As soon as Joe had taken the things out of the carriage John called him to stand by the horses, while he went on the platform. Poor Joe! he stood close up to our heads to hide his tears. Very soon the train came puffing up into the station; then two or three minutes, and the doors were slammed to, the guard whistled, and the train glided away, leaving behind it only clouds of white smoke and some very heavy hearts.

When it was quite out of sight John came back.

"We shall never see her again," he said – "never." He took the reins, mounted the box, and with Joe drove slowly home; but it was not our home now.

Lesson 79

1. Read chapters 22 and 23.
2. Take notes on major events.

22 Earlshall

The next morning after breakfast Joe put Merrylegs into the mistress' low chaise to take him to the vicarage; he came first and said good-by to us, and Merrylegs neighed to us from the yard. Then John put the saddle on Ginger and the leading rein on me, and rode us across the country about fifteen miles to Earlshall Park, where the Earl of W – – lived. There was a very fine house and a great deal of stabling. We went into the yard through a stone gateway, and John asked for Mr. York. It was some time before he came. He was a fine-looking, middle-aged man, and his voice said at once that he expected to be obeyed. He was very friendly and polite to John, and after giving us a slight look he called a groom to take us to our boxes, and invited John to take some refreshment.

We were taken to a light, airy stable, and placed in boxes adjoining each other, where we were rubbed down and fed. In about half an hour John and Mr. York, who was to be our new coachman, came in to see us.

"Now, Mr. Manly," he said, after carefully looking at us both, "I can see no fault in these horses; but we all know that horses have their peculiarities as well as men, and that sometimes they need different treatment. I should like to know if there is anything particular in either of these that you would like to mention."

"Well," said John, "I don't believe there is a better pair of horses in the country, and right grieved I am to part with them, but they are not alike. The black one is the most perfect temper I ever knew; I suppose he has never known a hard word or a blow since he was foaled, and all his pleasure seems to be to do what you wish; but the chestnut, I fancy, must have had bad treatment; we heard as much from the dealer. She came to us snappish and suspicious, but when she found what sort of place ours was, it all went off by degrees; for three years I have never seen the smallest sign of temper, and if she is well treated there is not a better, more willing animal than she is. But she is naturally a more irritable constitution than the black horse; flies tease her more; anything wrong in the harness frets her more; and if she were ill-used or unfairly treated she would not be unlikely to give tit for tat. You know that many high-mettled horses will do so."

"Of course," said York, "I quite understand; but you know it is not easy in stables like these to have all the grooms just what they should be. I do my best, and there I must leave it. I'll remember what you have said about the mare."

They were going out of the stable, when John stopped and said, "I had better mention that we have never used the check-rein with either of them; the black horse never had one on, and the dealer said it was the gag-bit that spoiled the other's temper."

"Well," said York, "if they come here they must wear the check-rein. I prefer a loose rein myself, and his lordship is always very reasonable about horses; but my lady – that's another thing; she will have style, and if her carriage horses are not reined up tight she wouldn't look at them. I always stand out against the gag-bit, and shall do so, but it must be tight up when my lady rides!"

"I am sorry for it, very sorry," said John; "but I must go now, or I shall lose the train."

He came round to each of us to pat and speak to us for the last time; his voice sounded very sad.

I held my face close to him; that was all I could do to say good-by; and then he was gone, and I have never seen him since.

The next day Lord W – – came to look at us; he seemed pleased with our appearance.

"I have great confidence in these horses," he said, "from the character my friend Mr. Gordon has given me of them. Of course they are not a match in color, but my idea is that they will do very well for the carriage while we are in the country. Before we go to London I must try to match Baron; the black horse, I believe, is perfect for riding."

York then told him what John had said about us.

"Well," said he, "you must keep an eye to the mare, and put the check-rein easy; I dare say they will do very well with a little humoring at first. I'll mention it to your lady."

In the afternoon we were harnessed and put in the carriage, and as the stable clock struck three we were led round to the front of the house. It was all very grand, and three or four times as large as the old house at Birtwick, but not half so pleasant, if a horse may have an opinion. Two footmen were standing ready, dressed in drab livery, with scarlet breeches and white stockings. Presently we heard the rustling sound of silk as my lady came down the flight of stone steps. She stepped round to look at us; she was a tall, proud-looking woman, and did not seem pleased about something, but she said nothing, and got into the carriage. This was the first time of wearing a check-rein, and I must say, though it certainly was a nuisance not to be able to get my head down now and then, it did not pull my head higher than I was accustomed to carry it. I felt anxious about Ginger, but she seemed to be quiet and content.

The next day at three o'clock we were again at the door, and the footmen as before; we heard the silk dress rustle and the lady came down the steps, and in an imperious voice she said, "York, you must put those horses' heads higher; they are not fit to be seen."

York got down, and said very respectfully, "I beg your pardon, my lady, but these horses have not been reined up for three years, and my lord said it would be safer to bring them to it by degrees; but if your ladyship pleases I can take them up a little more."

"Do so," she said.

York came round to our heads and shortened the rein himself – one hole, I think; every little makes a difference, be it for better or worse, and that day we had a steep hill to go up. Then I began to understand what I had heard of. Of course, I wanted to put my head forward and take the carriage up with a will, as we had been used to do; but no, I had to pull with my head up now, and that took all the spirit out of me, and the strain came on my back and legs. When we came in Ginger said, "Now you see what it is like; but this is not bad, and if it does not get much worse than this I shall say nothing about it, for we are very well treated here; but if they strain me up tight, why, let 'em look out! I can't bear it, and I won't."

Day by day, hole by hole, our bearing reins were shortened, and instead of looking forward with pleasure to having my harness put on, as I used to do, I began to dread it. Ginger, too, seemed restless, though she said very little. At last I thought the worst was over; for several days there was no more shortening, and I determined to make the best of it and do my duty, though it was now a constant harass instead of a pleasure; but the worst was not come.

23 A Strike for Liberty

One day my lady came down later than usual, and the silk rustled more than ever.

"Drive to the Duchess of B – – 's," she said, and then after a pause, "Are you never going to get those horses' heads up, York? Raise them at once and let us have no more of this humoring and nonsense."

York came to me first, while the groom stood at Ginger's head. He drew my head back and fixed the rein so tight that it was almost intolerable; then he went to Ginger, who was impatiently jerking her head up and down against the bit, as was her way now. She had a good idea of what was coming, and the moment York took the rein off the terret in order to shorten it she took her opportunity and reared up so suddenly that York had his nose roughly hit and his hat knocked off; the groom was nearly thrown off his legs. At once they both flew to her head; but she was a match for them, and went on plunging, rearing, and kicking in a most desperate manner. At last she kicked right over the carriage pole and fell down, after giving me a severe blow on my near quarter. There is no knowing what further mischief she might have done had not York promptly sat himself down flat on her head to prevent her struggling, at the same time calling out, "Unbuckle the black horse! Run for the winch and unscrew the carriage pole! Cut the trace here, somebody, if you can't unhitch it!" One of the footmen ran for the winch, and another brought a knife from the house. The groom soon set me free from Ginger and the carriage, and led me to my box. He just turned me in as I was and ran back to York. I was much excited by what had happened, and if I had ever been used to kick or rear I am sure I should have done it then; but I never had, and there I stood, angry, sore in my leg, my head still strained up to the terret on the saddle, and no power to get it down. I was very miserable and felt much inclined to kick the first person who came near me.

Before long, however, Ginger was led in by two grooms, a good deal knocked about and bruised. York came with her and gave his orders, and then came to look at me. In a moment he let down my head.

"Confound these check-reins!" he said to himself; "I thought we should have some mischief soon. Master will be sorely vexed. But there, if a woman's husband can't rule her of course a servant can't; so I wash my hands of it, and if she can't get to the duchess' garden party I can't help it."

York did not say this before the men; he always spoke respectfully when they were by. Now he felt me all over, and soon found the place above my hock where I had been kicked. It was swelled and painful; he ordered it to be sponged with hot water, and then some lotion was put on.

Lord W — — was much put out when he learned what had happened; he blamed York for giving way to his mistress, to which he replied that in future he would much prefer to receive his orders only from his lordship; but I think nothing came of it, for things went on the same as before. I thought York might have stood up better for his horses, but perhaps I am no judge.

Ginger was never put into the carriage again, but when she was well of her bruises one of the Lord W — — 's younger sons said he should like to have her; he was sure she would make a good hunter. As for me, I was obliged still to go in the carriage, and had a fresh partner called Max; he had always been used to the tight rein. I asked him how it was he bore it.

"Well," he said, "I bear it because I must; but it is shortening my life, and it will shorten yours too if you have to stick to it."

"Do you think," I said, "that our masters know how bad it is for us?"

"I can't say," he replied, "but the dealers and the horse-doctors know it very well. I was at a dealer's once, who was training me and another horse to go as a pair; he was getting our heads up, as he said, a little higher and a little higher every day. A gentleman who was there asked him why he did so. 'Because,' said he, 'people won't buy them unless we do. The London people always want their horses to carry their heads high and to step high. Of course it is very bad for the horses, but then it is good for trade. The horses soon wear up, or get diseased, and they come for another pair.' That," said Max, "is what he said in my hearing, and you can judge for yourself."

What I suffered with that rein for four long months in my lady's carriage it would be hard to describe; but I am quite sure that, had it lasted much longer, either my health or my temper would have given way. Before that, I never knew what it was to foam at the mouth, but now the action of the sharp bit on my tongue and jaw, and the constrained position of my head and throat, always caused me to froth at the mouth more or less. Some people think it very fine to see this, and say, "What fine spirited creatures!" But it is just as unnatural for horses as for men to foam at the mouth; it is a sure sign of some discomfort, and should be attended to. Besides this, there was a pressure on my windpipe, which often made my breathing very uncomfortable; when I returned from my work my neck and chest were strained and painful, my mouth and tongue tender, and I felt worn and depressed.

In my old home I always knew that John and my master were my friends; but here, although in many ways I was well treated, I had no friend. York might have known, and very likely did know, how that rein harassed me; but I suppose he took it as a matter of course that it could not be helped; at any rate, nothing was done to relieve me.

Lesson 80
1. Read chapters 24, 25, and 26.
2. Take notes on major events.

24 The Lady Anne, or a Runaway Horse

Early in the spring, Lord W – – and part of his family went up to London, and took York with them. I and Ginger and some other horses were left at home for use, and the head groom was left in charge.

The Lady Harriet, who remained at the hall, was a great invalid, and never went out in the carriage, and the Lady Anne preferred riding on horseback with her brother or cousins. She was a perfect horsewoman, and as gay and gentle as she was beautiful. She chose me for her horse, and named me "Black Auster". I enjoyed these rides very much in the clear cold air, sometimes with Ginger, sometimes with Lizzie. This Lizzie was a bright bay mare, almost thoroughbred, and a great favorite with the gentlemen, on account of her fine action and lively spirit; but Ginger, who knew more of her than I did, told me she was rather nervous.

There was a gentleman of the name of Blantyre staying at the hall; he always rode Lizzie, and praised her so much that one day Lady Anne ordered the side-saddle to be put on her, and the other saddle on me. When we came to the door the gentleman seemed very uneasy.

"How is this?" he said. "Are you tired of your good Black Auster?"

"Oh, no, not at all," she replied, "but I am amiable enough to let you ride him for once, and I will try your charming Lizzie. You must confess that in size and appearance she is far more like a lady's horse than my own favorite."

"Do let me advise you not to mount her," he said; "she is a charming creature, but she is too nervous for a lady. I assure you, she is not perfectly safe; let me beg you to have the saddles changed."

"My dear cousin," said Lady Anne, laughing, "pray do not trouble your good careful head about me. I have been a horsewoman ever since I was a baby, and I have followed the hounds a great many times, though I know you do not approve of ladies hunting; but still that is the fact, and I intend to try this Lizzie that you gentlemen are all so fond of; so please help me to mount, like a good friend as you are."

There was no more to be said; he placed her carefully on the saddle, looked to the bit and curb, gave the reins gently into her hand, and then mounted me. Just as we were moving off a footman came out with a slip of paper and message from the Lady Harriet. "Would they ask this question for her at Dr. Ashley's, and bring the answer?"

The village was about a mile off, and the doctor's house was the last in it. We went along gayly enough till we came to his gate. There was a short drive up to the house between tall evergreens.

Blantyre alighted at the gate, and was going to open it for Lady Anne, but she said, "I will wait for you here, and you can hang Auster's rein on the gate."

He looked at her doubtfully. "I will not be five minutes," he said.

"Oh, do not hurry yourself; Lizzie and I shall not run away from you."

He hung my rein on one of the iron spikes, and was soon hidden among the trees. Lizzie was standing quietly by the side of the road a few paces off, with her back to me. My young mistress was sitting easily with a loose rein, humming a little song. I listened to my rider's footsteps until they reached the house, and heard him knock at the door. There was a meadow on the opposite side of the road, the gate of which stood open; just then some cart horses and several young colts came trotting out in a very disorderly manner, while a boy behind was cracking a great whip. The colts were wild and frolicsome, and one of them bolted across the road and blundered up against Lizzie's hind legs, and whether it was the stupid colt, or the loud cracking of the whip, or both together, I cannot say, but she gave a violent kick, and dashed off into a headlong gallop. It was so sudden that Lady Anne was nearly unseated, but she soon recovered herself. I gave a loud, shrill neigh for help; again and again I neighed, pawing the ground impatiently, and tossing my head to get the rein loose. I had not long to wait. Blantyre came running to the gate; he looked anxiously about, and just caught sight of the flying figure, now far away on the road. In an instant he sprang to the saddle. I needed no whip, no spur, for I was as eager as my rider; he saw it, and giving me a free rein, and leaning a little forward, we dashed after them.

For about a mile and a half the road ran straight, and then bent to the right, after which it divided into two roads. Long before we came to the bend she was out of sight. Which way had she turned? A woman was standing at her garden gate, shading her eyes with her hand, and looking eagerly up the road. Scarcely drawing the rein, Blantyre shouted, "Which way?" "To the right!" cried the woman, pointing with her hand, and away we went up the right-hand road; then for a moment we caught sight of her; another bend and she was hidden again. Several times we caught glimpses, and then lost them. We scarcely seemed to gain ground upon them at all. An old road-mender was standing near a heap of stones, his shovel dropped and his hands raised. As we came near he made a sign to speak. Blantyre drew the rein a little. "To the common, to the common, sir; she has turned off there." I knew this common very well; it was for the most part very uneven ground, covered with heather and dark-green furze bushes, with here and there a scrubby old thorn-tree; there were also open spaces of fine short grass, with ant-hills and mole-turns everywhere; the worst place I ever knew for a headlong gallop.

We had hardly turned on the common, when we caught sight again of the green habit flying on before us. My lady's hat was gone, and her long brown hair was streaming behind her. Her head and body were thrown back, as if she were pulling with all her remaining strength, and as if that strength were nearly exhausted. It was clear that the roughness of the ground had very much lessened Lizzie's speed, and there seemed a chance that we might overtake her.

While we were on the highroad, Blantyre had given me my head; but now, with a light hand and a practiced eye, he guided me over the ground in such a masterly manner that my pace was scarcely slackened, and we were decidedly gaining on them.

About halfway across the heath there had been a wide dike recently cut, and the earth from the cutting was cast up roughly on the other side. Surely this would stop them! But no; with scarcely a pause Lizzie took the leap, stumbled among the rough clods and fell. Blantyre groaned, "Now, Auster, do your best!" He gave me a steady rein. I gathered myself well together and with one determined leap cleared both dike and bank.

Motionless among the heather, with her face to the earth, lay my poor young mistress. Blantyre kneeled down and called her name: there was no sound. Gently he turned her face upward: it was ghastly white and the eyes were closed. "Annie, dear Annie, do speak!" But there was no answer. He unbuttoned her habit, loosened her collar, felt her hands and wrist, then started up and looked wildly round him for help.

At no great distance there were two men cutting turf, who, seeing Lizzie running wild without a rider, had left their work to catch her.

Blantyre's halloo soon brought them to the spot. The foremost man seemed much troubled at the sight, and asked what he could do.

"Can you ride?"

"Well, sir, I bean't much of a horseman, but I'd risk my neck for the Lady Anne; she was uncommon good to my wife in the winter."

"Then mount this horse, my friend – your neck will be quite safe – and ride to the doctor's and ask him to come instantly; then on to the hall; tell them all that you know, and bid them send me the carriage, with Lady Anne's maid and help. I shall stay here."

"All right, sir, I'll do my best, and I pray God the dear young lady may open her eyes soon." Then, seeing the other man, he called out, "Here, Joe, run for some water, and tell my missis to come as quick as she can to the Lady Anne."

He then somehow scrambled into the saddle, and with a "Gee up" and a clap on my sides with both his legs, he started on his journey, making a little circuit to avoid the dike. He had no whip, which seemed to trouble him; but my pace soon cured that difficulty, and he found the best thing he could do was to stick to the saddle and hold me in, which he did manfully. I shook him as little as I could help, but once or twice on the rough ground he called out, "Steady! Woah! Steady!" On the highroad we were all right; and at the doctor's and the hall he did his errand like a good man and true. They asked him in to take a drop of something. "No, no," he said; "I'll be back to 'em again by a short cut through the fields, and be there afore the carriage."

There was a great deal of hurry and excitement after the news became known. I was just turned into my box; the saddle and bridle were taken off, and a cloth thrown over me.

Ginger was saddled and sent off in great haste for Lord George, and I soon heard the carriage roll out of the yard.

It seemed a long time before Ginger came back, and before we were left alone; and then she told me all that she had seen.

"I can't tell much," she said. "We went a gallop nearly all the way, and got there just as the doctor rode up. There was a woman sitting on the ground with the lady's head in her lap. The doctor poured something into her mouth, but all that I heard was, 'She is not dead.' Then I was led off by a man to a little distance. After awhile she was taken to the carriage, and we came home together. I heard my master say to a gentleman who stopped him to inquire, that he hoped no bones were broken, but that she had not spoken yet."

When Lord George took Ginger for hunting, York shook his head; he said it ought to be a steady hand to train a horse for the first season, and not a random rider like Lord George.

Ginger used to like it very much, but sometimes when she came back I could see that she had been very much strained, and now and then she gave a short cough. She had too much spirit to complain, but I could not help feeling anxious about her.

Two days after the accident Blantyre paid me a visit; he patted me and praised me very much; he told Lord George that he was sure the horse knew of Annie's danger as well as he did. "I could not have held him in if I would," said he, "she ought never to ride any other horse." I found by their conversation that my young mistress was now out of danger, and would soon be able to ride again. This was good news to me and I looked forward to a happy life.

25 Reuben Smith

Now I must say a little about Reuben Smith, who was left in charge of the stables when York went to London. No one more thoroughly understood his business than he did, and when he was all right

402

there could not be a more faithful or valuable man. He was gentle and very clever in his management of horses, and could doctor them almost as well as a farrier, for he had lived two years with a veterinary surgeon. He was a first-rate driver; he could take a four-in-hand or a tandem as easily as a pair. He was a handsome man, a good scholar, and had very pleasant manners. I believe everybody liked him; certainly the horses did. The only wonder was that he should be in an under situation and not in the place of a head coachman like York; but he had one great fault and that was the love of drink. He was not like some men, always at it; he used to keep steady for weeks or months together, and then he would break out and have a "bout" of it, as York called it, and be a disgrace to himself, a terror to his wife, and a nuisance to all that had to do with him. He was, however, so useful that two or three times York had hushed the matter up and kept it from the earl's knowledge; but one night, when Reuben had to drive a party home from a ball he was so drunk that he could not hold the reins, and a gentleman of the party had to mount the box and drive the ladies home. Of course, this could not be hidden, and Reuben was at once dismissed; his poor wife and little children had to turn out of the pretty cottage by the park gate and go where they could. Old Max told me all this, for it happened a good while ago; but shortly before Ginger and I came Smith had been taken back again. York had interceded for him with the earl, who is very kind-hearted, and the man had promised faithfully that he would never taste another drop as long as he lived there. He had kept his promise so well that York thought he might be safely trusted to fill his place while he was away, and he was so clever and honest that no one else seemed so well fitted for it.

It was now early in April, and the family was expected home some time in May. The light brougham was to be fresh done up, and as Colonel Blantyre was obliged to return to his regiment it was arranged that Smith should drive him to the town in it, and ride back; for this purpose he took the saddle with him, and I was chosen for the journey. At the station the colonel put some money into Smith's hand and bid him good-by, saying, "Take care of your young mistress, Reuben, and don't let Black Auster be hacked about by any random young prig that wants to ride him – keep him for the lady."

We left the carriage at the maker's, and Smith rode me to the White Lion, and ordered the hostler to feed me well, and have me ready for him at four o'clock. A nail in one of my front shoes had started as I came along, but the hostler did not notice it till just about four o'clock. Smith did not come into the yard till five, and then he said he should not leave till six, as he had met with some old friends. The man then told him of the nail, and asked if he should have the shoe looked to.

"No," said Smith, "that will be all right till we get home."

He spoke in a very loud, offhand way, and I thought it very unlike him not to see about the shoe, as he was generally wonderfully particular about loose nails in our shoes. He did not come at six nor seven, nor eight, and it was nearly nine o'clock before he called for me, and then it was with a loud, rough voice. He seemed in a very bad temper, and abused the hostler, though I could not tell what for.

The landlord stood at the door and said, "Have a care, Mr. Smith!" but he answered angrily with an oath; and almost before he was out of the town he began to gallop, frequently giving me a sharp cut with his whip, though I was going at full speed. The moon had not yet risen, and it was very dark. The roads were stony, having been recently mended; going over them at this pace, my shoe became looser, and as we neared the turnpike gate it came off.

If Smith had been in his right senses he would have been sensible of something wrong in my pace, but he was too drunk to notice.

Beyond the turnpike was a long piece of road, upon which fresh stones had just been laid – large sharp stones, over which no horse could be driven quickly without risk of danger. Over this road, with one shoe gone, I was forced to gallop at my utmost speed, my rider meanwhile cutting into me with his whip, and with wild curses urging me to go still faster. Of course my shoeless foot suffered dreadfully; the hoof was broken and split down to the very quick, and the inside was terribly cut by the sharpness of the stones.

This could not go on; no horse could keep his footing under such circumstances; the pain was too great. I stumbled, and fell with violence on both my knees. Smith was flung off by my fall, and, owing to the speed I was going at, he must have fallen with great force. I soon recovered my feet and limped to the side of the road, where it was free from stones. The moon had just risen above the hedge, and by its light I could see Smith lying a few yards beyond me. He did not rise; he made one slight effort to do so, and then there was a heavy groan. I could have groaned, too, for I was suffering intense pain both from my foot and knees; but horses are used to bear their pain in silence. I uttered no sound, but I stood there and listened. One more heavy groan from Smith; but though he now lay in the full moonlight I could see no motion. I could do nothing for him nor myself, but, oh! how I listened for the sound of horse, or wheels, or footsteps! The road was not much frequented, and at this time of the night we might stay for hours before help came to us. I stood watching and listening. It was a calm, sweet April night; there were no sounds but a few low notes of a nightingale, and nothing moved but the white clouds near the moon and a brown owl that flitted over the hedge. It made me think of the summer nights long ago, when I used to lie beside my mother in the green pleasant meadow at Farmer Grey's.

26 How it Ended

It must have been nearly midnight when I heard at a great distance the sound of a horse's feet. Sometimes the sound died away, then it grew clearer again and nearer. The road to Earlshall led through woods that belonged to the earl; the sound came in that direction, and I hoped it might be some one coming in search of us. As the sound came nearer and nearer I was almost sure I could distinguish Ginger's step; a little nearer still, and I could tell she was in the dog-cart. I neighed loudly, and was overjoyed to hear an answering neigh from Ginger, and men's voices. They came slowly over the stones, and stopped at the dark figure that lay upon the ground.

One of the men jumped out, and stooped down over it. "It is Reuben," he said, "and he does not stir!"

The other man followed, and bent over him. "He's dead," he said; "feel how cold his hands are."

They raised him up, but there was no life, and his hair was soaked with blood. They laid him down again, and came and looked at me. They soon saw my cut knees.

"Why, the horse has been down and thrown him! Who would have thought the black horse would have done that? Nobody thought he could fall. Reuben must have been lying here for hours! Odd, too, that the horse has not moved from the place."

Robert then attempted to lead me forward. I made a step, but almost fell again.

"Halloo! he's bad in his foot as well as his knees. Look here -his hoof is cut all to pieces; he might well come down, poor fellow! I tell you what, Ned, I'm afraid it hasn't been all right with Reuben. Just think of his riding a horse over these stones without a shoe! Why, if he had been in his right senses he would just as soon have tried to ride him over the moon. I'm afraid it has been the old thing over again. Poor Susan! she looked awfully pale when she came to my house to ask if he had not come home. She made believe she was not a bit anxious, and talked of a lot of things that might have kept him. But for all that she begged me to go and meet him. But what must we do? There's the horse to get home as well as the body, and that will be no easy matter."

Then followed a conversation between them, till it was agreed that Robert, as the groom, should lead me, and that Ned must take the body. It was a hard job to get it into the dog-cart, for there was no one to hold Ginger; but she knew as well as I did what was going on, and stood as still as a stone. I noticed that, because, if she had a fault, it was that she was impatient in standing.

Ned started off very slowly with his sad load, and Robert came and looked at my foot again; then he took his handkerchief and bound it closely round, and so he led me home. I shall never forget that night walk; it was more than three miles. Robert led me on very slowly, and I limped and hobbled on as well as I could with great pain. I am sure he was sorry for me, for he often patted and encouraged me, talking to me in a pleasant voice.

At last I reached my own box, and had some corn; and after Robert had wrapped up my knees in wet cloths, he tied up my foot in a bran poultice, to draw out the heat and cleanse it before the horse-doctor saw it in the morning, and I managed to get myself down on the straw, and slept in spite of the pain.

The next day after the farrier had examined my wounds, he said he hoped the joint was not injured; and if so, I should not be spoiled for work, but I should never lose the blemish. I believe they did the best to make a good cure, but it was a long and painful one. Proud flesh, as they called it, came up in my knees, and was burned out with caustic; and when at last it was healed, they put a blistering fluid over the front of both knees to bring all the hair off; they had some reason for this, and I suppose it was all right.

As Smith's death had been so sudden, and no one was there to see it, there was an inquest held. The landlord and hostler at the White Lion, with several other people, gave evidence that he was intoxicated when he started from the inn. The keeper of the toll-gate said he rode at a hard gallop through the gate; and my shoe was picked up among the stones, so that the case was quite plain to them, and I was cleared of all blame.

Everybody pitied Susan. She was nearly out of her mind; she kept saying over and over again, "Oh! he was so good – so good! It was all that cursed drink; why will they sell that cursed drink? Oh Reuben, Reuben!" So she went on till after he was buried; and then, as she had no home or relations, she, with her six little children, was obliged once more to leave the pleasant home by the tall oak-trees, and go into that great gloomy Union House.

Lesson 81
1. Read chapters 27, 28, and 29.
2. Take notes on major events.

27 Ruined and Going Downhill

As soon as my knees were sufficiently healed I was turned into a small meadow for a month or two; no other creature was there; and though I enjoyed the liberty and the sweet grass, yet I had been so long used to society that I felt very lonely. Ginger and I had become fast friends, and now I missed her company extremely. I often neighed when I heard horses' feet passing in the road, but I seldom got an answer; till one morning the gate was opened, and who should come in but dear old Ginger. The man slipped off her halter, and left her there. With a joyful whinny I trotted up to her; we were both glad to meet, but I soon found that it was not for our pleasure that she was brought to be with me. Her story would be too long to tell, but the end of it was that she had been ruined by hard riding, and was now turned off to see what rest would do.

Lord George was young and would take no warning; he was a hard rider, and would hunt whenever he could get the chance, quite careless of his horse. Soon after I left the stable there was a steeplechase, and he determined to ride. Though the groom told him she was a little strained, and was not fit for the race, he did not believe it, and on the day of the race urged Ginger to keep up with the foremost riders. With her high spirit, she strained herself to the utmost; she came in with the first three horses, but her wind was touched, besides which he was too heavy for her, and her back was strained. "And so," she said, "here we are, ruined in the prime of our youth and strength, you by a drunkard, and I by a fool; it is very hard." We both felt in ourselves that we were not what we had been. However, that did not spoil the pleasure we had in each other's company; we did not gallop about as we once did, but we used to feed, and lie down together, and stand for hours under one of the shady lime-trees with our heads close to each other; and so we passed our time till the family returned from town.

One day we saw the earl come into the meadow, and York was with him. Seeing who it was, we stood still under our lime-tree, and let them come up to us. They examined us carefully. The earl seemed much annoyed.

"There is three hundred pounds flung away for no earthly use," said he; "but what I care most for is that these horses of my old friend, who thought they would find a good home with me, are ruined. The mare shall have a twelve-month's run, and we shall see what that will do for her; but the black one, he must be sold; 'tis a great pity, but I could not have knees like these in my stables."

"No, my lord, of course not," said York; "but he might get a place where appearance is not of much consequence, and still be well treated. I know a man in Bath, the master of some livery stables, who often wants a good horse at a low figure; I know he looks well after his horses. The inquest cleared the horse's character, and your lordship's recommendation, or mine, would be sufficient warrant for him."

"You had better write to him, York. I should be more particular about the place than the money he would fetch."

After this they left us.

"They'll soon take you away," said Ginger, "and I shall lose the only friend I have, and most likely we shall never see each other again. 'Tis a hard world!"

About a week after this Robert came into the field with a halter, which he slipped over my head, and led me away. There was no leave-taking of Ginger; we neighed to each other as I was led off, and she trotted anxiously along by the hedge, calling to me as long as she could hear the sound of my feet.

Through the recommendation of York, I was bought by the master of the livery stables. I had to go by train, which was new to me, and required a good deal of courage the first time; but as I found the puffing, rushing, whistling, and, more than all, the trembling of the horse-box in which I stood did me no real harm, I soon took it quietly.

When I reached the end of my journey I found myself in a tolerably comfortable stable, and well attended to. These stables were not so airy and pleasant as those I had been used to. The stalls were laid on a slope instead of being level, and as my head was kept tied to the manger, I was obliged always to stand on the slope, which was very fatiguing. Men do not seem to know yet that horses can do more work if they can stand comfortably and can turn about; however, I was well fed and well cleaned, and, on the whole, I think our master took as much care of us as he could. He kept a good many horses and carriages of different kinds for hire. Sometimes his own men drove them; at others, the horse and chaise were let to gentlemen or ladies who drove themselves.

28 A Job Horse and His Drivers

Hitherto I had always been driven by people who at least knew how to drive; but in this place I was to get my experience of all the different kinds of bad and ignorant driving to which we horses are subjected; for I was a "job horse", and was let out to all sorts of people who wished to hire me; and as I was good-tempered and gentle, I think I was oftener let out to the ignorant drivers than some of the other horses, because I could be depended upon. It would take a long time to tell of all the different styles in which I was driven, but I will mention a few of them.

First, there were the tight-rein drivers – men who seemed to think that all depended on holding the reins as hard as they could, never relaxing the pull on the horse's mouth, or giving him the least liberty of movement. They are always talking about "keeping the horse well in hand", and "holding a horse up", just as if a horse was not made to hold himself up.

Some poor, broken-down horses, whose mouths have been made hard and insensible by just such drivers as these, may, perhaps, find some support in it; but for a horse who can depend upon his own legs, and who has a tender mouth and is easily guided, it is not only tormenting, but it is stupid.

Then there are the loose-rein drivers, who let the reins lie easily on our backs, and their own hand rest lazily on their knees. Of course, such gentlemen have no control over a horse, if anything happens suddenly. If a horse shies, or starts, or stumbles, they are nowhere, and cannot help the horse or themselves till the mischief is done. Of course, for myself I had no objection to it, as I was not in the habit either of starting or stumbling, and had only been used to depend on my driver for guidance and encouragement. Still, one likes to feel the rein a little in going downhill, and likes to know that one's driver is not gone to sleep.

Besides, a slovenly way of driving gets a horse into bad and often lazy habits, and when he changes hands he has to be whipped out of them with more or less pain and trouble. Squire Gordon always kept us to our best paces and our best manners. He said that spoiling a horse and letting him get into bad habits was just as cruel as spoiling a child, and both had to suffer for it afterward.

Besides, these drivers are often careless altogether, and will attend to anything else more than their horses. I went out in the phaeton one day with one of them; he had a lady and two children behind. He flopped the reins about as we started, and of course gave me several unmeaning cuts with the whip, though I was fairly off. There had been a good deal of road-mending going on, and even where the stones were not freshly laid down there were a great many loose ones about. My driver was laughing and joking with the lady and the children, and talking about the country to the right and the left; but he never thought it worth while to keep an eye on his horse or to drive on the smoothest parts of the road; and so it easily happened that I got a stone in one of my fore feet.

Now, if Mr. Gordon or John, or in fact any good driver, had been there, he would have seen that something was wrong before I had gone three paces. Or even if it had been dark a practiced hand would have felt by the rein that there was something wrong in the step, and they would have got down and picked out the stone. But this man went on laughing and talking, while at every step the stone became more firmly wedged between my shoe and the frog of my foot. The stone was sharp on the inside and round on the outside, which, as every one knows, is the most dangerous kind that a horse can pick up, at the same time cutting his foot and making him most liable to stumble and fall.

Whether the man was partly blind or only very careless I can't say, but he drove me with that stone in my foot for a good half-mile before he saw anything. By that time I was going so lame with the pain that at last he saw it, and called out, "Well, here's a go! Why, they have sent us out with a lame horse! What a shame!"

He then chucked the reins and flipped about with the whip, saying, "Now, then, it's no use playing the old soldier with me; there's the journey to go, and it's no use turning lame and lazy."

Just at this time a farmer came riding up on a brown cob. He lifted his hat and pulled up.

"I beg your pardon, sir," he said, "but I think there is something the matter with your horse; he goes very much as if he had a stone in his shoe. If you will allow me I will look at his feet; these loose scattered stones are confounded dangerous things for the horses."

"He's a hired horse," said my driver. "I don't know what's the matter with him, but it is a great shame to send out a lame beast like this."

The farmer dismounted, and slipping his rein over his arm at once took up my near foot.

"Bless me, there's a stone! Lame! I should think so!"

At first he tried to dislodge it with his hand, but as it was now very tightly wedged he drew a stone-pick out of his pocket, and very carefully and with some trouble got it out. Then holding it up he said, "There, that's the stone your horse had picked up. It is a wonder he did not fall down and break his knees into the bargain!"

"Well, to be sure!" said my driver; "that is a queer thing! I never knew that horses picked up stones before."

"Didn't you?" said the farmer rather contemptuously; "but they do, though, and the best of them will do it, and can't help it sometimes on such roads as these. And if you don't want to lame your horse you must look sharp and get them out quickly. This foot is very much bruised," he said, setting it gently down and patting me. "If I might advise, sir, you had better drive him gently for awhile; the foot is a good deal hurt, and the lameness will not go off directly."

Then mounting his cob and raising his hat to the lady he trotted off.

When he was gone my driver began to flop the reins about and whip the harness, by which I understood that I was to go on, which of course I did, glad that the stone was gone, but still in a good deal of pain.

This was the sort of experience we job horses often came in for.

29 Cockneys

Then there is the steam-engine style of driving; these drivers were mostly people from towns, who never had a horse of their own and generally traveled by rail.

They always seemed to think that a horse was something like a steam-engine, only smaller. At any rate, they think that if only they pay for it a horse is bound to go just as far and just as fast and with just as heavy a load as they please. And be the roads heavy and muddy, or dry and good; be they stony or smooth, uphill or downhill, it is all the same – on, on, on, one must go, at the same pace, with no relief and no consideration.

These people never think of getting out to walk up a steep hill. Oh, no, they have paid to ride, and ride they will! The horse? Oh, he's used to it! What were horses made for, if not to drag people uphill? Walk! A good joke indeed! And so the whip is plied and the rein is chucked and often a rough, scolding voice cries out, "Go along, you lazy beast!" And then another slash of the whip, when all the time we are doing our very best to get along, uncomplaining and obedient, though often sorely harassed and down-hearted.

This steam-engine style of driving wears us up faster than any other kind. I would far rather go twenty miles with a good considerate driver than I would go ten with some of these; it would take less out of me.

Another thing, they scarcely ever put on the brake, however steep the downhill may be, and thus bad accidents sometimes happen; or if they do put it on, they often forget to take it off at the bottom of the hill, and more than once I have had to pull halfway up the next hill, with one of the wheels held by the brake, before my driver chose to think about it; and that is a terrible strain on a horse.

Then these cockneys, instead of starting at an easy pace, as a gentleman would do, generally set off at full speed from the very stable-yard; and when they want to stop, they first whip us, and then pull up so suddenly that we are nearly thrown on our haunches, and our mouths jagged with the bit – they call that pulling up with a dash; and when they turn a corner they do it as sharply as if there were no right side or wrong side of the road.

I well remember one spring evening I and Rory had been out for the day. (Rory was the horse that mostly went with me when a pair was ordered, and a good honest fellow he was.) We had our own driver, and as he was always considerate and gentle with us, we had a very pleasant day. We were coming home at a good smart pace, about twilight. Our road turned sharp to the left; but as we were

410

close to the hedge on our own side, and there was plenty of room to pass, our driver did not pull us in. As we neared the corner I heard a horse and two wheels coming rapidly down the hill toward us. The hedge was high, and I could see nothing, but the next moment we were upon each other. Happily for me, I was on the side next the hedge. Rory was on the left side of the pole, and had not even a shaft to protect him. The man who was driving was making straight for the corner, and when he came in sight of us he had no time to pull over to his own side. The whole shock came upon Rory. The gig shaft ran right into the chest, making him stagger back with a cry that I shall never forget. The other horse was thrown upon his haunches and one shaft broken. It turned out that it was a horse from our own stables, with the high-wheeled gig that the young men were so fond of.

The driver was one of those random, ignorant fellows, who don't even know which is their own side of the road, or, if they know, don't care. And there was poor Rory with his flesh torn open and bleeding, and the blood streaming down. They said if it had been a little more to one side it would have killed him; and a good thing for him, poor fellow, if it had.

As it was, it was a long time before the wound healed, and then he was sold for coal-carting; and what that is, up and down those steep hills, only horses know. Some of the sights I saw there, where a horse had to come downhill with a heavily loaded two-wheel cart behind him, on which no brake could be placed, make me sad even now to think of.

After Rory was disabled I often went in the carriage with a mare named Peggy, who stood in the next stall to mine. She was a strong, well-made animal, of a bright dun color, beautifully dappled, and with a dark-brown mane and tail. There was no high breeding about her, but she was very pretty and remarkably sweet-tempered and willing. Still, there was an anxious look about her eye, by which I knew that she had some trouble. The first time we went out together I thought she had a very odd pace; she seemed to go partly a trot, partly a canter, three or four paces, and then a little jump forward.

It was very unpleasant for any horse who pulled with her, and made me quite fidgety. When we got home I asked her what made her go in that odd, awkward way.

"Ah," she said in a troubled manner, "I know my paces are very bad, but what can I do? It really is not my fault; it is just because my legs are so short. I stand nearly as high as you, but your legs are a good three inches longer above your knee than mine, and of course you can take a much longer step and go much faster. You see I did not make myself. I wish I could have done so; I would have had long legs then. All my troubles come from my short legs," said Peggy, in a desponding tone.

"But how is it," I said, "when you are so strong and good-tempered and willing?"

"Why, you see," said she, "men will go so fast, and if one can't keep up to other horses it is nothing but whip, whip, whip, all the time. And so I have had to keep up as I could, and have got into this ugly shuffling pace. It was not always so; when I lived with my first master I always went a good regular trot, but then he was not in such a hurry. He was a young clergyman in the country, and a good, kind master he was. He had two churches a good way apart, and a great deal of work, but he never scolded or whipped me for not going faster. He was very fond of me. I only wish I was with him now; but he had to leave and go to a large town, and then I was sold to a farmer.

"Some farmers, you know, are capital masters; but I think this one was a low sort of man. He cared nothing about good horses or good driving; he only cared for going fast. I went as fast as I could, but that would not do, and he was always whipping; so I got into this way of making a spring forward to keep up. On market nights he used to stay very late at the inn, and then drive home at a gallop.

"One dark night he was galloping home as usual, when all of a sudden the wheel came against some great heavy thing in the road, and turned the gig over in a minute. He was thrown out and his arm broken, and some of his ribs, I think. At any rate, it was the end of my living with him, and I was not sorry. But you see it will be the same everywhere for me, if men must go so fast. I wish my legs were longer!"

Poor Peggy! I was very sorry for her, and I could not comfort her, for I knew how hard it was upon slow-paced horses to be put with fast ones; all the whipping comes to their share, and they can't help it.

She was often used in the phaeton, and was very much liked by some of the ladies, because she was so gentle; and some time after this she was sold to two ladies who drove themselves, and wanted a safe, good horse.

I met her several times out in the country, going a good steady pace, and looking as gay and contented as a horse could be. I was very glad to see her, for she deserved a good place.

After she left us another horse came in her stead. He was young, and had a bad name for shying and starting, by which he had lost a good place. I asked him what made him shy.

"Well, I hardly know," he said. "I was timid when I was young, and was a good deal frightened several times, and if I saw anything strange I used to turn and look at it – you see, with our blinkers one can't see or understand what a thing is unless one looks round – and then my master always gave me a whipping, which of course made me start on, and did not make me less afraid. I think if he would have let me just look at things quietly, and see that there was nothing to hurt me, it would have been all right, and I should have got used to them. One day an old gentleman was riding with him, and a large piece of white paper or rag blew across just on one side of me. I shied and started forward. My master as usual whipped me smartly, but the old man cried out, 'You're wrong! you're wrong! You should never whip a horse for shying; he shies because he is frightened, and you only frighten him more and make the habit worse.' So I suppose all men don't do so. I am sure I don't want to shy for the sake of it; but how should one know what is dangerous and what is not, if one is never allowed to get used to anything? I am never afraid of what I know. Now I was brought up in a park where there were deer; of course I knew them as well as I did a sheep or a cow, but they are not common, and I know many sensible horses who are frightened at them, and who kick up quite a shindy before they will pass a paddock where there are deer."

I knew what my companion said was true, and I wished that every young horse had as good masters as Farmer Grey and Squire Gordon.

Of course we sometimes came in for good driving here. I remember one morning I was put into the light gig, and taken to a house in Pulteney Street. Two gentlemen came out; the taller of them came round to my head; he looked at the bit and bridle, and just shifted the collar with his hand, to see if it fitted comfortably.

"Do you consider this horse wants a curb?" he said to the hostler.

"Well," said the man, "I should say he would go just as well without; he has an uncommon good mouth, and though he has a fine spirit he has no vice; but we generally find people like the curb."

"I don't like it," said the gentleman; "be so good as to take it off, and put the rein in at the cheek. An easy mouth is a great thing on a long journey, is it not, old fellow?" he said, patting my neck.

Then he took the reins, and they both got up. I can remember now how quietly he turned me round, and then with a light feel of the rein, and drawing the whip gently across my back, we were off.

I arched my neck and set off at my best pace. I found I had some one behind me who knew how a good horse ought to be driven. It seemed like old times again, and made me feel quite gay.

This gentleman took a great liking to me, and after trying me several times with the saddle he prevailed upon my master to sell me to a friend of his, who wanted a safe, pleasant horse for riding. And so it came to pass that in the summer I was sold to Mr. Barry.

Lesson 82

1. Read chapters 30, 31, and 32.
2. Take notes on major events.

Vocabulary

1. Write a synonym, a word of similar meaning, for each of the following words. (Answers) (Hint: Your vocabulary words might come in handy.)
   - interruption, disorderly, eagerness, full, understand, echoing, increasing, knobby, trench

30 A Thief

My new master was an unmarried man. He lived at Bath, and was much engaged in business. His doctor advised him to take horse exercise, and for this purpose he bought me. He hired a stable a short distance from his lodgings, and engaged a man named Filcher as groom. My master knew very little about horses, but he treated me well, and I should have had a good and easy place but for circumstances of which he was ignorant. He ordered the best hay with plenty of oats, crushed beans, and bran, with vetches, or rye grass, as the man might think needful. I heard the master give the order, so I knew there was plenty of good food, and I thought I was well off.

For a few days all went on well. I found that my groom understood his business. He kept the stable clean and airy, and he groomed me thoroughly; and was never otherwise than gentle. He had been an hostler in one of the great hotels in Bath. He had given that up, and now cultivated fruit and vegetables for the market, and his wife bred and fattened poultry and rabbits for sale. After awhile it seemed to me that my oats came very short; I had the beans, but bran was mixed with them instead of oats, of which there were very few; certainly not more than a quarter of what there should have been. In two or three weeks this began to tell upon my strength and spirits. The grass food, though very good, was not the thing to keep up my condition without corn. However, I could not complain, nor make known my wants. So it went on for about two months; and I wondered that my master did not see that something was the matter. However, one afternoon he rode out into the country to see a friend of his, a gentleman farmer, who lived on the road to Wells.

This gentleman had a very quick eye for horses; and after he had welcomed his friend he said, casting his eye over me:

"It seems to me, Barry, that your horse does not look so well as he did when you first had him; has he been well?"

"Yes, I believe so," said my master; "but he is not nearly so lively as he was; my groom tells me that horses are always dull and weak in the autumn, and that I must expect it."

"Autumn, fiddlesticks!" said the farmer. "Why, this is only August; and with your light work and good food he ought not to go down like this, even if it was autumn. How do you feed him?"

My master told him. The other shook his head slowly, and began to feel me over.

"I can't say who eats your corn, my dear fellow, but I am much mistaken if your horse gets it. Have you ridden very fast?"

"No, very gently."

"Then just put your hand here," said he, passing his hand over my neck and shoulder; "he is as warm and damp as a horse just come up from grass. I advise you to look into your stable a little more. I hate to be suspicious, and, thank heaven, I have no cause to be, for I can trust my men, present or absent; but there are mean scoundrels, wicked enough to rob a dumb beast of his food. You must look into it." And turning to his man, who had come to take me, "Give this horse a right good feed of bruised oats, and don't stint him."

"Dumb beasts!" Yes, we are; but if I could have spoken I could have told my master where his oats went to. My groom used to come every morning about six o'clock, and with him a little boy, who always had a covered basket with him. He used to go with his father into the harness-room, where the corn was kept, and I could see them, when the door stood ajar, fill a little bag with oats out of the bin, and then he used to be off.

Five or six mornings after this, just as the boy had left the stable, the door was pushed open, and a policeman walked in, holding the child tight by the arm; another policeman followed, and locked the door on the inside, saying, "Show me the place where your father keeps his rabbits' food."

The boy looked very frightened and began to cry; but there was no escape, and he led the way to the corn-bin. Here the policeman found another empty bag like that which was found full of oats in the boy's basket.

Filcher was cleaning my feet at the time, but they soon saw him, and though he blustered a good deal they walked him off to the "lock-up", and his boy with him. I heard afterward that the boy was not held to be guilty, but the man was sentenced to prison for two months.

31 A Humbug

My master was not immediately suited, but in a few days my new groom came. He was a tall, good-looking fellow enough; but if ever there was a humbug in the shape of a groom Alfred Smirk was the man. He was very civil to me, and never used me ill; in fact, he did a great deal of stroking and patting when his master was there to see it. He always brushed my mane and tail with water and my hoofs with oil before he brought me to the door, to make me look smart; but as to cleaning my feet or looking to my shoes, or grooming me thoroughly, he thought no more of that than if I had been a cow. He left my bit rusty, my saddle damp, and my crupper stiff.

Alfred Smirk considered himself very handsome; he spent a great deal of time about his hair, whiskers and necktie, before a little looking-glass in the harness-room. When his master was speaking to him it was always, "Yes, sir; yes, sir" – touching his hat at every word; and every one thought he was a very nice young man and that Mr. Barry was very fortunate to meet with him. I should say he was the laziest, most conceited fellow I ever came near. Of course, it was a great thing not to be ill-used, but then a horse wants more than that. I had a loose box, and might have been very comfortable if he had not been too indolent to clean it out. He never took all the straw away, and the smell from what lay underneath was very bad; while the strong vapors that rose made my eyes smart and inflame, and I did not feel the same appetite for my food.

One day his master came in and said, "Alfred, the stable smells rather strong; should not you give that stall a good scrub and throw down plenty of water?"

"Well, sir," he said, touching his cap, "I'll do so if you please, sir; but it is rather dangerous, sir, throwing down water in a horse's box; they are very apt to take cold, sir. I should not like to do him an injury, but I'll do it if you please, sir."

"Well," said his master, "I should not like him to take cold; but I don't like the smell of this stable. Do you think the drains are all right?"

"Well, sir, now you mention it, I think the drain does sometimes send back a smell; there may be something wrong, sir."

"Then send for the bricklayer and have it seen to," said his master.

"Yes, sir, I will."

The bricklayer came and pulled up a great many bricks, but found nothing amiss; so he put down some lime and charged the master five shillings, and the smell in my box was as bad as ever. But that was not all: standing as I did on a quantity of moist straw my feet grew unhealthy and tender, and the master used to say:

"I don't know what is the matter with this horse; he goes very fumble-footed. I am sometimes afraid he will stumble."

"Yes, sir," said Alfred, "I have noticed the same myself, when I have exercised him."

Now the fact was that he hardly ever did exercise me, and when the master was busy I often stood for days together without stretching my legs at all, and yet being fed just as high as if I were at hard work. This often disordered my health, and made me sometimes heavy and dull, but more often restless and feverish. He never even gave me a meal of green food or a bran mash, which would have cooled me, for he was altogether as ignorant as he was conceited; and then, instead of exercise or change of food, I had to take horse balls and draughts; which, beside the nuisance of having them poured down my throat, used to make me feel ill and uncomfortable.

One day my feet were so tender that, trotting over some fresh stones with my master on my back, I made two such serious stumbles that, as he came down Lansdown into the city, he stopped at the farrier's, and asked him to see what was the matter with me. The man took up my feet one by one and examined them; then standing up and dusting his hands one against the other, he said:

"Your horse has got the 'thrush', and badly, too; his feet are very tender; it is fortunate that he has not been down. I wonder your groom has not seen to it before. This is the sort of thing we find in foul stables, where the litter is never properly cleaned out. If you will send him here to-morrow I will attend to the hoof, and I will direct your man how to apply the liniment which I will give him."

The next day I had my feet thoroughly cleansed and stuffed with tow soaked in some strong lotion; and an unpleasant business it was.

The farrier ordered all the litter to be taken out of my box day by day, and the floor kept very clean. Then I was to have bran mashes, a little green food, and not so much corn, till my feet were well again. With this treatment I soon regained my spirits; but Mr. Barry was so much disgusted at being twice deceived by his grooms that he determined to give up keeping a horse, and to hire when he wanted one. I was therefore kept till my feet were quite sound, and was then sold again.

32 A Horse Fair

No doubt a horse fair is a very amusing place to those who have nothing to lose; at any rate, there is plenty to see.

Long strings of young horses out of the country, fresh from the marshes; and droves of shaggy little Welsh ponies, no higher than Merrylegs; and hundreds of cart horses of all sorts, some of them with their long tails braided up and tied with scarlet cord; and a good many like myself, handsome and high-bred, but fallen into the middle class, through some accident or blemish, unsoundness of wind, or some other complaint. There were some splendid animals quite in their prime, and fit for anything; they were throwing out their legs and showing off their paces in high style, as they were trotted out with a leading rein, the groom running by the side. But round in the background there were a number of poor things, sadly broken down with hard work, with their knees knuckling over and their hind legs swinging out at every step, and there were some very dejected-looking old horses, with the under lip hanging down and the ears lying back heavily, as if there were no more pleasure in life, and no more hope; there were some so thin you might see all their ribs, and some with old sores on their backs and hips. These were sad sights for a horse to look upon, who knows not but he may come to the same state.

There was a great deal of bargaining, of running up and beating down; and if a horse may speak his mind so far as he understands, I should say there were more lies told and more trickery at that horse fair than a clever man could give an account of. I was put with two or three other strong, useful-looking horses, and a good many people came to look at us. The gentlemen always turned from me when they saw my broken knees; though the man who had me swore it was only a slip in the stall.

The first thing was to pull my mouth open, then to look at my eyes, then feel all the way down my legs, and give me a hard feel of the skin and flesh, and then try my paces. It was wonderful what a difference there was in the way these things were done. Some did it in a rough, offhand way, as if one was only a piece of wood; while others would take their hands gently over one's body, with a pat now and then, as much as to say, "By your leave." Of course I judged a good deal of the buyers by their manners to myself.

There was one man, I thought, if he would buy me, I should be happy. He was not a gentleman, nor yet one of the loud, flashy sort that call themselves so. He was rather a small man, but well made, and quick in all his motions. I knew in a moment by the way he handled me, that he was used to horses; he spoke gently, and his gray eye had a kindly, cheery look in it. It may seem strange to say – but it is true all the same – that the clean, fresh smell there was about him made me take to him; no smell of old beer and tobacco, which I hated, but a fresh smell as if he had come out of a hayloft. He offered twenty-three pounds for me, but that was refused, and he walked away. I looked after him, but he was gone, and a very hard-looking, loud-voiced man came. I was dreadfully afraid he would have me; but he walked off. One or two more came who did not mean business. Then the hard-faced man came back again and offered twenty-three pounds. A very close bargain was being driven, for my salesman began to think he should not get all he asked, and must come down; but just then the gray-eyed man came back again. I could not help reaching out my head toward him. He stroked my face kindly.

"Well, old chap," he said, "I think we should suit each other. I'll give twenty-four for him."

"Say twenty-five and you shall have him."

"Twenty-four ten," said my friend, in a very decided tone, "and not another sixpence – yes or no?"

"Done," said the salesman; "and you may depend upon it there's a monstrous deal of quality in that horse, and if you want him for cab work he's a bargain."

The money was paid on the spot, and my new master took my halter, and led me out of the fair to an inn, where he had a saddle and bridle ready. He gave me a good feed of oats and stood by while I ate it, talking to himself and talking to me. Half an hour after we were on our way to London, through pleasant lanes and country roads, until we came into the great London thoroughfare, on which we traveled steadily, till in the twilight we reached the great city. The gas lamps were already lighted; there were streets to the right, and streets to the left, and streets crossing each other, for mile upon mile. I thought we should never come to the end of them. At last, in passing through one, we came to a long cab stand, when my rider called out in a cheery voice, "Good-night, governor!"

"Halloo!" cried a voice. "Have you got a good one?"

"I think so," replied my owner.

"I wish you luck with him."

"Thank you, governor," and he rode on. We soon turned up one of the side streets, and about halfway up that we turned into a very narrow street, with rather poor-looking houses on one side, and what seemed to be coach-houses and stables on the other.

My owner pulled up at one of the houses and whistled. The door flew open, and a young woman, followed by a little girl and boy, ran out. There was a very lively greeting as my rider dismounted.

"Now, then, Harry, my boy, open the gates, and mother will bring us the lantern."

The next minute they were all standing round me in a small stable-yard.

"Is he gentle, father?"

"Yes, Dolly, as gentle as your own kitten; come and pat him."

At once the little hand was patting about all over my shoulder without fear. How good it felt!

"Let me get him a bran mash while you rub him down," said the mother.

"Do, Polly, it's just what he wants; and I know you've got a beautiful mash ready for me."

"Sausage dumpling and apple turnover!" shouted the boy, which set them all laughing. I was led into a comfortable, clean-smelling stall, with plenty of dry straw, and after a capital supper I lay down, thinking I was going to be happy.

Lesson 83

1. Read chapters 33 and 34.
2. Take notes on major events.

33 A London Cab Horse

Jeremiah Barker was my new master's name, but as every one called him Jerry, I shall do the same. Polly, his wife, was just as good a match as a man could have. She was a plump, trim, tidy little woman, with smooth, dark hair, dark eyes, and a merry little mouth. The boy was twelve years old, a tall, frank, good-tempered lad; and little Dorothy (Dolly they called her) was her mother over again, at eight years old. They were all wonderfully fond of each other; I never knew such a happy, merry family before or since. Jerry had a cab of his own, and two horses, which he drove and attended to himself. His other horse was a tall, white, rather large-boned animal called "Captain". He was old now, but when he was young he must have been splendid; he had still a proud way of holding his head and arching his neck; in fact, he was a high-bred, fine-mannered, noble old horse, every inch of him. He told me that in his early youth he went to the Crimean War; he belonged to an officer in the cavalry, and used to lead the regiment. I will tell more of that hereafter.

The next morning, when I was well-groomed, Polly and Dolly came into the yard to see me and make friends. Harry had been helping his father since the early morning, and had stated his opinion that I should turn out a "regular brick". Polly brought me a slice of apple, and Dolly a piece of bread, and made as much of me as if I had been the "Black Beauty" of olden time. It was a great treat to be petted again and talked to in a gentle voice, and I let them see as well as I could that I wished to be friendly. Polly thought I was very handsome, and a great deal too good for a cab, if it was not for the broken knees.

"Of course there's no one to tell us whose fault that was," said Jerry, "and as long as I don't know I shall give him the benefit of the doubt; for a firmer, neater stepper I never rode. We'll call him 'Jack', after the old one – shall we, Polly?"

"Do," she said, "for I like to keep a good name going."

Captain went out in the cab all the morning. Harry came in after school to feed me and give me water. In the afternoon I was put into the cab. Jerry took as much pains to see if the collar and bridle fitted comfortably as if he had been John Manly over again. When the crupper was let out a hole or two it all fitted well. There was no check-rein, no curb, nothing but a plain ring snaffle. What a blessing that was!

After driving through the side street we came to the large cab stand where Jerry had said "Good-night". On one side of this wide street were high houses with wonderful shop fronts, and on the other was an old church and churchyard, surrounded by iron palisades. Alongside these iron rails a number of cabs were drawn up, waiting for passengers; bits of hay were lying about on the ground; some of the men were standing together talking; some were sitting on their boxes reading the newspaper; and one or two were feeding their horses with bits of hay, and giving them a drink of water. We pulled up in the rank at the back of the last cab. Two or three men came round and began to look at me and pass their remarks.

"Very good for a funeral," said one.

"Too smart-looking," said another, shaking his head in a very wise way; "you'll find out something wrong one of these fine mornings, or my name isn't Jones."

"Well," said Jerry pleasantly, "I suppose I need not find it out till it finds me out, eh? And if so, I'll keep up my spirits a little longer."

Then there came up a broad-faced man, dressed in a great gray coat with great gray cape and great white buttons, a gray hat, and a blue comforter loosely tied round his neck; his hair was gray, too; but he was a jolly-looking fellow, and the other men made way for him. He looked me all over, as if he had been going to buy me; and then straightening himself up with a grunt, he said, "He's the right sort for you, Jerry; I don't care what you gave for him, he'll be worth it." Thus my character was established on the stand.

This man's name was Grant, but he was called "Gray Grant", or "Governor Grant". He had been the longest on that stand of any of the men, and he took it upon himself to settle matters and stop disputes. He was generally a good-humored, sensible man; but if his temper was a little out, as it was sometimes when he had drunk too much, nobody liked to come too near his fist, for he could deal a very heavy blow.

The first week of my life as a cab horse was very trying. I had never been used to London, and the noise, the hurry, the crowds of horses, carts, and carriages that I had to make my way through made me feel anxious and harassed; but I soon found that I could perfectly trust my driver, and then I made myself easy and got used to it.

Jerry was as good a driver as I had ever known, and what was better, he took as much thought for his horses as he did for himself. He soon found out that I was willing to work and do my best, and he never laid the whip on me unless it was gently drawing the end of it over my back when I was to go on; but generally I knew this quite well by the way in which he took up the reins, and I believe his whip was more frequently stuck up by his side than in his hand.

In a short time I and my master understood each other as well as horse and man can do. In the stable, too, he did all that he could for our comfort. The stalls were the old-fashioned style, too much on the slope; but he had two movable bars fixed across the back of our stalls, so that at night, and when we were resting, he just took off our halters and put up the bars, and thus we could turn about and stand whichever way we pleased, which is a great comfort.

Jerry kept us very clean, and gave us as much change of food as he could, and always plenty of it; and not only that, but he always gave us plenty of clean fresh water, which he allowed to stand by us both night and day, except of course when we came in warm. Some people say that a horse ought not to drink all he likes; but I know if we are allowed to drink when we want it we drink only a little at a time, and it does us a great deal more good than swallowing down half a bucketful at a time, because we have been left without till we are thirsty and miserable. Some grooms will go home to their beer and leave us for hours with our dry hay and oats and nothing to moisten them; then of course we gulp down too much at once, which helps to spoil our breathing and sometimes chills our stomachs. But the best thing we had here was our Sundays for rest; we worked so hard in the week that I do not think we could have kept up to it but for that day; besides, we had then time to enjoy each other's company. It was on these days that I learned my companion's history.

34 An Old War Horse

Captain had been broken in and trained for an army horse; his first owner was an officer of cavalry going out to the Crimean war. He said he quite enjoyed the training with all the other horses, trotting together, turning together, to the right hand or the left, halting at the word of command, or dashing forward at full speed at the sound of the trumpet or signal of the officer. He was, when young, a dark, dappled iron-gray, and considered very handsome. His master, a young, high-spirited gentleman, was very fond of him, and treated him from the first with the greatest care and kindness. He told me he thought the life of an army horse was very pleasant; but when it came to being sent abroad over the sea in a great ship, he almost changed his mind.

"That part of it," said he, "was dreadful! Of course we could not walk off the land into the ship; so they were obliged to put strong straps under our bodies, and then we were lifted off our legs in spite of our struggles, and were swung through the air over the water, to the deck of the great vessel. There we were placed in small close stalls, and never for a long time saw the sky, or were able to stretch our legs. The ship sometimes rolled about in high winds, and we were knocked about, and felt bad enough.

"However, at last it came to an end, and we were hauled up, and swung over again to the land; we were very glad, and snorted and neighed for joy, when we once more felt firm ground under our feet.

"We soon found that the country we had come to was very different from our own and that we had many hardships to endure besides the fighting; but many of the men were so fond of their horses that they did everything they could to make them comfortable in spite of snow, wet, and all things out of order."

"But what about the fighting?" said I, "was not that worse than anything else?"

"Well," said he, "I hardly know; we always liked to hear the trumpet sound, and to be called out, and were impatient to start off, though sometimes we had to stand for hours, waiting for the word of command; and when the word was given we used to spring forward as gayly and eagerly as if there were no cannon balls, bayonets, or bullets. I believe so long as we felt our rider firm in the saddle, and his hand steady on the bridle, not one of us gave way to fear, not even when the terrible bomb-shells whirled through the air and burst into a thousand pieces.

"I, with my noble master, went into many actions together without a wound; and though I saw horses shot down with bullets, pierced through with lances, and gashed with fearful saber-cuts; though we left them dead on the field, or dying in the agony of their wounds, I don't think I feared for myself. My master's cheery voice, as he encouraged his men, made me feel as if he and I could not be killed. I had such perfect trust in him that while he was guiding me I was ready to charge up to the very cannon's mouth. I saw many brave men cut down, many fall mortally wounded from their saddles. I had heard the cries and groans of the dying, I had cantered over ground slippery with blood, and frequently had to turn aside to avoid trampling on wounded man or horse, but, until one dreadful day, I had never felt terror; that day I shall never forget."

Here old Captain paused for awhile and drew a long breath; I waited, and he went on.

"It was one autumn morning, and as usual, an hour before daybreak our cavalry had turned out, ready caparisoned for the day's work, whether it might be fighting or waiting. The men stood by their horses waiting, ready for orders. As the light increased there seemed to be some excitement among the officers; and before the day was well begun we heard the firing of the enemy's guns.

422

"Then one of the officers rode up and gave the word for the men to mount, and in a second every man was in his saddle, and every horse stood expecting the touch of the rein, or the pressure of his rider's heels, all animated, all eager; but still we had been trained so well that, except by the champing of our bits, and the restive tossing of our heads from time to time, it could not be said that we stirred.

"My dear master and I were at the head of the line, and as all sat motionless and watchful, he took a little stray lock of my mane which had turned over on the wrong side, laid it over on the right, and smoothed it down with his hand; then patting my neck, he said, 'We shall have a day of it to-day, Bayard, my beauty; but we'll do our duty as we have done.' He stroked my neck that morning more, I think, than he had ever done before; quietly on and on, as if he were thinking of something else. I loved to feel his hand on my neck, and arched my crest proudly and happily; but I stood very still, for I knew all his moods, and when he liked me to be quiet, and when gay.

"I cannot tell all that happened on that day, but I will tell of the last charge that we made together; it was across a valley right in front of the enemy's cannon. By this time we were well used to the roar of heavy guns, the rattle of musket fire, and the flying of shot near us; but never had I been under such a fire as we rode through on that day. From the right, from the left, and from the front, shot and shell poured in upon us. Many a brave man went down, many a horse fell, flinging his rider to the earth; many a horse without a rider ran wildly out of the ranks; then terrified at being alone, with no hand to guide him, came pressing in among his old companions, to gallop with them to the charge.

"Fearful as it was, no one stopped, no one turned back. Every moment the ranks were thinned, but as our comrades fell, we closed in to keep them together; and instead of being shaken or staggered in our pace our gallop became faster and faster as we neared the cannon.

"My master, my dear master was cheering on his comrades with his right arm raised on high, when one of the balls whizzing close to my head struck him. I felt him stagger with the shock, though he uttered no cry; I tried to check my speed, but the sword dropped from his right hand, the rein fell loose from the left, and sinking backward from the saddle he fell to the earth; the other riders swept past us, and by the force of their charge I was driven from the spot.

"I wanted to keep my place by his side and not leave him under that rush of horses' feet, but it was in vain; and now without a master or a friend I was alone on that great slaughter ground; then fear took hold on me, and I trembled as I had never trembled before; and I too, as I had seen other horses do, tried to join in the ranks and gallop with them; but I was beaten off by the swords of the soldiers. Just then a soldier whose horse had been killed under him caught at my bridle and mounted me, and with this new master I was again going forward; but our gallant company was cruelly overpowered, and those who remained alive after the fierce fight for the guns came galloping back over the same ground. Some of the horses had been so badly wounded that they could scarcely move from the loss of blood; other noble creatures were trying on three legs to drag themselves along, and others were struggling to rise on their fore feet, when their hind legs had been shattered by shot. After the battle the wounded men were brought in and the dead were buried."

"And what about the wounded horses?" I said; "were they left to die?"

"No, the army farriers went over the field with their pistols and shot all that were ruined; some that had only slight wounds were brought back and attended to, but the greater part of the noble, willing creatures that went out that morning never came back! In our stables there was only about one in four that returned.

"I never saw my dear master again. I believe he fell dead from the saddle. I never loved any other master so well. I went into many other engagements, but was only once wounded, and then not seriously; and when the war was over I came back again to England, as sound and strong as when I went out."

I said, "I have heard people talk about war as if it was a very fine thing."

"Ah!" said he, "I should think they never saw it. No doubt it is very fine when there is no enemy, when it is just exercise and parade and sham fight. Yes, it is very fine then; but when thousands of good brave men and horses are killed or crippled for life, it has a very different look."

"Do you know what they fought about?" said I.

"No," he said, "that is more than a horse can understand, but the enemy must have been awfully wicked people, if it was right to go all that way over the sea on purpose to kill them."

Lesson 84
1. Read chapters 35 and 36.
2. Take notes on major events.

35 Jerry Barker

I never knew a better man than my new master. He was kind and good, and as strong for the right as John Manly; and so good-tempered and merry that very few people could pick a quarrel with him. He was very fond of making little songs, and singing them to himself. One he was very fond of was this:

> "Come, father and mother,
> And sister and brother,
> Come, all of you, turn to
> And help one another."

And so they did; Harry was as clever at stable-work as a much older boy, and always wanted to do what he could. Then Polly and Dolly used to come in the morning to help with the cab – to brush and beat the cushions, and rub the glass, while Jerry was giving us a cleaning in the yard, and Harry was rubbing the harness. There used to be a great deal of laughing and fun between them, and it put Captain and me in much better spirits than if we had heard scolding and hard words. They were always early in the morning, for Jerry would say:

> "If you in the morning
> Throw minutes away,
> You can't pick them up
> In the course of a day.
> You may hurry and scurry,
> And flurry and worry,
> You've lost them forever,
> Forever and aye."

He could not bear any careless loitering and waste of time; and nothing was so near making him angry as to find people, who were always late, wanting a cab horse to be driven hard, to make up for their idleness.

One day two wild-looking young men came out of a tavern close by the stand, and called Jerry.

"Here, cabby! look sharp, we are rather late; put on the steam, will you, and take us to the Victoria in time for the one o'clock train? You shall have a shilling extra."

"I will take you at the regular pace, gentlemen; shillings don't pay for putting on the steam like that."

Larry's cab was standing next to ours; he flung open the door, and said, "I'm your man, gentlemen! take my cab, my horse will get you there all right;" and as he shut them in, with a wink toward Jerry, said, "It's against his conscience to go beyond a jog-trot." Then slashing his jaded horse, he set off as hard as he could. Jerry patted me on the neck: "No, Jack, a shilling would not pay for that sort of thing, would it, old boy?"

Although Jerry was determinedly set against hard driving, to please careless people, he always went a good fair pace, and was not against putting on the steam, as he said, if only he knew why.

I well remember one morning, as we were on the stand waiting for a fare, that a young man, carrying a heavy portmanteau, trod on a piece of orange peel which lay on the pavement, and fell down with great force.

Jerry was the first to run and lift him up. He seemed much stunned, and as they led him into a shop he walked as if he were in great pain. Jerry of course came back to the stand, but in about ten minutes one of the shopmen called him, so we drew up to the pavement.

"Can you take me to the South-Eastern Railway?" said the young man; "this unlucky fall has made me late, I fear; but it is of great importance that I should not lose the twelve o'clock train. I should be most thankful if you could get me there in time, and will gladly pay you an extra fare."

"I'll do my very best," said Jerry heartily, "if you think you are well enough, sir," for he looked dreadfully white and ill.

"I must go," he said earnestly, "please to open the door, and let us lose no time."

The next minute Jerry was on the box; with a cheery chirrup to me, and a twitch of the rein that I well understood.

"Now then, Jack, my boy," said he, "spin along, we'll show them how we can get over the ground, if we only know why."

It is always difficult to drive fast in the city in the middle of the day, when the streets are full of traffic, but we did what could be done; and when a good driver and a good horse, who understand each other, are of one mind, it is wonderful what they can do. I had a very good mouth – that is I could be guided by the slightest touch of the rein; and that is a great thing in London, among carriages, omnibuses, carts, vans, trucks, cabs, and great wagons creeping along at a walking pace; some going one way, some another, some going slowly, others wanting to pass them; omnibuses stopping short every few minutes to take up a passenger, obliging the horse that is coming behind to pull up too, or to pass, and get before them; perhaps you try to pass, but just then something else comes dashing in through the narrow opening, and you have to keep in behind the omnibus again; presently you think you see a chance, and manage to get to the front, going so near the wheels on each side that half an inch nearer and they would scrape. Well, you get along for a bit, but soon find yourself in a long train of carts and carriages all obliged to go at a walk; perhaps you come to a regular block-up, and have to stand still for minutes together, till something clears out into a side street, or the policeman interferes; you have to be ready for any chance – to dash forward if there be an opening, and be quick as a rat-dog to see if there be room and if there be time, lest you get your own wheels locked or smashed, or the shaft of some other vehicle run into your chest or shoulder. All this is what you have to be ready for. If you want to get through London fast in the middle of the day it wants a deal of practice.

Jerry and I were used to it, and no one could beat us at getting through when we were set upon it. I was quick and bold and could always trust my driver; Jerry was quick and patient at the same time, and could trust his horse, which was a great thing too. He very seldom used the whip; I knew by his voice, and his click, click, when he wanted to get on fast, and by the rein where I was to go; so there was no need for whipping; but I must go back to my story.

The streets were very full that day, but we got on pretty well as far as the bottom of Cheapside, where there was a block for three or four minutes. The young man put his head out and said anxiously, "I think I had better get out and walk; I shall never get there if this goes on."

"I'll do all that can be done, sir," said Jerry; "I think we shall be in time. This block-up cannot last much longer, and your luggage is very heavy for you to carry, sir."

Just then the cart in front of us began to move on, and then we had a good turn. In and out, in and out we went, as fast as horseflesh could do it, and for a wonder had a good clear time on London Bridge, for there was a whole train of cabs and carriages all going our way at a quick trot, perhaps wanting to catch that very train. At any rate, we whirled into the station with many more, just as the great clock pointed to eight minutes to twelve o'clock.

"Thank God! we are in time," said the young man, "and thank you, too, my friend, and your good horse. You have saved me more than money can ever pay for. Take this extra half-crown."

"No, sir, no, thank you all the same; so glad we hit the time, sir; but don't stay now, sir, the bell is ringing. Here, porter! take this gentleman's luggage – Dover line twelve o'clock train – that's it," and without waiting for another word Jerry wheeled me round to make room for other cabs that were dashing up at the last minute, and drew up on one side till the crush was past.

"'So glad!' he said, 'so glad!' Poor young fellow! I wonder what it was that made him so anxious!"

Jerry often talked to himself quite loud enough for me to hear when we were not moving.

On Jerry's return to the rank there was a good deal of laughing and chaffing at him for driving hard to the train for an extra fare, as they said, all against his principles, and they wanted to know how much he had pocketed.

"A good deal more than I generally get," said he, nodding slyly; "what he gave me will keep me in little comforts for several days."

"Gammon!" said one.

"He's a humbug," said another; "preaching to us and then doing the same himself."

"Look here, mates," said Jerry; "the gentleman offered me half a crown extra, but I didn't take it; 'twas quite pay enough for me to see how glad he was to catch that train; and if Jack and I choose to have a quick run now and then to please ourselves, that's our business and not yours."

"Well," said Larry, "you'll never be a rich man."

"Most likely not," said Jerry; "but I don't know that I shall be the less happy for that. I have heard the commandments read a great many times and I never noticed that any of them said, 'Thou shalt be rich'; and there are a good many curious things said in the New Testament about rich men that I think would make me feel rather queer if I was one of them."

427

"If you ever do get rich," said Governor Gray, looking over his shoulder across the top of his cab, "you'll deserve it, Jerry, and you won't find a curse come with your wealth. As for you, Larry, you'll die poor; you spend too much in whipcord."

"Well," said Larry, "what is a fellow to do if his horse won't go without it?"

"You never take the trouble to see if he will go without it; your whip is always going as if you had the St. Vitus' dance in your arm, and if it does not wear you out it wears your horse out; you know you are always changing your horses; and why? Because you never give them any peace or encouragement."

"Well, I have not had good luck," said Larry, "that's where it is."

"And you never will," said the governor. "Good Luck is rather particular who she rides with, and mostly prefers those who have got common sense and a good heart; at least that is my experience."

Governor Gray turned round again to his newspaper, and the other men went to their cabs.

36 The Sunday Cab

One morning, as Jerry had just put me into the shafts and was fastening the traces, a gentleman walked into the yard. "Your servant, sir," said Jerry.

"Good-morning, Mr. Barker," said the gentleman. "I should be glad to make some arrangements with you for taking Mrs. Briggs regularly to church on Sunday mornings. We go to the New Church now, and that is rather further than she can walk."

"Thank you, sir," said Jerry, "but I have only taken out a six-days' license,[1] and therefore I could not take a fare on a Sunday; it would not be legal."

"Oh!" said the other, "I did not know yours was a six-days' cab; but of course it would be very easy to alter your license. I would see that you did not lose by it; the fact is, Mrs. Briggs very much prefers you to drive her."

"I should be glad to oblige the lady, sir, but I had a seven-days' license once, and the work was too hard for me, and too hard for my horses. Year in and year out, not a day's rest, and never a Sunday with my wife and children; and never able to go to a place of worship, which I had always been

---

[1] A few years since the annual charge for a cab license was very much reduced, and the difference between the six and seven days' cabs was abolished.

used to do before I took to the driving box. So for the last five years I have only taken a six-days' license, and I find it better all the way round."

"Well, of course," replied Mr. Briggs, "it is very proper that every person should have rest, and be able to go to church on Sundays, but I should have thought you would not have minded such a short distance for the horse, and only once a day; you would have all the afternoon and evening for yourself, and we are very good customers, you know."

"Yes, sir, that is true, and I am grateful for all favors, I am sure; and anything that I could do to oblige you, or the lady, I should be proud and happy to do; but I can't give up my Sundays, sir, indeed I can't. I read that God made man, and he made horses and all the other beasts, and as soon as He had made them He made a day of rest, and bade that all should rest one day in seven; and I think, sir, He must have known what was good for them, and I am sure it is good for me; I am stronger and healthier altogether, now that I have a day of rest; the horses are fresh too, and do not wear up nearly so fast. The six-day drivers all tell me the same, and I have laid by more money in the savings bank than ever I did before; and as for the wife and children, sir, why, heart alive! they would not go back to the seven days for all they could see."

"Oh, very well," said the gentleman. "Don't trouble yourself, Mr. Barker, any further. I will inquire somewhere else," and he walked away.

"Well," says Jerry to me, "we can't help it, Jack, old boy; we must have our Sundays."

"Polly!" he shouted, "Polly! come here."

She was there in a minute.

"What is it all about, Jerry?"

"Why, my dear, Mr. Briggs wants me to take Mrs. Briggs to church every Sunday morning. I say I have only a six-days' license. He says, 'Get a seven-days' license, and I'll make it worth your while;' and you know, Polly, they are very good customers to us. Mrs. Briggs often goes out shopping for hours, or making calls, and then she pays down fair and honorable like a lady; there's no beating down or making three hours into two hours and a half, as some folks do; and it is easy work for the horses; not like tearing along to catch trains for people that are always a quarter of an hour too late; and if I don't oblige her in this matter it is very likely we shall lose them altogether. What do you say, little woman?"

"I say, Jerry," says she, speaking very slowly, "I say, if Mrs. Briggs would give you a sovereign every Sunday morning, I would not have you a seven-days' cabman again. We have known what it was to have no Sundays, and now we know what it is to call them our own. Thank God, you earn enough to keep us, though it is sometimes close work to pay for all the oats and hay, the license, and the rent besides; but Harry will soon be earning something, and I would rather struggle on harder than we do than go back to those horrid times when you hardly had a minute to look at your

429

own children, and we never could go to a place of worship together, or have a happy, quiet day. God forbid that we should ever turn back to those times; that's what I say, Jerry."

"And that is just what I told Mr. Briggs, my dear," said Jerry, "and what I mean to stick to. So don't go and fret yourself, Polly" (for she had begun to cry); "I would not go back to the old times if I earned twice as much, so that is settled, little woman. Now, cheer up, and I'll be off to the stand."

Three weeks had passed away after this conversation, and no order had come from Mrs. Briggs; so there was nothing but taking jobs from the stand. Jerry took it to heart a good deal, for of course the work was harder for horse and man. But Polly would always cheer him up, and say, "Never mind, father, never, mind.

> "'Do your best,
> And leave the rest,
> 'Twill all come right
> Some day or night.'"

It soon became known that Jerry had lost his best customer, and for what reason. Most of the men said he was a fool, but two or three took his part.

"If workingmen don't stick to their Sunday," said Truman, "they'll soon have none left; it is every man's right and every beast's right. By God's law we have a day of rest, and by the law of England we have a day of rest; and I say we ought to hold to the rights these laws give us and keep them for our children."

"All very well for you religious chaps to talk so," said Larry; "but I'll turn a shilling when I can. I don't believe in religion, for I don't see that your religious people are any better than the rest."

"If they are not better," put in Jerry, "it is because they are not religious. You might as well say that our country's laws are not good because some people break them. If a man gives way to his temper, and speaks evil of his neighbor, and does not pay his debts, he is not religious, I don't care how much he goes to church. If some men are shams and humbugs, that does not make religion untrue. Real religion is the best and truest thing in the world, and the only thing that can make a man really happy or make the world we live in any better."

"If religion was good for anything," said Jones, "it would prevent your religious people from making us work on Sundays, as you know many of them do, and that's why I say religion is nothing but a sham; why, if it was not for the church and chapel-goers it would be hardly worth while our coming out on a Sunday. But they have their privileges, as they call them, and I go without. I shall expect them to answer for my soul, if I can't get a chance of saving it."

Several of the men applauded this, till Jerry said:

"That may sound well enough, but it won't do; every man must look after his own soul; you can't lay it down at another man's door like a foundling and expect him to take care of it; and don't you see, if you are always sitting on your box waiting for a fare, they will say, 'If we don't take him some one else will, and he does not look for any Sunday.' Of course, they don't go to the bottom of it, or they would see if they never came for a cab it would be no use your standing there; but people don't always like to go to the bottom of things; it may not be convenient to do it; but if you Sunday drivers would all strike for a day of rest the thing would be done."

"And what would all the good people do if they could not get to their favorite preachers?" said Larry.

"'Tis not for me to lay down plans for other people," said Jerry, "but if they can't walk so far they can go to what is nearer; and if it should rain they can put on their mackintoshes as they do on a week-day. If a thing is right it can be done, and if it is wrong it can be done without; and a good man will find a way. And that is as true for us cabmen as it is for the church-goers."

Lesson 85
1. Read chapters 37, 38, and 39.
2. Take notes on major events.

37 The Golden Rule

Two or three weeks after this, as we came into the yard rather late in the evening, Polly came running across the road with the lantern (she always brought it to him if it was not very wet).

"It has all come right, Jerry; Mrs. Briggs sent her servant this afternoon to ask you to take her out to-morrow at eleven o'clock. I said, 'Yes, I thought so, but we supposed she employed some one else now.'"

"'Well,' said he, 'the real fact is, master was put out because Mr. Barker refused to come on Sundays, and he has been trying other cabs, but there's something wrong with them all; some drive too fast, and some too slow, and the mistress says there is not one of them so nice and clean as yours, and nothing will suit her but Mr. Barker's cab again.'"

Polly was almost out of breath, and Jerry broke out into a merry laugh.

"'Twill all come right some day or night': you were right, my dear; you generally are. Run in and get the supper, and I'll have Jack's harness off and make him snug and happy in no time."

After this Mrs. Briggs wanted Jerry's cab quite as often as before, never, however, on a Sunday; but there came a day when we had Sunday work, and this was how it happened. We had all come home on the Saturday night very tired, and very glad to think that the next day would be all rest, but so it was not to be.

On Sunday morning Jerry was cleaning me in the yard, when Polly stepped up to him, looking very full of something.

"What is it?" said Jerry.

"Well, my dear," she said, "poor Dinah Brown has just had a letter brought to say that her mother is dangerously ill, and that she must go directly if she wishes to see her alive. The place is more than ten miles away from here, out in the country, and she says if she takes the train she should still have four miles to walk; and so weak as she is, and the baby only four weeks old, of course that would be impossible; and she wants to know if you would take her in your cab, and she promises to pay you faithfully, as she can get the money."

"Tut, tut! we'll see about that. It was not the money I was thinking about, but of losing our Sunday; the horses are tired, and I am tired, too -that's where it pinches."

"It pinches all round, for that matter," said Polly, "for it's only half Sunday without you, but you know we should do to other people as we should like they should do to us; and I know very well what I should like if my mother was dying; and Jerry, dear, I am sure it won't break the Sabbath; for if pulling a poor beast or donkey out of a pit would not spoil it, I am quite sure taking poor Dinah would not do it."

"Why, Polly, you are as good as the minister, and so, as I've had my Sunday-morning sermon early to-day, you may go and tell Dinah that I'll be ready for her as the clock strikes ten; but stop-just step round to butcher Braydon's with my compliments, and ask him if he would lend me his light trap; I know he never uses it on the Sunday, and it would make a wonderful difference to the horse."

Away she went, and soon returned, saying that he could have the trap and welcome.

"All right," said he; "now put me up a bit of bread and cheese, and I'll be back in the afternoon as soon as I can."

"And I'll have the meat pie ready for an early tea instead of for dinner," said Polly; and away she went, while he made his preparations to the tune of "Polly's the woman and no mistake", of which tune he was very fond.

I was selected for the journey, and at ten o'clock we started, in a light, high-wheeled gig, which ran so easily that after the four-wheeled cab it seemed like nothing.

It was a fine May day, and as soon as we were out of the town, the sweet air, the smell of the fresh grass, and the soft country roads were as pleasant as they used to be in the old times, and I soon began to feel quite fresh.

Dinah's family lived in a small farmhouse, up a green lane, close by a meadow with some fine shady trees; there were two cows feeding in it. A young man asked Jerry to bring his trap into the meadow, and he would tie me up in the cowshed; he wished he had a better stable to offer.

"If your cows would not be offended," said Jerry, "there is nothing my horse would like so well as to have an hour or two in your beautiful meadow; he's quiet, and it would be a rare treat for him."

"Do, and welcome," said the young man; "the best we have is at your service for your kindness to my sister; we shall be having some dinner in an hour, and I hope you'll come in, though with mother so ill we are all out of sorts in the house."

Jerry thanked him kindly, but said as he had some dinner with him there was nothing he should like so well as walking about in the meadow.

When my harness was taken off I did not know what I should do first-whether to eat the grass, or roll over on my back, or lie down and rest, or have a gallop across the meadow out of sheer spirits at being free; and I did all by turns. Jerry seemed to be quite as happy as I was; he sat down by a bank under a shady tree, and listened to the birds, then he sang himself, and read out of the little brown book he is so fond of, then wandered round the meadow, and down by a little brook, where he picked the flowers and the hawthorn, and tied them up with long sprays of ivy; then he gave me a good feed of the oats which he had brought with him; but the time seemed all too short-I had not been in a field since I left poor Ginger at Earlshall.

We came home gently, and Jerry's first words were, as we came into the yard, "Well, Polly, I have not lost my Sunday after all, for the birds were singing hymns in every bush, and I joined in the service; and as for Jack, he was like a young colt."

When he handed Dolly the flowers she jumped about for joy.

38 Dolly and a Real Gentleman

Winter came in early, with a great deal of cold and wet. There was snow, or sleet, or rain almost every day for weeks, changing only for keen driving winds or sharp frosts. The horses all felt it very much. When it is a dry cold a couple of good thick rugs will keep the warmth in us; but when it is soaking rain they soon get wet through and are no good. Some of the drivers had a waterproof cover to throw over, which was a fine thing; but some of the men were so poor that they could not protect either themselves or their horses, and many of them suffered very much that winter. When we horses had worked half the day we went to our dry stables, and could rest, while they had to sit on their boxes, sometimes staying out as late as one or two o'clock in the morning if they had a party to wait for.

When the streets were slippery with frost or snow that was the worst of all for us horses. One mile of such traveling, with a weight to draw and no firm footing, would take more out of us than four on a good road; every nerve and muscle of our bodies is on the strain to keep our balance; and, added to this, the fear of falling is more exhausting than anything else. If the roads are very bad indeed our shoes are roughed, but that makes us feel nervous at first.

When the weather was very bad many of the men would go and sit in the tavern close by, and get some one to watch for them; but they often lost a fare in that way, and could not, as Jerry said, be there without spending money. He never went to the Rising Sun; there was a coffee-shop near, where he now and then went, or he bought of an old man, who came to our rank with tins of hot coffee and pies. It was his opinion that spirits and beer made a man colder afterward, and that dry clothes, good food, cheerfulness, and a comfortable wife at home, were the best things to keep a cabman warm. Polly always supplied him with something to eat when he could not get home, and sometimes he would see little Dolly peeping from the corner of the street, to make sure if "father" was on the stand. If she saw him she would run off at full speed and soon come back with something in a tin or basket, some hot soup or pudding Polly had ready. It was wonderful how such a little thing could get safely across the street, often thronged with horses and carriages; but she was a brave little maid, and felt it quite an honor to bring "father's first course", as he used to call it. She was a general favorite on the stand, and there was not a man who would not have seen her safely across the street, if Jerry had not been able to do it.

One cold windy day Dolly had brought Jerry a basin of something hot, and was standing by him while he ate it. He had scarcely begun when a gentleman, walking toward us very fast, held up his umbrella. Jerry touched his hat in return, gave the basin to Dolly, and was taking off my cloth, when the gentleman, hastening up, cried out, "No, no, finish your soup, my friend; I have not much time to spare, but I can wait till you have done, and set your little girl safe on the pavement." So saying, he seated himself in the cab. Jerry thanked him kindly, and came back to Dolly.

"There, Dolly, that's a gentleman; that's a real gentleman, Dolly; he has got time and thought for the comfort of a poor cabman and a little girl."

Jerry finished his soup, set the child across, and then took his orders to drive to Clapham Rise. Several times after that the same gentleman took our cab. I think he was very fond of dogs and horses, for whenever we took him to his own door two or three dogs would come bounding out to meet him. Sometimes he came round and patted me, saying in his quiet, pleasant way, "This horse has got a good master, and he deserves it." It was a very rare thing for any one to notice the horse that had been working for him. I have known ladies to do it now and then, and this gentleman, and one or two others have given me a pat and a kind word; but ninety-nine persons out of a hundred would as soon think of patting the steam engine that drew the train.

The gentleman was not young, and there was a forward stoop in his shoulders as if he was always going at something. His lips were thin and close shut, though they had a very pleasant smile; his eye was keen, and there was something in his jaw and the motion of his head that made one think he was very determined in anything he set about. His voice was pleasant and kind; any horse would trust that voice, though it was just as decided as everything else about him.

One day he and another gentleman took our cab; they stopped at a shop in R – – Street, and while his friend went in he stood at the door. A little ahead of us on the other side of the street a cart with two very fine horses was standing before some wine vaults; the carter was not with them, and I cannot tell how long they had been standing, but they seemed to think they had waited long enough, and began to move off. Before they had gone many paces the carter came running out and caught them. He seemed furious at their having moved, and with whip and rein punished them brutally, even beating them about the head. Our gentleman saw it all, and stepping quickly across the street, said in a decided voice:

"If you don't stop that directly, I'll have you arrested for leaving your horses, and for brutal conduct."

The man, who had clearly been drinking, poured forth some abusive language, but he left off knocking the horses about, and taking the reins, got into his cart; meantime our friend had quietly taken a note-book from his pocket, and looking at the name and address painted on the cart, he wrote something down.

"What do you want with that?" growled the carter, as he cracked his whip and was moving on. A nod and a grim smile was the only answer he got.

On returning to the cab our friend was joined by his companion, who said laughingly, "I should have thought, Wright, you had enough business of your own to look after, without troubling yourself about other people's horses and servants."

Our friend stood still for a moment, and throwing his head a little back, "Do you know why this world is as bad as it is?"

"No," said the other.

"Then I'll tell you. It is because people think only about their own business, and won't trouble themselves to stand up for the oppressed, nor bring the wrongdoer to light. I never see a wicked thing like this without doing what I can, and many a master has thanked me for letting him know how his horses have been used."

"I wish there were more gentlemen like you, sir," said Jerry, "for they are wanted badly enough in this city."

After this we continued our journey, and as they got out of the cab our friend was saying, "My doctrine is this, that if we see cruelty or wrong that we have the power to stop, and do nothing, we make ourselves sharers in the guilt."

39 Seedy Sam

I should say that for a cab-horse I was very well off indeed; my driver was my owner, and it was his interest to treat me well and not overwork me, even had he not been so good a man as he was; but there were a great many horses which belonged to the large cab-owners, who let them out to their drivers for so much money a day. As the horses did not belong to these men the only thing they thought of was how to get their money out of them, first, to pay the master, and then to provide for their own living; and a dreadful time some of these horses had of it. Of course, I understood but little, but it was often talked over on the stand, and the governor, who was a kind-hearted man and fond of horses, would sometimes speak up if one came in very much jaded or ill-used.

One day a shabby, miserable-looking driver, who went by the name of "Seedy Sam", brought in his horse looking dreadfully beat, and the governor said:

"You and your horse look more fit for the police station than for this rank."

The man flung his tattered rug over the horse, turned full round upon the Governor and said in a voice that sounded almost desperate:

"If the police have any business with the matter it ought to be with the masters who charge us so much, or with the fares that are fixed so low. If a man has to pay eighteen shillings a day for the use of a cab and two horses, as many of us have to do in the season, and must make that up before we earn a penny for ourselves I say 'tis more than hard work; nine shillings a day to get out of each horse before you begin to get your own living. You know that's true, and if the horses don't work we must starve, and I and my children have known what that is before now. I've six of 'em, and only one earns anything; I am on the stand fourteen or sixteen hours a day, and I haven't had a Sunday these ten or twelve weeks; you know Skinner never gives a day if he can help it, and if I don't work hard, tell me who does! I want a warm coat and a mackintosh, but with so many to feed how can a man get it? I had to pledge my clock a week ago to pay Skinner, and I shall never see it again."

Some of the other drivers stood round nodding their heads and saying he was right. The man went on:

"You that have your own horses and cabs, or drive for good masters, have a chance of getting on and a chance of doing right; I haven't. We can't charge more than sixpence a mile after the first, within the four-mile radius. This very morning I had to go a clear six miles and only took three shillings. I could not get a return fare, and had to come all the way back; there's twelve miles for the horse and three shillings for me. After that I had a three-mile fare, and there were bags and boxes enough to have brought in a good many twopences if they had been put outside; but you know how people do; all that could be piled up inside on the front seat were put in and three heavy boxes went on the top. That was sixpence, and the fare one and sixpence; then I got a return for a shilling. Now that makes eighteen miles for the horse and six shillings for me; there's three shillings still for that horse to earn and nine shillings for the afternoon horse before I touch a penny. Of course, it is not always so bad as that, but you know it often is, and I say 'tis a mockery to tell a man that he must not overwork his horse, for when a beast is downright tired there's nothing but the whip that will keep his legs a-going; you can't help yourself-you must put your wife and children before the horse; the masters must look to that, we can't. I don't ill-use my horse for the sake of it; none of you can say I do. There's wrong lays somewhere-never a day's rest, never a quiet hour with the wife and children. I often feel like an old man, though I'm only forty-five. You know how quick some of the gentry are to suspect us of cheating and overcharging; why, they stand with their purses in their hands counting it over to a penny and looking at us as if we were pickpockets. I wish some of 'em had got to sit on my box sixteen hours a day and get a living out of it and eighteen shillings beside, and that in all weathers; they would not be so uncommon particular never to give us a sixpence over or to cram all the luggage inside. Of course, some of 'em tip us pretty handsome now and then, or else we could not live; but you can't depend upon that."

The men who stood round much approved this speech, and one of them said, "It is desperate hard, and if a man sometimes does what is wrong it is no wonder, and if he gets a dram too much who's to blow him up?"

Jerry had taken no part in this conversation, but I never saw his face look so sad before. The governor had stood with both his hands in his pockets; now he took his handkerchief out of his hat and wiped his forehead.

"You've beaten me, Sam," he said, "for it's all true, and I won't cast it up to you any more about the police; it was the look in that horse's eye that came over me. It is hard lines for man and it is hard lines for beast, and who's to mend it I don't know: but anyway you might tell the poor beast that you were sorry to take it out of him in that way. Sometimes a kind word is all we can give 'em, poor brutes, and 'tis wonderful what they do understand."

A few mornings after this talk a new man came on the stand with Sam's cab.

"Halloo!" said one, "what's up with Seedy Sam?"

"He's ill in bed," said the man; "he was taken last night in the yard, and could scarcely crawl home. His wife sent a boy this morning to say his father was in a high fever and could not get out, so I'm here instead."

The next morning the same man came again.

"How is Sam?" inquired the governor.

"He's gone," said the man.

"What, gone? You don't mean to say he's dead?"

"Just snuffed out," said the other; "he died at four o'clock this morning; all yesterday he was raving – raving about Skinner, and having no Sundays. 'I never had a Sunday's rest,' these were his last words."

No one spoke for a while, and then the governor said, "I'll tell you what, mates, this is a warning for us."

Lesson 86
1. Read chapters 40, 41, 42 and 43.
2. Take notes on major events.

40 Poor Ginger

One day, while our cab and many others were waiting outside one of the parkswhere music was playing, a shabby old cab drove up beside ours. The horse was an old worn-out chestnut, with an ill-kept coat, and bones that showed plainly through it, the knees knuckled over, and the fore-legs were very unsteady. I had been eating some hay, and the wind rolled a little lock of it that way, and the poor creature put out her long thin neck and picked it up, and then turned and looked about for more. There was a hopeless look in the dull eye that I could not help noticing, and then, as I was thinking where I had seen that horse before, she looked full at me and said, "Black Beauty, is that you?"

It was Ginger! but how changed! The beautifully arched and glossy neck was now straight, and lank, and fallen in; the clean straight legs and delicate fetlocks were swelled; the joints were grown out of shape with hard work; the face, that was once so full of spirit and life, was now full of suffering, and I could tell by the heaving of her sides, and her frequent cough, how bad her breath was.

Our drivers were standing together a little way off, so I sidled up to her a step or two, that we might have a little quiet talk. It was a sad tale that she had to tell.

After a twelvemonth's run off at Earlshall, she was considered to be fit for work again, and was sold to a gentleman. For a little while she got on very well, but after a longer gallop than usual the old strain returned, and after being rested and doctored she was again sold. In this way she changed hands several times, but always getting lower down.

"And so at last," said she, "I was bought by a man who keeps a number of cabs and horses, and lets them out. You look well off, and I am glad of it, but I could not tell you what my life has been. When they found out my weakness they said I was not worth what they gave for me, and that I must go into one of the low cabs, and just be used up; that is what they are doing, whipping and working with never one thought of what I suffer – they paid for me, and must get it out of me, they say. The man who hires me now pays a deal of money to the owner every day, and so he has to get it out of me too; and so it's all the week round and round, with never a Sunday rest."

I said, "You used to stand up for yourself if you were ill-used."

"Ah!" she said, "I did once, but it's no use; men are strongest, and if they are cruel and have no feeling, there is nothing that we can do, but just bear it – bear it on and on to the end. I wish the end was come, I wish I was dead. I have seen dead horses, and I am sure they do not suffer pain; I wish I may drop down dead at my work, and not be sent off to the knackers."

I was very much troubled, and I put my nose up to hers, but I could say nothing to comfort her. I think she was pleased to see me, for she said, "You are the only friend I ever had."

Just then her driver came up, and with a tug at her mouth backed her out of the line and drove off, leaving me very sad indeed.

A short time after this a cart with a dead horse in it passed our cab-stand. The head hung out of the cart-tail, the lifeless tongue was slowly dropping with blood; and the sunken eyes! but I can't speak of them, the sight was too dreadful. It was a chestnut horse with a long, thin neck. I saw a white streak down the forehead. I believe it was Ginger; I hoped it was, for then her troubles would be over. Oh! if men were more merciful they would shoot us before we came to such misery.

41 The Butcher

I saw a great deal of trouble among the horses in London, and much of it might have been prevented by a little common sense. We horses do not mind hard work if we are treated reasonably, and I am sure there are many driven by quite poor men who have a happier life than I had when I used to go in the Countess of W – – 's carriage, with my silver-mounted harness and high feeding.

It often went to my heart to see how the little ponies were used, straining along with heavy loads or staggering under heavy blows from some low, cruel boy. Once I saw a little gray pony with a thick mane and a pretty head, and so much like Merrylegs that if I had not been in harness I should have neighed to him. He was doing his best to pull a heavy cart, while a strong rough boy was cutting him under the belly with his whip and chucking cruelly at his little mouth. Could it be Merrylegs? It was just like him; but then Mr. Blomefield was never to sell him, and I think he would not do it; but this might have been quite as good a little fellow, and had as happy a place when he was young.

I often noticed the great speed at which butchers' horses were made to go, though I did not know why it was so till one day when we had to wait some time in St. John's Wood. There was a butcher's shop next door, and as we were standing a butcher's cart came dashing up at a great pace. The horse was hot and much exhausted; he hung his head down, while his heaving sides and trembling legs showed how hard he had been driven. The lad jumped out of the cart and was getting the basket when the master came out of the shop much displeased. After looking at the horse he turned angrily to the lad.

"How many times shall I tell you not to drive in this way? You ruined the last horse and broke his wind, and you are going to ruin this in the same way. If you were not my own son I would dismiss you on the spot; it is a disgrace to have a horse brought to the shop in a condition like that; you are liable to be taken up by the police for such driving, and if you are you need not look to me for bail, for I have spoken to you till I'm tired; you must look out for yourself."

During this speech the boy had stood by, sullen and dogged, but when his father ceased he broke out angrily. It wasn't his fault, and he wouldn't take the blame; he was only going by orders all the time.

"You always say, 'Now be quick; now look sharp!' and when I go to the houses one wants a leg of mutton for an early dinner and I must be back with it in a quarter of an hour; another cook has forgotten to order the beef; I must go and fetch it and be back in no time, or the mistress will scold; and the housekeeper says they have company coming unexpectedly and must have some chops sent up directly; and the lady at No. 4, in the Crescent, never orders her dinner till the meat comes in for lunch, and it's nothing but hurry, hurry, all the time. If the gentry would think of what they want, and order their meat the day before, there need not be this blow up!"

"I wish to goodness they would," said the butcher; "'twould save me a wonderful deal of harass, and I could suit my customers much better if I knew beforehand – But there! what's the use of talking-who ever thinks of a butcher's convenience or a butcher's horse! Now, then, take him in and look to him well; mind, he does not go out again to-day, and if anything else is wanted you must carry it yourself in the basket." With that he went in, and the horse was led away.

But all boys are not cruel. I have seen some as fond of their pony or donkey as if it had been a favorite dog, and the little creatures have worked away as cheerfully and willingly for their young drivers as I work for Jerry. It may be hard work sometimes, but a friend's hand and voice make it easy.

There was a young coster-boy who came up our street with greens and potatoes; he had an old pony, not very handsome, but the cheerfullest and pluckiest little thing I ever saw, and to see how fond those two were of each other was a treat. The pony followed his master like a dog, and when he got into his cart would trot off without a whip or a word, and rattle down the street as merrily as if he had come out of the queen's stables. Jerry liked the boy, and called him "Prince Charlie", for he said he would make a king of drivers some day.

There was an old man, too, who used to come up our street with a little coal cart; he wore a coal-heaver's hat, and looked rough and black. He and his old horse used to plod together along the street, like two good partners who understood each other; the horse would stop of his own accord at the doors where they took coal of him; he used to keep one ear bent toward his master. The old man's cry could be heard up the street long before he came near. I never knew what he said, but the children called him "Old Ba-a-ar Hoo", for it sounded like that. Polly took her coal of him, and was very friendly, and Jerry said it was a comfort to think how happy an old horse might be in a poor place.

42 The Election

As we came into the yard one afternoon Polly came out. "Jerry! I've had Mr. B − − here asking about your vote, and he wants to hire your cab for the election; he will call for an answer."

"Well, Polly, you may say that my cab will be otherwise engaged. I should not like to have it pasted over with their great bills, and as to making Jack and Captain race about to the public-houses to bring up half-drunken voters, why, I think 'twould be an insult to the horses. No, I shan't do it."

"I suppose you'll vote for the gentleman? He said he was of your politics."

"So he is in some things, but I shall not vote for him, Polly; you know what his trade is?"

"Yes."

"Well, a man who gets rich by that trade may be all very well in some ways, but he is blind as to what workingmen want; I could not in my conscience send him up to make the laws. I dare say they'll be angry, but every man must do what he thinks to be the best for his country."

On the morning before the election, Jerry was putting me into the shafts, when Dolly came into the yard sobbing and crying, with her little blue frock and white pinafore spattered all over with mud.

"Why, Dolly, what is the matter?"

"Those naughty boys," she sobbed, "have thrown the dirt all over me, and called me a little raga − raga − "

"They called her a little 'blue' ragamuffin, father," said Harry, who ran in looking very angry; "but I have given it to them; they won't insult my sister again. I have given them a thrashing they will remember; a set of cowardly, rascally 'orange' blackguards."

Jerry kissed the child and said, "Run in to mother, my pet, and tell her I think you had better stay at home to-day and help her."

Then turning gravely to Harry:

"My boy, I hope you will always defend your sister, and give anybody who insults her a good thrashing – that is as it should be; but mind, I won't have any election blackguarding on my premises. There are as many 'blue' blackguards as there are 'orange', and as many white as there are purple, or any other color, and I won't have any of my family mixed up with it. Even women and children are ready to quarrel for the sake of a color, and not one in ten of them knows what it is about."

"Why, father, I thought blue was for Liberty."

"My boy, Liberty does not come from colors, they only show party, and all the liberty you can get out of them is, liberty to get drunk at other people's expense, liberty to ride to the poll in a dirty old cab, liberty to abuse any one that does not wear your color, and to shout yourself hoarse at what you only half-understand-that's your liberty!"

"Oh, father, you are laughing."

"No, Harry, I am serious, and I am ashamed to see how men go on who ought to know better. An election is a very serious thing; at least it ought to be, and every man ought to vote according to his conscience, and let his neighbor do the same."

43 A Friend in Need

The election day came at last; there was no lack of work for Jerry and me. First came a stout puffy gentleman with a carpet bag; he wanted to go to the Bishopsgate station; then we were called by a party who wished to be taken to the Regent's Park; and next we were wanted in a side street where a timid, anxious old lady was waiting to be taken to the bank; there we had to stop to take her back again, and just as we had set her down a red-faced gentleman, with a handful of papers, came running up out of breath, and before Jerry could get down he had opened the door, popped himself in, and called out, "Bow Street Police Station, quick!" so off we went with him, and when after another turn or two we came back, there was no other cab on the stand. Jerry put on my nose-bag, for as he said, "We must eat when we can on such days as these; so munch away, Jack, and make the best of your time, old boy."

I found I had a good feed of crushed oats wetted up with a little bran; this would be a treat any day, but very refreshing then. Jerry was so thoughtful and kind – what horse would not do his best for such a master? Then he took out one of Polly's meat pies, and standing near me, he began to eat it. The streets were very full, and the cabs, with the candidates' colors on them, were dashing about through the crowd as if life and limb were of no consequence; we saw two people knocked down that day, and one was a woman. The horses were having a bad time of it, poor things! but the voters inside thought nothing of that; many of them were half-drunk, hurrahing out of the cab windows if their own party came by. It was the first election I had seen, and I don't want to be in another, though I have heard things are better now.

Jerry and I had not eaten many mouthfuls before a poor young woman, carrying a heavy child, came along the street. She was looking this way and that way, and seemed quite bewildered. Presently she made her way up to Jerry and asked if he could tell her the way to St. Thomas' Hospital, and how far it was to get there. She had come from the country that morning, she said, in a market cart; she did not know about the election, and was quite a stranger in London. She had got an order for the hospital for her little boy. The child was crying with a feeble, pining cry.

"Poor little fellow!" she said, "he suffers a deal of pain; he is four years old and can't walk any more than a baby; but the doctor said if I could get him into the hospital he might get well; pray, sir, how far is it; and which way is it?"

"Why, missis," said Jerry, "you can't get there walking through crowds like this! why, it is three miles away, and that child is heavy."

"Yes, bless him, he is; but I am strong, thank God, and if I knew the way I think I should get on somehow; please tell me the way."

"You can't do it," said Jerry, "you might be knocked down and the child be run over. Now look here, just get into this cab, and I'll drive you safe to the hospital. Don't you see the rain is coming on?"

"No, sir, no; I can't do that, thank you, I have only just money enough to get back with. Please tell me the way."

"Look you here, missis," said Jerry, "I've got a wife and dear children at home, and I know a father's feelings; now get you into that cab, and I'll take you there for nothing. I'd be ashamed of myself to let a woman and a sick child run a risk like that."

"Heaven bless you!" said the woman, and burst into tears.

"There, there, cheer up, my dear, I'll soon take you there; come, let me put you inside."

As Jerry went to open the door two men, with colors in their hats and buttonholes, ran up calling out, "Cab!"

"Engaged," cried Jerry; but one of the men, pushing past the woman, sprang into the cab, followed by the other. Jerry looked as stern as a policeman. "This cab is already engaged, gentlemen, by that lady."

"Lady!" said one of them; "oh! she can wait; our business is very important, besides we were in first, it is our right, and we shall stay in."

A droll smile came over Jerry's face as he shut the door upon them. "All right, gentlemen, pray stay in as long as it suits you; I can wait while you rest yourselves." And turning his back upon them he walked up to the young woman, who was standing near me. "They'll soon be gone," he said, laughing; "don't trouble yourself, my dear."

And they soon were gone, for when they understood Jerry's dodge they got out, calling him all sorts of bad names and blustering about his number and getting a summons. After this little stoppage we were soon on our way to the hospital, going as much as possible through by-streets. Jerry rung the great bell and helped the young woman out.

"Thank you a thousand times," she said; "I could never have got here alone."

"You're kindly welcome, and I hope the dear child will soon be better."

He watched her go in at the door, and gently he said to himself, "Inasmuch as ye have done it to one of the least of these." Then he patted my neck, which was always his way when anything pleased him.

The rain was now coming down fast, and just as we were leaving the hospital the door opened again, and the porter called out, "Cab!" We stopped, and a lady came down the steps. Jerry seemed to know her at once; she put back her veil and said, "Barker! Jeremiah Barker, is it you? I am very glad to find you here; you are just the friend I want, for it is very difficult to get a cab in this part of London to-day."

"I shall be proud to serve you, ma'am; I am right glad I happened to be here. Where may I take you to, ma'am?"

"To the Paddington Station, and then if we are in good time, as I think we shall be, you shall tell me all about Mary and the children."

We got to the station in good time, and being under shelter the lady stood a good while talking to Jerry. I found she had been Polly's mistress, and after many inquiries about her she said:

"How do you find the cab work suit you in winter? I know Mary was rather anxious about you last year."

"Yes, ma'am, she was; I had a bad cough that followed me up quite into the warm weather, and when I am kept out late she does worry herself a good deal. You see, ma'am, it is all hours and all weathers, and that does try a man's constitution; but I am getting on pretty well, and I should feel quite lost if I had not horses to look after. I was brought up to it, and I am afraid I should not do so well at anything else."

"Well, Barker," she said, "it would be a great pity that you should seriously risk your health in this work, not only for your own but for Mary's and the children's sake; there are many places where good drivers or good grooms are wanted, and if ever you think you ought to give up this cab work let me know."

Then sending some kind messages to Mary she put something into his hand, saying, "There is five shillings each for the two children; Mary will know how to spend it."

Jerry thanked her and seemed much pleased, and turning out of the station we at last reached home, and I, at least, was tired.

Lesson 87
1. Read chapters 44 and 45.
2. Take notes on major events.

44 Old Captain and His Successor

Captain and I were great friends. He was a noble old fellow, and he was very good company. I never thought that he would have to leave his home and go down the hill; but his turn came, and this was how it happened. I was not there, but I heard all about it.

He and Jerry had taken a party to the great railway station over London Bridge, and were coming back, somewhere between the bridge and the monument, when Jerry saw a brewer's empty dray coming along, drawn by two powerful horses. The drayman was lashing his horses with his heavy whip; the dray was light, and they started off at a furious rate; the man had no control over them, and the street was full of traffic.

One young girl was knocked down and run over, and the next moment they dashed up against our cab; both the wheels were torn off and the cab was thrown over. Captain was dragged down, the shafts splintered, and one of them ran into his side. Jerry, too, was thrown, but was only bruised; nobody could tell how he escaped; he always said 'twas a miracle. When poor Captain was got up he was found to be very much cut and knocked about. Jerry led him home gently, and a sad sight it was to see the blood soaking into his white coat and dropping from his side and shoulder. The drayman was proved to be very drunk, and was fined, and the brewer had to pay damages to our master; but there was no one to pay damages to poor Captain.

The farrier and Jerry did the best they could to ease his pain and make him comfortable. The fly had to be mended, and for several days I did not go out, and Jerry earned nothing. The first time we went to the stand after the accident the governor came up to hear how Captain was.

"He'll never get over it," said Jerry, "at least not for my work, so the farrier said this morning. He says he may do for carting, and that sort of work. It has put me out very much. Carting, indeed!

445

I've seen what horses come to at that work round London. I only wish all the drunkards could be put in a lunatic asylum instead of being allowed to run foul of sober people. If they would break their own bones, and smash their own carts, and lame their own horses, that would be their own affair, and we might let them alone, but it seems to me that the innocent always suffer; and then they talk about compensation! You can't make compensation; there's all the trouble, and vexation, and loss of time, besides losing a good horse that's like an old friend-it's nonsense talking of compensation! If there's one devil that I should like to see in the bottomless pit more than another, it's the drink devil."

"I say, Jerry," said the governor, "you are treading pretty hard on my toes, you know; I'm not so good as you are, more shame to me; I wish I was."

"Well," said Jerry, "why don't you cut with it, governor? You are too good a man to be the slave of such a thing."

"I'm a great fool, Jerry, but I tried once for two days, and I thought I should have died; how did you do?"

"I had hard work at it for several weeks; you see I never did get drunk, but I found that I was not my own master, and that when the craving came on it was hard work to say 'no'. I saw that one of us must knock under, the drink devil or Jerry Barker, and I said that it should not be Jerry Barker, God helping me; but it was a struggle, and I wanted all the help I could get, for till I tried to break the habit I did not know how strong it was; but then Polly took such pains that I should have good food, and when the craving came on I used to get a cup of coffee, or some peppermint, or read a bit in my book, and that was a help to me; sometimes I had to say over and over to myself, 'Give up the drink or lose your soul! Give up the drink or break Polly's heart!' But thanks be to God, and my dear wife, my chains were broken, and now for ten years I have not tasted a drop, and never wish for it."

"I've a great mind to try at it," said Grant, "for 'tis a poor thing not to be one's own master."

"Do, governor, do, you'll never repent it, and what a help it would be to some of the poor fellows in our rank if they saw you do without it. I know there's two or three would like to keep out of that tavern if they could."

At first Captain seemed to do well, but he was a very old horse, and it was only his wonderful constitution, and Jerry's care, that had kept him up at the cab work so long; now he broke down very much. The farrier said he might mend up enough to sell for a few pounds, but Jerry said, no! a few pounds got by selling a good old servant into hard work and misery would canker all the rest of his money, and he thought the kindest thing he could do for the fine old fellow would be to put a sure bullet through his head, and then he would never suffer more; for he did not know where to find a kind master for the rest of his days.

The day after this was decided Harry took me to the forge for some new shoes; when I returned Captain was gone. I and the family all felt it very much.

Jerry had now to look out for another horse, and he soon heard of one through an acquaintance who was under-groom in a nobleman's stables. He was a valuable young horse, but he had run away, smashed into another carriage, flung his lordship out, and so cut and blemished himself that he was no longer fit for a gentleman's stables, and the coachman had orders to look round, and sell him as well as he could.

"I can do with high spirits," said Jerry, "if a horse is not vicious or hard-mouthed."

"There is not a bit of vice in him," said the man; "his mouth is very tender, and I think myself that was the cause of the accident; you see he had just been clipped, and the weather was bad, and he had not had exercise enough, and when he did go out he was as full of spring as a balloon. Our governor (the coachman, I mean) had him harnessed in as tight and strong as he could, with the martingale, and the check-rein, a very sharp curb, and the reins put in at the bottom bar. It is my belief that it made the horse mad, being tender in the mouth and so full of spirit."

"Likely enough; I'll come and see him," said Jerry.

The next day Hotspur, that was his name, came home; he was a fine brown horse, without a white hair in him, as tall as Captain, with a very handsome head, and only five years old. I gave him a friendly greeting by way of good fellowship, but did not ask him any questions. The first night he was very restless. Instead of lying down, he kept jerking his halter rope up and down through the ring, and knocking the block about against the manger till I could not sleep. However, the next day, after five or six hours in the cab, he came in quiet and sensible. Jerry patted and talked to him a good deal, and very soon they understood each other, and Jerry said that with an easy bit and plenty of work he would be as gentle as a lamb; and that it was an ill wind that blew nobody good, for if his lordship had lost a hundred-guinea favorite, the cabman had gained a good horse with all his strength in him.

Hotspur thought it a great come-down to be a cab-horse, and was disgusted at standing in the rank, but he confessed to me at the end of the week that an easy mouth and a free head made up for a great deal, and after all, the work was not so degrading as having one's head and tail fastened to each other at the saddle. In fact, he settled in well, and Jerry liked him very much.

45 Jerry's New Year

For some people Christmas and the New Year are very merry times; but for cabmen and cabmen's horses it is no holiday, though it may be a harvest. There are so many parties, balls, and places of amusement open that the work is hard and often late. Sometimes driver and horse have to wait for hours in the rain or frost, shivering with the cold, while the merry people within are dancing away to the music. I wonder if the beautiful ladies ever think of the weary cabman waiting on his box, and his patient beast standing, till his legs get stiff with cold.

I had now most of the evening work, as I was well accustomed to standing, and Jerry was also more afraid of Hotspur taking cold. We had a great deal of late work in the Christmas week, and Jerry's cough was bad; but however late we were, Polly sat up for him, and came out with a lantern to meet him, looking anxious and troubled.

On the evening of the New Year we had to take two gentlemen to a house in one of the West End Squares. We set them down at nine o'clock, and were told to come again at eleven, "but," said one, "as it is a card party, you may have to wait a few minutes, but don't be late."

As the clock struck eleven we were at the door, for Jerry was always punctual. The clock chimed the quarters, one, two, three, and then struck twelve, but the door did not open.

The wind had been very changeable, with squalls of rain during the day, but now it came on sharp, driving sleet, which seemed to come all the way round; it was very cold, and there was no shelter. Jerry got off his box and came and pulled one of my cloths a little more over my neck; then he took a turn or two up and down, stamping his feet; then he began to beat his arms, but that set him off coughing; so he opened the cab door and sat at the bottom with his feet on the pavement, and was a little sheltered. Still the clock chimed the quarters, and no one came. At half-past twelve he rang the bell and asked the servant if he would be wanted that night.

"Oh, yes, you'll be wanted safe enough," said the man; "you must not go, it will soon be over," and again Jerry sat down, but his voice was so hoarse I could hardly hear him.

At a quarter past one the door opened, and the two gentlemen came out; they got into the cab without a word, and told Jerry where to drive, that was nearly two miles. My legs were numb with cold, and I thought I should have stumbled. When the men got out they never said they were sorry to have kept us waiting so long, but were angry at the charge; however, as Jerry never charged more than was his due, so he never took less, and they had to pay for the two hours and a quarter waiting; but it was hard-earned money to Jerry.

At last we got home; he could hardly speak, and his cough was dreadful. Polly asked no questions, but opened the door and held the lantern for him.

"Can't I do something?" she said.

"Yes; get Jack something warm, and then boil me some gruel."

This was said in a hoarse whisper; he could hardly get his breath, but he gave me a rub-down as usual, and even went up into the hayloft for an extra bundle of straw for my bed. Polly brought me a warm mash that made me comfortable, and then they locked the door.

It was late the next morning before any one came, and then it was only Harry. He cleaned us and fed us, and swept out the stalls, then he put the straw back again as if it was Sunday. He was very still, and neither whistled nor sang. At noon he came again and gave us our food and water; this time Dolly came with him; she was crying, and I could gather from what they said that Jerry was dangerously ill, and the doctor said it was a bad case. So two days passed, and there was great trouble indoors. We only saw Harry, and sometimes Dolly. I think she came for company, for Polly was always with Jerry, and he had to be kept very quiet.

On the third day, while Harry was in the stable, a tap came at the door, and Governor Grant came in.

"I wouldn't go to the house, my boy," he said, "but I want to know how your father is."

"He is very bad," said Harry, "he can't be much worse; they call it 'bronchitis'; the doctor thinks it will turn one way or another to-night."

"That's bad, very bad," said Grant, shaking his head; "I know two men who died of that last week; it takes 'em off in no time; but while there's life there's hope, so you must keep up your spirits."

"Yes," said Harry quickly, "and the doctor said that father had a better chance than most men, because he didn't drink. He said yesterday the fever was so high that if father had been a drinking man it would have burned him up like a piece of paper; but I believe he thinks he will get over it; don't you think he will, Mr. Grant?"

The governor looked puzzled.

"If there's any rule that good men should get over these things, I'm sure he will, my boy; he's the best man I know. I'll look in early to-morrow."

Early next morning he was there.

"Well?" said he.

"Father is better," said Harry. "Mother hopes he will get over it."

"Thank God!" said the governor, "and now you must keep him warm, and keep his mind easy, and that brings me to the horses; you see Jack will be all the better for the rest of a week or two in a warm stable, and you can easily take him a turn up and down the street to stretch his legs; but this young one, if he does not get work, he will soon be all up on end, as you may say, and will be rather too much for you; and when he does go out there'll be an accident."

"It is like that now," said Harry. "I have kept him short of corn, but he's so full of spirit I don't know what to do with him."

449

"Just so," said Grant. "Now look here, will you tell your mother that if she is agreeable I will come for him every day till something is arranged, and take him for a good spell of work, and whatever he earns, I'll bring your mother half of it, and that will help with the horses' feed. Your father is in a good club, I know, but that won't keep the horses, and they'll be eating their heads off all this time; I'll come at noon and hear what she says," and without waiting for Harry's thanks he was gone.

At noon I think he went and saw Polly, for he and Harry came to the stable together, harnessed Hotspur, and took him out.

For a week or more he came for Hotspur, and when Harry thanked him or said anything about his kindness, he laughed it off, saying it was all good luck for him, for his horses were wanting a little rest which they would not otherwise have had.

Jerry grew better steadily, but the doctor said that he must never go back to the cab work again if he wished to be an old man. The children had many consultations together about what father and mother would do, and how they could help to earn money.

One afternoon Hotspur was brought in very wet and dirty.

"The streets are nothing but slush," said the governor; "it will give you a good warming, my boy, to get him clean and dry."

"All right, governor," said Harry, "I shall not leave him till he is; you know I have been trained by my father."

"I wish all the boys had been trained like you," said the governor.

While Harry was sponging off the mud from Hotspur's body and legs Dolly came in, looking very full of something.

"Who lives at Fairstowe, Harry? Mother has got a letter from Fairstowe; she seemed so glad, and ran upstairs to father with it."

"Don't you know? Why, it is the name of Mrs. Fowler's place – mother's old mistress, you know – the lady that father met last summer, who sent you and me five shillings each."

"Oh! Mrs. Fowler. Of course, I know all about her. I wonder what she is writing to mother about."

"Mother wrote to her last week," said Harry; "you know she told father if ever he gave up the cab work she would like to know. I wonder what she says; run in and see, Dolly."

Harry scrubbed away at Hotspur with a huish! huish! like any old hostler. In a few minutes Dolly came dancing into the stable.

"Oh! Harry, there never was anything so beautiful; Mrs. Fowler says we are all to go and live near her. There is a cottage now empty that will just suit us, with a garden and a henhouse, and apple-trees, and everything! and her coachman is going away in the spring, and then she will want father in his place; and there are good families round, where you can get a place in the garden or the stable, or as a page-boy; and there's a good school for me; and mother is laughing and crying by turns, and father does look so happy!"

"That's uncommon jolly," said Harry, "and just the right thing, I should say; it will suit father and mother both; but I don't intend to be a page-boy with tight clothes and rows of buttons. I'll be a groom or a gardener."

It was quickly settled that as soon as Jerry was well enough they should remove to the country, and that the cab and horses should be sold as soon as possible.

This was heavy news for me, for I was not young now, and could not look for any improvement in my condition. Since I left Birtwick I had never been so happy as with my dear master Jerry; but three years of cab work, even under the best conditions, will tell on one's strength, and I felt that I was not the horse that I had been.

Grant said at once that he would take Hotspur, and there were men on the stand who would have bought me; but Jerry said I should not go to cab work again with just anybody, and the governor promised to find a place for me where I should be comfortable.

The day came for going away. Jerry had not been allowed to go out yet, and I never saw him after that New Year's eve. Polly and the children came to bid me good-by. "Poor old Jack! dear old Jack! I wish we could take you with us," she said, and then laying her hand on my mane she put her face close to my neck and kissed me. Dolly was crying and kissed me too. Harry stroked me a great deal, but said nothing, only he seemed very sad, and so I was led away to my new place.

Lesson 88

1. Read chapters 46 and 47.
2. Take notes on major events.

Vocabulary

1. Try to match these root words with their meanings. (Answers)
2. The root is where the word came from. For example: bicycle comes from bi meaning two and cycle meaning any complete round that repeats over and over again.

3. If you are stuck, try to think of a word that begins with that root and think about its definition. Any time you come across a word you don't know, looking for familiar roots in the word can sometimes help you decipher the meaning.

1. biblio	A. make
2. carn	B. foot
3. fac	C. heat
4. anim	D. water
5. aqua	E. book
6. arbor	F. meat
7. pod	G. end
8. pop	H. tree
9. term	I. life
10. therm	J. people

46 Jakes and the Lady

I was sold to a corn dealer and baker, whom Jerry knew, and with him he thought I should have good food and fair work. In the first he was quite right, and if my master had always been on the premises I do not think I should have been overloaded, but there was a foreman who was always hurrying and driving every one, and frequently when I had quite a full load he would order something else to be taken on. My carter, whose name was Jakes, often said it was more than I ought to take, but the other always overruled him. "'Twas no use going twice when once would do, and he chose to get business forward."

Jakes, like the other carters, always had the check-rein up, which prevented me from drawing easily, and by the time I had been there three or four months I found the work telling very much on my strength.

One day I was loaded more than usual, and part of the road was a steep uphill. I used all my strength, but I could not get on, and was obliged continually to stop. This did not please my driver, and he laid his whip on badly. "Get on, you lazy fellow," he said, "or I'll make you."

Again I started the heavy load, and struggled on a few yards; again the whip came down, and again I struggled forward. The pain of that great cart whip was sharp, but my mind was hurt quite as much as my poor sides. To be punished and abused when I was doing my very best was so hard it took the heart out of me. A third time he was flogging me cruelly, when a lady stepped quickly up to him, and said in a sweet, earnest voice:

"Oh! pray do not whip your good horse any more; I am sure he is doing all he can, and the road is very steep; I am sure he is doing his best."

"If doing his best won't get this load up he must do something more than his best; that's all I know, ma'am," said Jakes.

"But is it not a heavy load?" she said.

"Yes, yes, too heavy," he said; "but that's not my fault; the foreman came just as we were starting, and would have three hundredweight more put on to save him trouble, and I must get on with it as well as I can."

He was raising the whip again, when the lady said:

"Pray, stop; I think I can help you if you will let me."

The man laughed.

"You see," she said, "you do not give him a fair chance; he cannot use all his power with his head held back as it is with that check-rein; if you would take it off I am sure he would do better – do try it," she said persuasively, "I should be very glad if you would."

"Well, well," said Jakes, with a short laugh, "anything to please a lady, of course. How far would you wish it down, ma'am?"

"Quite down, give him his head altogether."

The rein was taken off, and in a moment I put my head down to my very knees. What a comfort it was! Then I tossed it up and down several times to get the aching stiffness out of my neck.

"Poor fellow! that is what you wanted," said she, patting and stroking me with her gentle hand; "and now if you will speak kindly to him and lead him on I believe he will be able to do better."

Jakes took the rein. "Come on, Blackie." I put down my head, and threw my whole weight against the collar; I spared no strength; the load moved on, and I pulled it steadily up the hill, and then stopped to take breath.

The lady had walked along the footpath, and now came across into the road. She stroked and patted my neck, as I had not been patted for many a long day.

"You see he was quite willing when you gave him the chance; I am sure he is a fine-tempered creature, and I dare say has known better days. You won't put that rein on again, will you?" for he was just going to hitch it up on the old plan.

"Well, ma'am, I can't deny that having his head has helped him up the hill, and I'll remember it another time, and thank you, ma'am; but if he went without a check-rein I should be the laughing-stock of all the carters; it is the fashion, you see."

"Is it not better," she said, "to lead a good fashion than to follow a bad one? A great many gentlemen do not use check-reins now; our carriage horses have not worn them for fifteen years, and work with much less fatigue than those who have them; besides," she added in a very serious voice, "we have no right to distress any of God's creatures without a very good reason; we call them dumb animals, and so they are, for they cannot tell us how they feel, but they do not suffer less because they have no words. But I must not detain you now; I thank you for trying my plan with your good horse, and I am sure you will find it far better than the whip. Good-day," and with another soft pat on my neck she stepped lightly across the path, and I saw her no more.

"That was a real lady, I'll be bound for it," said Jakes to himself; "she spoke just as polite as if I was a gentleman, and I'll try her plan, uphill, at any rate;" and I must do him the justice to say that he let my rein out several holes, and going uphill after that, he always gave me my head; but the heavy loads went on. Good feed and fair rest will keep up one's strength under full work, but no horse can stand against overloading; and I was getting so thoroughly pulled down from this cause that a younger horse was bought in my place. I may as well mention here what I suffered at this time from another cause. I had heard horses speak of it, but had never myself had experience of the evil; this was a badly-lighted stable; there was only one very small window at the end, and the consequence was that the stalls were almost dark.

Besides the depressing effect this had on my spirits, it very much weakened my sight, and when I was suddenly brought out of the darkness into the glare of daylight it was very painful to my eyes. Several times I stumbled over the threshold, and could scarcely see where I was going.

I believe, had I stayed there very long, I should have become purblind, and that would have been a great misfortune, for I have heard men say that a stone-blind horse was safer to drive than one which had imperfect sight, as it generally makes them very timid. However, I escaped without any permanent injury to my sight, and was sold to a large cab owner.

47 Hard Times

My new master I shall never forget; he had black eyes and a hooked nose, his mouth was as full of teeth as a bull-dog's, and his voice was as harsh as the grinding of cart wheels over graveled stones. His name was Nicholas Skinner, and I believe he was the man that poor Seedy Sam drove for.

I have heard men say that seeing is believing; but I should say that feeling is believing; for much as I had seen before, I never knew till now the utter misery of a cab-horse's life.

Skinner had a low set of cabs and a low set of drivers; he was hard on the men, and the men were hard on the horses. In this place we had no Sunday rest, and it was in the heat of summer.

Sometimes on a Sunday morning a party of fast men would hire the cab for the day; four of them inside and another with the driver, and I had to take them ten or fifteen miles out into the country, and back again; never would any of them get down to walk up a hill, let it be ever so steep, or the day ever so hot – unless, indeed, when the driver was afraid I should not manage it, and sometimes I was so fevered and worn that I could hardly touch my food. How I used to long for the nice bran mash with niter in it that Jerry used to give us on Saturday nights in hot weather, that used to cool us down and make us so comfortable. Then we had two nights and a whole day for unbroken rest, and on Monday morning we were as fresh as young horses again; but here there was no rest, and my driver was just as hard as his master. He had a cruel whip with something so sharp at the end that it sometimes drew blood, and he would even whip me under the belly, and flip the lash out at my head. Indignities like these took the heart out of me terribly, but still I did my best and never hung back; for, as poor Ginger said, it was no use; men are the strongest.

My life was now so utterly wretched that I wished I might, like Ginger, drop down dead at my work and be out of my misery, and one day my wish very nearly came to pass.

I went on the stand at eight in the morning, and had done a good share of work, when we had to take a fare to the railway. A long train was just expected in, so my driver pulled up at the back of some of the outside cabs to take the chance of a return fare. It was a very heavy train, and as all the cabs were soon engaged ours was called for. There was a party of four; a noisy, blustering man with a lady, a little boy and a young girl, and a great deal of luggage. The lady and the boy got into the cab, and while the man ordered about the luggage the young girl came and looked at me.

"Papa," she said, "I am sure this poor horse cannot take us and all our luggage so far, he is so very weak and worn up. Do look at him."

"Oh! he's all right, miss," said my driver, "he's strong enough."

The porter, who was pulling about some heavy boxes, suggested to the gentleman, as there was so much luggage, whether he would not take a second cab.

"Can your horse do it, or can't he?" said the blustering man.

"Oh! he can do it all right, sir; send up the boxes, porter; he could take more than that;" and he helped to haul up a box so heavy that I could feel the springs go down.

"Papa, papa, do take a second cab," said the young girl in a beseeching tone. "I am sure we are wrong, I am sure it is very cruel."

"Nonsense, Grace, get in at once, and don't make all this fuss; a pretty thing it would be if a man of business had to examine every cab-horse before he hired it – the man knows his own business of course; there, get in and hold your tongue!"

My gentle friend had to obey, and box after box was dragged up and lodged on the top of the cab or settled by the side of the driver. At last all was ready, and with his usual jerk at the rein and slash of the whip he drove out of the station.

The load was very heavy and I had had neither food nor rest since morning; but I did my best, as I always had done, in spite of cruelty and injustice.

I got along fairly till we came to Ludgate Hill; but there the heavy load and my own exhaustion were too much. I was struggling to keep on, goaded by constant chucks of the rein and use of the whip, when in a single moment – I cannot tell how – my feet slipped from under me, and I fell heavily to the ground on my side; the suddenness and the force with which I fell seemed to beat all the breath out of my body. I lay perfectly still; indeed, I had no power to move, and I thought now I was going to die. I heard a sort of confusion round me, loud, angry voices, and the getting down of the luggage, but it was all like a dream. I thought I heard that sweet, pitiful voice saying, "Oh! that poor horse! it is all our fault." Some one came and loosened the throat strap of my bridle, and undid the traces which kept the collar so tight upon me. Some one said, "He's dead, he'll never get up again." Then I could hear a policeman giving orders, but I did not even open my eyes; I could only draw a gasping breath now and then. Some cold water was thrown over my head, and some cordial was poured into my mouth, and something was covered over me. I cannot tell how long I lay there, but I found my life coming back, and a kind-voiced man was patting me and encouraging me to rise. After some more cordial had been given me, and after one or two attempts, I staggered to my feet, and was gently led to some stables which were close by. Here I was put into a well-littered stall, and some warm gruel was brought to me, which I drank thankfully.

In the evening I was sufficiently recovered to be led back to Skinner's stables, where I think they did the best for me they could. In the morning Skinner came with a farrier to look at me. He examined me very closely and said:

"This is a case of overwork more than disease, and if you could give him a run off for six months he would be able to work again; but now there is not an ounce of strength left in him."

"Then he must just go to the dogs," said Skinner. "I have no meadows to nurse sick horses in – he might get well or he might not; that sort of thing don't suit my business; my plan is to work 'em as long as they'll go, and then sell 'em for what they'll fetch, at the knacker's or elsewhere."

"If he was broken-winded," said the farrier, "you had better have him killed out of hand, but he is not; there is a sale of horses coming off in about ten days; if you rest him and feed him up he may pick up, and you may get more than his skin is worth, at any rate."

Upon this advice Skinner, rather unwillingly, I think, gave orders that I should be well fed and cared for, and the stable man, happily for me, carried out the orders with a much better will than his master had in giving them. Ten days of perfect rest, plenty of good oats, hay, bran mashes, with boiled linseed mixed in them, did more to get up my condition than anything else could have done; those linseed mashes were delicious, and I began to think, after all, it might be better to live than go to the dogs. When the twelfth day after the accident came, I was taken to the sale, a few miles out of London. I felt that any change from my present place must be an improvement, so I held up my head, and hoped for the best.

Lesson 89

1. Read chapters 48 and 49.
2. Take notes on major events.
3. To talk or write about: What's your initial reaction to the book? What did you like or not like? What are your feelings about animal cruelty? Did your opinion change at all by this book and why?

48   Farmer Thoroughgood and His Grandson Willie

At this sale, of course I found myself in company with the old broken-down horses – some lame, some broken-winded, some old, and some that I am sure it would have been merciful to shoot.

The buyers and sellers, too, many of them, looked not much better off than the poor beasts they were bargaining about. There were poor old men, trying to get a horse or a pony for a few pounds, that might drag about some little wood or coal cart. There were poor men trying to sell a worn-out beast for two or three pounds, rather than have the greater loss of killing him. Some of them looked as if poverty and hard times had hardened them all over; but there were others that I would have willingly used the last of my strength in serving; poor and shabby, but kind and human, with voices that I could trust. There was one tottering old man who took a great fancy to me, and I to him, but I was not strong enough – it was an anxious time! Coming from the better part of the fair, I noticed a man who looked like a gentleman farmer, with a young boy by his side; he had a broad back and round shoulders, a kind, ruddy face, and he wore a broad-brimmed hat. When he came up to me and my companions he stood still and gave a pitiful look round upon us. I saw his eye rest on me; I had still a good mane and tail, which did something for my appearance. I pricked my ears and looked at him.

"There's a horse, Willie, that has known better days."

"Poor old fellow!" said the boy, "do you think, grandpapa, he was ever a carriage horse?"

"Oh, yes! my boy," said the farmer, coming closer, "he might have been anything when he was young; look at his nostrils and his ears, the shape of his neck and shoulder; there's a deal of breeding about that horse." He put out his hand and gave me a kind pat on the neck. I put out my nose in answer to his kindness; the boy stroked my face.

"Poor old fellow! see, grandpapa, how well he understands kindness. Could not you buy him and make him young again as you did with Ladybird?"

"My dear boy, I can't make all old horses young; besides, Ladybird was not so very old, as she was run down and badly used."

"Well, grandpapa, I don't believe that this one is old; look at his mane and tail. I wish you would look into his mouth, and then you could tell; though he is so very thin, his eyes are not sunk like some old horses'."

The old gentleman laughed. "Bless the boy! he is as horsey as his old grandfather."

"But do look at his mouth, grandpapa, and ask the price; I am sure he would grow young in our meadows."

The man who had brought me for sale now put in his word.

"The young gentleman's a real knowing one, sir. Now the fact is, this 'ere hoss is just pulled down with overwork in the cabs; he's not an old one, and I heerd as how the vetenary should say, that a six months' run off would set him right up, being as how his wind was not broken. I've had the tending of him these ten days past, and a gratefuller, pleasanter animal I never met with, and 'twould be worth a gentleman's while to give a five-pound note for him, and let him have a chance. I'll be bound he'd be worth twenty pounds next spring."

The old gentleman laughed, and the little boy looked up eagerly.

"Oh, grandpapa, did you not say the colt sold for five pounds more than you expected? You would not be poorer if you did buy this one."

The farmer slowly felt my legs, which were much swelled and strained; then he looked at my mouth. "Thirteen or fourteen, I should say; just trot him out, will you?"

I arched my poor thin neck, raised my tail a little, and threw out my legs as well as I could, for they were very stiff.

"What is the lowest you will take for him?" said the farmer as I came back.

"Five pounds, sir; that was the lowest price my master set."

"'Tis a speculation," said the old gentleman, shaking his head, but at the same time slowly drawing out his purse, "quite a speculation! Have you any more business here?" he said, counting the sovereigns into his hand.

"No, sir, I can take him for you to the inn, if you please."

"Do so, I am now going there."

They walked forward, and I was led behind. The boy could hardly control his delight, and the old gentleman seemed to enjoy his pleasure. I had a good feed at the inn, and was then gently ridden home by a servant of my new master's, and turned into a large meadow with a shed in one corner of it.

Mr. Thoroughgood, for that was the name of my benefactor, gave orders that I should have hay and oats every night and morning, and the run of the meadow during the day, and, "you, Willie," said he, "must take the oversight of him; I give him in charge to you."

The boy was proud of his charge, and undertook it in all seriousness. There was not a day when he did not pay me a visit; sometimes picking me out from among the other horses, and giving me a bit of carrot, or something good, or sometimes standing by me while I ate my oats. He always came with kind words and caresses, and of course I grew very fond of him. He called me Old Crony, as I used to come to him in the field and follow him about. Sometimes he brought his grandfather, who always looked closely at my legs.

"This is our point, Willie," he would say; "but he is improving so steadily that I think we shall see a change for the better in the spring."

The perfect rest, the good food, the soft turf, and gentle exercise, soon began to tell on my condition and my spirits. I had a good constitution from my mother, and I was never strained when I was young, so that I had a better chance than many horses who have been worked before they came to their full strength. During the winter my legs improved so much that I began to feel quite young again. The spring came round, and one day in March Mr. Thoroughgood determined that he would try me in the phaeton. I was well pleased, and he and Willie drove me a few miles. My legs were not stiff now, and I did the work with perfect ease.

"He's growing young, Willie; we must give him a little gentle work now, and by mid-summer he will be as good as Ladybird. He has a beautiful mouth and good paces; they can't be better."

"Oh, grandpapa, how glad I am you bought him!"

"So am I, my boy; but he has to thank you more than me; we must now be looking out for a quiet, genteel place for him, where he will be valued."

49 My Last Home

One day during this summer the groom cleaned and dressed me with such extraordinary care that I thought some new change must be at hand; he trimmed my fetlocks and legs, passed the tarbrush over my hoofs, and even parted my forelock. I think the harness had an extra polish. Willie seemed half-anxious, half-merry, as he got into the chaise with his grandfather.

"If the ladies take to him," said the old gentleman, "they'll be suited and he'll be suited. We can but try."

At the distance of a mile or two from the village we came to a pretty, low house, with a lawn and shrubbery at the front and a drive up to the door. Willie rang the bell, and asked if Miss Blomefield or Miss Ellen was at home. Yes, they were. So, while Willie stayed with me, Mr. Thoroughgood went into the house. In about ten minutes he returned, followed by three ladies; one tall, pale lady, wrapped in a white shawl, leaned on a younger lady, with dark eyes and a merry face; the other, a very stately-looking person, was Miss Blomefield. They all came and looked at me and asked questions. The younger lady – that was Miss Ellen – took to me very much; she said she was sure she should like me, I had such a good face. The tall, pale lady said that she should always be nervous in riding behind a horse that had once been down, as I might come down again, and if I did she should never get over the fright.

"You see, ladies," said Mr. Thoroughgood, "many first-rate horses have had their knees broken through the carelessness of their drivers without any fault of their own, and from what I see of this horse I should say that is his case; but of course I do not wish to influence you. If you incline you can have him on trial, and then your coachman will see what he thinks of him."

"You have always been such a good adviser to us about our horses," said the stately lady, "that your recommendation would go a long way with me, and if my sister Lavinia sees no objection we will accept your offer of a trial, with thanks."

It was then arranged that I should be sent for the next day.

In the morning a smart-looking young man came for me. At first he looked pleased; but when he saw my knees he said in a disappointed voice:

"I didn't think, sir, you would have recommended my ladies a blemished horse like that."

"'Handsome is that handsome does'," said my master; "you are only taking him on trial, and I am sure you will do fairly by him, young man. If he is not as safe as any horse you ever drove send him back."

I was led to my new home, placed in a comfortable stable, fed, and left to myself. The next day, when the groom was cleaning my face, he said:

"That is just like the star that 'Black Beauty' had; he is much the same height, too. I wonder where he is now."

A little further on he came to the place in my neck where I was bled and where a little knot was left in the skin. He almost started, and began to look me over carefully, talking to himself.

"White star in the forehead, one white foot on the off side, this little knot just in that place;" then looking at the middle of my back – "and, as I am alive, there is that little patch of white hair that John used to call 'Beauty's three-penny bit'. It must be 'Black Beauty'! Why, Beauty! Beauty! do you know me? – little Joe Green, that almost killed you?" And he began patting and patting me as if he was quite overjoyed.

I could not say that I remembered him, for now he was a fine grown young fellow, with black whiskers and a man's voice, but I was sure he knew me, and that he was Joe Green, and I was very glad. I put my nose up to him, and tried to say that we were friends. I never saw a man so pleased.

"Give you a fair trial! I should think so indeed! I wonder who the rascal was that broke your knees, my old Beauty! you must have been badly served out somewhere; well, well, it won't be my fault if you haven't good times of it now. I wish John Manly was here to see you."

In the afternoon I was put into a low park chair and brought to the door. Miss Ellen was going to try me, and Green went with her. I soon found that she was a good driver, and she seemed pleased with my paces. I heard Joe telling her about me, and that he was sure I was Squire Gordon's old "Black Beauty".

When we returned the other sisters came out to hear how I had behaved myself. She told them what she had just heard, and said:

"I shall certainly write to Mrs. Gordon, and tell her that her favorite horse has come to us. How pleased she will be!"

After this I was driven every day for a week or so, and as I appeared to be quite safe, Miss Lavinia at last ventured out in the small close carriage. After this it was quite decided to keep me and call me by my old name of "Black Beauty".

I have now lived in this happy place a whole year. Joe is the best and kindest of grooms. My work is easy and pleasant, and I feel my strength and spirits all coming back again. Mr. Thoroughgood said to Joe the other day:

"In your place he will last till he is twenty years old – perhaps more."

Willie always speaks to me when he can, and treats me as his special friend. My ladies have promised that I shall never be sold, and so I have nothing to fear; and here my story ends. My troubles are all over, and I am at home; and often before I am quite awake, I fancy I am still in the orchard at Birtwick, standing with my old friends under the apple-trees.

The End.

Lesson 90

1. The conflict in the novel is Black Beauty being passed from one owner to another. How is the conflict resolved in the novel? What happens in the end? How is Black Beauty at the end of the novel?

2. What were the most surprising, exciting, scary and sweet moments in the plot?

ANSWERS

Lesson 1
teeming-to be full of
fathom-understand
reverberating-echoing
cumulative-increasing

Lesson 2
gnarled-knobby
trajectory-path of a flying object
baritone-adult male singing voice, second lowest pitch
furrows-rut or trench

Lesson 3
full-teeming, knobby-gnarled, increasing-cumulative, content-satisfied, admire-respect, cautious-careful, understand-fathom, echoing-reverberating

Lesson 4
Nature

Lesson 6
foliage-lots of plant leaves together
flecked- marked or dotted with color
knoll-small hill

Lesson 7
miscellany- a collection of different items
interposed-interruption or place between two things
tumultuous- excited, disorderly, loud and confused noise
keen- eagerness, interest in
subdue-bring under control
dilating-make or become wider, larger
sanctify-set apart as holy

Lesson 8
russet-redish borwn color, rustic
profane-degrade, desecrate
peck-an amout of food, strike with a beak, light kiss
acquainted-to come to know, have a fair knowledge of
luminary-artificial light, someone who inspires
Vocabulary: 1K, 2I, 3A, 4E, 5F, 6N, 7D, 8L, 9H, 10B, 11J, 12C, 13G, 14O, 15M

Lesson 10
2. leaf, Eden (as in Garden of Eden), dawn (as in the sunrise)
The rest of these answers don't have to be precise as long as they reflect the right idea
3. the leaf looks gold in the morning sun (or you could say the leaf is dying and will be replaced by another), grief/sin ruined the perfection of Eden, the sun rises and makes a new day
4. somber

5. He's pessimistic. He generalizes and says nothing gold can last just because some things don't.
Vocabulary: 1F, 2J, 3E, 4I, 5H, 6B, 7D, 8C, 9G, 10A

Lesson 11

2. They can be unjust and unkind. That they could learn from the animals.

Lesson 16

Mowgli is the protagonist; Sher Khan and the jackal are the antagonists.

Lesson 17

He did not obey the caste. He was different. The people did not understand his relationship with the animals.

Lesson 18

1.	sanctify	set apart or declare holy
2.	peck	an amount of food, strike with a beak, light kiss
3.	rued	bitterly regret
4.	profane	degrade or desecrate
5.	diffuse	spread or cause to spread over a wide area
6.	acquainted	to come to know, have a fair knowledge of
7.	russet	redish brown color, rustic
8.	luminary	artificial light, someone who inspires
9.	fragmentary	consisting of small parts, incomplete
10.	agitated	feeling troubled

Lesson 19

He is angry and worried his son might become an elephant hunter and live near the jungle.

Lesson 23

Kipling to his son

Lesson 25

students wanting America to go to war with different countries just because they've heard of them, American students don't know geography

Lesson 26

American's aren't free when they are bound to pay taxes on everything. Even the tombstone in the graveyard had a tax price tag on it.

Lesson 27

TR is giving the old way of spelling the boot. He's kicking the old dictionary character out of the White House. (He made an order that in the White House simplified spelling had to be used. bil for bill, thro for throw, etc. It didn't stick.)

Lesson 28

TR is watching while the trusts are literally having the money squeezed out of them. You can see that the trusts are seen by the cartoonists as being "fat" with money and that TR has sent the other character (secretary of the treasury, Cortelyou) to "squeeze" the money out of them.

Lesson 46

A thunderbolt overthrows, breaks, and rends bodies that do not permit electricity to circulate freely.

This is an implied main idea: It's abnormal to venture out in the rain, but the positive results can be well worth it.
http://testprep.about.com/od/readingtesttips/l/Finding_Main_Idea_2_Answers.doc.pdf

Lesson 47

Now there are two distinct kinds of electricity, which are present in equal quantities in all bodies and remain neutralized unless separated.

This is an implied main idea: Technology is pervasive in today's classrooms, and although critics doubt its use in education, their viewpoint is faulty.
http://testprep.about.com/od/readingtesttips/l/Finding_Main_Idea_2_Answers.doc.pdf

Lesson 48

2nd: There is a lot to learn about plants people eat, such as how to grow them and how to prepare them for eating.

3rd: If you don't know about foods and plants, you can make a big mistake.

4th: Some plants actually help keep people safe, for example, cloves.

Whole: The more you know about plants and foods, the healthier you will be.

Lesson 49

2nd: Badger always had a good day—he never complained and always turned a problem into an opportunity.

3rd: Badger helped everyone build their burrows.

4th: Badger was lonely because the other animals never stopped to be with him.

Whole: Badger wasn't appreciated until he was needed.

Lesson 54

He had the idea and in the same instant acted on it. He snatched up the overalls and put them on.

Lesson 57

Iscariot refers to Judas Iscariot in the Bible. He was the traitor; he was "treacherous." How can your mind turn against you?

Lesson 63

2. Just like how you can tell in a movie how everything is going to end up right in the end, this is saying how in books you always know how the fight between the good guy and bad guy is going to take place and how it will turn out in the end. He says everyone loves to read this type of story.

3. expurgator: a person who edits a text by removing obscene or offensive words or passages; he says there won't be much left after the expurgator gets through with it which means there was a lot of foul talk and action in the fight.

Lesson 65

The irony is that she is calling him a horrible boy and says he'll come to no good and is thinking he'll be a criminal when he grows up, but he says he's going to be a minister who is someone who should always be doing what is good and right.

Lesson 68

1A, 2D, 3A, 4D, 5B, 6A, 7A, 8B, 9A, 10B, 11B, 12B, 13D, 14C, 15D, 16 D, 17B, 18C

Lesson 82

interposed-interruption, tumultuous-disorderly, keen-eagerness, teeming-full, fathom-undestand, reverberating-echoing, cumulative-increasing, gnarled-knobby, furrows-trench

Lesson 88

1E bibliography, 2F carnivore, 3A factory, 4I animated, 5D aquarium, 6H arboretum, 7B podiatrist, 8J population, 9G terminate, 10C thermometer (You didn't have to write example words. I just wrote them to help you in case you got any wrong.)

About Easy Peasy All-in-One Homeschool

Easy Peasy All-in-One Homeschool is a free, complete online homeschool curriculum. There are 180 days of ready-to-go lessons for every level and every subject. It's created for your children to work as independently as you want them to. Preschool through high school is available as well as courses ranging from English, math, science and history to art, music, computer, thinking, physical education and health. A daily Bible lesson is offered as well. The mission of Easy Peasy is to enable those to homeschool who otherwise thought they couldn't.

Made in the USA
Las Vegas, NV
11 May 2024

89830499R00260